A SOCIAL AND ECONOMIC HISTORY OF BRITAIN

1760–1972

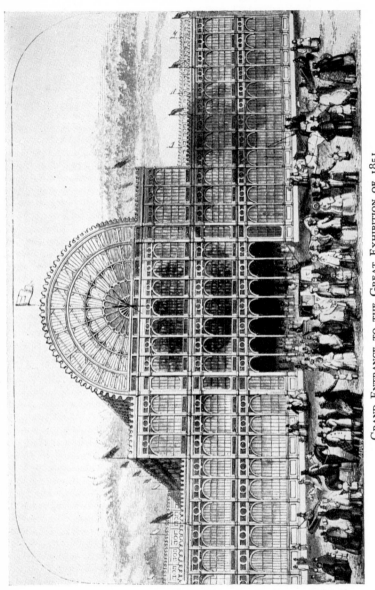

GRAND ENTRANCE TO THE GREAT EXHIBITION OF 1851

[See p. 288]

A
SOCIAL AND ECONOMIC HISTORY OF BRITAIN
1760–1972

PART I: THE RISE OF THE MIDDLE CLASSES
PART II: THE RISE OF THE WORKING CLASSES
PART III: A CENTURY OF SOCIAL REFORM
PART IV: THE AGE OF AFFLUENCE

by
PAULINE GREGG
PH.D. B.SC. (ECON.)

Seventh Edition Revised

HARRAP   LONDON

First published in Great Britain 1950
by GEORGE G. HARRAP & CO. LTD
182–184 High Holborn, London WC1V 7AX

Reprinted: 1952; 1954

Second Edition Revised 1956
Reprinted: 1957; 1960; 1961

Third Edition Revised 1962

Fourth Edition Revised 1964

Fifth Edition Revised 1965

Reprinted: 1967; 1969

Sixth Edition Revised 1971

Seventh Edition Revised 1973

ISBN 0 245 51899 1

*Printed in Great Britain by
Redwood Press Limited, Trowbridge, Wiltshire*

To

MY MOTHER AND FATHER

PREFACE

In this book I have tried to meet a need felt by myself and others, as students and as teachers, for a social and economic history of modern Britain which, while giving a broad review of the period, would serve as a practical introduction to the original sources. I have therefore quoted freely from contemporary writings and particularly from the nineteenth-century Blue Books, which are so much more exciting than is commonly supposed by those who have never read them. To the Select Committees and Royal Commissions of the century I record my thanks.

In common with all historians of the period I owe a debt to the Webbs, the Hammonds, and to Sir John Clapham, which I acknowledge in full. I wish also to thank Russell Meiggs, Fellow of Balliol College, for the help he gave me in correcting proofs.

PAULINE GREGG

HOLYWELL MANOR,
  OXFORD

  November 1949

NOTE TO THE SIXTH EDITION

THE decision to end this book at the present day entails frequent revision, and I am glad that a new edition gives me the opportunity of again bringing it up to date. The five years that have passed since the last edition, ending with the change from Labour to Conservative rule, make 1970 a convenient point for a fresh appraisal. Tables, dates, and the Index have been revised, and a new chapter has been added.

PAULINE GREGG

OXFORD
November 1970

NOTE TO THE SEVENTH EDITION

IN the two years of Conservative Government that have passed since the last edition of this book, events have moved so rapidly that a full new Chapter is called for. This is incorporated as Chapter XXVIII 'Into the Seventies'. Tables, Appendices and the Index have again been brought up to date.

PAULINE GREGG

GARSINGTON
July 1972

CONTENTS

PART I: 1760–1851
THE RISE OF THE MIDDLE CLASSES

PART II: 1851–1950

THE RISE OF THE WORKING CLASSES

PART III: 1851–1950

A CENTURY OF SOCIAL REFORM

PART IV

THE AGE OF AFFLUENCE

ILLUSTRATIONS

TABLES, GRAPHS, AND DIAGRAMS

PART I

1760–1851

THE RISE OF THE MIDDLE CLASSES

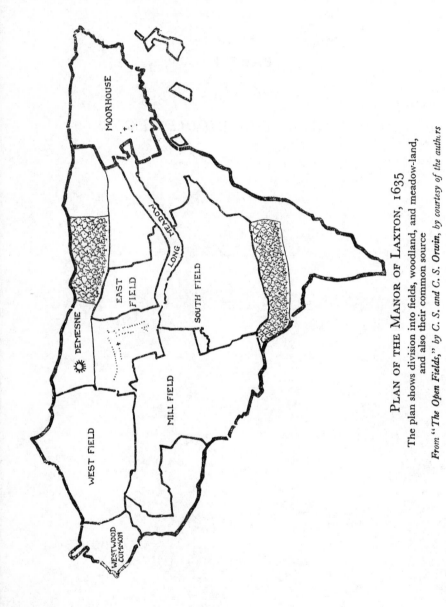

PLAN OF THE MANOR OF LAXTON, 1635

The plan shows division into fields, woodland, and meadow-land,
and also their common source

From "The Open Fields," by C. S. and C. S. Orwin, by courtesy of the authors

CHAPTER I

THE AGRARIAN REVOLUTION

(a) THE ECONOMIC CHANGES

CHANGE or development is continuous in the history of any nation. In some conditions development is so slow that the pattern of society barely seems to change in the course of centuries. At other times circumstances combine to alter social and economic life so rapidly that the change can be noted in the life of an individual. After centuries of comparatively slow development Britain, from the middle of the eighteenth century, became involved in a series of rapid agrarian and industrial changes which both to contemporaries and to after generations appeared revolutionary. These changes, their causes and results, and their ramifications throughout the social fabric of Britain form the vital core of British history during the last two hundred years. In agriculture the external sign of the change was the disappearance of the open hedgeless fields which had endured for centuries over a large part of the country, especially in the centre and south. For at the opening of the eighteenth century at least half the arable land in England was still farmed on the open-field or three-field system. The appearance of the open-field villages was much as it had been in feudal times. Round each village were three large arable fields, a portion of common pasture-land, on which the cattle and sheep of the villagers fed, some meadow-land to be cut for hay, probably some woodland in which firewood could be gathered, and beyond—waste land.

Of the three arable fields, two only were cultivated each year, while the third lay idle, or fallow. So a field might grow wheat or rye the first year, oats or barley the second, and lie fallow the third. There would be a spring sowing in one field, an autumn sowing in the other. The apparent wastefulness of leaving one-third of the land idle each year was due largely to ignorance of scientific methods of manuring. Each year's crop robs the soil of some of the properties essential to plant growth, and no method of treatment was known other than that of letting the land 'rest' one year in three, to restore itself slowly and naturally.

Most of the villagers were landholders, holding their land as they had held it in feudal times, in scattered strips in each of the three big fields, each strip being about 220 yards by 22 yards. The division of holdings among the fields ensured that the farmers shared each crop and bore their proportion of fallow each season. The strip system in each field gave each man in turn the benefit of approximately one day's work by the plough, and also served the purpose of dividing both good and bad land among different people.

The open-field economy as a whole was a mixture of the co-operative principle and the individualistic. A man had to farm in accordance with the custom of the village, sowing and reaping the same crops at the same time as his neighbours. The implements he used—the plough, for example—were often the joint property of the village or of groups of villagers, being too expensive for an individual to own. The team of oxen or horses which drew the plough was rarely the property of one man. On the other hand, each man looked after his own individual acre strip, and its product was his own. Meantime his cattle and sheep were put to feed on common and fallow, and after harvest were allowed on to the arable fields. Perhaps he owned a pig or chickens, which fed on the waste, where, too, he had rights of collecting firewood and cutting turf.

The system had both drawbacks and advantages, the former largely economic, the latter largely social. The farmer lost time and money in walking and cartage from one field to another; the farm buildings were at the village, perhaps a mile away from his strip; drainage improvement was difficult, for his system might be blocked by the next man's. He suffered many inconveniences through the carelessness or bad work of a neighbour. Custom, for example, gave a man the right, in turning his plough, to encroach on to the neighbouring strip. If a man was late with his ploughing his neighbour had either to delay his sowing or see his seeds destroyed by the turning of the heavy plough. In addition, the open, hedgeless fields were unprotected from straying animals and from the traveller who sometimes chose them as preferable to the miry lanes. As a result growing corn for twenty yards on either side of the track was often spoiled.

The most fundamental criticism of the open-field system, however, lay in its rigidity. Change of any kind was almost impossible without the consent of all landholders, and the pace of advance, consequently, was that of the slowest. Most of the open-field farmers, cut off by lack of communication from influences outside the village, performing age-old tasks by methods hallowed by tradition, became resistive of change; and the fact that the early part of the eighteenth century was an age of comparative prosperity for them wedded them the more firmly to their old ways. They continued sowing seed by scattering it broadcast with the hand, gathering crops by hand, using a hand-plough and implements which were crude and inefficient, and leaving each year a third of their land lying fallow and practically useless.

While cattle and sheep were allowed on the fallow field, and on the arable and meadow-land after the crops were gathered, their chief pasture was on the common, held, as its name implies, communally. Here the condition of the most unhealthy animals was likely to set the standard for all, for diseases are easily caught by animals pasturing together. Moreover, years of unscientific management of commons, frequently over-loaded with stock, had often reduced their feeding value, so that even in good seasons there was scarcely enough grass to keep the animals alive, while in bad they died for want of nourishment. To make matters worse, one of the stronger or richer farmers sometimes turned out more animals on to the common than custom allowed, so depriving his neighbours of food for their beasts. Scientific breeding was quite impossible with such a mixture of animals.

Thus, economically, the open-field system was difficult to justify, the work being heavy, the yield of the land low, the standard of living of the farmers often extremely meagre. Yet socially the system had the inestimable advantage that few countrymen were completely landless. The farmers had their strips, and even the 'squatters,' who had no rights in the open fields, were by custom permitted to clear and settle upon a piece of the waste.

The open-field community could be divided into different classes in accordance with the method of land-tenure. There were, broadly speaking, five classes connected with the land. There was the lord of the manor, who in the eighteenth century was generally the squire, in most cases the largest landowner in the village and the legal owner of the waste. The amount of land which the squire cultivated himself varied: on the one hand was the 'gentleman farmer' taking pride in the cultivation of his own acres; on the other was the absentee landlord, whose only interest in his land was the rent he received from his tenants.

The second class on the land were the freeholders, varying downward from men as substantial as the squire himself. Since Tudor times they had been noted for their sturdy independence, and were considered the backbone of England.

The third group consisted of people who held their land by varying tenures, but who all paid rent for it. Those who held by a legally fixed rent were fairly secure on their holding. Those who held by ancient copyhold tenure were less secure. In most cases the court roll which recorded the details of their holding was either lost or not available for consultation, and the terms of their lease depended merely on custom. Even less secure were the tenants-at-will. The terms upon which they held their land were governed simply by the will of the lord or squire.

Fourth were the squatters and cottagers. These for the most part had no land in the open fields, though a cottager might occasionally own or rent a strip. Custom, however, gave them the right to build cottages on the waste land, to feed a pig there, perhaps to pasture a cow on the common, to gather firewood from the woodland and cut turf from the waste.

Finally there were the farm servants and labourers who worked for the farmers. Between these and the others, however, there was not always a strictly defined line. Many smaller landholders spent part of their time as labourers, working for larger landholders. The amount of time a man spent working for another was generally dependent on the size of his own holding; rarely, however, was he a completely landless labourer.

This was the system in operation over most of Central and Southern England in the middle of the eighteenth century. Here, on the agricultural plain land, the impact of the Enclosure movement was most severe. In the hilly districts of the North of England and Scotland small individual holdings, added to by reclamation from the waste, were general. The

Scots for the most part farmed on a two-field system, an infield and an outfield, the former being cultivated incessantly, the latter occasionally. Wales was largely pastoral, and the South-west of England had already, in the sixteenth and seventeenth centuries, suffered its Enclosure movement for sheep-farming.

Inside the open-field system itself modifications were being made. Stretches of waste land were gradually being taken into cultivation, and never formed part of the open-field system. Sometimes 'strip-swapping' was practised by small owners, who thus secured their land in one piece, instead of scattered in the several fields. More important, the lord of the manor, or squire, frequently did the same thing on a larger scale, securing his holdings in one continuous piece by buying out or evicting tenants, and perhaps adding to his acres a stretch of waste. The consolidated piece was generally 'enclosed' or fenced, and thus the name 'enclosure' was applied to this method of superseding the open-field farm. Sometimes the landowner received sanction of Parliament for his action in what was known as an Enclosure Act.

Enclosure of this kind had been going on slowly for centuries. About 1750, however, the whole process quickened. Some indication of the speed of increase is given by the fact that between 1700 and 1760 there were just over 200 Enclosure Acts, while between 1760 and 1840 there were over 3500 Acts. The acreage enclosed between 1700 and 1760 was about 312,000; between 1760 and 1840 over 5,500,000.[1]

The reason for the rapid acceleration of the Enclosure movement in the second half of the eighteenth century is to be found in the threefold value of land—political, social, and economic.

Land was a necessary qualification for election to Parliament and, in the counties, for the right to vote. Political power consequently rested with the landed class, and Parliament was controlled by landowners. In the second place the most important man locally was the Justice of the Peace—generally the squire. He combined political and social power in his position as magistrate and as leader of local society. Thirdly, the owner of land could make a profit either by selling its produce or by leasing it at a high rental to tenant farmers.

These considerations were given fresh weight in the eighteenth

[1] J. L. and B. Hammond, *The Village Labourer, 1760-1832*, p. 17.

century in two ways. In the first place the growing wealth of traders led them to buy land as an investment and as a means to political power and social ostentation. In the former case particularly they would wish to gather as much as possible of the open fields and the waste into their own hands and to farm scientifically. There was also another set of factors at work in the second half of the eighteenth century. The growth of population meant more people to feed; the growth of trade and industry meant more people who provided directly no part of their food.

There were two methods by which the home supply of food could be increased. More land could be brought under cultivation or a larger crop obtained from each acre. An obvious method of effecting the former was to take more of the waste land into use. This was done to the extent of about two million acres in the eighteenth century. When the waste was in good condition the task was comparatively simple. In other cases— for example, in the Fenland—extensive and expensive drainage was necessary, and none but the rich man or company could undertake the task. Land thus obtained was naturally not farmed under the open-field system, but was kept in one piece, the property of the persons who reclaimed it, and generally enclosed.

To obtain a higher return from each acre better methods of farming were necessary. The drag on progress constituted by the open-field system was felt the more since scientific improvements were becoming known, and were being practised by some of the more enlightened landlords. By the mid-eighteenth century the way to such improvements had already been pointed. In 1645 Sir Richard Weston, having lived in and studied the methods of Flanders and Brabant, published his *Discourse upon Husbandry*, urging, above all, the use of clover and root crops such as turnips. Both these were invaluable for 'cleaning' the soil, and obviated the wasteful necessity of letting land lie fallow every third year. In addition, these crops were excellent cattle food, and provided the means of keeping cattle alive during the winter. The prevailing practice was to kill them off at the end of the summer and salt their carcasses for human food. With winter feeding they could be killed when required, so that there became available a supply of fresh meat instead of salt, with obvious advantages to health. Yet farmers were not only slow to use these crops, they strongly opposed their introduction, terming them 'gentlemen's crops' which would not pay. This strange-sounding denunciation of the humble turnip was based on a certain amount of rationality. It was the richer farmers and landowners who were the first to enclose and try the new methods. It was they who had the capital to do so and could take the risk of loss. Smaller men, working on the margin of their resources, dared not risk experiment. Many years' demonstration by great land-owners (foremost among them Lord Townshend—"Turnip Townshend"—of Norfolk) were needed to convince the farmers of the practicability of turnips, clover, and even potatoes.

Besides new crops the replacement of the old crude methods of husbandry was essential to agricultural progress. To this again opposition was fierce and unreasonable. Jethro Tull, another 'gentleman farmer,' was the principal teacher. He learned to distinguish good seeds from bad and to sow in straight lines, with the seeds at uniform depth. But when he required his labourers to do likewise, rather than use so new and strange a method they struck in a body. To overcome this setback Tull set to work and invented the first drill for the planting of seeds. Tull also taught the necessity of keeping the earth between the rows of plants well raked so that air and moisture could penetrate to the roots. He experimented with manures. He improved drainage methods. These principles and others he laid down in his book *Horse-hoeing Husbandry*, published in 1733. Though Tull's methods were at first derided, his principles were ultimately responsible for a wide-spread improvement in tillage.

While the benefits of the new husbandry were being demon-strated by Tull, Robert Bakewell was experimenting with scientific stock-breeding. Taking advantage of the improved feeding which root crops and clover provided, and practising in-and-in breeding, he nearly trebled the weight of sheep and lambs and doubled that of beeves.

But the knowledge of improved methods possessed by a few men was not sufficient to ensure a revolution in agricultural technique. In an age when communications were so bad that Kensington was for part of the year virtually cut off from London one part of Britain often literally did not know what other parts were doing, and news of improved methods of tillage and of new crops took long to reach isolated country districts; and then it had to contend with the conservatism of the open-field farmer. Adequate scientific instruction in the new methods was generally impossible. One of the great educators and popularizers was Arthur Young, who in 1767 set out on a series of horseback journeys through the country, and in his published *Tours* gave detailed accounts of agricultural conditions. In 1784 he began the publication of the *Annals of Agriculture* in order to circulate information. He created farmers' clubs and agricultural societies, sponsored ploughing matches and agricultural shows. In 1793 further assistance was given to agriculture by the foundation of the Board of Agriculture (not, however, a Government department), of which Arthur Young was first secretary. Among other activities the Board published surveys and statistical accounts of agricultural experiments, and appointed lecturers to spread detailed information.

But even the popularization of the new technique was not in itself sufficient to effect an agrarian revolution. Capital was a prime necessity. In agriculture, as in industry, the application of capital was worth while only on a large scale. A necessary concomitant of new methods of farming was therefore a change in the system of landholding. Apart from conservatism or obstinacy on the part of the small open-field farmer, it was useless to talk to him of large-scale improvements which required several hundreds of pounds for their introduction. Arthur Young and other agricultural reformers recognized this, and repeatedly urged that the open-field system must go. And go it did before the twin requirements of a growing population which had to be fed and a landlord class which desired profit.

Thus agriculture had its eighteenth-century revolution. The process was piecemeal; its speed varied from county to county and from village to village, but on the whole it was slow and uncertain. Until the third decade of the nineteenth century there was more crude farming than scientific. It was not until the end of the thirties that the period of 'high farming' began.

(b) THE DESTRUCTION OF THE PEASANT VILLAGE

The Agrarian Revolution was economically justifiable: its social effects were disastrous. Scores of thousands of peasants suffered complete ruin. The small farmer, the cottager, the squatter, were driven off the soil, and their cottages were often pulled down. The land they had worked was enclosed, and became part of the park or plough-land of a large estate. Thus the English peasant village was destroyed, and the countryside became as Goldsmith described it in *The Deserted Village:*

> Ill fares the land, to hastening ills a prey,
> Where wealth accumulates, and men decay:
> Princes and lords may flourish, or may fade;
> A breath can make them, as a breath has made;
> But a bold peasantry, their country's pride,
> When once destroyed, can never be supplied.

Enclosure was generally set in train by petition to Parliament for permission to enclose. Such a petition need bear one signature only. Thereupon a Bill of Enclosure was read twice in the House of Commons and then turned over to a Committee. If the Committee reported favourably the Bill became law, and Commissioners proceeded to supervise the enclosure of the land in question.

The crucial point of the procedure was, it is clear, the Committee. Yet, following the usual practice of the time, the Committee consisted of one of the Members who had sponsored the Bill, such Members as he chose from the House, and others connected with the county concerned or adjacent counties. Consisting mostly of interested parties, the Committee generally reported favourably upon enclosure if three-quarters to four-fifths of the *property* concerned approved the project. Thus a few big landowners could override the wishes of a large number of small farmers.

The report of the Committee was followed by the Enclosure Act and the Commissioners took over. Far from being appointed as guardians of the interests of the small land-holders threatened by enclosure, these consisted of a representative of the lord of the manor (until 1801 the lord himself could act as Commissioner), a representative of the tithe-owner, and a representative of the majority—in *value*, not in *numbers*—of the owners. These Commissioners, "vested with despotic power," as Arthur Young bears witness, thus represented the very people who had introduced the Bill.

What could the poorer landholders do against the determination of these more substantial neighbours to enclose the land? After 1774 it became legally necessary to post on the church doors of parishes concerned notices of proposed enclosures; before that date it might happen that a man knew nothing of an enclosure scheme until Commissioners arrived to eject him from his land. The posting of a notice, however, was little more than a formality, since the promoters had made their arrangements long before. The poorer landholders could attend a public meeting and protest—but words had little effect. They could riot—but their opponents commanded superior force. They could petition the House of Commons, but this was an expensive and lengthy process, and the petition more often than not laid aside by the House. Almost the only anti-Enclosure petitions which had effect were those few which came from wealthy interests.

In 1801, 1836, and 1845 General Enclosure Acts were passed. Their aim was to facilitate and cheapen the process of enclosure, and they were consequently opposed by attorneys and other small officers who made money out of the process. The 1801 Act applied chiefly to commons. That of 1836 applied to open fields, and allowed two-thirds of the farmers, in number and value, to nominate Commissioners and enclose, or seven-eighths in number and value to enclose entirely on their own account. The Act of 1845 replaced the Parliamentary Committee who examined Enclosure Bills by Enclosure Commissioners, who, instead of sitting at Westminster, proceeded to the spot. Each year the Enclosure Commissioners presented their findings to Parliament in the form of a General Bill for passage into law.

The result of enclosure varied with the classes concerned. The squire was able to consolidate his holdings, adding to them the land of ejected tenants and probably stretches of common land and waste. The larger freeholders generally maintained their claims and often increased their holdings. With the smaller freeholders, however, the story was different.

An Enclosure Bill could not drive a freeholder off the land, because he had a legal claim to his holding. There were, however, aspects of the enclosure which hit him hard. First he had to pay his share of the expenses of enclosure, which was a costly process, varying from about £200 to nearly £5000. If he had insufficient money he had to sell the plot of land awarded him —he had to pay for the privilege of being ruined. If he survived this first blow he had to pay for the hedges and fences which every owner was compelled to make round the new fields; if he could not do so the land would be sold or mortgaged. If he managed to cling to his freehold he found himself deprived of the fallow and stubble pasture, and of the common grazing land and waste, almost as indispensable to him as the land he cultivated. On those pastures he had perhaps kept a cow or two, or a few geese or poultry. Now he could do so no longer. Similarly he lost the rights of cutting fuel and turf from the commonable waste and woodland.

The fortunes of the small freeholders who sold out varied. Some became tenant farmers, renting land instead of farming their own. Though many were compelled by sheer hardship to do this, some found it profitable to sell their small holding and rent a larger acreage, where rationalized methods could more economically be practised. Others who sold out abandoned the country, and put the proceeds of the sale into an industrial concern. Very many realized too little for either of these alternatives, and were forced to work either as labourers on the lands they had once owned or as 'hands' in one of the new factories. Some emigrated. Some sought the alehouse, and in desperation drank the small proceeds of the land of their fathers.

The leasehold tenant was in a position similar to the freeholder, but his rights were even more difficult to establish.

Finally there were the cottagers and squatters. Their rights depended upon custom, not law, and were rarely considered. Like the others, they lost their rights of waste and woodland and, in addition, the ancient customary right of gleaning. Their cottages, being built on the waste, were generally pulled down. Only when a detailed statement in writing, and in exact legal form, was made within a certain time to the Commissioners did the question of customary rights arise. But the ignorant and probably frightened cottagers, mostly illiterate, were generally unable to conform to such a requirement. In most cases they lost their customary rights and their home.

In addition the little 'village bureaucracy' was swept away

All those people whose livelihood had been provided by the communal life of the open-field village were no longer wanted —the common shepherd, the chimney sweeper, the pinder, who had charge of the pound.

There was resistance, bitter and often violent—in the case of Otmoor, near Oxford, long and determined. But all to no purpose. The ruling class rode roughshod over the peasants. Land became concentrated into fewer hands, and the great estate took the place of peasant farms. Farming was rationalized by capitalistic methods. Technique was improved, output increased, profits rose, rents soared. But the peasants were destroyed. A landless proletariat was created, divorced from the land, owning no means of production, often workless as well as landless.

The condition of the farm labourer was meantime worsening. He no longer lived on the farm and ate at the board of the farmer. This was partly because many farmers were becoming 'gentlemen,' building themselves parlours in which their wives and daughters drank tea instead of working in dairy or kitchen. The 'living-in' system also declined, because in a period of rising prices the farmer preferred to pay his servants in money rather than in board and lodging—especially since the labourers were prodigious eaters. "Why," asked Cobbett, "do not farmers now *feed* and *lodge* their work-people as they did formerly? Because," he answered, "they cannot keep them *upon so little* as they give them in wages."

The wages of agricultural labourers fell to less than 8s. a week. Their condition was pitiful. Having no land, they could now obtain neither eggs, meat, nor milk by keeping poultry, pigs, or cows, nor grow vegetables or cereals. They had to buy food at the shops, where prices were high. They could buy so little that numbers died outright of starvation. Their chief diet was bread and tea.

They could not even keep themselves warm. Many died of cold. They had no money for clothes. As a clergyman wrote, "It is but little that the belly can spare for the back." And they had lost the right to take fuel from the waste land, now enclosed—a hardship which had the further effect of preventing many of them from cooking the little food they were able to obtain.

To crown all, the Settlement Laws prevented an **English**

worker from leaving the village where he was settled unless provided with a certificate that the parish accepted full responsibility for him should he become chargeable to the rates. Settlement was determined by birth; sometimes, though with difficulty, by residence. Thus, as was said in 1851, by "the Settlement Laws, 15,535 parishes were made the gaols of their own poor people, and fortresses against all others."[1] An Act of 1795 amended the law so that a man was not removable until he actually became chargeable. Before that date he could be removed directly he appeared in a village not his own. The Act of 1795 allowed, for example, the countryman to go to work in the factory town in times of brisk trade. But when trade slumped he was promptly passed back to the parish where he was 'settled,' to add to the sum of confusion and destitution in the countryside.

What then could the agricultural labourers do? They could die; many did. Many resorted to the same expedient as the young man breaking stones by the road in Surrey. When asked how he could live upon half a crown a week his answer was simple: "I don't live upon it. . . . I *poach*."

Poaching was such an obvious and tempting solution to his problems. In preserved woods he could catch glimpses of the carefully protected birds and animals, destined for a barbarous 'sport,' which could save his family from starvation. This game, preserved for the amusement of wealthy landowners, was by the Game Laws protected from the half-starved labourers who wanted it for food. Landowners the annual value of whose land exceeded £100, tenants with leases for life who paid a rent of at least £150 a year, the sons or heirs apparent of esquires or persons of higher rank, were permitted to shoot game. Others were termed poachers if they tried to catch a hare for the stewpot of a starving family.

These poachers were unemployed men, agricultural labourers, miners, ribbon-weavers. Sometimes they worked in gangs organized by men who served the London market. Though the law forbade the sale of game, fashionable London regularly bought it from the poulterers. The poulterers got part of their supplies from poachers. While the fashionable world thus condoned the practice of poaching, the half-starved labourers

[1] Quoted by S. and B. Webb, *English Poor Law History: The Last Hundred Years*, vol. i, p. 348.

who joined a gang for the sake of the money they could not otherwise earn risked life and limb and liberty in defiance of the law their patrons helped to make. When it became clear that in face of the misery of their condition even the ferocity of the Game Laws could not deter able-bodied Englishmen from poaching, English gentlemen scattered over the great estates man-traps and spring-guns to mutililate the limbs and break the spirits of men made desperate, but not cowed, by hunger.

Sentences for poaching convictions included imprisonment, whipping, hard labour, transportation, and death. To be caught with a gun when poaching meant fourteen years' transportation. To be convicted of violence meant death by hanging. The fact that the local magistrates were themselves the very landowners who delighted in hunting and shooting assured the poacher that he would find little mercy. Only when a case got as far as quarter-sessions, where a jury had to be impanelled, had poachers a chance of getting fair treatment. The victims were typified by the brothers Lilley. The elder was twenty-eight, with a wife and two children. He was unable to find work, and was given 7s. a week relief, out of which he had to pay three guineas a year rent. His unmarried brother, aged twenty-two, received for his work 6d. a day. Convicted of firing on and wounding a keeper while poaching, the two brothers were hanged in the spring of 1829.

Efforts to reform the Game Laws broke against the stern front of the 'sportsmen' who bred bright-plumaged birds for the pleasure of killing them, and who fought their half-starved labourers with transportation, death, and man-traps. The game thus preserved at the expense of working-men's lives and liberties played havoc with the farmer's crops during its brief spell of pampered life. So

> The merry brown hares came leaping
>   Over the crest of the hill,
> Where the clover and corn lay sleeping
>   Under the moonlight still.
>
> Leaping late and early,
>   Till under their bite and their tread
> The swedes and the wheat and the barley
>   Lay cankered and trampled and dead.

"Turnip Townshend"
School of Kneller
[See p. 25]
National Portrait Gallery

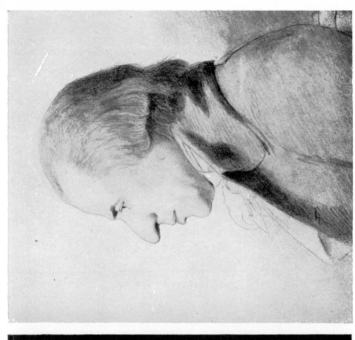
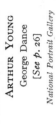

Arthur Young
George Dance
[See p. 26]
National Portrait Gallery

REPLICA OF
HARGREAVES'S
SPINNING JENNY
(1750–57)
[See p. 44]

Crown Copyright.
From an exhibit in the
Science Museum, South
Kensington

And the poacher's widow spoke to the squire:

> There's blood on your new foreign shrubs, squire,
>   There's blood on your pointer's feet;
> There's blood on the game you sell, squire,
>   And there's blood on the game you eat.
>
> You have sold the labouring-man, squire,
>   Body and soul to shame,
> To pay for your seat in the House, squire,
>   And to pay for the feed of your game.
>
> You made him a poacher yourself, squire,
>   When you'd give neither work nor meat,
> And your barley-fed hares robbed the garden
>   At our starving children's feet.[1]

There remained the parish and the Poor Law. In Tudor times the State had energetically organized the poor. Wages were fixed by local magistrates. The destitute were sent to houses of correction and there provided with work. The system broke down under the strain of the Civil Wars, and in the eighteenth century the State was lax in performing its duties to the poor. The stern but strictly regulated house of correction became the almost wholly unregulated mixed workhouse. Here, regardless of age, sex, physical or mental condition, without inquiry into the cause of their destitution or attempt to remedy it, were housed the poor. The horrors of the parish poorhouse have been painted indelibly by Crabbe:

> There, in yon house, that holds the parish poor,
> Whose walls of mud scarce bear the broken door;
> There, where the putrid vapours, flagging, play,
> And the dull wheel hums doleful through the day—
> There children dwell, who know no parents' care;
> Parents, who know no children's love, dwell there!
> Heartbroken matrons on their joyless bed,
> Forsaken wives, and mothers never wed;
> Dejected widows with unheeded tears;
> And crippled age with more than childhood fears;
> The lame, the blind, and, far the happiest they!
> The moping idiot, and the madman gay.
> Here too the sick their final doom receive,
> Here brought, amid the scenes of grief, to grieve,
> Where the loud groans from some sad chamber flow,

[1] Charles Kingsley, from the novel *Yeast*.

Mix'd with the clamour of the crowd below,
Here, sorrowing, they each kindred sorrow scan,
And the cold charities of man to man.[1]

By the end of the eighteenth century, augmented by Enclosure and industrial change, destitution had become a problem
of more severe dimensions than the parish workhouse could
embrace. Occurring at a time when the influence of the French
Revolution was strong, the mass pauperism of the time constituted a serious menace to national security. So humanity
and public interest combined to direct public attention to the
problem of the poor.

It was not, however, the State, but a group of Berkshire
magistrates who provided a solution. At their memorable
meeting on May 6, 1795, in the Pelican Inn, Speenhamland,
near Newbury, they discussed "the insufficiency of the
labourers' wages for the necessary support of an industrious
man and his family." It was at first proposed to fix a minimum
wage. Instead the justices of the peace at the Pelican Inn took
the tragically mistaken decision not to fix wages, but to make
them up out of the rates to an agreed minimum, which should
be the price of three gallon loaves a week for a man, and of
one and a half loaves for his wife and for each child. The
gallon loaf (8½ lb.) cost then about 1s. So a single man was to
receive 3s. a week, a married couple 4s. 6d., and so on. This
was not just their bread allowance. It was their total income
for food, clothing, fuel, rent, and everything else. The plan was
adopted by every county in England except Northumberland.
Although never receiving the sanction of law, the Speenhamland system received the stamp of common acceptance.

The check to unemployment caused by the Napoleonic wars
served to obscure for a few years the worst features of the
scheme. After the wars unemployment figures again soared,
and the numbers on relief grew, though it was not until the
Poor Law Commissioners made their famous Report in 1834
that there was revealed the extent of the degradation caused
by the Speenhamland system.

Thus in the process of the Agrarian Revolution—tragically
and unnecessarily—the English peasantry were destroyed, with
scarcely a hand raised to help them. The Poor Law, the Law

[1] *The Village*, Book I.

of Settlement, the Game Laws, as well as Enclosure itself, combined with a disregard of the condition of the poor to depress the agricultural labourer into virtual serfdom. Apart from two brief flickers of hope, it would be a century before the agricultural workers again lifted their heads.

SELECT BIBLIOGRAPHY

ASHLEY, W. J.: *The Economic Organization of England* (Longmans, 1914).

CHAMBERS, J. D. AND MINGAY, G. E.: *The Agricultural Revolution, 1750–1880* (Batsford, 1966).

ERNLE, LORD: *English Farming, Past and Present* (Longmans, 1912; revised edition, 1961).

FUSSELL, G. E.: *The Farmer's Tools, 1500–1900* (Melrose, 1952).

——: *The English Rural Labourer from Tudor to Victorian Times* (Batchworth Press, 1949).

HAMMOND, J. L. AND B.: *The Village Labourer, 1760–1832* (Longmans, 1911).

MARSHALL, J. D.: *The Old Poor Law, 1795–1834* (Studies in Economic History, Macmillan, 1968).

MINGAY, G. E.: *Enclosure and the Small Farmer in the Age of the Industrial Revolution* (Studies in Economic History, Macmillan, 1968).

ORWIN, C. S. AND C. S.: *The Open Fields* (Oxford University Press, 1938; third edition, 1967).

ORWIN, C. S.: *A History of English Farming* (Nelson, 1949).

CHAPTER II

THE INDUSTRIAL REVOLUTION

(a) THE ECONOMIC CHANGES

THE second series of changes which gained momentum in the second half of the eighteenth century were those associated with the Industrial Revolution.

Until the middle of the eighteenth century woollen manufacture was England's chief industry. It was practised in the West Riding of Yorkshire, where cloths of medium quality were produced; in East Anglia, where coarser fustians were made; and in the South-west of England, which specialized in fine, good-quality cloth.

Originally the weaving of cloth had been carried on in the homes of the people for household needs. But the stage was soon reached when the cloth was taken to market and sold for use in other parts of the country or for export. So important did the export of woollen cloth become that the industry was closely regulated. The export price of cloth was fixed as early as the tenth century, and special measures were taken to prevent the export of the raw wool.

In the eighteenth century production in the West Riding and East Anglia was still in the hands of small masters. They produced the cloth with the help of their families and their neighbours, and themselves rode off to market it at the nearest town. It was near Halifax that Daniel Defoe found, in the early eighteenth century, the busy community of domestic workers which so impressed him. Each of the more prosperous of these manufacturers kept one or two horses to fetch his wool and his provisions from market and to carry back the finished product. On the two or three pieces of enclosed land round his house he kept a cow or two and grew his vegetables. In one of the larger houses Defoe saw "a house full of lusty fellows, some at the dye-vat, some dressing the cloths, some in the loom . . . all hard at work." Often the spinning was done by another family, and in the smaller cottages Defoe saw the women and children all busily carding and spinning—"hardly any thing above four years old, but its hands are sufficient to itself."[1]

An interesting comparison is provided by Samuel Bamford's description of a cotton-weaver's cottage in Lancashire at the end of the century. It consisted, he said,

> of one principal room called "the house"; on the same floor with this was a loom-shop capable of containing four looms, and in the rear of the house on the same floor, were a small kitchen and a buttery. Over the house and loom-shop were chambers; and over the kitchen and buttery was another small apartment, and a flight of stairs. The whole of the rooms were lighted by windows of small square panes, framed in lead, in good condition; those in the front being protected by shutters. [Inside] were a dozen good rush-bottomed chairs, the backs and rails bright with wax and rubbing; a handsome clock in mahogany case; a good chest of oaken drawers; a mahogany snap-table; a mahogany corner cupboard, all well polished; besides tables, weather-glass, cornice, and ornaments.[2]

When Bamford wrote the domestic system was in process of being superseded. His uncle, whose house he described, was employed chiefly by a near-by firm. Broadbent's were middlemen from whom the raw material was collected and to whom the finished product was returned. Samuel described his uncle, a typical weaver,

> a stick in his hand, his green woollen apron twisted round his waist, his clean shirt showing at the open breast of his waistcoat, his brown silk handkerchief wrapped round his neck, a quid of tobacco in his mouth, and a broad and rather slouched hat on his head.

Arrived at Broadbent's, they generally found

> some half-dozen weavers and winders, waiting for their turn to deliver in their work and to receive fresh material; and the business betwixt workman and putter-out was generally done in an amicable, reasonable way. . . . If the work were really faulty, the weaver was shown the fault, and if it were not a serious one he was only cautioned against repeating it; if the length or the weight was not what it should be, he was told of it, and would be expected to set it right, or account for it, at his next bearing-home, and if he were a frequent defaulter he was no longer employed.[3]

---

[1] *A Tour through England and Wales* (Everyman), ii, 195.
[2] *Passages in the Life of a Radical and Early Days*, i, 93–94. [3] *Ibid.*, i, 106–107.

In the woollen districts of the South-west a more advanced form of capitalism was already superseding the cottage industry. As the market for woollen cloth expanded the possession of capital and the control of credit became of great importance. The cottage workers had no capital with which to buy large quantities of raw material, nor could they afford to sell the finished product on credit or to market it far from their homes. Middlemen consequently emerged who undertook the function of supplying numbers of workers with raw material, and of marketing the product of numbers of cottage industries. These middlemen thus came between the workers and their raw material on the one hand, and between the worker and his market on the other. Although they fulfilled a useful function, they creamed off a substantial profit, and were much hated. Thousands of pamphlets issued during the Tudor period are a sign of the great outcry against these men who crept, as one writer said, "between the bark and the tree."

By the eighteenth century there were three kinds of capitalist in the woollen industry. The wool-dealer acted as middleman between the grazier and the cottagers who spun and wove the cloth. He procured the raw wool (sometimes advancing money to the grazier), transported it to the cottagers, and gave it out to them on credit. Secondly there was the clothier, who bought the woven cloth from the cottagers and marketed it. Finally there was the man who acted as distributor to the consumers. When he operated in the home market only he was at first known as a 'draper.' When he exported the cloth he belonged to the wealthy company of Merchant Adventurers, who had the monopoly of the cloth-export trade. Here again credit played an important part, the clothier often not receiving his money until the cloth had been paid for by the consumer.

Gradually the second of these classes of middlemen—the clothiers—had taken over the function of the wool-dealer, and to some extent that of the draper, so that the clothiers and the Merchant Adventurers were by the eighteenth century the two chief capitalist groups in the woollen industry.

The clothier was a capitalist engaged in large-scale business. Sometimes he had as many as 800 or 1000 persons working for him.[1] His capital was merchant capital. It was not sunk in factories and plant and machines, but employed in supplying

[1] E. Lipson, *The Economic History of England*, ii, 18.

credit to grazier, worker, and merchant, and in making the necessary transport and marketing arrangements. He bought in advance the wool-clip of a number of graziers. His agents handed out the fleeces to the spinners, collected the yarn from them and redistributed it to the weavers (unless both processes were done in the same family), and finally collected the cloth and took it to market at Blackwell Hall, in London, or sold it to the Merchant Adventurers for export.

The spinners and weavers continued for some time to own the spinning-wheels and looms. But soon a combination of causes deprived them of the ownership of the means of production—they had to rent their looms from the capitalist clothiers. Scattered over the countryside, unorganized in guilds, owning neither the raw materials nor the product, having no access to the market, not even owning the instruments of their trade, the cottage workers were in a precarious position. From independent craftsmen they had become proletarians, or workers who owned none of the means of production, but were paid wages for their work.

Thus, before the Industrial Revolution, a highly organized form of capitalism existed in the woollen industry of the Southwest. It was associated not with industrial capital, but with merchant capital. A few factories existed, but they were of small industrial importance and quite unlike the modern factory. They consisted of a number of looms or spindles collected together in the house of the master or in a shed near by. Their significance lay in the fact that the workers could no longer perform their work at home, but had to congregate in a place owned by the employer.

In another industry, however—the silk industry—there were already half a dozen factories of a modern type. The story of what was probably the first modern factory in England is one of romance and adventure rather than sober industrial history.

The story goes that John Lombe was sent to Italy by his brother Thomas to discover the method of spinning and weaving fine silk, then known only to the Italians, who jealously guarded their secret. John Lombe reached Piedmont in disguise, and by a series of deceptions obtained entrance to a silk factory. He made himself familiar with the construction and working of the machinery, and finally escaped from Italy with plans of the machinery and workmen to assist in its erection, arriving home in 1717. Vengeance followed him, however. Furious at the deception practised, the Italians sent a woman to Derby to make her way into Lombe's confidence and to kill him. It is said that her expedition to England was as successful as John Lombe's journey to Piedmont, and that Lombe died a lingering and agonizing death from poison in 1723. But he had lived to see the establishment in 1719 of his brother's silk factory, which stood on an island in the river Derwent at Derby, and attracted travellers from far afield. By 1765 there were seven such silk mills in England, employing hundreds of people, mostly women and children.[1]

Iron and coal are examples of industries which were capitalist in a different sense by the eighteenth century. Each required heavy expenditure for the actual process of production, and had been capitalist from their inception. Workers in each industry were wage-earners, working for a master, and not themselves owning the forge or the iron-ore or the coalmine. There were also numbers of comparatively small industries, like the soap, brewing, glass, and salt-making industries, which so early as the seventeenth century were becoming capitalist, the small independent master being replaced by the man who owned an expensive plant and employed wage-labour.

Eighteenth-century Britain, nevertheless, was still far from being a country of capitalist enterprise. In only one of the three parts of the country in which the woollen industry was located had the capitalist form developed on a large scale. Cotton was in an intermediate stage. The iron and coal industries employed comparatively few people, and other capitalist enterprises were not typical. The agricultural interest was still dominant, and the handicraftsman was more important than the industrial or commercial capitalist.

It was not until the second half of the eighteenth century that the change towards large-scale industry quickened, becoming so rapid as to appear revolutionary. A number of interconnected causes produced this acceleration. There was a growth of population, creating an increased demand for goods. There was improved transport, making possible the carrying of finished commodities to markets and raw materials to centres of production. There were the great mechanical inventions,

---

[1] E. Lipson, The Economic History of England, ii, 103.

new materials, and improved chemical processes, which quickened and cheapened production. It is useless to try to assign priority to any of these factors; together they comprised the Industrial Revolution.

It was impossible for the roads of the early eighteenth century to carry the materials of an expanding industrial system. Not only had new markets to be served with finished goods, but the new methods of production themselves created a demand for heavy goods, like coal and iron, which could not be carried in quantities by horses over tracks several feet deep in mud. Either roads had to be improved or some other form of highway developed before industry could expand. Sea and river transport had, of course, long been in use. London received her coal by sea from Newcastle, and much of her wheat by sea from East Anglia. Rivers, so far as they were navigable, were important distributing channels, but served part of the country only. One way of improving transport was by widening and dredging the rivers. But more generally useful was found the scheme of digging new artificial waterways, or canals, which could be constructed where they were most needed.

There is no doubt as to the impetus behind the cutting of the canals. The Bridgewater Canal, opened in 1761, was designed to bring the Duke of Bridgewater's coal from Worsley to the cotton town of Manchester. Later the pottery and salt manufacturers of the Midlands financed the extension of this canal to the Mersey and Trent, thus forming the system known as the Grand Trunk Canal. In 1763 the extension of the Bridgewater Canal to Runcorn, at the mouth of the Mersey, was begun. By the time it was finished, ten years later, the canal era was well on the way. In the nineties 'canal mania' was at its height, and by 1830 a network of canals covered the Black Country, the Potteries, Lancashire, and the West Riding of Yorkshire, linking the chief rivers and connecting London with the Provinces. There were, among others, the Grand Junction, linking London with the Midlands; the Oxford Canal, which brought Midland coal to Oxford and other Thames-side towns; the Kennet and Avon, joining Thames and Severn and providing a waterway from the Irish Sea to the North Sea. Along these new highways moved bulky barges with their cargoes, not only of coal and iron and pottery and clay, but of corn and flour and potatoes, the transport charges being a quarter, or less, than they would have been by road.

The canals, with two exceptions (the Caledonian and the Crinan), were entirely private ventures. Canal companies raised loans, financed the construction of canals, received payment from canal-users, and paid the shareholders what dividends they could. The canal companies merely provided the water highway for the transit of goods. They did not themselves do the carrying. Anyone could use the canals who paid the fee. It followed that the people who constructed the canals were interested primarily in their own particular stretch of water, and had little interest in through traffic. As a consequence the canals varied in gauge, depth, level, and many other particulars, and goods had to be many times transhipped in the course of a single journey.

Greatest of the canal-builders was James Brindley. He was foreman to the Duke of Bridgewater, largely illiterate, and in wages received £1 1s. a week. Yet it was Brindley's brains which wrestled with the many problems of canal-construction in a country where there was nobody of experience to give guidance.

Though canal transport had the disadvantages of slowness and troublesome transhipment, its cheapness was the all-important factor, and canals held their own until killed by the railway competition of the thirties. They were the arteries which carried the coal and iron which was the life-blood of industrialism, and which carried the food required by a growing industrial population. Though they were superseded as the blood flowed faster through the industrial system, it was largely their initial service which gave life to the early stages of the Industrial Revolution.

Transport could also be improved by the building of better roads; it was obvious that wheeled vehicles could never travel safely until the roads were properly constructed. The chief difficulty was to fix the responsibility for their improvement and upkeep, neither the Government nor the local authorities being anxious for the task. Parliament attempted to solve the question by settling their maintenance on turnpike trusts. These were companies, generally of local people, who by Act of Parliament became responsible for the construction and

maintenance of a given length of road. They then levied toll
on the traveller by stopping him for a fee at the turnpike gate.
Thus there were no through roads, and within a mile radius
of London alone there were at one time a hundred turnpike
gates. The great service of the turnpike trusts was in their
employment of salaried surveyors and engineers who applied
scientific methods to road construction. Greatest of these were
John Metcalfe—"Blind Jack of Knaresborough"—Thomas
Telford, and John Loudon Macadam. Telford used a system
of firm foundation and drainage. Macadam advocated a strong
surface through which water could not soak to the subsoil.
Parliament in 1827 made him Surveyor General of Roads.

In this way by 1830 there were approximately 22,000 miles
of turnpike road, of which about half was fairly good. Outside
the turnpike trusts, however, there remained five times this
length of road in various degrees of repair under the control of
the parish authorities.

The great era of road-making (1760–1830) coincided with
that of canal-construction. That these are also roughly the
dates of the great mechanical inventions serves to emphasize
the interrelation of transport and industry. Neither could
improve or expand without corresponding changes in the other.
The question of priority is insoluble. The circle was not so
much broken at one point as worn away in many places by a
growth of population and towns and an increasing specialization
of function which induced men to exchange the products of
one locality for those of another.

While the transport of coal and iron was becoming possible
on a large scale, in the textile industry were being introduced
those methods of production for which the coal and iron were
required. It was in the newer industry, cotton, that the
textile inventions made most headway. The older established,
prosperous, and therefore more conservative, woollen industry
was slower to move. The era of inventions was heralded in
1733, when John Kay's method of weaving with a flying
shuttle was made known. Long before Kay's time a device
had enabled the weaver to raise every alternate thread of his
warp, so making a lane through which the shuttle with the
weft thread attached could be passed; after which the alternate warp threads were raised and the weft thread passed

again, so that the weft was actually woven in and out of the warp. If the cloth were wider than the span of a man's arms an assistant had to be employed to stand at the opposite end of the loom and return the shuttle. Kay's invention enabled the weaver to throw his shuttle through the warp and to return it to his hand by jerking a thread with one hand only. It doubled the work that one man could do, made possible wider cloth, and dispensed with the services of an assistant.

The two branches of the industry, spinning and weaving, have a supply-and-demand relationship to each other, equilibrium being achieved when the amount of yarn needed by the weaver equals the amount which the spinner can supply. The textile inventions can be regarded as an attempt to attain this equilibrium on an ever higher level as invention succeeded invention. So when Kay's flying shuttle doubled the amount of cloth a man could weave the demand for yarn increased. As a consequence inventions to improve spinning followed. About four years after Kay's invention Lewis Paul and John Wyatt announced their device of spinning by rollers, a method by which the thread, as it was spun, was both drawn out and twisted at the same time. In this invention was the germ of the present system, which still consists in drawing out and twisting threads in one operation. Neither invention came into general use until about 1760. In the history of invention the important date is seldom the time of the actual announcement, but the year when that discovery is first widely applied. The dates rarely coincide, for people as a whole are loath to take advantage of, and are even hostile to, new methods of production. The workers are suspicious because they fear unemployment, the employers because they fear the loss of money invested in old methods. Kay, for example, met with such opposition in England that he was forced to emigrate to France and seek the protection of the French Government. His case is not exceptional, but typical of many.

Exceptional rather was the spinning jenny, invented by Hargreaves and called after his wife. It could spin many threads at once—at first eight, later eighty. This was introduced in 1767, and immediately adopted all over the country. Arkwright's water-frame, driven by water instead of hand, and Crompton's 'mule,' which combined the jenny and the water-frame, and spun a thread so fine that it could be used for muslin, followed in 1769 and 1779 respectively, but did not win immediate popularity. By this time the spinning-wheels were turning out more yarn than the weavers could use. Then the power loom, driven by water or steam instead of being operated by hand, was introduced by Cartwright in 1785. The two branches of the industry again drew level, and a new temporary equilibrium was achieved.

Two important developments which proceeded side by side with the invention of new methods of spinning and weaving were the use of new power to drive the machinery and of new materials in its manufacture. It was these changes which created the unprecedented demand for coal and iron. Wooden machinery turned by hand or by animals, and later by water, was replaced by iron machinery driven by steam. Coal became doubly important: in the generation of steam and in the smelting of iron.

The question of driving machinery by some force more effective than the human hand and less capricious than wind or animals was solved at first by the use of water-power. The principle of the mill-wheel driven by the mill-stream was applied to machinery on a larger scale. At this period, consequently, the textile industry began to move to the rushing streams of the Pennines and the Derbyshire hills, cotton taking the lead. At the end of the century, cotton again leading, the textile industries were once more changing their location. This time it was from the swift-flowing streams of the countryside to the coal areas. The reason for the second move was that water-power was being supplanted by steam-power. Steam-engines—notably those of Newcomen and later of James Watt —had since the early eighteenth century been used for pumping water from mines, but the vertical movement associated with pumping was inappropriate to machinery, the wheels of which needed to be driven *round*. In 1782 James Watt at last provided a steam-engine with a *rotary* movement, and from that date the application of steam-power to machinery became practicable. Since, to produce steam, coal was necessary, the great industrial centres of Britain henceforth had to be near coalfields.

Wooden machinery could not stand up to the strain of steam, and iron began to replace it. Iron had been smelted by wood until a threatened timber famine caused Abraham Darby, early

in the eighteenth century, to make the experiments which led
to his discovery of smelting with coal. So the use of iron
machinery entailed the bringing together of coal and iron, and
how effective the canals were in this connexion has already
been seen. Since the demand for iron was increasing, further
improvements began to be made in its production. In 1740
Huntsman had made cast steel, and in 1783 Cort and Oliver
Onions simultaneously discovered the method of puddling iron,
a process which increased output fifteen times, as well as improving the product. The fact that two men simultaneously
and independently produced the same invention indicates that
their discovery was no accident, but a response to a definite
need. In 1828 Neilsen introduced a hot-air blast for the
smelting of iron, so reducing the amount of fuel required.

The use of improved methods of spinning and weaving
brought with it also improvements in other branches of the
textile industry—in bleaching, dyeing, printing, finishing—and
this involved a development of chemical processes in which the
great modern chemical industries were born.

The Industrial Revolution, it is clear, was made up of many
strands: the development of transport, of metallurgy, of
engineering, of chemistry, the invention of new machines, and
the harnessing of new sources of power. It is also apparent
that the Industrial Revolution did not burst upon an astonished
world overnight. It was the outcome of a movement begun
centuries earlier when the discoveries of new lands in the
fifteenth and sixteenth centuries opened the possibilities of
increased trade and commerce. In the eighteenth century this
movement gathered speed, until, between about 1760 and
1830, change was so rapid as to deserve the term 'revolutionary.'
There was an expansion of markets, of production, of population. Figures relating to production form one of the simplest
indices of the change. In 1760 about 8000 tons of raw cotton
were being used in British mills; in 1800 about 25,000 tons; in
1830 about 100,000 tons.[1] The output of iron in Great Britain
in 1835 was 1,000,000 tons, as against one-quarter of that
figure at the beginning of the century.[2] The production of coal
in Great Britain in 1830 was nearly four times that of 1770.[3]

[1] Sir John H. Clapham, *An Economic History of Modern Britain*, i, 241.
[2] *Ibid.*, i, 425.   [3] *Ibid.*, i, 431.

THE FIRST STAGE OF THE INDUSTRIAL
REVOLUTION IN GREAT BRITAIN

Year	Consumption of Raw Cotton
1760	8,000 tons
1800	25,000 tons
1830	100,000 tons
	Iron Output
1800	250,000 tons
1835	1,000,000 tons
	Coal Production
1770	6,000,000 tons
1830	23,000,000 tons
	Population, in Millions
1760	8·0
1801	10·5
1831	16·0

Who was buying these great quantities of coal, iron, and cotton goods? The textile industry was, of course, the indirect purchaser of great quantities of coal and iron for the making of machinery, and the direct purchaser of coal to make the steam-power to drive it. Other industries, such as pottery and hardware, were using increasing quantities of coal; and for the great bridges which spanned canal and river much iron was used. Coal was also being more widely used as a domestic fuel. Most of the coal was used in some form or other in the home market until after the repeal in 1834 of the general export duty. The export of unmanufactured iron began, however, to increase rapidly about 1825, 73,000 tons being exported in 1829, 191,000 tons ten years later.[1] But until 1843 the export of machinery was forbidden or possible only under licence, for manufacturers tried to prevent their secrets being known abroad. There were many evasions of the law, however, and much smuggling of machinery and machine parts out of the country. Textiles had a growing market abroad as well as at home.

[1] *Ibid.*, i, 483.

Above all the rapidly increasing population, which grew from an estimated 8,000,000 in 1760 to 10,500,000 in 1801 and 16,000,000 in 1831, absorbed an increasing amount of goods of all kinds, particularly of cotton. In manufacturing areas towns grew at an astonishing rate. Birmingham, Sheffield, Glasgow, the cotton towns of England, all grew more rapidly between 1821 and 1831 than before or since.

In the period 1760–1830, although there was no doubt of the great mechanical development of some industries, change was piecemeal, fluctuating between industry and industry, place and place. The inventions spread slowly and unevenly through the different industries, the pace of development of the fastest, cotton, being by no means typical of industry as a whole. And even in the cotton industry there were still in 1830 an estimated 240,000 hand-looms as against 60,000 power-looms,[1] although spinning was almost entirely a steam-factory operation. Wool was in a less advanced condition, and its weaving still largely a domestic industry. Outside the textile industries manufacture was still mostly carried on in the literal sense of the word—making things by hand; much machinery was still made of wood; railways were still in the future; and, although the first steamship had plied on the Forth and Clyde Canal in 1802, sailing-ships still maintained their supremacy. Mining was affected comparatively slightly by the new technique; the potteries, although developing in skill and organization, owed little to mechanical power; shipbuilding was evolving slowly with the metal engineering industries; boots and shoes were still mostly made by hand on the outwork system, although power-driven machinery was introduced into some boot factories in Kettering. Clothing, hardware, leather, rope-making, cutlery, carpet-making, were still non-mechanized in 1830. When it is remembered that four of the largest occupational groups in the country—agriculture (the largest of all), building, domestic service, and shoemaking—included not a single mechanized industry, it is clear that the extent of the early Industrial Revolution must not be over-emphasized.

Between 1760 and 1830 there was an enormous general increase in production, by far the greatest in those industries

[1] Sir John H. Clapham, *An Economic History of Modern Britain*, i, 72.

RICHARD ARKWRIGHT

After the engraving by J. Jenkins of the portrait by Joshua Wright
[See pp. 52, 53]

By courtesy of the Director of the Science Museum, South Kensington

SAMUEL CROMPTON

After the engraving by James Morrison of the portrait by Allingham
[See p. 53]

REPLICA OF CROMPTON'S MULE (1774–79)

[See p. 53]

THE CROPPERS: SHEARING AFTER RAISING

[See p. 49]

By courtesy of the Director of the Science Museum, South Kensington

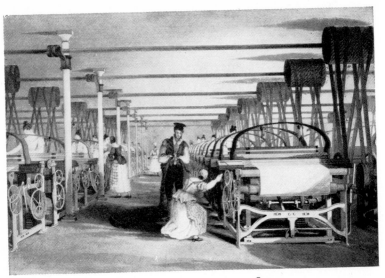

POWER-LOOM WEAVING IN 1835
By courtesy of the Director of the Science Museum, South Kensington

CALICO PRINTING IN 1835
By courtesy of the Director of the Science Museum, South Kensington

which adopted iron machinery and steam-power. But, great as were these increases, they were to be dwarfed by the figures of development subsequent to 1830. Seen in its true perspective, the period 1760–1830 is but the *first phase* of an Industrial Revolution, the period in which the new and startling inventions were made. It was not until the following decades that the full implications of large-scale industry were realized, and only in the second half of the century that Britain ceased to be primarily agricultural and became the world's leading industrial country.

(b) THE OLD INDUSTRIAL CLASSES: LUDDISM

As the mechanization of industry developed the handworkers were left to fight a losing battle against the machine. Some accepted the inevitable, and went to work in the new factories. Those who maintained their independence did so at the cost of a steadily depressed standard of life. Their numbers declined, until by the middle of the nineteenth century comparatively few remained. Some made their protest at the beginning of the century in the Luddite and other movements. Many later marched with the Chartists.

Handworkers naturally saw their enemy in the machine itself, and sought either to prevent its introduction or to destroy it. The first method was tried in Wiltshire and the South-west from 1802 to 1809, when woollen-cloth workers strove in vain to prevent the use of the gig-mill, a machine for raising the nap on woollen cloth. The Luddites, who operated in the North and Midlands from 1811, burned the factories and smashed the machines they hated.

The Lancashire Luddites were hand-loom weavers. They succeeded at the third attempt in burning the steam-loom factory at West Houghton in April 1812. For this four men were hanged. Seventeen were transported for seven years for similar attempts.

In Yorkshire it was the croppers who were the Luddites. These were highly skilled shearmen who cut the nap off the woollen cloth. Against the use of a shearing frame which did the work of four men they protested by going round in bands and smashing the frames with a hammer which they called "Great Enoch." After some success they planned to attack on the night of April 11, 1812, William Cartwright's mill at Rawfolds, Liversedge, where shearing frames were in use. But Cartwright was lying in wait for the Luddites with nine men, including five soldiers, armed with guns. The Luddites numbered about 150, and had a few guns, with some hammers and other heavy weapons. There was a sharp encounter, during which one of Cartwright's soldiers refused to fire—an insubordinate act for which he was afterwards tried by court-martial and sentenced to receive 300 lashes. The Luddites were driven back, leaving two mortally wounded men before the mill. These men, Samuel Hartley, aged twenty-four, and John Booth, aged nineteen, dying slowly and in great agony, their opponents endeavouring to wring from them the names of their fellows, yet died without saying a word which would betray one Luddite. The story of the attack on the mill is told from the employer's standpoint in Charlotte Brontë's *Shirley*. The more human story of the men who made the attack is told by J. L. and Barbara Hammond in *The Skilled Labourer*. An unsuccessful attempt was subsequently made on Cartwright's life, and on April 28 William Horsfall, of Marsden, another manufacturer who used shearing-frames, was shot and killed by four men as he rode home from market.

For the Luddite risings in Yorkshire fourteen men were hanged, including four for the attack on the mill. The faith and loyalty of Booth and Hartley had not been universal. But of the murderers of Horsfall not one was ever discovered.

In Nottingham, Leicestershire, and Derbyshire Luddism assumed a slightly different form, though it was from here that the movement started and derived its name. These Luddites were stockingers working on hand-frames in their own homes. The industry had become capitalist in the sense that several big masters had emerged, owning many hundreds of frames for which the workers paid rent. In 1810 the master hosiers, in face of a trade depression, began to lower wages and to make their stockings on wider frames. The wider material was not shaped in the making, but cut up afterwards and sewn into stockings. This inferior product, known as a 'cut-up,' was much resented by the stockingers, for it lowered both their reputation and their wages; so bands of them went round smashing up frames which made 'cut-ups' or whose owners underpaid their stockingers. They issued letters signed by "King

Lud," or "Ned Lud," and so gave the movement of machine-breaking its name. In nearly a year, from March 1811 to February 1812, they broke over a thousand frames, but only by accident touched one of a friendly master. Sympathy with them was general. The frames being in private houses, it was easy to break them, and with the help of the householder to get away at the back or over the roof-tops. There were no executions for machine-breaking in Nottinghamshire, but seven young men, including two of sixteen and two of seventeen years of age, were sentenced to transportation for seven or fourteen years.

In its efforts to stem Luddism the Government used spies, provocative agents, police, cavalry, infantry, and yeomanry, and in 1812 raised the penalty for frame-breaking from fourteen years' transportation to death by hanging. During the debate in the Lords on this Bill Lord Byron made his maiden speech —an impassioned attack on the Bill and defence of the workers. The attacks of the workmen, he said,

> have arisen from circumstances of the most unparalleled distress: . . . nothing but absolute want could have driven a large, and once honest and industrious, body of the people, into the commission of excesses so hazardous. . . . You call these men a mob. . . . Are we aware of our obligations to a mob? It is the mob that labour in your fields and serve in your houses, that man your navy, and recruit your army, that have enabled you to defy all the world, and can also defy you when neglect and calamity have driven them to despair. . . . I have traversed the seat of war in the peninsula, I have been in some of the most oppressed provinces of Turkey, but never under the most despotic of infidel governments did I behold such squalid wretchedness as I have seen since my return in the very heart of a Christian country. And what are your remedies? After months of inaction, and months of action worse than inactivity, at length comes forth the grand specific, the never failing nostrum of all state physicians, from the days of Draco to the present time . . . death. . . . Is there not blood enough upon your penal code, that more must be poured forth to ascend to Heaven and testify against you? . . . Are these the remedies for a starving and desperate populace?[1]

The Lords considered that the Bill *was* the remedy, and proceeded to pass it.

[1] February 27, 1812 (Hansard, xxi, 966–972).

(c) THE NEW INDUSTRIAL CLASSES

While the handworkers were being slowly superseded the new order was producing other classes. There were the owners of the new factories, the inventors of the new machinery, the investors and speculators, and the men, women, and children who worked in the factories.

The new employers, who adventured with new methods of production and obtained profits far exceeding the wildest dreams of earlier generations, were mostly men with the acquisitive instinct highly developed. But they were not successful capitalists *because* they had strong acquisitive instincts. There is no reason to believe that this particular characteristic was more developed in Richard Arkwright than in "Jack of Newbury," though the former amassed the larger fortune. But in the nineteenth century the circumstances were favourable to an unprecedented expansion in which man's acquisitive instinct could be given full play. Generally it was not the big landowners and the capitalist clothiers of the South-west who were the first to seize the opportunities offered. The men who built up the first great centres of industry were of a different type—'self-made.' Sometimes, like Richard Arkwright, they exploited a series of wealthy partners; sometimes, like James Watt, they found a partner willing to link wealth and business ability with their own impecunious and unbusinesslike genius. Many of these new industrialists came from families of farmers or handicraftsmen. Some were of the small yeoman type. The grandfather of Sir Robert Peel, the Prime Minister, farmed his own land and produced woollen stuffs and cotton goods in his own house. His son, concentrating on industry, made his fortune in a few years, bought for £132,000 the double-seated Parliamentary constituency of Tamworth, became Member of Parliament, and was awarded a baronetcy for financial help given to the Government during the Napoleonic wars.

William Radcliffe's family was driven off the land and nearly ruined by Enclosure, and consequently turned to weaving. William used his practical knowledge and scanty savings to such account that in a few years he was employing over a thousand weavers. In 1780 Joshua Fielden was a typical peasant, working the family holding. He set up two or three looms in his house; then he brought some spinning jennies and set his family to work them. By 1800 he owned a five-storied factory, and his son became not only the owner of works which were among the largest in the world, but Member of Parliament.

Robert Owen was apprenticed to a draper in Stamford. At the age of twenty he was manager of one of Manchester's largest factories, and finally became partner in the great Scottish mills of New Lanark. Arkwright was a barber who became a wealthy factory-owner, was knighted and made sheriff of his county.

The engineers and inventors were mostly practical, self-educated men like George Stephenson, the son of a colliery fireman. Hargreaves and Crompton were practical craftsmen, Brindley was illiterate. In the welter of fortune-making the inventor rarely prospered like the business-man. Certainly all successful business-men were not bad, nor all inventors good. Owen and Fielden alone dispose of that generalization. Yet there was a general difference between the two types. Arkwright stands out as typical of the unscrupulous, self-made *entrepreneur* who exploited other people's ideas, and combined them with his own powers of leadership and business organization to make a fortune. Samuel Crompton, the inventor of the 'mule,' represents the other type. In his father's house near Bolton he worked from 1744 to 1779 perfecting the invention whose product combined extreme fineness of thread with strength. Though he had little business ability, he started a small cloth workshop. Neighbouring manufacturers, jealous of the fineness of his cloth, tried to discover his methods, spying upon him by placing ladders up to his windows and boring holes in his walls. Crompton *gave* his invention to the world, but, although the manufacturers who benefited from it had promised him compensation, he died penniless. A French historian commented on the portraits of the two men:

> Arkwright, with his fat, vulgar face, his goggling, heavy-lidded eyes . . . the vigorous line of the brow . . . the cunning lips. . . . Crompton, with his refined and emaciated profile, his fine forehead . . . the austere line of his mouth. . . . Together they represent invention and industry, the genius which creates revolutions and the power which possesses itself of their results.[1]

People such as the Peels, Arkwright, Wedgwood, Boulton, and Watt were not only the instruments of the Industrial

[1] P. Mantoux, *The Industrial Revolution in the Eighteenth Century*, p. 242.

Revolution, but were reared up on its back to form a new and powerful class of industrial capitalists. Their position was bound up with the prosperity of industry, and their importance grew as industry expanded. Later in the century they were to attain political power and mould the policy of the State to their will.

Meantime what of the factory workers whose labour helped to build up the fortunes of the industrial middle class? When factories used water-power and were built in the country labour was scarce. But since machines needed little skilled attention the cheap labour of children could be used. So the mill-owners entered into contracts with the Poor Law authorities of the towns for supplies of pauper children between the ages of seven and twenty-one. The Poor Law officials were only too glad to get rid of their child paupers, whom they were bound by law to apprentice, and contracts were made for batches of fifty, eighty, or a hundred to be sent to the cotton mills. In one case at least the stipulation was included that for every twenty children one idiot child should be taken. Generally these pauper apprentices travelled long distances from London and the South, where the pauper population was largest, to the North. If a mill closed the unwanted children were simply tipped out on to the roads and left alone to make their way as best they could. To the cotton master they were as much his property as the machines they tended. Kind treatment did not pay. It was more economical to work one batch out and then get another. Frequently, therefore, the children worked in shifts of twelve, fifteen, or more hours, so that work, while the mill-stream ran, never ceased. This had the additional advantage of reducing the number of beds required. As one lot of children, half asleep, were forced out to the factory others dropped into their still warm beds.

The factories themselves, especially the smaller ones, were generally dirty, unhealthy, ramshackle affairs. The apprentice houses in which the children were lodged—usually long, low sheds adjoining the factory—were worse. Both were entirely free from outside supervision or regulation. More often than not they were dens of fever and vice. Both sexes and all ages up to twenty-one were indiscriminately herded together in the 'prentice houses, with resultant depravity and degradation.

The stories of the treatment of the children while at work are sickening. They suffered constant flogging to keep them awake. One boy as a punishment was hung by his wrists over moving machinery, so that he was compelled to hold his legs up to avoid mutilation. Some of the apprentices tried to escape. One girl managed to do so by throwing herself into the mill-stream. Another, a girl of eighteen, was not so fortunate. She was pursued by her employer on horseback, captured, dragged back, flogged, and sentenced to work for a longer period than the original term of indenture. Many apprentices died of fever and ill-treatment. On Sundays those who were not cleaning the machinery were sent to church, so that it might appear that Christian training was not lacking.

A severe outbreak of putrid fever at Radcliffe in 1784 (one of many) brought the condition of the apprentices before the public eye. But it was not until 1802 that Sir Robert Peel the elder, the wealthy manufacturer who employed nearly a thousand of these children, was brought by Robert Owen to admit that he himself was shocked by the condition of the children in his own mills. Peel then introduced the Health and Morals of Apprentices Act. This Act limited hours of work to twelve, forbade night work, and provided for instruction in reading, writing, and arithmetic. Boys and girls were to sleep in separate rooms, and not more than two to a bed. Inspection was to be by a magistrate and a clergyman appointed by the local justices of the peace. This method of inspection proved totally inadequate, since the inspectors were generally well disposed to the mill-owner, if not factory-owners themselves. An Act of 1816 was likely to have been more effective. This prohibited the apprenticing of pauper children more than forty miles from their parish. Since most factories in water-power days were remote from towns where there was the biggest pauper population, this Act might have ended the feeding of factories with the parish poor. The interesting point, however, is that efforts to pass it earlier had failed, and that it was not passed until other factors had ended the misery of these apprentices. It was not legislation, but the change from water- to steam-power, which solved the problem of the factory apprentices by transforming it into one of free-labour children living with their parents in the factory towns. Their story comes a little later. The initial impact of the Industrial

Revolution was upon three groups of people—the handi-craftsmen, flung high and dry between the tides of the old and the new industry; the manufacturers who rose to wealth, and whose sons would ride to power, on the back of the Industrial Revolution; and the little pauper apprentices, whose labour guided the machinery of the early stages of industrialism.

SELECT BIBLIOGRAPHY

ASHLEY, W. J.: *The Economic Organization of England* (Longmans, 1914).

ASHTON, T. S.: *The Industrial Revolution, 1760–1830* (Oxford University Press, Home University Library, 1948).

BAMFORD SAMUEL: *Autobiography*, vol. i, *Early Days*, vol. ii, *Passages in the Life of a Radical*, edited with an introduction by W. H. Chaloner (Frank Cass, 1967).

BEALES, H. L.: *The Industrial Revolution, 1750–1850* (Longmans, 1928).

CLAPHAM, SIR JOHN H.: *An Economic History of Modern Britain*, vol. i, *The Early Railway Age, 1820–1850* (Cambridge University Press, 1930).

HADFIELD, CHARLES: *British Canals* (Phoenix House, 1950).

HAMILTON, H.: *The Industrial Revolution in Scotland* (Oxford University Press, 1932).

HAMMOND, J. L. AND B.: *The Skilled Labourer, 1760–1832* (Longmans, 1919).

——: *The Town Labourer, 1760–1832* (Longmans, 1917)

HARTWELL, R. M.: *The Industrial Revolution in England*, Historical Association Pamphlet No. G 58 (The Historical Association, 1966; reprinted 1972).

KAY, F. G.: *Pioneers of British Industry* (Rockliff, 1952).

KNOWLES, L. C. A.: *The Industrial and Commercial Revolutions in Great Britain during the Nineteenth Century* (Routledge, 1921).

MANTOUX, P.: *The Industrial Revolution in the Eighteenth Century* (J. Cape, 1928).

PEEL, FRANK: *The Risings of the Luddites, Chartists and Plug-Drawers* (1880; fourth edition, Frank Cass, 1968).

PINCHBECK, I.: *Women Workers and the Industrial Revolution, 1750–1850* (Routledge, 1930).

RAISTRICK, A.: *Dynasty of Ironfounders: The Darbys and Coalbrookdale* (Longmans, 1953).

WEBB, S. AND B.: *The Story of the King's Highway* (Longmans, 1913)

CHAPTER III

WAR AND DEPRESSION

(a) ECONOMIC CONDITIONS

In the years when the Agrarian and Industrial Revolutions were gathering momentum Britain was involved in three wars. The Seven Years War ended in 1763; the War of American Independence lasted from 1775 until 1783. Ten years later Britain again went to war with France. The Revolutionary and Napoleonic wars lasted until 1815. For more than twenty vital years British economic development was distorted by the need for fighting France.

War gave an artificial stimulus to industry. British cotton and British leather clothed and shod the British Army and the armies of the Coalition, while even the armies of Napoleon sometimes marched in British cloth. Demands for armaments kept the heavy industries feverishly busy. Prices rose, and, though it helped the manufacturer, this was doom to the workman; and even the manufacturer found his profits partially offset by the heavy war taxation. Britain subsidized the Coalition on land. At sea, with great energy and at great expense, she fought Napoleon virtually alone. The attention of thinking men, which might otherwise have been turned to the problems of industry, was set on the war. It was Britain's misfortune, and particularly her workers' misfortune, that the Industrial Revolution and the war with France so nearly coincided.

Upon British agriculture fell the task of providing food for the population, which, in spite of the war, was growing rapidly. Not only was Europe too preoccupied to export corn, but Napoleon attempted to fight with economic as well as military weapons, and by the Continental System tried to dislocate the whole of Britain's economy, and to deprive her of food in the process. The result was a virtual monopoly for British agriculture, which, with the higher demand, caused the price of British corn to reach unprecedented heights. Between 1760 and 1792 it had varied between an average of 28s. and 59s. a

57

quarter. In the following twenty-three years of rapidly rising population, industrial revolution, and foreign war it fluctuated between an average of 43s. and 126s. a quarter.[1]

Land of every description, whether suitable or not, was ploughed up to meet the demand for corn. As a result of the "war enclosure fever" over 1500 Enclosure Acts were passed between 1795 and 1812.[2] Marsh and waste were reclaimed; grass was hastily converted into arable; much unsuitable land was put under the plough. As the demand for land increased rents soared. Napoleon, as Byron pointedly told in *The Age of Bronze*, proved to be the patron saint of the agricultural interest:

> his vices
> Destroyed but realms, and still maintained your prices;
> He amplified to every lord's content
> The grand agrarian alchymy, high *rent*.

Consequently the English country gentlemen were

> The last to bid the cry of warfare cease,
> The first to make a malady of peace.
>
> True, blood and treasure boundlessly were spilt,
> But what of that? The Gaul may bear the guilt;
> But bread was high, the farmer paid his way,
> And acres told upon the appointed day.
>
> Safe in their barns, these Sabine tillers sent
> Their brethren out to battle—Why? for rent!
> Year after year they voted cent. per cent.
> Blood, sweat, and tear-wrung millions—why?—for rent
> They roared, they dined, they drank, they swore they meant
> To die for England—why then live?—for rent!

But with peace all was changed. After a brief period of speculative activity the "false and bloated prosperity" of the war, as Cobbett called it, gave way to depression and gloom.

The size of factories and plant had been adapted to temporary conditions. Now they had to be contracted, and the process was painful. Capital, which had been attracted by temporary boom conditions, was left "high and dry, unemployed and wasted." Falling profits and unemployed capital were accompanied by unemployed labour. Returned soldiers and sailors added to the unemployed, depression became

---

[1] Lord Ernle, *English Farming, Past and Present*, pp. 440-441. [2] *Ibid.*, p. 264 n.

general, and stagnation settled upon industry. For a time it seemed as if the Industrial Revolution had been checked in mid-career. With falling profits improvements in iron and steel technique were impossible. The demand created by the war had masked many defects. After the war, when in face of a decreased demand efficiency and cheapness were imperative, the inefficiency and high costs of the heavy industries stood revealed; but the capital necessary to effect improvements was lacking.

Textiles presented the same picture of arrested development. Though cotton-spinning was mainly a steam-factory process, weaving was still largely left to the hand-loom weavers. Their long and slow absorption into the expanding system was made more painful by the dislocation following 1815.

The agricultural position was similar. With peace came large supplies of corn from the Continent. The price of corn fell. Cheap bread—a blessing to consumers—was the nightmare of the farmers. Their profits fell. Tenants could not pay their rents. Insolvency became general. Land that had so easily been ploughed up for arable could not so simply be converted to pasture. Consequently much of it decayed and ran to waste. In the face of falling profits improvements were neglected. In the absence of improved methods of farming, competition with foreign wheat was impossible. The home market was injured by the industrial depression, prices fell still further, the agricultural depression in its turn reacted upon industry, and the vicious circle continued.

Reports of Parliamentary Committees in 1820, 1821, 1822, 1833, and 1836 witness to the serious view of the situation taken by the Government, and the minutes of evidence paint an almost uniformly bleak picture of agricultural despair. In 1833 there was said to be not a solvent tenant in the whole Weald of Sussex and Kent, though rent reductions were considerable. Cobbett reported from Lincoln that the greater part of the farmers in the district, if sold up, would be found to be insolvent.[1] To falling receipts had been added the burdens of debt and mortgage. Savings were exhausted or diminished, improvements in methods of farming and proper care of the soil were impossible, and much land practically abandoned. Sheep-rot added to the distress. Property was

[1] *Rural Rides*, April 19, 1830.

sinking fast into decay. Even reduced rents could not be met. The reluctance to buy or rent land became more marked. As the farmers' returns decreased the burden of numerous rates —the poor rate, the county rate, the highway rate—increased. Even the richer property-owners began to feel alarmed, and the poorer ones were "fast falling into the rank of paupers."

Though the Select Committee of 1833 reported that the agricultural labourers in full employment were better off than in any other period, it admitted much unemployment, and other contemporary writing pictured the labourers' conditions as exceedingly bad. "They are, everywhere, miserable," said Cobbett of the Eastern counties, a married man often earning but 12s. or less weekly.[1] With violent fluctuations in the price of bread, wages seldom bore a just relation to the cost of living. The Poor Law, the Law of Settlement, the Game Laws, were causes of distress more bitter than statistics can show. Emigration, where movement was possible, was resorted to. But, far from improving the situation, the 1833 Committee reported that it was the strongest who left the land or the country, the poorest and least efficient who remained. Cobbett from his own observations reported the same: "It is not the *aged*, the *halt*, the *ailing*; it is not the *paupers* that are going; but men with from £200 to £2,000 in their pocket!"[2] At Hull he watched a farmer embark with his five sons and £1500.[3] So, while property depreciated, those who were able abandoned the soil, and ill-kept land was worked by the least efficient of the labouring population.

The depression was widespread geographically and socially. Even in a "very highly-favoured county" like Suffolk Cobbett found that distress pervaded "all ranks and degrees."[4] It also communicated itself to the county towns, where tradesmen lost their customers, and where the decline of playhouse audiences witnessed to the financial discomfort of the middle classes.[5] "I have come," wrote Cobbett in May 1830, "through the counties of corn and meat and iron and coal, and from the banks of the Humber to those of the Severn I find all the people ... in a state of distress."[6] The only exception, Cobbett found, were the fundholders (holders of war loan). These

---

[1] *Rural Rides*, April 19, 1830.
[2] *Ibid.*, April 13, 1830.
[3] *Ibid.*, ii, 258.
[4] *Ibid.*, March 22, 1830.
[5] *Ibid.* April 19, 1830.
[6] *Ibid.*, May 18, 1830.

were prosperous, but at the expense of the taxpayers. The National Debt had reached the figure of £780,000,000 by 1827,[1] and the already disorganized financial system could manage to meet the interest on it only by increasing the burden on the shoulders of the groaning and expostulating taxpayers. William Cobbett directed some of his best broadsides against the "fundholders who retire to be country squires." He pointed out to people the "absurdity of grumbling at the six millions a year given in relief to the poor, while they were silent and seem'd to think nothing of the sixty millions of taxes collected by the government at London."[2]

The complaints of farmers and landowners were bitter. Wrote Byron:

> The peace has made one general malcontent
> Of these high-market patriots; war was rent!
> Their love of country, millions all misspent,
> How reconcile? By reconciling rent!
> And will they not repay the treasures lent?
> No; down with everything, and up with rent!
> Their good, ill, health, wealth, joy, or discontent,
> Being, end, aim, religion—*rent—rent—rent!*[3]

In these circumstances the landlord Parliament attempted one measure of relief only. It tried to protect the landlords and the farmers by the Corn Law of 1815. This was designed to raise the price of English wheat and preserve the English farmers' monopoly by prohibiting the import of foreign wheat until the price of English had reached 80s. a quarter. With the exception of the landowners and larger farmers, nearly all sections of the population were affected by this deliberate attempt to raise the price of bread. There was furious rioting in Parliament Square while the Bill was being read, but, in spite of fierce opposition outside, it became law. Nevertheless the price of wheat in the next few years was often well below the 80s. maximum, and the landed interest grew restless. The Government therefore substituted a sliding scale for the sharp prohibition at 80s. of the 1815 Corn Law. Then, as the price of corn began again to rise, renewed agitation against the landlords grew. Finally a new sliding scale was fixed in 1828 with a duty of 1s. a quarter when the price of corn was 73s. Between

---

[1] Sir John H. Clapham, *An Economic History of Modern Britain*, i, 318.
[2] *Op. cit.*, March 28, 1830, ii, 232.   [3] *The Age of Bronze*.

1828 and 1831 harvests were bad and corn was imported. In the better years which followed, the price of corn kept low, and the Corn Law agitation died down, while agriculture began to emerge from the depression.

(b) POPULATION

Population meantime, in spite of the war and trade vicissitudes, was growing rapidly. From 10,500,000 in 1801, the year of the first census, it had grown to nearly 12,000,000 ten years later. In 1821 the 14,000,000 mark was passed; there were over 16,000,000 people in Britain in 1831; and by 1851 there would be nearly 21,000,000, the population having doubled itself in half a century.

The growth of population over the country as a whole can be determined by any or all of three factors—the birth-rate, the death-rate, and migration. For long it was held that a high birth-rate was the main cause of the increase from the middle of the eighteenth century, but the figures belie this. Between 1710 and 1810 the birth-rate was slowly rising; it fell slightly to 1840; and then dropped sharply. That it stood relatively high until 1840 is probably connected both with the Speenhamland system of poor relief and with the demand for factory labour. Since the birth-rate fell after 1810, however, it clearly cannot account for the rapidity of the population increase. In this respect the death-rate is more significant. In the middle of the eighteenth century, when the pernicious gin-drinking was at its height, the death-rate was in some years higher than the birth-rate. But from about 1750 the death-rate declined, between 1780 and 1815 falling sharply, in spite of the casualties of the war. The fall was less sharp after 1815, but there was no return to the very high death-rate of the previous century. Statistics for this period are not by any means reliable, yet all sufficiently bear out this trend to make it possible to assign to the falling death-rate the reason for the growth in population during the period of the Industrial Revolution. The third factor, migration, influenced negatively the growth of population, since movement was in the opposite direction, there being considerable emigration from Scotland and some from England in the years 1800–50.[1]

[1] A. Redford, *Labour Migration in England*, p. 12.

The declining death-rate was due to greater personal clean-liness, improved public hygiene, and the development of medical science. It is difficult to conceive the attitude of even cultured people towards elementary personal hygiene in the eighteenth century. Many people who were accustomed to wash their hands and faces regularly rarely washed their bodies. The benefits of soap and water and the necessity for fresh air had to be urged upon unwilling and often hostile citizens. Part of the advance in medical practice in the eighteenth century consisted simply in the successful applica-tion of a few simple rules of hygiene. The famous "cool regimen" which doctors began to advocate was merely the opening of windows to allow the passage of fresh air.

At the same time easily washed and comparatively cheap cotton clothes were replacing heavy and expensive woollens, though women still wore numerous long petticoats and dresses that trailed the dirt. Even women in factories wore the same kind of garments, which were both dirt-traps and a source of danger where there was unfenced running machinery.

Public hygiene was improved, especially in London, by some street-paving, improved drainage, and a better water-supply—though this barely touched the fringe of the problem of cleaning the towns. Attention was also turned to the hospitals, where the sanded floors were filthy, the bed-linen rarely changed, the beds verminous, the patients never washed, and fresh air never permitted. Towards the middle of the eighteenth century the rebuilding of hospitals began. Between 1730 and 1753 Bart's was rebuilt; in 1752 the London Hospital. Cotton bed-fabrics, which could be easily washed, replaced the heavy, never-washed woollens. Iron bedsteads, which resisted germs, replaced the wooden germ-ridden ones. Floors were regularly cleaned, and rules of hygiene applied to patients.

At the same time the dispensary movement was developing. The first dispensary, opened in Red Lion Square in 1769, was for the Infant Poor. The following year the first general dis-pensary was opened. Doctors saw patients at the dispensary and visited them in their homes.

Meanwhile the science and practice of modern medicine was growing. Edinburgh led the way with its famous school of medicine and its infirmary. In London, though there was no organized school of medicine, medical men were putting into practice some of the new ideas. Much of the new knowledge is associated with two men whose attendance upon the Army and the Navy gave them opportunities of observing certain diseases. Sir John Pringle, who became President of the Royal Society, found that dysentery was spread among the troops by inadequate sanitary arrangements. He discovered that marsh-land induced malaria and that fresh air often cured it. James Lind, a Navy surgeon trained at Edinburgh, was led to investigate the causes of scurvy, from which large numbers of sailors suffered on every voyage. Lind traced its cause to lack of fresh meat and vegetables, and found that orange or lemon juice was a certain preventive.

The use of antiseptics and disinfectants, the need for segregation in certain cases, began to be understood. Inoculation and vaccination were advocated, although the latter was not generally introduced into England until the early nineteenth century.

Perhaps the most important development of all concerned the improvements in the science of midwifery. The death-rate of mothers in childbirth and of infants had been extremely high in the early eighteenth century. Between 1730 and 1749 nearly three-quarters of the children born had died before they were five years old.[1] From the middle of the century more maternity hospitals were opened and increased attention given to midwifery. The work of William Smellie in particular was responsible for spreading greater knowledge, and resulted in the training of midwives who regarded their profession as a science. Deaths of mothers in childbirth declined, and between 1810 and 1829 the number of children dying before the age of five years had fallen to less than 32 per cent.[2]

The share of the growth of population borne by some of the towns was startlingly great, and particularly in the manufacturing North. Only London could compare with the rapid growth of Glasgow, Birmingham, Sheffield, Manchester, Leeds, Bradford. The period of most rapid growth was between 1821 and 1831.[3] By 1831 Manchester had 238,000 inhabitants, Leeds 123,000, Liverpool 202,000, Glasgow 193,000.

---

[1] M. Buer, *Health, Wealth, and Population in the Early Days of the Industrial Revolution*, p. 30.

[2] *Ibid.*, p. 30.   [3] Redford, *op. cit.*, p. 54.

CARDING, DRAWING, AND ROVING IN 1835
By courtesy of the Director of the Science Museum, South Kensington

MULE-SPINNING FACTORY IN 1835
By courtesy of the Director of the Science Museum, South Kensington

THOMAS PAINE

After the engraving by W. Sharp of the portrait by Auguste Millière

[See pp. 79–80]

National Portrait Gallery

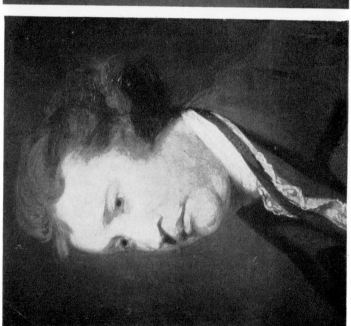

EDMUND BURKE

Sir Joshua Reynolds

[See pp. 79–80]

The growth of towns was caused both by the general growth of population and by immigration from the countryside. The latter was not a direct transfer from agricultural districts to towns, from the South to the North. It was short-distance migration, which proceeded, in spite of the Settlement Laws, in a series of short hops from rural districts to the nearest town. Each industrial centre acted as a magnet which drew immigrants from the districts around. Manchester drew upon North Lancashire, Yorkshire, Cumberland, North Wales; the woollen towns of the West Riding of Yorkshire upon North-east Yorkshire and Lincolnshire; Birmingham upon Staffordshire and Warwickshire. London was the great centre of attraction to the East and South-east, Glasgow attracted Highland immigrants and those from rural Lowland districts. A typical case is one reported by an inhabitant of Glasgow in 1838:

> Taking Glasgow as the centre, there are persons who have come to it from all sides, within a circuit of sixty miles. My father originally came from the Lothians, and had been a country farmer; he was driven out by the improvements in farming, became a mechanic, and settled in Glasgow. . . . When the extinction of small farms took place, and the cottiers were driven in from their agricultural and pastoral employments, they first collected in villages, and then gradually inclined to the large towns, especially to Glasgow, from the Lothians.[1]

Frequently the process seems to have been from village to small county town, from county town to industrial town. Sometimes it continued from town to town.

Census returns show that the growth of towns was not accompanied by a depopulation of the countryside. The outcry against the Speenhamland system pointed to the same conclusion. Though contemporaries like William Cobbett believed that the countryside was being drained by the towns, the fact was that the agricultural population as a whole was growing, although slowly when compared with the growth of towns. Some regions were an exception, and showed a positive decline in population. These were areas of upland pasture or districts where the enlargement or consolidation of farms was marked, such as the Highlands of Scotland, East Wales, Devon, the Chiltern Hills, and Marlborough Downs. Agricultural areas specializing in corn or mixed agriculture, and those

[1] *Ibid.*, p. 57.

where waste land had been enclosed and taken into cultivation, showed increases in population.

Though the spectacular rise in population was in large measure due to a lowered death-rate, which in turn was due to improved medicine and hygiene, the condition of British towns and the public-health record remained shocking. There was probably a deterioration in the early nineteenth century, as fresh people crowded in on the inadequate accommodation provided by existing towns. Then would go up hurriedly the back-to-back houses supplied by the speculative builders for the new factory hands. Then cellars and garrets were filled beyond capacity. Then dirt and vermin and disease spread rapidly. It was not until the thirties and forties of the nineteenth century that these conditions were officially described in the pages of Government Reports, and not until 1848 that an Act of Parliament assumed partial responsibility for the health of the nation.

(c) INDUSTRIAL STRUGGLE: THE COMBINATION LAWS AND CO-OPERATION

The political and insurrectionary activity of the working classes during the Napoleonic wars and the depression which followed won no success.[1] An important industrial victory, however, was achieved by the repeal of the Combination Acts in 1824. By this repeal the workers won the right to form trade unions.

The permanent combination of workmen in a trade union is a product of the Industrial Revolution, though temporary combination is much older. While the guild system lasted conditions were not favourable to permanent trade unionism. The line between employer and journeyman and apprentice was not so rigidly defined as to be impassable. The journeyman became a master. The apprentice, if he did not always marry his master's daughter, was accepted as part of the household. The workman owned his tools. His master frequently worked by his side. The journeymen guilds, which were the precursors of the trade unions, were consequently largely Friendly Societies, providing sick-benefit for their

[1] See Chapter IV.

members and taking part in the festivities of public holidays. Not until a growing capitalism deprived the worker of the tools of his trade, and a growing discrepancy of wealth separated him from his master, did the workman attempt united action with his fellows to preserve his standard of life.

The trade unions which began to be formed in the eighteenth century were still in the direct tradition of the craft guilds. They still looked to the State for protection. Until the middle of the eighteenth century Parliament consisted almost entirely of landowners who had little sympathy with the new industrial and commercial capitalists. When there was a dispute between employers and workers Parliament often supported the workers. When workmen petitioned against low piece-rates, or the introduction of new processes which were reducing their standard of living, or being put off work in time of trade depression, Parliament in some cases ordered wages to be raised, or prohibited or limited the use of new methods, or even commanded the employers to keep their men at work in slack periods. It also empowered magistrates to fix wages for certain industries at the quarter-sessions.

From about 1750 onward a change came over the attitude of Parliament. On the one hand, the Industrial Revolution caused such changes in industrial organization, and together with wars caused such violent fluctuations in prices, that the old system of wage regulation broke down. On the other, landowners were themselves being drawn more into industry and commerce, and began to have the same interests as the general body of employers. Moreover, wealthy manufacturers bought land in order to qualify for election to Parliament, and when there they formed a nucleus of strong opposition to the workers' interests. In consequence workers found it increasingly useless to appeal to the State for protection, and tried instead what their united trade-union efforts might do. The State replied by prosecution under the Conspiracy Acts, and later by special Acts forbidding combination in particular industries. In 1786, when the London bookbinders struck for the reduction of working hours from twelve to eleven, the five leaders were convicted under the law of conspiracy and sentenced to two years' imprisonment.[1] In 1799 two shoemakers of York were convicted of the crime of "refusing to make shoes under a

[1] S. and B. Webb, *The History of Trade Unionism*, p. 79.

certain price."[1] Hatters, papermakers, and shoemakers were among those specifically prohibited from combining.

Finally, under pressure from the employers and the panic aroused by the French Revolution, Parliament in 1799 passed a general prohibition of all trade unions. This notorious Combination Act was hurried through all its stages in both Houses in twenty-four days. As a result workmen had no time to organize petitions against the Act. By its provisions all combinations for increase in wages or decrease of hours, or any meeting for the same object, or any attempt to influence a man to act with this object in view, were forbidden under penalty of three months' imprisonment or two months' hard labour in a house of correction. Even attending a meeting with a similar object, or persuading another workman to do so, or collecting money for the purpose was subject to the same penalties. Moreover, a single magistrate—who might even be the accused's employer —was competent to commit. Yet, in spite of this anomaly, a further clause in the Act aimed at hampering the legal defence of a person charged under it, by prohibiting subscriptions towards his expenses. Appeal against commitment was possible only if the accused could provide surety for £20—a sum well outside the resources of a workman. Technically the Act applied to employers as well as to workmen, but, although many employers' associations existed, there is no case on record of an employer's being prosecuted under the Act.[2]

In the following year there descended on the House of Commons such a deluge of protests and petitions against the Combination Act as could hardly be ignored. This gave the liberal-minded Members their chance, and Sheridan reopened the case for the workers against what he termed a "foul and oppressive" Act. As a result, though the principle of the 1799 Act remained, certain changes were introduced into the 1800 Combination Act. Not one magistrate only, but two, were necessary to secure a conviction; no magistrate who was a master in the trade concerned could act; and certain arbitration clauses were added, by which workmen and employers could name arbiters, and, if these failed to agree, could take the case before a justice of the peace as final arbitrator.

The Combination Acts, as the Hammonds have pointed

---

[1] S. and B. Webb, *The History of Trade Unionism*, p. 80.
[2] *Ibid.*, p. 73.

out,[1] involved an important principle, quite new in the State's industrial legislation. Hitherto in theory, and to some extent in practice, the State regulated industry. Combinations of workmen were unlawful because they challenged this authority. After 1800 it was to protect the authority of the employers, and not of the State, that the law was enforced.

This, then, was the policy, and these were the laws, which made all trade unionists criminals. The nature of the situation was made still clearer a few years later. In 1808 Whitbread's proposal for a Minimum Wage Act was defeated in the Commons. In 1813 and 1814 the Elizabethan laws regulating wages and conditions of apprenticeship were repealed. So the old protection was withdrawn and new safeguards were denied at a time when the State had closed against the workmen the avenue of legal industrial protest. They were left with no alternative but submission or illegal activity. That in many cases they preferred the latter is clear from the numerous prosecutions of workmen under the Combination Acts.

It was chiefly in the new textile industries and among the miners that the most crushing weight of the Acts was felt. The half-literate operatives clung to the idea of combination, but, not daring to assemble openly, developed an underground organization hedged around with secret ritual, mystic oaths, buried records, and midnight meetings in the countryside.

In 1808 despair at the rejection of the Minimum Wage Bill drove the cotton operatives of Lancashire into strike action which, in spite of the Combination Acts, was temporarily successful. In 1810 the mining districts of the North of England, in 1818 the textile districts again, were convulsed with strikes, but the outbursts were short-lived.

The effect of the Combination Acts on the skilled and better-organized trades, such as shoemakers, compositors, and shipwrights, was less distressing. Their trade unions did not go underground, but instead were organized with greater care and efficiency, their members showing a commendable degree of audacity in continuing to stake their claims and refusing to suffer encroachment. Journeymen shoemakers of Lombard Street refused to work in face of a threat of half-pay, and were sentenced to fourteen days' hard labour. Coachmakers, cabinet-makers, cutlers, and many others were sentenced under

[1] *The Town Labourer, 1760–1832*, p. 113.

the Combination Acts. In 1810 the Acts were invoked against the compositors of *The Times*, who were brought to trial before Sir John Silvester, known as "Bloody Black Jack." "Prisoners," declared this judge,

> you have been convicted of a most wicked conspiracy to injure . . . those very employers who gave you bread. . . . The frequency of such crimes among men of your class of life . . . demand . . . that a severe example should be made of . . . such daring and flagitious combinations.[1]

The compositors received sentences ranging up to two years' imprisonment.

After the Napoleonic wars trade unionism had to struggle not only against the Combination Acts, but against severe trade depression, and was beaten down both by the law and by unemployment. It is surprising that from this period of depression dates the first attempt at the formation of a general union of all trades, in place of separate unions for each trade. John Gast, secretary of the London shipwrights, was the leading spirit in the organization, and in 1818 the general union was established under the curious name of the Philanthropic Hercules. The venture was ill-timed, however. The workers were not even ready for strong organization in their own trades, and, since the existence of even a small vigorous union was difficult while the Combination Acts remained on the Statute Book, a large general union was out of the question. Little is heard of the Philanthropic Hercules beyond the articles of its formation. More important was the foundation by Gast of the first trade-union newspaper, *The Gorgon*, which did excellent service in spreading propaganda for the repeal of the Combination Acts.

Trade unions remained illegal for twenty-five years. Both objective and subjective conditions were unfavourable in that quarter-century to a widespread movement for repeal of the Acts. On the one hand, trade languished after 1815, and the repressive grip of the Government continued, paralysing movement. On the other, the workers had no clear consciousness of their aim and no strong leader to point the goal. They fluctuated between spasmodic strike action (in spite of the Combination Acts), attempts at political reform, machine-

---

[1] G. Wallas, *Life of Francis Place*, p. 200.

smashing and wild schemes of insurrection, and some sober attempts at Owenite co-operation.[1] After 1820 the wave of panic repression subsided, and, although there arose no mass movement, two men with clearness of purpose and singleness of aim took charge of the movement for the repeal of the Combination Acts.

Francis Place was a tailor, who worked his way through very hard times from apprentice to master. While unemployed he taught himself mathematics, read not only English literature and philosophy, but the classics, and became the close friend of Jeremy Bentham and the Mills. The little parlour at the back of his shop in Charing Cross became the acknowledged meeting-place of Radicals. In 1810 the master tailors attempted to get a special law passed to prohibit workmen's unions in their trade, and a Parliamentary Committee was formed to investigate the question. Place opposed the other master tailors, insisted upon being called as witness before the Committee, and, largely through his influence, the master tailors' plea was rejected. From this time dates his unflagging work for repeal of the Combination Acts. His procedure is a model of thorough and tireless devotion to a task which took him fifteen years.

He first set himself to note every dispute between masters and men of which he could obtain knowledge. He intervened as often as he could by writing letters to trade societies requesting information, and to local newspapers giving accounts of the disputes. In this way he collected information that filled eight thick volumes, and gave valuable publicity to the cause of repeal.

He soon began a more ambitious Press campaign, writing to *The Chronicle* and *The Star* and *The Times*. He tried to win the assistance of key people rather than to spread his propaganda in a more general way. This direct approach won the useful sympathy of several editors, including the powerful M'Culloch, the economist and editor of *The Scotsman*. Together with Joseph Hume, Radical Member of Parliament, Place also made a special approach to Members of Parliament and to the Prime Minister. He gave financial assistance to the small working-class paper, *The Gorgon*. He wrote for it himself, prepared material for the editor, and made it the mouthpiece of his

[1] *Infra*, pp. 74–77.

propaganda. Copies of the paper were sent to trade societies, employers, workmen, newspapers, and Members of Parliament. Place often visited half a dozen trade groups in a single day, and persuaded workmen to contribute a penny a week towards sending delegates to a Parliamentary Committee on the Combination Acts at whose appointment he aimed.

In 1824 the careful work among Members of Parliament bore fruit. Hume's motion for the appointment of a Committee to consider the Combination Acts was carried. This was only the beginning, however. The Committee had now to be induced to recommend the repeal of the Acts. Employers' evidence had to be immediately refuted; workmen had to be taught to put their case adequately and to resist intimidation. Place, refused permission to act as Hume's assistant in the Committee because he was "neither a member of the honourable House nor even a gentleman," had to work from outside. His help was essential to Hume, and so began that elaborate work of co-operation which has become a classical tale.

In Place's own words:

Both masters and men sent up deputations to give evidence. The delegates from the working people had reference to me, and I opened my house to them. Thus I had all the town and country delegates under my care. I heard the story which every one of these men had to tell. I examined and cross-examined them; took down the leading particulars of each case, and then arranged the matter as briefs for Mr Hume; and, as a rule, for the guidance of the witnesses, a copy was given to each. This occupied days and nights, and occasioned great labour. . . . Each brief contained the principal questions and answers. That for Mr Hume was generally accompanied by an appendix of documents, arranged in order with a short account of such proceedings as was necessary to put Mr Hume in possession of the whole case. Thus he was enabled to go on with considerable ease, and to anticipate or rebut objections.[1]

In this way the workmen's case was so skilfully handled and the employers' evidence so completely rebutted that the Committee was compelled to declare itself favourable to repeal. But Place and Hume were in dread of the searchlight of Parliamentary speechmaking, and for that reason arranged that

[1] Wallas, *op. cit.*, p. 213.

the Committee should not report, but simply propose resolutions to the House, in the fewest possible words. In securing
his Committee Hume had skilfully managed that it should
deal, not with the Combination Acts only, but also with the
Act prohibiting the emigration of artisans, the repeal of which
few opposed. Thus, the two being coupled together and the
House having taken little interest in the proceedings of the
Committee, Hume's motion for the repeal of the Combination
Acts passed almost unnoticed, and the formation of trade
unions became legal. Incredible as it seems, both the Prime
Minister and the Lord Chancellor later stated that they had
been quite unaware of the passing of the 1824 Act of Repeal.[1]

Skilful as had been their work in engineering the repeal of
the Combination Acts, the conception of both Place and Hume
as to the results of repeal was completely erroneous. They
deplored strike action, but argued that when men were free
to bargain collectively they would not need to resort to the
strike weapon. Events proved them wrong. Repeal came at a
time of improving trade, and workmen in many parts of the
country took advantage of their right to combine to strike on
the rising market.

In consequence the implications of Hume's Committee and
the hastily passed repeal of 1824 became apparent, and the
anger of the ruling classes, intensified by fear, broke out.
Parliament felt it had been tricked. Under pressure from
deputations of indignant employers Huskisson, the President of
the Board of Trade, appointed another Committee, packed this
time by the manufacturing interest. Only Hume, whose detailed knowledge of the working of the Combination Acts could
not be overlooked, represented the workmen.

The co-operation between Place and Hume began again.
Working-class bodies were circularized, personal contacts made
or renewed, a permanent central committee was formed, a
pamphlet distributed. Place "laid everything aside" to fight
to maintain the 1824 Act. The workmen, for their part, formed
committees in London, Manchester, Sheffield, Glasgow, Newcastle, and poured their petitions in to both Houses and to the
Government Committee. Place has described how the passages
to the Committee room were packed with workmen demanding
to be heard. Members could hardly make their way into the

[1] Webb, *op. cit.*, p. 105, *n*. 2.

room without being besieged by offers on the part of the workmen to rebut evidence given by masters.

In spite of its efforts at secrecy, the Committee found that
every point made by an employer was known outside and
promptly answered. In the Committee room Hume con-
sistently supported the case of the men, not all of whom could
be denied a hearing. The Committee was quite unscrupulous,
paying the expenses of masters, but refusing to pay those of
workmen, or sometimes, when pressed, paying but a fraction
of what was due. It is a magnificent tribute to the courage and
organization of the men that they nevertheless insisted upon
coming to London to be heard.

Thus, through sheer dogged determination and hard work,
the attempt to reimpose the Combination Act was defeated.
The Act of 1825, however, was harsher than that of 1824.
Combination remained a legal right, but was hedged and
restricted in many ways. Workmen, for example, were no
longer protected from prosecution for conspiracy. Nevertheless, although leaving much to be desired, the Act of 1825
maintained the workman's right to join a trade union. The
important principle of combination had been won and retained.

There was again a period of bad trade from 1825 to 1829,
and on the falling market trade-union activity was slight, and
the effect of repeal not immediately apparent. It was not until
1829 that there began that forward movement which culminated in the trade-union activity of the thirties.

The part played by Francis Place in the repeal of the Combination Acts has been both overemphasized and decried. He
himself has left the most detailed account of the work of repeal,
and, since he was not a man to underestimate his own importance, there has been a tendency by posterity to go to the other
extreme and fail to give just value to his work. In a completely
unfavourable atmosphere—say, five years earlier—neither
Place nor anyone else could have achieved repeal. On the
other hand, without the organizing ability and devotion of
Francis Place the Combination Acts might well have remained
operative for many more years.

Besides trade-union activity, industrial reformers at the
opening of the nineteenth century were beginning to think in
terms of co-operative enterprise. The idea behind co-operation

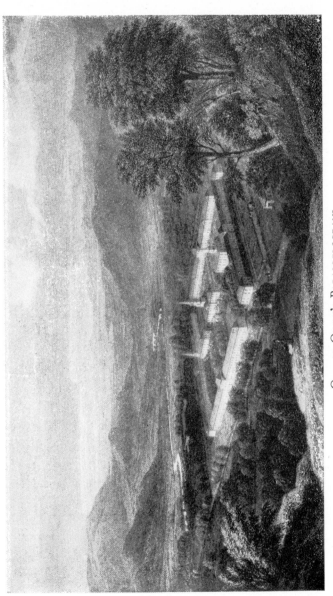

ONE OF OWEN'S PARALLELOGRAMS

[*See p.* 75]

74

ANTHONY ASHLEY COOPER, SEVENTH
EARL OF SHAFTESBURY

G. F. Watts

National Portrait Gallery

was twofold. It would immediately raise the standard of living by freeing the workers from their dependence upon capitalist producers; and it would slowly and surely spread, and with very little friction supersede the capitalist system of production and exchange.

There were two kinds of co-operation. In co-operative exchange the workers would seek to buy and sell without the intervention of middlemen. In co-operative production they would go a step farther back and themselves make the goods, which they would then use or sell. The latter was the more ambitious object, for it entailed ownership of tools, machines, and factories, and ultimately of mines, minerals, and of the land itself. Thus would come about the Socialist or Co-operative Commonwealth.

The prophet of the Co-operative movement was Robert Owen. He himself was a successful cotton-mill owner, and introduced many reforms into his factories. He believed in industrialism, but not in capitalism, his aim being to transfer to the workers the control of production which was vested in the capitalist class.

It was in the dark days of post-war depression that Owen first advanced his scheme for 'villages of co-operation.' His immediate object was to put the unemployed to work on the land and at some subsidiary manufacture. He estimated that about 500 to 1500 people could be housed in a 'village,' and would require about 1000 to 1500 acres of land. He reckoned the cost at £80 a head, which the workman would pay back at the rate of £4 a year. Meantime he would work and maintain his family, who would—and this was essential to the Owenite scheme—be educated in accordance with Socialist principles at the community centre. In the villages of co-operation the houses were built in the form of squares round open spaces, in the centre of which were the communal buildings. 'Owen's parallelograms,' they were commonly called.

The idea was unpopular at the time with the workers, and some initial middle-class support soon drifted away. Not one of Owen's parallelograms ever came to life. But Owen's teaching was falling on better ground than he knew. It was received with enthusiasm by many intellectuals, and several ambitious books put forward his views in different form. George Mudie founded *The Economist*, a Co-operative newspaper which ran from January 1821 to January 1822. Abram Combe, a prosperous leather manufacturer, lost his entire fortune in various Co-operative schemes. The first was a Co-operative store in Edinburgh, which had a successful start, over five hundred families joining; a dishonest storekeeper, however, caused the break-up of the enterprise.

In 1825 Abram Combe determined on a more ambitious experiment. He bought the estate of Orbiston, near Motherwell, and planned to establish there a Co-operative colony. He intended to avoid friction by a gradual change-over from private property to communal, and in so doing incurred the antagonism of those who would have all or nothing in twenty-four hours. At the same time he naturally antagonized capitalist interests. To the accompaniment of this double-barrelled hostility, Combe pursued his plan with such devotion and energy that he fell ill in August 1826, and died twelve months later, having spent £20,000 on Orbiston, and leaving his family penniless. By the end of 1827 the Orbiston experiment was at an end.

In 1826, the year after Combe bought Orbiston, the London Co-operative Society was formed, and shortly afterwards William Lovett became storekeeper. Similar Co-operative trading societies were being formed in other parts of the country, and when they appealed to London for information the British Association for Promoting Co-operative Knowledge was founded. When local societies asked that there might be some central depot where they could deposit their goods for sale a Co-operative Bazaar was formed. Lovett has described the aim and methods of these early Co-operative societies:

> The members subscribed a small weekly sum for the raising of a common fund, with which they opened a general store, containing such articles of food, clothing, books, etc. as were most in request among workmen; the profits of which were added to the common stock. As their fund increased some of them employed their members; such as shoemakers, tailors, and other domestic trades: paying them journeymen's wages, and adding the profits to their funds. Many of them were also enabled by these means to raise sufficient capital to commence manufactures on a small scale; such as broadcloth, silk, linen, worsted goods, shoes, hats, cutlery, furniture, etc.[1]

[1] *Life and Struggles*, pp. 41–42.

None of these early societies nor the British Association lasted for more than three or four years. Most important of the causes of failure in Lovett's view was the fact that these societies at that time had no legal protection for their funds. Dishonest storekeepers and others—of which there were many—could ruin a society without fear of prosecution. Lovett then mentions the reluctance of women to buy all their goods from one store; and finally there were religious difficulties caused by Owen's insistence on making known his atheistic beliefs from the public platform.

Owen himself had been out of the country while his doctrines were thus taking root. Despairing at gaining support in Britain, he went to America in 1824, and there founded the Co-operative community of New Harmony. It was 30,000 acres in extent, and Owen settled about 900 persons on it. There was friction, however; the settlers were not of a good type, any who wished to join being admitted, and the experiment lasted only three years. In 1829 Owen was back in England. At first he was cool towards what he considered trading associations, and declared that mere buying and selling formed no part of his Co-operative scheme. But when he saw how working-men and intellectuals alike were embracing his ideals, how the very trading associations were aiming also at production, he found fresh hope, and in the following decade threw himself again into the movement in Britain.

SELECT BIBLIOGRAPHY

BEER, MAX A.: *History of British Socialism*, vol. i (Bell, 1919).

ʿBUER, M. C.: *Health, Wealth, and Population in the Early Days of the Industrial Revolution* (Routledge, 1926).

COBBETT, W.: *Rural Rides* (1830; Penguin edition 1967).

COLE, G. D. H.: *Life of Robert Owen* (Macmillan, 1925).

ERNLE, LORD: *English Farming, Past and Present* (Longmans, 1912; revised edition, 1961).

FAY, C. R.: *Great Britain from Adam Smith to the Present Day* (Longmans, 1928).

LOVETT, W.: *Life and Struggles*, edited by R. H. Tawney (Bell, 1920).

PODMORE, F.: *Robert Owen, a Biography* (Hutchinson, 1906).

REDFORD, A.: *Labour Migration in England, 1800–1850* (Longmans, 1926; second edition, edited by W. H. Chaloner, 1964).

OWEN, ROBERT: *Life of Robert Owen written by Himself* (Knight, 1971).

CHAPTER IV

THE CRUSHING OF BRITISH RADICALISM

(a) THE FRENCH REVOLUTION AND THE WAR WITH FRANCE

THE American War of Independence broke out in 1775, the French Revolution in 1789. Both these events—particularly the second, since it was nearer—made a deep impression in Britain, especially on the British Radical movement. Their significance was heightened by the fact that in the very years when Americans and Frenchmen were pronouncing the doctrines of liberty and democracy Britain was in the throes of the Industrial and Agrarian Revolutions. The American Declaration of Independence, with its noble assertion "that all men are created equal," that "Life, Liberty and the pursuit of Happiness" are "inalienable rights," and that "whenever any form of Government becomes destructive of these ends, it is the Right of the People to alter or to abolish it, and to institute new Government"; the French Declaration of the Rights of Man, with its pronouncement that all men are born equal and remain equal in rights—these opened a wide vista of hope to British Radicals and to the British working classes.

But while the fire of revolutionary France seemed to the workers of Britain to light the way back to a lost freedom, to their rulers it lit the dangerous path of sedition and revolution. On the one hand it engendered hope; on the other it created a form of panic repression quite out of proportion to the desperate but ineffectual efforts of the workers and Radicals to assert their independence.

In the seventies of the eighteenth century the cause of Parliamentary Reform had become fashionable. The younger Pitt, the Duke of Richmond, and Fox were among those who advocated Reform, and Radical societies flourished. The opening events of the French Revolution were followed with sympathy by nearly all classes.

> Bliss was it in that dawn to be alive,
> But to be young was very heaven!

exclaimed Wordsworth. Southey, Coleridge, and Hazlitt fervently agreed.

The Bastille was stormed on July 14, 1789, and though Fox's comment, "How much the greatest event that has happened in the world, and how much the best!" was regarded by his class as over-enthusiastic, no marked cooling off began for some months. It was only as the Revolution grew more violent that there was a marked defection. The poets and intellectuals abandoned it. The ruling class grew particularly alarmed when the French peasants began to burn their lords' chateaux and divide up the manorial lands. They were even more agitated when the French began to send propaganda beyond their own frontiers. On November 19, 1792, the French Convention offered "assistance to all people who wish to recover their liberty." In December a French Minister announced aid for the British Radicals: "We will fly to their succour," he said. "We will make a descent in the island. We will lodge there 50,000 caps of Liberty. The tyranny of their Government will soon be destroyed."[1] This incitement of the working classes of other countries to revolt was one of the three reasons given by Pitt for breaking off relations with France in January 1793. The following month France declared war against Britain, and the Revolutionary and Napoleonic wars began.

Two books typify the sentiments of the rival British factions at this time. Burke's *Reflections on the Revolution in France*, published on November 1, 1790, is the classic of conservatism. Eloquent, forceful, rich in sonorous passages of rhetoric, passionately loyal to the ideals of chivalry and aristocracy, it lamented the passing of the French nobility and denounced the French Revolution. Of the forty published replies to the *Reflections* the greatest was Tom Paine's *The Rights of Man*. The first part of this was published in March 1791, only four months after the *Reflections*, the second part in February 1792. Uncompromising and unrhetorical, direct and forceful, the book was a contrast in style as well as in sentiment to Burke's. It was reprinted dozens of times; in 1793 alone 200,000 copies were sold, and more in the following years as the Radical societies continued to issue cheap editions.

Burke, in one of his most famous passages, recalled his sight

[1] J. Holland Rose, *William Pitt and the Great War*, p. 102.

of Marie-Antoinette at the Court of Versailles, and lamented the passing of what appeared to him as the age of chivalry:

> It is now sixteen or seventeen years since I saw the Queen of France, then the dauphiness, at Versailles; and surely never lighted on this orb, which she hardly seemed to touch, a more delightful vision. I saw her just above the horizon, decorating and cheering the elevated sphere she just began to move in,— glittering like the morning-star, full of life, and splendour, and joy. Oh! what a revolution! and what a heart must I have, to contemplate without emotion that elevation and that fall! .. little did I dream that I should have lived to see such disasters fallen upon her in a nation of gallant men, in a nation of men of honour, and of cavaliers. I thought ten thousand swords must have leaped from their scabbards to avenge even a look that threatened her with insult.
>
> But the age of chivalry is gone. That of sophisters, economists, and calculators, has succeeded; and the glory of Europe is extinguished for ever. Never, never more shall we behold that generous loyalty to rank and sex, that proud submission, that dignified obedience, that subordination of the heart, which kept alive, even in servitude itself, the spirit of an exalted freedom. The unbought grace of life, the cheap defence of nations, the nurse of manly sentiment and heroic enterprise is gone! It is gone, that sensibility of principle, that chastity of honour, which felt a stain like a wound, which inspired courage whilst it mitigated ferocity, which ennobled whatever it touched, and under which vice itself lost half its evil, by losing all its grossness.[1]

Paine replied:

> Through the whole of Mr Burke's book I do not observe that the Bastille is mentioned more than once, and that with a kind of implication as if he were sorry it was pulled down, and wished it were built up again. . . .
>
> Not one glance of compassion, not one commiserating reflection that I can find throughout his book, has he bestowed on those who lingered out the most wretched of lives, a life without hope in the most miserable of prisons. It is painful to behold a man employing his talents to corrupt himself. Nature has been kinder to Mr Burke than he is to her. He is not affected by the reality of distress touching his heart, but by the showy resemblance of it striking his imagination. He pities the plumage, but forgets the dying bird. Accustomed to kiss the aristocratical hand that hath purloined him from himself, he degenerates into a composition of

[1] *Reflections on the Revolution in France* (University Tutorial Press, 1927), pp. 78–79.

art, and the genuine soul of nature forsakes him. His hero or his heroine must be a tragedy-victim expiring in show, and not the real prisoner of misery, sliding into death in the silence of a dungeon.[1]

Radical ideas, meantime, were flourishing. Old Reform 'clubs' revived and new 'associations' sprang into vigorous life. The Friends of the People, with mainly middle-class Whig supporters and a subscription of two and a half guineas a year, was the most conservative. Its objects were political reform; its members included the tried Reformer Major Cartwright, Erskine, Charles Grey, Sheridan, and Whitbread. More Radical was the Society for Constitutional Information, founded in 1791. Besides the reform of Parliament it recommended the publication of a cheap edition of *The Rights of Man*, and appointed a committee for foreign correspondence. Its members included Romney the painter, Holcroft, Horne Tooke, and Thelwall.

More characteristic of the period were the 'corresponding societies.' The London Corresponding Society was formed in 1792, with eight members and funds of 8*d*. and Thomas Hardy as secretary. As it grew and prospered other societies were formed. Members were divided into groups of thirty, and delegate meetings from the groups were held. The societies' aim was political reform, which they believed could be achieved by education rather than agitation. They issued pamphlets, corresponded with one another and with groups in France, and called one another 'citizen,' after the mode in France. The members were mainly skilled artisans: Thomas Hardy, for example, was a shoemaker. He was unflinching in his support of Radicalism, and would never, in spite of the attacks of excited hooligans, illuminate his windows for a victory over the French.

There were many other Reform societies. The Manchester Constitutional Society was formed in 1790. The Friends of Universal Peace and the Rights of Man was founded at Stockport in 1792. A Sheffield Society was formed in the same year, with the aim of "a radical Reform of the country, consistent with the Rights of Man."[2] The Sheffield Association was concerned as much with the price of food as with the Rights of Man. It discussed "the enormous high price of provisions"

---

[1] *The Rights of Man* (Thinker's Library), pp. 13-15.   [2] Rose, *op. cit.*, p. 25.

and "the waste . . . of the public property by placemen, pensioners, luxury and debauchery."[1] Many societies reprinted and circulated *The Rights of Man*, which was translated into Welsh, Gaelic, and Erse, and sold for sixpence a copy or less.

In opposition to Radicals, who were generally also Dissenters, 'Church and King' clubs were formed. While Radicals were celebrating the anniversary of the fall of the Bastille Church and King mobs rioted in Birmingham in July 1791, and made their way to the house of Dr Priestley, the famous scientist and well-known Radical. Priestley escaped, and afterwards left the country; but his valuable laboratory was wrecked, his house set on fire, his cellars raided by the mob, who celebrated their victory by a drunken orgy. Whitbread's motion in the Commons for an inquiry into the riot was rejected by 189 votes to 46.

With the very bad harvest of 1792 discontent increased. There were bread riots in various parts of the country, a dock strike at Liverpool, a coal stoppage at Wigan. At Pocklington, in Yorkshire, villagers threatened to burn magistrates in their houses. In North Cornwall tinworkers marched to Padstow harbour to prevent the export of corn. Spitalfields weavers in London petitioned for relief. There were anti-Enclosure riots near Sheffield. In Liverpool the press gang was out. The ugly situation in Manchester and Sheffield caused the Government to send troops to keep order; but these became disaffected and sent a petition for higher pay. Unrest even invaded the prisons. At the end of 1792 was found nailed to the chapel door in the Fleet Prison a placard saying, "The republic of France having rooted out despotism, their glorious example and success against tyrants, renders infamous bastiles no longer necessary in Europe." For this offence Patrick William Duffin, who posted it up, and Thomas Lloyd, an attorney, who read it aloud, were tried and found guilty. Lloyd was pilloried outside the Royal Exchange before a great concourse of people.[2]

Repression began in earnest when, in December 1792, Tom Paine was prosecuted for sedition. Paine was an elected member of the French Convention and out of England, but he was tried in his absence and formally banished. Prosecutions came thick and fast for circulating *The Rights of Man*, and for

---

[1] Rose, *op. cit.*, pp. 21–22. [2] *State Trials*, xxii, 318–358.

sedition' in other forms. The Reformers persisted. The London Corresponding Society prophesied the speedy formation of a Revolutionary Convention in England. On December 11, 1792, a Convention of the Friends of the People was held at Edinburgh. Though the resolutions passed were pacific, the authorities took alarm. Thomas Muir was arrested, and tried in August 1793 before the notorious Judge Braxfield. Muir was a young Edinburgh advocate, the son of a Glasgow tradesman and Vice-President of the Glasgow branch of the Friends of the People. He was sincere, impetuous, and able. The jury was packed against him. Braxfield was unashamedly biased, and after a trial full of irregularities Muir was found guilty, in spite of the eloquent three-hour speech he made in his own defence. He received the shocking sentence of fourteen years' transportation to Botany Bay.

In the same year in Dundee, where the population consisted largely of poor weavers, the high price of food was causing grave discontent. The Government, anxious to make an example, traced an *Address to the People* to a Unitarian minister, Thomas Fyshe Palmer, and he was sentenced to five years' transportation.

The sentences on Muir and Palmer did not damp the Scottish Reformers. At the end of 1793 delegates from forty-five Reform societies, including those of Ireland and London, met at Edinburgh. Joseph Gerrald and Maurice Margarot came from the London Corresponding Society, Sinclair and York from the Society for Constitutional Information. Gerrald, Margarot, Sinclair, and Skirving, the secretary of the convention, were arrested. Sinclair turned informer, the rest were charged with attending meetings "of a dangerous and destructive tendency." Braxfield in his summing up declared them guilty of sedition, and they each were sentenced to fourteen years' transportation.

The demeanour and defence of the prisoners made a profound impression on the crowds who thronged the court. Gerrald made a magnificent defence. "By heavens!" exclaimed the poet Campbell, who had tramped from Glasgow for the trial, "that is a great man." "Yes, Sir," replied his neighbour, "he is not only a great man himself, but he makes every other man feel great who listens to him."[1]

---

[1] Rose, *op. cit.*, p. 183.

The ruthless persecution of the Scottish Reformers and the monstrous bias of Braxfield had an effect opposite to that intended. Unrest simmered, and "The sow's tail to Geordie!" became the popular Scottish cry. In the South the London Corresponding Society was planning a general Convention of the People for the spring of 1794. On May 12 the Government arrested Hardy at his shop in Piccadilly and seized the books and papers of the L.C.S.; the shock of the raid on her house caused Mrs Hardy to die in premature childbirth. Thelwall and Horne Tooke, of the Society for Constitutional Information, and other members of both societies were also imprisoned. Still unsatisfied, the Government hurriedly suspended Habeas Corpus by a vote carried at 3.30 A.M., and appointed a Committee of Secrecy to inquire into the condition of the country. Though this Committee reported on plots and insurrections in various stages of readiness, nothing could be proved against the men in prison. After a masterly defence by Erskine and Gibbs, Hardy, Thelwall, and Horne Tooke were acquitted, and the cases against the others quietly dropped. The verdicts are a high tribute to the integrity of the London jury who returned them.

Reports from other parts of the country meantime justified to some extent the fears of the Committee of Secrecy. At Norwich, Birmingham, Sheffield, Manchester, Edinburgh, there were further disturbances and trials. Economic conditions continued to foment the insurrection so dreaded by Pitt and his colleagues. The poor harvest of 1794 was followed by a summer of great cold in which all available food stocks were exhausted. And again the harvest was small. Prices soared, and the war kept out the foreign corn which might have fed the hungry. In the summer of 1795 hundreds of Birmingham men cried for "a large loaf." "Are we to be starved to death?" they demanded.[1] In July there was rioting in London at Charing Cross, a recruiting station in Lambeth was demolished, and Pitt's windows in Downing Street were smashed. On October 27, 1795, the London Corresponding Society mustered nearly 150,000 at a great meeting in Copenhagen Fields, which protested against the war and demanded annual Parliaments and universal suffrage. Two days later angry crowds hissed and booed the King as he proceeded to

[1] Rose, *op. cit.*, p. 288.

the opening of Parliament. Along the route people cried for peace and bread; the royal carriage was pierced by what appeared to be a shot; it was struck by a stone. At St James's, when the King alighted on his return, the crowd set on the carriage and considerably damaged it.[1]

Pitt once more turned to the legislature. On November 10 Grenville in the Lords piloted into law the Treasonable Practices Bill, while Pitt in the Commons did likewise for the Seditious Meetings Bill. The former laid down heavy penalties for all who acted, spoke, or wrote against the Constitution. The latter, which was to remain effective for three years, made impossible any meeting of which the magistrates disapproved. Demonstrations of protest numbering hundreds of thousands of people were unavailing. Meetings were henceforth limited to forty-five persons. Delegates of the London Corresponding Society who went to Birmingham were there arrested, the Society's membership diminished, its propaganda declined. By the end of 1796 it was in debt.

In the following year, however, the Government had a new danger to deal with. Insurrectionary handbills were discovered at Chatham Barracks, and there was open mutiny in the Fleet. At the Nore and Spithead sailors demanded better conditions, and this revolt in the very citadel caused such alarm that the Government granted a small pay increase as well as executing Parker, the leader of the Nore mutiny. In the same year a rising in North Ireland, assisted by a small French force, was suppressed; the laws against the Press tightened. In 1799 the Corresponding Act prohibited all corresponding societies and similar bodies. Combinations of workmen were prohibited by the Combination Acts of 1799 and 1800.

Against such vigorous action the Reformers had little chance. A black night of repression had fallen. Every little effort of Reform was countered by legislation, by packed juries, unscrupulous judges, and severe sentences. Since there was as yet no police force, the Government had to rely upon the soldiery to keep order. When these were found too ready to sympathize with the people the yeomanry—picked troops of the landowning class—were used instead. Finally it was felt to be too dangerous to leave the soldiery billeted on the people. And so, for the first time in British history, barracks appeared

[1] *Ibid.*, p. 282.

all over Northern England and in some of the Eastern counties, so that the soldiers could be segregated from a discontented populace.

For the next fifteen years there was no working-class political activity, though the discontent which was its cause broke out in various ways. In April 1812 food rioting was combined with machine-smashing in Lancashire. Crowds in Manchester, Bolton, Ashton, and Oldham seized groceries and flour from provision carts and shops, sometimes appropriating the food, sometimes selling it at what they considered a fair price. At Manchester a woman named Hannah Smith was prominent. Having led a mob which seized potatoes, she was heard to cry, "We will not be satisfied with potatoes!" and afterwards she jumped upon a butter-cart and sold the stock for the 'fair' price of 1s. a pound. For this exploit she was hanged.[1] These, too, were the years of Luddism, and there was intermittent strike action. But not until 1815 did the Radical movement again raise its head. In this respect Pitt's Government had done its work well.

It is hard to excuse Pitt for repression so ruthless, so out of proportion to the moderate requests of the men he crushed. By social and political reform he could have removed the just grievances which made them rebels against his government. It was unemployment, hunger, and frustration, aggravated by war, as much as abstract ideas of the Rights of Man which caused the revolutionary ferment of the war years. The masses were ignorant and unarmed, their leaders sometimes Radicals who deserted them when they threatened insurrection, sometimes working-men who were promptly imprisoned or transported or executed, sometimes young intellectuals whose enthusiasm for the Rights of Man lent a temporary voice to a discontented people, before they too were silenced by law. Nowhere and at no time during the Napoleonic wars was there a revolutionary situation; there was no protest which a moderate reform would not have converted into acclamation for the Government. At every turn it was the legislature which made the revolution out of its own fears, and which magnified the riots of hungry men into an incipient French Revolution.

[1] J. L. and B. Hammond, *The Skilled Labourer, 1760–1832*, pp. 287–294.

(b) THE POST-WAR DEPRESSION

In the acute economic distress which followed the Napoleonic wars discontent broke out afresh. This new wave of revolt was treated as ruthlessly as the earlier, and was characterized by the use not only of Government informers, but of the abominated provocative agent, who himself planned and encouraged the 'plots' which he then disclosed to the Government. Juries were packed with Government supporters, sentences of death and transportation executed on men known to be the dupes of *agents provocateurs*, armed cavalry used to intimidate and to break up peaceful meetings. Finally, the notorious Six Acts of 1819 attempted to block every avenue of working-class expression through speech, meeting, or writing.

After the collapse of the London Corresponding Society the little group of Spencean Philanthropists, formed in 1812, for a while focused the activities of the more politically conscious of the workers. Its leader was Thomas Spence, its doctrine the socialization of the land without compensation.

After the war William Cobbett and "Orator" Hunt gave a fresh urgency to political reform. Cobbett's *Political Register* was printed in cheap form and eagerly read by thousands of working-class families. Dozens of other cheap, working-class papers followed its lead. Francis Place and Sir Francis Burdett drew in the skilled workers and the Radicals. Major Cartwright revived the Hampden Clubs of the nineties, which, at a penny a week membership, soon spread over the country. They had plenty of material to work on. The Corn Law Bill of 1815 became law only in face of grave opposition. Rioting developed in many parts of the country. Agricultural labourers demanded higher wages and a fixed maximum price for bread. In the Eastern counties in 1816 they smashed machines, set fire to barns and ricks and even houses, and marched under a banner inscribed, "Bread or Blood." Yeomanry, dragoons, and militia were called out to suppress them. At Littleport, in the Isle of Ely, two rioters were killed and seventy-five taken prisoner. Of the latter five were hanged, nine transported, and ten imprisoned for twelve months.[1] There were angry demonstrations by hand-loom weavers, stockingers, and col-

[1] J. L. and B. Hammond, *The Village Labourer, 1760–1832*, pp. 153–154.

liers. Factory workers followed suit. Birmingham, Nottingham, Norwich, Lancashire, were affected. Local magistrates lined up in opposition backed by yeomanry and troops. Unemployed coalminers made their way through England dragging their coal-carts behind them. In London there were angry meetings in Spa Fields and processions of unemployed in which the Tricolour and caps of liberty were prominent.

The middle-class manufacturers—without the vote, in spite of their wealth—sought to further their own interest in political reform by making common cause with the Radicals. Even the Whigs, willing to make party capital out of the situation, joined forces against the Government. Before the year 1816 was over the Government was faced with a formidable coalition of agricultural labourers, factory workers and handworkers, miners, skilled artisans, Radicals, the Spencean Socialists, the manufacturers, and the Whigs.

On November 15, 1816, the Spencean Society organized a great meeting in Spa Fields, addressed by "Orator" Hunt. The meeting resolved upon a petition to the Prince Regent, who was acting ruler during the King's insanity. The petition, demanding instant Government action for relief and reform, was to be presented by Hunt, and a public meeting fixed for December 2, when he was to report on his reception.

The group of Spenceans, however, had resolved to make December 2 the occasion of a great rising of the populace, who would take the Tower of London and overthrow the British Government as the Paris rebels had stormed the Bastille and overthrown the French. But the British Government actually had one of its creatures, John Castle, on the secret committee organizing the rising, and acting not only as spy, but as provocative agent. The plans he helped to lay were ambitious. When all was complete a Committee of Public Safety was to be formed and the Government of the country taken over. In execution, however, the Spencean plot was nothing but a small riot. There were several arrests, and one man was tried for his life. That he was found not guilty was due to the complete exposure of Castle, the chief witness, as a spy, provocative agent, bigamist, and forger.

Sidmouth, the Home Secretary, was in close touch with the affected areas. It was not until an assault on the Prince Regent in January 1817, however, that he took strong action.

His seeming inertia had been sound wisdom. While *The Times* was crying "Revolution" and the mob were rioting in the City the Radicals were silently withdrawing from the contest, regarding their own cause of Parliamentary Reform as lost by the unbridled passions of the populace and the popular leaders. With the others—the manufacturers, merchants, and financiers of the middle class—who had a quarrel with the Government, and with the Whig Opposition, satisfaction at the discomfiture of the Government gave way to the realization that in the fight between property and poverty their place was at the side of law and order. With them lined up all the little shopkeepers of the City, whose shops were in danger of being looted, and all who had or thought they had an interest in the preservation of existing property relationships. The old cry "Property in danger!" had been raised. So, silently at first, the forces of counter-revolution worked. And when the Government struck it delivered a blow well backed by Whig and Tory and middle classes alike. Within a week of the opening of Parliament Habeas Corpus was suspended. Other Acts, relating to the personal safety of the Prince Regent, limiting the right of public meeting, declaring the Spencean Society illegal, prohibiting federation of political societies, easily became law. Cobbett fled to America to avoid prosecution and imprisonment for unpaid stamp duties. Hunt and Burdett and Place and the other colleagues of the previous year were in a condition of mutual exasperation. A meeting at Spa Fields could muster only twenty people. "It seemed as if the sun of freedom were gone down and a rayless expanse of oppression had finally closed over us," wrote Samuel Bamford of this time.

In the dark days of early 1817 the idea was conceived in the North and Midlands of personally presenting to the Prince Regent a petition telling the grievances of the workers and requesting the remedy of universal suffrage. The weavers and spinners had little to lose by marching to London, and considerable support was gained for the venture. Each man was to carry his petition wrapped in brown paper and tied to his right arm by a piece of tape. Blankets were to be carried for the six nights of the march to London, and so the marchers came to be called "Blanketeers."

The organization was careful and detailed. The marchers

were divided into groups of a hundred, and these again into
tens, each ten and each hundred having its leader. There was
also a special group to deal with provisions. Different societies
of workers and those who remained behind were to make
contributions, according to their means, to the support of the
marchers and their families.

The march was organized in good faith, and strict order
was intended, the police actually being invited to attend.
Fear, however, gave birth to rumours of the insurrectionary
character of the marchers. Consequently, on March 10, 1817,
when they and their well-wishers gathered in St Peter's Fields,
Manchester, troops arrived to arrest them before they could
set out. Many of the Blanketeers had started before the
Dragoons arrived, but Bagguley and Drummond, the leaders,
were arrested, and soldiers, yeomanry, and special constables
set off after the rest. About 160 men were arrested on the
Stockport road; others got as far as Macclesfield; some reached
Ashbourne, only to turn back when they found the bridge
over the Dove occupied by yeomanry. A few straggled into
Derby and Loughborough. One man, Abel Couldwell, of
Stalybridge, actually reached London and presented his
petition to Lord Sidmouth for the Prince Regent.

Having arrested them, the Government was at a loss what
to do with the unarmed and harmless Blanketeers they had
lodged in goal. For some nights the men were packed into
prisons, already over-full, and then all who admitted repentance were released. Most of the marchers, mindful of the fate
of political prisoners, obtained their release in this way.
There were nine of them, however, who insisted that they had
done nothing wrong and who refused to accept bail. These
were to be sent for trial to the August Assizes. But even with
these few the Government was not quite sure of the wisdom of
prosecution. Finally it decided, in the words of the Under-
Secretary of State, that it would be "more prudent . . . to
make a merit of letting them off."[1]

Thus ended the affair of the Blanketeers. It was perhaps
the first 'hunger march' to be organized in England, with the
exception of the unemployed miners who had toured England
the previous year. The Blanketeers were for the most part
young, inexperienced, and full of a naive belief in the powers

---

[1] J. L. and B. Hammond, *The Skilled Labourer, 1760–1832*, p. 349.

both of political representation and of the Prince Regent. The nine who remained in prison, risking death or transportation, when a word of repentance would have secured their release, are among the obscure heroes of the working class.

A few months later there was again talk of insurrection in the North. This time violence really was intended, and on June 9, 1817, pikes and guns were distributed in the Pentridge district of Derbyshire in preparation for a march on Nottingham. But twenty cavalrymen were sufficient to disperse the insurrectionists, who fled without firing a shot. Forty-eight of them were captured, and their leader, Jeremiah Brandreth, was betrayed by a spy in whose house he sought refuge. For months the prisoners were kept on bread and water, and then brought to trial before a jury carefully selected by the Government. Brandreth and two others were executed. Eleven were transported for life, three for fourteen years.

How came it that poor men, so timid in action, conceived so grand a plot for "levying war against the king," as the prosecution put it? The answer is devastatingly simple. It was the work of Oliver, the spy, one of the most despicable creatures ever employed by a craven Home Office. It was he who worked upon the feelings of hungry men and built up the little plots which step by step he betrayed to his master, Lord Sidmouth. Like Castle before him, Oliver was discovered and denounced by diligent reformers as spy, provocative agent, bigamist, and forger. But it was too late to save Brandreth and his friends.

Things were quieter as the summer of 1817 passed. The harvest was good and trade improved. With the recurrence of depression in 1818 strikes broke out afresh, and the defeat of a big strike in Lancashire left the workers in a mood when they were willing to try anything. Mass meetings were taking place at the end of the year, and the cries were for universal suffrage and the repeal of the Corn Laws. The workers' old allies were early on the scene. Hunt and Cartwright addressed great meetings in Lancashire and Scotland in June 1819, the ferment spreading south through the Midlands. The climax came with "Peterloo" on August 16, 1819. This had little in common with the insurrections of the previous years, but was an orderly demonstration of men, women, and children, some 80,000 strong, which marched to St Peter's Fields, Manchester, to listen to "Orator" Hunt making demands for political reform. The organizers took the utmost care that there should be no violence, but the days before the meeting were full of tension and suspicion on the part of the authorities. Rumour and counter-rumour were rife; the legality of the coming meeting was questioned; yeomanry was held ready for action.

Early in the morning of the great day crowds began to converge on St Peter's Fields. Men, women, and children marched along, banners flying, in orderly fashion. Samuel Bamford, who led 3000 people from Middleton, has described how he instructed his contingent to show their enemies that the working classes were not a mere rabble. Only the aged and infirm were allowed to carry sticks. In order to make certain that there would be no trouble Hunt offered to give himself up to the authorities before the meeting. His offer, however, was refused, and the demonstrators were allowed to assemble. Then, while Hunt was addressing a vast but silent crowd, the magistrates decided that the meeting was illegal, and sent a contingent of yeomanry to arrest Hunt. What happened is not very clear. The mounted soldiers forced their way through the dense crowd to the platform, and Hunt allowed himself to be arrested. The crowd seem to have been quiet enough, though the passage of cavalrymen through the tightly packed mass of people must have caused a stir.

Then, either panic at being surrounded by a crowd 80,000 strong, or deliberate vindictiveness, or preconceived design caused the yeomanry to raise the cry, "Have at their flags!" and to strike out right and left with their swords. Hussars were at once sent to their assistance by the magistrates. Terrible confusion followed, in which the main thought of the crowd seems to have been escape. Within ten minutes the field was cleared. There remained only dead and wounded men and women, mutilated banners, women's bonnets, torn shawls. Among 80,000 unarmed and closely packed people, many of them women and children and old persons, mounted horsemen with drawn swords had been let loose. Over 400 people were wounded, 113 being women. Eleven died, including two women and a child. Of the wounded over a quarter were injured by the sword.

It was an unprovoked attack by a Government using armed force upon unarmed people exercising the right to meet together and make in peaceful and dignified manner a few plain demands in the name of justice. It was not a case of alarmed or over-zealous local authorities acting on impulse. On the orders of the Government careful preparation had been made, and after the event Lord Sidmouth sent a letter of congratulation to the local authorities of Manchester.

The "Peterloo" massacre drew a protest from all classes of society; indignation and horror stimulated the Reform movement. The days after Peterloo were uneasy days for the Government. Manchester itself was in a state bordering upon hysteria. Cobbett, opportunely returning from America, was at Liverpool met by a huge crowd, and his journey to London was a triumphal progress. Burdett and Cartwright led the Westminster Radicals into the general agitation. Even the Common Council of London, with its Tory Lord Mayor, yielded to the popular clamour so far as to address a letter of protest to the Prince Regent. Hunt, who had been arrested at "Peterloo," was released on bail, and in September made a spectacular entry into London. He was met by a crowd of about 250,000, headed by Watson, Preston, and Thistlewood, the Spencean Communists. New revolutionary journals appeared, such as *The Cap of Liberty* and *The Republican*.

In 1816 Sidmouth had found that wisdom lay in waiting for discord to develop among the Reformers before presenting his Coercion Acts to the House. But in 1819 it was apparent that time was consolidating the forces opposed to the Government. The sequel was inevitable. An extraordinary session of Parliament was called to approve an increase of the Army by 10,000 and Six Acts of severe repression. The first and second of these Acts were approved immediately, the third only after opposition from the Whigs.

The first of the Six Acts prohibited meetings for the purpose of drilling and military exercises under penalty of a maximum of seven years' deportation or two years' imprisonment for the instructor, and two years' imprisonment for any participator The second Act prohibited the carrying of arms, and empowered magistrates on their own authority to seize arms, to arrest any person possessing arms and release him only on bail, and also to enter private houses at any time of the day or night in search of arms.

A third Act consisted of forty clauses restricting the right of public meeting under penalty of seven years' transportation. The fourth, fifth, and sixth Acts were aimed at the Press. The fourth was designed "for the more effectual Prevention and Punishment of Blasphemous and Seditious Libels." It gave a court the authority to seize every copy of a condemned pamphlet, even though an appeal were pending. The fifth Act was directed against cheap working-class periodicals, all the liabilities to which newspapers were subject being extended to political periodicals costing less than sixpence. The sixth and last Act regulated procedure and minimized delays in prosecution.

Of those who opposed the measures none spoke more eloquently than Earl Grey in the House of Lords:

> He had heard strong observations on the progress of sedition and treason, and on the necessity of adopting measures of coercion calculated to avert the danger which threatened the country. But he had as yet heard no recommendation to avert the danger, by relieving the people from some part of the heavy burthens which oppressed them.

He reminded his hearers that in 1817 similar restrictive laws had been passed.

> The same complaints were then made of the existence of disaffection and discontent, and the same means of resorting to force were suggested. Did those measures produce the effects which were promised? . . . The effect of these measures was, in his opinion, the cause of a great portion of the discontent which now prevailed. . . . The natural consequence of such a system, when once begun, was, that it could not be stopped; discontents begot the necessity of force; the employment of force increased discontents: these would demand the exercise of new powers, till by degrees they would depart from all the principles of the constitution.[1]

Even after the passage of the Six Acts the work of the spies and provocative agents continued, and there were still reformers whom they could dupe and betray.

[1] November 23, 1819 (Hansard, xli, 4–21). Grey was speaking on the Address from the Prince Regent.

The Cato Street Conspiracy of 1820 was no less than a desperate attempt to assassinate the whole Cabinet, who were held responsible for the repression of the time. The leader of the plot was Arthur Thistlewood, who had been prominent in the Spencean plot. Then, in 1816, he had been betrayed by the spy Castle. Now, in 1820, he fell into the toils of Edwards. Thistlewood had meantime been imprisoned for twelve months for libelling the Prince Regent. Two months after his release occurred the massacre of Peterloo. "I resolved," said Thistlewood, "that the lives of the instigators should be the requiem to the souls of the murdered innocents. In this mood I met with George Edwards."

Edwards was fertile in the suggestion of plans and liberal in supplying money. Thistlewood turned down all plans which would involve the innocent as well as the guilty, and Edwards finally brought forward a scheme for assassinating the Ministers at a Government dinner. It was while completing their plans in a loft in Cato Street, Edgware Road, that the soldiery arrived. Thistlewood, after hand-to-hand fighting, escaped, only to be again betrayed by Edwards, who had offered to help him. On May Day 1820 Arthur Thistlewood and four others were hanged in front of Newgate Gaol.

Edwards, like Castle and Oliver, was shortly afterwards exposed. But none of these wretched creatures met the fate he deserved. Edwards was never found to answer for his villainy, Oliver was assisted by the Government to the post of Inspector of Government Buildings in South Africa, where he died in 1827. Of Castle nothing more is known.

The period of Peterloo and Cato Street was a time of ferment in Scotland also, where hatred of the Government was fanned to white heat by unemployment, especially in the textile trades, by dear bread, and by the Six Acts. There was an outburst of rebel journalism and pamphleteering, and once again could be seen the sinister figure of the provocative agent. On Sunday morning, April 20, 1820, placards appeared in and round Glasgow calling a general strike. Although Radical leaders denounced this proclamation as the work of spies, so ready for action were the people that on the following day they ceased work almost to a man. It was rumoured that arms were being manufactured, that hundreds were drilling in preparation for a great rising, that terrified citizens were fleeing from the countryside into Glasgow for safety. Certain it is that there was much alarm, and that on the Wednesday morning spies induced about eighty Glasgow men to march on the Carron ironworks at Falkirk. The spies slunk off, the workmen marched straight into a waiting detachment of the 10th Hussars at Bonnymuir. There followed the "battle of Bonnymuir," in which the men fought desperately, though hopelessly, against the cavalry. Nineteen of the rebels were captured, some killed, nearly all wounded. Andrew Hardie, a young weaver, and John Baird, the village blacksmith, were hanged, drawn, and quartered, and eighteen others transported for life.

In Paisley, meantime, the military had fired on the crowd. In Greenock the gaol was stormed and five Radical prisoners were set free. In Lanarkshire men from Strathaven were duped into marching to an imaginary rendezvous at Cathkin Braes, near Rutherglen. Among them marched an old Strathaven weaver, James Wilson, carrying a banner with the words, "Scotland free or a desert." He was captured and hanged and given a pauper's grave. But in the night his daughter and niece came to the place and carried his body back to Strathaven, where he belonged. Once more repression had triumphed. Not for ten years did Scotland produce another mass movement for political reform.[1]

Spasmodic plots and insurrections lasted from 1816 until 1820. Then, losing hope of the speedy overturning of the Government, the Reformers turned to political and trade-union action.

The unhappy years from 1816 to 1820 were marked on the one hand by the uncoordinated and blind protests of the working classes, ignorant of all but the fact of their misery. They were marked on the other hand, not by any vestige of reform, but by repression distorted by fear into a harsh and evil system of espionage and tyranny. This not only routed out the least sign of insurrection, but made the word whispered in the market-place or the conversation at the hearth into evidence of a plot. To make the evidence more convincing Government agents themselves supplied the details of the schemes to the

[1] T. Johnston, *History of the Working Classes in Scotland*, pp. 238-244.

WILLIAM COBBETT
National Portrait Gallery

FRANCIS PLACE
Daniel Maclise
[See pp. 71–74]
Victoria and Albert Museum, London

unhappy men who alone would never have dared, and could hardly have conceived, the plots which the Government then punished with imprisonment, transportation, and death.

Revolution was no nearer between 1816 and 1820 than in the war years. There was the same unharnessed discontent and unhappiness, due largely to economic depression and the effects of industrial and agrarian change. Revolution existed chiefly in the mind of the Government, who itself fanned the flame of the insurrection it then turned to crush. As Earl Grey said:

> The march of spies and informers, who were employed by the executive ministers of the Crown—were themselves the instigators of mischief, were themselves the originators of plans of treason, and were themselves the primary cause of an unconstitutional attack upon the liberties of the people.[1]

Ministers such as Pitt, Eldon, Castlereagh, and Sidmouth could understand the voice of repression, but not that of reform. The social results of their rule were summarized by Cobbett: "Gaols ten times as big as formerly; houses of correction; treadmills; the hulks; and a country filled with *spies* of one sort and another!"

[1] November 23, 1819 (Hansard, xli, 17).

SELECT BIBLIOGRAPHY

BURKE, E.: *Reflections on the Revolution in France,* edited by H. P. Adams: various editions.

DARVALL, F. O.: *Popular Disturbances and Public Order in Regency England* (Oxford University Press, 1934).

DUGAN, JAMES: *The Great Mutiny* (André Deutsch, 1966).

HAMMOND, J. L. AND B.: *The Skilled Labourer, 1760–1832* (Longmans, 1919).

JOHNSTON, T.: *History of the Working Classes in Scotland* (Forward Publishing Co., 1923).

MACCOBY, S.: *English Radicalism, 1762–1785: The Origins* (Allen and Unwin, 1955).

MARLOW, JOYCE: *The Peterloo Massacre* (Panther paperback, 1971).

PAINE, T.: *The Rights of Man* (Watts, Thinker's Library, 1937).

STANHOPE, J.: *The Cato Street Conspiracy* (Cape, 1962).

WALMSLEY, ROBERT: *Peterloo: the case re-opened* (Manchester University Press, 1969).

CHAPTER V

ECONOMIC DEVELOPMENT

THE period 1760–1830 was the first phase of the Industrial
Revolution. It was characterized by the great inventions, by
improved transport on roads and canals, a changing organization of production, a greatly increased output, a growth of
population, and an expansion of towns.

In the period 1830–50, which marked the second phase of
the Industrial Revolution, there were no inventions whose
effects on production were so profound as those which transformed the textile industries in the first period. Of the two
inventions which did most to increase the output of iron, the
first, the hot-air blast, was made known in 1828. Nor was the
increase of population nor the growth of towns so rapid in the
second period. The population of Great Britain, which had
increased by 50 per cent. between 1801 and 1831, increased by
little more than 25 per cent. between 1831 and 1851. London,
the ports, and the iron centres continued to grow rapidly, but
Glasgow, Birmingham, Sheffield, and the cotton towns had all
passed their maximum rate of growth.

The two main characteristics of the second phase of the
Industrial Revolution were, however, sufficiently significant.
They were the rapid construction of railways over the whole
country, and an increase of output so vast that that of 1760–
1830 was dwarfed by comparison.

(a) RAILWAYS AND THE NAVVIES

In 1830 there was little passenger transport other than coach
or horse, and heavy goods were conveyed slowly along the
great canals. In the forties Chartist delegates travelled to their
meetings by railway, and the canal as a highway for goods was
losing its supremacy to the iron road. While roads and canals
served the earlier stages of capitalism, railways were the instrument of capitalism in its prime. They opened markets, conveyed raw materials, reduced the cost of transport, created a

demand for iron and steel and labour. By supplying fields of investment, at home and later abroad, by mobilizing capital, including small savings, and by rewarding the contractor and speculator with fortunes, they helped to consolidate the resources of the middle class. By stimulating industry and agriculture both directly and indirectly they helped the country to emerge from the depression of the post-war years. At the same time they encouraged the mobility of men and ideas. People travelled more easily and made more visits for business and pleasure. Newspapers, books, and periodicals, as well as the mail, travelled by rail. Foodstuffs were carried quicker, with less decay and wastage.

The first public railways, like the first canals, were built to facilitate the marketing of coal or to link it with supplies of iron. In 1825 the Stockton–Darlington line was opened to provide an outlet for Durham coal. In 1830 followed the Liverpool–Manchester, for which Stephenson designed his *Rocket*, to bring raw materials and food to Manchester; in 1833 came the Leicester–Swannington, another coal line, which formed the beginning of the Midland system; in 1838 the London–Bath–Bristol, the beginning of the Great Western, and the London–Birmingham line. By this time 500 miles of railway were operating.[1] Ten years later 5000 miles of railway existed in the United Kingdom, including the East and West coast routes to Scotland and the London–York line.[2]

Railway development brought to light both the obstinacy of vested interests in resisting change and the conservatism of ordinary men and women, who at first regarded the "locomotive monster" with awe and dread:

What was to be done with all those who have advanced money in making and repairing turnpike roads? What was to become of the coach-makers and harness-makers, coach-masters, coachmen, inn-keepers, horse-breeders and horse-dealers? The beauty and comfort of country gentlemen's estates would be destroyed by it. Was the House aware of the smoke and the noise, the hiss and the whirl which locomotive engines, passing at the rate of ten or twelve miles an hour, would occasion? Neither the cattle ploughing in the fields or grazing in the meadows could behold them without dismay. Lease-holders and tenants, agriculturists,

[1] Sir John H. Clapham, *An Economic History of Modern Britain*, i, 387
[2] *Ibid.*, i, 391–392.

graziers and dairy-men would all be in arms. . . . Iron would be raised in price one hundred per cent., or, more probably, it would be exhausted altogether. It would be the greatest nuisance, the most complete disturbance of quiet and comfort in all parts of the kingdom, that the ingenuity of man could invent.[1]

In face of opposition many railways had to follow round-about routes or pay large sums for the purchase of land, or compensate landowners for the possible destruction of rural amenities. In addition, the process of getting Parliamentary permission in the form of an Act to lay down a railway was long, cumbersome, and expensive. As a result the cost of British railway construction was among the heaviest in the world, and all the costs were, of course, loaded into freight and passenger charges.

Until 1840 canals were still the chief carriers of goods, and many were still paying excellent dividends, while railways were concerned chiefly with passengers—partly because their engines were still too small and weak for heavy loads, partly because passengers pay better. Since their object was profit, the railways at first paid little attention to the third-class traveller, and even second-class passengers travelled in open carriages. It was not until 1844 that Parliament prescribed the famous 'Parliamentary train'—one train daily stopping at each station if required and carrying third-class passengers at a penny a mile. At the same time waiting-rooms and buffets were being built for the convenience of travellers.

By this initial preponderance of passenger traffic on the railways the canals were lulled into a false security, and therefore made little preparation for railway competition, except by cutting their rates in the few cases where railways actually opened in competition. When railways began to multiply rapidly in the forties and to carry more freight the canals were unprepared. Some organized Parliamentary opposition to Railway Bills, some amalgamated with a railway, some sold out to the railways at good prices, some at less good, others lingered on with falling trade and little profit. A few, on favourable routes, maintained, or even, like the Manchester–Liverpool, increased their traffic.

The turnpike roads similarly lost to the railway. Unlike the canals, they had no heavy goods traffic to keep them going,

[1] J. Francis, *A History of the English Railway* (1851), i, 119–120.

and most passenger- and mail-coaches ceased to run in the forties as travel by train became more popular. Tom Brown must have taken one of the last journeys of the *Tally Ho* when he travelled up to school at Rugby from London in the cold dawn of a day in the later thirties. Some steam-carriages were actually designed—notably one by Goldsworthy Gurney, intended to serve the London–Bath road—but no one was enthusiastic except the promoters. Only the horse-drawn traffic that fed the railways grew. But this was generally not on the turnpike roads, which mostly ran parallel to the railways, but on the local roads which intersected them.

The story of railway finance and the great railway speculators—foremost among them George Hudson, the linen-draper of York, who became "the Railway King"—is a fascinating though disreputable passage in nineteenth-century history. The first railways were financed by local people for one reason or another interested in a local railway. But after an initial period of general distrust, and when the high profits of the Liverpool–Manchester Railway became known, the general public went railway-mad. Intoxicated with the vision of high profits, oblivious of difficulties, promoters rushed in with plans for building railways all over the country. This was the 'little railway mania' of 1836–37. In 1838 there was a check. But in the forties the pace again became feverish. By 1846 'railway mania' was at its height. A 'railway party' in the House of Commons, headed by George Hudson himself, and a Prime Minister favourable to railways silenced opposition. It was no longer necessary to invest thousands of pounds; anyone with savings, however small, was welcomed by the railway promoters. The small investor had come into the field, and with him the small savings of the country were for the first time mobilized. This was a remarkable achievement, the causes of which were many. In the thirties and forties money was a little easier than it had been. People had a little more to spend, or to save, or to invest. The field of investment was in any case not wide, and when the Government began converting 4 per cent. loan to $3\frac{1}{2}$ per cent. and, in 1844, to $3\frac{1}{4}$ per cent., there was every inducement to change to railways. The move to railway investment was encouraged by the high dividends paid by some lines. Finally, when in 1844 Gladstone's Bill embodying a measure of

Government control of railways was mutilated in its passage, there was a flux of railway enthusiasm, investors gaining fresh confidence in the railway's freedom for expansion and profits. Thus the boom gathered its strength, and thousands of miles of railways were recklessly and wildly launched. There were 805 additional miles sanctioned in 1844; 2700 additional miles in 1845. There were schemes for railways in places possible and impossible. There were many projects for one and the same line—for example, five projected lines from London to Brighton. New lines were subscribed before old ones were complete and before capital had been set aside for depreciation. No account was taken of possible capital expenditure and high running expenses on existing lines. Dividends could not remain as high as the public demanded without eating up essential reserves. Money became tighter in the middle forties, prices were beginning to rise, the Bank of England raised its discount rate. New capital could not be raised when vitally required. And so in 1847 the boom broke. Interest was reduced or not paid at all. Capital was lost on worthless lines. Thousands of little investors were ruined as well as many men of substance. The Railway King himself fell from his eminence two years later when it was discovered that many of his dealings were fraudulent and his own fortune built up by dubious dealings with stocks and shares.

But, in spite of the pricked bubble of Hudson and the railway boom, the railway age had arrived.

Railway promotion in Britain was carried on entirely by private enterprise. Although six major Government Committees discussed railway policy between 1839 and 1853, *laissez-faire* had bitten deeply, and only one of these Committees—Gladstone's of 1844—recommended even a gradual taking over of railways by the State. So this important service was left to grow up haphazard, at the whim of private profit. While in France and Germany the railway system was planned, in Britain there existed no system, but simply many miles of railway lines, for the most part following existing lines of communication. Thomas Grey, who had visualized a system of radiating main lines with London as the centre, was looked upon as a fanatic. It was not until the second half of the century that the State even attempted to define its attitude towards the railway system, which by that time had become part of civilized life.

Meanwhile what of the people who built the railways? The workmen were known as 'navvies.' As a distinct species the navvy came into existence during the days of canal construction, the men who cut the channel for the ships being called 'navigators,' or 'navvies' for short. But his great days, when he became a social problem and even the subject of a Parliamentary Report, were those of the railway boom. The navvies proper were skilled workmen engaged on railway construction —hardworking daredevils, risking life and limb in blasting and tunnelling, well paid for it and matching hard work with hard drinking and eating and whatever other pleasures they could contrive.

The railway navvies were employed by railway contractors, in the boom years about 200,000 of them being at work in different parts of the country. The contractor was the man who undertook to see the job through from start to finish. Generally he made a fortune; frequently, like Thomas Brassey, Samuel Morton Peto, or Isambard Brunel, he obtained a contract for a foreign railway, exporting not only his iron rails, but his navvies and himself for the job. The story was current of the amazement of the French at the prodigious powers of work and the enormous appetite of the British navvy taken to France for railway construction.

Generally the contractor gave some of the work to a subcontractor; even sub-subcontracting was usual. The subcontractor, so Brunel told the Committee of 1846, was a man with a capital of about £1000 or £1500. He sublet his brickwork to small master bricklayers, and his earth-work usually to excavator gangs. The 'gangs' were of two kinds—'butty gangs,' where the men worked on a co-operative system, sharing the price of the work between them; or of a semi-capitalist type, one man contracting for the work, employing and paying the men, and making a profit for himself. The more critical undertakings, however, were generally not sublet.

The navvies were often local men, as on the South Devon line, where Dorset and Somerset men worked their way south and west with the railway, being joined later by Devonshire workers. On the other hand, navvy gangs frequently consisted of 'foreigners,' many having worked their way long distances from their homes, others being immigrant Irish or Scots. Considerable movements of workers were thus an accompaniment of railway construction.

The task of finding food and accommodation for them all was no light one. Villagers regarded with horror the prospect of some hundreds of navvies descending upon them for food and lodging, and were often completely unable to meet the onrush. Near the Woodhead Tunnel the company built stone cottages for the men; but accommodation was rarely as good as this. Sometimes the contractor would run up wooden huts or barracks. The roughest accommodation generally sufficed. The question of food was frequently solved by the tommy-shop, run by the contractor, the ganger, or some one who paid for the privilege. This, often the only shop for miles round, could charge what it wished and sell what it cared to. Even when village shops were near the men were often driven to the tommy-shop by having their wages paid irregularly and infrequently. Peto, a moderately enlightened contractor, operated an alternative scheme in inaccessible districts of the Fen country, where he notified village shopkeepers in advance of pay-day so that they sent carts with goods or men for orders.

The navvies built up a complete world of their own. Their work required much endurance and physical strength. They needed stamina beyond the average to stand up to the exposure to wind and rain and to sleeping quarters often cold and wet. The blasting of tunnels, often carried through at dangerous speed and with inadequate safety devices, exacted a high toll in injured and dead. When disabled or unfit for work these men knew they would most likely be cast aside to die—like the navvy in Patrick McGill's poem. Relaxation from such difficult and dangerous work was often rather terrifying. Eating, drinking, quarrelling, as ready to risk their lives outside working hours as in them, indulging in wild orgies when pay-day came, bringing their women with them or picking them up as they went along, with little regard for the law, making their own sport with dogs, pigeons, and fighting, the navvies were regarded with a kind of horrified awe by most of their fellows, and lived as outcasts from society. They had a reputation for swagger, bluster, and conceit, being better paid than most workers, not troubling to save money, and liking to display themselves in velvet trousers and bright plush waist-coats. But one rarely heard of a navvy's refusing to help a comrade. They had no trade unions, but sick clubs—essential on such dangerous work—provided help in time of sickness or disablement. Of orthodox religion they had little or none.

The problem of these 200,000 navvies began to exercise public opinion and the Government. In 1846 a Government Committee considered not only their housing accommodation, wages, food, extent and nature of accidents and compensation, but also their morals and political opinions. "Do you believe that many of them are Socialists?" was asked.

The evidence concerning accidents revealed a picture of mangled limbs, of pain heroically borne, and of death—with the company often refusing compensation, on the grounds of "unnecessary carelessness" on the men's part. But evidence showed that the opposite was too often the case. In the blasting of the Summit Tunnel on the Manchester–Sheffield railway, to give one example only, devices essential to the men's safety were omitted. The Committee challenged the companies and contractors to prove that "these great industrial undertakings are necessarily accompanied by so large a sacrifice of human life and limb," and that this was "part of the necessary price at which we purchase great national works." It suggested that companies be made civilly responsible for accidents.

Recommendations included the application of the Truck Acts to the railway labourers, and the provision of a police force under the direction of the local authorities and paid for by the companies. The railway navvies were so far a com-munity on their own, and were such a dangerous centre of potential disorder, that it was felt to be wisdom for the State and the companies to combine to make special arrangements to keep them in order.

The navvy was violent, intemperate, often vicious. Yet he was fearless and loyal. His place in English history, though remarkable, is not large, yet he is remembered with admiration and sometimes with compassion. In the words of Patrick McGill:

> He lived like a brute as the navvies live, and went as the cattle go,
> No one to sorrow and no one to shrive, for heaven ordained it so—
> He handed his check to the shadow in black, and went to the misty lands,
> Never a mortal to close his eyes or a woman to cross his hands.

(b) THE DEVELOPMENT OF INDUSTRY AND AGRICULTURE

The second characteristic of the period 1830–50 in Great Britain was a greatly increased output. This was due not so much to new inventions as to the wider application of methods already known, as well as to the great stimulus, direct and indirect, afforded by railways.

The application of steam-power to the textile industry continued at greater speed after 1830 than before. By 1830 cotton-spinning was almost entirely a steam-powered factory operation. After 1830 power was also rapidly applied to weaving. The number of power looms jumped from 60,000 in 1830 to 100,000 by 1834 and to 250,000 by 1850.[1] Of about 225,000 hand-looms in 1830 only 40,000 or 50,000 remained in 1850.[2] Similarly with the woollen industry. Spinning had become a power operation by 1830, while weaving was still largely done by hand. Silk-weaving in 1830 was also largely a manual operation organized on the outwork system, though silk-spinning was located in small power factories. Linen was in the same intermediate position. Between 1830 and 1850 the weaving of these three textiles, like that of cotton, became steam-factory processes, but the rate of change was slower. The 2000 woollen power looms of 1835, for example, grew to only 9000 by 1850,[3] and many hand-looms remained in all three industries.

Most of the finishing processes of the textile industries meanwhile—fulling, shearing, printing, glazing—had become mechanized, while chemical discoveries were improving the processes of dyeing and bleaching.

The period 1830–50, though not marking the complete mechanization of textiles, saw nevertheless a great increase in their product. The cotton industry, which was using 100,000 tons of raw cotton in 1830, consumed more than three times that amount in 1850. Imported raw wool rose from 11,000 tons to 33,000 tons between 1830 and 1850.[4]

The figures for iron production were perhaps the most spectacular of all, growing from 700,000 tons in 1830 to 1,000,000 tons in 1835, to 1,500,000 tons in 1840, and to over 2,000,000 tons by 1850.[5] In this industry two new devices

[1] Clapham, *op. cit.*, i, 554.   [2] *Ibid.*, i, 554.
[3] *Ibid.*, i, 554.   [4] *Ibid.*, i, 478.   [5] *Ibid.*, i, 425.

were used. The hot-air blast—made known in 1828—was the technical basis of the increased output, enabling the Scottish ores in particular to be used in great quantities, so that it was from Scottish mines that the greatest increases came. Eleven years later the steam-hammer greatly quickened production. Most of the increase came from comparatively few firms working on a much larger unit of production than formerly. The typical firm still ran two, three, or perhaps four small furnaces.[1] The figures of increased output are an index not of change over the whole industry, but of the remarkable expansion of a few firms.

The production of coal ran parallel to that of iron. There was a steady increase from an output of about 21,000,000 tons in 1826 to 30,000,000 tons in 1836, a sharper increase to 44,000,000 tons in 1846, and a much sharper rise to 65,000,000 tons in 1856.[2]

THE SECOND STAGE OF THE INDUSTRIAL REVOLUTION IN GREAT BRITAIN

Year	Consumption of Raw Cotton
1830	100,000 tons
1850	300,000 tons
	Iron Output
1835	1,000,000 tons
1840	1,500,000 tons
1850	2,000,000 tons
	Coal Production
1830	23,000,000 tons
1846	44,000,000 tons
1856	65,000,000 tons
	Population, in Millions
1831	16·0
1841	18·5
1851	21·0

[1] *Ibid.*, i, 430.   [2] *Ibid.*, i, 431.

The increased supplies of coal and iron were used largely by the railways both for home and foreign construction and running. Railways created a double demand for coal. Coal was needed both for smelting the iron used in railway construction and for the actual running of the locomotives. Demand for coal and iron came also from industry generally, and grew as steam-power and mechanization became more general between 1830 and 1850. There was also a higher domestic consumption of coal.

The export of manufactured goods played an increasingly important rôle in these years. Not only coal and iron for foreign railways, but heavy goods of all kinds, cotton goods, woollen goods, were exported in ever-growing quantities. The total value of exports nearly doubled between 1830 and 1850.

In face of these enormous increases in output and the apparently changing structure of British economy the figures of the occupational census of 1851 are unexpected. They reveal agriculture as still the greatest industry, employing 1,790,000, out of a total population over ten years old of 15,771,000. Domestic service was still numerically second, as it had been in 1831, employing 1,039,000 men and women. Cotton-workers had replaced builders in third place, with 527,000 operatives, builders coming fourth with 443,000. Wool-workers were in the seventh place (284,000), coalminers ninth (219,000), iron-workers seventeenth (80,000). Though the actual figures are a little uncertain, the occupational census of 1851[1] makes a number of facts abundantly clear: agriculture employed more persons than all the textile and heavy industries put together; there were more people in domestic service than in cotton and wool; handicraft blacksmiths were still more numerous than the workers in the great ironworks; more men were employed with horses on the roads than on the whole of the railway system.

This seeming discrepancy between a greatly increased industrial output and the figures of the occupational census is largely accounted for by the enormously increased output from each worker and each machine. Nor does it follow that the majority of men and women whose occupations were not mechanized were untouched by the developments of the time. What the occupational census of 1851 does emphasize is that,

[1] Clapham, *op. cit.*, ii, 24: "Principal Occupation Groups in Britain in 1851."

though the years 1830 to 1850 saw an unparalleled increase in Britain's production of heavy goods and textiles, Britain was far from being an industrial state.

Apart from the striking increase in production, there were at least two other directions in which progress was significant though not yet outstanding in the first half of the century. One was the development of the steamship and of the iron ship.

In 1802 the first steamship had sailed on the Forth and Clyde Canal. Fifteen years later a similar ship appeared on the Thames. Coastal and channel trips by steamboat began, but were not important until the thirties. In 1837 a steamship service was started between Falmouth and Gibraltar. In the following year an Atlantic steamship service began. In 1840 the Falmouth–Gibraltar line was extended to Egypt, and later to India and the Far East. In 1845 the first iron ship crossed the Atlantic.

The other important development which had its small beginnings in the first half of the century was the electric telegraph. Electrical engineering was not born as a science until 1831, the year in which Faraday advanced his theory of electromagnetic induction. The electric telegraph was one of the important inventions which developed from Faraday's theory. In 1839 the first electric telegraph was installed by the Great Western Railway between Paddington and West Drayton.

For agriculture the period 1830–50 started in acute depression. In face of the depressed condition of the country generally, only an improvement in agricultural technique and a general 'rationalization' could save agriculture from stagnation. Yet standing in the way of improvement were several factors. There was little capital available; an uneconomic preponderance of wheat production at the expense of mixed farming was encouraged by the Corn Laws, which, at the same time, gave an artificial protection to agriculture in place of the real protection of scientific farming; the general depression prevented the increased demand for agricultural produce which alone could have stimulated the agricultural interest to fresh efforts. So the most difficult land, particularly the heavy clay soils, deteriorated through want of care and capital.

Animals were badly and unscientifically housed. Farm buildings decayed. There were a few outstandingly good farms,
whose farmers were applying the newest knowledge to their
work, but these were not typical. The Government, meantime, though it appointed several Committees to inquire into
the matter, could think of nothing to apply to a failing agriculture but the then universal specific of *laissez-faire*. "Although
it is in the power of the legislature to do much evil," stated the
Select Committee of 1833, "yet it can do little positive good by
interference in agricultural industry."

In the middle of the thirties the vicious circle of restricted
markets, bad farming, and lack of capital was broken. The
beginnings of industrial revival, and in particular railway
development, acted as general stimuli. Greater industrial
prosperity was reflected in an increased demand for agricultural produce. Railways not only helped agriculture indirectly,
but directly. They opened new markets for agricultural produce, they safely conveyed goods which otherwise would have
perished in transit. They conveyed without loss of weight
animals which formerly lost pounds as they journeyed on foot
from the fattening pastures to the big cities. They brought
agricultural implements, manures and chemicals, and agricultural journals; they spread knowledge, popularized new ideas,
and removed many farms from virtual isolation. In addition,
the New Poor Law of 1834 and the Tythe Commutation Act
of 1836 relieved farmers of burdens which had previously fallen
heavily upon them. The poor rate alone fell from £7,000,000
in 1832 to £4,000,000 in 1837.[1]

In these more favourable circumstances agriculture took on
a new lease of life. Landlords began to supply some of the
capital needed to effect improvements, and by the end of the
thirties a definite advance towards more careful, scientific
farming was apparent. The final stimulus to 'high farming'
was, however, provided by the repeal of the Corn Laws in
1846. These protective laws had provided some comfort to the
farmer in the blackest years of depression. The knowledge of
their removal did more to stimulate him into a reorganization
of his farming methods than either the depression itself or the
propaganda of reformers. Caird's maxim, "High farming the
best Substitute for Protection," was widely adopted, with

[1] Lord Ernle, *English Farming, Past and Present*, p. 350.

respect both to the application of capital and to the rationalization of agriculture.

The use of machinery and of artificial manures became more
general, drainage was improved, there were better farm
buildings, more adequate provision for farm animals, greater
care of livestock. There was a more careful balancing of arable
against pasture. Animal manure was scientifically utilized for
the land, while swedes and mangel-wurzels, which store better
than turnips, were grown for the express purpose of maintaining
animals during the winter.

The Royal Agricultural Society—"the heart and brain of
agriculture"—founded in 1838, acted as clearing-house for new
ideas and adviser to the farmers. The Government also stepped
in to assist development. Its first drainage loan of £2,000,000
in 1846 was evidently intended as a slight compensation to the
landed interest for the abandonment of protection. Another
£2,000,000 loan followed in 1850, and Drainage and Improvement Acts provided Government supervision. As agriculture
continued to move steadily towards the 'high farming' period
of the mid-nineteenth century two characteristics became
apparent—a growth in the size of holdings and a movement
towards permanent pasture and away from large wheat farms.

The size of the unit of cultivation, though on the whole it
increased, showed great variety both from county to county
and within the same county. In East Anglia, the chief grain
district, farms were large. The sheep-walks on the Sussex
Downs were large; but in other parts of Sussex quite small
farms existed; while in Kent and the South-east there were
many really small holdings of ten to fourteen acres. Essex
compassed the whole range from the large-scale to the very
small market garden. In the West the dairying and mixed
farms were generally small; in the neighbourhood of towns
small mixed farms catered for the local market. In Norfolk
and the Fen district were many large farms and numbers of
small ones, including some where a few small owners continued
to work their land.

These yeoman farmers were exceptional. The decline of
their class had been a feature of the Enclosure movement.
The high prices of the war period had temporarily arrested
their decline, but in the slump they were virtually extinguished.
The small tenant farmer, though his numbers also were

reduced, continued in some parts of the country to farm his small holding, and the census of 1831 revealed the existence of quite a number of farms under 100 acres.

The increase in permanent pasture at the expense of the large wheat farms was a natural sequel to Corn Law repeal and a necessary preliminary to good mixed farming. It had gone so far by the mid-century that a French observer estimated in 1854 that half of the land of England was under pasture.

So between 1830 and 1850 British agriculture was responding to a diffusion of scientific knowledge and to the application of capital, the size of the unit of cultivation was growing, and there was an increase in permanent pasture. Agriculture as a whole was improving in methods and results and moving steadily towards the period of 'high farming.'

(c) THE FREEING OF TRADE

Meanwhile a revolution ancillary to the Industrial and Agrarian revolutions was in progress.

The relics of three centuries' practice of restrictive mercantilism still survived at the opening of the nineteenth century. The British East India Company preserved the monopoly of the India and China trades. The course of trade was still partially prescribed by the Navigation Acts. Laws forbade the export of machinery or the emigration of artisans. There was a nominal wage regulation under the Elizabethan Statute of Artificers. Taxes on imported corn protected British farmers, but raised prices for British consumers. There were tariffs on the import of manufactured goods, taxes on the export of raw materials. There were various revenue taxes on consumption whose range and number had grown exorbitant during the stress of the Napoleonic wars. In 1820 Sydney Smith was writing in *The Edinburgh Review*:

> Taxes upon every article which enters into the mouth, or covers the back, or is placed under the foot—taxes upon everything which it is pleasant to see, hear, feel, smell or taste—taxes upon warmth, light, and locomotion—taxes on everything on earth, and the waters under the earth—on everything that comes from abroad or is grown at home—taxes on the raw material—taxes on every fresh value that is added to it by the industry of man— taxes on the sauce which pampers man's appetite, and the drug

THE OPENING OF THE STOCKTON AND DARLINGTON RAILWAY, 1825

[See p. 99]

By courtesy of the Director of the Science Museum, South Kensington

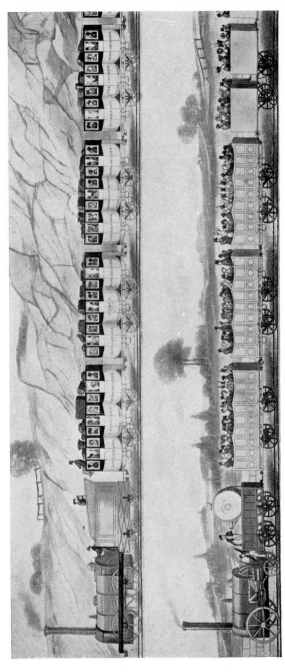

TRAVELLING ON THE LIVERPOOL AND MANCHESTER RAILWAY

[See p. 99]

By courtesy of the Director of the Science Museum, South Kensington

NAVVIES AT WORK, EXCAVATING ON THE LIVERPOOL
AND MANCHESTER RAILWAY

[See pp. 103–105]

By courtesy of the Director of the Science Museum, South Kensington

GURNEY'S STEAM COACH, 1827

[See p. 101]

By courtesy of the Director of the Science Museum, South Kensington

that restores him to health—on the ermine which decorates the judge, and the rope which hangs the criminal—on the poor man's salt, and the rich man's spice—on the brass nails of the coffin, and the ribands of the bride—at bed or board, couchant or levant, we must pay:—The school-boy whips his taxed top—the beardless youth manages his taxed horse, with a taxed bridle on a taxed road:—and the dying Englishman pouring his medicine, which has paid seven per cent., into a spoon that has paid fifteen per cent.—flings himself back upon his chintz bed which has paid twenty-two per cent.—makes his will on an eight pound stamp, and expires in the arms of an apothecary who has paid a licence of £100 for the privilege of putting him to death. His whole property is then immediately taxed from two to ten per cent. Besides the probate, large fees are demanded for burying him in the chancel; his virtues are handed down to posterity on taxed marble; and he is then gathered to his fathers,—to be taxed no more.[1]

Finally, during the Napoleonic wars, Pitt introduced an income-tax to help meet the mounting national expenditure. The burden of war debt was immense. An annual revenue of £74,500,000—four times the size of the pre-war budget[2]—was required to meet the debt and other expenditure. Hence the multiplication of taxes. Hence also the need of any reform to justify itself by continuing to supply the national exchequer to equal or greater extent. There were indeed reasons enough for reform. The system was so complicated that it often defeated its own ends. Officials made excusable mistakes or were frankly ignorant; smuggling and other forms of evading the tariff were rife; the excise frequently cost as much to collect as it yielded; there were

a great army of excise-men and irksome restrictions on traders. At the head of the army were the Collectors, 55 in all in 1835; under them the County Supervisors; under them the Ride Officers for country districts, the Footwalk Officers for towns, the Special London Officers for London. Every dealer in an excisable article had to take out a licence for it and to enter every sale in books provided by the Department. No articles subject to excise could be removed, except in very small quantities, from one place to another without a written permit. Once a month the office took an account of the stock of every retailer.[3]

[1] January 1820, vol. 33, pp. 77-78.
[2] W. Cunningham, *Growth of English Industry and Commerce: Modern Times,* Part II, p. 833.
[3] C. R. Fay, *Great Britain from Adam Smith to the Present Day,* p. 61.

Adam Smith had already enunciated the doctrine that free trade benefited both buyers and sellers, enabling each to dispose of his surplus and acquire what he needed, and that in both international trade and internal the unfettered free enterprise of individuals made for the maximum public good. But mercantilist theory and practice was finally discredited because it restricted the development of British commercial and industrial interests. Merchants with opportunities of expanding trade and commerce, yet cut off from the lucrative markets of the East by the East India Company, required freedom to trade where they wished. The cotton-manufacturers demanded that the duty on raw cotton be removed. Landowners objected to the restriction of their market for raw wool. Manufacturers and their workpeople cried for cheap bread and the abolition of the Corn Laws. Shopkeepers and merchants supplying the home market asked for nothing more urgently than freedom to sell to the public at prices that the public could pay; while the public wanted cheap articles and no taxation. The only interests still defending taxation were the landowners, who fought tooth and nail until 1846 for the right to tax imported corn.

The basic fact underlying the outcry for the reform of the fiscal system was that British industry and commerce no longer needed protection. The home market was expanding. The Napoleonic wars had provided protection sufficient to enable British industry to outstrip the industries of a war-ravaged Europe. British shipping interests emerged from the wars strong enough to face foreign competition. Britain wanted cheap raw materials and unlimited markets, cheap bread for the masses (to keep down wages and therefore costs of production), and sufficient imports to enable the foreigner to pay for British exports. She wanted all her ships to travel with merchandise all over the world; she wanted to choose the cheapest ships for her goods; she welcomed raw materials and essential foodstuffs, so long as they were cheap, in the ships of any nations. Finally, she would no longer restrict her home market by a multiplicity of excise duties. Revenue the Government must have, but careful and scientific taxation, and even a small income-tax, could supply the place of the duty on thousands of articles of everyday use. The voice that thus cried was the voice of the industrialist, of the middle class.

But it was also the voice of sound common sense, the voice of the workers, of the bankers, of the Government. The repeal of the Corn Laws was the only Free Trade measure which caused a major clash of interest.

In 1813 the Indian trade was opened to all British subjects. Twenty years later the China trade was similarly freed. The East India Company's monopoly was, after over two hundred years, overthrown; anyone was free to lend a hand in forcing open China's door. In 1839 and 1856 the Government backed British merchants in this policy in the notorious Opium wars. Finally, in 1849, the survivals of the Navigation Acts were repealed amid a weak protest from shipowners.

The work of fiscal reform was begun by Pitt, but interrupted by the Napoleonic wars. He fought smuggling by substituting for the tariff a series of excise duties. The duty on goods taxed at a port could be evaded by the goods being smuggled past the port and on to the middleman. There was no such opportunity for evading the excise, a tax paid by the consumer on purchase of the goods and handed over by the producer or importer.

A systematic reduction of taxation was initiated by Huskisson. The years 1822–28 were comparatively prosperous, and the Government felt able to forgo some of the taxation revenue. The duties on many raw materials were lowered, those on copper, zinc, tin, and wool being halved; in general, Huskisson made 30 per cent. the limit of taxation on raw materials and semi-finished goods, and reduced much of the high taxation on foreign manufactured goods. The import of foreign silk, for example, was permitted on payment of a 30 per cent. duty. Export bounties and export prohibitions were withdrawn, with the exception of wool, where an export tax of 1d. per pound was substituted for complete prohibition of export. Taxes on windows, shops, horses, carriages and servants, the excise duty on salt, spirits, leather, candles, starch, sweets, were reduced or withdrawn. The wine excise was abolished in 1825, the tea excise in 1833, the beer tax in 1830, the tobacco excise in 1840. The transit duties on coal were reduced, the law prohibiting the emigration of artisans was repealed in 1824; the export of machinery was permitted under licence.

Still many taxes remained. The general principle which lay behind Peel's great budgets of 1842–46 was that of obtaining money by an income-tax and a tax on the export of coal, so still further relieving the tariff and the excise and thereby lowering the cost of living. Imports he divided roughly into three classes with maximum duties: raw materials had to pay a maximum duty of 5 per cent.; partly manufactured goods a maximum duty of 12 per cent.; fully manufactured goods a maximum duty of 20 per cent. The export of machinery was completely freed in 1843, and the following year the export duty on wool, which Huskisson had reduced to 1d. a pound, was abolished altogether. Peel abolished the excise duties on livestock, meat, and potatoes; he reduced those on sugar, cheese, and butter. Gladstone's budgets of 1853 and 1860 completed the work, and Britain was virtually a Free Trade country. The repeal of the Corn Laws Peel also achieved as spokesman of the Anti-Corn Law League and at the cost of his position as leader of the Tory Party. The fight on the Corn Law issue and the defeat of the landed interest marked the triumph of Free Trade and the supremacy of the industrial interest. Its significance is so great that it is treated separately in a later chapter.

(d) BANKING AND CURRENCY

The development of industry, the growth of railways, the payment of wages, buying and selling, all on a scale unprecedented, required a corresponding expansion of the various means of payment, without which the multiple transactions of modern economy were impossible. At the same time heavy war expenditure, the increasing note issue, and high prices caused apprehension and uncertainty. After the war it was obviously necessary to ensure that sufficient means of payment were available for the smooth working of the economic machine and to provide a stable currency.

The use of cheques had been growing since the seventeenth century, and eased the transactions between business-men. But at the beginning of the Industrial Revolution an acute shortage was felt in ready cash with which to pay wages. When agricultural labourers who had been paid chiefly in kind became factory workers with a weekly wage the demand for money was clearly much increased. The precious metals, even when supplemented by Bank of England notes, were insufficient. The strain was instanced by the prevalence of truck, the employer still seeking to pay either in kind or in tallies. That his motive was often gain and intimidation does not alter the fact that a real money shortage existed.

The Bank of England had been founded in 1694, and various private banks also existed. Means of payment were cheque, gold, silver, Bank of England notes, and notes issued by private banks. Gold was the basis of the currency, silver being mere 'change' and legal tender for amounts up to 40s. only. Bank of England notes were exchangeable at the Bank for gold, and their value was thus strictly their face value until 1797, during the Napoleonic wars, when the Government authorized the Bank to suspend cash payment for its notes. Suspension was continued until 1821. During the period of suspension the Bank of England notes were made legal tender, and it was compulsory to accept them as a means of payment equivalent to gold. Both Bank of England notes and the notes of country banks, generally £2 and £1 notes, were the chief medium of exchange during the suspension period. When cash payments were resumed in 1821 notes ceased to be legal tender, until the Act of 1833 made them so for all purposes except at the Bank of England itself. Other banks were compelled to redeem their notes in legal tender—gold or Bank of England notes.

In 1816 Britain tied her currency definitely to gold by adopting a gold standard, which meant simply that the pound sterling was said to be worth a given quantity of gold. In practice this meant that gold bullion could be coined into gold at the Bank of England at the rate of £3 17s. 10½d. an ounce, and that it could be exported. In 1819 bullion and coin were allowed freely in and out of the country, a move which paralleled the development of Free Trade in commodities.

Meantime the questions of credit and security of investment were equally important to an expanding capitalist economy. Banks were all allowed to issue notes without limit, the number they issued being determined by the state of trade and of demand generally. In the depression after the Napoleonic wars issues were small, and many country banks failed. In the speculative mania which followed, particularly for investment in the South American states, the issue of banknotes increased enormously, and when the widespread demand came in 1825 for their redemption in gold many country and London banks went out of business.

To remedy an over-issue of notes an Act of 1826 tried both to increase the size of banks and to decrease their note issue. The monopoly of the Bank of England had prevented the opening of banks on a joint-stock basis. Now joint-stock banks were permitted to open for the issue of notes outside a radius of sixty-five miles from London. In 1833 the Bank Charter Act allowed the joint-stock banks within the sixty-five-mile radius. Crises nevertheless recurred, and in 1844 Peel by the Bank Charter Act attempted a more drastic regulation of the great machine of currency and credit, which was becoming more ponderous and more dangerous to the stability of the country.

The main feature of the Act of 1844 was the regularization and restriction of the issue of paper money. In the London area the Bank of England was given the sole right of issuing notes, and any joint-stock bank which opened a London house or amalgamated with a London house automatically surrendered its right of issue; if a private bank increased its partners to more than six it similarly forfeited its right of issue; no new bank of issue was to be established; and if an issue was voluntarily surrendered the Bank of England automatically acquired the right of printing up to two-thirds of the lapsed issue. The Bank of England itself was authorized to issue notes uncovered by gold to the value of £14,000,000—the fiduciary issue. After that each note needed to be backed pound for pound by gold in coin or bullion. In these ways an excessive note issue and the accompanying evil of inflation were expected to be controlled. The joint-stock banks gradually amalgamated, or otherwise forfeited their right of issue, and so the Bank of England became the only important note-issuing agency.

To finance industry on the scale necessary to the Industrial Revolution it remained necessary to mobilize the savings which still lay in banks or which were hoarded at home. The high interest paid, particularly by the railways, was partially successful in making available this capital. Later the reform of company organization would still more effectively bring into use the small and large savings necessary for capitalist development.[1]

[1] See Chapter XIV (a).

SELECT BIBLIOGRAPHY

Report of Select Committee on Railway Labourers, 1846, XIII.

BAINES, SIR EDWARD: *History of the Cotton Manufacture in Great Britain* (1835).

CHAMBERS, J. D. AND MINGAY, G. E.: *The Agricultural Revolution, 1750–1880* (Batsford, 1966).

CLAPHAM, SIR JOHN H.: *An Economic History of Modern Britain*, vol. i, *The Early Railway Age, 1820–1850* (Cambridge University Press, 1930).

ERNLE, LORD: *English Farming, Past and Present* (Longmans, 1912; revised edition, 1961).

FAY, C. R.: *Great Britain from Adam Smith to the Present Day* (Longmans, 1928).

FLINN, M. W.: *British Population Growth 1700–1850* (Studies in Economic History, Macmillan, 1970).

FRANCIS, J.: *A History of the English Railway* (Longmans, 1851).

JACKMAN, W. T.: *The Development of Transportation in Modern England*, 2 vols. (Cambridge University Press, 1916).

JERVIS, F. R. J.: *The Evolution of Modern Industry* (Harrap, 1960).

KNOWLES, L. C. A.: *The Industrial and Commercial Revolutions in Great Britain during the Nineteenth Century* (Routledge, 1921).

LAMBERT, RICHARD S.: *The Railway King, 1800–1871* (Allen and Unwin, 1934).

LIPSON, E.: *The Growth of English Society*, Part III (fourth edition, Black, 1959).

ORWIN, C. S.: *A History of English Farming* (Nelson, 1949).

SHERRINGTON, C. E. R.: *A Hundred Years of Inland Transport. 1830–1933* (Duckworth, 1934).

CHAPTER VI

WORKING CONDITIONS

(a) INDUSTRY AND TRADE

WHEN steam superseded water-power, 'free-labour' children and their parents took the place of the pauper apprentices who had worked in the first textile mills. When factories moved to the coalfield towns the labour of whole families became abundant. These new recruits were forced into the factories by a double pressure. The Enclosure movement drove them off the land and deprived them of their customary rights. At the same time the development of machine industry rendered their own handicrafts of little commercial value. By slow stages (there were as yet no railways) increasing numbers made their way to the nearest town and thence to the industrial Midlands and North, their ranks being swollen by poverty-stricken immigrants from Ireland and Scotland.

Children and adults of both sexes were employed in the factories, six or seven being the admitted age of starting work, though children sometimes began at three and four years old. Parents were frequently compelled by economic pressure to send their children to the mill; in some cases they were unemployed themselves, and were refused parish relief if they had children who could work; sometimes adults were refused work unless they brought their children with them. The consequences were reflected not only on the unfortunate child labourers but on the parents, whose wages were forced down by their own children.

The lot of the free-labour children was little better than that of the pauper apprentices, save that they slept at home. Hours ranged from twelve a day to as many as nineteen in busy periods. Discipline was in the hands of overseers who were bound to exact a full quota of work or be penalized themselves. Brutality, including whipping and beating, was said to be necessary to keep the children awake, who otherwise, from sheer fatigue, sometimes fell into the moving machinery, to be killed or maimed. Parents were known themselves to beat their

children to save them from a worse fate at the overseer's
hands. The children had frequently to clean the machinery
while taking their food, and often while it was moving, with
the result that their lungs were filled with dust and flue, and
they ran the danger of mutilation. A rigid discipline was
enforced on adults and children alike. Beating and loss of
wages were the penalties for arriving late at work. For opening
a window (the temperature was 80–84 degrees) the penalty
was a fine of 1s.; for keeping the gas burning too long into the
morning the operative was fined 2s.; for washing himself 1s.;
if he was able to raise his spirits so far as to whistle while at
work he was fined 1s. In one mill near Manchester operatives
were not allowed a drink of water, and even the rainwater
was locked up.[1]

The tale of these unfortunate factory workers has been told
many times. But their own stories of their lives, told unemo-
tionally to Government Committees, remain the most eloquent
testimony to their wrongs. Here is the story told by the father
of two mill girls to the Committee on Factory Children's
Labour of 1832. The witness is Samuel Coulson, and the
questions are numbered as in the original report:

5047. At what time in the morning, in the brisk time, did those
girls go to the mills?
In the brisk time, for about six weeks, they have gone at
3 o'clock in the morning, and ended at 10, or nearly half-
past at night.

5049. What intervals were allowed for rest or refreshment during
those nineteen hours of labour?
Breakfast a quarter of an hour, and dinner half an hour,
and drinking a quarter of an hour.

5051. Was any of that time taken up in cleaning the machinery?
They generally had to do what they call dry down;
sometimes this took the whole of the time at breakfast or
drinking, and they were to get their dinner or breakfast
as they could; if not, it was brought home.

5054. Had you not great difficulty in awakening your children
to this excessive labour?
Yes, in the early time we had them to take up asleep and
shake them, when we got them on the floor to dress them,
before we could get them off to their work.

[1] List published by spinners at Manchester during a strike. Quoted by J. L.
and B. Hammond: *The Town Labourer, 1760-1832*, pp. 19-20.

5059. What was the length of time they could be in bed during those long hours?

It was near 11 o'clock before we could get them into bed after getting a little victuals, and then . . . my mistress used to stop up all night, for fear that we could not get them ready for the time. . . .

5060. What time did you get them up in the morning?

In general me or my mistress got up at 2 o'clock to dress them.

5061. So that they had not above four hours' sleep at this time?

No, they had not.

5062. For how long together was it?

About six weeks. . . .

5063. The common hours of labour were from 6 in the morning till half-past eight at night?

Yes.

5065. Were the children excessively fatigued by this labour?

Many times; we have cried often when we have given them the little victualling we had to give them; we had to shake them, and they have fallen to sleep with the victuals in their mouths many a time.

5066. Had any of them any accident in consequence of this labour?

Yes, my eldest daughter when she went first there; . . . the cog caught her forefinger nail and screwed it off below the knuckle, and she was five weeks in Leeds Infirmary.

5068. Were her wages paid during that time?

As soon as the accident happened the wages were totally stopped. . . .

5072. Did this excessive term of labour occasion much cruelty also?

Yes, with being so very much fatigued the strap was very frequently used.

5073. Have any of your children been strapped?

Yes, every one. . . .

5080. What was the wages in the short hours?

Three shillings a week each.

5081. When they wrought those very long hours what did they get?

Three shillings and sevenpence-halfpenny.

5082. For all that additional labour they had only $7\frac{1}{2}d$. a week additional?

No more.

5083. Could you dispose of their wages, when they had received them, as you wished? . . .

The children have said, "If we do not bring some little from the shop I am afraid we shall lose our work." And sometimes they used to bring a bit of sugar or some little oddment, generally of their own head.

5084. That is, they were expected to lay out part of their wages under the truck system?
Yes.

5086. Had your children any opportunity of sitting during those long days of labour?
No. . . .

5118. At the time they worked those long hours, would it have been in their power to work a shorter number of hours, taking the 3s.?
They must either go on at the long hours, or else be turned off.[1]

Secondly, let us hear Elizabeth Bentley, a little doffer, whose task was to remove the full bobbins from the spinning-machine, and supply empty ones:

5127. What age are you?
Twenty-three.

5128. Where do you live?
At Leeds.

5129. What time did you begin to work at a factory?
When I was six years old.

5131. What kind of mill is it?
Flax mill.

5132. What was your business in that mill?
I was a little doffer.

5133. What were your hours of labour in that mill?
From five in the morning till 9 at night, when they were thronged.

5134. For how long a time together have you worked that excessive length of time?
For about half a year.

5214. You are considerably deformed in your person in consequence of this labour?
Yes, I am.

5215. At what time did it come on?
I was about 13 years old when it began coming, and it has got worse ever since; it is five years since my mother died, and my mother was never able to get me a pair of

<hr>

[1] *Report of Select Committee on Factory Children's Labour*, 1831–32, XV, 192 *et seq.*

good stays to hold me up, and when my mother died I had
to do for myself, and got me a pair.

5216. Were you perfectly straight and healthy before you worked
at a mill?

Yes, I was as straight a little girl as ever went up and
down town.

5217. Were you straight till you were 13?

Yes, I was.[1]

In spite of such evidence, people argued then, and are still
arguing now, as to whether factory slavery was any worse than
the domestic system in which whole families, including children
of three and four years old, laboured from morning until night.
In their cottage homes workers were at least not subject to the
whip of the overseer or the fine for leaving a window open;
nor was "the animal machine chained fast to the iron machine,"
and beyond their cottage door was always the fresh air of
garden or field where they could refresh themselves. Contrast
this with the lack of home life, the stifling atmosphere of the
factory, the increasingly foul conditions of the town beyond,
the mutilation of children, and it is not surprising that only
after a prolonged period of struggle were handworkers driven
into the factory.

Nor were wages such as to attract people to the factories.
Though employers in 1818 quoted wages as high as 30s. to
40s. a week, these figures were convincingly disproved by the
men. *The Gorgon* for September 12, 1818, gave the total wages
of a spinner and three piecers as £3 3s. 4d. Out of this the
piecers received their wages ranging from 5s. 8d. to 9s. 2d. a
week, and the spinner paid for candles and sick benefit and
incidental expenses. He was left with 18s. 4d. to keep himself
and his family for a week.[2] For children the cases of the
Coulson children show that wages of 3s. and 3s. 6d. a week
were usual. It was in the several strikes of the period that the
question of wages was brought to the fore. The factory-reform
movement directed attention more to hours and conditions of
work than to wages.

Factory reform was slowly and painfully won. It began
with the cotton mills, taking nearly fifty years to achieve a

[1] *Report of Select Committee on Factory Children's Labour*, 1831–32, XV, 195 *et seq.*
[2] J. L. and B. Hammond, *The Skilled Labourer, 1760–1832*, pp. 97–99.

nominal ten-hour day. Partial regulation had spread to other textiles by 1833, but not until 1861 were other trades included. The movement was sponsored by one of the strangest medleys which ever agreed upon one political measure. First, there were many humane manufacturers; some themselves introduced reforms into their factories, others were willing to do so if the law compelled all manufacturers to do likewise. Secondly, members of the Church of England, Evangelical Christians and others, were moved by philanthropic and religious sentiments to support factory reform. Thirdly, the Tory landowners were glad when considering the factory children to give full scope to those feelings of sympathy which rarely overflowed towards the wretched agricultural labourers dwelling on their own estates. With the landowners went most of the Tory Press and also *Punch*. Finally, there were the adult workers themselves. They were organized in 'Short-time Committees,' which attempted to enforce the factory laws already in existence and to further the Ten Hours movement.

Individuals prominent in the agitation were John Doherty, the energetic trade-union organizer; Robert Owen, whose influence and example were vital forces in the early days of factory reform; John Fielden, Radical cotton-spinner, whose works were among the largest in the world and who introduced a ten-hour day into his own factory: John Wood, Bradford worsted-spinner and Evangelical Christian, who gave £40,000 towards the factory-reform campaign; G. S. Bull, vicar of Brierley, near Bradford; Richard Oastler, land agent and Tory, whose fiery eloquence on behalf of the factory workers was rivalled only by that of the Wesleyan minister, Tory, and Chartist, John Raynor Stephens; Michael Sadler, Member of Parliament for Leeds, Tory, banker, Evangelical Christian, and Sunday-school superintendent; Anthony Ashley, later Earl of Shaftesbury, Tory landowner and Evangelical Churchman.

Opposing this group of reformers stood many of the manufacturers. They resisted factory legislation on the double ground that it would increase their costs and that it was an unwarrantable interference with private property. So urgent were they in pushing the first claim that it seemed as though all the prosperity of industrial Lancashire and Yorkshire must depend on some hundreds of little children. "Hitherto," exclaimed William Cobbett in the House of Commons, we have been told that our navy was the glory of the country, and that our maritime commerce and extensive manufactures were the mainstays of the realm. We have also been told that the land had its share in our greatness, and should justly be considered as the pride and glory of England. The Bank, also, has put in its claim to share in this praise, and has stated that public credit is due to it; but now, a most surprising discovery has been made, namely, that all our greatness and prosperity, that our superiority over other nations, is owing to 300,000 little girls in Lancashire. We have made the notable discovery, that, if these little girls work two hours less in a day than they now do, it would occasion the ruin of the country; that it would enable other nations to compete with us; and thus make an end to our boasted wealth, and bring us to beggary![1]

Many of the manufacturers who opposed factory reform—notably John Bright—were active in the movement for the abolition of negro slavery. This anomaly evoked from Richard Oastler in 1830 the *Letters on Yorkshire Slavery*, in which he pointed to "the little white slaves of the factories." It drew from John Fielden the exclamation, "What a pity that these 35,000 factory children happen to be white instead of black!"

In spite of the fact that many manufacturers opposed and many landowners supported factory legislation, it was the Whigs who passed the most important Factory Acts. Lord Ashley, himself a Tory, lamented that he received more support in this cause from his political opponents than from his own party. The difficulty of drawing any clear-cut line between parties on this issue is demonstrated by the fact that first Sadler, the Tory banker, then Ashley, the Tory landowner, then Fielden, the Radical manufacturer, led the cause of factory reform in Parliament. The campaigns were often marked by confusion and cross-loyalties. "The discussions and divisions on the Factory Bill have been of the most confused and almost ludicrous kind," wrote *The Leeds Times* of the 1844 debates.[2] "I never remember," wrote Greville of the same debates,

a more curious political state of things, such intermingling of parties, such a confusion of opposition . . . so much zeal, asperity, and animosity, so many reproaches hurled backwards and for-

[1] Quoted by John Fielden, *The Curse of the Factory System* (1836), p. 48.
[2] Quoted by Hutchins and Harrison, *A History of Factory Legislation*, p. 69.

wards. The Government . . . have been abandoned by nearly
half their supporters. . . . The Opposition were divided. . . . It
has been a very queer affair.[1]

A further characteristic of the factory-reform movement was
the number of Committees which examined the question of
factory labour. But this is a common feature of nineteenth-
century procedure, and of invaluable service to the historian.

The Health and Morals of Apprentices Act of 1802 was a
dead letter, and in any case applied only to the pauper apprentices of the water-mills. It was again Robert Owen who directed
Peel's attention to the condition of the steam-mills. In 1815 a
Bill proposing reform met with such opposition that three
Committees—those of 1816, 1818, and 1819—were required
before any legislation was permitted. Two of these Committees
flatly contradicted each other. That of 1818 produced medical
men to testify—rather strangely—that there was nothing amiss
with the condition of the factory children: that of 1819 refuted
this evidence. After this the Factory Act of 1819 was passed.
It applied to cotton mills only, where it prohibited the labour
of children under nine years of age, and limited the hours of
persons under sixteen to twelve a day. It required no evidence
of a child's age, and provided for no adequate inspection,
enforcement of the law remaining with the justices of the peace.
Consequently, niggardly as it was, the Act of 1819 remained,
like its predecessor, largely inoperative.

Other Acts followed in 1825 and 1831. But meantime the
operatives were forming Short-time Committees with the
object of more effective reform. Since the children under
thirteen employed in the factories formed a high proportion
of the total number of operatives, it was thought impossible to
shorten the children's hours without reducing adults'. The
agitation for factory reform began, consequently, to concentrate
on the children.

The battle for the ten-hour day was joined when in December
1831 Sadler introduced a Ten Hours Bill in the House of
Commons. In March 1832 it received a second reading, but
only on condition that a Select Committee examined the whole
question of the condition of the factories. This famous Committee, with Sadler as chairman, heard Oastler and others give

[1] *Memoirs*: March 31, 1844; ii, 236–237 (1885 edition).

evidence. Many operatives themselves told the tales of their lives and their physical deformities. It was to Sadler's Committee that the little doffer told her story and before whom Samuel Coulson described the lives of his children. And many more came with their simple and tragic stories. The accumulation of such evidence, which has made the Report of Sadler's Committee a classic document, was largely due to the tireless energy and resource of Sadler himself, and his name is for ever associated with the attempt to reduce this catalogue of wrongs. By some the Committee was considered biased, because it gave more time and weight to the evidence of the operatives than to that of their employers. But the evidence given has never been refuted.

At this point other events impinged upon the cause of factory reform. While the operatives were demanding the ten-hour day, and Sadler was pressing their case in the Commons, the Reform Bill agitation was shaking Parliament and country. In December 1832 the first election under the new franchise was held, and Sadler was unseated by Macaulay. It was then that the Short-time Committees asked Lord Ashley to be their spokesman in the House. Ashley accepted, and began the long and finally victorious campaign with which his name is inseparably linked.

When Ashley brought the Ten Hours Bill again before the House many Members were openly hostile. A motion that more information was needed was carried by seventy-four votes to seventy-three—in spite of Fielden's remark that he had worked since the age of ten, and could not imagine why people wanted evidence to convince them that children of this age were unfit to work twelve or fourteen hours a day. The workers recognized this as a delaying manœuvre, and angrily demonstrated against the Commissioners who visited the textile towns to take evidence. At Huddersfield a great protest meeting expressed its

> disgust and indignation at having been threatened with a visit from an inquisitorial itinerant to inquire whether our children shall be worked more than ten hours a day; we are at once and for all determined that they shall not.[1]

At Bradford Commissioners were surrounded by children singing the popular chorus:

[1] *Leeds Intelligencer*, June 22, 1833. Quoted by Hutchins and Harrison *op. cit.* p. 54.

We will have the Ten Hours Bill;
That we will, that we will.[1]

Nevertheless the Commissioners were in earnest. They included two energetic Benthamites—Southwood Smith and Edwin Chadwick—and completed their work in four months.

Their Report followed Benthamite lines. Bentham aimed at happiness. Adult workers were old enough to know whether their happiness was best served by working fourteen hours, and therefore ought to be allowed to do so if they wished. So, in the name of freedom, no Factory Code for adults! But children were too young to understand the requisites of happiness, so needed State protection.

In face of the Report Ashley had no alternative but to surrender his own Ten Hours Bill in favour of the Government's new Factory Act.

The Factory Act of 1833 was in two respects an advance on existing legislation: it was extended from cotton to other textiles,[2] and it provided for four whole-time, paid Government inspectors to enforce the law. Here the influence of Chadwick is perceived. Although the number was clearly inadequate for the whole country, the concession of the principle of Government inspection was important, and some of the men who became inspectors, notably Leonard Horner, did great service to the cause of factory reform. They were tireless in examining factory conditions, in submitting reports, in suggesting improvements in the Acts, in seeking to prevent evasion of the spirit of the law.

Besides appointing inspectors the new Act prohibited night work to all under eighteen years of age in all textile mills except lace; it repeated the provision that no child under nine years of age should work in any mill except a silk mill; it limited the hours of work of children under thirteen to nine a day, or ten in silk mills, and of young persons over thirteen to twelve a day, to be worked between 5.30 A.M. and 8.30 P.M.

A further clause raised great opposition from the workers. It permitted the working of two sets of children for a maximum period of eight hours each. This, it was asserted, was a device for keeping adults at work for fifteen or sixteen hours a day. There was a great protest meeting, over 100,000 strong, on the

---

[1] Quoted by J. L. and B. Hammond, *Lord Shaftesbury*, p. 28.
[2] Woollen, worsted, hemp, flax, tow, linen, and silk.

moors near Bradford on July 1, 1833. There were big meetings in the spring of 1834, addressed by Doherty and others. Fielden and Owen called for a strike for a forty-eight-hour week. The enthusiasm for this project fused with the feverish excitement generated by Owen's Grand National Consolidated Trades Union. As a result the factory question was engulfed in the despair which followed the trade depression and the collapse of the Grand National in 1833. So far from striking, the workers found themselves presented with the 'document'[1] by their employers. The Short-time Committees had to content themselves with carefully watching the operation of the 1833 Act.

The next few years were a period of depression. Chartism was distracting the country, and the factory reformers lost three of their leaders. Sadler died in 1835. One of his fiery speeches brought Stephens in 1839 a sentence of eighteen months' imprisonment. Oastler's service to the working class caused his dismissal from his post, and shortly afterwards he was in a debtors' prison, where he remained from 1840 until 1843. In the Factory Act campaign there were few more notable incidents until 1840.

About this time the Short-time Committees changed their tactics. They had first demanded the regulation of the hours of children. Then, after the passage of the 1833 Act, they emphasized the need to limit the working hours of machinery. They then began to concentrate on the regulation of women's labour. There was an advance when a Government Bill in 1844 classed women of all ages as young persons, with a working day of twelve hours. Ashley tried to go a step farther and turn the Government Bill into a Ten Hours Bill by moving the substitution of 6 P.M. for 8 P.M. as the time for finishing work. Working hours would then be between 6 A.M. and 6 P.M., with two hours for meals. Ashley won by 161 votes to 153. But when it came to Clause 8 of the Bill, which specified the number of hours to be worked, Ashley's amendment for ten hours was narrowly defeated.

In face of this anomalous position the Government withdrew its Bill altogether, and in April introduced a new one. This time the ten-hour clause was decisively defeated. The leading Whigs—Lord John Russell, Macaulay, Palmerston, Grey—

[1] See p. 170.

voted with Ashley; so did the already somewhat rebellious Tory Benjamin Disraeli.

Though the ten-hour day was still to be won, the Act of 1844 marked a step in the right direction. Various provisions aimed at making inspection more effective; children's hours were reduced to six and a half a day, and the twelve-hour day for women and young persons, to be worked between 5.30 A.M. and 8.30 P.M. remained. In order to prevent their being worked in relays it was required that the labour of all protected persons should begin simultaneously. Finally, there were provisions concerning education and the fencing of machinery.

The last was of great importance. A Select Committee which reported in 1841 had exposed the dangers resulting from unfenced machinery and from the practice of operatives' cleaning machinery which was in motion. Factory inspectors pointed out the danger caused by clothes—particularly women's clothes —being caught in the machinery. A girl at Stockport was carried by her clothing round an upright shaft; her thighs were broken, her ankles dislocated.[1] A boy's shirt caught in a machine he was helping an overlooker to repair, his arm was torn off and his head injured.[2] The Act of 1844 made compulsory the fencing of all machinery, and prohibited any woman, child, or young person from cleaning a moving machine.

Equally significant were the clauses concerning education. The 1833 Act provided for two hours' education a day for every child in the cotton, wool, worsted, and flax industries. If a suitable school were lacking it enjoined the inspectors to "establish or procure the establishment" of such a school. The proof of a child's attendance at school was to be a certificate signed by the schoolmaster. The inspectors had been zealous in fulfilling their task, and in many Reports told of the difficulty in enforcing the law. While children were working eight hours a day they were rarely free at the time a public school was open, and had therefore to depend on a school provided by the millowner. He was rarely helpful. "I have myself," wrote Inspector R. J. Saunders in 1843, "(and I believe others have done the same,) used every exertion, but without any success,

---

[1] *Report of Select Committee on the Regulation of Mills and Factories*, 1841, IX, 25–26,
[2] *Report of Inspectors of Factories . . . on Frequency of Accidents in Factories*, 1841. X, 19.

to induce mill occupiers to subscribe for the establishment of special factory schools."[1]   The Government grant towards education was of little use, for at this time it was given in proportion to voluntary subscriptions, and the districts from which the factory children came were poor.   As for schools in the factories themselves, Leonard Horner was able in 1839 to report an excellent school in the factory of M'Connel and Co., of Manchester; and also a school where the teacher's certificate was signed by the fireman of the factory and where Horner found the little factory schoolchildren in the coal-hole, with a few books as black as the coal, and the fireman 'schooling' them in the intervals of stoking the furnace.[2]   Meanwhile the Church of England and the Nonconformists were quarrelling to such effect over the religious aspects of teaching the little factory workers that, because of their disagreement, the Government had been compelled to drop the educational clauses of its 1843 Factory Bill.

The inspectors, particularly Horner, had been urging a half-time system for children by which they worked morning or afternoon and went to school in the other part of the day. But this, Horner pointed out, would have to be enforced by law, for otherwise parents might—as in cases which he knew —withdraw their children from a mill which ran on the half-time system to send them elsewhere to get higher wages. It was the Act of 1844 which enjoined the half-time system for children, the factory inspectors being given the important right of inspecting factory schools and of disqualifying incompetent teachers.

In January 1846 Ashley introduced a new Ten Hours Bill. Then the Corn Law issue flared to a head. When the Tory Prime Minister repealed the Corn Laws Ashley felt compelled to resign.   He was Member for an agricultural constituency which was strongly Protectionist, and felt in honour bound to leave a Government which had abandoned the tax upon corn. The decision was not an easy one for Ashley to take, for it meant abandoning the Ten Hours Bill which he had just piloted through its first reading.   Fielden moved the second

---

[1] *Report upon the Establishment of Schools in the Factory Districts*, August 1843, XXVII, 4.
[2] *Report on Educational Provisions of the Factories Act*, 1839, XLII, 5–6.

reading, and, though Ashley paced outside in the lobby in an agony of suspense, the Bill was well received. Macaulay, in particular, uttered one of his most famous passages in support of the Bill:

> Never will I believe that what makes a population stronger, and healthier, and wiser, and better, can ultimately make it poorer. You try to frighten us by telling us that, in some German factories, the young work seventeen hours in the twenty-four, that they work so hard that among thousands there is not one who grows to such a stature that he can be admitted into the army; and you ask whether, if we pass this bill, we can possibly hold our own against such competition as this? Sir, I laugh at the thought of such competition. If ever we are forced to yield the foremost place among commercial nations, we shall yield it, not to a race of degenerate dwarfs, but to some people pre-eminently vigorous in body and in mind.[1]

Against this the antagonism of Bright, not only to the Bill, but to Ashley himself, was notable. The Bill was defeated by ten votes: 203–193.

A few months later the Tory Government fell, and a Whig Government, more sympathetic to the Ten Hours Bill, took its place. Simultaneously came revived agitation in the North, with Stephens and Oastler again at liberty; in September a new weekly paper, *The Ten Hours Advocate*, was started in Manchester. Ashley was out of Parliament, but Fielden introduced another Ten Hours Bill in January 1847. This time the second reading was carried by 195 to 87 votes. Two manufacturers, Fielden and Brotherton, were tellers for the Bill. It was supported by the Whigs Russell and Grey; by Tories who opposed Peel on the Corn Law issue—Bentinck and Disraeli and Lord John Manners by many of the Radicals—Duncombe and Wakley and Sir Charles Napier. Opposing it were the chief Peelites and Peel himself; and some of the Radicals, including Roebuck and Bright. Three years afterwards Ashley commented in his diary that those who gave victory to the Bill "were governed, not by love to the cause, but, by anger towards Peel and the Anti-Corn Law League. Had not these passions interposed," he wrote, "there would have been no unusual 'humanity.'"[2]

[1] May 22, 1846 (Hansard, third series, lxxxvi, 1028–1044).
[2] Quoted by J. L. and B. Hammond, *Lord Shaftesbury*, p. 143.

The third reading passed uneventfully in May 1847, and the Ten Hour provision for women and young persons became operative twelve months later—nearly half a century after the passage of the first Factory Act. Its effect was at first masked by a trade depression. But by 1849 trade had revived, and employers began to feel the limitation irksome. They therefore took advantage of ambiguities in the law to evade the new Act. On the one hand, no Act yet limited men's labour. On the other, the provision that machinery could run between 5.30 A.M. and 8.30 P.M. still remained operative. It was therefore still possible to work women and young persons in shifts in order to keep the men at work for as long as fifteen hours a day. The Act of 1844 had intended to prohibit the shift system, on which such exploitation depended, yet it was so ambiguous that in a case before the Court of Exchequer in 1850 Mr. Justice Parke gave judgment for the employers. "The Ten Hours Act, nullified," wrote Ashley in his diary. "The work to be done all over again."[1]

While the Short-time Committees also set to work again, the Government proposed a compromise. It would raise the working day for women and young persons to ten and a half hours, but would insist on the outside limits of 6 A.M. and 6 P.M. The operatives spurned the proposal. Ashley, on the other hand, believing he could get support in the House for nothing more favourable, agreed to the compromise. The factory workers were aghast. Ashley was accused of treachery. It soon became apparent, indeed, that in the Government's proposal was a reservation which nullified any possible benefit: children were not to be included in the 'normal day.' The factory machinery could be kept working after those hours by relays of children and the labour of men thus extended.

That the men lost heavily by the new Act was proved by the reports of factory inspectors. In 257 mills in 1850, they reported, children were being used as assistants to men after the women and young persons had left off work.[2] This was remedied three years later when the House of Commons extended the normal day to children. Even so factory inspectors continued to report 'nibbling' by the masters, who started the mills a little before 6 A.M., ended a little after 6 P.M., and took a few

[1] Quoted by J. L. and B. Hammond, *Lord Shaftesbury*, p. 136.
[2] P. Papers, XLII 477, quoted by Hutchins and Harrison, *op. cit.*, p. 108.

minutes from meal-times, so making up perhaps an extra month's work in the year with little fear of detection, for the practice was extraordinarily hard to prove.

Thus, stubborn, unscrupulous, and grasping, manufacturers who in their private lives were often kind fathers and husbands and sometimes, like John Bright, devout Christians, had so successfully resisted the reform of their factories that even by the middle of the nineteenth century, when Britain was proud of being the world's leading industrial country, she had passed no effective Ten Hours Act, and still sent children of nine years old to work in her factories.

Perhaps one of the strangest aspects of the campaign for a ten-hour day, and one which significantly illumines contemporary thought, is that no one before 1850 directly asked for a ten-hour day for adult male workers. Certainly the men hoped, through the regulation of women's and children's labour, to reduce their own hours of work: but the affront to public opinion in the *laissez-faire* age would have been too great if the regulation of adult male labour had been directly demanded.

In the event the reduction of hours nowhere proved the fatality to production and profits that the manufacturers had feared. Ten hours' labour was as productive as twelve. Profits multiplied. British industry led the world. Nevertheless it was only slowly that the scope of the Factory Acts was extended.

In 1847 the existing Factory Acts applied wholly to textiles other than silk and lace, and partially to silk and lace mills. In 1840 Ashley had obtained a Royal Commission to examine conditions of children outside the scope of the Factory Acts, but he was unsuccessful in trying to extend the 1833 Act to cover silk and lace factories. The Reports of the Children's Employment Commission which followed in 1843 described conditions in the calico-printing, lace, hosiery, metal, earthenware, glass, paper, and tobacco manufactures. It told of children beginning work at three or four years old in their own homes and at five in the manufactories, and of being in regular employment by the age of seven or eight. The hours of work were twelve in many instances, fifteen, sixteen, and eighteen hours consecutively being common, the children generally working as long as the adults. In the majority of cases examined by the Commissioners the places of work were "very defective in drainage, ventilation, and the due regulation of temperature," while "little or no attention" was paid to cleanliness.[1] Where deleterious substances were used there was generally no accommodation for washing or for changing clothes. The privies were disgusting, often the same for male and female.[2] In the case of metal, earthenware, and glass manufacture the work was positively injurious, reported the Commissioners.[3]

The Report was received coldly. The utmost that Ashley could secure was a limited Act applying to calico-print works. The Print Works Act of 1845 prohibited night-work for women and young persons under thirteen, prohibited the employment of children under eight, and required children under thirteen to attend school for thirty days in each half-year. All other trades and industries were left unregulated until well into the second half of the century.

The Report of 1843 described, too, the objectionable system of apprenticeship in operation in many trades. Children, who were frequently orphans apprenticed by boards of guardians, or the children of very poor parents, were legally bound as early as seven years old to serve until they were twenty-one. There was frequently no skill to be acquired; often they made one part of an article over and over again, at the end of their term being incapable of making any complete article of what was supposed to be their trade. They suffered often "great hardship and ill-usage," and frequently received no wages for their labour, but only food and clothing, whose quantity and quality varied considerably. Yet to leave such employment meant gaol, for they were held to be legally indentured.

Among these bound apprentices were the little chimney-sweeps, little boys and sometimes little girls who, in accordance with the barbarous practice which still prevailed in Britain in the middle of the nineteenth century, were compelled to climb up into the flues of chimneys in order to sweep them.

> When my mother died I was very young,
> And my father sold me while yet my tongue
> Could scarcely cry "'weep! 'weep! 'weep! 'weep!"
> So your chimneys I sweep, and in soot I sleep.[4]

[1] *Second Report of Children's Employment Commission*, 1843, XIII, 196.
[2] *Ibid.*, XIII, 196.   [3] *Ibid.*, XIII, 196–197.
[4] William Blake, *Songs of Innocence*.

Nearly every one is familiar with little Tom, the chimney-sweep of Kingsley's *Water Babies*. His story, but for its happy ending, might be an account of the life of any one of these little climbing boys.

The boys were selected for their smallness and their ability to climb the narrowest and most difficult chimneys. Sometimes they were purchased for as much as £5 apiece, sometimes kidnapped. They were still actually bought and sold as late as the sixties, and the smaller the boy the bigger the price. Nottingham boys, who were known to be good and adept, were sometimes stolen for shipment to France. When they became too big for climbing they were unfit for other work, and generally had no alternative but a life of the lowest pauperism. They formed one of the most neglected classes of the community being illiterate and rarely attending Sunday school. They worked with their masters for from twelve to sixteen hours a day in the large towns. They began work at about six years old—"a nice trainable age," as one master said.

When the boys first started climbing their knees and elbows were rubbed with strong brine close by a hot fire to harden them. At first they came back from their work "with their arms and knees streaming with blood, and the knees looking as if the caps had been pulled off."[1] Then more brine was applied. Sheer terror of their masters drove them up the chimneys; sheer terror of the dark, sooty chimneys, where in places they could squeeze only with difficulty, and which often were hot from newly extinguished or still burning fires, urged them to come down. Their masters kept them up, sometimes by kindly encouragement, more often by threats, by sticks, by pins stuck in their bare feet, or even by lighting straw below them.

Washing was not considered necessary for these little boys. Often they 'slept dirty' from one year's end to another, using the blankets in which they caught soot from the chimneys as their bed coverings at night, so encouraging the disease known as 'sooty wart' or 'sooty cancer.'

In 1773 Jonas Hanway had drawn attention to the plight of the little chimney-sweeps. Efforts to prohibit the use of climbing boys had been made early in the nineteenth century by Henry Grey Bennet, but had met with fierce opposition.

[1] *Children's Employment Commission*, 1863; Minutes of Evidence, XVIII, 297–298,

In 1834 an Act prohibited the apprenticeship of a child under ten to a chimney-sweep, and forbade the employment by a chimney-sweeper of any child under fourteen who was not an apprentice. In 1840 a further Act prohibited the climbing of chimneys by all under twenty-one, or the apprenticing of children under sixteen to sweeps. Both Acts contained provisions for improving the construction of chimneys. Both failed to name a responsible authority for enforcing the law, and the number of climbing boys continued to increase.

Sometimes a little sweep would die in the chimney, suffocated or burnt or wedged so that he could not extricate himself. Then there was an inquiry, and sometimes a newspaper or a Member of Parliament took the matter up. But, short of this, very little notice was taken of the climbing boys, except when they tried to run away; then they were brought back and sometimes imprisoned for breaking their indenture.

Why did people permit the use of boys in the sweeping of their chimneys? Because the construction of many chimneys was so complicated and the flues were so narrow, with so many bends, that it was believed that mechanical implements could not clean them effectively. The most difficult chimneys were in public buildings and the mansions of the rich. In the latter, an architect told a Committee of the House of Lords in 1818, were flues which were constructed solely in order to provide the occupants with greater comfort and luxury. They often objected to the use of a 'trap' on the grounds that it would disfigure their rooms, and refused the small expense necessary to alter the flue. Even in the case of easy chimneys master sweeps were known to persuade their customers that the mechanical method was dirty and ineffective, while the boys were clean, speedy, and thorough. Thus, with the connivance of many householders, little boys were sentenced to lives of terror, to fearful diseases caused by the soot and dirt, and to agonizing deaths.

(b) MINES

There were a few industries to which the Industrial Revolution made little difference. The most important of these was the mining industry. The steam-pump was used in mines, and the steam-engine for raising the coal from the shaft bottom, and large winding engines were in operation in the forties.

But generally the great mechanical inventions were of no use. Wire ropes were used in the mid-thirties, and towards the mid-century ventilation began to be improved. Above-ground, improved haulage and transport made the marketing of the coal more efficient. But the actual hewing and the cartage below-ground remained much as they had done for centuries.

The increased demand occasioned by the Industrial Revolution was met both by working existing mines deeper and more extensively and by bringing new or abandoned mines into use, with the consequent application of more capital and labour.

In the North of England and in most parts of Scotland the miners were in the direct employ of a mining company or mine-owner, and were subject to the yearly bond. They were hired for the year, and contracted to work for that period without absence or strike. They were paid generally by the piece, so their wage depended upon their luck in striking a good seam. Often the 'butty' system of hire was in operation. 'Butties' contracted to have the coal hewn and brought to the foot of the shaft, the proprietor then making himself responsible for raising it to the surface. The proprietor paid the butty, who in turn paid the hewers and other workers below-ground. This method was common in Warwickshire, South Staffordshire, and Shropshire. Sometimes the butty was a small capitalist and quite well off. In South Staffordshire, said the Commissioners of 1842, "His business requires capital, as he provides the tools for the men, also the cars and the horses, in the pits, and is often at a considerable outlay for wages in the necessary preparations." In such a case he might lay out a capital of £500. But this was exceptional. The greater number of butties were "in very limited circumstances."[1] In Lancashire, Cheshire, and the West Riding the hewer or 'getter' himself undertook to deliver the coal at a fixed rate at the foot of the shaft, employing such assistants as were necessary. It was here that by far the greater number of children were employed.

Payment was not always made entirely in money. The iniquitious truck system was stronger in mining districts than anywhere else. Wages were often paid partly in the form of tickets for goods upon the tommy-shop, where prices were generally about 25 per cent. higher than elsewhere. Even

[1] *Children's Employment Commission, Reports and Evidence,* 1842, XVI, 2.

when full money wages were paid a miner who wished to keep his job would spend part of his wages at the tommy-shop. The practice of paying the men at irregular and long intervals encouraged this system. Miners' wives who had to wait two, four, or six weeks for their husbands' wages would be driven to take goods on credit at inflated prices from the tommy-shopkeeper. Such fury against the tommy-shop often broke out as Disraeli depicted in *Sybil*.

Wages and hours of work varied considerably. In general miners were better paid, and therefore better clothed and housed, than other workpeople. Children received anything from 2s. 6d. to 7s. a week, the little trappers getting about 6d. a day. The older boys and girls, who acted as putters, could get in South Durham as much as 40s. or 44s. fortnightly if they could manage the loads themselves and were not compelled to share with another child. In the West Riding of Yorkshire were adults getting 30s. a week, and this was considered good and above the average. Sometimes they worked for fourteen or more hours at a stretch rarely for as few as, eleven. In some districts night-work was common.[1]

Little was known of the miner and his way of life. He was noted for recklessness, hard living, and degradation. There were tales current of the lawless debauchery which took place in the 'subterranean galleries' where he spent so much of his life. Both inside the mine and outside it the miner was said to live like a savage. But not until the searchlight of a Government Commission lit the dark places of the mine in 1842 was there revealed a true picture of the life going on beneath the soil of a country which was congratulating itself that its rising assets were being balanced by an equivalent growth of humanitarianism.

The Report of 1842 told of the extensive use of women and children below-ground. Children began work as early as four years of age, eight or nine being the common age for starting. They worked below-ground for twelve, thirteen, fourteen hours, and even longer. The youngest—mere babies of four years old and upward—were usually employed as 'trappers.' They sat with a string in their hands pulling it to open the 'traps' when a coal-cart passed, and closing it afterwards. Though not in itself difficult or arduous, it was work of great importance,

[1] *First Report of Children's Employment Commission*, 1842, XV, *passim*.

because upon it the ventilation of the mine depended. For this reason the trapper had to be at his post from the opening of the mine until its closing. In most cases the trappers were in total darkness all the time and quite alone. "Were it not," said the 1842 Report, "for the passing and repassing of the coal-carriages," this would "amount to solitary confinement of the worst order."[1] Many of these children never saw the daylight for months at a stretch: it was dark when they descended the pit, dark below, and dark when they ascended. Hear Sarah Gooder, eight years old, speak:

> I'm a trapper in the Gauber Pit. I have to trap without a light, and I'm scared. I go at four and sometimes half-past three in the morning, and come out at five and half-past, I never go to sleep. Sometimes I sing when I've light, but not in the dark; I dare not sing then. I don't like being in the pit. I am very sleepy when I go sometimes in the morning.[2]

From six years of age the children took their places with the women, and began their work of pushing and dragging and carrying the coal from the place where it was hewn to the main roads of the pit or the bottom of the shaft.

There were several methods of carting or 'putting.' In South and North Wales and parts of Scotland the 'trace and chain' method was in use, by which women and children were actually harnessed to the carts. A leather girdle was put round the waist. Attached was a chain which passed between the legs and was then fastened to the cart. Sometimes, where the passages were very low, the putters crawled on all fours, like animals; sometimes they walked bent nearly double to take the strain.

Margaret Hipps, seventeen years old, was a putter at Stoney Rigg Colliery, Stirlingshire. "My employment, after reaching the wall-face," she said,

> is to fill a bagie, or slype, with 2½ to 3 cwt. of coal. I then hook it on to my chain, and drag it through the seam, which is 26 to 28 inches high, till I get to the main-road—a good distance, probably 200 to 400 yards. The pavement I drag over is wet, and I am obliged at all times to crawl on hands and feet with my bagie hung to the chain and ropes. It is sad sweating and sore fatiguing work, and frequently maims the women.[3]

[1] *Ibid.*, XV, 256.　　　[2] *Ibid.*, XV, 71.　　　[3] *Ibid.*, XV, 95.

Sometimes the women and girls actually carried the coal on their backs. They were known to carry as much as 2½ to 3 cwt. at a time in this way. The Commissioners gave a detailed account of this manner of coal-bearing in East Scotland, together with illustrations of the work in progress.

The girl, they say,

has first to descend a nine-ladder pit to the first rest, even to which a shaft is sunk, to draw up the baskets or tubs of coals filled by the bearers: she then takes her creel (a basket formed to the back, not unlike a cockle-shell flattened towards the neck, so as to allow lumps of coal to rest on the back of the neck and shoulders), and pursues her journey to the wall-face. . . . She then lays down her basket, into which the coal is rolled, and it is frequently more than one man can do to lift the burden on her back. The tugs or straps are placed over the forehead, and the body bent in a semicircular form, in order to stiffen the arch. Large lumps of coal are then placed on the neck, and she then commences her journey with her burden to the pit bottom, first hanging her lamp to the cloth crossing her head. In this girl's case she has first to travel about 14 fathoms (84 feet) from wall-face to the first ladder, which is 18 feet high: leaving the first ladder she proceeds along the main road, probably 3′ 6″ to 4′ 6″ high, to the second ladder, 18′ high, so on to the third and fourth ladders till she reaches the pit-bottom, where she casts her load, varying from 1 cwt. to 1½ cwt. into the tub. This one journey is designated a rake; the height ascended, and the distance along the roads added together, exceed the height of St Paul's Cathedral; and it not unfrequently happens that the tugs break, and the load falls upon those females who are following.[1]

One of these coal-bearers was Margaret Leveston, six years old, a "most interesting child, and perfectly beautiful." "The work is na guid," she said; "it is so very sair. I work with sister Jesse and mother; dinna ken the time we gang; it is gai dark."[2] Small wonder at the exclamation of a woman seen groaning under an excessive weight of coals: "I wish to God that the first woman who tried to bear coals had broke her back, and none would have tried it again!"[3]

In East Scotland and in the West Riding of Yorkshire women worked equally with men in all the work of the mine. In the

---

[1] *First Report of Children's Employment Commission*, 1843, XV, 91–92.
[2] *Ibid.*, XV, 91.   [3] *Ibid.*, XV, 94.

West Riding the Commissioners found a girl of fourteen in boy's clothes lying on her side in a place not two feet high, picking coals with the men.[1]

Not only debauchery, but brutality was common in the pit. The boys were often in the sole charge of butties who worked the lads as hard as they could and often ill-treated them. Most of the miners wore a leather strap round the waist, which they could apply to the boys if they thought necessary. James Robinson, for example, aged fourteen, was often beaten by the man he called "the corporal," who

> kicked him when he was down, pulled his ears and hair, and threw coals at him; he dare not tell his masters then, or he believes the corporal would have killed him. His brothers, one ten, the other thirteen years old, . . . are beaten until they can hardly get home, and dare not tell for fear of worse usage, and they and their father losing their work.[2]

Accidents frequently occurred, for there were many mines without the most elementary safety precautions. Some of the most vital safety-points—for example, the ventilation doors—were in the sole control of small children. In Derbyshire and Lancashire it was common for boys to be at the engine by which the workpeople were drawn up and let down the shaft. Once, when a little boy of nine was distracted by a mouse while at this work, three or four boys who were travelling in the cage were killed.[3] Sometimes chairs or baskets on ropes would simultaneously let people up and down the mine. Two of these came into contact under an assistant inspector's eyes, and a child of ten was hurled sixty yards to the bottom of the pit and dashed to pieces.[4]

There were so many ways in which accidents might occur. Besides falling down the shaft, which might happen in a number of ways, there was the risk of falling coal, of being crushed by the coal-carts, of suffocation, burning, or drowning. In South Staffordshire accidents were so frequent that, said an Assistant Commissioner, "we might consider the whole population as engaged in a campaign."[5] In Lancashire and Cheshire, reported another, accidents were a "daily occurrence in almost every mine where numbers are employed, and so common that a record of them is seldom kept."[6] In truth, in the dark,

[1] *Ibid.*, XV, 74.   [2] *Ibid.*, XV, 127.   [3] *Ibid.*, XV, 144.
[4] *Ibid.*, XV, 14.   [5] *Ibid.*, XV, 37.   [6] *Ibid.*, XV, 141.

unregulated mine, where strapping and brutality were known to be common, who was to give reliable evidence of the way in which a person met his death? Besides genuine accidents, many a private quarrel may have seen its end in the pit. What kind of evidence could be obtained from indifferent owners and illiterate miners—some of them frightened, some of them knowing too much?

Apart from accidents, the mine in other ways took toll of its workpeople. The smallness of the passages, the excessively hard work at an early age, resulted in an abnormal development of some of the muscles of the body, while growth was stunted and the workers often crippled and distorted. To the women, and particularly to the expectant mothers who worked until a late date in their pregnancies, the injury was even more serious. Finally there were the diseases of the lungs which work in the coal-dust-laden atmosphere frequently produced.

Perhaps it is small wonder that the miner lived less like a civilized man than like a savage, that he seized what moments of exhilaration he could at the alehouse or at his favourite sport of cock-fighting, and that he was often brutal and vicious. Yet, in spite of the hideous burden of their working lives, the miners even then produced some of the finest types of British workmen and trade unionists—men, for example, like Tommy Hepburn, the Northumberland miner. The proud spirit of the miners who, in the depression following the Napoleonic wars, toured England with their coal-carts and the placard "Willing to work, but none of us will beg" came not from a beaten class, but from a breed of dogged fighters.

It was the idea of Dr Southwood Smith, one of the Commissioners, to illustrate the Report of 1842. Many Members of Parliament, who had probably not read the Report, were clearly struck by the illustrations, and the passage of the Mines Bill which Ashley introduced into the House of Commons on June 7, 1842, was made easier. It passed its first and second readings without a division. But the House of Lords, which contained most of the mine-owners, and particularly Lord Londonderry, one of the richest of them, heavily criticized and amended the Bill. Londonderry persuaded the Lords to strike out the clause which gave inspectors the power of reporting on the state and conditions of the mines. It was more than sufficient, their lordships deemed, that inspectors should report

'HURRYING' COAL IN THE HALIFAX DISTRICT

The girl in the picture is drawing a weight of between 2 and 5 cwts.

[See p. 141]

From the "Report of the Children's Employment Commission, 1842"

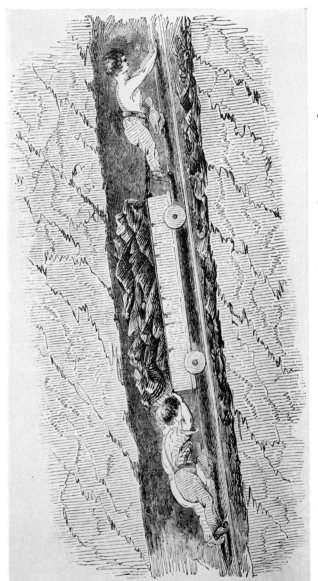

THREE CHILDREN TAKING A LOADED WAGON OF COAL UP AN INCLINE IN THE LANCASHIRE AND CHESHIRE DISTRICT

[See pp. 140–141]

From the "Report of the Children's Employment Commission, 1842"

BEARING COAL IN EAST
SCOTLAND

[See p. 142]

*From the "Report of the Children's Employment
Commission, 1842"*

ROBERT OWEN

on the state and condition of the people in the mines. "Never," wrote Ashley, "have I seen such display of selfishness, frigidity to every human sentiment, such ready and happy self delusion."[1] The Act prohibited the work of women and girls and of boys under ten years old. The binding of parish apprentices was still allowed between the ages of ten and eighteen. Hours remained unrestricted, though children worked longer hours in the mines than in the mills. Eight years later, after several serious and large-scale mining accidents, an Act extended the power of inspectors to report on the condition of mines and machinery and compelled owners to submit plans of the workings of their collieries. Lord Londonderry was again in opposition, although the majority of mine-owners offered no objection.

In each case—factories, workshops, and mines—reform was carried out only after a long and painful struggle against the resistance of interested parties and the indifference of the uninterested. Not in textile mills, nor in mines, nor in workshops, was even moderate reform complete by the middle of the nineteenth century. The textile workers had not won an effective ten-hour day. Miners' hours were unlimited. No Act protected the workers in thousands of 'sweat-shops.' The number of little climbing boys was increasing. Yet even the partial assumption by the State of responsibility for its workpeople was a new thing to the nineteenth century, though by no means new to the earlier history of Britain. It is a matter for consideration as to whether, in interpreting the social legislation of the first half of the century, the emphasis should be on the State's partial reassumption of industrial regulation, or whether the significant fact is not its extreme slowness to realize its responsibilities.

[1]Diary, quoted by J. L. and B. Hammond, *Lord Shaftesbury*, p. 80.

SELECT BIBLIOGRAPHY

Report of Select Committee on Factory Children's Labour (Sadler's Committee), 1831–32, XV.

First Report of Children's Employment Commission, Mines, 1842, XV.

DRIVER, C.: *Tory Radical: The Life of Richard Oastler* (Oxford University Press, 1947).

HAMMOND, J. L. AND B.: *Lord Shaftesbury* (Longmans, 1923).

HUTCHINS, B. L. AND HARRISON, A.: *A History of Factory Legislation* (P. S. King, 1903; revised edition, 1911).

PINCHBECK, I.: *Women Workers and the Industrial Revolution, 1750–1850* (Routledge, 1930).

THOMAS, M.W.: *The Early Factory Legislation* (Thames Bank, 1948).

CHAPTER VII

ARISTOCRACY VERSUS MIDDLE CLASSES

THE Reform Act of 1832 and the repeal of the Corn Laws in 1846 were alike the result of hard struggle between the middle-class manufacturing interests and the landlords. The Reform Act gave the middle classes the semblance of political power: that it withheld the reality is demonstrated by the fact that ten years later they were fighting what Bright himself described as a class battle for the repeal of the Corn Laws. Both struggles were severe. That a revolution did not occur in 1832 was not because the middle classes were not revolutionary, but because they were so well organized for revolution that the Tories gave way. In the Corn Law struggles the middle classes fought with the power they already had in the House of Commons and with their enormous wealth, putting hundreds of thousands of pounds into the campaign. "Let us," said Cobden, "invest part of our property, in order to save the rest from confiscation."[1] The landowners' chief weapon—that of intimidating voters—was of little avail against the propaganda and organization and wealth of the Anti-Corn Law League. The year 1846 was the complement of 1832. For a quarter of a century thereafter there was nothing to stop the triumphal progress of the middle classes.

(a) THE REFORM ACT OF 1832

At the opening of the nineteenth century Britain was still ruled by landowners. In spite of the fact that the industrial middle classes were growing wealthy, important, and powerful, landowners controlled the three organs of government—the legislature, the judiciary, and the executive. The judiciary and the executive they controlled as magistrates and judges, as officers in the Army and in the militia. The legislature they controlled through their hereditary membership of the House of Lords and by the system which gave them control of the

---

[1] J. Morley. *Life of Cobden*, (one volume edition, 1905) p. 146.

House of Commons. It was this control which the manufacturers set out to break in the early nineteenth century. To do so they had to reform an out-of-date and inequitable electoral system, which was expensive, which lacked uniformity, which was open to abuse and corruption, and which yet strongly resisted amendment.

Until 1832 there was no electoral law which applied to the whole country, but nearly everywhere it was preponderantly on the side of the landowner. In the counties every forty-shilling freeholder had the vote. In counties like Shropshire, where there were a number of small and medium-sized estates, this made possible some expression of middle-class opinion, but in most cases the counties were dominated by a single landowner or a few powerful families. Of the forty county constituencies only seven could be counted as independent.[1]

In the boroughs there was less uniformity, but no more independence. In 'nomination' boroughs the whole estate was owned by one man, who had the sole right of nominating a Parliamentary candidate. In 'close' boroughs the electorate was restricted to a small number of office-holders. There were several kinds of close boroughs, of which the most important were burgage, corporation, and Freemen boroughs. In the thirty-seven burgage boroughs the voters were the owners or tenants of holdings by burgage tenure—a feudal tenure by which the tenant performed certain fixed services for the lord of the manor. Two examples of burgage boroughs were Old Sarum and Haslemere. The first was the almost uninhabited site of an ancient town; but as purchaser of the hereditary burgage holdings the Earl of Caledon had the right of nominating and returning two Members of Parliament.

At Haslemere Lord Lonsdale owned forty burgage freeholds, each of which gave its occupier the vote. In order to secure beyond doubt the votes of the occupiers Lonsdale brought from Northumberland forty of his miners and gave them lodging and 10s. 6d. a week each for the sole service of recording their votes for his candidates.[2]

In the thirty-six corporation boroughs the right to vote was vested in members of the corporation, who themselves had the

---

[1] Oldfield, *Representative History*, iv, 54, quoted by E. Halévy, *A History of the English People in 1815*, i, 109.
[2] Halévy, *op. cit.*, i, 120.

right of co-opting fresh members. The electors were often not more than ten, and rarely exceeded one hundred in number. Often the members of the corporation were the tenants, or otherwise under the influence, of a big landowner. Sometimes they openly sold their support to the highest bidder. Sometimes the Government itself bought the seat.

In the seventy-seven Freemen boroughs the electorate consisted of members of guilds and City Companies and all who had the freedom of the City. It varied in size from a mere handful to several thousands. In most Freemen boroughs the corporation also had the right to vote and, more importantly, had the right of creating honorary Freemen. In cases where the corporation was under the control of a landowner the rights of the original Freemen could in this way be abrogated. In Carlisle, for example, Lord Lonsdale again brought his miners into play. Lonsdale was master of the corporation of Carlisle, where there were 700 electors. In order to secure the election of his nominees he induced the corporation to grant the honorary Freedom of the City to 14,000 miners, who thus acquired the right to vote.[1] In many of the boroughs with a larger electorate, however, such as Bristol, the City of London, Norwich, and Nottingham, the Freemen boroughs retained a considerable independence.

The 'pocket' boroughs were frequently and openly put up to sale by the controlling landowner. Camelford was in 1812 sold by the Duke of Bedford for £32,000.[2] The two seats at Tamworth were bought by Sir Robert Peel the elder for £132,000.

In a few 'open' boroughs the franchise was nominally wider. There were thirteen 'potwalloper' or 'potwaller' constituencies, where all the inhabitants able to 'keep their pots boiling'—that is, to support themselves without recourse to the rates—were entitled to vote. There were also thirty-six 'scot-and-lot' boroughs, where every payer of taxes scot-and-lot had the vote. In a few boroughs all the freeholders or all the forty-shilling freeholders had the vote. In Preston all the inhabitants, without exception, were enfranchised.

The fate of these open boroughs varied in accordance with their size. Camelford was theoretically an open borough, but the nine electors were controlled by the Duke of Bedford, so

---

[1] Halévy, op. cit., i, 125.   [2] Ibid., i, 114.

that it was virtually a nomination borough. At Gatton, a scot-and-lot borough, the existing six houses belonged to Sir Mark Wood, who occupied one himself, performed the functions of magistrate, churchwarden, collector of taxes—all of which he paid himself—and, thus being the only voter, returned two Members to Parliament.[1]

In many of the boroughs, both close and open, the number of electors was so small that every one could be bribed. Votes were openly auctioned, and very high prices paid. As much as £700 or £1000 was said to have been paid for a single vote at Wycombe.[2] Even where the electors were numerous bribery sometimes determined their choice. Election feasts and beer-drinking at Westminster, a scot-and-lot borough, for example, were notorious. Lord John Townshend's election for the constituency in 1788 cost him £50,000. Lord Castlereagh's election for County Down cost £60,000. The King himself set aside £12,000 at each general election from the Civil List to ensure the return of Tory candidates.[3]

Apart from the injustice and corruption of the franchise, there was another set of anomalies due to the maldistribution of seats. While many small towns and hamlets returned one or two Members of Parliament, populous industrial districts had no representation at all. Appleby, a burgage tenure consisting of nothing but pigsties, sent a Member to Parliament; Birmingham, Leeds, Manchester, and Sheffield returned none at all. The whole county of Durham returned only four, Nottinghamshire eight, and Lancashire fourteen Members, while Suffolk returned sixteen and Cornwall forty-two. It is clear that such proportions entirely ignored the growth of industry and the redistribution of population effected by the Industrial Revolution. Lancashire with its factories, Nottinghamshire with its weavers, Durham with its miners, were clearly entitled to more Members than thinly populated Cornwall.

The House of Commons, as described by *The Black Book* of 1820, was "unconstitutional . . . glaringly absurd and ridiculous: . . . founded on no rational principle of either population, intelligence, or property."[4]

---

[1] *The Black Book*, p. 414.
[2] Fitzmaurice, *Life of Lord Shelburne*, ii, 362–363, quoted by Halévy, *op. cit.*, i, 126 *n*. 2.
[3] Halévy, *op. cit.*, i, 116.   [4] *The Black Book*, p. 413.

The allies in the campaign for political reform were the middle classes, most of whom were wealthy industrialists with no direct representation in the House of Commons; the Whigs, most of whom were landed aristocracy with seats in both Houses and some of whom had direct ties with industry; the Radicals, of whom a few were Members of Parliament and many of whom were in close touch with the workers; and the working classes themselves, who hoped to gain through political reform that higher standard of living which industrial activity and insurrection had failed to bring.

The motives of the middle classes, the Radicals, and the workers were simple. They were shut out from direct political power, and they sought to redress the balance. The position of the Whigs was more complicated. They were strong in both Houses of Parliament, and the great Whig families were accustomed to power and high office. Yet in the eighteenth century they had begun a movement for Parliamentary Reform, involving chiefly the disfranchisement of certain rotten boroughs and overrepresented counties in favour of a more equitable distribution of seats. This was chiefly to counteract the power of the Crown. George III hated the Whigs and their influence, which was strong when he came to the throne. To balance it he gathered round himself—largely by means of the bribery and corruption to which the representative system was open—a party of "King's Friends." The Whigs' answer was to press Parliamentary Reform in the House of Commons and through various Reform Societies. The burst of Radical Reform in Britain which followed the French Revolution silenced them for a while, but as that fear receded the Whigs again appeared as leaders in Parliament of the Reform movement. This time they had a double motive—to consolidate their own power against monarch and Tories and to provide a bulwark against the demands of the Radicals and the workers for any further reform. Most of the industrialists already in the House were Whigs, so there seemed good reason for believing that the middle-class vote would strengthen the Whig Party. But reform should go no further than the admission of the middle classes to the vote. It should be no instalment of reform, but a definitive measure which would consolidate the ruling classes against disorder from below.

In spite of these adequate reasons for desiring Parliamentary

Reform the effective pressure which drove the Whigs to carry through the Reform Bill when, faced with the opposition of the Tories and the King they would gladly have dropped it, was provided by forces outside Parliament.

The middle classes, though shut out from direct political power, had not been slow to exert all the influence their wealth commanded. They bought land and acquired votes or themselves stood for Parliament. They bought 'pocket' boroughs and nominated M.P.'s. They intermarried with the aristocracy, who in turn invested money in industry and commerce. Wealthy landowners of 1830 were often but cotton lords one generation removed. The very corruption of the 'borough-mongering' landowners was thus a means of admitting their class opponents to a share in power.

Nevertheless the political power of the middle classes fell far short of their requirements, and in their fight against the aristocratic state they used other weapons than permeation. That they stopped short of revolution in 1832 was due, not so much to the fact that they feared to drive the issue so far, as that the Government, seeing further resistance useless, itself gave way.

One of the weapons they used was economic power in its more direct forms, ranging from a threatened run on the banks to the raising of funds for the purchase of forty-shilling free-holds—buying votes just as they sometimes bought whole boroughs.

In addition, the middle class recruited as its allies in the political struggle the proletariat, the very people whom in industry it was fighting day after day. The workers joined forces with their capitalist masters against the landed aristocracy for the simple reason that in 1832 all other methods of improving their condition had failed. Machine-smashing, insurrection, hunger-marching, carefully laid plot, even trade-union action, had so far achieved next to nothing for the working classes. Men like Henry Hunt and Cobbett had for years been urging that only through political representation could the grievances of the workers be redressed. At the beginning of the thirties, in a period of disillusionment, this counsel prevailed, and the workers were swept uncritically into the Reform movement. They could not tell that the middle classes alone would reap the reward of the struggle and that the moment of victory would be also the moment of betrayal.

In July 1830 news came to England of the revolution in France which replaced the reactionary Charles X by Louis-Philippe, the "bourgeois king." England was wildly excited, the example of France fanning into flame her own smouldering movement for Parliamentary Reform. Even the Whigs were infected. In order to secure popular support and provide themselves with a stick to beat the Tories they publicly announced themselves in favour of Parliamentary Reform, and in November 1830, after the Tory Government had been defeated on a minor issue, took office under Earl Grey.

In the country economic unrest and political excitement were growing. Middle-class 'political unions' sprang up as they had done a generation earlier. Thomas Attwood in Birmingham founded the Birmingham Political Union. Cobbett and Hunt returned to the fray. The Metropolitan Political Union for Radical Reform was formed in March 1830 by Hunt, O'Connell, Carlile, and Hetherington. The National Union of the Working Classes under the influence of Lovett held large meetings at the Rotunda. Place with the National Political Union of 1831 tried to bring together the middle classes and the Rotundanists. There were many new Radical journals, including Hetherington's *Poor Man's Guardian* and Cobbett's *Twopenny Trash*. Large demonstrations were frequent in London, and in December 1830 over 10,000 skilled workmen demonstrated outside St James's Palace. The movement for Reform was soon far in advance of the party in office.

The Whig Government in March 1831 produced its first Reform Bill. In the boroughs the franchise was to be extended to include all householders rated at £10 per annum or over. In the counties certain leaseholders and copyholders, as well as the freeholders, were to be enfranchised. The estimated increase in the electorate was from about 500,000 to 1,000,000. A more equitable representation was proposed by the abolition of 168 seats in overrepresented constituencies and in boroughs of less than 2000 inhabitants, and the creation of 107 new seats for large towns and populous counties. Manchester and Birmingham, for example, were to gain two seats each. Yorkshire would return six instead of four Members, Scotland would gain five seats.

Though not wholly satisfactory to the Radicals, the Bill was generally considered by all but the Tories as a worth-while measure of reform. One of the strongest speakers for it was Lord Macaulay, who admirably expounded the point of view of many of the Reformers—that Parliamentary Reform, by admitting the wealthy industrial classes into an active share in Government, would consolidate the forces of the State against revolution. "Unless the plan proposed be speedily adopted," Macaulay said,

> great and terrible calamities will befall us. . . . At present we oppose the schemes of revolutionists with only one-half, with only one-quarter of our proper force. . . . We do more. We drive over to the side of revolution those whom we shut out from power. . . . Turn where we may, within, around, the voice of great events is proclaiming to us, Reform, that you may preserve![1]

The first reading passed by a show of hands; the second, after an all-night session and a dramatic count at 3 A.M. on March 23, 1831, was found to have been carried by one vote: 302–301. When, however, the House reassembled in April the Tories returned to the attack, and during the third reading gained a majority for an amendment which the Government had declared a matter of confidence. For the Whigs there remained the alternatives of resignation and dissolution. The first entailed handing the Government over to the Tories, the second a general election. For the latter the consent of the King was necessary. But William IV opposed Reform, and while he was considering the matter stormy debates continued in both Houses. On April 22 the King gave way and came to Westminster in person to dissolve Parliament.

Throughout the ensuing short and feverish election the Reformers fought on the cry, "The Bill, the whole Bill, and nothing but the Bill!" The result was an overwhelming majority for the Whigs, who were thus returned for the express purpose of carrying the Reform Bill. The Tory opposition was led by the Duke of Wellington.

On June 24, 1831, the introduction of the second Reform

[1] House of Commons, March 2, 1831 (Hansard third series, vol. ii, 1190–1250, *passim*).

Bill inaugurated the fight that continued throughout the summer.

The Commons finally passed the Bill. On September 21 Lord John Russell took it to the Lords. It passed its first reading, and then for a fortnight there was silence. At last, after an all-night sitting, the Lords rejected the second Reform Bill on the morning of October 8.

The masses were furious. At Derby prisoners were released from gaol. At Nottingham the castle of the Duke of Newcastle was burned. There were serious riots at Bristol, where the gaols were broken open, the town hall fired, and the bishop's palace burned to the ground. Troops were called in to keep order, twelve people were killed, and ninety-four wounded. Many must have remembered Macaulay's words. When it was suspected that the Commons might compromise with the Lords the Westminster Radical politicians, headed by Francis Place, marched at night to Lord Grey's house and awakened him to demand a statement of his intentions. There is also a story, related by William Lovett but lacking confirmation, of a fund of £1000 to be used to kidnap the wives and daughters of peers who continued their opposition to the Bill, to convey them to Scotland and hold them as hostages until the Bill was passed.

It became apparent that, as Macaulay said, in "peace or in convulsion, by the law or in spite of the law, through the Parliament or over the Parliament, Reform must be carried."[1]

On December 12 Russell presented the Bill a third time. It passed the Commons by a two-to-one majority on the 18th. What would the Lords do? It was not until four months later that, by a majority of nine, they approved the second reading. Then began discussion of the clauses; and on an amendment the Government was again defeated by 116 to 101. On May 8, 1832, Lord Grey asked the King to do the only thing that could save the situation—create peers. This could have been done at the time of the Lords' rejection of the second Reform Bill, but both the King and the Whig lords themselves were opposed to it as a cheapening of their order. Now there seemed no alternative. But the King refused the necessary permission.

The news at once caused a spontaneous and widespread stoppage of work. Shops and factories closed, business on the

---

[1] House of Commons, December 16, 1831 (Hansard, third series, ix, 391).

Exchanges was negligible, workmen and employers stood idle. The National Political Union, the City of London, Manchester, Birmingham, and other towns and cities sent petitions to the House of Commons urging them to stop supplies, as a House of Commons had once before done to an autocratic King. The middle classes declared they would pay no taxes until the Reform Bill became law. "No taxes paid here until the Reform Bill is passed," said placards which appeared in many Birmingham windows. In London a Committee of Public Safety was to be formed. In the Provinces political-reform societies were to take over local government and barricade the towns, while the threat of disturbance in London kept the troops in the South. Many people had firearms hidden in readiness, and it was widely believed that a large number of soldiers of all ranks would side with the people. A Lambeth meeting resolved to address the King, "praying that if he had not resolution to check a proud and selfish aristocracy he would abdicate his throne."[1] The Queen was reminded of the fate of Marie-Antoinette. Then, on Saturday, May 12, a meeting at Place's shop in Charing Cross planned the wholesale withdrawal of deposits from the banks. The next day London was plastered with the slogan: "To stop the Duke go for gold." And as an indication of what could be done £2000 was actually withdrawn from the Savings Bank in Birmingham and several hundred thousand pounds from the Bank of England.[2] Meanwhile the Reformist Press continued its propaganda, insulting and reviling the King and the royal family and all who failed to support the Bill.

In this atmosphere many Tories deserted Wellington, and Grey once again became Prime Minister. It was not until four days later, however, after the King had given a written promise to Grey to create sufficient peers to ensure the passage of the Bill through the Lords, that Wellington gave an undertaking to abandon active resistance to the Reform Bill.

The third Reform Bill became law on June 4, 1832, without the creation of peers. Although embodying a few amendments, it remained substantially the same as the first Reform Bill. Its passage had been secured by the economic pressure which the middle classes put upon the Government—the threat to

---

[1] J. R. M. Butler, *The Passing of the Great Reform Bill*, p. 404.
[2] *Ibid.*, p. 396, p. 403.

stop all business, to create a run on the banks, to cease the granting of supplies and the payment of taxes—and by the careful organization of men like Francis Place who were in close touch with the working classes and who had worked out a careful scheme of resistance.

In practice the Reform Act was not the disaster to the Tories that they had feared: though their numbers dropped, their chief leaders were all returned to the first Reformed Parliament. The working classes were bitterly disappointed: working men were not enfranchised, and no hope was offered of a further measure of reform. Even the middle classes were dissatisfied: the Reformed Parliament and its Cabinet were predominantly aristocratic. The real gainers were the Whigs, who held over 500 out of the 658 seats in the new House. A little leavening —of greater significance, perhaps, than its size indicates—was provided by a group of the followers of Bentham, the "Philosophic Radicals," and by certain outstanding individuals. John Fielden, the Radical factory-owner, Thomas Attwood, who had played a leading part in the Birmingham Political Union, and William Cobbett, the people's champion, all took their seats by the side of the aristocratic majority.[1]

There were both confusion and anomaly in the Reform Bill campaign. It was a middle-class measure, yet was sponsored by a Cabinet with a majority of peers. It was intended to benefit the manufacturers and industrialists, yet was supported by the very workers to whom they begrudged the Factory Acts. The peers hoped it would prevent revolution; the workers expected it to be followed by reform. In the event it produced Chartism, feared by middle classes and aristocracy alike, and the Factory Acts, which most of the industrialists detested, while leaving the middle classes still to fight their biggest battle against the landlords—that for the repeal of the Corn Laws.

(b) THE REPEAL OF THE CORN LAWS

In the second big struggle between middle classes and landowners—for the repeal of the Corn Laws—the workers for the most part remained outside the conflict, although it was they

---

[1] See Halévy, *History of the English People*, iii, 62–68, for a description of the first Reformed Parliament.

who suffered directly from dear bread. The Anti-Corn Law League was a predominantly middle-class organization, with ample funds at its disposal and in marked contrast to the London Working Men's Association and the Chartist movement, which were flourishing at the same period. The Chartists were split over the question of supporting the League. With the memory of what they termed the 'Great Betrayal' in mind, most of them opposed it as a deliberate attempt to divert the energy of the workers from the struggle for the franchise. Some, however, like Ebenezer Elliot, supported the League. "I am for your Charter," said Elliot, "but I am not for being starved to death first."

The manufacturers opposed the Corn Laws because a reduction in the import of corn meant a reduction in the export of manufactured goods, and this in turn would throw on other countries the necessity of manufacturing for themselves the goods which Britain might otherwise have supplied. Higher bread prices also meant a greater compulsion to higher wages, which in turn would raise the price of manufactured goods and restrict their market. The manufacturers amplified their case with the orthodox Free Trade doctrine of comparative costs. "Let each country," they said, "produce what it best can. We will supply the world with manufactured goods, they will send us food." Thus, once again, it seemed as though self-love and social, patriotism and internationalism, were to prove the same.

The manufacturers' resolution to obtain the repeal of the Corn Laws was strengthened by the very bad trade of the early forties, in which they saw themselves going bankrupt within a few months. It was then that they followed Cobden's advice and poured their money into the Anti-Corn Law League "because they knew that the rescue of their capital depended on the opening of markets from which the protection on corn excluded them."[1] They even marched in procession in London, these sober business-men from the North, when in February 1842 Peel refused to hear their demand for repeal.

> Arm in arm they tramped down the Strand and Parliament Street, a column of 500 well-dressed but angry citizens, each a man of note in some northern town. . . . Arrived at Palace Yard they stood around the entrance door, scuffling with the blue-coated

[1] J. Morley, *Life of Cobden* (one volume edition, 1905), p. 250.

"Peelers" and shouting "Total Repeal" and "Cheap Food."
Finally, they marched back up Parliament Street and, meeting
Peel's carriage, shouted angrily: "No Corn Law, Down with the
Monopoly, Give Bread and Labour!"[1]

Against the middle classes stood farmer, landlord, and parson,
to whom the Corn Laws meant higher prices, higher rents,
and higher tithes. They fought by intimidating their tenants,
so that farmers sometimes had to travel forty miles from their
own districts to hear a League speaker. At Arundel the mayor
refused the use of the town hall, the landlord refused the use
of his large room.[2]

It was a class struggle, as Bright himself made clear. On
December 19, 1845, addressing a crowded meeting in Covent
Garden Opera House, he said:

> Notwithstanding the hope that my friend [Cobden] . . . has
> expressed, that it may not become a strife of classes, I am not sure
> that it has not already become such, and I doubt whether it can
> have any other character. I believe this to be a movement of the
> commercial and industrious classes against the lords and great
> proprietors of the soil. . . .
> We have had landlord rule longer, far longer than the life of
> the oldest man in this vast assembly, and I would ask you to look
> at the results of that rule. . . . The landowners have had unlimited
> sway in Parliament and in the provinces. Abroad, the history of
> our country is the history of war and rapine: at home, of debt,
> taxes, and rapine too. . . . We find them legislating corruptly:
> they pray daily that in their legislation they may discard all
> private ends and partial affections, and after prayers they sit
> down to make a law for the purpose of extorting from all the
> consumers of food a higher price than it is worth, that the extra
> price may find its way into the pockets of the proprietors of land,
> these proprietors being the very men by whom this infamous
> law is sustained. . . .
> Two centuries ago the people of this country were engaged in
> a fearful conflict with the Crown. A despotic and treacherous
> monarch assumed to himself the right to levy taxes without the con-
> sent of Parliament and the people. That assumption was resisted.
> This fair island became a battlefield, the kingdom was convulsed,
> and an ancient throne overturned. And if our forefathers two
> hundred years ago resisted that attempt—if they refused to be the
> bondmen of a king, shall we be the born thralls of an aristocracy
> like ours? Shall we, who struck the lion down, shall we pay the

[1] G. M. Trevelyan, *Life of John Bright*, p. 70.   [2] Morley, *op. cit.*, p. 153.

wolf homage? Or shall we not, by a manly and united expression of public opinion, at once, and for ever, put an end to this giant wrong?[1]

In 1839 the Anti-Corn Law League was formed. Its leaders were Richard Cobden and John Bright. Cobden was a Manchester cotton manufacturer, consciously middle class, incorruptible, and of extraordinary ability as debater and organizer. Bright, a Rochdale carpet manufacturer, was a Quaker who regarded his political activities as part of his religious duties, and whose forceful and often moving orations were those of a crusader.

The defeat of the landlords was not easy, and the effort put out by the League was prodigious. They were helped by the penny postage, by railways, and, above all, by money. They sent missionaries and lecturers all over the country, including Cobden and Bright themselves. Within five days Bright addressed meetings at Kirkcaldy, Dundee, Perth, Stirling, Glasgow, Hawick, and Newcastle. All the great towns, and particularly Manchester, had big and enthusiastic meetings. In twelve weeks 150 meetings were held in London alone. The League, with great expenditure of money and care in organization, sent a little library of Free Trade tracts to every elector in the kingdom. Total annual subscriptions in 1839 were £5000; they rose to £8000 the following year, to £50,000 in 1843, to between £80,000 and £90,000 in 1844, when the League was spending at the rate of £1000 a week. At a meeting in Manchester at the end of 1845 more than £60,000 was subscribed in two hours. This is what is meant by the command of economic resources. Even agricultural workers and small farmers were converted to Free Trade in the campaign the League began in 1843. The hungry forties were a strong ally. Bright was able to make great play with the fact that

a fat and sleek dean, a dignitary of the Church and a great philosopher, recommends for the consumption of the people . . . swede, turnips and mangel-wurzel; and the Hereditary Earl Marshal of England . . . recommends hot water and a pinch of curry-powder.[2]

1 *Speeches of John Bright* (1868), edited by J. E. Thorold Rogers, vol. ii, pp 275–278.
2 *Ibid*, p. 284.

But the most effective speech of the whole campaign was that of the farm labourer who said simply, "I be protected and I be starving."

The League also used the power which the Reform Act had put into their hands. They organized sympathetic votes in the constituencies, put pressure on Parliamentary candidates, sometimes put forward their own candidates, and maintained incessant pressure from the floor of the House. This was their tactic particularly when, in 1845 and 1846, better harvests and better trade had removed the extremest sting of poverty, and consequently taken the edge off their propaganda. They did more. Since the possession of freehold land to the annual value of 40s. gave the owner a vote, they organized the buying of such freehold properties by Free Traders. The response was enthusiastic. In the Northern counties 5000 votes were obtained in this way by the beginning of 1845, and not less than £250,000 was invested in forty-shilling freeholds in these counties.[1] Bright described this tactic as "the *ulterior measure* of our contest."

In the autumn of 1845 it became certain that the potato crop in Ireland had failed and that phenomenal rain was ruining the wheat crop in England. What was to be done? Sir Robert Peel, the Tory Prime Minister, wished to open the ports to foreign corn for a limited period. But his Cabinet was divided. Lord John Russell, the leader of the Whigs, on the other hand, in an open letter from Edinburgh to his constituents came out strongly for total repeal of the Corn Laws. The League held excited meetings all over the country. "Our meetings are everywhere gloriously attended. There is a perfect unanimity among all classes; not a syllable about Chartism or any other *ism*," wrote Cobden to his wife, "and not a word of dissent."[2] Peel, unable to lead a divided Cabinet, resigned. Lord John Russell's attempt to form a Cabinet failed, and Peel came back as Prime Minister, his conversion to Free Trade, which had been proceeding slowly for years, finally accomplished by the potato famine in Ireland, the threat of famine in England, and the outcry of public opinion led by the Anti-Corn Law League. "It was those rotten potatoes," said the Duke of Wellington, "that put Peel in his damned fright." But fright was not the word. Peel had greater honesty and

---

[1] Morley, *op, cit.*, p. 306.   [2] *Ibid.*, p. 342

courage than the party he led, and he committed political suicide by declaring for Free Trade.

After Governmental changes and Parliamentary intrigue, on the evening of June 25, 1846, the Bill repealing the Corn Laws was passed by the House of Commons. On the same night the Government was defeated on another issue, and five days later Peel resigned. The effects of repeal were nowhere as disastrous as the landed interests had feared, the price of corn, through a variety of reasons, keeping at a steady average of about 52s. a quarter for over twenty years.

In a struggle that was even more clearly a class issue than the fight over the Reform Bill the middle classes had won. For nearly a century middle and upper classes would together govern the country with little effective opposition.

SELECT BIBLIOGRAPHY

BARNES, D. G.: *A History of the English Corn Laws from 1660–1846* (Routledge, 1930).

BUTLER, J. R. M.: *The Passing of the Great Reform Bill* (Longmans, 1914).

FAY, C. R.: *The Corn Laws and Social England* (Cambridge University Press, 1932).

HALÉVY, E.: *A History of the English People in 1815* (Unwin, 1924).

McCORD, NORMAN: *The Anti-Corn Law League 1836–1846* (second edition, paperback, Unwin University Books, 1968).

MORLEY, J.: *Life of Cobden* (Chapman, 1881).

SEYMOUR, C.: *Electoral Reform in England and Wales* (Milford, 1916).

TREVELYAN, G. M.: *Life of John Bright* (Constable, 1925).

CHAPTER VIII

WORKING-CLASS STRUGGLE: 1829-34

THE period 1829-34 is one of great significance in British working-class history. Between 1829 and 1834, and particularly after 1832, there were many factors making for energetic industrial action. Trade, which had been bad since the repeal of the Combination Acts, revived in 1829. There were strikes on the rising market, and new and ambitious trade unions were formed, including an attempted general union of all trades. Robert Owen, returning to England in 1829 after the failure of New Harmony, found that his gospel had been making headway, and he determined to waste no time in transforming British capitalist society into a Co-operative Commonwealth. For part of the time the industrial movement ran parallel with the Reform movement: for part of the time it developed as a reaction against the 'Great Betrayal' of 1832. It seemed at one point as though the trade-union and Co-operative movements would fuse into a triumphant coalition of workers. But by the end of 1834 these high hopes were dead. The employers and the State had united against the workers, and the working-class movement lay crushed by the catastrophe of the 'Black Year.'

(a) CO-OPERATION

The Co-operative movement held steadily to its course despite the more vocal agitation for the Reform Bill. The 300 Co-operative Societies of 1830 had grown to nearly 500 by 1832, and in 1831 the first national Co-operative Congress was held.

These Co-operative Societies were of three types. Some were purely educational, aiming at spreading the Owenite ideal by propaganda, holding meetings, and circulating literature. Others were trading concerns, engaged in practical experiments in storekeeping, like the London store of which Lovett was in charge. Here the aim was the simple one of eliminating the profit of the middleman. Goods were bought wholesale,

and the profit on their sale was generally put to some Co-operative purpose, such as building up a fund to establish a Co-
operative community. It was comparatively easy to open a
little store and sell goods to your fellow-workmen. Far more
ambitious was the third type of Co-operative enterprise, which
consisted in Co-operative production—making, without the
help of the capitalist, the goods which would be sold in the
Co-operative store. Handicraftsmen could make articles on a
small scale, but in most cases capital equipment, raw materials,
and time—all beyond the reach of the workman—were needed.
Nevertheless, of the 500 Co-operative Societies of 1832 many
were little producing societies, consisting mainly of small-scale
handicraftsmen. Co-operative production on a big scale
developed only in the second half of the century, when Co-
operative trading concerns had accumulated sufficient capital
to finance production on their own account.

The first tasks of Owen after his return in 1829 were to
get control of the energy which the masses were putting into
the Reform Bill agitation, and to guide the development of the
Co-operative enterprises which already existed. Like the
Co-operative Societies which were founded upon it, Owenism
had three lines of development. There was education. Owen
had founded excellent schools at his factories in New Lanark;
he urged the inclusion of education clauses in the Factory Acts;
he was the inspiration of Co-operative Societies, like the
National Union of the Industrious Classes, and of middle-class
societies like the Society for National Regeneration, in which
educational aims ranked high. There was storekeeping. But
over Co-operative stores Owen was not very enthusiastic,
regarding mere storekeeping as paltry compared with his great
schemes for regenerating society. Finally, there was Co-operative production, which was at the very heart of Owenism.

Owen's big chance came after the disillusionment of June
1832. But already in December 1831 he had begun a campaign
which, besides immediate propaganda, had as its object the
founding of labour exchanges or labour bazaars, in which the
workers were to exchange the products of their labour without
the intervention of middlemen. Co-operative production
and Co-operative exchange were thus to join hands. Some
premises in Gray's Inn Road, London, were lent for the purpose, and for nearly twelve months there was ceaseless propa-

ganda. There were meetings and lectures, and a weekly paper, *The Crisis*, which began in April 1832. For its third biennial Congress, held in April 1832, the Co-operative Congress assembled at the premises in Gray's Inn Road, and Owen took the opportunity of spreading his gospel of exchange bazaars. In September 1832 the first exchange bazaar was opened in Gray's Inn Road. Soon there was a branch in Blackfriars Road. Early in 1833 the parent exchange moved there also, owing to disagreement between Owen and the owner of the Gray's Inn Road premises. In May it moved to Charlotte Street, Tottenham Court Road, and in June 1833 a new exchange was opened in Birmingham, to be followed by others in Liverpool, Glasgow, and other towns.

The goods in the bazaar were priced in accordance with the cost of their raw materials and the amount of labour incorporated in them. Current rates of pay per hour in different industries were accepted, and thus differences in the value of labour were allowed for. A commission of one penny in the shilling was then added to meet the expenses of the labour bazaar. Finally the whole sum was divided by 6*d*.—6*d*. being taken as an average or basic cost of labour per hour—in order to ascertain the price of the article in labour hours. Specially appointed valuers made these calculations, which might go something like this:

Cost of a Pair of Shoes

Cost of raw materials	4*s*. 6*d*.
Number of hours worked to make shoes	ten
Cost of labour at 9*d*. an hour	7*s*. 6*d*.
	12*s*.
Commission at 1*d*. in 1*s*.	1*s*.
Total cost of shoes	13*s*.
Cost in labour hours $\frac{156}{6}$	26.

As a medium of exchange special 'labour notes' were printed expressing, in place of a number of shillings or pounds, a number of labour hours. Thus if a shoemaker deposited two pairs of shoes, one valued at twenty-six labour hours, the other at twenty labour hours, he would get labour notes to the value of forty-six labour hours, and could buy goods of corresponding **value.**

In the first weeks there was a rush of depositors, especially of tailors, cabinet-makers, and shoemakers—the traditional independent handicraftsmen who could produce without a large capital or the intervention of a capitalist. The building in which the bazaar was housed was in the form of an open quadrangle with rooms and galleries running round—eminently suited for the display and storage of goods. The public, as well as the Co-operators themselves, readily bought goods, and local shopkeepers even accepted the labour notes across their counters. The bazaar itself was ready to start customers by exchanging money for labour notes.

But soon the impracticability of the scheme was manifest. The prices at the bazaar were not always in accordance with commercial prices. Where they were lower the goods were quickly sold; where higher they remained on the hands of the organizers. Poorer workers could not afford the initial outlay to make their goods; even better-off ones could not do so unless they were assured of a quick valuation, which was not always possible when goods piled up quickly. Moreover, the scope of the exchange bazaar was very limited. Clearly only small articles, requiring relatively little capital, could in this way be made and exchanged. The pricing of the goods depended upon the workman's own estimate of the number of hours he had worked. Owen had not discovered the later concept of 'socially necessary labour time,' which struck the mean between the slow worker and the very quick worker.

Apart from these inherent causes of failure there were certain extraneous causes. Owen's quarrel with the owner of the Gray's Inn Road premises was unfortunate; the two moves of the London Exchange Bazaar within twelve months caused lack of confidence; and Owen himself was spreading his energies in other directions—to the formation of the Builders' Gild and to a general union of the working classes.

(b) THE INDUSTRIAL WORKERS' REVOLT

One of the areas of early trade-union activity was Northumberland. The first definite union of the Northumberland and Durham miners was in 1825, a year after the repeal of the Combination Acts. It was revived in 1830 as the Pitmen's Union of the Tyne and Wear, under the leadership of Tommy

Hepburn, of Hetton. Early in 1831 there were big meetings at Black Fell, Durham, and on the Newcastle Town Moor. The miners denounced the yearly bond and the wages and tied cottages attached to it, the colliery tommy-shops, the fines inflicted by the viewers (the owners' agents), and they objected to the length of time worked underground by boys of twelve. The miners refused to sign any yearly bond until these grievances had been redressed. Meantime they held protest meetings, and subscribed 6d. a week each to send a deputation and petition to Parliament. The owners agreed not to work boys more than twelve hours a day and to allow the pitmen to spend their pay where they pleased. But on the questions of fines and the yearly bond they were adamant. When the yearly bond expired on April 5 the men therefore left work.

Tommy Hepburn led the strike, and under his guidance there was little violence. At one colliery the pitmen called on the viewer and took everything they could eat or drink; at another they put the mines temporarily out of action by throwing corves and rolleys down the shafts. The mine-owners called in the Army, the yeomanry, marines, and London police, but by the middle of June they had given way on all points except the right to fine. The victory was short-lived. It was less than a year later that the struggle began which in a few months broke the miners' union. This time the owners took the offensive, and in many pits they refused to employ trade unionists. The men, again led by Hepburn, decided to stand by the union. There were big meetings on Bolden Fell and Newcastle Town Moor. Men in pits not locked out for many weeks contributed 6s. out of every £1 they earned to help the others. The owners used police to break up meetings; they brought blacklegs from Wales and Staffordshire and Yorkshire. Under the protection of cavalry, London police, and special constables, they evicted hundreds of miners' families from their homes. At Friar's Goose Collieries an ejection caused a pitched battle, after which dozens of miners were indiscriminately dragged to prison. Tension rose. A blackleg was killed, and the four men accused of the murder were loudly cheered by the populace. A justice of the peace was fatally wounded, and a miner executed for the crime. A special constable shot dead a miner who was doing nothing violent and received only six months' imprisonment.

More and more blacklegs were introduced. Miners in employment could not keep up their heavy contributions to the unemployed. Evicted families were living in the open fields, cold and hungry. Gradually the miners gave way. The owners were exultant. Tommy Hepburn, the last to give in, wandered homeless, workless, and alone for months, trying to sell packets of tea. Finally he too was driven to ask for work. He got it—but only after promising never again to take part in trade-union activity. He kept his word.

Among the cotton-spinners the period of action was opened in 1829 by a strike at Hyde, near Manchester. After six months the strikers were driven back to work convinced that their failure was due to lack of co-ordination with other centres of the industry. There followed a meeting at Ramsey, Isle of Man, at which delegates from the spinners of England, Ireland, and Scotland were present. Largely under the inspiration of John Doherty, an Irishman who was secretary of the Manchester cotton-spinners, a single union for male cotton-spinners and piecers was established in December 1829 under the title of the Grand General Union of all the Operative Spinners of the United Kingdom. In addition to their subscriptions to their local societies members were to pay one penny a week to the central organization, which was to consist of three national committees, a secretary (Doherty), and two organizers.

From this single organization for male spinners Doherty advanced to the more ambitious idea of a single union embracing many trades. More than ten years previously the curiously named Philanthropic Hercules had the same intentions. In July 1830 Doherty launched the National Association for the Protection of Labour, a general union of which he himself became secretary, with its own journal, entitled, *The United Trades Co-operative Journal*. An entrance fee of £1, together with 1s. for each member of the affiliating society, and a weekly subscription of one penny a member was required. In spite of these high contributions the project was vastly popular. At least 150 separate unions enrolled immediately, and by the beginning of 1831 the membership was about 100,000 and still growing.[1] In April 1831 a delegate meeting of 9,000 coalminers resolved to join, Belfast trades enrolled,

[1] S. and B. Webb, *The History of Trade Unionism*, p. 123.

Leeds woollen workers formed the Leeds Clothiers' Union and affiliated to the National Association. There was a Potters' Union, which Doherty helped to start; there were unions of millwrights, blacksmiths, mechanics. In London a federation of trades formed the Metropolitan Trades Union, and was in touch with the National Association for the Protection of Labour.

The success of the N.A.P.L. seems to have overshadowed the cotton-spinners' General Union. The latter met at Manchester in December 1830 at the time of a strike of cotton-spinners at Ashton-under-Lyne. Doherty appears to have abandoned the secretaryship, and nothing further is heard of of the Grand General Union.

The United Trades Co-operative Journal, the original newspaper of the N.A.P.L., failed shortly after its inception because of the high newspaper tax of 4*d*. per copy. But a fund, of which Francis Place was treasurer, was raised in order to finance *The Voice of the People*, which started in January 1831, with Doherty as editor. Its object was "to unite the productive classes of the community in one common bond of union." It paid the stamp duty, and consequently cost 7*d*. It reached, nevertheless, the surprisingly high circulation of 30,000 copies weekly.[1]

Neither the N.A.P.L. nor *The Voice of the People* outlasted 1831. There were quarrels, recrimination when one section refused to support another, and by the beginning of 1832 the general union had disappeared, and Doherty was working on another working-class paper, *The Poor Man's Advocate*. In this year interest shifted to another section of the working class—the builders—who for two years maintained the lead in trade-union organization.

In 1832 the builders formed a great national union, which they called the Operative Builders' Union. It was a federation of the seven trades or crafts concerned in building. In the localities each craft met in its own separate lodge; no bricklayer, for example, could attend a carpenters' meeting without invitation. Each lodge sent a delegate to an annual central conference known as the Grand Lodge, or the Builders' Parliament. This body elected the President and other officials, laid down rules, decided questions of policy, and determined the

[1] *Ibid.*, p. 123.

advisability of a strike. Subject to the ruling of the Builders' Parliament, the separate lodges remained autonomous and elected representatives to quarterly district meetings, which formed district executive centres. The general secretary of the Union, however, required monthly returns of their membership and financial position, while the whole Union was subject to a levy for the purpose of maintaining the executive and for financing the annual Builders' Parliament.

In its meetings the Builders' Union maintained much of the ritual of the days when trade unions were illegal. There were secret initiation ceremonies and solemn oaths of secrecy, accompanied by the singing of hymns and the use of much theatrical paraphernalia, such as white shrouds, death's-heads, and skeletons, intended to impress the incoming member. The impression made must have been considerable, for the Builders' Union spread rapidly, and in 1833 had 30,000 members.

Both Builders' Union and Builders' Parliament were under the influence of Owen. There was good reason for this. The builders suffered much at the hands of middlemen and contractors who creamed off a substantial profit without performing any useful function that the builders themselves could not undertake. Owen's doctrine of Co-operative production by the workers for the workers was bound to appeal to the builders. Moreover, in the building trade there was little fixed capital—no heavy machinery, no factory, no mine. It was comparatively easy for the workmen themselves to eliminate the middlemen and make direct contracts for work. When in 1833 Owen was urging the various national trade unions to form guilds to take over the whole of industry, the builders acted.

In Liverpool they launched a large-scale attack upon contractors. The small masters were at first sympathetic, but the initial success of the operatives brought them into line with other employers, who all decided to fight the Builders' Union. This they did by what became the notorious practice of 'presenting the document.' Every worker was required to sign a printed pledge that he would neither belong to a trade union nor assist a trade unionist. The Operative Builders' Union replied by calling out all their members. The struggle spread. In Manchester "not a brick was laid for sixteen weeks." In Birmingham a bitter struggle was started in August 1833 by Messrs Walthen, one of the largest contractors, who discharged every Union man from their employ. The struggle was proceeding vigorously when in September 1833 the annual Builders' Parliament assembled at Manchester. To this meeting of 270 delegates, representing 30,000 operatives, Owen outlined his scheme for taking over the whole of industry. As a result the Grand National Gild of Builders was formed "to render the employer superfluous."

This body was to build directly for the public, abolishing employers and middlemen of all kinds. It was not only itself founded on the Co-operative principle, but it planned to wipe out all competition by liquidating private builders. These might join the Gild on equal terms, but they were not to be allowed to secure workmen to carry on their old practices. The Gild would accept all contracts, provide the materials and labour, and estimate the price based on the cost of these. Each craft lodge would elect its own foreman, the foremen together would elect their superintendent. There was to be sickness, old-age, and accident insurance.

There were thus in existence two organizations—the Operative Builders' Union, struggling to improve workers' conditions under capitalism, and the Grand National Gild of Builders, struggling to eliminate capitalism. Their fate was in turn to be influenced by the Grand National Consolidated Trades Union. The Gild secured a few small contracts, mostly from political sympathizers, but its biggest undertaking was the construction of the Birmingham Guildhall. On November 28 the builders' crafts of the city, headed by the local band and with banners flying, marched to Broad Street, where the foundation stone was laid.

The Union was still engaged in the conflicts which had broken out before the formation of the Gild, and which still continued. But by the end of 1833 the builders in Liverpool, Manchester, and Birmingham had all been defeated. The remaining centre of Union strength was London, and here also the men were involved in a long and bitter and somewhat curious struggle. In July 1834 a firm of brewers—Combe, Delafield and Company—refused to employ any Union men. The employees of Cubitt's, a large firm of master builders, thereupon retaliated by refusing to drink any of Combe, Delafield's beer. Cubitt's retorted by prohibiting all beer except Combe, Delafield's from being brought into their yards.

The men defied this order and attempted to take in other beer. They were then locked out. The dispute spread to questions of wages and the employment of non-Unionists, and the employers 'presented the document.' The men were solid until September, but by November their resistance was broken. They had to consent to the employment of non-Unionists; they failed to obtain uniform wages. Nevertheless they had compelled the employers to withdraw the document.

But other forces of disruption were at work. The secretary of the Operative Builders' Union absconded with the Union funds. There was dissension within their ranks. Some 'exclusives' objected to including the whole industry in one union, and instead demanded that each craft union should be autonomous. At the September Grand Lodge meeting the 'exclusives' carried their resolution. So, without funds and without unity, the Operative Builders' Union, at the end of 1834, passed out of existence, the constituent bodies falling apart and going their own ways. The Gild perished simultaneously, the unfinished Gild Hall being sold to a private merchant, who used it as a warehouse.

The Builders' Union had held the stage for two years, but there had been other bursts of trade-union activity. The Leeds Clothiers' Union, for example, outlived Doherty's National Association for the Protection of Labour, of which it was a constituent, and in 1833 had a lively exchange with employers. The Potters' Union was another active body, also owing its origin to Doherty. In 1833 it reached a membership of 8000, chiefly in Staffordshire. It was at this period also that the cotton-spinners were pressing for their Ten Hour Bill, and early in 1834 Fielden and Owen were demanding a strike for an eight-hour day for all.

Meantime a new tactic, that of the general strike, had been elaborated in a pamphlet in January 1832 by a disciple of Owen's named William Benbow, who, like so many of these early Socialists, was a shoemaker and a coffee-house keeper. There were two theories attached to the general strike. One was that it would precipitate revolution, the other that it would be the instrument for peacefully effecting the change from capitalism to Socialism. "There will not be insurrection, . . ." wrote *The Trades Union Gazette*.

The men may remain at leisure; there is, and can be, no law to compel them to work against their will. They may walk the streets . . . with their arms folded . . . and what happens in consequence? . . . capital is destroyed, the revenue fails, . . . government falls into confusion, and every link in the chain which binds society together is broken in a moment by this inert conspiracy of the poor against the rich.[1]

The idea of the general strike, or 'national holiday' as it was called, did not materialize. It was popular with the Chartists, among whom it was known as 'the Sacred Month,' but it was not until nearly a century later that a general strike actually occurred. Meantime, in 1834, the interest shifted back to Owen.

Owen, like Doherty, believed that the ineffectiveness of working-class activity in the thirties was partly the result of lack of co-ordination. He therefore made a further effort to bring all the widespread but disparate industrial activity of the time under the ægis of one big union. The object of such a union would be nothing less than the ending of the capitalist system. Owen announced that all individual competition would cease and that industry would be carried on by 'national companies.' He called upon all trades to organize themselves into lodges and associations of lodges, on the pattern of the builders. The grand union of all the trades would then follow. The idea spread like wildfire, the proposals were adopted enthusiastically, and at a conference early in 1834 the Grand National Consolidated Trades Union was formed. It was a federation of trades or lodges, and there were 'miscellaneous' lodges and 'female miscellaneous' lodges to ensure the inclusion of all workers. Each lodge was to have its own sick, funeral, superannuation, and other benefits; the oath and the initiation ceremonies were retained. There was apparently no regular subscription to central funds, but there was to be a general levy of all members to acquire land and to set up Co-operative workshops. The trades would thus begin the acquisition of capital, and would at the same time be able to provide work for strikers and the unemployed.

Missionaries toured the country. The G.N.C.T.U. reached the half-million membership mark in a few weeks. Unions

[1] Quoted by Max Beer, *A History of British Socialism*, i, 333.

sprang up almost overnight throughout the country and hastened to affiliate. Chimney-sweeps and shop-assistants, cabinet-makers, ploughmen, shearmen—all pressed in. So did the women. Operative bonnet-makers, female tailors, female gardeners, formed lodges. There was also a Lodge of Ancient Virgins, subsequently distinguished for its members' militancy in an Oldham riot.

The aim appears to have been a form of Syndicalist Government founded on a pyramid system of representation from local lodge to district, and so on to the Trades Parliament. The alarm caused both to employers and to the State was considerable. "We considered much," wrote Lord Melbourne, ". . . as to whether the arrangements of these unions, their meetings, their communications, or their pecuniary funds could be reached or in any way prevented."[1] The Government found several ways. Although it could not legally prosecute men who combined to raise wages or reduce hours, it could prosecute under the laws concerning master and servant; it could punish for 'molestation,' 'obstruction,' or 'intimidation'; it could construe peaceful picketing as one of these. Under such pretexts many peaceful trade unionists were imprisoned. It was in the case of the Dorchester Labourers, however, that the Government played its trump card, charging the men under the Act prohibiting illegal oaths.

At the same time employers were busily 'presenting the document' and locking out from work members of the Grand National who refused to submit. Leicester hosiers, Glasgow builders, calico-printers, engineers, and cabinet-makers were all in trouble with their employers, and some at least were supported from Grand National funds. At Derby 1500 workers were locked out during the winter of 1833–34 for refusing to abandon their union. The Grand National made a levy of 1s. per head per week of its members. But the heavy toll lasted for four months only, after which the operatives returned to work on the employers' terms. In March 1834 Westminster was for several days in partial darkness through a strike of gas-stokers. In May a levy of 1s. 6d. per member throughout the country was intended chiefly to support the 20,000 London tailors on strike. Leeds clothing workers were defeated, the cotton-spinners first postponed and then abandoned their strike

---

[1] Quoted by Webb, *op. cit.*, pp. 141–142.

for an eight-hour day. The builders had been beaten in Lancashire and Birmingham, and in July came their great London lock-out and strike, which in December ended in their defeat.

(c) THE REVOLT OF THE LAND WORKERS

Meantime, in the countryside, another act of the same drama was being played. The first scene was in 1830. There were no unions of agricultural labourers, and the protest against the starvation conditions of that year—in which no surprise was occasioned when four men were found under a hedge dead of starvation—was spontaneous and unorganized. In Kent and Sussex, in Essex, in Hampshire, and finally over the whole of the South and South-west, bands of agricultural labourers, seemingly unconnected, went about from village to village, marching sometimes to the squire, sometimes to the assembled justices, sometimes round the local farms. Sometimes they demanded a wage of 2s. 3d. a day for a married man; they often asked for a small sum as immediate 'satisfaction.' They frequently destroyed threshing machines, though this was often done at the instigation of the farmers themselves. Where a parson was aggressively rich they demanded a reduction of tithes—in which also they had the support of the farmers. Where a farmer was particularly unpopular his ricks were fired. In two cases the local workhouse was destroyed. Often these acts were carried out by a mysterious "Captain Swing," reminiscent of "King Lud." Sometimes the labourers were joined by local craftsmen. A young carpenter was strangely outspoken: "You gentlemen have been living long enough on the good things, now is our time, and we will have them," he said. "You gentlemen would not speak to us now, only you are afraid and intimidated."[1]

The crowds were on the whole disciplined and orderly. There was little violence, but much fear of the labourers and not a little sympathy with them. Consequently, for several weeks the labourers were in control of a large part of Kent and part of East Sussex. The larger landowners and the Government were at first indignant and then alarmed. The Duke of Buckingham said that the country was in the hands of the

---

[1] Quoted by J. L. and B. Hammond, *The Village Labourer, 1760–1832*, p. 240.

rebels. Cavalry, infantry, and dragoons were hurried to the
scenes of the disturbances. A much smaller display of force
would have sufficed. The labourers were not only unorganized,
they were weak with hunger and unused to asserting themselves. They quickly relapsed into an apathy and despair all
the more bitter for the brief hope they had held of being treated
like human beings. But the ruling class would not let them sink
back quietly. As their fear had been out of proportion to the
revolt, so their vengeance was tragically disproportionate to
the wrongdoing of the labourers they now brought before their
courts of justice. A special Commission of Assize was appointed,
and thousands of villagers, helpless and afraid, were dragged
off to 'justice.' The rest watched—cowed, perhaps, but
magnificently incorruptible. Even the reward of £1000 offered
by the Crown to these starving wretches brought no information
against any labourer. Some who had not been arrested came
forward voluntarily with evidence which they hoped might
help a comrade, though warned that it would also incriminate
themselves. But nothing the agricultural labourers were able to
do could mitigate the severity of the punishment on which their
rulers were set. The shuddering sigh that went through the
court-room and through the villages as the savage sentences
were pronounced can still be heard. Nine men were hanged,
457 men and boys were transported, hundreds more imprisoned
in England.

This was the "Last Labourers' Revolt," and this the
'justice' that followed. Beaten and stunned, the labourers
took no part in the Reform Bill agitation, but when the excitement of Owen's Grand National Consolidated Trades Union
swept the country there stirred again, very faintly, the hope of
the agricultural labourer for a few extra shillings a week.

From Hampshire, in 1832, the Duke of Wellington reported
that the labourers were forming societies which appeared to be
affiliated to some national union. Wages rose, and in the
Dorsetshire village of Tolpuddle the farmers promised that
wages should be the same as in other districts. This meant a
rise to 10s. a week. Subsequently, however, the employers
deducted one shilling and then another, until wages stood at
7s. a week. Then the men were told a further reduction to 6s.
was necessary. They "consulted together what had better be

done, as they knew it was impossible to live honestly on such scanty means." As a result the Tolpuddle workers wrote to the Grand National asking for advice. In reply the Grand National sent two delegates and a copy of the rules and instructions for organizing trade unions.

Living in Tolpuddle was George Loveless, twenty-eight years old, with a wife and three children. He was paid 7s. a week as an agricultural labourer, and yet had contrived to gather together a small collection of theological works, for he was a Wesleyan and a local preacher. Loveless, his brother James, and four others followed the advice of the Grand National, and in 1833 formed a trade union, the Friendly Society of Agricultural Labourers, "to maintain the wages of farm servants." The entrance fee was a shilling, with a weekly contribution of one penny. A ritual and initiation ceremony were adopted. The village painter made a life-size figure of a skeleton. James Loveless clothed himself in a white surplice, intending members were blindfolded, took an oath of secrecy, and pledged themselves to carry out the aims of the union. Sufficient labourers joined the union to alarm the authorities, but, since joining a trade union was no longer a crime, they had to devise some other pretext for prosecution. The same problem was arising all over the country. The Grand National was spreading, and trade unions were springing up everywhere. Though in themselves they were legal, there existed an Act, passed in 1797 at the time of the Nore mutiny, and re-enacted as one of the Six Acts of 1819, which prohibited "unlawful oaths." This was sufficient for the purpose. If trade unions could not be prohibited, they could be prosecuted as bodies indulging in unlawful oaths. The union selected for an example was the little Tolpuddle Labourers' Union.

Consequently on February 24, when he arose at daybreak to go to his work, George Loveless was arrested, and with five others taken to Dorchester. The six trade unionists were tried at the Assizes in March. The only document discovered by the prosecution was a copy of the rules for the General Society of Labourers. It prohibited drunkenness and obscene language at lodge meetings, and forbade violence or any breach of the law. The accused had neither practised nor meditated violence. They had neither struck work nor even asked for higher wages. On the testimony of their employers they were "good labouring servants." All this availed nothing. The judge openly displayed his prejudice. The jurymen were farmers and millers. George Loveless, asked if he had anything to say, handed in to the Court a written statement, in which he said:

> My Lord, if we have violated any law it was not done intentionally. We have injured no man's reputation, character, person, or property. We were meeting together to preserve ourselves, our wives, and our children, from utter degradation and starvation. We challenge any man, or number of men, to prove that we have acted, or intended to act, different from the above statement.

Important as this was to the accused, it was mumbled so that it was practically unintelligible to the Court. The sentence was seven years' transportation for each of the prisoners.

Petitions for pardon or retrial poured in to the Home Secretary. The Grand National organized a great agitation. A London Dorchester Committee was formed. By April 21 it had secured nearly 250,000 signatures to a petition, and for that day planned a great protest demonstration. For days *The Times* had been publishing alarmist leading articles. Lord Melbourne refused to receive either the marchers or their petition. To deal with the demonstrators special constables were sworn in and troops called out. But Robert Owen had shrewdly hired the ground at Copenhagen Fields, where the procession assembled, and the police did not dare to break it up. The marchers, numbering according to *The Times* 30,000 and estimated by trade unionists as between 100,000 and 200,000, each wore a red ribbon and followed the thirty-three banners of the Metropolitan trade unions.[1]

All this failed to save the six. While their friends were protesting against their sentence the Dorchester labourers were on their way to exile. On September 4 the brothers Loveless were landed at Hobart, Tasmania, and put to work with the chain gangs. The other four reached Botany Bay in August. The London Dorchester Committee, a group of about sixteen working-men, never ceased its efforts, and in 1836 the remainder of the prisoners' sentence was remitted. It was not until 1838, however, that they were brought back to England. About £1300 had been collected by the indefatigable London

---

[1] Webb, *op. cit.*, pp. 47–48.

Dorchester Committee, and this money was used to provide the Tolpuddle martyrs with small farms. Five settled with their families in Essex; the sixth returned to his native village.

Just at the time when internal dissension was wrecking the Grand National the prosecution of the Dorchester Labourers threatened the whole trade-union world with similar attacks. Neither the Grand National nor the separate unions could withstand the calamities of 1834. The exchange bazaars had failed in 1833; in 1834 the Builders' Gild and the Grand National both fell to pieces in an atmosphere of bleak despair. The Grand National had lasted for less than twelve months. Industrial activity was useless. Once again the swing of the pendulum took the workers to political action. But this time —and for the first time—it was to be an independent working-class movement. Out of the 'Great Betrayal' of 1832 and the 'Black Year' of 1834 arose Chartism.

SELECT BIBLIOGRAPHY

BEER, MAX: *A History of British Socialism* (Bell, 1919), vol. i.

COLE, G. D. H.: *Life of Robert Owen* (Macmillan, 1925).

——: *Attempts at General Union* (Macmillan, 1953).

COLE, MARGARET: *Robert Owen of New Lanark, 1771–1858* (Batchworth Press, 1953).

FUSSELL, G. E.: *The English Rural Labourer from Tudor to Victorian Times* (Batchworth Press, 1949).

HAMMOND, J. L. AND B.: *The Village Labourer, 1760–1832* (Longmans, 1911).

HOBSBAWM, E. J. AND RUDE, G.: *Captain Swing* (Lawrence and Wishart, 1969).

MARLOW, JOYCE: *The Tolpuddle Martyrs* (Deutsch, 1972).

PODMORE, F.: *Robert Owen, a Biography* (Hutchinson, 1906).

WEBB, S. AND B.: *The History of Trade Unionism* (Longmans, 1894; revised edition, 1920).

CHAPTER IX

THE POOR LAW AND PUBLIC HEALTH

(a) THE POOR LAW

ONE of the first questions to which the Reformed Parliament turned its attention was the Poor Law. It had been observed that the Labourers' Revolt of 1830 occurred in the Southern counties where the Speenhamland system was most widely practised, and the belief gained ground that lavish poor relief led to insubordination and violence. This point of view was reinforced by dissatisfaction over the alarming rise in the poor rates. There had been Committees of Inquiry from 1817 onward, and in February 1832, before the passage of the Reform Act, a Royal Commission had been appointed. One of the Assistant Commissioners, who afterwards became Commissioner, was Edwin Chadwick, a prodigious worker, an ardent Benthamite and favourite disciple of the master. Chadwick not only drew up a long and influential Report of his observations as Assistant Commissioner, but probably also drew up the final Report of the Commission, which was then refined upon by Nassau Senior.

The Poor Law Report was published in 1834. In its pages were revealed for the first time the degradation and inefficiency of a system which had flourished over the greater part of the country for nearly forty years.

The outstanding features of the Speenhamland system were its almost entire dependence on out-relief and its habit, not merely of relieving the unemployed, but of making up low wages to a level deemed sufficient for maintenance. The Commissioners of 1834 heavily condemned both practices, which, they declared, demoralized the poor by making them insolent, lazy, thriftless, and immoral. They were insolent because they had grown to regard parish relief as a right, and exhibited a reprehensible spirit of "independence." "The bread money is hardly looked upon by the labourers in the light of parish relief. They consider it as much their right as the wages they receive from their employers," reported Mr Russell, Magistrate of Swallowfield, Berks, with resentment.[1] It made them lazy because they received the same amount of money whether in work or out, the relief payments becoming a bounty upon idleness. They became thriftless because they were generally refused relief until their savings had been exhausted. The system made them immoral because the allowance for each child encouraged the breeding of illegitimate children. It "is considered," reported an Assistant Commissioner, "a good speculation to marry a woman who can bring a fortune of one or two bastards to her husband."[2] Finally the Commissioners condemned the Speenhamland system because it was not a deterrent. It neither made pauperism a "badge of shame" nor compelled the segregation of those who were in receipt of public relief.

There was, however, another side to this picture of the independent, dissolute pauper insolently claiming his 3s. a week from the parish. Farmers, knowing that wages would be made up to a subsistence level out of the rates, often threw the cost of maintaining their labourers on to the parish, and wages fell to such fantastically low levels as 2s. 6d. a week. But as the price of all goods, and not bread alone, rose during and after the Napoleonic wars, the Speenhamland bread scale became insufficient for bare existence.

Frequently paupers were disposed of by some variant of the 'roundsman' system. They were sometimes billeted in turn on parishioners, who were then free to exact labour from them. Sometimes they were sent round from door to door, with a ticket from the parish, to offer themselves for work. Sometimes, singly or in gangs, they were actually put up to auction and knocked down to the highest bidder, for whom they had to work for the ensuing day or week. At Yardley Hastings, for example, ten men were knocked down at one time to a farmer for 5s.[3] Sometimes they were sent to break stones on the road or perform other parish work. But this method of disposal was not much favoured. "It was among these gangs, who had scarcely any other employment or amusement than to collect in groups and talk over their grievances, that the riots of 1830 ... originated," it was remarked.[4] In short, paupers were

---

[1] Report of the Royal Commission for inquiring into the Administration and Practical Operation of the Poor Laws, 1834, XXVII, 16.
[2] Ibid., XXVII, 95.   [3] Ibid., XXVII, 19.   [4] Ibid., XXVII, 21.

driven down to a position of complete and degrading dependence in which their maintenance was regarded as charity and
a premium was put on complete destitution. "When a man
has his spirit broken, what is he good for?" asked one witness
of the Commissioners.

Meantime the countryside decayed. Farmers frequently
awaited the arrival of the 'ticket man,' whom they were either
bound to employ or could employ for next to nothing, according
to the custom of the parish. Work was meanwhile held up.
In other cases the pressure of the poor rates compelled the
abandonment of farms, and even of whole parishes.

Administratively the chief weakness of the system was its
lack of centralization, its dependence upon parish initiative,
the absence of responsible authority. This administrative
anarchy had created a mass of petty interests riddled with
corruption. The overseers who administered the relief were
not paid officials, but local men selected to serve for a year
without payment. Few were imbued with a spirit of public
service. The best generally regarded the task as a nuisance;
the worst made it a means of feathering their own nests. The
Commission brought to light many scandalous practices of
these overseers. Some, owning house property, raised the
rents to their destitute tenants, and then, as relief to the tenants,
paid the rent from the parish fund. William Hughes, for
example, an overseer in North Wales, himself signed on behalf
of his parish a promise to pay to himself the sum of £1 5s.
yearly, being the rent of A. Jones, pauper of the parish.[1]
Sometimes overseers who were shopkeepers paid relief money
across their own counters. Recipients who failed to take the
hint were liable to have their allowance reduced.

Most striking, perhaps, to the middle classes was the rapid
rise in the rates brought about by the Speenhamland system
of poor relief. Expenditure on relief by the local authorities
rose from about £2,000,000 in 1784 to nearly £8,000,000 at
the peak point in 1818, when the country was commonly
declared to be on the verge of bankruptcy and ruin. Since the
levy of local rates for all purposes never exceeded £10,000,000,
or 3d. per week per head of population, such talk was clearly
nonsense. Yet the burden of the poor rate was heavy. Its
incidence was unequal, many towns being lightly assessed,

[1] *Ibid.*, XXIX, 174 *a*, Assistant Inspector Walcott on North Wales.

while some rural parishes paid 20*s.* or even 30*s.* in the pound.[1]
Many farms were abandoned, and "the derelict parish of
Cholesbury" became a nightmare which haunted the imagina-
tions of the Poor Law Commissioners as typical of the dire
consequences of lavish poo, relief.

So the results of the system ァ ıaugurated by the Berkshire
magistrates in 1795 were unsatisfactory to the labourers, who
were permanently pauperized without receiving adequate
maintenance; to the countryside, whose cultivation decayed;
to the general body of ratepayers, whose burdens increased
without seeming to guarantee them against revolution; and
unsatisfactory also from the point of view of administrative
efficiency. What were the remedies proposed?

The two principles which the Poor Law Report recommended
for subsequent legislation were in accordance with the spirit
of the Report and with the beliefs of the time. They were the
principles of the "Workhouse Test" and "Less Eligibility."
By the first, all out-relief to able-bodied persons and their
families was to be abolished. No able-bodied man should be
granted assistance unless he and his whole family entered the
workhouse. In the words of the Report, "All relief whatever
to able-bodied persons or to their families, otherwise than in
well-regulated workhouses . . . shall be declared unlawful."
In accordance with the second principle, the condition of any
workhouse inmate was to be "less eligible"—that is, more
miserable—than that of the lowest-paid labourer. In the words
of Chadwick:

> By the workhouse system is meant having all relief through the
> workhouse, making this workhouse an uninviting place of whole-
> some restraint, preventing any of its inmates from going out or
> receiving visitors, without a written order to that effect from one
> of the overseers, disallowing beer and tobacco, and finding them
> work according to their ability: thus making the parish fund the
> last resource of a pauper, and rendering the person who adminis-
> ters the relief the hardest taskmaster and the worst paymaster
> that the idle and the dissolute can apply to.[2]

[1] S. and B. Webb, *English Poor Law History: The Last Hundred Years*, i, 1–3.
[2] *Report of the Royal Commission for inquiring into the Administration and Practical
Operation of the Poor Laws*, 1834, XXVII, 146.
[3] *Ibid*, XXIX, iii, 29.

With the horrors of the mixed workhouses in mind, the Commissioners also advised segregation in separate workhouses, according to age and sex.

On the administrative side the Commissioners recommended a central board to control the administration of the Poor Laws, with power to appoint Assistant Commissioners and to frame and enforce such regulations as might be necessary and, as far as possible, to obtain uniformity throughout the country.

The influence of the Benthamites is clear in all these proposals—centralization, uniformity, a stern justice that made little allowance for men's weakness, that would keep them alive indeed if they fell on evil days, but only under conditions of severe regimentation.

The Report was received in Parliamentary circles with great enthusiasm. Its underlying assumptions were quite in accord with the spirit of the time. To Malthus and his followers and to most of the Benthamites—who were, indeed, in most cases one and the same—poverty was a condition to be relieved publicly only as a matter of last resort, for public relief would hinder it from finding its own level. Left alone, the poor would of necessity stop breeding when they were destitute, or, if they did not, death and misery would redress the balance. Poverty would thus be its own natural check. Give poor relief to the destitute and they would multiply, by their own actions thus increasing their numbers and reducing themselves again to destitution. Poor relief was thus a disservice to the poor, for it created a vicious circle of expanding population, lower wages, and pressure upon subsistence, and so destitution and further poor relief; it was a drain on the rich, who paid for it out of the rates; it was a danger to the State, for it bred a growing population of potential revolutionaries. Far better was private charity, which of its goodness relieved necessitous cases and had the discrimination to pass over the idle and dissolute. The labouring population would thus be kept down to the level at which there was work for all, and a sequence of work, wages, and contentment would be set in train, with the unavoidably needy relieved by the charitable rich.

In these beliefs religion, economics, and political philosophy nicely blend. The teaching of Adam Smith, Malthus, and

Bentham, as well as a good smattering of Elizabethan views on society, goes to their making.

There is first the idea of a natural order in society in which the poor are intended to labour. This was the Elizabethan 'degree.' "How," asked Shakespeare,

> could communities,
> Degrees in schools, and brotherhoods in cities,
> Peaceful commerce from dividable shores,
> The primogenitive and due of birth,
> Prerogative of age, crowns, sceptres, laurels,
> But by degree, stand in authentic place?
> Take but degree away, untune that string,
> And, hark, what discord follows! . . .[1]

It was the same spirit that inspired the Victorian hymn:

> The rich man in his castle,
> The poor man at his gate,
> God made them, high or lowly,
> And ordered their estate.

Similar were the views of many Benthamites and near Benthamites. The Rev. Joseph Townsend, a friend of Bentham, wrote in 1785 a *Dissertation on the Poor Laws* in which he pressed the point not only that the poor must always be present to do the less agreeable work, but that there must always be an overhanging punishment to urge them to do so. This punishment was hunger. "Hunger will tame the fiercest animals; it will teach decency and civility, obedience and subjection to the most brutish, the most obstinate, and the most perverse," he wrote.[2]

The economists, as represented by Adam Smith, had a slightly different version of the theme. Each man had to work, not in the position to which God and birth had called him, but in the place into which his own exertions had brought him. Supervising his efforts and ensuring that the sum total of all such activity in the community would result in the greatest possible good was an "Invisible Hand." So, in place of God and birth, the economists substituted the Invisible Hand and competition, which, in the long run, came to the same thing. For all were agreed that the poor should work for the rich and that lavish poor relief was a mistake.

The Report of 1834 tacitly assumed these beliefs. It did not

---

[1] *Troilus and Cressida*, Act I, Scene 3.　　[2] Quoted by Webb, *op. cit.*, i, 11.

give, and no one asked for, a supplementary inquiry into the causes of unemployment and poverty, nor for a classification of the thousands of men, women, and children to whom the Report referred as paupers. Poverty, the Commissioners believed, was no organic disease, nor "principally the result of unavoidable distress," but arose from "fraud, indolence or improvidence." They therefore made no mention of trade fluctuations or of unemployment caused by machinery. To the Commissioners there was one kind of pauper only, and little reference was made to the nature of his poverty. Subsequent experience proved this lack of classification to have been a profound error. There were many kinds of paupers, among whom the sick, infirm, imbecile, orphans, infants in arms, and widows predominated. Able-bodied men and women were a minority. Yet, to deter this minority, the Report explicitly avowed its intention of making pauperism a condition of shame. Nor did it give much attention to the Settlement Laws, which had been in operation far longer and which were an integral part of the current method of poor relief. Years later the secretary to the Commission wrote that "the maladministration of relief . . . was only the most glaring effect of the disease, but not the disease itself. *The disease lay in the settlement laws.*"[1] But the Commissioners concentrated their attention on the system of granting relief.

Consequently, although invaluable as a collection of particular instances and as a general description of the working of the Speenhamland system, as a diagnosis the Report of 1834 was inadequate. The Commissioners regarded their investigation merely as an examination of a system of poor relief, and made no inquiry into the nature and causes of the poverty which made that relief necessary. The result of wide and careful investigation, invaluable as a source book, fascinating to read, exercising much influence on public opinion, the Report of 1834 as a basis for legislation was practically valueless, both because of its failure to deal with causes and because of its fatal lack of classification or statistical detail. It remains, in Professor Tawney's words, a "brilliant, influential and wildly unhistorical Report."[2]

The Poor Law Amendment Act which became law on

---

[1] Quoted by S. and B. Webb, *English Poor Law History: The Old Poor Law*, p. 34.
[2] *Religion and the Rise of Capitalism* (1926 edition), p. 272.

August 14, 1834, adopted the spirit and principles of the Report without very clearly defining them. Its outstanding feature was not the principles of legislation it laid down, but the administrative machinery it created. In place of the unpaid parish officers provision was made for three paid Government Commissioners and a paid secretary, who would constitute a Central Poor Law Department. From this department would issue the orders and regulations which would guide the local Poor Law officers in their administration of the law. Neither the nature of the orders nor the principles which should determine them were clearly stated in the Act, in which there were many permissive clauses, but few imposing compulsory action on the Commissioners. It was implied, however, that the Commissioners would act in accordance with the principles of the Workhouse Test and Less Eligibility. Edwin Chadwick was appointed secretary.

To carry out their work the Poor Law Commissioners were empowered to appoint Assistant Commissioners and clerical staff. In the localities their orders were to be carried out, not by the overseers, but by boards of guardians elected by the ratepayers of parishes grouped together for the purpose. The Commissioners were in a somewhat anomalous position. Although endowed with powers extensive, albeit lightly defined, they were to have no representative in Parliament. They were to be under neither its direct control nor its protection.

The significance of centralizing responsibility for Poor Law administration by granting such wide powers to an extra-Parliamentary body was very great. The Act in this respect was based on the Report, and was no mean triumph for the Benthamites, whose influence is clear in the proposal. They argued that a group of three Commissioners would settle many matters expeditiously and effect alterations in the light of experience, would provide ready access to local information and opinion, and be altogether more flexible than a department tied to Parliament. The proposal was regarded with suspicion sufficient to limit the group's initial period of office to five years. But no other modification of the original proposal was accepted.

When the Commissioners began their work it was clear that, although it had been a Parliamentary success, the Poor Law Amendment Act was by no means popular. They began by dividing the country into nine divisions, for each of which they appointed an Assistant Commissioner. The Assistant Commissioners were to group the parishes into unions and arrange for the election of boards of guardians. Local feeling was at once outraged. Many revered the parish as an ancient unit of local government. Many regarded with abhorrence the substitution of the familiar local Poor Law authority by three remote impersonal Commissioners in London. The latter were considered a dictatorial bureaucracy, compared with which the old parish administration appeared a benevolent patriarchate.

Nevertheless, in the agricultural counties, where the Speenhamland system had been most general and total pauperism widespread, and where the most opposition had been feared, the new arrangements met with little resistance. Fine summers and good harvests in 1834, 1835, and 1836 took the edge off the hardships of poor relief; wages rose a little as parish relief was gradually stopped, and railway construction was providing a fresh outlet for the unemployed. At the same time the refusal of out-relief was not so universal as had been feared. The Commissioners found it "not expedient absolutely to prohibit out-relief even to the able bodied."[1] It was frequently granted to the genuinely incapacitated and not always refused to the temporarily unemployed. In 1839 there were 98,000 paupers in workhouses, as against 560,000 receiving relief outside[2]— figures which read strangely against the sternness of the 1834 Report. These facts, however, had little weight with the industrial North of England. Here the simple principles of the Act were known and condemned by almost the whole working population. When in 1836 the Commissioners turned their attention to the Northern manufacturing districts they met a burst of angry protest against "the three kings of Somerset House," as they were called, and against the "Bastilles," or new union workhouses.

The latter were a complete disgrace and an unexplained departure from the principles of the 1834 Report, which had advocated the segregation of different groups of paupers in different buildings. The Commissioners, in carrying out their

---

[1] Circular of August 25, 1852, quoted by S. and B. Webb, *English Poor Law History: The Last Hundred Years*, i, 151, n. 1.
[2] *Report of Poor Law Commission*, 1840; p. 29; quoted by Webb, *op. cit.*, i, 148.

task after the passage of the Act, recommended a single work-house for all the paupers of the union. This was often a building erected specially for the purpose in a central position. Within it segregation of the sexes was to "be entire and absolute," and categories for the aged and infirm, children, and others were provided. There were, however, no classes for the sick, the lunatic, lying-in cases, and several others. Nor was it possible in a single building to enforce the rule of segregation when the work of the house had to be performed by the inmates them-selves. Moreover, a common dining-hall and chapel brought together several times a day all the inmates, from the idiot to the young child and the expectant mother. As a consequence the new union workhouses reproduced much of the horror of the old mixed workhouse—and on a larger scale, because they catered for larger districts.

Although complete destitution was not so general in the manufacturing districts as in the agricultural, most workers expected to require parish aid at some period of their lives. They could put by nothing from their weekly wages against times of unemployment, sickness, and old age. To go to the parish officer, who was probably acquainted with their circum-stances, for a little to tide them over difficult times had no stigma of shame. To be forced into such a workhouse on every occasion was a very different matter. For, whatever the figures proved, the belief was widespread that all persons receiving parish relief would be forced into the workhouse. Moreover, 1836, the year in which the Commissioners began their work in the North, was the last of the good trade years. Everywhere bad trade and unemployment made their task more difficult, as it brought closer to every worker the fear of the Bastille. The hand-loom weavers and the stockingers were hit immedi-ately, for their craft had already ceased to yield them a living, and they had been regularly assisted by the parish. The prospect of the workhouse was particularly galling to a craft of such traditional independence as that of the hand-loom weavers, and one, moreover, which in living memory had been so prosperous that weavers had been credited with walking about with five-pound notes stuck in their hatbands.

It was chiefly these workers who provided the raw material for what was almost a revolution in the North of England. The lead was taken by William Cobbett, who had been

returned Member of Parliament for Oldham in 1832, and had
been the most vigorous of the few Parliamentary spokesmen
against the Bill, by Fielden, the factory-owner, and by Oastler
and Stephens, already busy in the cause of factory reform.
Their general theme was that the neighbourliness of the Old
Poor Law had been sacrificed to the impersonal tyranny of
the three Commissioners at Somerset House. The real purpose
of the Bill was to compel the workmen to live on a coarser diet:
it was a Coarser Food Bill. It was the fruit of an evil bargain
between the employers and the Government. It was intended
to drive wages down until they were no higher than those of
the poorest Irish labourer.[1] At Huddersfield Oastler led the
opposition to such effect that proceedings under the 1834 Act
were held up for a year. At Todmorden Fielden's cotton firm
refused the payment of rates, and, though a riot directed against
newly elected boards of guardians was quelled by the arrival
of a military force, it was not until a generation later that a
workhouse was erected at Todmorden.

It was the burning resentment against the New Poor Law,
and to a lesser extent the demand for factory reform, which
prepared the ground for the Chartist movement, in which,
again, Oastler and Stephens were leading figures. From many
a Chartist platform they thundered out their denunciations of
the New Poor Law. Many Poor Law meetings recruited
indignant men and women for the Chartist movement. The
New Poor Law, said Stephens,

> was the law of devils . . . if vengeance was to come, let it come:
> it should be an eye for an eye, a tooth for a tooth, limb for limb,
> wife for wife, child for child, and blood for blood.[2]

If "this damnable law, which violated all the laws of God, was
continued," he cried at another meeting,

> and all means of peaceably putting an end to it had been made
> in vain, then, in the words of their banner, "For children and
> wife we'll war to the knife." . . . If the musket and the pistol,
> the sword, and the pike were of no avail, let the women take the
> scissors, the child the pin or needle. If all failed, then the fire-
> brand—aye, the firebrand,—the firebrand, I repeat. . . . If the
> cottage is not permitted to be the abode of man and wife, and if
> the smiling infant is to be dragged from a father's arms and a

---

[1] See Mark Hovell, *The Chartist Movement*, pp. 81–83.
[2] Quoted by Hovell, *op. cit.*, p. 90.

mother's bosom, it is because these hell-hounds of commissioners have set up the command of their master the devil, against our God.[1]

The New Poor Law had come to the working classes as the first-fruit of the Reform Act of 1832. In return for the common cause they had made with the middle classes they received nothing but the principle of the Workhouse Test, the Poor Law Bastille, and the declaration that poverty was the fault of the poor. It was this betrayal, more than anything else, that drove them into the demand for independent working-class action.

The Poor Law Commissioners went to work slowly and carefully, and by the exercise of tact gradually promoted the election of one board of guardians after another. By 1839 95 per cent. of the parishes of England and Wales belonged to unions, with elected boards of guardians,[2] though the establishment of union workhouses was often more difficult. The Commissioners won in the end because no one at that time had any practical alternative to the Poor Law Amendment Act, except a reversion to a system which had clearly become unworkable.

The Commissioners, appointed in the first place for five years, had their appointment renewed for three successive years. In 1842 it was renewed for five years. Before that term was up a new Poor Law Amendment Act of 1844 introduced improvements suggested by the Commissioners, and more or less confirmed the existing practice. In spite of this, a dispute at a workhouse at Andover provided a rallying ground for opponents of the New Poor Law which was strongly attacked in Parliament without having a direct representative in either House to speak for it. In face of this anomalous position, which had, indeed, been apparent for some time, the Government in 1847 replaced the Commissioners by a Poor Law Board. Policy remained unchanged. The importance of the Poor Law Board Act was that it created a body, the Poor Law Board, with a President who was to be a Member of the Government with a seat in Parliament, with an Under-Secretary also a Member of Parliament. To centralization was thus added power and control. How much the power and to what purpose it was used remained to be seen. It was the achievement of the 1847 Poor Law Board Act to establish

[1] *Ibid.*, p. 97.
[2] S. and B. Webb, *English Poor Law History: The Last Hundred Years*, i, 119.

effective machinery for administering the Poor Law on the lines already laid down by the Act of 1834.

(b) PUBLIC HEALTH

Within three years of its return to power the Reformed Parliament had amended the Poor Law, passed the first effective Factory Act and the Municipal Corporations Act of 1835. The Municipal Corporations Act was directed to the reform of local government in England and Wales. Town government showed great variety, corruption, and inefficiency, and the Act aimed at uniformity, democracy, and efficiency. The old historic boundaries were to be preserved—not altered as in the Poor Law Amendment Act—and a council was to be elected triennially by all ratepayers. The new borough councils, however, had little power, all health and sanitary services requiring a special local Act. Thus even the most enlightened town council found its efforts at local reform hampered and restricted. This was partly the reason for the scandalous lack of public health services which circumstances soon forced upon the Government's notice.

Having passed its three Acts of Factory, Poor Law, and Local Government Reform, Parliament sat back, fearful of further inroads upon the doctrine of *laissez-faire* and to a large extent ignorant of the need for making Britain clean. It was sixteen years before it acted, and nearly forty before it acted effectively. Yet in setting up the Poor Law Department in 1834 it had unconsciously created the instrument which was to open up the question of the health of the population.

Already medical men were urging the necessity for reform; now their plea was reinforced by the Poor Law Commissioners, who were compelled to state that it was impossible to administer the *deterrent* Poor Law successfully unless *preventive* measures against dirt and disease were taken. Pauperism, they found, was more often than not caused directly or indirectly by preventable disease. The secretary of the Poor Law Commissioners, Edwin Chadwick, with indomitable energy had been penetrating into the worst slums himself, enlisting support privately, and pressing for Government inquiries. Another and stranger ally of the reformers was the cholera. Alarmed by outbreaks in 1832 and 1837, the Government began to consider

A Labour Note

[See p. 165]

THE HOVELS OF THE POOR

From E. Chadwick's "Report on the Sanitary Condition of the Labouring Population"

MODEL HOUSES EXHIBITED AT THE GREAT EXHIBITION,
1851, BY THE PRINCE CONSORT

*From "A History of Everyday Things in England," by M. and C. H. B. Quennell,
by courtesy of Messrs B. T. Batsford, Ltd.*

193

their causes. In 1838 three medical men—Dr Southwood-Smith, Dr Arnott, and Dr Kay—submitted Reports dealing with the physical causes of fever in London, which included Southwood-Smith's terrible account of the slums of Bethnal Green and Whitechapel. Genuinely appalled, the Government called for wider investigation over the whole country, and two major Inquiries were set on foot. The one, the *Report of the Health of Towns Committee*, was published in 1840; the other, sponsored by the Poor Law Commission and written by Chadwick, was published in 1842 as the *Report on an Inquiry into the Sanitary Condition of the Labouring Population of Great Britain*. The questions of health and cleanliness were at last a public matter. But before the Government acted a Royal Commission was ordered which reported in 1844 and 1845 as the Health of Towns Commission.

These Blue Books revealed the startling fact that when Britain was leading the world in industrial development the living conditions of the majority of her people were so foul that the annual death-rate from typhus fever alone was double that of the fatalities of the allied armies at Waterloo.[1] The average age at death of workers in Rutlandshire was thirty-eight, in Manchester seventeen years; while the corresponding ages for the gentry were fifty-two and thirty-eight years respectively.[2] The expectation of life thus revealed a significant difference between class and class and between country and town. Obviously the fact that the rich had better food and houses than the poor, together with leisure and servants, and more opportunities for keeping themselves and their houses clean, accounted for the class difference; the geographical was due to the rapid concentration of population in the urban areas.

The evils of overcrowding became acute as the population multiplied round the factories. By 1840 there were 15,000 people in Manchester living in cellars. In Liverpool 39,000 people lived in 7800 cellars; in 2400 courts were a further 86,000 persons.[3] Describing some of these courts in Liverpool, a local physician said that there was generally only from nine to fifteen feet between the rows of houses—in one case only six feet.

[1] E. Chadwick, *Report on the Sanitary Condition o the Labouring Population*, 1842, p. 3.
[2] *Ibid.*, p. 157.
[3] *Report of the Select Committee on the Health of Towns*, 1840, XI, viii.

The backs of the houses in one court are built against the backs of houses in another court; at the further end there is generally an ash pit between two privies; they are in the most abominable state of filth. . . . The stench arising from these causes is such, in some of the courts, as to render it almost impossible to remain for any time in them.[1]

Thus in all the great towns the manufacturing population crowded in on existing accommodation, using cellars, garrets, rooms in houses, and finally corners of rooms, till every house in the factory area swarmed with people like ants, but less clean than ants. Here was the speculator's opportunity, and the speculative builder rushed in to make his money. There were virtually no laws to govern his building. On the smallest space he put as many houses as he could, generally made of the cheapest materials. His attitude was described to the Health of Towns Committee:

An individual who may have a couple of thousand pounds . . . wishes to lay it out so as to pay him the best percentage in money; he will purchase a plot of ground; . . . then what he thinks about is, to place as many houses on this acre of ground as he possibly can, without reference to drainage or anything, except that which will pay him a good percentage for his money.[2]

The result was too often like the "fever street," in Stockton, described by the Medical Officer of the Poor Law Board:

Shepherd's Buildings consist of two rows of houses with a street seven yards wide between them; each row consists of what are styled back and front houses—that is two houses placed back to back. There are no yards or out-conveniences; the privies are in the centre of each row, about a yard wide; over them there is part of a sleeping-room; there is no ventilation in the bed-rooms; each house contains two rooms, viz., a house place and sleeping room above; each room is about three yards wide and four long. In one of these houses there are nine persons belonging to one family, and the mother on the eve of her confinement. There are 44 houses in the two rows, and 22 cellars, all of the same size. The cellars are let off as separate dwellings; these are dark, damp, and very low, not more than six feet between the ceiling and floor. The street between the two rows is seven yards wide, in the centre of which is the common gutter, or more properly sink, into which all sorts of refuse is thrown; it is a foot in depth. Thus there is always a quantity of putrefying matter

[1] *Ibid.*, XI, viii.   [2] *Ibid.*, XI, vii. 89.

contaminating the air. At the end of the rows is a pool of water very shallow and stagnant, and a few yards further, a part of the town's gas works. In many of these dwellings there are four persons in one bed.[1]

The pressure on lodging houses increased correspondingly, and in many of these the same conditions of crowded and filthy tenements were repeated.

Overcrowding in itself was perhaps the least of the evils suffered by the town population. It was the dirt and the lack of all facilities for cleaning which made the great towns poisonous dens of filth and disease. The streets of all save the great thoroughfares were unpaved, water was available to only middle-class houses, there was no effective drainage or sewage disposal, the efforts of scavengers and muck-carts were haphazard and ineffectual, there was often no provision for removing the dead before their bodies further fouled the atmosphere. From almost any page of the great Reports can be taken descriptions of our great cities which are at once amazing and sickening.

Of part of Leeds the Health of Towns Committee reported:

> All the streets and dwellings in this ward are stated to be more or less deficient in sewerage, unpaved, full of holes, with deep channels formed by the rain intersecting the roads, and annoying the passengers, sometimes rendered untenantable by the overflowing of sewers and other more offensive drains, with ash-holes, etc., exposed to public view, and never emptied; or being wholly wanting, as is frequently the case, the refuse is accumulated in cellars, piled against the walls, or thrown into the streets.[2]

For London there is no better authority than Dr Southwood-Smith, whose untiring work of exposure, denunciation, and suggestion was largely responsible for bringing to the attention of an unheeding age the insanitary state of large areas of its great cities. He describes the Bethnal Green and Whitechapel districts:

> Uncovered sewers, stagnant ditches and ponds, gutters always full of putrefying matter, nightmen's yards, and privies, the soil of which lies openly exposed, and is seldom or never removed. It is not possible for any language to convey an adequate conception of the poisonous condition in which large portions of both

[1] *Report on the Sanitary Condition of the Labouring Population,* 1842, pp. 17–18.
[2] *Report of the Select Committee on the Health of Towns,* 1840, XI, xi.

these districts always remain, winter and summer, in dry and in rainy seasons, from the masses of putrefying matter which are allowed to accumulate.[1]

Even in Church-street, Bethnal-green, the main thoroughfare, there is no drain, the water runs off as it can, and now and then the parish authorities send round a mudcart to gather up what becomes so thick as to block up the way.[2]

These are not isolated instances. The absence of effective sewerage or drainage, of running water, of paving of surface cleansing, speaks for itself. Chadwick was provoked to declare that the condition of some of the great towns was "almost as bad as that of an encamped horde, or an undisciplined soldiery." Army Standing Orders do, however, he said, provide for sanitary precautions, but

> the towns whose population never change their encampment, have no such care, and whilst the houses, streets, courts, lands, and streams are polluted and rendered pestilential, the civic officers have generally contented themselves with the most barbarous expedients, or sit still amidst the pollution, with the resignation of Turkish fatalists, under the supposed destiny of the prevalent ignorance, sloth and filth.[3]

In districts such as these the poor had to fetch every pint of water they used—often from a considerable distance. "The whole family of the labouring man in the manufacturing towns," wrote Chadwick,

> rise early, before daylight in winter time, to go to their work; they toil hard, and they return to their homes late at night. It is a serious inconvenience, as well as discomfort to them to have to fetch water at a distance out-of-doors, from the pump or the river on every occasion that it may be wanted, whether it may be in cold, in rain, or in snow. The minor comforts of cleanliness are of course foregone, to avoid the immediate and greater discomforts of having to fetch the water.[4]

Often water was sold. In Hampstead, Highgate, and Hendon it was purchased by the bucketful.[5] At Hyde, near Manchester, the poor paid 1d. a day or 1s. a week to water-carriers for their water.[6]

---

[1] Ibid., XI, 3.   [2] Ibid., XI, 7.
[3] Report on the Sanitary Condition of the Labouring Population, 1842, pp. 43–44.
[4] Ibid., p. 70.   [5] Ibid., p. 65.
[6] Report of the Royal Commission for inquiring into the State of Large Towns and Populous Districts, 1844, XVII, 332.

Sometimes a stand-pipe was erected in a court, but the supply was rarely continuous. The water when turned on was insufficient for any but the most vital needs, and quarrels and altercations resulted. In Snow's Rents, Westminster, one of the filthiest of the courts, "16 houses are accommodated with one stand pipe in the court!" explained a witness to the Health of Towns Commission.

> On the principal cleaning day, Sunday, the water is on for about 5 minutes, and it is on also for three days in the week for one half-hour, and so great is the rush to obtain a modicum before it is turned off, that perpetual quarrelling and disturbance is the result, and water-day is but another name for dissension.[1]

"Many of the poor beg water,—many steal it," said a witness to the Commission.[2] With water scarce, even for drinking, impure water from stagnant ditches was used for cooking, and it is not surprising that floors went unwashed.

Another essential to cleanliness and health—fresh air—was also lacking. The air was never fresh in the close courts, where putrefying matter and stagnant ditches were always present. This could be true even of a healthy small town like Tiverton, in Devon, which suffered from fever because open drains and sewers ran in front and round the houses in one section of the town.[3] In any case the window tax reduced the number of windows to a minimum. At its highest in 1808 the window tax stood at about 8s. for houses with six windows and under, £1 for seven windows, £1 13s. for eight windows, and progressively for more. In 1825 houses with less than eight windows were exempted, and, though the duty on more than eight windows was lessened, it is clear that in the big tenements light and air were ruthlessly cut to lessen expense. Windows in stairways and privies were blocked in older buildings, or simply not put in in new buildings. Stairways were commonly said to be dark as night even at noonday.

The details of life in the slums of the great cities can be easily filled in—the flies, insects, and vermin that breed in filth, the evil condition of food kept in such conditions, the horror of hot days, which made the stench unbearable, and of wet days, which stirred the pestilential ditches to overflowing

---

[1] *Ibid.*, XVII, 419.   [2] *Ibid.*, Appendix, 189.
[2] *Report on the Sanitary Condition of the Labouring Population*, 1842, p. 5.

—no family bath night, no family wash-day—families rising
unrefreshed from sleep in the polluted atmosphere—returning
weary from work to the fetid courts, where the choice between
fetching water and remaining unwashed too often followed the
line of least resistance. This was how the poor lived in early
Victorian Britain in the slums where the Frenchman Faucher
felt a thousand leagues from the civilized world.[1]

The first conclusion which Chadwick and the reformers
drew from the Reports and urged repeatedly was that disease
was preventable, that drainage, sewage arrangements, the
cleansing of streets and roads, adequate ventilation, a supply
of fresh running water, were means by which cleanliness and
health could be secured at a cost to the country far less than
that expended on illness, unemployment, and destitution.
Chadwick yearned for the day when, as he wrote,

> man shall be brought to acknowledge that it is by his own hand,
> through the neglect of a few obvious rules, that the seeds of
> disease are most lavishly sown . . . when Governments shall be
> induced to consider the preservation of a nation's health an
> object as important as the promotion of its commerce or the
> maintenance of its conquests.[2]

Secondly, it was urged that bad physical conditions of life
bred bad moral habits. Chadwick claimed that his inquiry
into the sanitary conditions of the labouring population showed
"how strongly circumstances that are governable govern the
habits of the population, and in some instances appear almost
to breed the species of the population."[3] In the case of water,
for example, Chadwick maintained that the labour of bringing
home water from a distance acted as "an obstacle to the
formation of better habits." "I deem it an important principle to be borne in mind," he declared,

> that in the actual condition of the lower classes, conveniences of
> this description must precede and form the habits. It is in vain
> to expect of the great majority of them that the disposition, still
> less the habits, will precede or anticipate and create the con-
> veniences. Even with persons of a higher condition, the habits
> are greatly dependent on the conveniences, and it is observed,

[1] Léon Faucher, *Études sur l'Angleterre*, 2 vols. (1845), and *Manchester in 1844*
(Simpkin, 1845).
[2] *Report on the Sanitary Condition of the Labouring Population*, 1842, p. 143.
[3] *Ibid.*, pp. 94–95.

that when the supplies of water into the houses of persons of the middle class are cut off by the pipes being frozen, and when it is necessary to send for water to a distance, the house-cleansings and washings are diminished by the inconvenience; and every presumption is afforded that if it were at all times requisite for them to send to a distance for water, and in all weathers, their habits of household cleanliness would be deteriorated.[1]

It generally appeared, Chadwick maintained,

that the state of the conveniences gives, at the same time, a very fair indication of the state of the habits of the population in respect to household, and even personal cleanliness.[2]

In the third place the reformers believed that, once the evils were made known and the relationship between dirt, disease, and moral degeneration was established, there would be a willingness to repair the evil. "They would not, they could not be allowed to remain, if their nature were really understood, and if the ease with which the most urgent of them might be removed were known," said Southwood-Smith.[3] Fourthly, it was agreed that legislation was necessary to effect reform. "There do not appear to be any practicable means of removing them without legislative interference," wrote Southwood-Smith. If in London, he argued,

it be certain that conditions exist which are absolutely incompatible with the public health, and which conditions are to a very considerable extent removable; and if it shall be found that similar conditions exist in all the large towns in Great Britain, here would seem to be a proper and legitimate field for the exercise of legislative wisdom and power.[4]

The practical steps which a central body for protecting public health should take included the paving and drainage of streets, the removal of all refuse of habitations, streets, and roads, an improved supply of water to every house, and the construction of sewers upon the scientific principles which were already known if not applied. Independent district medical officers should be appointed, parks and public walks opened to give people fresh air and green surroundings and stimulate their desire to be clean and tidy when they walked abroad and met their friends.

[1] Ibid., pp. 69–70. [2] Ibid., p. 70.
[3] Report of the Select Committee on the Health of Towns, 1840, XI, vii.
[4] Ibid., XI, vii.

Some enlightened individuals and a few progressive towns had, indeed, demonstrated in a small way what preventive measures could do. Fever, for example, had been stopped in Portsmouth since the town had been paved in 1769.[1] At Hyde, Thomas Ashton, a manufacturer, had had water laid on to his workpeople's cottages. He testified emphatically to the greater cleanliness and better health of the people. The cost to the consumers was 3*d.* a week—about one-quarter the previous charge of the water-carrier.[2] Water was also supplied in pipes by private companies to the better parts of some towns. There was no uniformity, and a duplication of services increased costs. It was chiefly the middle classes who benefited, the owners of slums and tenements being loth to incur the expense of a water rate on their property. The Corporation of Liverpool in 1842 had opened baths and wash-houses where cold baths could be had for a penny, warm baths for 2*d.*, and where for a penny a tub and hot water for washing clothes were provided. There were private swimming-baths at Leeds and in Westminster, where the working classes could swim for 2*d.* or 3*d.*, and in Westminster the middle classes could go to a separate bath for 1*s.* and bathe in the water, which then ran into the mechanics' bath. In 1846 there was, moreover, a Bath and Wash Houses Act which authorized any town to establish baths and wash-houses out of the rates.

The question of sewers was rather different. Sewers had been constructed in the bigger towns, but their imperfect construction frequently resulted in nuisances as bad as those they were intended to end. Noxious gases escaped back into houses —generally the houses of the well-to-do—which were connected with the sewers, workmen were injured from explosions of accumulated gas, rivers and lakes into which the sewers emptied became open cesspools for the neighbourhood. They generally present, wrote Chadwick,

> only instances of varieties of grievous defects from incompleteness and from the want of science or combination of means for the attainment of the requisite ends. Thus ... expensive main-drains, which from ignorant construction as to the levels, do not perform their office, and do accumulate pestilential refuse; others, which have proper levels, but from the want of proper supplies

[1] *Report on the Sanitary Condition of the Labouring Population*, 1842, p. 37.
[2] *Report of the Royal Commission for inquiring into the State of Large Towns and Populous Districts*, 1844, XVII, 331–332.

of water do not act; others, which act only partially or by surface drainage, in consequence of the neglect of communication from the houses to the drains; others, where there are drains communicating from the houses, but where the house-drains do not act, or only act in spreading the surface of the matter from cesspools, and increasing the foetid exhalations from it in consequence of the want of supplies of water; others again, as in some of the best quarters of the metropolis, where the supplies of water are adequate, and where the drains act in the removal of refuse from the house, but where from want of moderate scientific knowledge or care in their construction, each drain acts like the neck of a large retort, and serves to introduce into the house the subtle gas which spreads disease from the accumulation in the sewers.[1]

In one or two parts of the country model houses or cottages for the working population had been built, like the excellent group at Harlaxton, near Grantham, in Lincolnshire. Plans for model houses were made for the *Report on the Sanitary Condition of the Labouring Population,* and the Prince Consort exhibited a model at the Great Exhibition in 1851. The fact that these allowed for air and sunshine and drainage served to throw into greater relief the actual hovels of the poor.

If acutely bad conditions are dated from the great population increase beginning in 1800, half a century of pestilential conditions had elapsed before any centralized attempt was made to deal with them. Why was this? It was partly because the health of towns was no one's special responsibility. So far as to anyone, it belonged to each individual town, but the towns were possessed of no powers wide enough to tackle the problem, and were, moreover, composed of so many separate vested interests that the supreme interest of all in public cleanliness and health was lost sight of. On the one hand, even the most enlightened towns were hampered by the necessity of obtaining an Act for each reform proposed and Treasury permission for any loan raised; on the other hand, there existed no method of compelling anyone or any authority to undertake sanitary measures, no means of preventing profit from insanitary conditions, no control of such services as private or local initiative might inaugurate. Where a private company supplied a public

---

[1] *Report on the Sanitary Condition of the Labouring Population,* 1842, p. 36.

service, like water, it was laid on to the parts of the town whose inhabitants could pay for it. Time and again the special interest or the question of cost—both of which should have been swept away by an overriding public authority—stood in the way of reform. With typhus periodically raging in West Ham, for example, owing to the presence of ditches into which privies and pigsties emptied, the Medical Officer called the matter to the attention of the vicar, the Board of Guardians, and the parochial officers. All admitted the evil, and wished to remedy it, but declared they had no funds.[1] Until water was laid on in houses it was essential to clear privies and carry away the refuse from houses and tenements. The cost of clearing a tenement was about £1 a time. Tenants could not afford to pay their shares, and the landlord would not pay for the whole, so tenements letting for as much as £30 or £40 per annum in all went for years without being cleared.[2] Sometimes improved modes of paving and efficient cleansing were opposed by parish officers because they wished to keep at their disposal the means of employing indigent persons as scavengers and street-sweepers.[3] Landowners objected that they would have to pay for improvements in towns when they themselves lived elsewhere. Water companies, burial companies, gas companies, builders, proprietors of slum dwellings, and others whose profits came from existing conditions opposed change. Property and business, including Disraeli and Cobden and Hudson, the Railway King, opposed reform. In addition, the Government was convinced that as a general rule a policy of *laissez-faire* was advisable, and it was, moreover, too preoccupied with the Corn Law controversy to be interested in much else except Chartism.

Of those in a position to act, Normanby, the Whig Home Secretary, was among the first to realize the need for Government action, having been convinced by visits paid to the slums of London under Southwood-Smith's guidance. The mutilation in Committee of his Bill of 1839 for regulating methods of building, however, gave an indication of the strength of vested interests bound up in insanitary tenements and back-to-back houses. Medical men, the Church, Members of Parliament, literary men like Dickens, a part of the Press, including *The Times*, and the Poor Law Commissioners, particularly

---

[1] *Ibid.*, 1842, p. 14.   [2] *Ibid.*, p. 45.   [3] *Ibid.*, p. 96.

Chadwick, continued to demand large-scale legislative action. In 1847 cholera again appeared, and did more than the arguments of men, the printed pages of Blue Books, and the evidence of the senses to secure health legislation. In 1847 a Public Health Bill was introduced, proposing a central Board of Health. At once the swarm of vested interests was set buzzing, and the Bill had to be abandoned. The following year another Bill was brought forward, and in spite of strong opposition became law as the Public Health Act of 1848. The vested interests, the devotees of *laissez-faire*, all who feared a rise in the rates, those who regarded the parish as the natural unit of government and feared bureaucratic centralism, were together strong enough to limit the Act to a term of five years.

Like the Poor Law Amendment Act, the Public Health Act appointed a Central Board, but with no responsible Member of Parliament. It was permissive and not compulsory. A local authority might adopt it, but only in certain circumstances was compelled to do so. The Board of Health was given powers of inspection, audit, and recommendation, but very limited powers of control. The local authorities of whom it was the loosely defined head consisted of town councils in municipal boroughs which adopted the Act, and of such other districts, whether towns, boroughs, or parishes, one-tenth of whose inhabitants made application for the establishment of a local board of health, or whose death-rate was more than 23 per 1000. In these districts the Central Board was empowered to authorize the election by all owners or occupiers of property, of local boards of health. Other districts, and municipal boroughs which did not adopt the Act, could proceed exactly as before.

The weaknesses of the Act are clear. It provided neither Parliamentary protection nor control, it was largely permissive, it followed the model of the extremely unpopular Poor Law Commission, and, as one of the three Public Health Commissioners, selected Edwin Chadwick, the man whose work as secretary to the Poor Law Board had made him undeservedly unpopular. The Act was, in fact, adopted by about two hundred local authorities. But this could not take the place of strong centralized policy enforcing a minimum standard of activity.

The outcry against the Board was considerable. *The Times,*

advocate of reform as it was, declared it would rather take its chance of cholera and the rest than be bullied into health by the Public Health Board. A picture was given of Britain suffering "a perpetual Saturday night"—Master John Bull being "scrubbed, and rubbed, and small-tooth-combed until the tears came into his eyes."[1] As a result, although the Board was given a further year of life, it was not renewed after 1854, when Chadwick was dismissed. The ultimate adoption of the principle of central control in a fuller and more satisfactory form was not achieved until later in the century.

[1] *The Times*, August 1, 1854.

SELECT BIBLIOGRAPHY

Report of the Royal Commission for inquiring into the Administration and Practical Operation of the Poor Laws, 1834, XXVII.

Report of the Select Committee on the Health of Towns, 1840, XI.

Report of the Royal Commission for inquiring into the State of Large Towns and Populous Districts, 1844, XVII.

CHADWICK, E.: *Report on the Sanitary Condition of the Labouring Population* (published by the Poor Law Commissioners), 1842.

ENGELS, F.: *The Condition of the Working Class in England* (1844; new edition with introduction by E. J. Hobsbawm, Panther paperback, 1969).

FINER, S. E.: *The Life and Times of Sir Edwin Chadwick* (Methuen, 1952).

HAMMOND, J. L. AND B.: *The Age of the Chartists, 1832–1854* (Longmans, 1930).

LAMBERT, ROYSTON: *Sir John Simon, 1816–1904* (MacGibbon and Kee, 1963).

LEWIS, R. A.: *Edwin Chadwick and the Public Health Movement, 1832–1854* (Longmans, 1952).

MARSHALL, J. D.: *The Old Poor Law, 1795–1834* (Studies in Economic History, Macmillan, 1968).

WEBB, S. AND B.: *English Poor Law History: The Last Hundred Years* (Longmans, 1929), vol. i.

CHAPTER X

CHARTISM

CHARTISM was a political movement based largely on economic grievances. A section of its supporters from the first advocated armed insurrection, and for four years, 1838–42, it kept the great industrial centres in an uproar, and in its final flare-up in 1848 so alarmed the Government that to prevent disturbance the Duke of Wellington was given command of London as formerly he had commanded at Waterloo. The strength of the Chartist movement fluctuated with movements of trade, and was apparently greatest in the peak months of unemployment. It was bitterly divided over tactics, its leaders quarrelled with one another, and misunderstandings arose between the London and Northern sections of the movement. Nevertheless Chartism presents one outstanding feature. It canalized the feeling behind a host of diverse discontents into one cry— the demand for the Charter. The specific aims of various sections of Chartists were widely different and in some cases incompatible. But every Chartist believed that the means to his end was the Charter.

The Charter originated with the London Working Men's Association, of which Willam Lovett was secretary. Thoughtful, well-read though self-educated, courageous, of irreproachable character, and of outstanding efficiency as secretary to one society after another, Lovett was one of the great working-class leaders of the nineteenth century.

The London Working Men's Association was formed in 1836. Its ultimate aims were political equality and social justice; its immediate objects included self-education, a cheap Press, and a national system of education. It marked a reaction against the political activity which had culminated in the 'Great Betrayal' of 1832 and the industrial activity which had collapsed in the 'Black Year' of 1834. The artisan section of the working class turned in upon itself and sought by education to fit itself for a share in government. Many of the London artisans, and Lovett chief among them, had an almost mystical belief in the power of education. The walls of privilege which stood so firmly against the attacks of unlettered labourers and ignorant factory hands would, they thought, come tumbling down before the reasoned arguments of an educated working class.

Its political demands the London Working Men's Association embodied in a Bill or Charter which it desired Parliament to pass into law. In Lovett's *Life* it fills twenty pages, but to the masses the Charter meant the famous Six Points which formed the kernel of the Bill. They were:

1. Universal adult manhood suffrage.
2. Annual Parliaments.
3. Vote by ballot.
4. Equal electoral districts.
5. Abolition of the property qualification for Members of Parliament.
6. Payment of Members.

The statement of Chartist aims, as embodied in these six points, was precise. This formal precision, however, concealed divergent aims and conflicting tactics.

There were three main sections to the Chartist movement. First, the Northern section, consisting of the most depressed ranks of society. These were the crowds who flocked to open spaces such as Kersal Moor and Hartshead Moor by torchlight at the end of 1838. They consisted largely of hand-loom weavers and stockingers, a decaying class being slowly but surely superseded by machinery. They were joined by factory workers who hated the conditions of their lives, by miners made desperate by underground conditions and the tommy-shop, by part-time workers and the temporarily unemployed.

The hand-loom weavers—about half a million of them in 1839—were the backbone of the Northern movement. Dragging out a painful existence as economic and social outcasts, they naturally desired the abolition of machinery and the return to a handicraft system. It followed that in the main the Chartist movement of the North of England was in this sense reactionary.

The second demand of the Northern Chartists was for the repeal of the Poor Law Amendment Act, a cry taken up by all whom lack of full-time work or ill health forced to the Poor Law for relief, and again including the hand-loom weavers.

There were many other demands, including factory reform and nationalization of the land. In 1838 in Sheffield Ebenezer Elliot demanded "Free trade, universal peace, freedom in religion and education for all," while another speaker was content with "good food and plenty of it."

The masses were powerfully worked upon by the two Tories Oastler and Stephens. Though they were subsequently superseded in leadership by Feargus O'Connor, their eloquence was not soon forgotten.

The second section of Chartism was represented by some middle-class currency reformers of Birmingham, under the leadership of Thomas Attwood, a Member of Parliament who had been prominent in the Reform Bill agitation. These middle-class Chartists traced the cause of trade depression to a flaw in the monetary system. By a reformed House of Commons, such as the Charter proposed, they hoped to have their currency reform implemented.

Lovett and the Chartists of the London Working Men's Association made up the third section. They regarded the Charter as of great constitutional importance, but to them also it was a means to an end. It was for the social change which he believed political reform would bring that Lovett valued the Charter. He wanted workmen to give up what he termed "their various hobbies of anti-poor-laws, factory bills, wages protection laws, and various others, for the purpose of conjointly contending for the Charter,"[1] and he warned them against getting involved in Anti-Corn Law agitation.

Lovett's almost naïve belief that change in the social content of the system would necessarily follow change in the form of representation was coupled with a conviction that education and moral permeation were the weapons with which Chartists must fight. The dependence on moral force differentiated the tactic of the London and Birmingham groups sharply from that of the Northern "O'Connorites," who in 1838 were openly arming and drilling with such weapons as they could acquire. It was paradoxical that the section which in tactic was revolutionary, in aim was reactionary, wishing to destroy industrialism rather than to create a new industrial society.

[1] Quoted by Hovell, op. cit., p. 204.

Thus, although to outward appearance the Chartists were united behind a concise political programme, yet beneath lay various, and sometimes conflicting, economic grievances. Moreover, the all-embracing mantle of the Charter hid vital differences of method and tactics. The North formed the left wing and prepared for violence. Birmingham was the constitutional right wing. The London Chartists opposed violence, but were less antagonistic than Birmingham to the North. The movement was further weakened by lack of support from two influential sections of the working class. Robert Owen and his followers, believing in economic methods of reform, despised the political agitation round the Charter and stood aside from it, while the trade unions officially gave no support.

As the Charter was the product of London, so the Charter Petition and the Convention originated in Birmingham. A great national petition supporting the Charter was to be drawn up, and when millions of signatures had been obtained was to be presented to Parliament. Meantime, a convention of delegates, elected at great public meetings in the chief Chartist centres, was to assemble in London for the opening of Parliament, arrange for the presentation of the Petition, and decide the steps to be taken if the Petition were rejected by Parliament.

Chartist agitation quickly developed in the spring of 1838, when London published the Charter and Birmingham published the Petition. In Glasgow a meeting of 150,000 approved the Petition. The Birmingham audience of Newhall Mill was estimated at 200,000, the Bradford meeting on Hartshead Moor at 100,000, and the great Manchester demonstration on Kersal Moor at the unbelievably high figure of 250,000.[1] In October 1838 the Northerners started midnight meetings by torchlight. Contingents were headed by banners with skulls painted on them. Others bore slogans such as: "More pigs, fewer priests," "Fight to the knife for child and wife," "Universal suffrage or universal revenge."

The speeches made at the meetings were equally incendiary. At Norwich 6000 workers were thus addressed by Stephens:

> I tell the rich to make their will. The people are with us, the soldiers are not against us. The working men have produced all

[1] Hovell, *op. cit.*, p. 105, p. 107, p. 119, p. 118.

the wealth and they are miserable. . . . The working man is the ground landlord of all the property in the kingdom. If he has it not he has a right to come down on the rich until he gets it.[1]

O'Connor and Harney were more explicitly insurrectionary. Their audiences were exhorted to arm themselves, and Chartists began to attend their meetings with muskets and pikes, and to fire pistol shots into the air for applause. More and more the speakers advocated a revolutionary class war.

Bad harvests and trade dislocation added fuel to the flames. Unemployed factory operatives, famished hand-loom weavers, and desperate colliers gave the Northern movement a ferocious intensity which the better-off artisans of London and Birmingham were slow to realize. Pikes were sharpened, bullets moulded, small arsenals collected. It seemed as though the class war were about to begin. This caused the quarrel within the movement to become more open. Said Lovett:

> The whole physical force agitation is harmful and injurious to the movement. Muskets are not what are wanted, but education and schooling of the working people. Stephens and O'Connor are shattering the movement. . . . Violent words do not slay the enemies but the friends of our movement. O'Connor wants to take everything by storm, and to pass the Charter into law within a year. All this hurry and haste, this bluster and menace of armed opposition can only lead to premature outbreaks and to the destruction of Chartism.[2]

From the other side came many replies. The neatest is, ironically enough, that given by the worker in the novel *Sybil*, by Benjamin Disraeli, the future Tory Premier:

> I should first of all like the capitalists to try a little moral force —then we should see how things would go on. If the capitalists give up their redcoats, I shall become an adherent of moral force to-morrow.

London, Birmingham, and Scotland supported Lovett. The North and probably South Wales were for O'Connor. The opponents were never reconciled, but in the earlier stages of the agitation the majority accepted a compromise which became the most famous of all the Chartist slogans: "Peacefully if we may, forcibly if we must."

[1] Quoted by Max Beer, *A History of British Socialism*, ii, 41.
[2] Quoted by Beer, *op. cit.*, ii, 42-43.

The Chartist Convention met on February 4, 1839, at the British Coffee-House, Cockspur Street, charged with the duty of superintending the presentation of the great Chartist Petition to Parliament. The delegates numbered fifty-three, but several did not attend. A quarter of them were from London, five from Birmingham. Less than half were working-men or artisans.[1] The Convention sat, with interruptions, until September 4. The date of the Assembly had been determined by that of Parliament, which was formally opened on February 5 by the Queen's speech. So had the meeting of the delegates of the Anti-Corn Law League, who on February 4 gathered at Brown's Hotel to superintend the bringing forward of their petition for Free Trade. Thus the representatives of the three classes met separately on the same day—those of the aristocracy in Parliament, of the middle classes in Brown's Hotel, of the working classes in the British Hotel.

Within the Convention was dissension. The extreme right wing opposed the left, Lovett attempted to mediate, and many members resigned. Two important decisions were nevertheless made. As only 600,000 signatures had been obtained to the Petition, the Convention decided to postpone the date of its presentation to Parliament and to send out 'missionaries,' fifteen at a time, to tour the country rousing enthusiasm and securing more signatures. Secondly, a Committee was appointed to consider the question of "ulterior measures," or action that should be taken if Parliament rejected the Petition.

The reports of the missionaries strengthened the revolutionary fervour of the left, for they brought stories of demonstrations and the collection of arms, and declared that the small Welsh town of Llanidloes had been occupied by armed revolutionaries. Nevertheless by May the delegates to the Convention were becoming anxious both for the fate of the Petition and for their own safety. The Petition had now been signed by 1,250,000 people; it weighed six hundredweight, was two miles long, and was placed on a huge wagon decorated with banners.[2] But the Government gave no sign of surrender or even perturbation. It had not been frightened into repressive acts, but had taken several strong precautionary measures.

The garrisons of the North of England were in April strengthened and placed under the command of General

[1] Hovell, *op. cit.*, pp. 121–122.　　[2] Beer, *op. cit.*, ii, 68.

Sir Charles Napier, a soldier of varied service. On May 3 Lord John Russell, the Home Secretary, authorized magistrates to suppress all meetings to which people came armed. Thirdly, he took the remarkable step of encouraging citizens to form a volunteer force for the protection of life, liberty, and property, offering to equip and arm them.

Feeling now ran high. The two best-selling pamphlets, which had phenomenal sales, were William Benbow's on the *National Holiday*, or general strike, and Colonel Francis Maceroni's on *Defensive Instructions for the People*, which dealt with the erection of barricades and the tactics of street fighting. In this atmosphere of growing tension the Convention resolved to remove to Birmingham, where the atmosphere was more favourable to Chartists than in London. It arrived there on May 13, and shortly afterwards its Committee on Ulterior Measures reported. Nine proposals were made for action if Parliament refused to grant the points of the Charter. These were the withdrawal of all bank deposits; the inauguration of the Sacred Month, or general strike; a refusal to pay rents, rates, and taxes; the procuring of arms in readiness for fighting; the support of Chartist candidates at general elections; the cessation of all commercial dealings with non-Chartists; a resistance to all rival agitators who would divert attention from Chartism; the refusal to read opposition newspapers; a pledge of obedience to the decisions of the majority of the Convention.

The resistance to rival agitators and the pledge of obedience to the Convention were matters of internal organization. The support of Chartist candidates at general elections was useful and not unconstitutional. The loss of the comparatively small sum which Chartists spent on 'opposition newspapers' was hardly likely to cause disquiet. The procuring of arms in readiness for fighting was an extension of the activity already proceeding, and would become important in proportion to the quantity of arms obtained and the use made of them. The cessation of commercial dealings with non-Chartists might injure small traders in districts where Chartism was widespread, but the impact of a commercial boycott by poor Chartists could hardly be sufficient to disturb the security of the country or compel the Government to pass the Charter. Similarly if all Chartists in the country withdrew all their bank deposits the effect would be trifling. There remained of the ulterior measures the refusal to pay rents, rates, and taxes, and the general strike. The former might have had some effect, but was never put to the test; for the general strike was the ulterior measure finally agreed upon.

It is clear that, with Owen and the trade unions standing for the most part outside the Chartist movement, the chance of the Government's being coerced by means of a general strike was small. The much talked-of ulterior measures amounted then to very little. The only ones of any potential force had been used in the Reform Bill agitation, and were being used in the Corn Law struggle with much greater effect because wielded by a rich and powerful class.

Meantime the presentation of the Petition was delayed again and again, and Attwood finally reported that it could not be presented until mid-June and not discussed until July. Five months would therefore have elapsed from the meeting of the Convention until the time when Parliament's decision was known. Inaction was breeding disappointment, which would soon be followed by lack of faith and disintegration. On May 18 the Convention took one of the wisest decisions of its career. It adjourned in order that its members might test the feeling of the masses on the question of ulterior measures and revive the flagging spirits of Chartist supporters.

The response to the meetings which followed was enthusiastic, particularly in the North. Many magistrates and employers were panic-stricken, and sent urgent appeals to Napier for troops to disperse meetings or repel threatened attacks. To most of these appeals Napier turned a deaf ear, being contemptuous both of the wisdom and of the courage of the magistrates. For Napier was a remarkable man. He was a Tory democrat and himself supported some of the Chartist claims. In 1839 he explained his position quite clearly in his diary:

> I am for a strong police, but the people should have universal suffrage, the ballot, annual Parliaments, farms for the people, and systematic education. I am opposed to landlordism and capitalism. . . . England has an abundance of bad laws, but is every man to arm against every law he thinks bad? No! Bad laws must be reformed by the concentrated reason of the nation

gradually acting on the legislature, not by pikes of individuals acting on the bodies of the executive.[1]

Given command of 6000 men and eighteen pieces of artillery, he concentrated his forces in strategic places in the North, where he provided barracks for the men in order to keep them from the civilian population. He attended Chartist meetings, argued with the speakers, and got to know the local leaders. When they declared the English artillery to be useless, as it had been out of action since Waterloo, he sent them invitations to a private display of gunnery practice, and demonstrated to them the prompt handling and quick firing of the guns. On the question of the Sacred Month he wrote:

> The Chartists say they will keep the sacred month. Egregious folly! They will do no such thing; the poor cannot do it; they must plunder, and then they will be hanged by the hundreds. . . .

As for physical force, Napier wrote:

> Physical force! Fools! *We* have the physical force, not they. They talk of their hundred thousands of men. Who is to move them when I am dancing round them with cavalry and pelting them with cannon-shot? What would their 100,000 men do with my rockets wriggling their fiery tails among them, roaring, scorching, tearing, smashing all they come near? And when in desperation and despair they broke to fly, how would they bear five regiments of cavalry careering through them? Poor men! How little they know of physical force![2]

The Convention reassembled in Birmingham on July 1, to the alarm of the Birmingham magistrates, who had already prohibited meetings in the Bull Ring, where the people of the town were accustomed to gather to listen to speeches and the reading of newspapers. On the reassembly of the Convention the mayor decided to take more stringent action. Himself travelling to London, he secured the services of a hundred of the new Metropolitan police force. Arriving in Birmingham on July 4, he marched straight to the Bull Ring, where a crowd was quietly listening to the reading of newspapers, and ordered the instant dispersal of the meeting. In the ensuing tussle, which went on intermittently all night and next day, ten policemen were wounded and many Chartists arrested. When

---

[1] Quoted by Beer, *op. cit.*, ii, 71–72.   [2] Quoted by Beer, *op. cit.*, ii, 74.

the Convention met the following morning Lovett immediately rose and moved a resolution of protest against the action of the authorities. This was carried unanimously, and was to be printed and placarded all over the town. All the delegates were willing to sign, but Lovett urged that one signature would suffice. It was not difficult to foresee the fate of the signatories, and it would be fatal if the movement were deprived of all its leaders at one blow. Lovett offered to sign, and accordingly, accompanied by one other delegate, Collins, took the manuscript to the printer. By the afternoon the Chartist resolution was placarded all over the town.

On the evening of the following day, July 6, Lovett and Collins were arrested; they were subsequently committed for trial and imprisoned in Warwick Gaol. The city remained under martial law in a condition of almost continuous disturbance.

Meanwhile, on July 12, the great climax of the Chartist agitation came. The National Petition, bearing 1,250,000 signatures and brought to the House in several vans, was presented to Parliament by Attwood and rejected by a vote of 235 to 46. While this decisive rejection added fuel to the indignation of the Birmingham men, the country as a whole had its eyes so firmly riveted on affairs in Birmingham that the rejection passed without serious disturbance. After a week's imprisonment Lovett and Collins were released on bail, and on July 15 crowds streamed out along the Warwick Road to give them a triumphal reception. To avoid possible trouble Lovett and Collins slipped into the town by a side-street, and the disappointed crowd surged back to the Bull Ring, where the growing rage of the past week finally had its vent in acts of violence—the second Bull Ring Riot.

Meantime there rested with the Convention, since Parliament had so decisively rejected the Charter Petition, the responsibility of calling for the General Strike, the ulterior measure it had decided to operate. On July 13 a discussion was opened which lasted several weeks and ended in the appointment of a Committee! But while the Convention deliberated the Government acted. A few months earlier, when the movement was on the up-grade, persecution would have strengthened the Chartist ranks and steeled their resolution. Now Government action would hasten disintegration. Accordingly Lord John

Russell declared the ulterior measures to be "illegal and sub-versive of the peace," and directed magistrates to arrest and prosecute all who agitated for them. In April arrests had begun. In July and August they increased, and hundreds of Chartists, including many of the leaders, were thrust into gaol.

Among those imprisoned was Henry Vincent, who had won Wales to Chartism and was something of a popular hero to the Welsh. The rejection of the Charter Petition, the harsh treat-ment of Welsh Chartists at Llanidloes, the failure of the Convention to issue a call to action, and finally the report of cruel treatment meted out to Vincent in Monmouth Gaol, roused the men of Newport to make one supreme effort to obtain justice.

Their leader was John Frost, a Newport draper. He had been a prominent Radical in the Reform agitation of 1830–32, and his fellow-citizens had elected him successively mayor, magistrate, and justice of the peace. When Vincent came to Wales in 1838 Frost unhesitatingly gave his support to Chartism, and allowed himself to be elected delegate to the Chartist Convention. This was unpardonable conduct in a J.P., and Frost was forced to resign his office.

Frost remained with the Convention until it dissolved, and then returned to Wales, where he knew feeling was running high. With William Jones, a journeyman watchmaker, and Zephaniah Williams, an innkeeper, plans were laid. On the night of November 3 over a thousand men and boys gathered on the hills above Newport. The intention was to occupy the mining village of Risca, six miles north-west of Newport, hold up the mails as a sign to other districts, and then to march on Monmouth to release Vincent. Though sentries had been posted to arrest strangers and prevent information getting through to the town, it was not long before terrified people were rushing to the mayor with news of strange happenings on the hills. Perhaps most fatal of all to the Chartist cause was the delay occasioned by the difficulty of conducting a thousand or more untrained men over the hills in the darkness.

It was already nine o'clock on the morning of the 4th when the three rebel columns converged on Newport, armed with old muskets, pikes, and clubs. Police and special constables were awaiting them, but retreated before the oncoming Chartists into the Westgate Hotel. Frost marched his men across the

Square with the intention of speaking to the Mayor, when from the windows of the hotel soldiery opened fire. For about twenty minutes the Chartists remained, by which time fourteen of their number lay dead and about fifty wounded, of whom ten subsequently died. Then the rest fled.

The Government made the insurrection an excuse for still further arrests. Not only were Frost, Jones, Williams, and others prominent on the night of November 3 arrested, but throughout the winter of 1839 and into the summer of 1840 wholesale seizure of Chartists continued. Sentences ranged from three months' imprisonment to transportation for life. Frost, Williams, and Jones were tried for high treason and sentenced to death.

In the weeks following the Newport rising the country was strangely agitated. There was talk of insurrection to free Frost, and of many intended outbreaks in which it is difficult to disentangle genuine Chartist activity from the work of *agents provocateurs*. The sentence on Frost and his comrades was, however, commuted to transportation for life to Botany Bay. Seventeen years later they were permitted to return.

The Newport rising, because it failed, is generally dismissed lightly as a kind of postscript to the events of 1839. But the fervent spirit of lads like eighteen-year-old George Shell is beyond the praise of after-generations. Before he left for the hills on the night of the insurrection George Shell had written to his parents:

PONTYPOOL
Sunday Night, Nov. 3, 1839
DEAR PARENTS, I hope this will find you well, as I am myself at this present. I shall this night be engaged in a glorious struggle for freedom, and should it please God to spare my life I shall see you soon; but if not, grieve not for me, I shall have fallen in a noble cause. Farewell!

Yours truly,
GEORGE SHELL[1]

George Shell was one of those left dead in the square before the Westgate Hotel.

Was Frost's rising an isolated attempt, or was it part of a wider scheme which miscarried? Frost is said to have spoken to his fellow-delegates before he left for Wales of the possibility

[1] Quoted by Beer, *op. cit.*, ii, 98.

of trouble. It is likely that a wider effort was discussed secretly by some of the delegates. But, if so, what happened to the rest of the schemes, and, above all, what rôle was played by O'Connor, the recognized leader of the movement since Lovett's imprisonment and, moreover, the chief advocate of armed insurrection? O'Connor himself disavowed all knowledge of any rising anywhere. But he cancelled a series of meetings in the North of England in order to go on a lecture tour in Ireland. Why? Some Chartists asserted that a wider plan had been made but was cancelled, and that Frost failed to receive news of the alteration; others that Frost was virtually swept into the plan by the spontaneous enthusiasm of the Welsh and that there were no further arrangements.

At all events November 1839 marks the end of the first phase of Chartism. By February 1840 Frost, Williams, and ones were on their way to exile; Vincent was sentenced to a further term of imprisonment; O'Connor was imprisoned for newspaper libel; of the leaders only Harney and MacDouall remained at liberty.

In the first period of Chartism, 1837–39, the slogan of "The Charter!" acted as a cloak for divergent aims and tactics. In the second period, 1839–42, the antagonisms of the Chartists were so open that there could be no pretence of a unified policy. The points of the Charter were still adhered to, but each Chartist supplied his own interpretation in terms of immediate policy. It was a period of sectionalism and local loyalties, each Chartist leader trying to bridge the period of disheartenment in his own way. Lovett and Collins concentrated on education, Vincent preached total abstinence, Scottish and Birmingham leaders adopted a kind of Christian Chartism. O'Connor wrote scathingly from York Prison of "Bible Chartism," "Teetotal Chartism," "Knowledge Chartism," and produced his own unworkable scheme. After several local societies had been formed, like the Metropolitan Charter Union of London, a conference met at Manchester in July 1840 and formed the National Charter Association, which was to work for the Charter by peaceful and constitutional means. Great stress was laid upon efficient organization, and as one of its first tasks the National Charter Association was to draw up a second Charter Petition to Parliament.

The next event of importance was the general election which was to be held in the summer of 1841. Immediately disagreement arose. In the majority of districts, where there was no Chartist candidate, to whom should Chartist support be given, the Liberal or the Tory? The Liberals were the hated industrial class, the perpetrators of the New Poor Law of 1834, the betrayers of 1832. But, on the other hand, it was they who voted for the Chartist Petition.

O'Connor, at the one extreme, declared against "the vile, bloody Whigs." On the other hand the London Chartists advocated support of those Radicals and Liberals who had voted for the Charter Petition. O'Brien meanwhile repudiated both forms of class collaboration, declaring they had nothing to expect from either the Tories or the Whigs, and must, therefore, make use of the elections mainly as a means for agitation.

The question of class collaboration was further exercised when Joseph Sturge, a middle-class Quaker of Birmingham, proposed the formation of a society of middle- and working-class members to work for universal suffrage. At the beginning of 1842 several Birmingham men joined with him to form the Complete Suffrage Union, and issued an appeal to the working classes. Many Chartists responded, including Lovett, Vincent, O'Brien, and all opposed to O'Connor.

Thus, by the beginning of 1842, not only was the Chartist movement split into groups owing different loyalties and supporting different aims, but there were in existence two main organizations whose object was the attainment of the six points of the Charter—the National Charter Association, of which O'Connor and his followers had control, and the Complete Suffrage Union, a combination of middle-class Liberals, Radicals, and Chartists.

The National Charter Association was pursuing its work of getting signatures for the second Charter Petition. It was claimed that over 3,000,000 people signed, and that the procession which bore it to the House stretched from Westminster to Oxford Circus. Duncombe presented it to the Commons on May 3, 1842, in an able speech, but the division resulted in 287 Noes and 49 Ayes. There was no question of ulterior measures this time, but events played right into the Chartists' hands.

Throughout 1841 economic distress had been deepening, trade declining, wages falling. In August 1842 workers at Stalybridge came out on strike, marching to Ashton, Hyde, and finally to Manchester, recruiting comrades as they went. From Manchester the strike spread over Lancashire, into Yorkshire, Staffordshire, the Potteries, Warwickshire, and Wales. In Scotland miners went on strike. Where operatives would not leave their work the strikers adopted the simple expedient of putting boilers out of action by removing the plugs. Thus the strike earned the name of Plug Plot.

Here at last was economic action on a considerable scale. Would the Chartists be able to utilize it? For a time they were. The workers took up the cry of "Cease work until the Charter becomes the law of the land!" At Manchester an appeal placarded on the walls of the town urged: "The trades of Great Britain carried the Reform Bill. The trades of Great Britain shall carry the Charter."[1] At last the trade unions and Chartism were marching together. Now, if ever, was the time for action.

But still irresolution and disagreement rent the Chartist ranks. Before they had decided upon a course of action the strike began to fail, and the men drifted back to work.

Chartism never again won such confidence, such numbers of supporters, or the adherence of 'the trades.' There were about 1500 arrests. What the Government really felt at the time was related afterwards by Sir James Graham, the Home Secretary:

We had . . . the painful and lamentable experience of 1842 . . . a year of the greatest distress, and, now that it is passed, I may say, of the utmost danger. What were the circumstances of 1842? . . . We had in this metropolis, at midnight, Chartist meetings assembled in Lincoln's Inn Fields . . . immense masses of people, greatly discontented, and acting in a spirit dangerous to the public peace. What was the condition of Lancashire? . . . a great combination existed to stop machinery. . . . It was my painful duty to consult with the Horse Guards almost daily as to the precautions that were necessary for the maintenance of the public peace . . . for some time troops were continually called on, in different parts of the manufacturing districts, to maintain public tranquillity . . . for three months, the anxiety which I and my Colleagues experienced . . . was greater than we ever felt before with reference to public affairs.[2]

[1] Beer, op. cit., ii, 144.   [2] February 1846 (Hansard, lxxxiii. 718).

If Government disquiet is a measure of Chartist hope 1842 was a lost opportunity indeed.

The collapse of 1842, like that of 1839, was followed by reorganization. But the power of Chartism as a revolutionary force was spent. Between 1842 and 1848 there are two developments to be followed—O'Connor's Land Scheme and the history of the third Charter Petition.

O'Connor was second only to Cobbett in his hatred of industrialism and the factory, and after 1842 his plans for social regeneration centred round a system of peasant proprietorship to which industrial activity would be subordinated. The National Charter Association supported him, and in April 1845 the Chartist Co-operative Land Society, later called the National Land Company, was formed to obtain money for the purchase of land. The money was to be raised by the sale of shares costing 26s. each, which could also be bought by instalments of 3d., 6d., and 1s. When the first piece of land had been purchased a ballot was to be held to determine which of the shareholders should settle it. Each fortunate settler was to have an allotment of about three acres, with a cottage and stock provided by the company, and the loan of capital sufficient to start operations. The land was to remain the property of the settlers, provided they paid a rent equal to 5 per cent. of the total capital expended on setting them up.

The scheme had an amazing, if short-lived, success. Unemployed and badly employed workmen raked together their pennies to pay instalments on shares that gave them the hope of a better livelihood. More prosperous artisans welcomed a project that promised to relieve the market of superfluous labour that drove down wages. Many felt again the call of the village life from which their parents or themselves had been rudely driven by Enclosure. As a result subscriptions mounted rapidly.

In 1846 the first estate, of about 100 acres near Watford, named O'Connorville, was opened amid much joyful enthusiasm, and the first families settled. On Chorley Wood Common near by O'Connor led a cricket eleven of bricklayers to victory against an eleven of carpenters and sawyers who were working on the estate.[1] In order to procure money to buy more land a

---

[1] Hovell, *op. cit.*, p. 279.

Land Bank was then opened which received deposits on the
security of the land already held, and paid the then high
interest of 4–4½ per cent. This money was to be lent to the
Land Company for the purchase of land. By 1848 five estates
were settled, there were 75,000 shareholders, 200,000 shares
had been issued, and £96,000 paid up.

The scheme was individualistic, small-scale, agrarian. It
was neither Socialist nor progressive, but technically and
socially reactionary. Arithmetically it had no chance of
success.[1] Lovett, O'Brien, Cooper, and their followers vigorously opposed the whole idea. Internal troubles, such as the
non-payment of rent, arose. Most of the settlers were towns-
men, unskilled in land work. In addition the law took a hand
in the company's destruction. In 1848 a Government Committee of Inquiry reported that it was registered neither as
Friendly Society nor joint-stock company, and was therefore
illegal; and that the Land Bank was also illegal. Examination
of the books revealed many irregularities. All these, however,
were to O'Connor's financial disadvantage, and it was evident
that he had lost large sums of money over his land scheme.
Such an accumulation of blows and difficulties caused the
company to be wound up in 1849. O'Connor had put more
vigorous work into the land scheme than into any other phase
of Chartism. As he himself said, he was "no Socialist and no
Communist." He was at heart an Irish squire holding the
ideal of an England of small peasant proprietors.

Meantime the surge of political excitement had been rising.
In 1847–48 trade again collapsed, and distress was acute. As
in the depressed years 1839 and 1842, now again the masses
eagerly adopted the Chartist slogan. Enthusiasm was increased
by the return of O'Connor as Member of Parliament for
Nottingham in 1847. In addition, European events provided
a strong stimulus to action. Continental revolutionaries, such
as Mazzini, Engels, and Marx, were living as refugees in
London, and were a constant inspiration to the Chartist movement. When news came of the widespread European revolts
of 1848 something of the spirit of ten years earlier swept the
English workers. There were bread riots and other disturbances
all over the country; and a third Charter Petition was launched.

[1] See Beer, *op. cit.*, ii, 156–516.

In April a new Charter Convention met in London to watch over the Petition. It was decided that on April 10 the masses should assemble at Kennington Common and then march with the Petition to Westminster to force its acceptance upon the House. Since it was estimated to have 5,500,000 signatures, optimism prevailed among the Chartists.

In Government circles apprehension grew as the 10th approached. As in 1789, events in Britain were reflected in the light of Continental revolution. Wellington, the Iron Duke, who in his prime had defended the country against Napoleon, now, in his old age, had charge of the defence of London against the Chartists. Artillery, troops, and marines were brought in to control strategic points, but were kept in the main quietly out of sight. It was left to the police and 170,000 special constables to guard the bridges over the river and the rest of the route the Chartists were expected to take.

On the morning of the 10th shops were shut in London, citizens carefully locked their doors, Chartists contingents began to converge on Kennington. The police, the special constables, the soldiers were at their posts. The Government and the whole populace were expectant, ready for any contingency. By eleven o'clock O'Connor and other speakers had arrived at Kennington with contingents from North and East London; so had the Petition itself, carried in a decorated wagon drawn by four horses.

Anticlimax came before the meeting had even begun. The Commissioner of Police, who was stationed in a public house near by, informed O'Connor that a procession to Westminster would be resisted as an illegal attempt to intimidate Parliament, an offence for which the Government would hold O'Connor personally responsible. O'Connor capitulated. He and other leaders addressed the crowd, and the majority followed O'Connor's advice and quietly dispersed, while O'Connor carried off the Petition in three cabs to Parliament.

A Committee of the House checked the signatures, and found that the boasted five and a half millions were less than two millions, many of the signatures being duplicates and others merely frivolous, like "the Duke of Wellington," "Queen Victoria," or "Pug-nose." The Petition was rejected by 222 votes to 17. The Chartists made no sign of further fight. Instead the Government dissolved the Convention, and arrests swept the country. Chartist crowds never again assembled under that name. Feargus O'Connor had to be removed from the House of Commons to a lunatic asylum in 1853, and died two years later. Only a few of the leaders—notably Ernest Jones—carried on the work, and by personal contact linked the Chartism of the past with the growing working-class movements of the future.

The Chartist movement failed first because it was largely the reactionary movement of an economically superseded and politically powerless class. True, neither the Members of the London Working Men's Association nor the Birmingham currency reformers were of this class, but the full strength of Chartism lay, not in Birmingham or the South, but in the North, among the hand-loom weavers and stockingers, whose only hope seemed to lie in passionate denial of the industrial system. Among them Chartism became a mass movement at once reactionary in aim and revolutionary in spirit and tactics. But capitalist industry was far too strongly entrenched to be turned back by negation, however strongly expressed. A reversal of development, such as the hand-workers wished to achieve, was impossible.

A second and allied reason for the failure of Chartism can be perceived in the way the movement waxed and waned with industrial fluctuations—even with the price of corn. The years 1839, 1842, 1848, the years of the peak achievements of Chartism, were also years of industrial depression and high corn prices. At the end of the forties trade improved and Britain entered the period of prosperity which lasted until the seventies. Wages rose, unemployment fell. Friendly Societies, savings banks, Co-operative Societies—even railway investment—were used by the workers as means to thrift and steady investment. They took a share in the general prosperity, and this in itself was sufficient to silence such a *cri de l'estomac* as Chartism.

The miners began to turn to industrial and legal action in the forties, while the textile workers won not only increased wages, but improved conditions by means of the Factory Acts. The hand-loom weavers themselves were absorbed into the expanding industry, declining from about half a million in 1838 to 50,000 in 1848, while the immigration of the turbulent

Irish declined sharply. The new generation became, not hand-workers like their parents of 1839, but railway navvies or factory hands. The peeling off of these three sections of working-class discontent—miners, textile workers, and hand-workers—deprived the Chartist movement of most of its backing. The irony of the situation was that the movement should finally have been broken by the too complete acceptance by the workers of industrialism.

The third reason why Chartism failed was that it had no co-ordinated purpose. The Charter was all-embracing, but it embraced too much. Its adherents were deeply divided, and the Charter could only pretend to bridge the gap.

Fourthly, Chartism lacked strong, agreed leadership. It was impossible to combine Lovett, O'Connor, O'Brien, Sturge, Stephens, Harney, Vincent, Cooper into one effective team. Temperaments clashed, tactics differed, aims conflicted. The movement was consequently split up by local loyalties, and had no centralized leadership.

Fifthly, Chartism failed because it had opposed to it the might of the middle classes—"the leading poachers" who, since 1832, had "turned gamekeepers." The temporary alliance of Attwood and his followers with Chartism had been on grounds of expediency, and was abandoned when it was apparent that the direction of the movement lay outside their control. The humanitarian 'Sturgeites' of the Complete Suffrage movement were dismayed when their organization was captured by Chartists, and they too faded from the picture.

The first Chartist Convention met on the same day as the first Anti-Corn Law League conference, and the Corn Law repeal agitation continued—in the wealth behind its organization and in its success a striking contrast to Chartism—to its triumphant conclusion in 1846. For eight years this agitation consumed all the energies of the middle classes. It was the playing of the last act of the drama of landowner versus industrialist, which, in spite of the temporary prominence of certain acts of Chartism, held the centre of the stage.

The middle-class industrialists emerged with political power and economic power, but each step of their struggle upward had, as Macaulay rightly saw, made the possibility of working-class victory more remote. Once there, it was not middle-class policy to assist another class into the seats of power, but, on the

WILLIAM LOVETT

The National Convention, as it met on Monday, February 4, 1839, at the British Coffee-house, Cockspur Street, London

[See p. 210]

contrary, to consolidate its position by alliance with the land-owners, and to present an unbroken front to the forces of change.

The sixth reason for the failure of Chartism can be found in the fact that neither the trade unions nor the Owenites supported the movement. The trade-union struggle was essentially one for the improvement of industrial conditions; Chartism, at bottom, was a revolt against industrialism itself. The two movements were thus fundamentally opposed to each other. There were, of course, many workers who supported the big trade-union offensive of 1834 and who, after its collapse, turned to Chartism, and others who, like Lovett, were co-operators as well as Chartists. But the steady core of the trade-union and Co-operative movements remained outside the Chartist movement. Nor was the Chartist movement a Socialist movement. Owen, the greatest Socialist of his time, was no Chartist: O'Connor, the Chartist leader, was no Socialist. No Socialist experiment would have followed the attainment of the six points of the Charter. O'Brien and, later, Harney and Jones were the only Socialist theorists of the movement. Lovett, though at heart a Socialist, accepted and planned within the capitalist order.

Chartism failed. It would be good to find in subsequent working-class movements some sign of Chartist revival. But there is little in the trade-union and Labour movements of the second half of the century to suggest continuity with Chartism. The Chartist movement must stand by itself as the product of a transition period in capitalist development. It failed. But all the important points of the Charter have since been won— universal suffrage, vote by ballot, payment of Members, the abolition of the property qualification for Members of Parliament. It failed. But it was a necessary step in working-class development. It was markedly more mature than the spasmodic outbreaks of the beginning of the century. And, although it left no direct heir, it has bequeathed a very real inspiration to subsequent generations.

SELECT BIBLIOGRAPHY

BEER, MAX: *A History of British Socialism* (Bell, 1920), vol. ii.
BRIGGS, ASA (ed.): *Chartist Studies* (Macmillan, 1959).
COLE, G. D. H.: *Chartist Portraits* (Macmillan, 1941).
GAMMAGE, R. G.: *The History of the Chartist Movement, 1837–1854* (Newcastle-on-Tyne, 1894).
HOVELL, MARK: *The Chartist Movement* (Manchester University Press, 1918; second edition 1925, reprinted 1950).
LOVETT, W.: *Life and Struggle*, edited by R. H. Tawney.
MATHER, F. C.: *Chartism*, Historical Association Pamphlet No. G 61 (The Historical Association, 1965; reprinted 1971).
PEEL, FRANK: *The Risings of the Luddites, Chartists and Plug-Drawers* (1880; fourth edition, Frank Cass, 1968).
READ, D. AND GLASGOW, R. C.: *Feargus O'Connor: Irishman and Chartist* (Arnold, 1961).
SCHOYEN, A. R.: *The Chartist Challenge: A Portrait of George Julian Harney* (Heinemann, 1958).
THORNE, C.: *Chartism* (Sources of History Series, Macmillan, 1965).
WEST, JULIUS: *A History of the Chartist Movement* (Constable, 1920).
WRIGHT, L. C.: *Scottish Chartism* (Oliver and Boyd, 1953).

CHAPTER XI

EDUCATION

THE Industrial Revolution, with its growth and concentration of population, created new problems concerning health and housing and factory conditions. It also raised more sharply than before the question of education. It seemed that industrialism was accompanied by a general deterioration of manners and culture. Town life, which often meant dirt, overcrowding, and a low standard of living, combined with the brutalizing effect of long hours in factory or mine to coarsen and degrade many sections of the population. Their work no longer gave the joy which the craftsman feels in creation, but was a monotonous exercise. Their clubs were the beer-house and the gin-shop. Their dingy and often pestilential houses offered no attractive alternative.

The countryman remained nearer to the sources of education —the woods and fields, the streams and hills, of the countryside. But his material degradation too often covered his native intellect with the dull apathy of indifference and closed his mind to the curiosity which is the stimulus to knowledge.

This was a generation living before the age of the popular theatre or cinema or wireless and after the age of the self-acted pageants and miracle plays. The country fair still remained, but was losing its vitality. 'Popular' literature was just beginning to be a factor in the lives of the working class. Here were a people whose traditional culture was largely gone, while in its place they realized only the dross, and none of the worth, of the new civilization.

There was no State educational system. That the Governments of the nineteenth century were so slow to accept any responsibility for education was partly because of their unwillingness to assume new burdens; partly because of the theories which sprang to conflict at the mention of education; partly because education is necessarily linked with the question of religious teaching, where fresh controversies bristled at each breath of reform. Nevertheless, by the end of the nineteenth century there existed a State system of education, albeit an imperfect one, and a population from whom illiteracy had been virtually wiped out.

For the working classes such instruction as existed at the end of the eighteenth century was supplied by private effort in schools of three kinds. First there were the profit-making schools, charging fees of about 4d. to 9d. a week and comprising schools for older children, generally termed 'common day schools,' and those for the little ones, known as dame schools. Anyone could set up such a school. There was inspection of neither teachers, building, nor equipment. No standard of ability, knowledge, or cleanliness was required. So it happened that those who turned to teaching frequently did so because they could get a living in no other way. From forty-seven common day schools in a district of South Wales, for example, ten masters only had received some kind of instruction with a view to teaching; four were Ministers of Dissent; one was the clerk of a parish church. Of the rest sixteen had been unsuccessful in retail trade, and eleven had been miners or labourers who had lost their health or met with accidents and subsequently 'got a little learning' to enable them to keep a school. The remaining five teachers were women.[1] Inefficient as they were, these schools were clearly not for the very poor, whose children were at work from morning till night, and for whom the payment of even a few coppers a week for education was impossible. In the Manchester district it was chiefly the mechanics, warehousemen, and small shopkeepers who sent their children, hoping they would learn reading, writing, and arithmetic—the essential requirements of their parents' trades.[2] In fact, very little of anything was learnt.

The dame schools were places not so much of instruction as of 'periodical confinement' where children were looked after, generally by old women, but sometimes by old men "whose only qualification for this employment," according to a contemporary report, was "their unfitness for every other."[3] The

---

[1] *Minutes of Committee of Council on Education*, 1840, XL, Part II, 1839–40, p. 210, Report of Mr Tremenheere, H.M.I.
[2] *Report of Manchester Statistical Society*, p. 9, quoted by Kay-Shuttleworth, *Four Periods of Education*, p. 104.
[3] *Ibid.*, p. 5, quoted by Kay-Shuttleworth, *Four Periods of Education*, p. 102.

aged teacher would sometimes be attending a shop, or sewing, or washing, while the children were in her care. The rooms in which the schools were held were often dirty, overcrowded, and unhealthy. In Manchester they were "frequently in close damp cellars, or old dilapidated garrets." It was in a small room in this town that investigators found eleven children 'at school,' the child of the mistress meantime lying ill in bed with measles, another child having died in the same room a few days earlier from the same disease.[1]

Sometimes a child was more fortunate. Thomas Cooper, for example, went to the school kept by aged Gertrude Arum— "Old Gatty," as she was usually called. Her schoolroom was the larger lower room of her two-storied cottage, and Cooper describes how "she was an expert and laborious teacher of the art of reading and spelling," so that Cooper could soon read the tenth chapter of Nehemiah "with all its hard names 'like the parson in the church'—as she used to say, and could spell wondrously."[2]

Then there were schools supported by private subscription, to which parents might or might not contribute. Most of these were run either by the British and Foreign School Society, founded in 1814 from the Lancasterian Society, which Joseph Lancaster had started in 1808, or by the National Society for Promoting the Education of the Poor in the Principles of the Established Church, founded in 1811 by Dr Bell. The name of the latter society speaks for itself. The former was its rival in that it stood for training children in the principles, not of the Church of England, but of Dissent. Both used the Bible as textbook and gave instruction in reading, writing, and arithmetic, with a smattering of geography or general knowledge. There was further rivalry between Bell and Lancaster, for they both claimed the credit for inventing the method of instruction known as the monitorial or mutual system. By this system a whole school could be run by one teacher in one room. The information for each lesson was given by the teacher to various boys called monitors. Each monitor then returned to his appointed group of schoolfellows and did his best to convey to it what had been crammed into him. At certain times the hubbub ceased for a few moments; then it started again as the

[1] *Ibid.*, p. 6, quoted by Kay-Shuttleworth, *Four Periods of Education*, p. 102.
[2] Thomas Cooper, *The Life of Thomas Cooper* (1897 edition), p. 7.

presiding master or the monitors tested the pupils by means of set questions, to which the class replied in chorus.

Pupils were admitted to these schools at any age from about six to fourteen, their stay being generally from one to three years; few left with a competent knowledge of reading and writing. The majority of those who could read did so mechanically, without understanding. Questions on subject-matter and the meanings of words were consequently introduced, and the chorus of children's voices told of the habits of ruminating animals and the growth of enamel on the teeth. The merits of the system were said to be not only its cheapness, but the excellent training it afforded the monitors and the stimulus it imparted to all pupils to become monitors themselves.

Discipline was largely in the hands of these monitors, who might be no more than seven years old. The classes were trained to obey them, and from them came the first reproofs or cautions, before the presiding master was notified of a fault. The rôle of the monitor was in part that of the præposter or prefect. Joseph Lancaster's attitude towards his monitors anticipated that of Dr Arnold at Rugby. "I have successfully convinced a number of the leading boys in my institution," he wrote,

> of the beauty, usefulness, and piety there is in ever speaking the truth; of the pernicious effects . . . not only as to lying, but swearing and various kinds of profaneness. These boys are bright examples, and give the lead to the whole school. . . . Thus the public spirit of the whole school is marshalled on the side of virtue; for what the elder boys do from conviction and principle, is followed by the minors from the force of example.[1]

The monitors may have improved a boy's moral standards: they did little to hasten his mental development. In 1842 classes were still so mechanically giving set answers to set questions that when a visiting inspector changed the order of the questions the answers were given in the original order, so making nonsense.[2] The monitorial system was "the division of labour applied to intellectual purposes."[3] And since the intellect is not merely mechanical, the system failed.

[1] *A Letter to John Foster, Esq.*, quoted by S. Trimmer, *A Comparative View of the New Plan of Education promulgated by Mr Joseph Lancaster* (1805), pp. 25–26.
[2] J. L. and B. Hammond, *The Age of the Chartists*, pp. 190–191.
[3] Thomas Bernard, *Of the Education of the Poor*, quoted by J. W. Adamson, *English Education*, p. 24.

Schools of a third type, the charity and Sunday schools, were mostly free. Charity schools had been conducted since the end of the seventeenth century by the Society for Promoting Christian Knowledge, whose avowed aims were to combat Popery and to teach the children of the poor to "keep their stations." They taught reading and writing, and the children were expected to learn the Catechism by heart as well as being "trained to some labour." The charity schools had much in kin with the workhouse schools, where children were "set on work." Similar also were the schools established by the Society for the Betterment of the Condition of the Poor. This society, established in 1796, regarded schools as part of a local service, which included also public hospitals, savings banks, and kitchens. Its surprisingly modern outlook is further indicated by its insistence that if parents could not meet school fees magistrates should do so. Similar, again, were the schools of industry. The aim of them all was to provide the basis of a trade, together with the rudiments of learning.

Mrs Sarah Trimmer was a typical supporter of these schools, raising subscriptions and writing school books. She was keenly if narrowly religious, and representative of her class and age in thinking that education should be given to each according to his station. She was almost frightened at her own temerity in advocating instruction in reading and writing for the lower orders, for "*Poor* boys sent into the world, without fixed principles, may in consequence of having been taught to write and read become very dangerous members of society."[1] The safeguard upon which she insisted was religious instruction according to the principles of the Church of England.

Most of the charity schools were connected with church or chapel, and there were frequent feuds between the schools of rival denominations. Fortunately these did not all reach the height of that in the St Giles district of London. Here were settled many Irish—some Roman Catholic, some Protestant. Mr Finnegan's Irish Free Schools in George Street used the Authorized Version of the Bible without religious comment, and taught no Creed or Catechism. Mr Gandolphy, a Roman Catholic priest, entered the schoolroom and demanded to teach the Roman Catholic Catechism. When denied, he preached a sermon to such good effect that a Roman Catholic

[1] S. Trimmer, *op. cit.*, p. 31.

mob stormed the school buildings, breaking the windows, pelting Mr and Mrs Finnegan with mud, and beating their child so that he was crippled for years.[1]

Sunday schools had existed in the early eighteenth century; in 1780 Robert Raikes founded his first Sunday school at Gloucester, and in 1785 the Sunday School Union began to spread schools over the whole of England. These were originally designed for the very poor and for the little factory workers whose labour prevented their attendance at school on weekdays. Raikes's chief aim was to prevent the hooliganism which took place in the streets on Sundays when the pin factory near Gloucester was closed. In spreading the idea of Sunday schools through the pages of his newspaper, *The Gloucester Journal*, he put the case thus:

> Farmers, and other inhabitants of the towns and villages' complain that they receive more injury to their property on the Sabbath than all the week besides: this, in a great measure, proceeds from the lawless state of the younger class, who are allowed to run wild on that day, free from every restraint.[2]

In 1785 Raikes professed himself as far less pleased with the fact that about 200 children had been taught to read in the Painswick Sunday school than that there was present in their manner "in a striking degree, a sense of subordination and of due respect to their superiors." Two hundred children from this Sunday school went out to service in four years, so it was clearly an all-round blessing to the superior classes.[3]

Hannah More was another enthusiastic advocate of Sunday schools; she used arguments similar to those of Raikes. There was nevertheless a deep sense of devotion to the poor in the earnestness with which she strove to win the rude miners of the Mendips and their families to a knowledge of the Bible. Though known as a wit and beauty, the friend of Garrick and Dr Johnson, she forsook the intellectual life of London for the task of Bible instruction near her native Bristol.

The Sunday schools normally aimed at teaching children to read the Bible. They were often far from unattractive to the children, though it is saddening to read that Sunday wakes and Sunday fairs declined with the growth of the Sunday

[1] *Report of the Select Committee on the Education of the Lower Orders of the Metropolis*, 1816, IV, Minutes of Evidence, p. 3.
[2] Alfred Gregory, *Robert Raikes* (1877), p. 78.   [3] *Ibid.*, p. 80.

school movement. The Sunday school at Middleton run by the Methodists was strenuous enough, starting at 8.30 A.M. and finishing at 4 or 4.30, and combining hymns and prayers with spelling lessons and reading at specially set-out desks. Men and women as well as boys and girls attended this school from distant parts. "Big collier lads and their sisters from Siddal Moor" tramped in; "groups of boys and girls with their substantial dinners tied up in clean napkins" came to spend the day at the school.[1]

In some districts there was an amazing duplication of schools. In Spitalfields, London, there were a parish school, a Methodist Sunday school, two other Sunday schools, of which one was run by the parish, a Protestant Dissenting school, and—by far the most popular—a Sunday school attached to Mr Evans's chapel. They were all free. Then there were Mrs Buxton's school, for which she charged 2*d.* a week, an adult school, and a free school which was held on Sunday evenings.[2] Together these schools could accommodate about two thousand people.

Nevertheless the net result of educational activity of all kinds in Great Britain in 1818 resulted in what an official Report described as a "lamentable deficiency" in education for the poor. Voluntary effort was confined almost entirely to the towns, so that country districts were wells of ignorance. But even in London there were districts where complete illiteracy engulfed half the population. Most investigators agreed that even the poorest and most dissolute possessed a genuine desire to educate their children. But poverty often compelled parents to keep their children away from school, sometimes through lack of clothing, sometimes because the children were used as more successful beggars than their parents, sometimes because they were sent to work instead of to school.

Richer people, meantime, were attaining to a stereotyped pattern for the education of their children. First there was the governess at home; then a private tutor or a private school or both. In the most intellectual families the instruction given at home might approach, but would rarely equal, that given by

[1] Samuel Bamford, *Passages in the Life of a Radical and Early Days*, i, 101.
[2] *Report of the Select Committee on the Education of the Lower Orders of the Metropolis*, 816, **IV**, 11–12.

James Mill to his son. John Stuart Mill was learning Greek
at the age of three, Latin at the age of eight; by the time he
was fourteen he was widely read in the classics, in history and
political economy, was well versed in logic and familiar with
mathematics and philosophy. He was also the little monitor
who taught his sisters their lessons and who suffered with them
for any fault, however trifling. James Mill was fortunate in
having children whom his methods did not break. Little John
Stuart had no childhood. But neither had those children whose
parents took as models such books as *The Fairchild Family*, by
Mrs Sherwood. The aim of this book was to inspire children
with the Christian virtues. It did so by portraying the deaths
of many people, young and old, and by such conversations
as this:

> "Indeed, mamma," said Lucy [aged nine], "I did not under-
> stand the sermon; it was all about besetting sins. What are they,
> mamma?"
>
> "You know, my dear," said Mrs Fairchild, "that our hearts
> are all by nature wicked?"
>
> "O yes, mamma; I know that," answered Lucy.
>
> "Do you recollect, my dear," said Mrs Fairchild, "what things
> our Lord says naturally proceed out of man's heart?"
>
> "Yes, mamma."

The child then quotes from Mark vii, 21–23, and Mrs Fairchild explains "that sin which a man feels himself most inclined
to is called his besetting sin."

> "Oh! now I know what besetting sins mean," answered
> Lucy.[1]

Or this from Mr Fairchild when Henry, aged between six
and seven, would not learn Latin:

> "Henry, listen to me; When wicked men obstinately defy and
> oppose the power of God, He gives them up to their own hard
> hearts. . . . I stand in the place of God to you, whilst you are a
> child; . . . therefore, if you cast aside my authority, and will not
> obey my commands, I shall not treat you as I do my other
> children. From this time forward, Henry, I have nothing to do
> with you; I will speak to you no more, neither will your mamma,
> or sisters . . . so go out of my study immediately."[2]

There were many books similar to *The Fairchild Family*,
which parents would make the basis of home instruction. Sarah

---

[1] Second edition, 1818, pp. 233–234. The book was first published in 1802.
[2] *Ibid.*, p. 269.

Trimmer wrote several, Mrs Barbauld wrote a nursery book for children from three to four years old. In lighter vein for older children were Elizabeth Turner's *The Daisy, or Cautionary Stories in Verse*, published in 1807 and reaching thirty editions by 1885. *The Cowslip* followed *The Daisy* in 1811, and reached its twenty-second edition by 1842. Here is a picture of *The Good Girl*, from *The Cowslip*:

> Miss Lydia Banks, though very young,
> Will never do what's rude or wrong,
> When spoken to, she always tries
> To give the most polite replies.[1]

And this is *The Dunce*, accompanied by an appalling picture of a girl in a hideous Punch-like mask:

> Miss Bell was almost seven years old,
> A shame to tell indeed!
> But when the real truth is told,
> She scarce could spell or read.
>
> But very much was she disgrac'd
> Deservedly at school;
> She wore an ugly mask, while plac'd
> Upon the dunce's stool.[2]

Most books for home instruction had a religious turn; some, like the *Peep of Day*, were simply Bible stories for the young. The annual *Juvenile Scrap Book*, and *Fireside Tales for the Young*, collected from various scrap-books, contained a variety of stories and poems, all strangely stiff and unyouthful. There were instructional pieces, many illustrations, and some fearful moral stories, like the one in the 1837 edition of *The Juvenile Scrap Book*. Two boys, against their parents' instructions, went to watch a burial service and were accidentally locked in a vault. After several hours of incarceration George, the ringleader, thinks that Edgar is dead, and cries out, "Oh, he is dead! . . . *I* tempted him to do evil; wretch that I was! and the wages of sin is death."[3] The standard nursery stories and such adventure tales as *Robinson Crusoe* were, of course, available, but it was not until rather later that children began to reap a full harvest suited to their years in the books of Kingsley, Christina Rossetti, and Lewis Carroll.

[1] P. 31.   [2] P. 37.   [3] P. 17.

The next stage in education was given at the grammar school or similar private school, sometimes a day school, sometimes a boarding establishment. These schools varied widely in quality. The grammar schools proper had been founded by endowment, mostly between the fourteenth and seventeenth centuries, as free schools for instructing poor boys of the district in Greek and Latin grammar. As prices rose throughout the sixteenth and seventeenth centuries and founders' bequests became insufficient for the upkeep of free schools the stress on paying pupils became greater and the number of free places less. The rich and the aristocracy began to claim the education of these schools for their sons, while tradesmen and small craftsmen ceased to send their children, partly because of the high fees charged, partly because the obligation laid by the terms of their foundation on the teaching of dead languages precluded the teaching of other subjects more suitable to the sons of working-men. So, instead of local schools for the poor, they became non-local schools for the rich, still, however, clinging tenaciously to their function of teaching Greek and Latin grammar. By the nineteenth century nine of these endowed schools had become famous as the public schools of England which nurtured the sons of the ruling class. With the exception of Merchant Taylors', St Paul's, and perhaps Shrewsbury, the bulk of each school had become, as later described by a Government Commission, "an accretion upon the original foundation," consisting of "boarders received by masters or other persons at their own expense and risk, and for their own profit."[1] Various instances of "neglect and abuse" of the terms of their endowment were cited by the Committee on Education of 1816–18. At both Eton and Winchester the Committee found that "considerable unauthorized deviations" had been made from the original plans of the founder; that those deviations had been dictated "more by regard to the interests of the Fellows than of the Scholars, who were the main objects of the foundations and of the founders' bounty."[2] Brougham told in the House of Commons in 1817 of a Lord of the Manor, who was also a rector, who managed the endowment of a school. He himself was the Principal, with a salary of £1500 *per annum*. He appointed his brother, another clergyman, school-

---

[1] *Report of Public Schools Commission*, 1864, XX, 8.
[2] *Third Report of Select Committee on Education*, 1818, IV, 58.

master at a large salary. The real work of teaching was done by a journeyman carpenter, who was called an assistant schoolmaster and was paid £40 a year.

Internally the public schools were amazing institutions. Little discipline was imposed either by the masters or by the boys themselves. By the fagging and prefectorial system the Sixth Formers ruled the rest of the school, using the younger boys as servants, practising corporal punishment, and often indulging in bad bullying. Masters occasionally descended to flog the boys, but for the most part took little interest in the school. Neighbouring fields, gardens, and orchards were regarded as fair game. On one occasion at Eton when the boys became completely out of hand the military were called in to quell the disturbance. Teaching was as rigid as discipline was loose. At the beginning of the nineteenth century all the public schools were adhering strictly to the laws of their foundations, and taught Latin and Greek only; it was pronounced illegal by Lord Eldon in 1805 for any endowed grammar school to do otherwise. Not only were other subjects excluded, but the classics were taught mechanically and inefficiently, schoolboys spending many hours attempting to compose Greek and Latin verse. It is evidence not so much of progress as of slowness to change that by 1860 every public school except Eton taught one modern language, and that three hours a week were generally given to mathematics and arithmetic. These subjects were completely subordinate to classics, and in some cases did not count for promotion or for prizes, and in others were given lower markings than classical studies. So, at the mid-century, in the words of Thomas Huxley,

> a boy might have passed through any one of the great public schools with the greatest distinction and credit and might never. . . . have heard of [modern geography, history, literature, science physical moral and social.] He might never have heard that the earth goes round the sun; that England underwent a great revolution in 1688, and France another in 1789; that there once lived certain notable men called Chaucer, Shakespeare, Milton, Voltaire, Goethe, Schiller.[1]

A vicious spiral of tradition was largely responsible for this state of affairs. Son followed father to Eton or Harrow or

[1] "A Liberal Education; and where to find it." An Address to the South London Working Men's College (*Collected Essays*, 1893 edition).

Winchester; the public-school boy returned, after an interval at the university, as master; the universities demanded a classical training as a condition of entry; in exhibitions and entrance examinations marks were given either exclusively or chiefly for classical subjects. It was the universities which, if they did not break this circle, helped to expose the inefficiency of the public schools in the very classical tuition upon which they specialized.

There was little reform of the public schools from outside in the first half of the nineteenth century, such enthusiasm as existed for educational reform being directed to the elementary system. But there were several headmasters whose zeal raised their schools from the general inefficiency of the early days of the century.

Outstanding were Samuel Butler, who was Headmaster of Shrewsbury from 1798 to 1836, and Thomas Arnold, who was Headmaster of Rugby from 1828 to 1842. Arnold's predecessors at Rugby had started the school on the upgrade, but even so Arnold inherited much of the atmosphere of hooliganism and licence which was typical of the public schools. First and foremost, Arnold felt himself as a moral reformer, and it was on this side of school life that his influence was most felt. Education for Arnold was bound up with religion, and his constant aim was to train a boy to be a Christian, a gentleman, and a scholar—in that order. His chief contact with the boys was in chapel on Sundays, where he delivered the sermon to the whole school. Next in importance was his belief that the senior boys of the Sixth Form could act as a leaven to imbue the whole school with the right moral atmosphere. He put his trust in the Sixth, with whom he had considerable personal contact, allowing them the full power which prefects normally had over the lower school, including that of corporal punishment. Flogging he retained, and he insisted on the right to expel any boys whose influence on the school he felt was bad. In studies Arnold continued the classical tradition, in which he was a firm believer, both on account of its intellectual discipline and of its 'humanity,' but he introduced modern history, geography, and modern languages. Rugby raised its 'tone' and to some extent its scholarship, and its example had effect beyond its own walls. Something of the influence of Arnold and his effect on his boys can be realized by the book which one of them wrote. *Tom Brown's Schooldays* is interesting as being written by Thomas Hughes, the Christian Socialist, and particularly for its account of Arnold's preaching in Rugby chapel, and the effect his sermon and his presence had on the small boy listening for the first time.

Below the public schools were the smaller grammar schools, many of them modelled upon the nine, others attempting to meet the needs of a wider public. It was Leeds Grammar School which in 1805, by trying to include non-classical subjects in its curriculum, drew the ruling from Lord Eldon that the innovation was illegal. In spite of his lordship's ruling, such subjects did begin to appear in the time-tables of the grammar schools. The classics were termed 'business'; other subjects were 'accomplishments' and taught at odd times like half-holidays. The most popular 'accomplishment' was at first arithmetic; later science and mathematics and history were added, and the place which these subjects assumed in school curricula loomed larger in response to demand. Further to meet the requirements of men whose sons would be moving in the world of trade and commerce, or who for other reasons wanted a wider education than the grammar schools provided, or who could not afford to pay the fees of the public schools, private and proprietary schools were being founded. The gibe that the former were "schools for the shop, the warehouse, the counting house and the manufactory"[1] is an indication of their usefulness. Their attraction was enhanced by the addition of music, dancing, fencing, and drawing to the curriculum.

The proprietary schools were brought into existence by groups of people anxious to obtain a higher education for their sons on lines similar to those provided by the public schools, yet less rigidly classical and less expensive. The headmasters were appointed by the owners of the school. Among the earliest of these schools were Cheltenham (1841), Marlborough (1842), and Rossall (1844). They gave a classical training, but paid far more attention to modern subjects than did most of the endowed schools.

So, while the public schools provided schooling for the aristocracy, the schools of the middle class were these numerous private and proprietary and smaller endowed schools, ranging

[1] Vicesimus Knox, headmaster of Tunbridge School, quoted by J. W. Adamson, *English Education, 1789-1902*, p. 48.

from a good, expensive school like Marlborough to what Matthew Arnold termed "the numberless obscure endowed schools and 'educational homes' of the country, some of them good, many of them middling, most of them bad." Some were as bad as the schools which Charles Dickens found in Yorkshire in the forties and typified in Dotheboys Hall and its villainous schoolmaster-owner, Squeers.

But, even where it was not vicious, English schoolteaching, from the monitorial schools to the public schools, was for the most part unimaginative and unproductive, reflecting little of the contemporary discussion and experiment which was drawing visitors from all over the world to Yverdon and Hofwyl, in Switzerland, to see the schools of Pestalozzi and von Fellenberg, and seemingly ignorant both of the accounts of the Swiss experiments given in the pages of *The Quarterly Journal of Education* by the Society for the Diffusion of Useful Knowledge between 1831 and 1835 and even of the English work on *Practical Education* by the Edgeworths. This remarkable book expressed many truths which, though simple enough, needed underlining to a generation which tended to regard the educational process as no less amenable to the division of labour than the production of a piece of cotton cloth. The Edgeworths, basing their conclusions on several generations of instruction in a large family, pointed out that "Play . . . is only a change of occupation," that "the instruction and amusements of children may be so managed as to coincide with each other." "We are not solicitous about the quantity of knowledge that is obtained at any given age," they said,

> but we are extremely anxious that the desire to learn should continually increase, and that whatever is taught should be taught with that perspicuity which improves the general understanding.[1]

The writers and selectors of school textbooks were far from realizing these simple truths. Two best-selling school textbooks of the period were Lindley Murray's *English Grammar*, which ran to forty-six editions between 1795 and 1832, and Mangnall's *Historical and Miscellaneous Questions for the Use of Young People*, which from its publication in 1800 achieved twelve editions by 1815. Both books were used chiefly by the private schools,

[1] Maria and R. L. Edgeworth, *Practical Education* (second edition, 1801), iii 292; iii, 309.

"ORATOR" HUNT

A. Buck

National Portrait Gallery

FEARGUS O'CONNOR

The background shows the farms of his land plan.

SARAH TRIMMER
H. Howard
[See p. 231]
National Portrait Gallery

ROBERT RAIKES
George Romney
[*See p.* 232]
National Portrait Gallery

HANNAH MORE

H. W. Pickersgill

[See p. 232]

National Portrait Gallery

and were pedestrian and lifeless methods of teaching by rote English grammar and history, the latter in the then popular form of question and answer. Probably more attractive to the young than Murray was the religious alphabet used in the Sunday schools:

> A stands for Angel, who praises the Lord;
> B stands for Bible, that teaches God's word;
> C stands for Church, to which righteous men go;
> D stands for Devil, the cause of all woe.[1]

But, from what is on the whole a dreary record of monotonous attempts to teach, there emerge one or two brighter pictures of happier places of learning. Such was the school kept by a master in Manchester, whose method of teaching consisted "in watching the dispositions of the children and putting them especially to that particular thing which they take to."[2] Was he consciously or unconsciously following the teaching of Rousseau or of Pestalozzi?

Robert Owen had greater opportunities of putting similar principles into practice. In 1816 he started a school at his cotton mills in New Lanark. To the preparatory section children went at the age of three, passing to the higher school at five or six and staying there until at ten they went into the mills. In both sections the overriding aim was to form good 'habits' and 'dispositions.' Here was the educational theory of the Utilitarians—that the child mind is a blank to be written on by the instructor of his earliest years. In Owen's school this was to be done chiefly by example and practice, Owen wisely recognizing that among the infants at any rate "precept was little comprehended." In addition the older children were taught reading, writing, and arithmetic, and the girls needlework. Throughout stress was laid upon exercise and fresh air, and the acquisition of knowledge by way of amusement—what we should call the 'play way' in education. Dancing, singing, and the playing of musical instruments were encouraged; classes were held whenever possible in the open air. If parents could afford to forgo the extra wages children could stay at the school until they were thirteen and obtain what Owen claimed was an education which well prepared them for any of the

---

[1] Quoted by Mr Gibson, House of Commons, June 20, 1839 (Hansard, third series, xlviii, 599).

[2] J. L. and B. Hammond, *The Age of the Chartists*, p. 171.

"ordinary active employments of life."[1] For those whom financial need compelled to work at ten, and for the adults, there was an evening school of about two hours' duration each night, for instruction, exercise, and amusement. On Sundays similar Sunday schools were open to all. Owen claimed a great success for "this combined system of instruction, exercise, and amusement," and his school became a place of pilgrimage. There were 300 children in the day school, and 400 persons in the evening school in the first year of the venture.

Then there were the schools organized by the Hill family at Hazelwood, near Birmingham, and at Bruce Castle, Tottenham, whose object was the important one of teaching "the arts of self-government and self-education." These schoolboy communities enacted their own laws through elected committees, subject to the veto of the headmaster, and learnt their lessons largely through questions and "copious explanations" from the master, "it being an object of great anxiety . . . that the pupil should be led to reason upon all his operations."[2]

Above the public schools, grammar schools, and others which together came to be loosely termed 'secondary schools' stood the universities.

The University . . . was, we may almost say, the chief charity-school for the poor, and the chief grammar-school in England, as well as the great place of education for Students of Theology, of Law, and of Medicine. The oldest of the great Public Schools was not yet founded. The Inns of Court and the Schools of Medicine had no existence, and many students from foreign Universities thought their education incomplete until they had visited the most celebrated seat of English learning.[3]

The education imparted there is not such as to conduce to the advancement in life of many persons, except those intended for the ministry of the Established Church.[4]

The first of these quotations is a description of Oxford University as it was in the thirteenth century; the second as it

[1] For a full account see Owen's evidence before the Select Committee on Education of the Lower Orders, 1816, IV, 240 *et seq.*
[2] M. D. and R. Hill, *Public Education*, 1822.
[3] *Report of the Royal Commission on the State of the University and Colleges of Oxford*, 1852, XXII, 19.
[4] *Ibid.*, XXII, 18.

was in the middle of the nineteenth century. Both statements were made by the Royal Commission which reported in 1852 on the state of the University. The extent of the deterioration of Oxford from its thirteenth-century eminence is measured by the fact that at the beginning of the nineteenth century an average of only 267 students matriculated each year. At Cambridge the numbers were higher, in spite of the fact that Oxford had more colleges and ampler revenue. This was partly because Oxford laid more restrictions on entry and graduation than Cambridge, though neither university was open to all talent.

Oxford was exclusively Anglican, only those who subscribed to the Thirty-nine Articles of the Church of England being admitted. At Cambridge the bar came at the later stage of graduation. At Oxford restrictions on Fellowships were in 1851 still so severe that of a total of 540 Fellowships scarcely 20 were open to general competition, and even these were not absolutely free. The rest were restricted by regulations as to locality, family (generally 'founder's kin'), and membership of a college. Most Fellows were Church of England clergymen, and all were bound to retire on marriage. At Cambridge there were more open scholarships and Fellowships, but the marriage bar remained. Oxford was governed by Laudian statutes, Cambridge by Elizabethan. In both universities the colleges were self-governing, and no effective co-ordinating body existed to act for the university as a whole.

At the opening of the nineteenth century classics were the chief subjects taught at Oxford, while Cambridge had no examination but the mathematical tripos. Teaching at both universities was chiefly by tutors, there being few public lectures. Examinations at the end of the eighteenth century were largely farcical, consisting of a formal 'disputation' which had become practically meaningless, and a series of questions crammed from 'schemes' which were handed down from generation to generation. General life at the universities was a continuation of that at the public schools, with even fewer restrictions. Wealthy students with their private tutors, who regarded the university as a club rather than as a place of learning, too frequently set the standard—both of expenditure and of learning—for the rest. So the highest places of learning in the land taught neither widely nor efficiently, yet reserved whatever benefit might accrue from their instruction for wealthy members of the Church of England.

The Scottish universities of Edinburgh, Aberdeen, Glasgow, and St Andrews were proceeding meanwhile on wider lines, without the restrictions of religious intolerance, cheaper, and consequently open to a wider section of the population. Instead of the tutorial method of teaching there were professorial lectures attended by big audiences. Standards of examination were low, the age of coming up younger than at Oxford and Cambridge. Though some schools, notably the medical school at Edinburgh, were justifiably held in high esteem, the standard of learning as a whole was not high. But John Stuart Mill's comparison with the English universities is noteworthy. "Youths come to the Scottish universities ignorant," he said, "and are there taught." But he added, "The majority of those who come to the English Universities come still more ignorant, and ignorant they go away."[1]

In the first half of the nineteenth century there was a little internal reform of the universities, chiefly concerning curriculum and examination. In 1800 for the B.A. degree at Oxford a written and an oral examination of some substance replaced the formal disputation. In 1807 mathematics and physics were separated from the other subjects, which became *Literæ Humaniores*, results being divided into first- and second-class honours. In 1809 a third class was added; in 1830 a fourth class was introduced and candidates for the ordinary pass degree were separated from the honours men. The ordinary degree, however, was of so narrow a range of interest, and the standard so low "as to leave all but the dullest and most ignorant unoccupied for the greater part of their academical course."[2] In the honours school, meanwhile, the range of classical reading became more limited, although ancient history and political philosophy were added to the examination for *Literæ Humaniores* in 1830. Mathematics failed to attract much talent, for scholarships and Fellowships continued to go to classics men, and the Professorships of Mathematics were so poorly endowed as to be untenable without private means.

At Cambridge a classical tripos was added to the mathe-

<hr>

[1] Rectorial Address at St Andrew's University, 1867.

[2] *Report of the Royal Commission on the State of the University and Colleges of Oxford*, 1852, XXII, 62.

matical in 1824, and in 1848 triposes in the natural and moral sciences. At the middle of the century University Commissioners noted with pleasure that such writers as Bacon and Newton were influencing for good the studies of Cambridge. The standards of the tripos examinations had been rising since the beginning of the century, and by 1850 the mathematical tripos, at least, had a deservedly high reputation.

External reform of the university system took the form of the creation of new colleges and universities. The Benthamites and other secularists were especially anxious to have a university of their own where secular instruction and scientific subjects could take the place of the Thirty-nine Articles and the classics. In 1828 their work resulted in the opening of University College, Gower Street, London, in whose entrance hall the figure of Jeremy Bentham still sits, giving an implied blessing to all who enter. They had raised the money for the building, their principles controlled its completely secular curriculum, which included not only languages and mathematics and history, but the more revolutionary political economy. There was naturally some opposition to the type of teaching given, and, to counterbalance "the godless institution in Gower Street," King's College was opened in London in 1831, under Church of England auspices. In 1836 the University of London, in which University College and King's College were incorporated, was created to confer degrees. Other universities and university colleges followed, the University of Durham in 1837 and others later in the century. All these universities were non-residential; most had hostels attached, but many students attended as day scholars. They were less expensive than the older universities, and thus university education became available to a wider class. Their more liberal syllabuses made them at the same time more attractive to students during whose lifetime startling mechanical inventions and revolutionary scientific theories were becoming subjects of popular interest.

It was the question of elementary education which attracted most public attention in the first half of the nineteenth century, chiefly because here the problem was very obviously bigger. A population increasing so rapidly as to double itself in half a century must be either educated or not educated. There is no shelving the problem. The effect of the decision, be it negative or positive, is certain to make its impact upon society as a whole. As the nineteenth century opened, the two outstanding questions, which comprised the rest, concerned the relation of the State and of religion to the educational issue. The first instinct of the State itself was against the education of its rapidly growing population. This was in line with the traditional view that assigned education to the upper classes and regarded knowledge for the poor as either mischievous or unnecessary. It would "be prejudicial to their morals and happiness; it would teach them to despise their lot in life";[1] it "might do a great deal of harm; it would enable them to read every thing that would tend to inflame their passions."[2] But at the same it was apparent that the ruling-class attitude was changing. The vice of ignorance was perhaps a more dangerous threat to public order than carefully managed enlightenment. Wrote the prosperous manufacturer Andrew Ure:

> The uneducated state of the 'lower orders'. . . is the dark den of incendiarism and misrule . . . which, if not cleared out, will give birth ere long to disastrous eruptions in every other province.[3]

A limited education might be a most effective bulwark against revolution. Not "Liberty, equality and fraternity," but

> God bless the squire and his relations,
> And keep us in our proper stations.

might be the theme of the educational process. A little education, as Mr Sharpe put it in the House of Commons, would form "many beneficial habits of an indelible nature; habits of submission and respect for their superiors."[4]

The Select Committee on Education of 1816–18 questioned its witnesses closely on the connexion between reading and Christianity and morals. "In what way does religious instruction tend to make children good members of society?" was the question put to the Rev. Daniel Wilson. He answered that it tends

> directly to lay in the children's minds the foundation of obedience to their governors in church and state, to make them contented with the station which Providence has appointed to them in the

---

[1] Mr Davies Giddy, House of Commons, July 13, 1807 (Hansard, 1807, ix, 798).
[2] *Report of Select Committee on the Education of the Lower Orders of the Metropolis,* 1816, IV, 301.
[3] *The Philosophy of Manufactures* (1861 edition), p. 404.
[4] April 24, 1807 (Hansard, ix, 544).

world, to teach them the subjugation of their passions . . . to make them worthy, respectable and virtuous persons in their stations.[1]

The Committee then asked whether the addition of reading would make the poor "discontented in their stations, or less obedient to their superiors?" "Unquestionably not," replied the minister. "The direct tendency of the two, when united, is to produce those principles that lead to submission, contentment, humility."[2] This was a pointer to the way in which educational opinion was changing. The Committee of Council on Education, eminent philanthropists like Lord Shaftesbury, Government Commissions, Church workers like Hannah More, Reports, articles, and speeches right through the century echo the sentiment again and again that a controlled education was a safeguard against social disorder. When the Poor Law Commissioners made their famous survey in 1834 most of them were struck as much by the potential revolutionary force in England as by the misery which caused it. The safeguard which Mr Cowell, an Assistant Commissioner, advised was education. He could not avoid coming to the conclusion that "education among the lower orders" was "connected with the development of those virtues which we desire to see them possess."[3]

Political reasons for teaching the rudiments became more obvious as political concessions outran educational opportunity. They were assessed by Whitbread early in the century: "Sir, in a political point of view, nothing can possibly afford greater stability to a popular government than the education of your people."[4] Roebuck, twenty-six years later, after the passage of the first Reform Bill, was more explicit. The mass of the population, he said,

will have power. In a very short time they will be paramount. I wish them to be enlightened, in order that they may use that power well which they will inevitably obtain.[5]

In 1870, after the passage of the third Reform Bill, Robert Lowe more tersely uttered a sentiment similar, but more acid: "Educate your Masters!"

[1] Fourth Report, 1816, IV, 279.   [2] Ibid., IV, 282.
[3] Report of the Poor Law Commission, 1834, Appendix A, Report of J. W. Cowell, 2nd Part, p. 644.
[4] House of Commons, February 19, 1807 (Hansard, viii, 877).
[5] House of Commons, July 30, 1833 (Hansard, third series, xx, 159).

An even more practical stand was taken by Earl Stanhope as early as 1807:

> In a manufacturing country, . . . when so much of excellence in our productions depended on a clear understanding and some degree of mathematical and mechanical knowledge, which it was impossible to attain without first receiving the rudiments and foundations [the three R's] . . . the superiority of workmen with some education, over those who had none, must be sensibly felt by all the great manufacturers in the country.[1]

The Government, in spite of its changing attitude towards education, would have been quite content to leave the work of providing it in the hands of private persons and the Church; but the Radicals and Utilitarians urged the matter as a national responsibility, and the private societies pressed for money. After many schemes had been defeated the Government in 1833 made its first gesture with a grant of £20,000 towards education. The money was for building purposes only. A school that could raise 50 per cent. of such cost could apply for the remainder from the Government fund. The result was that in richer areas, which could themselves afford half the cost, building took place, while the poorer districts suffered not only from their own poverty, but from the Government's discrimination. The fund was to be administered solely through the two religious societies—the National Society and the British and Foreign. In practice the bulk went to the National Society, and there was more Church of England building. Thus control of the first Government grant for education was exercised exclusively by religion, and mainly by the Established Church.

This brought to a head the question of the relationship of Church and State in educational matters. The most direct case for State control came from the Utilitarians, who regarded it as the duty of the State to supply an opportunity for the fullest possible development of all its citizens. The moderate Liberal case against State control was put by the Lord Chancellor in evidence before the Select Committee on Education of 1834. As the State took over the business of education, he said, the flow of voluntary contributions would be stemmed; education would become unpopular because of the increased

[1] House of Lords, August 11, 1807 (Hansard, ix, 1178).

taxation involved. English people would not like to be forced to educate their children, and "education would be made absolutely hateful in their eyes, and would speedily cease to be endured." Moreover, it would place in the hands of the Government—that is, of the Ministers of the day—the means of dictating opinions and principles to the people.[1] The last objection was the crux of the matter among many opponents of State control of education, from those who feared, like Disraeli, that "all would be thrown into the same mint, and all would come out with the same impress and superscription,"[2] to those who, like Sir Robert Peel, believed that "it must, almost of necessity, interfere with religious opinion."[3]

While those who opposed State control did so for various reasons, those who supported it also differed among themselves, especially on religious questions. "Education provided by the public," said John Stuart Mill, "must be education for all, and to be education for all it must be purely secular education."[4] Viscount Morpeth would have the State provide the widest possible toleration for all beliefs:

> As long as the State thought proper to employ Roman Catholic sinews and to finger Unitarian gold it could not refuse to extend to those by whom it so profited the blessings of education.[5]

Lord Ashley, on the other hand, was rigid in maintaining that "The State adopted the Church of England as the true Church, and if it did not enforce her tenets in education, it had no right to countenance others."[6] The religious bodies as a whole were united against the State in wanting to keep control in their own hands, but divided among themselves as to its apportionment. In the words of Brougham:

> the Sects were jealous of the Church, and the Church of the Sects; wherefore the people, both Churchmen and Dissenters, must go without instruction.[7]

Those in favour of a national system of education made

[1] *Report of Select Committee on Education*, 1834, IX, Minutes of Evidence, 220–222.
[2] House of Commons, June 20, 1839 (Hansard, third series, xlviii, 586).
[3] House of Commons, July 30, 1833 (Hansard, third series, xx, 173).
[4] Speech on Secular Education—not delivered—1849.
[5] House of Commons, June 14, 1839 (Hansard, third series, xlviii, 265).
[6] House of Commons, June 14, 1839 (Hansard, third series, xlviii, 279).
[7] *Works* (1872), vol. viii, On the Making and Digesting of the Law, p. 233.

several efforts to achieve their end, but each time were opposed and beaten either by the Church of England, the Dissenters, or by both. Roebuck's Bill of 1833, Brougham's of 1837, Graham's of 1843, were broken in the same manner. An attempt was also made to secure through the back door what could not be achieved by frontal attack, and the Factory Acts of 1801 and 1833 had education clauses attached. Inquiries by Government Committees were achieved in 1834, 1835, and 1837.

In 1837 Brougham taunted the House of Lords with the "opprobrium of having done less for the Education of the People than any one of the more civilized nations of the world." In England and Wales about one-tenth of the population went to school, in Prussia one-sixth to one-seventh, in Saxony one-fifth to one-sixth were at school; and, while the means of instruction were altogether inadequate, "the kind of education afforded," said Brougham, "was far more lamentably defective than its amount."[1]

In 1839 there was at last appointed a Government body to organize the distribution of public money for education. It was a small Committee of the Privy Council consisting of four Ministers of the Crown and a secretary. The first secretary was Dr James Phillips Kay, afterwards Sir James Kay-Shuttleworth, who had served on the Poor Law Commission and on the Manchester Board of Health. The Committee of Council was for sixty years the only body with any direct official interest in education. Though created as a financial control, it did, in fact, function almost like a Ministry of Education, being, at least, the only body with any pretence of seeing the education question as a whole. It proceeded by means of Minutes which became operative after they had received the approval of Parliament. Shortly after its creation the Committee of Council made several important proposals which in this way came before the House of Commons. It proposed, in the first place, to increase the Government grant for education to £30,000. Secondly, it proposed certain amendments in the method of allocating the money, which it thought should not necessarily be distributed solely through the two societies, and should not invariably be proportional to the amount of private

[1] *Speeches and Observations of Lord Brougham* . . . *in the House of Lords,* Thursday June 29, 1837, pp. 7–9.

subscriptions already raised. Instead the determining factor in the allocation of public money for education should be the reports of two Inspectors of Schools, whom the Committee proposed to appoint. The third proposal concerned a teachers' training college.

Each of these proposals met with violent opposition. By a majority of five votes a motion in the Commons to disband the Committee was defeated; by a majority of two votes only the educational grant was increased to £30,000. The House agreed to the appointment of inspectors so long as they were instructed not to interfere with religion; but the following year the Church won a complete victory when the appointment and dismissal of inspectors to Church of England schools became dependent upon the approval of the Archbishops. In 1843 Dissent won a corresponding victory and it became the practice to appoint laymen to Dissenting schools. After Roman Catholic schools became eligible for grant in December 1847 it was customary to appoint Roman Catholic inspectors to their schools, so that for the three types of school three groups of inspectors existed.

But the greatest opposition was to the teachers' training school. The need for more and more efficient teachers was urgent. The profession attracted little talent and less culture. It was held in such small esteem that in 1818 £24 a year had been suggested by a Government Committee as adequate salary for a schoolmaster.[1] While public men regarded the schoolmaster in this light, the master himself was apt to consider teaching as a sideline, and follow the example of Mr George Griffith, who was clerk to his parish and occupied the rest of his time as local undertaker, chorus singer, tutor to private pupils, and, finally, as master of St Catherine's Charity School.[2]

The two societies trained students as teachers from the ages of about fourteen to nineteen. The National Society reckoned on a training period of about five months; the British and Foreign regarded three months as a minimum. Mr Henry Dunn, the secretary to the British and Foreign, described to the Select Committee of 1834 the routine which these prospective teachers were expected to follow:

[1] *Third Report of Select Committee on Education*, 1818, IV, 57.
[2] *First Report of Select Committee on Education*, 1816, IV, 112.

They are required to rise every morning at 5 o'clock, and spend an hour before 7 in private study. They have access to a good library. At 7 they are assembled together in a Bible class and questioned as to their knowledge of the Scriptures; from 9 to 12 they are employed as monitors in the school, learning to communicate that which they already know or are supposed to know; from 2 to 5 they are employed in a similar way; and from 5 to 7 they are engaged under a master who instructs them in arithmetic and the elements of geometry, geography and the globes, or in any other branches in which they may be deficient. The remainder of the evening is generally occupied in preparing exercises for the subsequent day. Our object is to keep them incessantly employed from 5 in the morning until 9 or 10 at night.[1]

This was the position when the Committee of Council suggested a scheme for a residential Government training college for teachers. Attached to the training college were two schools for children from three to fourteen years old, one to serve as a model for the teachers in training, the other for their practice. The spirit of religion was to permeate all teaching in the school, but at periods of special religious instruction a chaplain was to instruct children of Church of England parents, while Dissenters' children might have their own ministers. From Anglicans and Dissenters alike arose a fierce protest against this spirit of toleration. The Bishop of London protested publicly against the presence of a Dissenting chaplain in a State school, while Nonconformists feared that the whole scheme was biased in favour of the wealthier and more influential Church of England. In the resultant storm the teachers' training college foundered.

In 1840 Kay-Shuttleworth started the Battersea Training College as a private venture, and six years later the Committee of Council returned to the task with a fresh scheme for training teachers. Children of thirteen and upward—the 'pupil teachers'—were attached for five years for training to a head teacher. They then sat a competitive examination for entrance to a training school, and if successful took a further examination at the end of a one year's, two years', or three years' course, on the result of which they were awarded a certificate.

By the middle of the nineteenth century public expenditure on education was rising. From the £20,000 of 1833 grants had

[1] *Report of the Select Committee on Education*, 1834, IX, Minutes of Evidence, 17.

risen to £100,000 in 1847, and to £125,000 in each of the following three years. In 1850 there were twenty-one Government Inspectors of Schools, comprising laymen, Church of England clergymen, and Roman Catholic priests. There were 4396 schools liable to inspection, and Inspectors' Reports came in regularly to the Committee of Council, and were regularly published, together with the Committee's minutes and other documents of interest, in annual volumes of many closely printed pages. Those who wished could read of the slow development of education for the people. The education of infants was still largely in the hands of 'dames,' and children passed to schools of the next grade ill equipped and "destitute of those preliminary elements of instruction" which the schools appeared to expect. Mining and manufacturing districts and some of the remoter agricultural areas were hostile to infant and public day schools, and only the evening school and the Sunday school had any appeal. Not more than a fraction of the children who should have done so attended works schools or factory schools. In districts where light domestic manufacture was still practised children were withdrawn wholesale in times of good trade, and schools at Hitchin and Leighton Buzzard were practically broken up in this way. In factory districts a boom frequently spelt the doom of the top classes of schools, as the older children went off to take their places in the factories.

It was not, however, merely a question of getting children to stay at school. It was a case also of improving school buildings and raising the standard of teaching so that the time spent at school was profitable. It was not a question only of developing the system begun into a universal system, but of seeing, as one inspector put it, that the instruction given was such as would make the boy a reasoning and an understanding man.[1]

So the mid-century was faced squarely with its problems: more schools and better schools, which meant more money, more trained teachers, more inspectors, better buildings, an end to the squabbles of all sectional interests, and a controlling body with more power than the Committee of Council.

[1] See Minutes of Committee of Council on Education and Reports of H.M.I., 1839–50, *passim*.

SELECT BIBLIOGRAPHY

Report of the Select Committee on the Education of the Lower Orders of the Metropolis, 1816, IV.

Report of the Royal Commission appointed to inquire into the Revenues and Management of Certain Colleges and Schools, and the Studies pursued and Instruction given there (the Clarendon Commission), 1864, XX.

Report of the Royal Commission on the State of the University and Colleges of Oxford, 1852, XXII.

ADAMSON, J. W.: *English Education, 1789–1902* (Cambridge University Press, 1930).

CURTIS, S. J.: *History of Education in Great Britain* (third edition), (University Tutorial Press, 1953).

CURTIS, S. J. AND BOULTWOOD, M. E. A.: *A Short History of Educational Ideas* (Chapters X or XI onward) (University Tutorial Press, 1953).

HAMMOND, J. L. AND B.: *The Age of the Chartists, 1832–1854* (Longmans, 1930).

JONES, M. G.: *The Charity School Movement* (Cambridge University Press, 1938).

CHAPTER XII

SELF-EDUCATION

(a) ADULT EDUCATION

THE Industrial Revolution in its first stages retarded the mental development of the working classes. A previous generation of humble folk had known their Bible, their Bunyan, their Milton, and had enjoyed *Tom Jones* and *Joseph Andrews* as well as a host of penny dreadfuls. In the nineteenth century many agricultural labourers and factory workers were unable to read or write. But it was a stimulating period. Sunday and day schools and adult education again turned the balance, so that there was a vigorous stratum of the working class, mostly self-educated, avid for books, information, and knowledge.

Adult education of the most elementary kind began when illiterate men and women started to attend classes to learn how to read the Bible. Hannah More was conducting such classes in Somerset at the end of the eighteenth century. At this time, too, in Wales men and women were with great enthusiasm attending Sunday schools. The adult poor were so anxious to learn, said the minister of Bala, Merionethshire, that they "flocked to the Sunday Schools in crowds," and "the shop-keepers could not immediately supply them with an adequate number of spectacles."[1] The problem of the Sunday schools was frequently the mixture of children and their parents, of young and old. In 1811, consequently, the Minister of Bala started a separate school for adults. The following year William Smith, a poor man who was doorkeeper at a Methodist chapel in Bristol, had a similar idea, and by energetic can-vassing interested his friends in an adult school for teaching the reading of the Bible. The first two pupils were William Wood, aged sixty-three, and Jane Burrace, aged forty.[2] Soon churches, chapels, and Friends' meeting-houses had their Sunday schools or adult schools attached to them.

Sometimes Sunday-school teachers tried to follow up the instruction of the young who had learnt to read at their hands.

[1] J. W. Hudson, *The History of Adult Education.* p. 3.   [2] *Ibid.*, p. 3.

For this reason Birmingham Sunday-school teachers formed in 1789 a Sunday Society to instruct young men in writing and arithmetic after they had left the Sunday schools. Subjects were extended, books were bought and lent out on payment of a small sum, and thus was established what was probably the first artisans' library in the country. In 1795 the subscription was fixed at a penny a week.

Rather more advanced self-education was being pursued by workmen in the mutual-improvement societies which at the end of the eighteenth century became common among young men whose desire for knowledge outstripped the means at their disposal. They lectured or read to one another, they contrived to buy or borrow the books they needed, meeting in one another's houses, in sheds or barns or any place where they could be quiet. One of these mutual-improvement societies was established in Birmingham before 1790, and in 1796 it amalgamated with the Sunday Society to form the Birmingham Brotherly Society, with an annual subscription of 2s. 6d. for lectures and library, and 3s. 6d. for lectures, library, and the use of a news-room. Declared the Society:

> The objects for improvement shall be Reading, Writing, Arithmetic, Drawing, Geography, Natural and Civil History, and Morals, or in short, whatever may be generally useful to a manufacturer, or as furnishing principles for active benevolence and integrity.[1]

This was a scheme more extensive than teaching the poor to read. It aimed at improving the knowledge and the skill and the morals of the tradesman and artisan class. It was the forerunner of modern adult education.

Meantime in Scotland Dr John Anderson, of Glasgow University, in 1796 bequeathed a sum of money for the founding of an institute to be known as Anderson's University. In 1799 George Birkbeck became its principal, and lectured there on scientific subjects which frequently required some apparatus for their elucidation. Local mechanics were employed to construct this apparatus, and Birkbeck was struck with the interest they displayed:

> I beheld, through every disadvantage of circumstances and appearance, such strong indications of the existence of the unquencheable spirit . . . that the question was forced upon me

[1] *Ibid.*, p. 30.

THE LONDON
MECHANICS'
INSTITUTE

After the engraving
by J. Westle of the
drawing by
L. Hebert

[See p. 257]

By courtesy of the
Governors of Birkbeck
College

This attempt to describe the effects of the Sublime & Wonderful is dedicated to M. G. Lewis Esq. M.P.

TALES of WONDER!

THE EFFECTS OF READING
TALES OF MYSTERY AND
HORROR
James Gillray

DRESS IN THE FORTIES

*Crown Copyright. Victoria and Albert
Museum, South Kensington*

257

—Why are these minds left without the means of obtaining that knowledge which they so ardently desire; and why are the avenues to science barred against them, because they are poor?[1]

Birkbeck therefore gave a free course in elementary science to these mechanics. The result was emphatic. "They came, they listened, and conquered," wrote Birkbeck.[2] He consequently opened to them a full course of lectures on physics and mechanics. Seventy-five workmen came to Birkbeck's first lecture; 200, 300, and 500 came to subsequent ones. In 1804 Birkbeck left Glasgow for London, and Andrew Ure took over his post at Anderson's University, adding a library in 1808. The numbers attending fluctuated. Finally there was a split in 1823, the Glasgow mechanics quarrelling with the management of Anderson's University. The former broke away and formed their own self-governing Glasgow Mechanics' Institute—the first of its kind.

In the same year the London Mechanics' Institute was formed, with Birkbeck as President. It was the fruit of much endeavour by enthusiasts like Hodgskin and Robertson, who were already editing a *Mechanics' Magazine*, but it owed its direct inspiration to the Glasgow Mechanics' Institute. Brougham and his friends were keen supporters; Francis Place collected £1500 in donations. Behind it were the intelligent artisans of London, known always for their ability and keenness to learn, and that enlightened section of the middle class to whom the education of the people meant progress and not revolution.

From the original small building the Institute moved to capacious premises in Southampton Buildings. There were a library, a museum, a workshop. Membership grew from 750 in 1824 to 1500 in 1826, the majority being weekly wage-earners. Women were admitted in 1830; Mechanics' Institutes spread over the whole country. After 1826 there was a decline in the membership of the London Institute, but by the mid-century there were nevertheless 622 Institutes in England and Wales, with a membership of 600,000.

They varied in the range of subjects taught. In the first few years of its life the London Mechanics' Institute held classes and lectures in mathematics, English, French, Latin, in chemistry, geometry, hydrostatics, and astronomy. The

[1] *Ibid.*, p. 33.   [2] *Ibid.*, p. 34.

Manchester Mechanics' Institute professed to be strictly practical. It was formed

> for the purpose of enabling Mechanics and Artisans . . . to . . . possess a more thorough knowledge of their business, acquire a greater degree of skill in the practice of it, and be qualified to make improvements and even new inventions in the Arts which they respectively profess.[1]

Some of the Institutes barred religious and political books and discussions, and there was an emphasis throughout on learning which was unlikely to have any impact on the social system. This, however, was far from the intention of at least two of the founders of the London Institute, for Hodgskin and Robertson had announced in *The Mechanics' Magazine* that the principal object of the Mechanics' Institutes would be to make their students acquainted not only with the facts of chemistry and of mechanical philosophy, but of the science of the creation and distribution of wealth.

The libraries were often—outwardly at least—impressive features of the Mechanics' Institutes. That at Birmingham had 3000 volumes, though many were much smaller. A few had a good selection of books. The London Institute started with £50 to spend on books. The majority had to rely on gifts, which meant that most of the volumes were unwanted books turned out of libraries because they were of no use. Where the ban on religious and political works existed many vital books were automatically excluded. George Dawson described a Mechanics' Institute library to the Committee on Public Libraries of 1849:

> Many of the books are gift books, turned out of people's shelves, and are never used, and old magazines of different kinds, so that, out of 1,000 volumes, perhaps there may be only 400 or 500 useful ones. The rest are, many of them, only annual registers and old religious magazines that are never taken down from the shelves.[2]

Francis Place had described with pleasure how at the opening of the London Mechanics' Institute he saw "from 800 to 900 clean, respectable-looking mechanics* paying most marked attention" to a lecture on chemistry.[3] Yet neither

---

[1] J. W. Hudson, *The History of Adult Education*, p. 56.
[2] *Report of the Select Committee on Public Libraries*, 1849, XVII, 79.
[3] Graham Wallas, *Life of Francis Place*, p. 113.

numbers nor enthusiasm nor the type of student remained unchanged. Numbers declined, recreation succeeded learning, and black-coated clerks replaced the fustian jackets. The workshops attached to the Institutes had the shortest careers. The chemical laboratories remained popular, but on the working models of machinery, the apparatus, the cabinets of minerals of the Institutes of London, Manchester, Leeds, and Glasgow, the dust early began to accumulate.[1]

The fate of lecture courses was sad but understandable. From ambitious courses of ninety lectures on a single branch of physics no more than three were given in each course. The most popular subjects became light literature, criticism, music, drawing. At the quarterly meetings the attorney's clerk out-talked and ultimately outvoted the working mechanic. In large towns, said Samuel Smiles in 1849, Mechanics' Institutes were for the most part not Institutes for the working classes, but for "the middle and respectable classes." Frequently less than half were working-men, and these the highly paid skilled workmen; "generally speaking," said Smiles, "they are not Mechanics' Institutes, and it is a misnomer to designate them as such."[2]

While it was commonly observed that artisans were giving way to clerks in the Mechanics' Institutes, it was also noticed that clerks were leaving the Athenæums, which had been their meeting-places, being succeeded by managers and employers of labour. The inference was that the black-coated workers sought a club where they would be free from the presence of their employers, and therefore invaded the Mechanics' Institutes, driving, in their turn, the mechanics from their original home. This, however, could have been but one of several reasons for the decline of the Mechanics' Institutes from their original purpose. The effort needed to concentrate upon a difficult and long course of lectures after the day's work is done is considerable and is rarely made. It is doubtful whether many lecturers had the gift of simple presentation. Counter-attractions were many, ranging from inactivity or a chat over a glass of beer to trade-union or political discussion. The ban on politics and religious discussion in many Institutes kept away the most active-minded. Fees were sometimes high.

[1] Hudson, *op. cit.*, p. 57.
[2] *Report of the Select Committee on Public Libraries*, 1849, XVII, 124.

Even the 6s. quarterly subscription together with 2s. 6d. entrance fee, to which the London Institute dropped in 1826, was a strain upon many an artisan. Or perhaps the author of *Tom Brown's Schooldays* was near the mark when he prophesied that no educational scheme would secure the allegiance of the men and boys of England unless it offered some equivalent for the games and sports of a previous century,

> something to put in the place of the back-swording and wrestling and racing; something to try the muscles of men's bodies, and the endurance of their hearts, and to make them rejoice in their strength. In all the new-fangled comprehensive plans which I see, this is all left out; and the consequence is that your great Mechanics' Institutes end in intellectual priggism.

But perhaps the chief reason for the decline of the Mechanics' Institutes was a fundamental difference in the conceptions of the founders. The Duke of Sussex took the chair at the opening in 1825 of the new lecture theatre of the London Institute. Subscriptions came from wealthy patrons; educated men gave their services as lecturers without payment. To Birkbeck himself, to Brougham and Place and their friends, all this was highly satisfactory. To Hodgskin and his supporters it detracted from the independence and therefore from the purpose of the Institutes. Many of the mechanics doubtless felt ill at ease under middle-class patronage, and, with the influx of black-coated workers, drifted off to some society composed solely of their fellows. The London Mechanics' Institute was transformed into Birkbeck College for adult students, and is now attached to the University of London. Similarly, most of the other Mechanics' Institutes gave way to the Working Men's Colleges, whose story belongs to the second half of the century.

There were other similar enterprises. In 1838 Lyceums opened in Manchester and other places. Their aim was lower than that of the Mechanics' Institutes, comprising little but elementary instruction and recreation. They were not successful. At Birmingham, however, in 1846 the People's Instruction Society was started with a penny a week subscription. This payment brought access to a reading-room with newspapers and periodicals, to a library of 1000 odd volumes, to weekly lectures, a chess-room, a debating society, and a refreshment-room where moderate prices were charged. For an additional penny a week instruction was given in the three R's, elocution, and singing. An average of sixty members attended the discussion class, and topics ranged widely, including monetary laws, juvenile delinquency, and distress in Ireland. Recreation was found in tea-parties and excursions. The founder of this interesting and successful experiment—which really brought instruction and entertainment to the poor at prices which they could pay—was a stockinger and Methodist named Brooks.

The London Working Men's Association was primarily educational in aim, and in 1841 under Lovett's directorship opened a National Hall in London where there was a library, where lectures and concerts were given, where coffee could be taken with talk and reading. A Sunday school and later a day school were started, where Lovett himself taught and for which he wrote textbooks. Thomas Cooper in 1841, among the Chartists of Leicester, ran an adult Sunday school for men and boys who were at work on weekdays, which extended to two or three meetings on week nights. Milton, Shakespeare, the Bible, geology, phrenology, were on the time-table.

There were Owenite Halls of Science, where dancing and excursions figured prominently. Coffee-houses, providing current periodicals, became a source of refreshment to both mind and body, and the centres of discussion. Itinerant lecturers, often self-educated men, carried their enthusiasm for their subjects all over the country, like the lecturer on astronomy who inspired Cooper and his friend to study the stars. Above all, there were more books, periodicals, and newspapers.

While educational opportunity was increasing the demand for reading matter of all kinds, mechanical developments were making possible more abundant and cheaper literature. Steam-printing, introduced in 1814, lowered costs; improved transport carried books and periodicals to all parts of the country. Whereas at the end of the eighteenth century Burke had estimated the number of readers over the whole country at 80,000, *The Penny Magazine* alone in 1832 claimed to sell 200,000[1] copies an issue, a figure which should be doubled or trebled to estimate the number who actually read it. And, as *The Penny Magazine* commented in 1832, the 200,000 copies not only were effectively distributed to the farthest parts of the

[1] Preface to the first bound volume, 1832-33.

kingdom, but were there delivered for no more than the penny which the Londoner paid. *The Penny Magazine* probably overestimated its own circulation. But 360,000 weekly was the estimate given by the printer of the joint circulation in 1836 of *The Penny Magazine, Chambers's Journal,* and *The Saturday Magazine*.[1]

Technical improvement continued throughout the first half of the century. Whereas in 1830 most country booksellers had a weekly parcel of books from the printer, by the mid-century they were getting as many as four. Public libraries were the most serious lack. There had been circulating libraries in London, Bath, and Southampton since 1740, but these were clearly for the leisured classes. Early in the nineteenth century there were book clubs and libraries for the gentry in most towns at an annual subscription of about £2 2s., while sometimes little shops had their library of general books for humble folk, like the one in the stationer's shop at Gainsborough discovered by Thomas Cooper. Sometimes book clubs were formed where each member subscribed a given sum quarterly for the purchase of books, which were afterwards sold to the highest bidder, the money so obtained being used to buy more books.[2] A few factory-owners provided libraries for their workpeople. Warrington in 1848, Salford in 1849, took advantage of an Act of 1845 relating to museums to create public libraries with the help of a half-penny rate, but not until 1850 did the Public Libraries Act specifically authorize towns of 10,000 inhabitants and over to use the half-penny rate for the purpose of establishing libraries. The Act followed the report in 1849 of the Select Committee on Public Libraries before which witness after witness had testified of the sore need of Britain for public libraries. She was worse served than any comparable country. The British Museum and the Chetham Library in Manchester, two of the few free national libraries, closed at four o'clock, before working-men had finished their day's work.[3] There were, of course, libraries attached to Mechanics' Institutes, to Oddfellows' Lodges, and other Friendly Societies, but for the most part the market and the 'number man' in the early part of the century took the place of the library. At the country fair

[1] J. L. and B. Hammond, *The Age of the Chartists*, p. 314.
[2] James Lackington, *Memoirs*, p. 243.
[3] *Report of the Select Committee on Public Libraries*, 1849, XVII, *passim*.

men and women could be seen arranging for the monthly delivery of the books of their choice, such as *Pamela*, *Joseph Andrews*, *History of Witchcraft*, or *Lives of the Highwaymen*. Around the towns and villages would come the 'number man,' like the one from whom Thomas Cooper bought a dictionary and a geography book in parts, while his mother arranged to take the monthly instalments of the *Dialogues between a Pilgrim, Adam, Noah, and Cleophas*. Though some of the books thus bought were standard works, many were mere trash, and their final cost when purchased by instalments inordinately high. Later, romances of many kinds were supplied in cheap editions, or in parts, through the regular booksellers.

The experience of working-men who educated themselves at the end of the eighteenth century and the beginning of the nineteenth is illuminating. It shows that working-men and their sons were reading what they could get, rather than getting what they wanted. Thomas Frost said:

> . . . the only books I ever saw in my father's house, besides the bible and a few old school books . . . were some odd numbers of Cobbett's *Register* . . . and a few pamphlets amongst which I can remember reports of the trial of the Cato Street conspirators.[1]

William Lovett, who was taught to read by his grandmother in Cornwall at the beginning of the nineteenth century, when there was not a bookshop in the town, was given Watts's *Hymns* as a first reading book, the Bible as a second. Otherwise he found a spelling book, a few religious works, and a few of the current romances. Samuel Bamford, who went to the free grammar school and to the Methodist Sunday school at Middleton at the end of the eighteenth century, was more fortunate than Lovett in having a bookshop in his town. There he was able to test his growing intellectual powers on *The Witches of the Woodlands*, *Fair Rosamond*, and the *Ballad of Chevy Chase*—all evidently products of Gothic taste. Later he came upon Pope's translation of the *Iliad* and a selection of Milton's works, both of which delighted him.

Outstanding among self-educated working-men was Thomas Cooper. His father died when he was small, his mother carried on a dyestuffs business in Gainsborough, on the Trent, in very poor circumstances. Cooper could read at three, and absorbed

---

[1] *Forty Years' Recollections* (1880), pp. 6-7.

every printed page he could get hold of. Again it was the
Bible, followed by penny story-books which his mother bought
him. At the day school he was able to borrow abridged
editions of Goldsmith's histories of England, Greece, and
Rome, *Robinson Crusoe*, and a few other books. Like Bamford
and Lovett, he found the current romances, highwaymen
stories, and *Chevy Chase*. Then, at the old lady's stationer's
shop in Gainsborough, Cooper discovered a circulating library,
and spent enthralled hours with *The Arabian Nights*, odd plays
of Shakespeare and Dryden, Cook's *Voyages*, and the romances
of Walpole and Ann Radcliffe. But the favourite reading of
his early years was *The Pilgrim's Progress*, with which he passed
"hours of wonder and rapture." Milton he read without much
enthusiasm; but when, at thirteen, some Byron fell into his
hands the works "seemed to create almost a new sense"
within him.

Cooper's history is remarkable for the help he got at every
turn from other self-educated working-men. Radical brush-
makers would lend him contemporary political works like
Hone's *Caricatures* and the *News Weekly*; his first master shoemaker lent him Burns's poems, many of which Cooper soon
got by heart, and spoke of Kemble and Young and Mrs
Siddons; a Methodist friend lent him various histories by
Robertson and Neal's *History of the Puritans*; Henry Whillock,
a grocer's apprentice, read with Cooper much of Byron and
Sibly's big work on astrology, their interest in the latter subject
having been aroused by a sixpenny lecture by Moses Holden
in Gainsborough. With John Hough, a draper, Cooper discussed philosophy, metaphysics, and history. Then came the
wonderful discovery of a bequest of a library to the town,
made many years earlier and buried in dust and cobwebs,
which revealed the standard works of philosophy.

It was when he read of Dr Samuel Lee, the self-taught
Professor of Hebrew at Cambridge University, that Thomas
Cooper was fired with the great ambition of his life, and
thereafter set himself to master the classics, modern languages,
religious commentary and philosophy, besides studying history
and literature. He learnt *Paradise Lost* by heart and the whole
of *Hamlet*, besides hundreds of lines of modern poetry, rising at
three or four in the morning, learning while plying his shoemaker's trade in the corner of his mother's kitchen. He read

Cæsar and Virgil in the original as well as a little Greek and Hebrew. Gibbon's *Decline and Fall* was taken in his stride. At his dear old lady's shop a book society for the gentry at £2 2s. a year was started, and the old friend allowed the young lad to take away Scott and Washington Irving, Mrs Shelley and *The London Magazine*. In the early hours of summer mornings he roamed the countryside, book in hand, so that people began to talk about "the remarkable youth that was never seen in the streets and was known to wander miles in the fields and woods, reading." In the winter, when his mother could not afford a fire until seven o'clock, Cooper wrapped himself in her old red cloak, determinedly reading until it was time for breakfast and a fire.[1]

Cooper, Lovett, Bamford, Place, are outstanding; but many men were teaching themselves and each other, too often without purpose or guidance. Lackington tells how at the end of the eighteenth century many a young man came to his bookshop with an inquiring mind but at a complete loss what to ask for and with no friend to advise. Charles Knight, another bookseller, with pity watched such an artisan spending his hardearned sixpence on an out-of-date history or geography, and determined both to meet the demand for books at prices which the poor could pay, and to guide the untutored in the choice of reading material.

Many of Knight's ventures were for the Society for the Diffusion of Useful Knowledge, whose aims are expressed in its cumbersome name, and which numbered many men eminent in politics and learning among its members. Among the most significant publications of Knight for the Useful Knowledge Society were *The Penny Magazine*, a weekly founded in 1832, and *The Penny Cyclopædia*, issued in weekly or bi-weekly sheets from 1833. There were also more expensive volumes, like the *Gallery of Portraits*, a series of illustrated biographies published in monthly numbers at 2s. 6d. each, and the illustrated geographical series, "The Land we live in." *The Penny Cyclopædia* was an excellent publication, with good, sound articles, well though somewhat crudely illustrated. *The Penny Magazine* was of unattractive format, double-columned, with article following article down each column with only a line between.

---

[1] T. Cooper, *The Life of Thomas Cooper*, *passim*.

Its contents aimed at giving each week a little sound knowledge on a variety of subjects—historical, geographical, zoological, literary, and so on; its illustrations were often crude, but sometimes apt and enlightening. Neither the *Cyclopædia* nor the *Magazine* was for the casual reader, though the latter was more popular in its appeal. Both, like all the publications of the Useful Knowledge Society, had to be self-supporting. Who were the probable half-million readers of *The Penny Magazine*? It had no news value, there was no comment on current political events to give it an immediate appeal, and its standard was at least as high, if not higher, than would be considered suitable in a popular publication to-day. The Society's intention was to reach as far as the working-man, who had often only just learned to read, and it believed it did so. While part of the large circulation was accounted for by middle-class buyers, a large part by artisans, whom all accounts of the period agree to have been intelligent and keen to learn, there is no reason to doubt that even humbler folk were eagerly seeking a concise form of knowledge. That a large market existed for this kind of monthly is certain. Besides the publications of the Useful Knowledge Society there were *Chambers's Journal*, a 1½d. weekly, started before *The Penny Magazine* and outlasting it; the popular *Family Herald*, which contained both stories and instruction and had a circulation of 125,000 weekly at the mid-century, and *Eliza Cook's Journal*, a moralizing periodical edited and largely written by the authoress who had professed such love for her *Old Arm Chair*, and which sold 50–60,000 weekly.

Besides educative periodicals, the men of the first half of the nineteenth century still perhaps glanced at the tracts of the religious societies, but in a world of stirring events these were dull matter. Far more exciting were those penny and even halfpenny 'romances' on Ann Radcliffe lines, which, as well as the educational Press, took advantage of cheaper printing and improved transport. One of the most popular editors to exploit this market was Edward Lloyd, who not only founded *Lloyd's News*, but in the early forties started a series of penny weeklies containing nothing but 'romances' of the approved type, some of which he also issued in serial form. G. W. M. Reynolds, the founder of another newspaper, himself wrote and issued more of these tales. Reynolds's

Mysteries of London was perhaps the worst of all the garbage that was served to the ignorant. The extent to which this kind of reading spread is surprising. Mr Imray found the vegetable hawkers of London prodigious readers of "horrible stories, with much of the marvellous and a good deal of the disgusting in them."[1] On the other hand, the growth of coffee-houses, like Potter's Coffee-house in Long Acre, where books and periodicals could be read over a cup of tea or coffee, was a distinct encouragement to a better type of reading.

No general statement can be made of the tastes of British workmen at the mid-century. Some knew Shakespeare by heart and read Milton, Froissart, and *The Anglo-Saxon Chronicle*; some spent hours before and after their work studying by candlelight. Others read not at all, while some turned from weary toil to *Varney the Vampire* or *Ada the Betrayed*. Dickens, of course, was writing, though it is doubtful how far he had penetrated to the working classes by 1850. What is certain is that far more literature of various kinds was being produced than ever before, and that the reading public was compassing the whole range from *The Mysteries of London*, through the more respectable romances of Robin Hood and various highwaymen, to Dickens, political economy and history, and English and foreign classics.

(b) NEWSPAPERS

A considerable section of the working class read also newspapers and political journals, but to obtain a free and cheap Press they had to fight against the laws and taxes which restricted its circulation and raised its price. Whigs, Radicals, working class, and intellectuals were in alliance to this end against various Governments. The reformers included at different times Sheridan, Roebuck, Whitbread, Hume, Bright, Cobden, and Milner Gibson, Leigh Hunt and Henry Hunt, Richard Carlile, Place, Birkbeck, Lovett, Collet, and Hetherington.

The period of the Industrial Revolution was one of intellectual ferment in which the need for news and comment was stimulated as it had not been since the English Civil Wars of the seventeenth century. Steam-printing and improved transport had a double effect on the newspaper, for they not only

---

[1] *Report of the Select Committee on Public Libraries*, 1849, XVII, 208.

cheapened the cost and increased the area of distribution, but brought news more quickly and certainly to editors and journalists.

But while technical factors made possible a larger circulation, political considerations forbade the full utilization of technical skill. The ruling class operated the laws of libel, sedition, and blasphemy to prosecute the writers, printers, publishers, and vendors of unwelcome publications. It also made use of a control inherited from the Stuart monarchy and rigorously enforced the device of the licence. This had originally applied to all publications, but was carried on into the eighteenth and nineteenth centuries as a newspaper control. Every copy of each periodical coming under the category of newspaper had to obtain licence by paying a tax, in return for which the newspaper was duly stamped. The first of these regulations applying particularly to newspapers was contained in the Act of June 1712. In 1789, in the agitation caused by the French Revolution, the newspaper tax was raised by Pitt to 2d. a sheet, and in 1815 it became 4d. In addition there were taxes upon the advertisements which newspapers carried, and a tax on the paper on which they were printed. Consequently, although some of our great modern daily and weekly newspapers came into being under the shadow of the Stamp Acts—*The Morning Post* in 1772, *The Times* in 1785—their price was high, *The Times*, for example, costing 7d. between 1815 and 1836. Thus, not only directly through the licence, but indirectly through their high cost, the number and circulation of newspapers were much smaller than technical developments warranted.

The Government, having started on a campaign of restriction, found itself compelled to make further regulations and to exact fresh penalties for evasion. There were soon in existence a confusing number of Acts regulating the Press. Fines for evading the Stamp Act were as high as £100, sellers of unstamped newspapers could be taken into custody by anyone and condemned by any justice of the peace to the house of correction for three months, while the mere possession of an unstamped newspaper was punishable by a fine of £20. And all the time the laws of blasphemy, sedition, and libel were operated with increasing violence.

In the confusion of Acts and regulations which applied to the Press, two of the notorious Six Acts of 1819 were conspicuous. The Blasphemous and Seditious Libels Act tightened the administration of the laws of blasphemy and sedition. Magistrates and constables were empowered not only to seize all copies of offending publications, but to enter any premises whatsoever, using force if necessary, in their search. Secondly, this Act laid down most severe penalties for second offences, with the object of thus deterring from a first offence. Banishment was the penalty for those wealthy enough to remove themselves from the kingdom; transportation for those unable to get away at their own expense.

The Publications Act extended the tax on newspapers to cover all periodicals which contained news and which were published more frequently than once a month and cost less than 6d., or which were similar in format to a newspaper. This Act at once hit those journals which had previously been treated as periodicals and were so exempt from tax. Under the new regulation the last remnant of the middle- and working-class Press was driven underground. The majority of people had no legal newspaper, daily or weekly. The law deprived them of news and one of their sources of general knowledge. The high-priced papers which existed catered for a wealthy class whose interests their reports and comments for the most part served. So long as the stamp lasts, declared Richard Cobden,

there can be no daily press for the middle or working-class. Who below the rank of a merchant or wholesale dealer can afford to take in a daily paper at fivepence? Clearly it is beyond the reach of the mechanic and the shopkeeper. The result is that the daily press is written for its customers—the aristocracy, the millionaires, and the clubs and news-rooms. The great public cannot have its organs of the daily press, because it cannot afford to pay for them.[1]

The battle for the freedom of the printed word was waged on two fronts. There were prosecutions both for blasphemy and sedition and for evasion of the stamp duty. Each aspect of the fight had its own figureheads, its own obscure enthusiasts and sufferers. The Hunts published a weekly journal, *The Examiner*. It paid the stamp duty, and bore on its title-page, "Paper and print 3½d.; Taxes on Knowledge 3½d.; price 7d." The Hunts were frequently infringing, or near infringing, the laws of libel. It was Leigh Hunt who wrote in *The Examiner* of the Prince

[1] John Morley, *Life of Cobden* (one volume, 1905), p. 885.

Regent as "a man who has just closed half a century without one single claim on the gratitude of his country."

Greatest, perhaps, of all the political pamphleteers of the period was William Cobbett. His weekly *Political Register*, beginning on January 16, 1802, paid the stamp duty. Although it was consequently too expensive for individual workers, many clubbed together to buy it, and it found a circulation among wealthier Radicals and an appreciative audience in public houses and other places where it was read aloud. In the hard-hitting style in which Cobbett excelled it attacked the Government, urged Parliamentary Reform, indulged in violent invective against the Industrial Revolution, the war debt, paper money, the borough mongers, the 'wen' of London. Wanting his writing to reach a wider public, Cobbett started a new *Register*, in the form of a small magazine, not liable to stamp duty and selling therefore at 2*d*. *Twopenny Trash* sold 50,000 copies a week. So great was its influence that the Publications Act of 1819 was directed largely against it, and such periodicals as *Twopenny Trash* were made liable to stamp duty. "And now, Twopenny Trash, dear little twopenny trash," wrote Cobbett, "go thy ways! Thou hast acted thy part in this great drama."[1]

After the Napoleonic wars Radical publications had become more numerous. Wooller started *The Black Dwarf*, a miner's paper, in 1817. John Gast was responsible for *The Gorgon*, the first trade-union newspaper, in 1818. Carlile took over *The Republican*. Richard Carlile was a tinplate worker from Cornwall, born in 1790. He began hawking pamphlets when working half-time, and then borrowed the money with which to turn publisher. He had a passionate belief in the power of print. "My whole and sole object, from first to last, from the time of putting off my leather apron to this day," he wrote in *The Republican*, "has been a Free Press and Free Discussion."[2] Of his integrity the austere John Stuart Mill was convinced. "He is a man of principle," Mill declared, "and a man who will stand to his principles though he should stand alone."[3]

Carlile's first imprisonment was an eighteen weeks' stretch in 1817 for publishing two parodies by William Hone. Hone himself carried his wit with him into the witness-box and was

[1] W. H. Wickwar, *The Struggle for the Freedom of the Press, 1819–1832*, p. 158.
[2] *Ibid.*, p. 75.   [3] *Speech on the Church*, 1829.

acquitted after several long speeches in which he recited un-published parodies. Carlile then developed an intense en-thusiasm for Thomas Paine, whose works he began to publish. In 1819 he was charged with blasphemous libel for publishing *The Age of Reason*, and in his defence read the book in court and attempted to comment on the Bible. He was sentenced to three years' imprisonment with a £1500 fine. But the circula-tion of *The Republican* rose to 15,000, 2000 copies of *The Age of Reason* were sold in six months, and £500 was taken by Jane Carlile in the shop during the week of her husband's trial. Carlile also published the '*Proceedings*' of what he terms his "mock trial," and sold 10,000 copies. Newspapers widely reported the trial, to such good effect that the Tsar restricted the entry into Russia of all newspapers carrying such reports, as likely to inflame his subjects.[1] So much the Government lost and the Reformers gained by the trial and sentence of Carlile. On the other hand, Carlile's shop was forcibly closed and his stock of 70,000 publications, many of them legal, was seized. This was a blow more crippling to Carlile than the fine imposed on him.

Carlile's wife, who gave birth to a child while the bailiffs were in the house, nevertheless opened up shop again. She was prosecuted and found guilty of selling a *Life of Paine*, but released because of a technical flaw in the indictment. A year later she was found guilty and imprisoned for selling *The Republican*. Thereupon Mary Ann, Carlile's sister, took over the nominal publishing of *The Republican*. In 1821 she too was imprisoned, her crime being blasphemous libel.

At the same time prosecutions of all vendors of Carlile's publications were proceeding. They were mostly humble folk, some of them selling from principle, most simply in order to make a living—like the old shoemaker, who supplemented his meagre earnings by selling pamphlets. Sentences on these men and women ranged from four to six weeks' imprisonment.

Meanwhile one of the most remarkable dramas in the history of the Press was being played. Dozens of workmen volunteers came forward to sell Carlile's publications and to keep his shop open while the three Carliles were in prison. Again in February 1822 police entered Carlile's shop in Fleet Street and took everything they could; six weeks later Carlile's shopmen

[1] Wickwar, *op. cit.*, pp. 94-95.

opened up a shop a few doors away; after repeated prosecutions they moved to a shop in the Strand. Sentences were as high as three years' imprisonment. Two of the men went to hard labour for two years, and were put to flax-beating. Mrs Wright, a Nottingham lace-worker with a six-months-old baby, was sentenced to eighteen months' imprisonment. "This game shall never cease," announced Carlile to the Government, "as long as you cease to be ashamed of having such cases before you."[1]

In November 1825, after six years in prison, Carlile was released, his wife and sister being already at liberty. Little more than five years later he was sentenced to a further term of two years for his printed address to the agricultural labourers on their revolt of 1830. Many working-class newspapers appeared during these years, including a second *Twopenny Trash* by Cobbett in 1830; there were many more prosecutions, but none more spectacular than those which centred round Hetherington.

On July 9, 1831, Hetherington started the unstamped *Poor Man's Guardian*. Said the opening number:

> Defiance is our only remedy . . . we will try, step by step, the power of right against might, and we will begin by protecting and upholding this grand bulwark of all our rights, this key to all our liberties, the freedom of the press.

Instead of the red Government stamp the *Guardian* bore a black stamp inscribed "Knowledge is Power," and at the head of each copy were the bold words: "Established contrary to law to try the power of right against might."[2]

Hetherington was twice for terms of six months imprisoned in Clerkenwell Gaol, and once for twelve months in the King's Bench Prison. He faced persecution undismayed, though his printing business was practically ruined by his persistence in publishing an illegal newspaper.

Since most bookshops would not stock an unstamped and therefore illegal paper, it was necessary to find sellers of the *Guardian* willing to risk persecution and imprisonment. Volunteers sold it in clubs and workshops, it was sent about the country in chests of tea, packets of shoes, and other parcels.[3] In the fourth number of the *Guardian* an advertisement appeared

[1] Wickwar, *op. cit.*, p. 223.
[2] H. R. Fox Bourne, *English Newspapers: Chapters on Journalism*, ii, 57.
[3] *Ibid.*, ii, 57.

asking for "some hundreds of poor men" to sell the paper. Hundreds responded. Hundreds were prosecuted and imprisoned, but more took their places. It was the story of Carlile's shopmen over again. Most showed a spirit of determination and defiance in the dock. Joseph Swann, who already had served four and a half years in Chester Castle for selling *The Republican*, was in 1841 brought before the magistrates of Stockport on the charge of selling *The Poor Man's Guardian* and other unstamped papers. Asked why he did so, Swann replied, "I sell them for the good of my countrymen." He was committed to three months' hard labour, but told the Bench that when he came out he would again hawk unstamped newspapers. For nearly four years the fight went on. The fund established for meeting fines proved inadequate, and some 500 persons were imprisoned for selling the *Guardian*.

By 1833, in spite of motions in the House of Commons for the reduction of the various newspaper taxes, the only concession won had been a reduction in the advertisement tax. In the following year Hetherington was again summoned on the charge of publishing *The Poor Man's Guardian*. He defended himself and stated the case of his paper before Lord Lyndhurst and a special jury. To the surprise of every one, the *Guardian* was declared to be a strictly legal publication. The inference behind the verdict was that the paper was too slight a thing to attract the attention of the censors. Lord Lyndhurst probably intended to put a stop to the free advertisement which persecution had given the *Guardian*. To the friends of the 'Unstamped' the judgment was a great step towards Reform.

Three years later a further concession was won which for nineteen years marked the limit of the success of the 'Unstamped.' The Act of 1836 maintained the principle of the taxation of the Press, though its actual burden was reduced from 4*d.* to 1*d.* In return for the penny tax the free postage of newspapers was allowed. This was of great benefit to the high-priced newspaper, which was able to reduce its price from 7*d.* to 4*d.* or 5*d.* The blessing, however, was a one-sided one, for the law against unstamped publications was by the same Act tightened. The unstamped Press had, in spite of the Stamp Acts, achieved a considerable circulation, one illegal paper having a print of 40,000 copies a week. If a more rigorous prosecution of the law now forced all these publications to pay even a penny tax their price would rise and their working-class readers would no longer be able to afford them. Unstamped papers were therefore faced with the alternatives of continuing to try evasion in the face of stiffer resistance, or of paying the tax and losing most of their customers.

The champions of the 'Unstamped' remained determined to secure a complete repeal of the newspaper tax, though they showed little activity for some years. A campaign against a penny tax, which receives a return in free postage, is more difficult to wage than one against a 4d. tax without free postage.

Meantime by 1839 *The Northern Star*, the Chartist newspaper, selling at 4½d., had achieved the astonishing circulation of nearly 24,000, and new newspapers were coming into being, among them the *Daily News*, founded in 1846 under Charles Dickens's editorship and priced at 5d. Later under Cadbury's proprietorship, it was to become a leading Liberal newspaper.

With the decline of Chartism after 1848 the abolition of the newspaper stamp came once more to the fore. The last meeting of the Chartist Conference in 1849 passed a unanimous resolution for the abolition of the taxes on knowledge, and Chartists were among those who in 1849 formed the Newspaper Stamp Abolition Committee. "Give, then," said the Chartists, "to the farmer his untaxed beer, let the shopkeeper enjoy his cheap tea, and the householder open his windows to the air and light of heaven; give us, Chartists, untaxed knowledge."[1] Not only was the newspaper stamp attacked, but also the duties on paper and advertisements. The last steps in reform were carried by the Association for the Repeal of the Taxes on Knowledge formed by Cobden, Bright, Milner Gibson, Francis Place, Collet, and many other well-known Radicals of the working and middle classes. Pamphlets, meetings, petitions, deputations to Members of Parliament, a Committee of Inquiry, were the orthodox means by which repeal was finally carried. In 1853 the advertisement duty was repealed. In 1855 the compulsory newspaper stamp was at last abolished; coupled with the repeal were special postage rates for printed papers to compensate for the loss of free postage to those papers which had paid the stamp. Finally the paper duty went in 1861. *The Daily Telegraph* in 1855 became the first penny newspaper;

---

[1] C. D. Collet, *History of the Taxes on Knowledge*, p. 45.

The Times and *The Daily News* came down to 3*d*. in 1861. The campaign against the "taxes on knowledge" had been long; it brought much suffering to ordinary men and women; its end was unspectacular. But the principle established was fundamental.

SELECT BIBLIOGRAPHY

Report of the Select Committee on Public Libraries, 1849, XVII.
BOURNE, H. R. FOX: *English Newspapers: Chapters on Journalism* (Chatto, 1887).
COLLET, C. D.: *History of the Taxes on Knowledge* (Watts, Thinker's Library, 1933).
COOPER, T.: *The Life of Thomas Cooper* (Hodder, 1872–80).
DOBBS, A. E.: *Education and Social Movements, 1700–1850* (Longmans, 1919).
HUDSON, J. W.: *The History of Adult Education* (Longmans, 1851).
KNIGHT, C.: *Passages of a Working Life during Half a Century*, 2 vols. (Bradbury, 1864–65).
WICKWAR, W. H.: *The Struggle for the Freedom of the Press, 1819–1832* (Allen and Unwin, 1928).

CHAPTER XIII

THE AGE OF THE MIDDLE CLASSES

A RECURRING theme in the social and economic history of Britain between 1760 and 1850 concerns the middle class—its rise to power, its political and economic struggles. As we cross the mid-century, passing the period of endeavour to the period of achievement, let us look at the beliefs, tastes, and fashions of the age in which the middle class had become paramount.

Victoria had come to the throne in 1837, and in 1840 had married a German prince—Albert of Saxe-Coburg—thereafter setting the example of rigid family life which was one of the characteristics of the age. She married in the year in which John Frost, the Chartist, was transported for life. The Corn Law issue raged during the first years of her married life. There was no Public Health Act; children and women were working unrestricted in the mines and with a minimum of control in the factories. Her Government could spend less in a year on education than on her horses' stables. Cholera still reared its head in her capital city. But, for all this, British goods were becoming supreme the world over, and the solid phalanx of the British ruling class on which her Government rested after the Reform Act would be, after the repeal of the Corn Laws and the defeat of Chartism, a more secure basis than any other in the world.

The middle-class merchants and manufacturers who had been assimilated by the aristocracy, or had themselves done the digesting, had their own beliefs, which gave rise to much discussion and writing, especially in the field of political economy and political philosophy; they had their own tastes, which brought about a change in houses and furniture; even in art and literature there were developments which coincided with the rise to power of the middle class.

(a) POLITICAL ECONOMY AND PHILOSOPHY

Among the earliest economists to identify himself with the new industry was Adam Smith, who gave his chief work the significant title: *An Inquiry into the Nature and Causes of the Wealth of Nations*. Adam Smith explained and justified *laissez-faire* and all that the middle-class industrialists stood for. Individual prosperity and national, he taught, are indissolubly linked, so that business-men, pursuing their own advantage, inevitably advance the general prosperity. So certain in its operation is the law of the reaction of individual upon general economic good that it acts like an "invisible hand," to promote an end not necessarily envisaged by the agent. "Every individual," said Adam Smith,

> is continually exerting himself to find out the most advantageous employment for whatever capital he can command. It is his own advantage, indeed, and not that of the society, which he has in view. But the study of his own advantage naturally, or rather necessarily leads him to prefer that employment which is most advantage to the society.

After Adam Smith came Malthus. His observations of increasing population and increasing poverty led him to enunciate the theory that, whereas population increases in geometric ratio, the means of subsistence increase only in arithmetic ratio. The population is therefore constantly outstripping its means of support, and is kept in check only by such 'natural' means as disease and war and by abstention from large families. This, of course, did not apply to the rich, who had no need to practise the economy of small families. Hence the sternness to the poor, who, it was said, could improve their condition by keeping down their birth-rate; hence the New Poor Law. The teaching of Malthus went very deep. The greater economists embodied it in their work, it was taken up by most of the thinking middle class, the powerful intellectual group of Utilitarians believed it, the Radicals and the Whigs supported it. Left to oppose it were the Tories, who did so rather lamely; some who said with little conviction, after a glance at the poverty of the masses, that with every mouth God sends a pair of hands; some, though not all, of the working class themselves; and notably Cobbett, who hated "Parson Malthus" with one of his major hates.

Following hard on Malthus was David Ricardo, the high priest of the manufacturers. Building on Malthus, he pointed out that, as the population grew, poorer land had to be taken into cultivation to supply its increasing needs. The cost of living therefore rose. But the use of more factors of production—labour and capital—tended to bring down their price per unit, and wages and profits therefore rose not at all or disproportionately. Rent alone, which was comparatively fixed, would remain unchanged. While, therefore, the worker never rose above subsistence level and profits fell, the landowning class drew a rent whose total increased as more land came into cultivation. Here was the class weapon *par excellence*, and the Ricardian theory of rent became the accepted economic doctrine of the middle classes. Like the Malthusian doctrine, it was widely believed, and opposition to it was lame. Adam Smith, Malthus, and Ricardo were the economic Paladins of *bourgeois* Britain. For those not ready to essay the often ponderous and sometimes obscure work of the masters themselves there was a little book published by Jane Marcet in 1816, in which their doctrines were analysed in the form of *Conversations on Political Economy*.

The Industrial Revolution produced also its own philosophy—called, after its leader, Benthamism and, after its leading principle, Utilitarianism.

In politics the Utilitarians formed a connecting link between Whig and Radical, with advocates in both these parties as well as among working-class groups. Their influence was felt far outside parties, however, and there is scarcely a movement for reform in the nineteenth century that does not owe something to the influence of the Benthamites. They contributed the philosophy to the great movement for the freeing of trade which began in the thirties; their teaching helped to achieve freedom of movement and freedom of contract and some measure of freedom of combination. The New Poor Law of 1834 was Utilitarian in both conception and execution. The education movement was actively helped by Bentham and his friends; public-health reform was undertaken by the Benthamite Edwin Chadwick; the passage of the first Reform Bill owed much to Jeremy Bentham's teaching and influence. Law reform was one of his chief passions, and to prison reform he contributed among other things the idea of the panopticon, or circular prison-house, which he later advocated as a model building for schools.

Behind this practical work was a distinct ethical code which said that the Greatest Happiness of the Greatest Number was the end to which all human conduct should be directed. In enunciating his ethic Bentham started from the premise that men desire happiness or pleasure and avoid pain. Pleasure and pain are thus the determinants of behaviour. But Bentham also, to use his own words, fastened the standards of right and wrong to their throne, so that the attainment of pleasure and avoidance of pain became moral acts. Pleasure and pain thus became both the determinants and the criteria of conduct. To resolve the seeming paradox that men would then always do what was right Bentham pointed out that desires were not always harmonious and that men must decide between alternative courses of action. The principle that recognizes the subjection of mankind to pleasure and pain Bentham called the Principle of Utility, and claimed that by it every action should be judged. It should be applied, Bentham emphasized, not only to every action of every individual, but to every measure of government. Yet there was a gap to be crossed before theory could thus be translated into practice: egoistic hedonism must become social hedonism. The Utilitarians attempted to bridge the gap in several ways, of which two were important. The first of these depended upon Adam Smith's "invisible hand," thus linking economic theory and Utilitarianism. The free working of the wills of many individuals towards their own happiness, it was said, would naturally produce a general happiness. Secondly, the Utilitarians claimed that Government legislation could canalize the individual's desire for happiness into channels which would effect the greatest happiness of the greatest number. Thus were the Benthamites faced with the necessity of influencing legislation; thus law reform and political reform became important to them; thus they came to insist on the absolute supremacy of the legislature. Since, according to their theory, "everybody is to count for one and nobody for more than one," they were led to favour a democracy, and most Utilitarians advocated universal suffrage. But a democracy must know what it is talking about, and so the Utilitarians became educational reformers.

Although they believed that the right kind of legislation could increase the sum of happiness, the Benthamites never overemphasized the power of the State. On the contrary, they believed that the State should interfere with private interests as little as possible, and *laissez-faire* became with them a powerful doctrine.

Upon the Utility principle the Benthamites had thus erected two canons of government. One asserted the power of the State to advance the general happiness, the other deplored State action as an interference with private rights. Formally the two beliefs could be reconciled. In fact, the emphasis of the Utilitarian teaching was on *laissez-faire*. In practice the Benthamites supported State action in public-health and Poor Law legislation, gave only partial support to factory legislation, and claimed complete freedom in trade and commerce. In each instance, they claimed, it was the touchstone of the Utility principle which determined their action.

Whether or not their beliefs were sound philosophically or whether or not practice always reflected principle, the fact remains that the Benthamites in general spoke and acted for their age. The era of prosperity into which Britain turned at the end of the forties made it appear that the mid-Victorians had, in fact, discovered the formula for giving the greatest happiness to the greatest number.

As well as its exponents the New Order produced its critics. These fall, broadly, into two groups—those who condemned industrialization and sought to restore Britain's 'original state' of agrarian happiness, and those who accepted the Industrial Revolution, but condemned the particular form which industrialism in Britain had assumed. Among the first group were Godwin, Paine, Cobbett, Spence, and Charles Hall. The second group contained co-operators like Robert Owen.

It is noteworthy that in the early part of the nineteenth century the anti-industrialists were the more vocal. The importance of their doctrine, though reactionary in the sense of being contrary to the march of progress, is measured by the support it won. It was taken up by the starving hand-loom weavers, by workers aching under the discipline of factory slavery, by dispossessed landholders driven off the land by Enclosure. It appeared in the social unrest of the post-war years, it ran right through Chartism, and, indeed, through all branches of social reform except the Co-operative. The Co-operative writers sought reform within the framework of an industrial, though not a capitalist, society; their works find a place in the chapter on Co-operation. Here, therefore, only the representative agrarian or non-industrial writers are mentioned.

Thomas Spence, whose followers were prominent in the disturbances of 1816–20, advocated a democratic republic composed of farmers. He proposed that all land should belong to the parishes, who would then lease it to farmers at a reasonable rent. This rent would be used to defray all the expenses of government, no other tax being necessary. This was the famous 'single tax' which was the basic doctrine of the Spenceans.

Thomas Paine, though best remembered by *The Rights of Man*, also wrote *Agrarian Justice*, in which he urged a 10 per cent. death duty on all estates, from the proceeds of which each propertyless person who reached the age of twenty-one was to be paid £15 in compensation for his lost heritage, and £10 as an annual old-age pension for life.

Spence and Paine based their cases on the theory of natural law or natural rights, which asserted that originally, as his natural heritage, every man had a share in the land, but that his birthright had been stolen from him. Charles Hall was more the deductive critic. He pointed out that the power of wealth made freedom of contract largely illusory. He showed how useless 'wealth' is without labour: "Wealth, without labour to fertilise it, represents a harmless heap of goods, giving no power to its possessor." He maintained that the capitalist system could not be mended, and must therefore be abolished, and demanded nationalization of the land and its settlement by small farmers. In Hall's work there is a deep revolutionary feeling allied to the expression of class revolt, which places him closer to the later social rebels than to his contemporaries.

Spence's single tax, Paine's death-duty, Hall's nationalization of the land—all these were concrete suggestions for reform. Yet the man whose influence was widest was William Cobbett, who offered no plan, but owed his popularity to his stinging pen and his trenchant criticism. He was an ardent agrarian reformer, a burning opponent of industrialism, a keen social critic, and a writer of some of the best prose in the English language. As such his name appears again and again in the pages of this book.

While Cobbett was the man of the masses, among a smaller group William Godwin was the leader. Godwin was an anarchist who ranks neither as agrarian reformer nor as industrial reformer. He opposed all forms of government and disclaimed the use of force, believing that the power of reason could replace both. In modern society the chief evil, besides government, was inequality of private property. If reason prevailed government could be abolished and equality "established by persuasion and the reasoned consent of all." Godwin's influence among the intellectuals was very great; even Shelley for long sat at his feet. Yet the fact that his book, *Political Justice*, cost three guineas indicates an influence that was deep rather than wide.

(b) ART AND LITERATURE

Towards the middle of the eighteenth century, while industrial change was quickening, conflicting elements appeared in the stream of artistic development. It was as though industrialism not only broke up the routine of farm life and cottage industry, but disrupted the comparative calm of the artistic world. The classical architecture of the early eighteenth century became more self-conscious and pompous. Then a Chinese influence appeared, brought to England by Sir William Chambers, who published a book on Chinese buildings in 1753 and who designed the Chinese pagoda at Kew. Chinese wallpapers, carpets, and decoration became popular. Goldsmith published a book of essays purporting to have been written by a Chinese visitor to England.

At the same time Gothic was rediscovered and became far stronger than the Chinese or any other influence both in building and in literature. It turned for its inspiration, not to the ancient world, but to the Middle Ages. In architecture Gothic art attempted to recapture the nobility of the medieval cathedrals. In literature it took the form of historical novels, an interest in ballads and old English forms of speech and rhyme, and a love of the romantic. On the stage Garrick revived Shakespeare, which played to enthusiastic audiences.

In both architecture and literature the name of Horace Walpole is associated with Gothic. At Strawberry Hill, Twickenham, he built a great pseudo-Gothic house. He wrote the *Castle of Otranto* in 1764, the first of the series of sham historical novels which led the way for Jane Porter and Ann Radcliffe, whose stock-in-trade comprised ruined castles, sinister monks, heroic deeds, and beauty and innocence in mute distress; their popularity was tremendous at the turn of the century. These women were imitated by hosts of smaller writers whose stories filled the sixpenny novelettes and penny magazines which were soon thick upon the market, and which undoubtedly owed their popularity to that awful pleasure in the supernatural common to all half-literate people. These truly dreadful publications must be read to be believed: they at least make credible the picture of the servant girl, hair standing on end, eyes glued to the magazine, fingers convulsively clutching its pages, oblivious to the calls of the mistress. We should like to know who else read these horrific stories. The prices of a penny and sixpence, and even a halfpenny, suggest humble folk, and Charles Knight, the bookseller, confirms this out of his own experience. The books of Ann Radcliffe not only were more expensive, catering for a middle-class audience, but had in them something more elaborate. There was a long and intricate plot, an attempt at characterization, much description of scenery, of which a great deal was overdone both in detail and cumulative effect, but which nevertheless gave the impression that here was something the writer cared about. Ann Radcliffe's handling of these 'Gothic' themes was undoubtedly more skilled than Walpole's. There is even a contemporary review which nicely balances the merits of Mrs Radcliffe and Sir Walter Scott. The Waverley novels, indeed, are essentially of the same stock, owing their popularity to the same interest in the Middle Ages and to the receptivity of audiences prepared by Ann Radcliffe. Scott himself was an admirer of Mrs Radcliffe, and wrote in 1824 a Prefatory Memoir to the Collected Works of this "mighty enchantress," as he called her. The very name The Mysteries of Udolpho, he said, was fascinating, and the public, who rushed upon it with all the eagerness of curiosity, rose from it with unsated appetite. When a family was numerous the volumes flew, and were sometimes torn, from hand to hand, and the complaints of those whose studies were interrupted were a general tribute to the genius of the writer.

Scott, however, raised the historical novel to a plane where fiction was played against a background of something approaching historical reality, and became the most popular novelist of his day.

In poetry young Thomas Chatterton in 1764 had forged some ballads which he tried to tell the world were genuine medieval work, and committed suicide at the age of eighteen when he was not believed. In 1765 Bishop Percy published the *Reliques*, genuinely medieval though considerably edited by the Bishop. Gray translated from the Norse, the Gaelic aroused interest and drew men back to observe nature, and so literature became "emancipated . . . from the chatter of the coffee-house and the tavern," and the way was open for Wordsworth and Coleridge, Byron, Keats and Shelley, and the great names of the early nineteenth century.

In painting Gainsborough was the first real landscape painter and the first to dispense with the sham nymphs of the classical school. Morland painted horses and hounds and stables against their natural background. The historical-novel school meanwhile was paralleled by pictures of ruins by moonlight and medieval castles with appropriate scenery.

In other directions the craze for nature and the Middle Ages led to strange results. Out of doors formal gardens were destroyed to make way for 'picturesque' and carefully planned wildness, with a manufactured 'ruin' to add the touch of 'romance.' One landscape gardener used to plant a dead tree here and there for greater 'naturalness.' The craze reached its apogee in the building of a ruined abbey at Fonthill in 1795. In place of 'elegant' and 'classical' the favourite adjectives of praise were 'romantic' and 'picturesque.'

There were reactions against Gothic. Gothic was not the architecture associated with the Regency (1811–20). Many of the houses in Brighton, which became a fashionable resort at this time, are in the classical tradition, and the Pavilion, though a decided departure from the classical, is Chinese or Indian in its inspiration, and not English medieval.

Early in the nineteenth century, however, the Gothic cult received a fresh impetus. Among architects Augustus Welby Pugin became a fervent disciple of Gothic, and published his book *Contrasts* in 1836 to show how far more magnificent were medieval buildings than their modern counterparts. It was partly Pugin's influence which gave to the Houses of Parliament, begun by Barry in 1840, their Gothic appearance. A further set of *Contrasts* would be interesting to show nineteenth-century mock Gothic against its medieval prototype.

By the mid-nineteenth century Gothic was rampant. It was a reaction against the rules of classicism, against simple buildings, planned gardens, unemotional writing. At worst it was a sham, producing mock abbeys, false history, a manufactured antiquity, a planned wilderness. It substituted one kind of artificiality for another. At best—and this was particularly apparent in literature—it broke away from the classical form, leaving art free to contact nature, to develop new forms, and to become the unashamed vehicle of all human emotions.

The sham histories of Ann Radcliffe are of interest to the social historian in marking a phase of popular taste. Other novelists there were who also wrote with a complete indifference to public affairs, yet frequently with the merit of describing in detail a life typical of some section of the community. If the lives of the Emmas and Mr Knightleys of Jane Austen's novels moved equally calmly whether France beheaded a king or a new civilization developed in the North of England, this was because, in fact, public affairs touched but lightly the circle of well-to-do county families in which Miss Austen moved.

Some writers were directly concerned with the social developments of their time. Few outside the ranks of the political economists and philosophers were anything but critical. Oliver Goldsmith, moved by the destruction of his native village, gave in the *Deserted Village* an account of what Enclosure signified. George Crabbe described the mixed workhouse before the Act of 1834; William Blake sang of the chimney sweep. The French Revolutionary doctrine of liberty, equality, fraternity, evoked a wide response. Coleridge proposed the establishment of a Communist colony, which he and Southey christened Pantisocracy. Both, however, abandoned their youthful ideals, and became instead the supporters of a democratic conservatism. William Hazlitt alone remained true to the French Revolution, even so far as remaining the equally ardent admirer of Napoleon, whom he loved "for putting down the rabble of Kings."

For scathing condemnation there is no poem in the language to surpass *The Age of Bronze*, Byron's immortal attack on the stay-at-home landowning profiteers who made money out of the high price of corn during the Napoleonic wars. Maria Edgeworth, at a time when rack-renting and Enclosure were proceeding apace, gave in *Castle Rackrent* the story of four generations of Irish squires who lived up to their name of Rackrent, and Charles Kingsley's *Yeast* presented a never-to-be-forgotten study of the agricultural labourer.

Factory life also began to be a theme of the novelists. Mrs Gaskell published *Mary Barton*, a moving story of life in the squalid industrial North. In Charlotte Brontë's *Shirley* the hero is a factory-owner, and one of the themes of her tale his attempt to introduce new machinery into his mill in spite of the opposition of his employees. The climax comes with the attack on the mill by people to whom machines meant unemployment, and their repulse by the owner. It is the story, from a different angle, of the attack on Cartwright's mill. Elizabeth Barrett Browning was much moved by the plight of the child labourers, and her poem *The Cry of the Children* should be compared with Andrew Ure's *Philosophy of Manufactures*. Ure described the pleasure it gave him to see "the lively elves" at work. Mrs Browning saw otherwise:

> They look up with their pale and sunken faces,
>   And their looks are sad to see,
> For the man's hoary anguish draws and presses
>   Down the cheeks of infancy.

Not all the misery of wretched, underpaid work was shut up in the factory. Kingsley's story of *Alton Locke* tells of the pestilential garrets in which London tailors plied their trade. Thomas Hood throws a brief light on the weary woman who made shirts in her home:

> With fingers weary and worn,
>   With eyelids heavy and red,
> A woman sat, in unwomanly rags,
>   Plying her needle and thread—
> Stitch! stitch! stitch!
>   In poverty, hunger, and dirt,
> And still with a voice of dolorous pitch
>   She sang the "Song of the Shirt!"

But while other writers might describe and criticize social conditions, the life and works of Percy Bysshe Shelley were one passionate revolt against a civilization which he hated. He was both philosopher and poet, making Godwin his philosophical master, calling himself anarchist and atheist, and preaching the power of reason and the doctrines of Ultimate perfectibility and of Communism. Some of Shelley's earlier works are in part poetical renderings of Godwin's book *Political Justice*. In *Queen Mab*, for example, Shelley speaks of the time

> when Reason's voice
> Loud as the voice of Nature, shall have waked
> The Nations.

His passion for justice and his intolerance of the despotic power of capitalism grew into a fine fury of indignation against tyranny of every kind. His was then the doctrine of revolt. "To suffer, to give, to love, but above all, to defy—that was for Shelley the whole duty of man."[1] How he hated the idle aristocracy!

> Those gilded flies
> That, basking in the sunshine of a court,
> Fatten on its corruption!

He saw, on the other hand, the degradation of poverty, making the life of the poor man one of "misery, and fear, and care." Yet, despite his sensitiveness to the world's wrongs, Shelley refused to believe that the triumph of Evil could be anything but temporary. In the *Revolt of Islam* Cythna, one of the children of Justice and Truth, converts a section of the workers to revolt. She depicts the misery of their position, but tells them

> This need not be; ye might arise and will
> That gold should lose its power and thrones their glory.

The same idea is brought out forcibly in *The Mask of Anarchy*, written after the "Peterloo" Massacre of 1819:

> Men of England, heirs of Glory,
> Heroes of unwritten story,
> Nurslings of one mighty Mother,
> Hopes of her, and one another;
>
> Rise like Lions after slumber
> In unvanquishable number,
> Shake your chains to earth like dew
> Which in sleep had fallen on you—
> Ye are many—they are few.

When they rose in their power the workers would will Freedom, which to Shelley is the substance of life. "What art thou Freedom?"

> For the labourer thou art bread,
> And a comely table spread.
>
> Thou art clothes, and fire, and food
> For the trampled multitude.

[1] H. N. Brailsford, *Shelley, Godwin and their Circle.*

In his *Song* addressed *To the Men of England* Shelley asked them:

> Men of England, wherefore plough
> For the lords who lay ye low?
> Wherefore weave with toil and care
> The rich robes your tyrants wear?

His advice?

> Sow seed,—but let no tyrant reap;
> Find wealth,—let no imposter heap;
> Weave robes,—let not the idle wear;
> Forge arms,—in your defence to bear.

A practical incitement to revolt.

By the middle of the century such giants among the novelists as Dickens and Thackeray were writing, both reflecting a section of life which they knew—Dickens the working world of the lower middle class and working class, Thackeray the world of snobbery and fashion. In *Sybil* Disraeli wrote of the "two nations" of rich and poor. Carlyle thundered his fulminations in many essays. "What means this bitter discontent of the Working Classes?" "Is the condition of the English working people wrong; so wrong that rational working men cannot, will not, and even should not rest quiet under it?" he asked in *Chartism*. "Legislative interference, and interferences not a few are indispensable," he wrote in *Past and Present*,

> a lawless anarchy of supply-and-demand . . . cannot longer be left. . . . There are already Factory Inspectors. . . . Perhaps there might be Mine-Inspectors too: might there not be Furrowfield Inspectors withal, and ascertain for us how on seven and sixpence a week a human family does live!

(c) THE GREAT EXHIBITION

The material prosperity of the mid-nineteenth century was demonstrated by the Great Exhibition of 1851. In a great glass building erected in Hyde Park—the "Crystal Palace"—which was later removed to South London, over 7000 British exhibitors took over 200,000 superficial feet of space to demonstrate their products. So sure were they of their position that the Exhibition was open to all lands, and as many foreigners, occupying as much space, brought their goods for display. The official catalogue of the Exhibition comprised four large volumes. Two hundred and forty-five designs were submitted

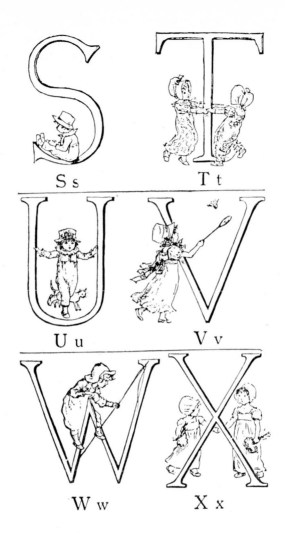

S s T t

U u V v

W w X x

A Page of Letters by Kate Greenaway, from
W. F. Mavor's "The English Spelling-book" (1885)
[See p. 529]
By courtesy of Frederick Warne and Co., Ltd.

One of Pugin's Contrasts:
Towns

Top: A Town in 1440
Bottom: The Same Town in 1840

[*See p.* 284]

From "Contrasts," by A. Welby Pugin

for the building itself, and finally Paxton's Crystal Palace was erected for £80,000. The result was a large and striking building in the heart of London, 1848 feet long, 68 feet high, without counting the semicircular vault of glass over the top. Inside, thousands of exhibits were divided into thirty classes and classified under four main heads: raw materials, machinery, manufactures, fine arts. Not only professionals but private people lent to the Exhibition, from the Queen downward. The conception of the Exhibition had, indeed, been the Prince Consort's, his was the choice of site, and he sat as President of the Royal Commission which planned the Great Exhibition of 1851. Besides the exhibits there were refreshment-rooms, but alcohol was barred. After the first few days the entrance fee was reduced to 1s., and the railway companies co-operated by reducing fares to bring people from all over the country to see the sights. Queen Victoria was delighted. Disraeli called it

that enchanted pile which the sagacious taste and the prescient philanthropy of an accomplished and enlightened Prince have raised for the glory of England and the delight of two hemispheres.

The year 1851 was certainly no bad peak from which to look back with complacency over the period of half a century. Chartism appeared to have flickered out, all-round prosperity had virtually solved the problem of labour unrest. The stream of great inventions was continuing to feed industrial life. Technical journals and technical societies were spreading new scientific knowledge. Medicine was developing, particularly with the use of chloroform in the forties, and the general practitioner was winning a place of respect and responsibility in the general life of the community.

In 1829 the Metropolitan Police Act had given a police force to London, with a Commissioner and headquarters at Scotland Yard, and the local authorities were following suit. A minor revolution had occurred in 1840 when the penny post was introduced by Rowland Hill. Families and friends could communicate easily and cheaply, business could be conducted quickly without expense. All the amenities of life were increasing—and not for the rich only. There were more materials of all kinds, for building, furnishing, dressmaking. The first match had been used in 1827. Railway travel was getting cheaper, making an annual holiday by the sea a possibility for many people. The growing Continental holiday traffic induced John Murray to start publishing his "Guide Books" in 1836.

Travel in the main thoroughfares of the chief towns was easier. Main streets were paved and better cleaned, and at night the small tin bowls of bad quality whale-oil, with cotton twist for wick, suspended from horizontal rods or stuck on poles set at long intervals apart, were replaced by gas-lighting, and petroleum-lighting was just coming into use. Street-lighting, and the London policeman who replaced the night watchman, did much to render London safe for the night traveller. More coaches and carriages, the omnibus, several bridges over the Thames, made him more mobile.

It was these general amenities as well as the great solid achievements of increased production and growing wealth which the Great Exhibition represented. It also revealed the taste of mid-Victorian Britain. In countless everyday articles of furniture there is the same lack of simplicity, the same desire for over-ornamentation. The craze for papier mâché is shown in several articles, for use as well as for ornamentation. This fashion was, indeed, one of the few frivolities which the early Victorian allowed himself in his domestic affairs. For the most part his taste was for solidity, heaviness, and weighty orna-mentation. In furniture, upholstery, plate, china, jewellery, he sought solid comfort but not elegance. His taste fitted well with Gothic architecture and long historical novels. The Victorian age drew attention not so much to its wealth, as it might have done by the beauty or extravagance of its way of life, but to its security, which it did by the solid worth of its heavily carved furniture, its heavily ornamented plate, its heavy Gothic buildings.

Its amusements were similarly more sober than those of the previous century. It had its dinner parties, its balls; its men rode to hounds and met at clubs, but there was a serious under-current not detected, say, in the time of the Regency. The working classes similarly were losing something of the spon-taneity and gaiety of the time when football was played up and down the Strand, when men and girls danced on the green at the May fair, and families made excursions in spring to see the hawthorn flowering along the Tottenham Court Road, and drank tea and beer with buns at the village of Kentish Town or at Paddington or Marylebone.

All classes were at the same time losing some of the brutality of an earlier age. Bear-baiting, bull-baiting, and cock-fighting were almost dead. William Lovett, when he came up to London at the end of the eighteenth century, saw "the working classes of London flocking out into the fields on a Sunday morning, or during a holiday, in their dirt and dishabille, deciding their contests and challenges by pugilistic combats. It was no uncommon thing," he said, "on taking a Sunday morning's walk, to see about twenty of such fights."[1] In 1850 the artisan was much more likely to take his family to an exhibition. It was one of his complaints that the British Museum and other galleries were shut on Sundays and that the fees for admission to Westminster Abbey and St Paul's Cathedral were too high.

Looking at the long line of exhibits at the Great Exhibition, the more thoughtful visitor might congratulate the country on the care it took of the workpeople who made them—on its Factory and Mines Acts, its Public Health Act, its provision for education. The humanitarian spirit which had helped all these reforms, and which was typified in Lord Shaftesbury, was indeed one of the most remarkable developments of an age whose general characteristic was laissez-faire-and-devil-take-the-hindmost, and an achievement for which pride was more justifiable than for most others.

But a visitor who looked a little deeper would see that reform had only scratched the surface, that beneath the façade of peace and plenty there still existed squalor and ignorance, poverty and degradation, sweat-shops and slums—that the industrial achievement of the first half of the nineteenth century had far outdistanced its humanitarianism and its sense of social justice.

Meanwhile, with minds perhaps deadened by material prosperity to the need for further social change, the middle classes and the upper classes were settling down to a life more serious than they had known, in which a somewhat sharply defined humanitarianism combined with a literal and stern religion to regulate family life and social duty. The sober dress of all classes and both sexes was perhaps an unconscious reflection

[1] W. Lovett, Life and Struggles, pp. 32–33.

of this spirit. Clothes had earlier reflected classical taste and the romantic movement. Now they were heavy, sombre, and voluminous. The crinoline did not arrive until 1854, so women created the necessary size of skirt by wearing as many as seven petticoats, one often being of thick red flannel. Even working-women were hampered by long and heavy skirts. Men, mean-time, still wore tight trousers and long coats, cut away in front, with side-whiskers and top-hats, but they no longer allowed themselves anything but the most sombre hues, except for sport or country wear, when a lighter-coloured suit or jacket would be allowed.

Thus it was that all classes ushered in the Prosperity era with due gravity and sense of duty. It was to be an era of Prosperity, indeed, but not one of extravagance or even of much gaiety.

SELECT BIBLIOGRAPHY

BEER, MAX: *A History of British Socialism*, vols. 1 and 2 (Bell, 1919–1920).

BRAILSFORD, H. N.: *Shelley, Godwin and their Circle* (Williams and Norgate, Home University Library, 1913).

CRUSE, A.: *The Englishman and his Books in the Early Nineteenth Century* (Harrap, 1930).

DICEY, A. V.: *Law and Public Opinion in England during the Nineteenth Century* (Macmillan, 1905).

FAY, C. R.: *Life and Labour in the Nineteenth Century* (Cambridge University Press, 1920).

——: *Palace of Industry, 1851* (Cambridge University Press, 1951).

GRETTON, R. H.: *A Modern History of the English People, 1880–1922* (Secker, 1930).

HEARNSHAW, F. J. C. (Ed.): *The Social and Political Ideas of Some Representative Thinkers of the Age of Reaction and Reconstruction, 1815–65* (Harrap, 1932).

LAVER, J.: *Fashions and Fashion Plates, 1800–1900* (Penguin, 1943).

——: *Taste and Fashion from the French Revolution to the Present Day* (Harrap, revised edition, 1945).

QUENNELL, MARJORIE AND C. H. B.: *A History of Everyday Things in England*, vol. iii, 1733–1837 (1933); vol. iv, 1851–1942 (1942) (Batsford).

STEPHEN, LESLIE: *The English Utilitarians*, 3 vols. (Duckworth, 1900).

YOUNG, G. M. (Ed.): *Early Victorian England, 1830–1865*, 2 vols. (Oxford University Press, 1934).

PART II

1851–1950

THE RISE OF THE WORKING CLASSES

CHAPTER XIV

'VICTORIAN PROSPERITY': 1851-73

(a) INDUSTRY

THE Great Exhibition of 1851 ushered in an age of prosperity which lasted virtually unbroken until 1873. Those twenty-two years were marked by a continued increase in population, which in Great Britain grew from 21,000,000 in 1851 to 26,000,000 in 1871; by Free Trade, mounting imports and exports, increasing production, an expanding transport system, greater capital investment abroad; and by changing forms of business and commercial organization. They were marked also by very great wealth for a few and at the same time by a substantial fringe of that poverty and degradation which had been present all through the Industrial Revolution. Bad luck, inefficiency, and weakness still cut off a section of the population from the benefits of national prosperity.

In the fifties and sixties the last vestiges of Protection were removed. In the fifties silk and paper were among the few manufactured articles for which protective duties still existed, and the highest of these, that on silk, was only 15 per cent. Most of these dutiable goods came from France, but in 1860 Cobden negotiated a French treaty as a result of which the paper and silk duties lapsed. Most raw materials were coming in free by the fifties, though foreign-hewn timber still paid an *ad valorem* duty which gave preference to Colonial timber. In 1860 the preference went, and in 1866 the timber duties were withdrawn entirely.

A few registration duties on food—on corn, flour, rice, sago, tapioca, and vermicelli—remained until 1869, and a revenue tax on sugar and kindred goods lasted until 1874, but otherwise all the food duties had already gone. Britain remained a virtually Free Trade country until the twentieth century.

The value of her imports mounted as her industries expanded, her population grew, and her standard of living rose. Net United Kingdom imports between 1854 and 1872 rose from

£133,000,000 to £297,000,000. Exports climbed rapidly in the same period from £97,000,000 to £256,000,000.[1] Invisible exports mounted no less rapidly, and Britain acquired substantial credit balances overseas. She did most of her own carrying and much of that of the rest of the world. Her tonnage grew from 3,600,000 in 1851 to 5,700,000 in 1871; the tonnage of British shipping cleared in the foreign trade in United Kingdom ports rose from 9,800,000 in 1851 to 28,000,000 in 1871.[2] Her overseas lending was larger in the period than before or since.

Britain's chief imports between 1851 and 1873 were raw cotton, largely from the U.S.A., raw wool, largely from the Colonies, and wheat—of which about a quarter of the total consumption was imported in 1851 and a half by the end of the seventies.[3] The imports of other foodstuffs were small in 1851, but growing larger. Apart from cotton, raw wool, and timber, Britain was virtually self-sufficient in raw materials in the fifties. Her dependence on American raw cotton led to the only real setback of the period, when the American Civil War cut off Lancashire's supply, causing the "cotton famine" of 1861-63 and the resultant unemployment and destitution of half a million people.

Of coal and iron and steel Britain was the world's greatest producer, sending to all parts of the earth, especially for railway construction. The coal exported rose from between 3,000,000 and 4,000,000 tons a year in the early fifties to 20,000,000 tons a year in the early eighties. Iron and steel exports, from less than 500,000 tons in 1850, rose to 3,500,000 tons in 1872. Cotton goods and yarns to the value of £30,000,000 were exported in 1853; the figure in 1872 was £80,000,000.[4] The £10,000,000 of woollen goods and yarn of 1850 had become £27,000,000 in 1870.[5]

Behind these exports were the great industries themselves, feeding each other and the home population as well as the

---

[1] *Memoranda, Statistical Tables, and Charts prepared in the Board of Trade with Reference to Various Matters bearing on British and Foreign Trade and Industrial Conditions*, 1903, LXVII (the *Fiscal Blue Book of* 1903), p. 403.
[2] *United Kingdom (Trade, Commerce, and Condition of the People) Return to the House of Commons, July* 1914; 1914, LXXVIII.
[3] Sir John H. Clapham, *An Economic History of Modern Britain*, ii, 218.
[4] *Ibid.*, ii, 226–228.
[5] L. C. A. Knowles, *The Industrial and Commercial Revolutions in Great Britain during the Nineteenth Century*, p. 141.

export trade. The iron-ore mined rose from 9,000,000 tons in 1855 to 15,000,000 tons in 1875. The amount of pig-iron produced in a year doubled between 1855, when it was 3,000,000 tons, and 1875.[1] In 1856 65,000,000 tons of coal were produced, in 1870 110,000,000 tons.[2] The cotton industry used an annual average of 826,000,000 lb. of raw cotton in the years 1850-54; between 1870 and 1874 the annual average had nearly doubled, standing at 1,524,000,000 lb. The woollen industry showed an intake of raw material that had more than trebled; between 1850 and 1854 the average annual quantity of raw wool imported was 95,000,000 lb.; between 1870 and 1874 it was 307,000,000 lb.[3]

'VICTORIAN PROSPERITY'

YEAR	
	CONSUMPTION OF RAW COTTON
1850	300,000 tons
1870	600,000 tons
	IRON OUTPUT
1850	2,000,000 tons
1875	6,000,000 tons
	COAL PRODUCTION
1856	65,000,000 tons
1870	110,000,000 tons
	POPULATION, IN MILLIONS
1851	21·0
1861	23·0
1871	26·0

Nearly everywhere the industrial unit was expanding—collieries, mills, shipyards, ironworks, employed more people in larger premises than before. One of the most striking examples of expansion was an ironworks which in 1850 was producing 120 tons of pig-iron a week, and in 1880 was turning out 500 tons a day.[4] In no industry and in no part of the country, however, was development uniform. In the iron and steel industries many great works in which the steam-hammer

[1] Clapham, op. cit., ii, 49.　　　　　[2] Knowles, op. cit., p. 141.
[3] Clapham, op. cit., ii, 225.　　　　[4] Ibid., ii, 50.

did the work of many men, in which the latest processes were used, and which compassed the whole range from the raw iron to the finished article stood side by side with the small business of two or three blast furnaces, or even rubbed shoulders with small domestic industries. Birmingham was notable in this respect. Beside her great heavy engineering works there flourished the cutlery trade—generally a small, non-mechanized concern even in the second half of the nineteenth century—and many other industries, such as jewellery and tinned ware, small-arms and nail-making, which were conducted in small factories or even parts of houses. Round High Wycombe and Luton parts of the chair industry and the straw-hat industry were still domestic; all over the country shoemakers were still plying their craft outside the factory; there were few industries where outwork of some kind did not continue. At the same time even such domestic tasks as brewing and baking were beginning to yield to steam-powered mills and breweries.

Parallel to this uneven development was an incomplete mechanization of industry. Even in the textile industries, while output was increasing both absolutely and per operative, mechanization was not even yet complete. This was partly because the inventions known were not all in use, partly because the important inventions had not yet all been made. There was not even a successful wool-combing machine until the fifties. Cotton-spinning was most nearly mechanized all through its processes. Nevertheless British spinners still kept mainly to their billies in spite of the fact that a mechanical condenser had been in use in America since the thirties. Nor was the spinner's mule completely mechanized. He still pulled his mule by his own strength to draw out and twist the thread, and then pushed it to wind it on to the bobbin. The work was heavy, but a self-acting mule invented in the twenties was expensive, and at first fit only for coarser work. Not until the fifties was it at all widely used.

In cotton-weaving the 300,000 power looms of 1856 grew to 560,000 by 1885, and only a few hundred hand-loom weavers were left. But in textiles as a whole there still remained 44,000 hand-loom weavers of all kinds scattered over the country in 1871, chiefly in Scotland, East Anglia, and Yorkshire.[1]

In lace and hosiery the application of power was still in its

[1] Clapham, *op. cit.*, ii, 118-119.

early stages and spreading slowly. Flax, jute, and hemp were moving rapidly towards complete mechanization.

In the mining industry technical advance on the whole was small. In the fifties and the sixties coalmines were being sunk deeper to meet the increasing demand for coal. Improvements were made in the ventilation of mines and in winding engines, in carrying the miner to and from the coal face, in conveying the hewn coal mechanically, in substituting metal for the old wicker cages and corves which had carried both the miners and the coal, in using steel ropes for haulage. But the fundamental process of hewing was still done by hand.

It was in the manufacture of iron and steel that the most significant developments of the period occurred, when a series of three inventions revolutionized the industry by substituting for malleable iron the substance known as mild steel.

Of these three inventions the first in order of time was Henry Bessemer's hot-air blast. Bessemer was working under the patronage of the Emperor Napoleon III, trying to find a material harder and more suitable than iron for the manufacture of cannon, when, as he watched his furnace, the idea occurred to him of driving an air blast through the molten iron. He discovered that by doing this he could produce steel at less than one-third of the existing cost of malleable iron. After reading a paper on his method in 1856 to the British Association Bessemer opened his own works in Sheffield. In the sixties he was meeting large orders for steel rails, tools, steel wire for ropes, and similar articles.

The importance of the invention lay in the quality of steel itself—harder and truer and more durable than iron—and in the great economies it effected, especially in the use of coal. There was one disadvantage, however, in Bessemer's method: it could not eliminate phosphorus from the ores upon which it operated; and steel will not form in the presence of phosphorus. The Bessemer method could be used, therefore, only with phosphorus-free ores.

Meanwhile William Siemens had been experimenting with a different method of making steel, and in 1861 tried out the open-hearth process. It was not until the end of the sixties, about ten years later than Bessemer's process, that it was working on a large scale, when Siemens founded the Siemens Steel Company at Landore, near Swansea. From that time it grew

steadily in importance, even when the popularity of the
Bessemer process began to decline in the eighties. Like the
Bessemer process, the open-hearth method was cheap; and it
had the advantage of being more easily controllable than the
hot-air blast.

Bessemer's basic process and Siemens's open-hearth both
required iron-ore free from phosphorus. To Britain this was
not highly important. Not only was much of the British ore
non-phosphoric, but Swedish non-phosphoric ore was easily
imported and worked conveniently at works near the ports.
To countries like Germany and Luxemburg, with large deposits
of phosphoric ore, a severe problem was presented. Many
people the world over were consequently trying to solve the
problem of using the hot-air blast or the open-hearth with
phosphoric ores. Curiously it was two Englishmen, Gilchrist-
Thomas, a clerk in the Thames Police Court, and his cousin
Percy Gilchrist, an ironworks chemist, who in the late seventies
solved the problem. The Gilchrist-Thomas 'basic' method
was first applied to the Bessemer converter, but by the end of
the eighties was being used with the open-hearth system also.
Great quantities of German and Luxemburg phosphoric ores
were as a consequence of the basic method brought into production cheaply and efficiently. This was excellent for the world
as a whole and for Germany in particular. But for Britain it
meant a quickening of the competition whose breath was
already beginning to blow.

By the end of the eighties four steel-making processes were in
operation in Great Britain—the Bessemer process, cheap, using
non-phosphoric iron ore; the basic method, refining on the
Bessemer process and enabling phosphoric ores to be used; the
open-hearth process, cheap, easily controlled, but again suitable for phosphorus-free ores only; and the basic method in
conjunction with the open-hearth.

Steel was not immediately used in place of iron. Several
steamers in the sixties were built of steel, but not until the
eighties was steel shipbuilding firmly established. It was only
a little earlier that the railways were changing from iron to
steel rails. The reasons for tardiness in the adoption of a
demonstrably superior and far cheaper material were, in the
first place, that many interests were bound up with the making
of iron—labour, skill, capital; secondly, that the change was

accompanied by an initial expense; and thirdly, that both ships and railways were still involved in other structural changes. The Prosperity Period saw only the beginnings of the Age of Steel. The inventions fundamental to Britain occurred in the period, but the absolute supremacy of steel came only at the end of the century.

Scarcely less important than the use of steel was the development of precision-tool making by Whitworth and Armstrong. Their aim was to make tools and machine-parts uniform and perfect to one ten-thousandth part of an inch. The Great Exhibition had shown the beginnings of the industry. In 1885 it was said that every marine engine and every locomotive in the country had the same screw for every given diameter, and that the Whitworth system had been adopted throughout the world wherever engines and machinery were manufactured, the dies for producing the whole series having been originally furnished from Whitworth's works at Manchester.[1]

The use of new materials and the new use of old were being pursued with enthusiasm and skill during the period. Spun silk was being developed from pieces originally cast aside, shoddy of all kinds was being made from waste cloth, new machinery was patiently tearing up rags for paper; glue was being extracted from bones, which were also being made into manure. Cement, particularly Portland cement, began to be widely used, and two quite new materials, indiarubber and gutta-percha, were found to have immense possibilities in a wide range of uses, from surgical bandages to mackintoshes and hose-pipes. Indiarubber and gutta-percha had been known in the twenties, but their general importance did not begin until the fifties. Even by the mid-seventies the range and importance of rubber was barely perceived.

The products of Britain's expanding economic system were carried overseas by a growing tonnage of steam-ships made of steel. At home, from ports and raw-material areas to factory sidings, the heavy materials of industry were carried, and the finished products taken away by rail. The railway mileage open in Britain grew from 4600 in 1848 to 13,600 in 1870.[2] For passengers travel became more comfortable. Open third-class

[1] Jeans, *Creators of the Age of Steel*, p. 224, quoted by Clapham, *op. cit.*, ii, 75.
[2] Clapham, *op. cit.*, ii, 181.

carriages disappeared, seats became softer; sleeping-cars came in the seventies, though dining-cars not until the eighties. From 1872 the Midland Railway began to supply third-class carriages on all its trains, and other lines followed suit. Improvements were made to the permanent way, rails being made of steel instead of iron; but, in spite of various experiments with metal, wood still proved better for sleepers. Attention was paid to braking. A Royal Commission of 1874 recommended the use of the absolute block system, by which not more than one train was allowed in any given block section at the same time. Various brake trials were held the following year, and the block system was generally adopted. Better signalling was devised. In 1842 the Board of Trade had become responsible for examining new railway lines, forbidding their opening if they appeared unsafe, and reporting upon accidents. By the Regulation of Railways Act of 1871 they were given power to compel information from the railway companies. All this kept the standard of safety comparatively high and made possible the higher speeds of the eighties.

The chief concern of the public and of the trading interest in particular was with railway amalgamations and agreements and with freight rates. The amalgamations which had been going on since Hudson's time culminated in the North-eastern in 1854, the Great Eastern in 1862, and the big Scottish amalgamations of 1865-66. Throughout the sixties agreements and annexations continued. All kept alive the ever-present fear of a monopoly which would hamper and dictate to industry. Freight rates which were sometimes high, which sometimes gave preferential treatment to imported goods, and which were notoriously erratic exasperated the trading community. If railway amalgamations could be attacked as contrary to the prevailing spirit of *laissez-faire*, however, the remedy of State control could be similarly criticized and equally feared. The position was difficult. Many Committees and Commissions examined various aspects of railway amalgamation, railway rates, and State control. A Royal Commission sat from 1865 to 1867, a Select Committee to deal specifically with Railway Companies Amalgamation met in 1872. In the event little was done. A Railway and Canal Commission was set up in 1873 for five years, and was thereafter renewed annually until 1888, but was ineffective. The development of the railway system continued to be the result of private enterprise given form where necessary by Private Bill. However much it might be criticized, it was a system outstandingly successful in unifying the country into an economic whole. The mileage growth was impressive. There were through routes from the South to Scotland by both East and West coasts. The railways were efficient carriers of goods; they took the business-man to his appointment, the statesman to his conference, the trade unionist to his meeting, the holidaymaker to the country and the sea.

Canals continued to decline. The main roads of the country were only very slowly improved, and only slowly the turnpike trusts died out, the last London toll being taken in 1871. An occasional stagecoach could still be seen, like the *Old Times*, which plied the London–Brighton road. Specialized carrying firms, like Pickfords, began to undertake business, their vans, like the stagecoach, being horse-drawn. A steam-roller and a steam traction-engine both appeared on the roads in the sixties. Gurney's steam-coach was but a memory, but another invention fraught with great social as well as industrial importance was being developed.

Various rudimentary types of bicycle had been known since the beginning of the century, but bicycle-making did not develop as an industry, nor bicycling as a major means to sport, pleasure, or business until the seventies, when geared wheels of equal size were connected by a chain and the modern bicycle was born. The natural location of the industry was the Birmingham–Coventry district. Here tools, machinery, and skill were all to hand. In Coventry, in a period of distress about 1870–71, the watchmakers of the district had turned their skill to sewing-machine making, and had recruited the out-work silk-workers to help them. Ten years later they were turning their ability to bicycles and bicycle parts, which were then produced with the precision made possible by Whitworth's tools in the hands of trained workers.

In the towns the hansom cab (introduced in the thirties) and the brougham (introduced in the forties) and various kinds of landau were all in use. The victoria, a cab phaeton, was popular in the seventies. These were for private use. But in 1829 George Shillibeer had introduced the omnibus from

France. It ran between Paddington and the Bank, drawn by three horses, and fares were 6*d*. and 1*s*. There were seats upstairs and downstairs, those on top being of the back-to-back, 'knifeboard' pattern. Several attempts were made to use steam propulsion, but with little success. The Great Exhibition caused a great increase of traffic, the number of omnibuses grew, and at the end of 1851 the first penny fares were introduced.

As an alternative to buses tramways were started. These needed lines for running on, and, like the buses, were drawn by horses. They were more popular in the Provinces than London, the lines of the first London tramway being taken up almost immediately, as the flanged rails were considered dangerous. By the seventies several tramway services were operating in London and the Provinces, but not until the eighties were tramways popular or numerous.

While ships and railways were carrying the business-man, his cargoes, his letters, and his bills of lading all over the world he was beginning to send his instructions far more quickly, by means of the telegraph. Not only did telegraphic communication come into general use at home in the second half of the century, but, following the experiments by Morse in America with long-distance communication, a cable for carrying messages was laid under the English Channel in 1851. The laying of an Atlantic cable was more difficult; but, after several costly failures, a cable was laid on July 27, 1866, and telegraphic communication triumphantly established between Britain and the U.S.A.

The expanding capitalism of the mid-nineteenth century was insatiable in its demand for capital. Yet, side by side with markets and inventions clamouring to be exploited and industries straining to expand, there existed the anomaly of capital unemployed. The reason for this is to be found largely in the laws governing business enterprise, especially those relating to joint-stock companies and limited liability.

The enterprises of high capitalism had to be operated on a scale surpassing that of private fortunes. Partnership or joint stock was needed. Yet partnerships or joint-stock enterprise, except in special cases, had to be carried on under the severe disadvantage of unlimited liability. Unlimited liability meant simply that a man or woman with the smallest possible investment in an enterprise, and even though a sleeping partner, was nevertheless responsible to the full extent of his property for any debt of the company, even though the existence of that property was unknown to the creditor, and though it was in consequence property on the credit of which not one farthing could have been advanced. People could be, and were, rendered penniless and propertyless overnight by the failure of a company in which they had invested a nominal sum. Persons of small means were the chief victims. In the words of the first Report of the Select Committee on Joint-stock Companies of 1844:

> The extent of the evil is to be measured rather by the circumstances of the victims than by the amount of the plunder. They are usually persons of very limited means, who invest their savings in order to obtain the tempting returns which are offered. . . . Old people, governesses, servants and persons of that description, are tempted to invest their little all, and when the concern stops, they are ruined.[1]

This same Committee epitomized the prevailing state of mind concerning joint-stock companies in the headlines of itt Report: "The Modes of Deception Adopted, The Amouns and Distribution of the Plunder, The Circumstances of the Victims, The Impunity of the Offenders."

Private partnerships were the greatest sufferers. Not only did they suffer unlimited liability, but there was also great difficulty in dissolving a partnership. The law generally acted on the assumption of once a partner, always a partner, being suspicious of partners endeavouring to divest themselves of responsibility just at the time when their business was ceasing to be profitable. So unlimited liability tended to hang like a millstone round the neck of unhappy partners who could foresee their fate but were powerless to free themselves.

The law relating to joint-stock companies was more complicated. Financial speculation had led to the 'Bubble Act' of 1719, which pronounced unincorporated joint-stock companies to be illegal. But the law was frequently evaded, and in 1825 the Bubble Act was repealed. The law of partnership,

[1] 1844, VII, xi.

including the burden of unlimited liability, applied to joint-stock companies, though they had none of the advantages of close personal contact which a private company provided. In 1837 the Chartered Companies Act gave them the opportunity of obtaining limited liability and the rights of suing and being sued at the discretion of the Minister. Hopes of normally obtaining limited liability in this way were frustrated both by the Minister's reluctance to grant charters and by the high cost and great delay involved.

There remained the corporation. This form of joint-stock enterprise was created either by charter or by private Act of Parliament, a procedure which was lengthy, cumbersome, expensive, and uncertain. When created its liability was strictly limited to its own assets, and it could sue and be sued in its corporate name.

There was a last possibility of obtaining limited liability. This was by having a special clause inserted in a contract to that effect. But only the strongest companies were in fact able to achieve limited liability in this way, and then it applied to a single contract only.

So when the mid-century had passed there were still only three ways of obtaining limited liability—by becoming an incorporated company by Crown Charter or Act of Parliament, by obtaining a charter under the 1837 Act, or by special clause inserted in an agreement. The methods were apparently designed to deter any group of individuals from limiting their liability. The assumption was that the normal (or, as a witness in 1851 said, the "natural") way of doing business was with unlimited liability.

The reason for this persistence of an anachronistic legal form was partly the weight of inertia which attaches to any established law, partly a muddled feeling that amendment by the State would constitute interference with natural forms, and partly a preference for individual enterprise over joint stock, and a consequent reluctance to bother with the troubles of companies. Joseph Parkes explained to the Committee on Joint Stock Companies:

> There never can be that spirit of cautious enterprise, and that skill and competition, which individuals carry on against one another . . . where they are conducted by public companies.[1]

[1] First Report, 1844, VII, 238.

But, whatever the views of individuals, it was clear that only joint-stock enterprise could shoulder the gigantic capital burdens of large-scale industry. Robert Lowe and others easily showed that true *laissez-faire* lay in the granting of limited liability and the opening of investment to all degrees of wealth, in building

> upon the only firm foundation on which the law can be placed—the right of individuals to use their own property, and make such contracts as they please, to associate in whatever form they think best, and to deal with their neighbours upon such terms as may be satisfactory to both parties . . . not to throw the slightest obstacle in the way of limited companies being formed . . . but to allow them all to come into existence, and when difficulties arise to arm the courts of justice with sufficient powers to check extravagance or roguery in the management of companies, and to save them from the wreck in which they may be involved.[1]

The middle-class business-men who for practical reasons wanted limited liability were joined by the Benthamites (often one and the same), who wanted to sweep away the anomalies of the existing law. Law reform had always been a leading anxiety of the Benthamites, joint stock, in particular, being termed "exceedingly barbarous and defective." It was a "mass of confusion." "Never was such an infliction."

But, above all, it was economic developments which were responsible for the reform of the law. No serious opposition stood in the way of the middle classes when they turned to amend the company laws. Through the Reform Act and by other means they had been steadily moulding the legal forms of the State to their will—the repeal of the restrictions on trade and commerce, the repeal of the Corn Laws, the reform of the House of Commons. Here was another battle to be fought. Without limited liability insufficient capital could be mobilized to finance their business enterprise. The Company and Joint-stock Laws acted, as they themselves put it, as "fetters on commercial freedom." They summoned their energies, as they said, for "unfettering the energies of trade."

They had a second reason for wanting reform. They needed to mobilize the small savings of the working classes, and this again for two reasons. The first was their need for every available shilling of capital to feed the insatiable demand of capitalist

[1] House of Commons, February 1, 1856 (Hansard, third series, 1856, cxl, 130-131).

enterprise; the second was their shrewd belief that, given a
stake in capitalism, the workers would become its devoted
slaves, and that the spectre of revolution, never for long absent
since 1789, would be finally laid. John Howell, described as
the largest warehouseman in London, told a Select Committee
in 1851 that the "effect of a change would be to bring the
interest of the working man into closer identity with that of
the capitalist."[1] As the Report of the Select Committee on
the Law of Partnership expressed it, it

> would be desirable to remove any obstacles which may now
> prevent the middle and even the more thriving of the working
> classes from taking shares in such investments, under the sanction
> of . . . their richer neighbours; as thereby their self-respect is
> upheld . . . and an additional motive is given to them to preserve
> order and respect the laws of property.[2]

The Chairman of the Committee of 1850 on the Savings of
the Middle and Working Classes asked J. M. Ludlow:

> You are decidedly of opinion that facilities given for such
> purposes, within the law [*i.e.*, for limited liability and co-operative
> production], would create content among those classes, and tend
> to foster habits of forethought and providence?

To which the reply came:

> I cannot say that I know of any more powerful means of
> increasing the security of the country.[3]

With such pressure behind it the movement for limited
liability went forward to certain success. The 1844 Act for
registration, incorporation, and regulation of joint-stock companies gave suing capacity to partnerships and unincorporated
companies. After the Select Committees of 1850 and 1851 the
question never cooled. In 1855 limited liability was given by
registration, subject to a number of conditions, apparently
intended as safeguards, and vexatious rather than onerous.
The 1856 Joint Stock Companies Act granted the fullest possible limitation upon liability, only slightly modified with
regard to publicity, processes concerning winding up of companies and similar matters by the 1857 Act. In 1862, when a
consolidating Act was passed, 2479 companies had registered

---

[1] *Report of the Select Committee on the Law of Partnership*, 1851, XVIII, 25.
[2] *Ibid.*, XVIII, vi–vii.
[3] *Report of the Select Committee on Investments for the Savings of the Middle and Working Classes*, 1850; XIX, 10.

under the Act.[1] In 1858 and 1862 similar Acts were applied to banking companies and insurance companies.

The law of joint stock and limited liability had developed, as Lowe said in the House of Commons, from prohibition to privilege, and now became a right. It was a right, as he assured the House, which in no way increased the authority of the State, but which, in enabling people to deal how and with whom they chose without risking their entire fortunes, ensured the largest possible measure of liberty.[2]

Besides being required at home, capital was in demand by all the concerns of rising foreign capitalism. Limited liability, by giving security against overwhelming loss, provided the final incentive to large-scale overseas investment.

At the beginning of the century Britain had made rehabilitation loans to Prussia, Russia, and Austria. She also lent to Spain, South America, and Greece, largely financing their wars. Then, after the disastrous collapse of the South American market in 1825, came a period of quiet, followed by the beginnings of railway investment in the early thirties. Lending to the U.S.A. in particular rapidly increased as America developed her transport system and the planters of the Southern states looked for more capital. So matters went forward to the collapse of 1841-42, when nine states defaulted on their debts and the U.S. Bank suspended payment and went into liquidation.

By this time British loans were already going to the Continent for Belgian and French railways. The Paris-Rouen line, begun in 1840, was actually under contract to a British firm, and Britain provided some of the capital, all the navvies, the iron and other materials. In the general expansion of the fifties and sixties British capital financed railway projects in Russia, Austria, Spain, Switzerland, Piedmont, Denmark, Portugal, Brazil, Turkey and the Near East, and the U.S.A. British iron and steel, sometimes British contractors and labourers, did the work. Economic and political motives, immediate and long-term advantages, moved the investors. Forging an overland route to India, ousting a rival state, developing an area whose raw materials or whose purchasing

---

[1] H. A. Shannon, "The Coming of General Limited Liability," *Economic Journal* (Economic History Supplement) (1932), p. 290.
[2] Hansard, third series, 1856, cxl, 131.

power was needed by Britain, or bringing home an immediate high percentage were all important. The area of investment spread farther afield as political alignments changed, new spheres of interest developed, and nationals controlled their own enterprises. By the seventies British capital was already going to India and Japan. In all, the years 1850–73 were the period of Britain's greatest capital export. Her far-flung overseas investment matched—indeed, was essential to—her great export trade, her enormous intake of raw materials, the growth of her production, and the prosperity of her people.

(b) AGRICULTURE

This prosperity was shared by agriculture. The actual population on the land between 1851 and 1873 was about stationary, although its proportion to the rest of the working population declined. The building of the great estate was proceeding steadily, and by 1870 there was a pronounced concentration of land-ownership on the one hand with landlessness on the other that was unique in Western Europe. The "Doomsday Enquiry" of 1874, though imperfect in its details, showed that about a quarter of the land of England had passed into the hands of some 1200 people.[1] At the same time a few smallholders still existed, mainly in the Fenlands, in Cumberland, Westmorland, and Yorkshire. Enclosure had ceased to be a live issue, as most suitable land had already been enclosed.

The outstanding characteristic of the period of 'high farming' into which Britain now passed was the balance between arable and pasture. Agriculture for the first time was regarded as a whole. After the excessive wheat cultivation of the Napoleonic wars period there was a gradual turning to pasture, especially after the Corn Law repeal had left bad arable farming with no protection. Lavergne in 1854 had already been struck with the extent of pasture in Britain. By the end of the sixties about 43 per cent. of the cultivated land was under grass.[2] Lavergne was also astounded at the "enormous" consumption of milk among the English, while the "quantities of butter and cheese manufactured throughout the whole extent of the British Isles," he said, "exceed all belief."[3]

---

[1] Clapham, op. cit., ii, 253.   [2] Ibid., ii, 274.
[3] Léonce de Lavergne, Rural Economy of England, Scotland and Ireland, p. 34.

British sheep, he remarked, were superior to French; British cattle also, although not in so marked a degree. Twenty years later he would have found a greater acreage of pasture and even better sheep and cattle. One of the features of the period was the skilful breeding and care of stock. Cattle were carefully bred for milk and meat, sheep for meat and wool. The shorthorns, Herefords, and Devons, the Leicesters, Cotswolds, and Southdowns, were supplemented by Jersey and Sussex cattle, by Lincoln and Shropshire sheep. There were better buildings for the animals, clean and dry, no longer ramshackle and tumbledown. Instead of existing during the winter as "bags of skin and bone" on the oddments of the fields they were given good imported feeding stuffs. Veterinary surgeons gave skilled attention to sick animals. By 1874 there were over 6,000,000 cattle and over 30,000,000 sheep in Great Britain in excellent condition.[1]

The gain to the farmer was incalculable. He had more and better meat and milk, he had manure to enrich his soil. Farmyards were carefully drained and all muck scientifically used on the fields. The laboratory was brought in to supplement nature. Liebig in Germany, Sir John Lawes and Sir Henry Gilbert at Rothamsted, in England, put manuring on a scientific basis and showed the effect of feeding upon the meat, milk, and manure of animals. Following this came the use of artificial manures to supplement dung. Fertilizers like soot and bones had been in use in the thirties, but now their application was systematized, and little-known fertilizers were popularized. Nitrate of soda, Peruvian guano, superphosphates, muriate of potash, sulphate of ammonia, basic slag, were used. As Lord Ernle points out, the artificial manures had the double advantage of extending fertilizing to more distant fields where dung could not easily be carried, and of inducing care in the farmer, for a man rarely wastes what he has bought at £10 a ton.[2]

Implements were improved, although their introduction was piecemeal and erratic. A locomotive steam threshing-machine was in fairly general use by the seventies; steam-ploughs, mowing-machines, haymakers, elevators, assisted the harvesters. There were corn and seed and manure drills. Machines cut and prepared animal food. Not only were there turnipcutters, but machines pumped the farmer's water, "ground his

---

[1] Lord Ernle, *English Farming, Past and Present*, p. 373.   [2] *Ibid.*, p. 367.

corn, crushed his cake, split his beans, cut his chaff, pulped his turnips, steamed and boiled his food."[1] Innumerable jobs on the farm which had employed many men at the beginning of the century could now be done more efficiently by machine.

The farmer, then, improved his stock and his farmland, his farm buildings and his implements; he also improved the home farm and the farm roads. Neater, stronger, better buildings, good sound roads, again helped his farming and added to the appearance of general prosperity. In his home Lavergne observed that the most perfect order reigned, everything being conducted "with that habitual regularity which indicates long usage."[2]

The period of 'high farming' was made possible by a variety of causes. The gold discoveries raised prices, the prosperity of industry reacted on agriculture. There was money to spend, and agriculture, like everything else, benefited accordingly. The development of transport helped the farmer to market his product. A growing scientific knowledge was at his disposal. The end of Protection had put him on his mettle. The sun shone at the right time, the rain came when wanted. With the exception of the year 1860 the seasons were favourable and the harvests good. Moreover, the general attitude to farming in Britain was important, not only landowning but farming itself being an occupation of social distinction. At Sandringham and Windsor the Royal Farms were scientifically farmed. The position was put succinctly by Lavergne: "In France, when a proprietor is ambitious of playing a part, he must come away from his estates; in England he must remain upon them."[3]

---

[1] *Ibid.*, p. 370. [2] Lavergne, *op. cit.*, p. 86. [3] Lavergne, *op. cit.*, p. 125.

SELECT BIBLIOGRAPHY

Report of the Select Committee on Joint-stock Companies, 1844, VII.

Report of the Select Committee on Investments for the Savings of the Middle and Working Classes, 1850, XIX.

Report of the Select Committee on the Law of Partnership, 1851, XVIII.

Debates in the House of Commons on Joint Stock Companies and Limited Liability, Hansard, 1856, third series, cxl.

BRIGGS, A.: *Victorian People, 1851–1867* (Odhams, 1954).

——: *Victorian Cities* (Odhams, 1963).

CAIRD, J.: *The Landed Interest and the Supply of Food* (Cassell, 1878).

CHAMBERS, J. D.: *The Workshop of the World: British Economic History, 1820–80*. Home University Library (Oxford University Press, 1961).

CHAMBERS, J. D. AND MINGAY, G. E.: *The Agricultural Revolution, 1750–1880* (Batsford, 1966).

CLAPHAM, SIR JOHN H.: *An Economic History of Modern Britain*, vol. ii, *Free Trade and Steel, 1850–1866* (Cambridge University Press, 1932).

DUNCAN, H. O.: *The World on Wheels* (Author, 1926).

ERNLE, LORD: *English Farming, Past and Present* (Longmans, 1912; revised edition, 1961).

JACKMAN, W. T.: *The Development of Transportation in Modern England*, 2 vols. (Cambridge University Press, 1916).

JENKS, L. H.: *The Migration of British Capital to 1875* (Knopf, 1927).

JERVIS, F. R. J.: *The Evolution of Modern Industry* (Harrap, 1960).

JONES, E. L.: *The Development of English Agriculture 1815–1873* (Studies in Economic History, Macmillan, 1968).

KAY, F. G.: *Royal Mail* (Rockliff, 1951).

KNOWLES, L. C. A.: *The Industrial and Commercial Revolutions in Great Britain during the Nineteenth Century* (Routledge, 1925).

LAVERGNE, L. DE: *Rural Economy of England, Scotland, and Ireland* (Blackwoods, 1855).

LEVI, L.: *History of British Commerce and of the Economic Progress of the British Nation, 1763–1870* (Murray, 1872).

LIPSON, E.: *The Growth of English Society*, Part III (fourth edition, Black, 1959).

PERKIN, HAROLD: *The Age of the Railway* (paperback, David and Charles, 1971).

ROBBINS, MICHAEL: *The Railway Age* (Penguin, 1965).

ROBINSON, H.: *Britain's Post Office* (Oxford University Press, 1953).

SHANNON, H. A.: "The Coming of General Limited Liability," *Economic Journal* (Economic History Supplement), 1932.

SHERRINGTON, C. E. R.: *A Hundred Years of Inland Transport, 1830–1933* (Duckworth, 1934).

CHAPTER XV

SELF-HELP IN THE PERIOD OF 'VICTORIAN PROSPERITY'

WORKING-CLASS movements in the period of 'Victorian Prosperity' were dominated by two complementary virtues enshrined in middle-class hearts and common to all classes in this period of harmony. 'Thrift' and 'Self-help' they were commonly called. They were manifest in the growth of Friendly Societies of many types, in the spirit of cautious husbanding of funds which characterized the trade unions, and in the development of Co-operative Societies paying a dividend to their customers. The Friendly Societies and the Co-operative Societies quite easily obtained the sanction of the State for their enterprises, which were, indeed, applauded by all ranks of society. The ruling classes were more sceptical about trade unions, which had a vivid revolutionary past to live down, but after solemn protestations of sobriety the trade unions also obtained their charter of recognition as legal bodies.

Nowhere are the virtues of thrift and self-help more carefully extolled than in Samuel Smiles's books. *Self-help* was published in 1859, *Thrift* not until 1875, though it admirably expounds the values of the preceding twenty-five years. The success of both books—particularly of *Self-help*—clearly shows that the advice given was popular. *Self-help* ran to four editions in the month of publication, and until 1885 (with the exception of the year 1865) was reprinted at least once a year—sometimes twice or three times.

The theme of *Self-help* is that a man needs the minimum of State intervention in his affairs—that by his own efforts he can provide for his family and educate himself. Says Smiles:

> That there should be a class of men who live by their daily labour in every state is the ordinance of God, and doubtless is a wise and righteous one; but that this class should be otherwise than frugal, contented, intelligent, and happy is not the design of Providence, but springs solely from the weakness, self-indulgence, and perverseness of man himself. The healthy spirit of

self-help created amongst working people would more than any other measure serve to raise them as a class, and this, not by pulling down others, but by levelling them up to a higher and still advancing standard of religion, intelligence, and virtue.

These sentiments were echoed by the working class, applauded by the ruling class, and given expression first and foremost through the Friendly Society.

(a) FRIENDLY SOCIETIES

Friendly Societies had an early origin. Medieval guilds had their schemes of mutual help; Friendly Societies, so called, began to operate by the middle of the seventeenth century; at the end of the eighteenth century began the line of legislation concerning them; the second half of the nineteenth century was their heyday; their decline corresponded with the taking over by the State of social insurance as a national responsibility.

Friendly Societies existed for mutual help in times of sickness, unemployment, death, or other trouble. They also provided good cheer in friendly clubs where members could meet, sometimes drinking a glass of beer out of the funds, sometimes, indeed, spending more than they should on dinners to the members, but sometimes merely providing a pretext for a social gathering which might be held in a public house, a schoolroom, or a near-by hall. Many of the big societies of the second half of the nineteenth century were strictly teetotal, but the same spirit of enjoyment was there.

The characteristic of the Friendly Society was saving out of income for a rainy day. It is therefore clear that only people above the absolute poverty line could join. Consequently the Friendly Society meant not only pleasure and profit, but a certain social standing to the self-respecting worker. As the 'poor man's club' it had already been described by Crabbe in the eighteenth century:

> The poor man has his club; he comes and spends
> His hoarded pittance with his chosen friends;
> Nor this alone,—a monthly dole he pays
> To be assisted when his health decays;
> Some part his prudence, from the day's supply,
> For cares and troubles in his age, lays by;

The printed rules he guards with painted frame,
And shows his children where to read his name:
Those simple words his honest nature move,
That bond of union tied by laws of love;
This is his pride, it gives to his employ
New value, to his home another joy;
While a religious hope its balm applies
For all his fate inflicts and all his state denies.[1]

The first Act of Parliament relating to Friendly Societies
was that of 1793, called, after its sponsor, Rose's Act. This
allowed persons to combine to raise funds for mutual advantage, provided their rules were approved by a justice of the
peace. Between 1793 and the big consolidating Act of 1875
nineteen Acts relating to Friendly Societies were passed, there
were four Select Committees of the House of Commons, one
of the House of Lords, and one Royal Commission directly
concerned with them. During the period of the Revolutionary
and Napoleonic wars they came under suspicion, but remained
the only legal working-class organizations. They used the
ritual and the oaths common to working-class societies of the
time, and were often indistinguishable from trade unions. It
was therefore common for trade unions to proceed under the
cover of Friendly Society functions even after the Acts of 1799
and 1800.

In 1801 the number of Friendly Societies was estimated at
over 7000 in England and Wales, with a membership of between 600,000 and 700,000.[2] Their growth continued slowly
through the century, and by 1872 there were nearly 2,000,000
members in Great Britain. In the next two years the increase
was astonishingly rapid, membership amounting to 4,000,000
in England and Wales alone, the number of persons interested
as wives, children, and other dependants being about 8,000,000.
The funds in hand of the 32,000 societies concerned were about
£11,000,000.[3]

The legislation which developed concerning Friendly
Societies protected them and gave them privileges as the most
favoured working-class organizations, while at the same time
it enabled the State to hold them with a guiding and, if necessary, controlling rein. The State's supervision of Friendly

---

[1] *The Borough*, Letter X.
[2] Sir John H. Clapham, *An Economic History of Modern Britain*, i, 296.
[3] *Fourth Report of the Committee appointed to inquire into Friendly and Benefit Building Societies*, 1874, XXIII, Part I, i, xvi, and Appendix, p. 1.

Societies was in line with its general policy. It had very clear reasons for guiding these voluntary bodies which came to control millions of pounds. One reason was the simple one that a great deal of money was involved, and that a Friendly Society which got into financial difficulties would involve many people and perhaps other institutions in its fall. Even big societies like the Oddfellows were not altogether safe, and the extent of their funds and membership—£340,000 annual income and a membership of 360,000 in 1848[1]—made their conduct of public interest. With small societies there was less at stake, but, because of insufficient funds and of reckless social expenditure, more likelihood of collapse.

The second reason for the State's care of Friendly Societies was its apprehension lest these large, well-organized bodies commanding large funds and widespread loyalty should become subversive. Speaking in 1848 of the Manchester Oddfellows, a Select Committee declared:

> So extensive an association became a powerful instrument of good or evil in proportion as its objects were useful or dangerous, and its members well or ill affected to the laws of the land.[2]

While the State was anxious to control the Friendly Societies, these Societies had their own motives for desiring State protection. Treasurers who absconded with Society funds were well known in all branches of the working-class movement. The Friendly Societies, in common with all bodies handling subscribed funds, wanted to be able to conduct legal proceedings, either against offenders or in their own defence, without jeopardizing their whole funds. They also wanted evidence, such as a Government guarantee would provide, to distinguish them from upstart and fraudulent societies with no security. It was these twin requirements of the State and the Societies which by the mid-seventies had produced legislation which covered the general body of Friendly Societies.

In 1817 Friendly Societies were accorded the privilege of safeguarding their funds by depositing them in savings banks. The next step was the registration of Friendly Societies not, as heretofore, by the local justices, but by the State. By 1855 a Registrar's Department had been created, and the Friendly Societies' Act of that year required the Registrar to make an annual Report to Parliament.

---

[1] *Ibid.*, Appendix, p. 4.   [2] *Ibid.*, Appendix, p. 4.

The first English Registrar was Tidd Pratt, who came to hold a unique position as friend and counsellor to the Friendly Societies. "For a society to be 'certified by Tidd Pratt,'" wrote E. W. Brabrook, a subsequent Registrar,

> was for a long time a kind of hall-mark of respectability in the eyes of many people in various parts of the country, and the name of Tidd Pratt was held up as a terror to managers suspected of evil designs, who were told "Tidd Pratt will never allow you to do this," or "if you do this, you will have Tidd Pratt upon you."[1]

An Act of 1875 consolidated the existing position, and also legalized the constitution which many of the bigger Societies had evolved. Friendly Societies could be established for insuring a sum of money not exceeding £200 to be paid on the death of a member, the birth of a member's child, the funeral expenses of a member's wife or child. They gave insurance against fire, loss of tools or implements of trade, and old age; and relief or maintenance during unemployment or sickness.

To be fully established all these Societies had to submit their rules to the Registrar and obtain his certificate that they were in conformity with the law. They had to make returns of the membership and general condition of the Society. All changes in rules had automatically to be deposited with the Registrar. Societies which granted annuities were required to adopt tables certified by an actuary.

In return the Friendly Societies so established obtained the valuable rights of holding property in the names of trustees; of suing and being sued in representative names; of proceeding against their officers in case of fraud or misconduct; of making provision for the settlement of disputes among their members by arbitration; of investing their funds in Government securities. They were exempt from stamp duties, and could be dissolved if they wished on cheap and easy terms. The Registrar was, moreover, available if required for advice to Societies framing rules and seeking registration.

The bulk of Friendly Societies were by 1875 financially sound, their transactions based on actuarial tables, their funds protected. They worked in full publicity, the State and the public as well as their own members having access to all their returns.

Two of them, the Oddfellows and the Foresters, stood head

---

[1] E. W. Brabrook, *Provident Societies and Industrial Welfare* (1898), p. 12.

and shoulders above the others. The Oddfellows were strongest in the Manchester area: in 1874, when there were 4,000,000 Friendly Society members in England and Wales, one-tenth were in the Manchester Unity. Its average yearly income was £560,000, its annual sickness and death payments were nearly £400,000, the value of the benefits for which it was liable was £11,000,000.[1]

The Oddfellows and the Foresters and a few similar Societies were known as Affiliated Societies, from their method of branch organization. They had branches in many towns and outlying districts all over the country and even abroad. In the Southwest of England Sir George Young in the seventies visited no town, and but a few large villages, in which a 'lodge' or 'court' of the Oddfellows or Foresters was not established. The members were mostly skilled workmen, earning from 18s. to 25s. a week, the agricultural and other unskilled labourers being excluded by the high rate of subscription.

There remained, but in decreasing numbers, the sociable little clubs of the villages and small towns. They served their locality only, and had few members and small funds. The old 'dividing societies' were mostly dying out—societies which met the obligations of death and sickness for a year or given period and then divided up the surplus between the members. Burial Clubs and societies remained very popular, but gradually they were being swallowed up by the big Orders. Said a contemporary observer:

> Everywhere that I have been I have heard the same story from the members of the older, or local clubs. "We cannot stand against the great orders." Wherever they penetrate, and they are penetrating year by year into more remote corners of the field, the majority of the existing clubs at once cease to enter young members, and within half a generation die out or break up.

Sick pay and accident benefit were the chief concern of the big Friendly Societies and their members, death and burial benefits being of secondary importance. The desire to guard against a pauper burial still, however, remained strong, and there came to meet the need in place of the little burial clubs the Collecting Society and the Commercial Society—which

[1] *Fourth Report of the Committee appointed to inquire into Friendly and Benefit Building Societies*, 1874, XXIII, Part I, xvi–xvii.

[2] *Committee appointed to inquire into Friendly and Benefit Building Societies*, 1874, XXIII, Part II, Report of Assistant Commissioner Sir George Young, 1.

were often one and the same thing. The success of the working-man's own movement brought the profit motive on the
scent, and in the fifties several of the big insurance companies,
notably the Prudential, started their gainful careers. The
Collecting Societies sent collectors round from door to door
collecting the weekly contribution. All the social intercourse
of the 'Friendly' was lost, and the gain was merely in a sick or
burial benefit, for which the terms were much higher in order
to cover the cost of collection and the profit of the Commercial
Society, but whose security was almost 100 per cent. The social
loss was lamented by Ludlow, the Registrar, in 1888:

> The simple act that contributions are collected from house to
> house, instead of being brought by the members to a centre, leads
> to a whole train of consequences which completely change their
> character from that of a friendly society. The main object for
> which a member seeks to meet his fellows, namely the payment
> of contributions, is gone; the members cease to know one another,
> and the collector becomes for them the only habitual embodiment
> of the society.[1]

Related to the Friendly Society was the savings bank. The
State promoted thrift by the encouragement of savings banks
where small deposits could be made upon sound security and
receive a small interest. The Post Office Savings Bank was
established by an Act of 1861, the State thereby standing
security for money deposited. Private or trustee savings banks
had been in existence since the beginning of the century. They
were actively supported by Bentham, who termed them fruga-
lity banks, and in 1817 the first Savings Bank Act was passed,
the rate of interest being fixed by law first at 4 per cent. and
then at 3½ per cent. The average deposit was estimated to be
about £34 in 1833,[2] a figure suggesting that it was people of
the small-tradesman class who made most use of them. Among
the working class there existed considerable distrust of them, a
fact mentioned by several witnesses to the Committee of 1850
on the Savings of the Middle and Working Classes.

By 1875 the worker could insure himself with Friendly
Societies or Commercial Societies against a variety of ills, or
with the State under the Annuities Acts of 1864. He could
choose between a variety of small investments for his savings,

[1] *Select Committee on Friendly Societies*, 1888, XII, Minutes of Evidence, p. 2, Q.8.
[2] Clapham, *op. cit.*, i, 300.

ANOTHER OF PUGIN'S CONTRASTS: PAROCHIAL CHURCHES

Left: All Souls', Langham Place, London
Right: Redcliffe Church, Bristol

[*See p.* 284]

From "Contrasts," by A. Welby Pugin

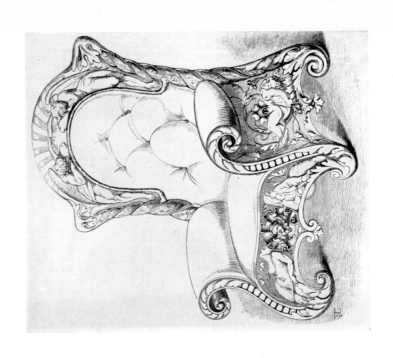

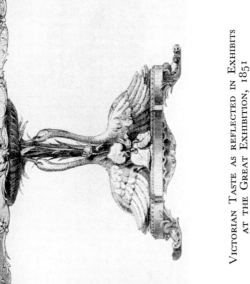

VICTORIAN TASTE AS REFLECTED IN EXHIBITS
AT THE GREAT EXHIBITION, 1851

Left: Ornamental Table
Right: An Easy Chair in Papier Mâché

[*See p.* 290]

THE EVOLUTION OF THE BICYCLE

Top: Johnson's 'Hobby Horse,' 1819
Bottom: 'Boneshaker' Bicycle, 1869

[*See p.* 303]

Crown Copyright. From exhibits in the Science Museum, South Kensington

The Evolution of the Bicycle

Top: Starley's 'Spider' Bicycle, 1872
Bottom: First Chain-driven Safety Bicycle, 1874

[*See p.* 303]

Crown Copyright. From exhibits in the Science Museum, South Kensington

including workers' co-operation; he could put them in a private savings bank or in the Post Office Savings Bank. And all these activities were protected by the State. He was encouraged to save, and complimented in proportion to his success in so doing. Expanding capitalism gave him the opportunity; the State provided the security and sometimes the means.

(b) CONSUMERS' CO-OPERATION

On October 24, 1844, the Rochdale Society of Equitable Pioneers was registered under the relevant Friendly Societies Acts. Its objects were:

The establishment of a store for the sale of provisions, clothing, etc.

The building, purchasing, or erecting a number of houses, in which those members, desiring to assist each other in improving their domestic and social condition, may reside.

The manufacture of such articles as the Society may determine upon, for the employment of such members as may be without employment, or who may be suffering in consequence of repeated reductions in their wages.

The Rochdale Pioneers announced also their intention to

purchase or rent an estate or estates of land, which shall be cultivated by the members who may be out of employment, or whose labour may be badly remunerated.

Above all, "as soon as practicable," they said, their Society should "proceed to arrange the powers of production, distribution, education, and government." As a sideline, but indicative of their general outlook on life, they decided that, "for the promotion of sobriety, a Temperance Hotel be opened in one of the Society's houses as soon as convenient."[1]

Of this grand scheme for regenerating society it was the first object, that of establishing a retail store, which won success and lasting fame.

The Rochdale Society of Equitable Pioneers was begun by seven flannel-weavers of Rochdale and their friends. All knew poverty and unemployment; all knew how the commercial shopkeeper by granting credit tied the poor man to his shop; all knew that the goods bought with hard-won wages were often

[1] G. J. Holyoake, *History of the Rochdale Pioneers*, pp. 11–12.

poor-quality or adulterated. All hated the spirit of competition, and desired, like Robert Owen, to establish friendly co-operation in production and exchange. They were simple men, teetotallers, and some at least shrewd and level-headed. They paid 2*d*. a week towards the projected store, increasing the subscription to 3*d*. as the fund mounted. Since the supporters of the scheme lived not only in Rochdale, but in outlying districts, the collector of the weekly pence had to walk as much as twenty miles on his weekly visit. The area was therefore divided into districts, and men took it in turn to take a district each on Sundays, collecting the money that was to found their store.

The money so collected was held in shares of £1. When sufficient was in hand the ground floor of a warehouse in Toad Lane was rented on a three years' lease at £10 a year. A certain amount of money had to be paid for fittings and preparation, and £14 or £15 was then left for stock. A little oatmeal, a little butter, and other goods in constant demand comprised the total, and on December 21, 1844, the Rochdale Equitable Pioneers opened their doors. Apprehension appears to have been the dominant feeling of the Pioneers themselves, and doubt and ridicule the reaction of the outside world. The little factory doffers came to jeer; a few friends came to purchase; many well-wishers were too far in debt to private shopkeepers to be able to change their custom. Nevertheless, three months later the store was sufficiently firmly established to apply for licences for the sale of tea and tobacco. The Toad Lane store steadily grew to the Rochdale Equitable Co-operative Society, Ltd, selling all the goods common to the modern big department store. By 1851 there were about 130 Co-operative Societies of the Rochdale type, with a membership of 15,000 persons. By 1862 there were 90,000 Co-operators in 450 Societies, with a share and loan capital of £450,000 and annual sales of £2,350,000.[1] By 1875 there were 437,000 Co-operators in 1266 stores in Great Britain, with a total capital of £4,412,000 and annual sales of over £13,000,000.[2]

The principle which Rochdale popularized, though it did not invent, was that of dividend upon purchases. Co-operators

---

[1] A. H. D. Acland and B. Jones, *Working-men Co-operators* (1884), quoting Returns made to Registrar by Co-operative Societies, p. 26.

[2] Beatrice Potter (Mrs Sidney Webb), *The Co-operative Movement in Great Britain*, Appendix IV.

had always tried, by eliminating the profit of middlemen, to reduce the cost of goods to the consumer. They had also endeavoured to give a return on their capital to the investors in Co-operative stores. The most popular method of achieving this had been by selling at market price and dividing the profit between the promoters of the concern. The dividend on purchases extended the benefits to all who bought goods at the shop. Without becoming involved in the difficulties of selling below market price the Rochdale Pioneers in fact gave their customers a cheaper article. Part of the profit was put back into the business, part was devoted to education and social services, the rest was returned to customers in proportion to the amount they had spent at the store.

As the retail stores grew they wanted, for their own benefit and to realize the grand ambition of the Rochdale manifesto, to avoid dealings with the commercial dealer and to wipe out the intermediate stages between producer and consumer, which add cost to the finished article without improving its quality. They wanted to avoid paying for the costs of competition between capitalist producers and to free themselves from the thraldom of capitalist monopoly. The first step towards this was the establishment of a single buying agency for the Co-operative retail stores. An English Co-operative Wholesale Society was started in 1863 and a Scottish in 1868. Branches of the English parent followed at Newcastle, Bristol, Cardiff, and London. The Wholesale supplied the retail stores with goods, as far as it was able, paying each store a dividend on its purchases in the same way as the stores paid dividends to their customers. Its growth was remarkably rapid, annual net sales rising from £52,000 in 1864 to over £1,500,000 in 1874.[1]

The chief function of the Wholesale Societies being to assemble goods for supply to the retail stores, the next step was the natural one of attempting to produce those goods themselves. At first the C.W.S. began by giving assistance to independent productive concerns, but when it lost money in this way it began itself to undertake the rôle of manufacturer. Its first venture was with biscuits in 1872 at Crumpsall, near Manchester, and the range thereafter extended.

The movement was strongest in the North of England and in the Lowlands of Scotland. It was least strong in big towns

[1] P. Redfern, *The New History of the C.W.S.*, p. 533.

like London and Birmingham, where people worked in their offices and dispersed to their homes at night. "London, the first to discuss co-operation, was the last to practise it."[1] It was strongest where some big concern, employing thousands of people, caused a spirit of solidarity to grow among the workers. They liked to patronize their own store; and Saturday night, when the shop was open until eleven o'clock or even later, was the time for gossip and banter, as the friendly customers flocked in with their wages to buy the week's stores.

The legal framework in which the Co-operative Societies could work was given by the extension to them of the relevant Friendly Society Acts. In 1846 legal recognition was given to Co-operative Societies as well as to Friendly Societies

> formed for the frugal investment of the savings of their members, for better enabling them to purchase food, firing, clothes or other necessaries, or the tools or other implements of their trade or calling, or to provide for the education of their children or kindred.[2]

In 1852 the Industrial and Provident Societies Act extended the rights of Friendly Societies to Co-operative Societies; stores were given the right to sell to non-members and the right of suing and being sued as legal personalities. Ten years later they were granted the right of limited liability, and in 1867 registered Co-operative Societies were given the right to invest in other societies up to any amount. The last provision made possible the establishment of Wholesale Societies on a Co-operative basis. In 1876 the Co-operative Societies were brought within the Friendly Societies Consolidating Act of the previous year. Thus, not without the sanction of the outer capitalist world, there developed what Lord Rosebery described as a "state within a state." Part of the reason for this approval—perhaps the price paid for legal recognition—was the steady concentration of the Co-operative Societies on their trading functions. Like most businesses, in the good years they prospered, and as they did so there faded from their programme the old ideals of social reform and even of educational service. Co-operative Congresses, which began to meet annually in 1869, were more concerned with trading details than with social regeneration. Of 400 Societies analysed in an appendix

---

[1] C. R. Fay, *Great Britain from Adam Smith to the Present Day*, p. 427.
[2] C. R. Fay, *Co-operation at Home and Abroad*, i, 278.

to a Congress Report of 1872 only 66 devoted funds to education.[1] Like other sections of the working-class movement, Co-operation prospered in the period of "Victorian Prosperity" not by opposition, but by absorption within that system which originally it had intended to supersede.

(c) CHRISTIAN SOCIALISM

About the middle of the nineteenth century there were a group of men—intellectuals, Christians, and Socialists in a limited sense—who gave to the working-class movement much practical help, legal, literary, and financial. They were also, because of their social connexions, excellent ambassadors of the working classes to other sections of the community.

The Christian Socialist group included F. D. Maurice, a Church of England clergyman who held the chair of theology at King's College, London, until dismissed for what were considered unorthodox beliefs, and Charles Kingsley, a Church of England clergyman, who would become more widely known as a writer of books which ranged from exciting historical novels like *Hereward the Wake* and *Westward Ho!* to social documents in novel form like *Yeast* and *Alton Locke*, and to charming children's books like *The Water Babies* and *The Heroes*.

The group included Thomas Hughes, a lawyer who became Member of Parliament and achieved fame through his account of Rugby in *Tom Brown's Schooldays*, and J. M. Ludlow, a lawyer who spent his early life in France and was much influenced by the Commune of 1848; he became Registrar of Friendly Societies in 1872. Friends and supporters included Professor Beesly, of Cambridge, Frederic Harrison, a lawyer who sat with Hughes and Ludlow on several Government Inquiries, and Vansittart Neale, the man among them who put most energy and money into the formation of various working societies for Co-operative production.

These Co-operative workshops form an interesting though premature development of working-class Co-operative production. There had been various experiments in the early part of the century, but all failed. In 1849 the Christian Socialists again took up the idea.

---

[1] Carr-Saunders, Florence, Peers, and others, *Consumers, Co-operation in Great Britain*, p. 36.

The story goes that Kingsley had come to London for the Kennington Common Chartist demonstration, and had there met Ludlow for the first time. Both men were relieved at the absence of violence, but unhappy about the future of working-class activity. They repaired to Maurice's house for discussion, and the next day the first placard of Christian Socialism appeared.

The group began its work with *Politics for the People*, a series of weekly tracts, the first of which appeared in May 1848, the last in July of the same year. Maurice in the first number announced their intention to consider the question of the extension of the suffrage, of the relation of the capitalist to the labourer, of finding work or giving maintenance to the poor. Kingsley, as "Parson Lot," spoke to the Chartists: "I think you have fallen into . . . the mistake of fancying that *legislative* reform is *social* reform, or that men's hearts can be changed by act of parliament."[1]

A little over a year later, in the autumn of 1849, appeared a series of articles in *The Morning Chronicle* on the tailoring and other distressed industries. This gave the group a further impetus. Parson Lot wrote the famous *Cheap Clothes and Nasty*, which did as it intended, and gave a severe shock to the complacency of the well-dressed well-to-do by exposing "the slavery, starvation, waste of life, year-long imprisonment in dungeons narrower and fouler than those of the Inquisition, which goes on among thousands of free English clothes-makers at this day." Kingsley's novel *Alton Locke* appeared in 1850, and the effect was the greater because of the piling up of horror which the length of the book permitted. The tract and the book between them not only drew a picture of sweat-shop and garret and cellar where consumptive men and women plied their trade, but showed the shivering wretches using the garments they were stitching to cover their naked limbs. The spread of consumption and fever and skin diseases hardly needed emphasis. Boycott sweat-shops, go only to reputable makers, and pay if necessary more money for your clothes, was the demand of the Christian Socialists to the public.

But they also had a project of immediate practical importance. In the last week in December 1849 ten of them, including two working-men, met to draw up a scheme. In

---

[1] *Politics for the People: Letter to Chartists*, p. 28.

early January 1850 they were ready to start Co-operative production. They began with the tailoring trade, partly because it was the subject of such scandalous abuses, partly because they were in touch with several working tailors, including a man of ability and integrity whom they planned to make manager of their first venture, and partly because tailoring needs a comparatively small capital expenditure and is a trade easily helped by personal orders. The tailors themselves resolved that "individual selfishness, as embodied in the competitive system, lies at the root of the evils under which English industry now suffers." They had a big meeting at the Mechanics' Institute, and there resolved:

> That the remedy for the evils of competition lies in the brotherly and Christian principle of co-operation—that is, of joint work with shared or common profits; and that this principle might be widely and readily applied in the formation of "Tailors' Working Associations."[1]

It was these tailors' working associations and similar Co-operative enterprises that the Christian Socialists were ready to start with money and advice. Developments were rapid. Premises at 34 Castle Street, Oxford Street, London, were leased on January 18, 1850, and £350 was advanced by the Promoters, as the group of Christian Socialists called themselves, to what became known as the Working Tailors' Association. The house was furnished and equipped in consultation with the man who was to become the manager of the Association.

Benefiting from the number of lawyers in their ranks, the Promoters drew up a detailed constitution for the Working Tailors' Association. The Promoters were to receive no profits, but the tailors (termed the Associates) were to repay quarterly from their profits the rent of the premises, an interest of 4 per cent. per annum on the money advanced, and an instalment of the capital which was to be not less than £10 per annum. After one-third of the net profits had been put aside for expansion the rest of the profit was to be used by the Associates as they thought fit. All moneys repaid by the Associates to the Promoters would be used for the extension of Co-operative production.

The manager of the workshop was to be the *liaison* between

[1] *Cheap Clothes and Nasty: Postscript*, p. 32.

Associates and Promoters; all work was to be executed on the premises, there was to be no Sunday work, all transactions were to be strictly for cash, accounts were to be made up once a week and be always open to the inspection of the Promoters and of customers.

At 7 A.M. on February 11, 1850, work began. There were twelve members of the Working Tailors' Association and for the first month they worked nine and a half hours a day for six days in the week, and received £1 a week each. During the second month they worked ten hours a day for six days, and received £1 2s. 6d. a week each. The manager meanwhile received a constant £2 a week. By the end of April they had twenty-four, by May thirty-four, men working. At the end of three months, after paying all expenses, they had a profit of £77, from which they paid back a proportion of the borrowed capital, increased their stock, and then divided the balance among the workmen. Said the manager:

> We were full of enthusiasm, and, I doubt not, of good intentions. . . . We called each other brothers, sang songs about "labour's social chivalry," and did wonders in the way of work and profit.[1]

The Christian Socialist Promoters meantime had elaborated their own constitution, and were embarking on fresh ventures "to show by what machinery the objects of Christian Socialism" could be achieved.

The whole group of organizers and workers were known as the "Society for Promoting Working Men's Associations." The Council of Promoters was the active body, consisting of a President, twelve ordinary members, and an unlimited number of honorary and corresponding members. Their object was to "diffuse the principles of Co-operation, as the practical application of Christianity to the purposes of trade and industry." To this end they collected and administered funds, kept accounts, published quarterly balance sheets and an annual report.

The workers in the Co-operative enterprises were to be represented by a Central Board, consisting of the manager and one delegate from each Association, and having a secretary appointed and paid by the Council of Promoters.

Up to July 1852 the S.P.W.M.A. had expended £397 on

---

[1] Quoted by B. Jones, *Co-operative Production*, p. 113.

propaganda and had lent £1222 to five workmen's Associations. Other money had been advanced as private loans. There were in all twelve Associations—three tailors', two builders', three shoemakers', one piano-makers', one printers', one smiths', one bakers'—and a Needlewomen's and Ladies' Guild.

The Christian Socialists were also publishing tracts on Christian Socialism at 1d. and 2d. each. In No. IV Ludlow described the S.P.W.M.A. and the Working Tailors. In 1852 the one and only Report of the Promoters was published.

The S.P.W.M.A. lasted for three or four years. One by one the associated bodies broke up. The tailors of Castle Street lasted for a few months only, and dissolved when times became slack and what its manager described as "those terrible evils, jealousy and disunion," prevailed. The Promoters assessed their failure with the tailors fairly enough in their first Report:

> We assumed that all the slop-workers of London must be alive to the evils of their position, and ready to try patiently and meekly any plan which offered a deliverance. We did not therefore take any pains to select the men for our experiment.[1]

Individual Christian Socialists continued to finance various enterprises, while the S.P.W.M.A. itself turned back to education. The Christian Socialists had always been largely missionary in aim, and in 1848 had had several slum schools in London. Now they founded the Working Men's College in Great Ormond Street, where Tom Hughes conducted one class for the study of the Bible and another for teaching the art of boxing.

The Christian Socialists themselves attributed the failure of their Co-operative workshops largely to their too casual selection of personnel. Others attributed it to over-assistance from the top—money too readily available, rules and organization ready-made, in place of a careful collection of funds by the workmen and a planning of their own organization, a too rigid control exercised by the Promoters, as, for example, their appointing and paying the secretary of the representative Council of the Associates. In this respect the success of Rochdale, with its laboriously collected pence, its carefully thought-out rules, was a striking contrast. But the Rochdale experiment was in other ways essentially different from the experiments of

[1] Quoted by Jones, *op. cit.*, p. 112.

the Christian Socialists. It was concerned with the simple process of selling retail, it had a consumers' market on its doorstep of a size easily estimated, and stocks could be adjusted to demand with little loss. The tailors' and similar enterprises, on the other hand, were engaged in actual production, which entailed more time and more capital for a less certain market. The goods of a retail grocery store are bought each day. The demand for clothes is a limited one so far as each individual is concerned, and the market must therefore be wide to maintain a steady sale. The Christian Socialist experiment which lasted longest was made by some bakers, and baking is the enterprise which lies nearest to the retail store; it takes comparatively little time, and the demand for bread is regular and constant.

The striking fact is that, whereas Co-operative production failed, consumers' Co-operation succeeded. It was not until producers had a steady market for their goods in the Co-operative Retail Societies that Co-operative production was successful. It was when the need came from below and consumers said, "Let us have our own stores and do away with the retail profit-maker," that consumers' Co-operation of the Rochdale type succeeded. It was not until the Co-operative retail stores all over the country said, "Let us do away with the profit-making manufacturer and produce our own goods," that Co-operative production succeeded in the form of the English and Scottish Co-operative Wholesale Societies.

Of the Christian Socialists' Co-operative workshops none remained. But their purely legal work was undoubtedly successful. The Friendly Society Acts owe much to Ludlow. He and Neale were called to give evidence to the Committee on the Savings of the Middle and Working Classes in 1850, and they were largely instrumental in securing the extension of the Friendly Society Acts to Co-operative Societies by the Industrial and Provident Societies Act of 1852. These two services alone are of outstanding importance, for without the protection of the law neither Friendly Societies nor Co-operative Societies could have developed as they did. The burst of Co-operation in the North of England which followed the Act of 1852 speaks for itself. But, beyond this, Ludlow and his friends were constant in sitting on Committees and Commissions and in rendering all the advice and help which their trained legal minds could give to the working-class movement.

In 1854, perhaps as a result of the failure of the Co-operative workshops, the emphasis of the Christian Socialists was again on the Christian side of their teaching. *Tracts for Priests and People* contained little of purely social interest. Their social teaching was, indeed, the outcome of their Christian beliefs. But always Christianity was first because they believed it to be basic. Christianity, said Kingsley, "gives a ray of hope . , . such as no universal suffrage, free-trade, communism, organization of labour . . . can give . . . a future of science, of justice, of freedom."[1] Christian Socialism, indeed, was never equalitarian Socialism as Owen had taught it. The Christian Socialists urged a change in heart and mind rather than a change in the basis of society, although they were Socialists in hoping and believing that the spiritual change would peacefully bring about an improvement in material conditions. They differed among themselves as to the extent of the change they considered desirable or inevitable. Maurice, in the *Tracts on Christian Socialism*, told his readers:

> We would have you just what you are—tailors, shoemakers, bakers, printers; only we would have you in these positions be men feeling and sympathizing with each other. . . . We will help you in fighting against the greatest enemy you have, your own self-will and selfishness. . . . This is what is meant by Christian Socialism.

Ludlow believed a change in the class basis of society to be inevitable, but considered that Co-operative enterprise and not violent action was the method. To the Committee on the Savings of the Middle and Working Classes he went so far as to use the argument—strange in the mouth of a man who called himself a Socialist—that facilities given to the working class for such enterprises as Co-operative production "would promote their submission to things as they are."[2]

All the Christian Socialists held to the creed given in the first tract on Christian Socialism: "I seriously believe that Christianity is the only foundation of Socialism, and that a true Socialism is the necessary result of a sound Christianity."

Although their Co-operative enterprises failed, the Christian Socialists are important in the development of Socialism and the Labour movement for several reasons. The effect of their propaganda was considerable. They were all men of influence

[1] *Cheap Clothes and Nasty.*   [2] 1850, XIX, 10.

in the Church, in society, and in intellectual circles, and some had a more popular following. They were possessed of a burning faith, which burnt all the clearer because their numbers were sufficiently small to allow of close and frequent contact. Not only did they write well and reach a large public, but they reached a public barely touched by normal Labour or Socialist writers.

Second, the Christian Socialists are important because of the practical legal help which they gave to all sections of organized labour. Third, for the very reason that they were so largely responsible for legalizing the working-class movement, they set it upon the path of what proved to be a prosperous legality, when it might have been driven, through want of recognition, into illegal activity. They thus did much "to bring the social evolution of England into a peaceful way." To the revolutionary Socialist this was no service, but a disservice, diverting the working class, as Ludlow openly boasted, from the political subjects which had been engrossing their attention, to the *petit bourgeois* virtues of thrift and self-help. But when the Friendly Societies and Co-operative enterprises were growing there was no revolutionary force in Britain. The effective counter-revolution was being made, not by Christian Socialism, but by the expanding capitalist system.

SELECT BIBLIOGRAPHY

Fourth Report of the Committee appointed to inquire into Friendly and Benefit Building Societies, 1874, XXIII, Parts 1 and 2.
Report of the Select Committee on Friendly Societies, 1888, XII.
ACLAND, A. H. D. AND JONES, B.: *Working-men Co-operators* (Cassell, 1884).
BAERNREITHER, J. M.: *English Combinations of Working Men* (Sonnenschein, 1888).
BRABROOK, E. W.: *Provident Societies and Industrial Welfare* (Blackie, 1898).
CARR-SAUNDERS, A. M., FLORENCE, P. S., PEERS, R., AND OTHERS: *Consumers' Co-operation in Great Britain* (Allen and Unwin, 1938).
JONES, Benjamin: *Co-operative Production* (Frowde, 1894).

Politics for the People (Parker and Son, 1848).

POTTER, B. (MRS SIDNEY WEBB): *The Co-operative Movement in Great Britain* (Sonnenschein, 1891).

RAVEN, C. E.: *Christian Socialism, 1848–1854* (Macmillan, 1920).

REDFERN, P.: *The New History of the C.W.S.* (Dent, 1938).

SMILES, S.: *Self-help*: centenary edition with introduction by Asa Briggs (Murray, 1959).

——: *Thrift* (Murray, 1875).

Tracts on Christian Socialism (Bell, 1850).

WEBB, S. AND B.: *The Consumers' Co-operative Movement* (Longmans, 1921).

CHAPTER XVI

TRADE UNIONS IN THE 'PROSPERITY' PERIOD

AFTER the collapse of 1834 trade unionism remained dormant. In the hungry forties workers turned fiercely to Chartism, while the attenuated trade unions held aloof. But as economic conditions improved at the end of the forties the pendulum swung again from political to economic activity, and Chartism was left high and dry to wither away. A trade-union revival became perceptible in the middle forties. There were Unions of Potters and Cotton-spinners, National Societies of Tailors, Shoemakers, and Typographical Workers, and a Miners' Association of Great Britain and Ireland. The last was formed in 1841, after which the miners under Martin Jude took the centre of the trade-union stage. Much of their trouble arose from interpretations of the Master and Servant Act and from the old-established custom of the yearly bond, which virtually put them in the power of the master for twelve months, without protection from illegal usage or broken contract. To remedy this the miners began to take action at law, and soon the name of William Prowting Roberts, a young lawyer, became known for the number of successes he won for the miners of Northumberland and Durham. Shortly afterwards he was employed by the Miners' Association at a salary of £1000 a year. But, though broken contracts and illegal practices by the employers became fewer, wages did not rise, and many of the grievances remained.

There followed consequently the strike of 1844, when 30,000 Northumberland and Durham men remained out for many months. This great effort failed. Roberts continued to be engaged by various unions, but the Miners' Association never recovered from the defeat, and by 1848 had virtually ceased to exist.

Meantime the general movement of the trade-union world was towards the old idea of the general union. The National Association of United Trades for the Protection of Labour, formed in 1845, recalled Doherty and Owen. There was also a National United Trades Association for the *Employment* of Labour which was purely Owenite in aim. These Associations, however, unlike Doherty's "one big union," did not attempt to replace existing trade unions, but were intended to be complementary.

In the Miners' Association and the other unions of this period appeared several characteristics which became common features of the big unions of the fifties. There was the use of the existing law to the full extent that it would benefit the unions. Here the miners led the way. The second characteristic was a turning to education. The bookbinders and compositors had their library, the bookbinders a reading-room, stonemasons a debating society and a class for "mutual instruction." Union and trade journals multiplied. *The Flint Glass Makers' Magazine* urged, "If you do not wish to stand as you are and suffer more oppression we say to you get knowledge, and in getting knowledge you get power."[1] The third characteristic of trade-union policy, which began to appear in the later forties, was an attitude of conciliation. At a conference of united trades in London in 1845 there was talk of the mutual interests of employer and employed, and of the advantages of a good understanding between master and men. The fourth, and in line with the third, characteristic was a growing disinclination to strike. Stonemasons warned their members to keep from strikes as from "a ferocious animal that you know would destroy you."[2] London compositors turned instead to "the irresistible weapons of truth and reason."[3] Many unions laid stress on the limitation of apprentices, encouragement of emigration, and other measures intended to reduce the supply of labour and keep up wages.

In all this can be noted the gradual adjustment of the workman to the system, his acceptance of its values, his use of its language, his shifting of the argument on to its ground. At the same time the unions were searching for a more effective organization to further their ends and safeguard their funds, which began to rise as trade improved. It was the engineers who first effectively combined a new and efficient organization with a policy of conciliation and arbitration, the Amalgamated

---

[1] S. and B. Webb, *History of Trade Unionism*, pp. 197–198.
[2] *Ibid.*, p. 199.   [3] *Ibid.*, p. 198.

Society of Engineers, as the New Model, giving its name to the unionism of the period.

The A.S.E. was founded in January 1851. The largest and most important section of the Amalgamation was the Journeymen Steam-engine and Machine-makers' and Millwrights' Friendly Society, two of whose members, William Newton and William Allan, were the force behind the Amalgamation, Allan becoming its secretary. By October 1851 membership was 11,000, by 1858 over 15,000, by 1867 33,000. Membership was confined to legally apprenticed workmen. There was a subscription at the high rate of 1s. a week. The A.S.E. was thus a union of skilled workmen, and accumulated a large fund, which it spent as much on Friendly Society benefits as on trade objects. It was, in fact, as much a Friendly Society as a trade union, and its members were largely concerned with sickness, old-age, and burial benefits—with that security which a man seeks when he has risen above the poverty line. The relative importance of Friendly Society benefits and strike pay in the annals of the Engineers is shown by the fact that over a period of ten years they gave £459,000 to benefits and £26,000 to trade disputes.[1] They had nevertheless definite trade objects, primary among which was the seeking of their ends by arbitration and not by strikes.

The large funds of the Union and its extensive Friendly Society benefits necessitated a careful organization. The secretary of the Society was a paid full-time servant. Funds were not centralized, because there was no certain provision at law for their protection, and it was better to spread the risk of loss among the branches. A high degree of uniformity and control was nevertheless ensured by vesting in the central office the sole right to authorize strike payments and by permitting branches to pay Friendly Society benefits only in conformity with carefully prepared rules. A method of 'equalization' or 'balancing' ensured that each branch of the Union started each financial year with the same amount of money. The A.S.E. thus became a highly centralized body, with control largely in the hands of William Allan and a small group of leaders with headquarters in London.

---

[1] *Royal Commission appointed to inquire into the Organization and Rules of Trades Unions and other Associations*; Minority Report of Hughes and Harrison, 1868–69, XXXI, xxxv.

In spite of its policy of conciliation, the Engineers' Union supported a strike when the reasons were strong, and then it did so without stint. Its first testing was twelve months after its foundation. In the strike and lock-out that lasted from January to April 1852 the A.S.E. not only made liberal contributions to its own members, but also helped the unskilled non-Union machine-minders who had been thrown out of work. The men lost. But the A.S.E. gained prestige through its high rate of strike pay. Seven years later a builders' strike was supported by the A.S.E. to the extent of three weekly payments of £1000 each. Such an impressive contribution helped to decide the carpenters to model themselves on the A.S.E., and with William Allan's help the Amalgamated Society of Carpenters was formed in June 1860. Two years later Robert Applegarth became its secretary.

Meantime, under the stimulus of better trade and the leadership of Alexander Macdonald, but without modelling themselves on the A.S.E., the miners again stirred themselves. There were strikes and lock-outs all over the country from 1855 to 1863, the year when the Miners' National Association was formed under Macdonald's influence. Sectionalism and quarrels followed, exacerbated by the depression which fell on the coal industry in 1864–65. The conciliatory political outlook of Macdonald was challenged by the Amalgamated Association of Miners, which was formed in 1869, and which stood for a vigorous industrial policy. The Amalgamated took the lead in a series of strikes in South Wales and Lancashire, but was defeated, and by 1875 had ceased to exist. The Miners' National Association continued successfully until Macdonald's death in 1881, when it broke up.

Like the engineers, the miners for the most part sought improvement within the limits of the existing system, preferring arbitration to strike action. Owing to the peculiar conditions of their service they also sought specific legal reforms—the amendment of the law of Master and Servant, the appointment of checkweighmen, and a statutory eight-hour day.

The law of Master and Servant affected many trades. Its very name was obnoxious. But on none did it press more heavily than the miners. Masters easily secured convictions against men who left their employment without due notice, who left work unfinished, or who perpetrated any similar 'crime' against their employer. Conviction could be secured on the verdict of a single justice of the peace, who might himself be an employer, and the penalty was always imprisonment, for breach of contract on the part of the worker was regarded as a criminal offence. The master, on the other hand, besides having the machinery of the law on his side, was liable to nothing more than damages for broken contract. In practice, while masters secured convictions against men, men who prosecuted their masters were rarely successful. The legal work of Roberts had done something to redress the balance, but now the miners began a strong campaign for the amendment of the law. The trades councils of the chief towns were circularized; in Leeds and elsewhere special trades councils were formed. A trade-union delegate conference—the first in history—was convened by the Glasgow Trades Council in 1864. Members of Parliament were vigorously lobbied, and a number promised support for an amendment of the obnoxious Act. There was a Select Committee, a Report, and finally an amending Act became law as the Master and Servant Act of 1867.

The position of the checkweighman was peculiar to the mining industry. Miners were paid according to their output, wages being computed at the pit-head office by means of tallies attached by the miner to each basket he filled. With only employers' representatives to compute his wages the possibilities of unfair treatment were many; a representative of the men to check the employers' calculations was essential. The campaign for the appointment of checkweighmen had been going on for a long while when, after the strikes in Yorkshire in 1859, some masters reluctantly agreed to accept checkweighmen in their pits. The following year, after great efforts by Macdonald and a hot debate in Parliament, an Act was passed legalizing the appointment of checkweighmen. The effect of the Act was vitiated, however, by a clause prescribing that the checkweighman had to be employed at the pit. It was consequently easy for unscrupulous employers to dismiss checkweighmen from their service. Although the men were supported by the courts, reinstatement took too long—in one case two years—for the advantage of the concession of checkweighmen to be reaped by the miners. In 1872 there was some improvement effected by the Mines Regulation Act, but it was not until 1887 that the full rights of appointing checkweighmen were explicitly granted to the men. One interesting result of this legislation is pointed out by the Webbs. Checkweighmen had necessarily to be men familiar with work at the coal-face, yet quick with figures, unperturbed and calm if the masters' representatives tried to rush them, tenacious in a dispute. These were the desirable qualities for a trade-union representative, and the ranks of the checkweighmen have, in fact, contributed some of the most efficient of the miners' leaders.

The miners' struggles are important for the stress they laid upon improving their position by means of the law. The Act of 1867 amending the law of Master and Servant, the Checkweighmen's Acts, were in this respect pointers to the way the whole trade-union world was moving.

Like the miners, the cotton operatives continued their own type of organization. To the centralization of the Amalgamated Societies the cotton-workers opposed their traditional federal structure, with autonomy for the various branches of the federation. This looser organization allowed more initiative, and therefore variety, to the branches, with the result that the cotton-workers were not as a whole so conservative nor so opposed to strike action as the engineers. Political action they approached in a spirit similar to that of the miners, seeking from the law specific reforms to improve working conditions. Campaigns to reduce working hours by law, for example, had long been a feature of the cotton industry, and it was the first industry to have its hours legally regulated.

As checkweighmen among miners were a valuable and highly trained class, so among cotton operatives the union representatives needed particular skill and quickness in negotiating wage-rates. In the cotton industry price-lists are used for the calculating of wages which are paid by the piece. The lists are extremely detailed, entailing different rates for type of yarn, width of frame, species of cloth, with dozens of variations understood only by the skilled worker. The union man had to be quick to see what rates would most benefit his members, which reductions must be avoided at all costs. He had to see the effect on a week's wages of fractional decreases or increases in various piece-rates. Like the checkweighman, he had to be quick, calm, with a good head for figures, and skilled in the intricacies of his trade.

The builders also remained loosely organized according to

their crafts, and in 1859 there broke out one of their periodic disputes. Their demand for a nine-hour day was refused, and 24,000 of them were locked out. An important outcome of the dispute was a series of meetings of various trades in several towns, including London, to consider support for the builders. Such trades councils had had temporary existence from time to time in various places, but the London Trades Council in 1860 became a permanent and important body.

This trades council, being a London body, had close contacts with the Amalgamated Society leaders, and Odger of the London Trades Council, Allan of the Engineers, Applegarth of the Carpenters, Guile of the Ironfounders, and Coulson of the London Bricklayers, became a close committee of the trade-union world. These were the men termed by the Webbs the Junta. Their policy was arbitration, conciliation, non-strike activity, stress on Friendly Society functions, husbanding of funds, close central control of policy and finance. In the prosperous atmosphere of the sixties their leadership was accepted because it appeared successful, and also because they were men of outstanding character and ability. Different groups of workmen had at times produced capable leaders, but never before at one time had so powerful a group flourished as the Junta. The trade-union movement was doubly fortunate in that the purpose, drive, and organizing ability of these men were complemented by the qualities which the Christian Socialists contributed to the movement, providing just the balance and trained intelligence required by the largely self-educated trade unionists.

The conservatism of the Junta was encouraged in a number of ways. The weight of business which devolved upon the full-time secretaries of the big unions caused them to become immersed in administration. When they called in assistants it was generally to help with the Friendly Society side of the union, which, with increasing membership, grew disproportionately to other functions. Thus the most conservative side of union business received emphasis. At the same time, as funds increased, the fear of losing them through strike action became stronger; while the richer and more powerful they became, the more the trade unions were respected as bargaining bodies, the greater readiness was shown by employers to negotiate agreements.

It was into this comparatively peaceful world that the troubles of 1866–67 burst. From Sheffield public opinion heard in 1866 of the violent action of certain trade unionists against blacklegs. Members of the grinders and other instrument-making trades had been conducting a campaign against violators of trade-union law using such barbarous methods as putting kegs of gunpowder down their chimneys. Injury and death of workmen, their families and friends resulted. A public inquiry was called for, and the trade unions, so anxiously striving for approval, found themselves faced with a Government Commission which gave little promise of friendship and a public opinion decidedly hostile. At this moment another blow fell. The Society of Boilermakers prosecuted its secretary for withholding Society funds. In doing so it was acting in accordance with the generally understood provisions of the Friendly Society Act of 1855. This Act was thought to allow a trade union, by depositing its rules with the Registrar of Friendly Societies, to enjoy the privilege of proceeding against a defaulting member in cases such as this. But the Judge of Queen's Bench, who heard the case, ruled that trade unions were not within the scope of the Act, and could not bring a case at law against any of their officers. This meant that their funds were open to misappropriation and that no redress was possible. It was a serious position. Their extensive Friendly Society functions, their accumulated reserves, all their work as trade societies, were threatened. But worse followed. The Judge of Queen's Bench went out of his way to rule that, although a trade union was not exactly criminal, it was yet so far in restraint of trade as to be an illegal organization. The effect of this ruling of 1867 was shattering. After nearly fifty years of legality trade unions were once again outside the pale of the law. The work of Francis Place had to be done again in a far more complicated reach of currents and cross-currents. It was ironic that this blow should fall at just the moment when twenty years of rectitude had apparently won recognition.

Meantime a Commission of Inquiry had been appointed. It was originally intended as an examination into the Sheffield outrages, but its official terms of reference were much wider, covering the organization and rules of trade unions and the relations between workmen and employers. The appointment of the Royal Commission made clear the course of action of the unions. They must justify their existence before the Commission, and obtain an amendment of the law which would ensure their legality and protect their funds. To this end they must emphasize their Friendly Society functions and vigorously dissociate themselves from the small group responsible for the Sheffield outrages. The Junta met constantly and urgently, calling to its aid all who could be of use. The Manchester Trades Council the following year convened the congress of trade-union representatives which was destined to be the first of the long line of Trade Union Congresses. On the Royal Commission itself the unions were fortunate in having two able sympathizers out of a membership of eleven. Both their supporters were lawyers and Christian Socialists—Thomas Hughes and Frederic Harrison. Further, the trade unions were permitted to have a representative observer at the sittings of the Commission. Thus the Royal Commission opened its proceedings in March 1867, while the Junta met almost constantly outside, in close touch with the two friendly Commissioners. Many trade unionists were called before the Commission— Robert Applegarth, William Allan, George Howell, Daniel Guile, John Kane of the Ironworkers, Alexander Macdonald.

Most of the witnesses made a good showing with carefully prepared and reasoned answers. These were no ranting, illiterate revolutionaries, but sober, intelligent workmen, many of whom had acquired an education far beyond the requirements of their trade. Alexander Macdonald, for example, told the Commission that he had started work in an ironstone mine at the age of eight. Before that he had been to the parish school, but there was no provision for education at the pit. With his brother he therefore travelled some three or four miles after work at seven or eight o'clock in the evening to a village school for the children of farm labourers. Later he went to evening classes at Airdrie for Latin and Greek; and then, working in the summer only, he saved enough money for attendance at Glasgow University in the winter. Fees, books, lodging and living expenses he estimated at £55–£60 for the six months. He studied Latin, Greek, logic, and mathematics.[1]

Most of the witnesses in one form or another emphasized

---

[1] *Royal Commission appointed to inquire into the Organization and Rules of Trades Unions and other Associations*, Minutes of Evidence, 1867–68, XXIX (Seventh Report), pp. 40–41, *passim*.

the Friendly Society functions of their unions and disparaged strikes. Allan told the Commission that "all strikes are a complete waste of money."[1] Applegarth, evidently with an eye to public consumption, announced pompously:

> I would here take the liberty of explaining that I have always held that men have no right to strike, nor masters to lock-out, without first making the public acquainted with the causes that are likely to lead to a strike or lock-out, for I believe that the interests of the public are of much greater importance than either those of the masters or of the men.[2]

As quoted by him to the Commission, the objects of the Amalgamated Society of Carpenters were entirely Friendly.[3]

George Howell and Alexander Macdonald described in glowing terms the improving effect of trade unionism on men's characters. Howell described the "discipline of the lodge" on the bricklayer members:

> Neither drunkenness nor swearing is allowed in the lodge room, and there is a moral self-restraint necessary to be exercised in the room, and the exercise of that has a most beneficial effect on the members.[4]

Macdonald attributed the "beneficial change in the condition of the mining class in Scotland" both to the "progress of civilization" and to "the combinations of the men from time to time."

After an inquiry spreading over two years the Commissioners issued their Report in March 1869. Investigation of the Sheffield outrages, which had been the initial cause of the Inquiry, appeared as only a small section of the Report. Some startling confessions, made under the promise of indemnity, revealed the Saw-grinders, under their secretary, William Broadhead, as responsible for some of the worst outrages. Elisha Parker, a saw-grinder, for example, worked for a firm which employed two non-union men. Consequently his horse was killed, gunpowder was placed at his door, and finally he himself was roused one night, and, on going outside, was shot at and wounded in both arms. James Linley, a saw-grinder who kept apprentices contrary to the rules of the union, was

---

[1] *Ibid.*, Minutes of Evidence, 1867, XXXII (First Report), p. 37, Q. 827.
[2] *Ibid.* (First Report), p. 4, Q. 77.   [3] *Ibid.* (First Report), p. 1, Q. 12.
[4] *Ibid.* (First Report), p. 65, Q. 1731.

shot at, a can of gunpowder was thrown into the house of his brother-in-law's family, where he was living, and he was finally shot again and died. A non-union fender-grinder named George Wastnidge lived in Acorn Street with his wife, child, and a lodger. About one o'clock in the morning of November 23, 1861, a can of gunpowder was thrown into the house. It exploded, set fire to clothing and part of the house, and resulted in the death of the lodger and the serious injury of Mrs Wastnidge.[1]

These confessions naturally created a great stir among the public. But the Report made it clear that only about one-fifth of the Sheffield unions had ever been involved, and that outrages of this nature had been getting less frequent in the years preceding 1866. It was impossible to indict trade unions as a whole for the actions of so small a section, however outrageous. The main body of the Report consequently made little reference to them. Instead it made it clear that there would be no difficulty about legalizing the unions provided they were, in fact, as innocent of subversive activity and as little in restraint of trade and individual freedom as they had professed to the Commission.

Trade unions, as such, the Commissioners justified on economic grounds, arguing that combination was natural to an individual workman, who was far less able to bargain than an individual employer. Nevertheless the Commissioners refused to condone any action which interfered with the rights of others to do as they pleased. Consequently they condemned picketing.

> So far as related to members of the union promoting the strike, the pickets cannot be necessary if the members are voluntarily concurring therein; so far as relates to workmen who are not members of the union, picketing implies in principle an interference with their right to dispose of their labour as they think fit, and is, therefore, without justification; and so far as relates to the employer, it is a violation of his right of free resort to the labour market for the supply of such labour as he requires.[2]

The Commissioners therefore recommended that no combination should be illegal merely because in restraint of trade,

---

[1] *Report presented to the Trades Unions Commissioners by the Examiners appointed to inquire into Acts of Intimidation, Outrage, or Wrong alleged to have been promoted, encouraged, or connived at by Trades Unions in the Town of Sheffield*, 1867, XXXII, *passim*.
[2] *Eleventh and Final Report*, 1868–69, XXXI, xxii.

but that 'molestation' and 'obstruction' by means of picketing should remain offences at law.

On the important question of union funds, the Commission confirmed that, as the law then stood, these were not protected, since trade unions were outside the scope of the Friendly Society Acts. It therefore recommended the registration of trade unions under the Friendly Societies Acts on roughly the same conditions as applied to Friendly Societies—primarily that the Registrar should deem their rules unobjectionable. Objectionable rules would be those whose objects were to prevent or limit the employment of apprentices or machinery in any trade or manufacture, to interfere in any way with a man's work, or to try to prevent his working with non-unionists, or to interfere in any way with any dispute on which another union was engaged.

Besides the Majority Report, an important Minority Report was signed by the two trade-union supporters, Frederic Harrison and Thomas Hughes. This Report emphasized the extent and increase of trade unionism and what it termed "the high character" of the principal unions. It recommended an explicit statement in law relating to the legality of combinations, which would make clear that no combination in pursuance of a trade object would be indictable unless it were guilty of some action punishable under the ordinary criminal law. Protection of funds the Minority Report regarded as essential, and, like the Majority Report, recommended it should be by registration under the Friendly Society Acts upon deposit of rules and an annual statement. But the Minority Report denied to the Registrar the power to object to any trade-union rule or item of expenditure that was not actually of itself criminal. The trade unions, in return for legal recognition, should agree to the sole condition of accepting publicity in their administration.

Legislation followed the Majority Report. The Act of 1871 provided that a trade union should not be considered an illegal body merely because it was in restraint of trade. It allowed a union to register under the Friendly Society Acts provided its rules were not criminal. But in its original form the Act went on to prohibit certain practices which were deemed illegal. The chief of these was picketing of any kind, including peaceful picketing. The trade-union world was immediately in arms.

Picketing, it pointed out, was the essential weapon of a strike or lock-out. Without it the right to strike was valueless. The Act acknowledged the end, but denied the means.

The utmost the trade unions could achieve was the division of the Act into two parts and the satisfaction of seeing their supporters vote for the one and against the other. The Trade Union Act of 1871 legalized and protected the trade unions. The Criminal Law Amendment Act of the same year declared picketing and all allied activity to be illegal.

That the Criminal Law Amendment Act was to be no dead letter was soon made clear. In the very year of its passage seven women in South Wales were imprisoned for saying "Bah!" to one blackleg.[1] In 1872 six gas-stokers were prosecuted for conspiracy under the Act and sentenced to twelve months' imprisonment. For the next few years the chief object of the trade unions was the repeal of the obnoxious Act. Changing the law implies political action, though economic means can be used to this end. The trade unions of the seventies might have organized mass strikes and refused to work until the law was changed. But this would have jeopardized the hard-won position already reached and threatened their carefully husbanded funds. They preferred instead a political campaign.

In this they were helped by the Reform movement, which in the fifties and sixties carried on the campaign for Parliamentary Reform which had never quite died since the Great Betrayal of 1832, and which already, by the Act of 1858, had achieved the abolition of the property qualification for M.P.'s. On the one hand was a group in the middle-class Radical tradition who asked for household suffrage and vote by ballot. On the other were groups, including the London Trades Council and the Junta, which demanded complete manhood suffrage as well as the ballot. The various groups finally crystallized into the Radical National Reform Union of 1864, centred round John Bright, and the working-class Manhood Suffrage Association of 1865, centred round the Junta.

The second Reform Act actually became law in 1867 while the trade unions were on trial before the Royal Commission. Its passage owed much to the game of party politics, in which Disraeli was quick to seize a chance of playing for the support

[1] Webb, *op. cit.*, p. 284.

of the working classes against the Whigs. As might be expected, the Act merely conceded household suffrage, the effect of which was to give the vote to the town artisan while leaving the county franchise unchanged and the agricultural labourer still voteless. In 1872 the Ballot Act instituted vote by ballot, so that the secrecy of the vote was safeguarded and the fear of intimidation largely removed. It would seem that the way was now clear for the return of working-class candidates. Nevertheless it was typical of the contemporary attitude that the workers of Sheffield chose as their first Parliamentary candidate after their enfranchisement not a workman, but Anthony John Mundella, a wealthy and enlightened Nottingham manufacturer who stood as a Liberal. But at the general election of 1868 three trade-union candidates went to the poll, in the following year the Labour Representation League was formed, primarily for returning labouring men to Parliament, and in the by-elections of the next few years working-class candidates fought in Southwark, Bristol, and Norwich. The crisis of 1867 had pushed the Junta thus far. The passage of the Criminal Law Amendment Act of 1871 pushed them further. In 1872 a pamphlet, *The Direct Representation of Labour in Parliament*, was published over signatures including those of Macdonald. Allan, and George Howell of the builders. It said:

> We have been deluded with promised reforms, but those we most desire are neglected and unduly deferred, whilst measures affecting the welfare of the wealthy classes are constantly studied, actively promoted.

The practical effect of this development was seen in a profound dissatisfaction with the Liberal Party, who had passed the Act of 1871, and a swinging of the working-class vote in the election of 1874 from Liberals to Tories, which was partly responsible for the defeat of the Liberal Government and the return to office of the Tories. Fifteen working-men candidates also went to the poll in 1874. In spite of working-class distrust of the Liberals there were a few agreements between Liberal and Labour candidates, and in two cases where there was no Liberal opposition Labour men were returned to Parliament —the first working-men to sit in the House of Commons. They were Thomas Burt, returned for Morpeth, and Alexander Macdonald, returned for Stafford—both miners. Since there were only two parties in the House they sat with the Liberals, being rather a Radical tail to the Liberal Party than an independent group.

The period of Liberal-Labour collaboration—the era of the Lib-Labs—dates from this time. For the time being, however, a Tory Government had been returned, partly at least through Labour dissatisfaction with the legislation of 1871. The Conservative Government appointed a Commission, and at first appeared as though it might open up again the whole question of the legality of trade unions. Labour was very much alarmed. The trade unions boycotted the Commission; few working-men gave evidence before it; Thomas Burt refused a seat; Hughes and Macdonald finally agreed to sit, but Macdonald presented a Minority Report. The Majority Report proposed no real amendment of the Criminal Law Amendment Act, and angry agitation swept the country. In the event the Tories decided not to antagonize Labour, and brought forward two Bills which were a surprisingly complete acquiescence in all the trade unions had been demanding. The Criminal Law Amendment Act of 1871 was repealed and replaced by the Conspiracy and Protection of Property Act of 1875. This legalized peaceful picketing, and laid down that no act done in combination was to be a punishable offence unless it was so when committed by an individual. In the same year the Master and Servant Act of 1867 was repealed and replaced by the Employers and Workmen Act. The change in title was significant. Apart from a few exceptional cases, imprisonment for breach of contract was abolished, and employer and workman became legally equal partners to a civil contract.

So, by the Acts of 1871 and 1875 and a minor amending Act of 1876, the trade unions won their charter. They had been brought into line with the Friendly Societies and the Co-operatives, and were legally recognized elements of capitalist society.

While the workers were developing the organization oi Friendly Societies and Co-operative Societies, and adjusting their trade-union organization to the prosperous background of the mid-century, various reform movements of other kinds were also developing. The reform movements which continued through the "Prosperity" years were more intellectual and middle class, less bread-and-butter issues than the struggles of the forties. When the masses were annoyed they mobbed the gentry, as they did at Hyde Park on successive Sundays in 1855 when an attempt was made to close Sunday street markets, and they had their way and retained their Sunday markets. Again, in 1871 popular agitation saved the remains of Epping Forest for the people; and in 1872 the voice of the populace helped to modify the Public Parks Regulation Bill which regulated meetings in parks. But on the whole the demands of the fifties and sixties were philanthropic, intellectual, middle class, and very little class-conscious.

A section of the reform movement was aimed at the strict Sabbatarianism which kept not only entertainments, but even museums and picture galleries, closed on Sundays—the only day when working-men and their families could visit them. The workmen themselves were pressing for the opening of the Crystal Palace, the National Gallery, the British Museum, at least on Sunday afternoons. In February 1856 Sir Joshua Walmsley proposed in the House of Commons the opening of the British Museum and the National Gallery after morning service. Amid a great pulpit outcry the motion was lost. In April of the same year Sir Benjamin Hall, Commissioner of Works and Forests, ordered band concerts in parks on Sundays. The Archbishop of Canterbury was among the angry protestants who compelled the abandonment of the scheme. Sunday Band Committees were formed, and the National Sunday League, which had been founded in 1855, tried on a wider front to provide educational and social entertainment on Sundays. In 1877 Manchester opened its civic museum and library on Sundays. Birmingham and other towns followed. But not until 1896 were the museums and art galleries of London opened to the public on Sunday afternoons. The Sunday League by this time was organizing Sunday-evening concerts and Sunday excursions to the sea and other popular places in co-operation with the railways, which issued cheap day-excursion tickets.

Other sections of the reform movement covered demands for factory reform, an extension of education, university reform, Jewish emancipation, the reform of City Government, a revision of taxation, the further extension of the franchise including votes for women, and penal and prison reform.

After the scandals revealed by the Crimean War Army reform and Civil Service reform received a particular impetus. The demand for the abolition in the Army of promotion by purchase was strong, and in 1855 the Administrative Reform Association pledged itself to "destroy the aristocratical monopoly of power and place" in the Civil Service. There was a growing demand for the extension of municipal enterprise by the further provision of baths, washhouses, libraries, museums, hospitals; for the prevention of food adulteration and for cleanliness in its preparation and sale. Select Committees on the Adulteration of Food reported in 1856 and 1874 that many articles were adulterated both for the sake of cheapness and to improve their appearance. Plaster of Paris, for example, and highly poisonous colourings were used in the making of confectionery, alum in bread, and antiseptics were added to perishable goods. There were Reports on Bakehouses which showed the existence of dirty, dilapidated bakeries where bread was made close by defective drains and privies, where there was no ventilation, and where the bakers also slept.

The success of the reform movement is marked by the legislation of the period. In 1854 a Government Report was published on the Organization of the Civil Service which recommended entry by competitive examination. In the following year Palmerston established the Civil Service Commission, and competitive entry for all branches but the Foreign Office was established in 1870. Apart from educational reform, factory reform, and franchise reform, many smaller but important improvements in the law or its administration were made. In 1858 a Jewish M.P. was allowed to take a modified oath in either House, omitting "on the true faith of a Christian." In 1871 the practice of purchasing commissions in the Army was abolished by Royal Warrant after the Lords had turned down the Commons' Bill to that end. A Bakehouses Regulation Act was passed in 1863, an Adulteration of Food Act in 1872, a Sale of Food and Drugs Act in 1875. In 1876 the Merchant Shipping Act successfully concluded Samuel Plimsoll's agitation for limiting the amount of cargo a ship could carry. Henceforth no ship might be weighted down so that the 'Plimsoll line was below water.'

On the whole the demands and the Acts which met them show a wide range, reflecting the requirements of people above the poverty line. The working classes left most of the agitation for these reforms to the middle classes; the populace, in general, were more concerned with oppression abroad than with any that pressed on them at home. They were ardently for Polish nationalism and against Russian tyranny; they were enthusiastic supporters of a free Italy. There were demonstrations of great enthusiasm for Garibaldi when he came to London in 1864. "Nothing except foreign politics seems to occupy the attention of the people, press, or parliament," grumbled Cobden in 1864.[1] "The impulse to advance in Great Britain has almost always come from below," said *The National Review* in April 1863,

> but for some years past the masses have been singularly unwilling to move. . . . They have given up the Charter, given up voting to a most annoying extent, and turned with fresh interest and avidity to schemes for social improvement. . . . The middle class sympathize with the lower in their crave for physical comfort. They will not concede them power—are, indeed, on that point recklessly selfish and blind—but they will go to almost any length to improve their material condition. Every kind of benevolent project finds, and for thirty years has always found, the heartiest sympathy and support. Law after law has been passed to make the popular insurance system, the great but half-tried idea of benefit societies, more and more efficient. The vote for the education of the poor has become a visible item in the estimates. A tax which presses upon the poor is, when once that fact is recognized, a tax doomed. The State has broken its ordinary rules to establish a vast system of banks for the poor. . . . The masses, if not contented, have at least arrived at the conviction that they are not wilfully injured.[2]

By the seventies the reform movement found its chief impulse in the Radicalism which centred round Joseph Chamberlain and his demands for "Free Church, Free Schools, Free Land, and Free Labour," against the "wealthy legislators acred up to the eyes and consolled up to the chin."[3] But, though in a sense a class struggle, this was no class struggle like that the Chartists waged against their oppressors. The "Prosperity" years knew no such bitter strife.

---

[1] J. Morley, *Life of Cobden* (one volume, 1905), p. 911.
[2] Quoted by S. Maccoby, *English Radicalism, 1853–1856*, p. 82.
[3] Quoted by S. Maccoby, *op. cit.*, p. 188.

SELECT BIBLIOGRAPHY

The London Trades Council, 1860–1950: A History (Lawrence and Wishart, 1950).

Reports of the Royal Commission appointed to inquire into the Organization and Rules of Trades Unions and other Associations: especially, 1867, XXXII; 1867–68, XXXIX; 1868–69, XXXI, 1941.

COLE, G. D. H.: *British Working-class Politics, 1832–1914* (Routledge, 1941).

COLE, G. D. H. AND FILSON, A. W.: *British Working Class Movements: Select Documents, 1789–1875* (Macmillan, 1951).

GILLESPIE, F. E.: *Labour and Politics in England, 1850–67* (Cambridge University Press, 1929).

HOWELL, GEORGE: *Labour Legislation, Labour Movements, Labour Leaders* (Unwin, 1902).

MACCOBY, S.: *English Radicalism, 1852–86* (Allen and Unwin, 1938).

WEBB, S. AND B.: *The History of Trade Unionism* (Longmans, 1894; revised edition, 1920).

SAMUEL SMILES
Sir George Reid
[See p. 314]
National Portrait Gallery

THE SHOP IN TOAD LANE
Thomas Wakeman
[*See pp.* 321–323]
By permission of The Rochdale Art Gallery Committee

CHAPTER XVII

THE AGRICULTURAL LABOURER

SINCE 1834 the agricultural labourers had remained quiet. This quietness was not the mark of contentment, but of apathy or despair. Chartism made no mark on them. They could be glimpsed during the Corn Law agitation, afraid to go to meetings in their native villages, but sometimes tramping miles after the day's work to hear a League speaker elsewhere. Their masters could be heard refusing the use of village halls for Free Trade meetings, squire, parson, and publican—politics, morals, and business—being linked in the same interest.

As agriculture went into the "Prosperity" period the condition of the agricultural labourers improved a little, though they still appeared to be "swept like a heap of rubbish into a corner,"[1] and their low condition still showed itself in their small stature and slow gait.

They were considered dull-witted as well as slow of speech. But for all their seeming apathy there was a smouldering resentment within. There

> were hundreds who could speak out and up when they were by themselves, but who had learned the trade of mouth-shutting and teeth-locking as soon as they could talk, and before they knew what bird-scaring was. A man with the weight of many masters on him learns how to be dumb, and deaf, and blind, at a very early hour in the morning.[2]

Their condition varied considerably from county to county in accordance with the type of farming practised, the kind of work done, the conditions of hire, and the method of payment. Money wages, payment in kind, customary diet, garden or allotment, cottage accommodation—all have to be taken into account in assessing the agricultural labourer's position. Nowhere was he well off, though in the North of England, parts of Scotland, and near centres of industry which acted as

[1] Léonce de Lavergne, *Rural Economy of England, Scotland, and Ireland* (1854), p. 130.
[2] Joseph Arch, *Joseph Arch : The Story of his Life, told by himself*, p. 147.

353

competitors for his labour he was not uncomfortable. The South of England, the South-west, and the South-east were lamentably bad. Everywhere cottage accommodation was appalling. The few cases where enlightened landlords had re-built or repaired derelict cottages served but to emphasize the condition of the majority.

In the North, where conditions were happiest, the 'living-in' system widely prevailed. Labourers were hired by the year and paid, partly at least in kind, in sickness and in health. The children rarely went to work before eleven or twelve years old, and then merely for the summer. In the South wages were very low, eked out by payments in kind and by allotments, and the children went to work at six years old or even younger. There was an acute shortage of fuel, in contrast to the North, many families rarely having a fire, except at meal-times, even in the depth of winter.

Always the lowness of the condition of the agricultural labourer of the South was emphasized. He was mentally and physically inferior to the Northern labourer. Not only were his wages lower than elsewhere, but the food he ate was worse. In Anglesey and North Wales people were comparatively well fed on breadstuffs, milk, a moderate quantity of sugars and fats, and a small quantity of meat. In South Wales there was little meat, but cheese was plentiful. In Northumberland and Durham there was plenty of milk, meal, barley and peas, bread, butter, cheese, and vegetables, as well as home-fed bacon. In Scotland there was good porridge and milk, which was generally considered a diet making for healthy and strong men. In Lincolnshire there was less dairy produce but more meat. In the South, by contrast, the labourer's diet consisted almost entirely of bread, potatoes, and cheese, supplemented in the more fortunate families by a little pork. A lump of pork fat to go with the bread was a rare luxury, reserved for times of extra-hard work, like harvest, or for an annual celebration, like Christmas.

Everywhere, from a well-favoured county like Northumber-land to Kent, Dorset, and Devon, disgraceful cottage accom-modation existed. Inspectors who covered the whole country between 1867 and 1870 for the Royal Commission on Women and Children in Agriculture were deeply shocked, and all their Reports carry detailed accounts of the living conditions of the

rural poor. All were struck by the physical and moral degradation that ensued.

"The majority of the cottages that exist in rural parishes,"
said the Rev. J. Fraser, reporting on the Eastern counties,

> are deficient in almost every requisite that should constitute a
> home for a Christian family in a civilized community. They are
> deficient in bedroom accommodation; . . . they are deficient in
> drainage and sanitary arrangements; they are imperfectly sup-
> plied with water; such conveniences as they have are often so
> situated as to become nuisances; they are full enough of draughts
> to generate any amount of rheumatism; and in many instances
> are lamentably dilapidated and out of repair.

He concluded:

> It is impossible to exaggerate the ill-effects of such a state of
> things in every aspect—physical, social, economical, moral,
> intellectual.[1]

The agricultural labourer still had practically no land to
farm for himself. His garden was small or non-existent; allotments, although on the increase, were not favoured by most
farmers or publicans. They gave a man independence, an interest
outside his daily work, saved him money, and kept him from
spending his coppers at the public house. When a labourer had
a piece of land, either garden or allotment plot, it was often
bad and ill-conditioned, taking years of hard work before
giving a yield. The man might then be moved on to another
such piece, to begin the work over again if he had the heart.

The married agricultural labourer had always attempted
to solve the problem of low wages by putting his family out to
work. He continued to do so. In the worst-paid districts boys
went to work at six years old, bird-scaring, stone-picking, or
the like; at seven they might be following the dibble—dropping
peas and beans into holes already made. Often the children
were hungry. Their mothers, also hungry, neglected the home
to try to earn a few pence at weeding and harvest work. Sometimes it was part of the man's bargain with the farmer that his
wife should work too.

A specialized form of this women's and children's labour
comprised the ganging which was common in certain of the
Eastern counties. There were two kinds of gang—one generally

[1] *Royal Commission on the Employment of Children, Young Persons and Women in
Agriculture*, 1867–68, XVII, Report by Rev. J. Fraser, 35.

called the public gang, the other the private gang. The public gang worked under a gang-master, who contracted with a farmer to do a certain amount of work, and recruited and paid the women and children, who then worked under his supervision. The private gang was employed directly by the farmer under the immediate charge of some farm servant. In the Eastern counties ganging had become a common and highly organized practice since its origin at the beginning of the century. Most of the land was newly farmed in large enclosed areas. In order to avoid the burden of settlement and the payment of poor rates a few cottages had been built. Those that existed housed the labourers who were hired by the year, the casual labourers coming in from miles away. In addition, the youths, women, and children who comprised the gangs went out from the villages to do the general work of the farm.

The gangers' work was hard and dreary; the gang-masters were often brutal and coarse. Talk of immorality was soon rife. The public opinion that was being exercised by Ashley on behalf of children in industry turned to women and children in agriculture. The Children's Employment Commission, which had been sitting since 1862, was instructed to extend its scope, and in 1867 its sixth Report was published, on Organized Agricultural Gangs—that is, on the public gangs. In the following three years there appeared Reports on the private gangs and on women and children in agriculture generally.

The public gang existed almost exclusively in parts of Lincolnshire, Huntingdonshire, Cambridgeshire, Norfolk, Suffolk, and Nottinghamshire, with a few in Northamptonshire, Bedfordshire, Leicestershire, and Rutland. It was therefore a highly specialized form of employment, affecting in all perhaps some 7000 persons. There were generally from ten to forty people in a gang, about half of whom were children. All evidence as to the character of the gang-masters is unfavourable. The Report of 1867 described them as

> men whom the farmers are not willing to have in their regular employ; men who belong to the class of "catchwork labourers"; in most cases men of indolent and drinking habits, and in some cases men of notorious depravity; as a rule, unfit for the office they undertake.[1]

[1] *Children's Employment Commission* (1862). *Sixth Report of the Commissioners*: on Organized Agricultural Gangs, 1867, XVI, xi.

Their net earnings were rarely more than those of common labourers.

The gang worked at weeding, picking twitch, singling turnips, setting potatoes, picking stones, spreading manure, and similar wearying and back-breaking tasks. Since payment to the gang-master was by the piece, he kept them working hard. Including their journey to the fields each day, their hours of labour would often be from 5 A.M. to 7 P.M., sometimes later. They tramped as far as seven miles each way, rarely having any conveyance. Mrs Anthony Adams, a labourer's wife of Denton, Huntingdonshire, told how her children walked eight miles each way with a gang.

> In June, 1862, my daughters Harriet and Sarah, aged respectively 11 and 13 years, were engaged by a ganger to work on Mr Worman's land at Stilton. When they got there he took them to near Peterborough; there they worked for six weeks, going and returning each day. The distance each way is 8 miles, so that they had to walk 16 miles each day on all the 6 working days of the week, besides working in the field from 8 to 5 or 5.30 in the afternoon. They used to start from home at 5 in the morning, and seldom got back before 9. . . . Sometimes they were put to hoeing, sometimes to twitching, and they had 7d. a day. They had to find all their own meals, as well as their own tools (such as hoes). They (the girls) were good for nothing at the end of the six weeks.

It was a mixed gang that these girls were in, but Mrs Adams never heard of any impropriety. When the ganger asked for the services of little Susan, aged six, she consented, and the little girl

> walked all the way (8 miles) to Peterborough to her work, and worked from 8 to 5.30 and received 4d. She was that tired that her sisters had to carry her the best part of the way home— 8 miles, and she was ill from it for three weeks, and never went again.[1]

Several of the Report's recommendations were passed into law by the Gangs Act of 1868. No child under eight was to be employed at all, and women and girls only when a licensed gang-mistress went with the gang. Gang-masters had to be licensed by justices of the peace in petty session, who would

---

[1] *Ibid.*, xii–xiii.

satisfy themselves as to a man's character. Breaches of the law were to be punished by fine.

The Gangs Act was fairly effective. By the following year many of the worst gang-masters were no longer being licensed, and gang-mistresses were being appointed where necessary. Some of the public gangs were trying to avoid the Act by turning themselves into private gangs, but, even so, the Assistant Commissioner who visited the Eastern counties in 1867–68 found private gangs not so common as the earlier Report had believed. Many of them were on large farms and often well organized, involving no more hardship for the labourer than his agricultural work would in any case entail.

Moreover, an amendment in the Settlement Laws was somewhat changing the issue. The object of owners and farmers in not building cottages on the newly cultivated tracts of land in the Eastern counties was to avoid the possible burden of pauperism and high rates. The Poor Law Amendment Act of 1834 had left the law of settlement much as it had been before: the parish where a man had a settlement was responsible for his keep if he became destitute, settlement being established, broadly speaking, by birth or a specified length of residence. Now, after many attempts at reform, an Act of 1865 made the union, or geographical group of parishes, responsible for all the paupers within its boundaries. No longer did a parish gain from building no cottages, for it had to pay for the destitute living in neighbouring parishes. It reaped no advantage from its lack of housing accommodation, but rather disadvantage in the form of labour shortage. Farmers began to complain that their poor rates were leaping upward, while the only men that came in to them from the villages were enfeebled by the long walk to and from their homes.

While public opinion began to stir, the agricultural labourers themselves began to shake off a little of the apathy that, with brief breaks, their conditions of life had forced on them.

Right in the heart of England, in the little village of Barford, near Warwick, Joseph Arch lived with his parents. His father was an agricultural labourer living in a cottage without even a garden. Four times he was moved from the plot of land he was cultivating for his family just when he had cleared it and

prepared it for a good yield. Joseph's independent spirit early
brought him into contact with squire, parson, and magistrate.
He left Barford in order to gain experience. He did agricultural work of all kinds, and became a skilled hedger and
ditcher. He saw conditions all over agricultural England. He
saw the land when it was prosperous, he saw it when, in the
depression, thistles and docks were so firmly rooted that even
when mowers had cut down their tops the plough could not be
used. He talked to labourers up and down the country. He
grieved at their wretched lives—ill-clad, badly housed and
hungry, close to the land from which they wrested food which
was eaten mostly by others. "One old farmer used to say,"
recounted Joseph Arch in his old age,

> I was the most dangerous man that ever went on a farm, as I
> was always talking about combination to the labourers, and
> spreading discontent far and wide. So I was, and the farther I
> could spread it the better I was pleased. I would speak a few
> words to this man and a few to that, trying to stir them all up,
> and make them see where the only remedy for their misery lay;
> in season and out of season I was at them, dropping in the good
> seed of manly discontent; and I made sure, too, that most of it
> was not cast on to stony ground.[1]

Always as he went about his work Arch pondered the means
of raising the standard of life of the agricultural labourer. "I
had spent years thinking the matter well out," he said later.

> I had pondered over it when at work in the wood and the field; I
> had considered the question when I was hedging and ditching;
> I had thrashed it right out in my mind when I was tramping to
> and from my day's toil; and I had come to the conclusion that
> only organized labour could stand up, even for a single day,
> against employers' tyranny.[2]

At the end of the sixties there were signs. There were small
movements in Scotland in 1865, in Buckinghamshire and
Hertfordshire in 1867, and a more powerful movement in
Herefordshire in 1871. Early in 1872 came news that men in
Weston and Willey, in Warwickshire, were asking for higher
wages. Then at Wellesbourne, near Barford, the labourers
began to stir.

[1] Joseph Arch, *Joseph Arch, the Story of his Life, told by himself*, p. 66.
[2] *Ibid.*, pp. 67–68.

When the new year of 1872 opened . . . their poverty had fallen to starvation point, and was past all bearing. They began to raise their heads and look about them. . . . Oppression, and hunger and misery, made them desperate, and desperation was the mother of Union.[1]

Arch was by that time married and living in the cottage that had been his parents'. At the age of forty-six he was better off than most of his fellows—an experienced agricultural labourer in robust health, active in mind and body, master of his work in all its branches, in full employment and earning good money. In his living-room were his Bible and other religious books, coloured prints of Biblical scenes, and a Primitive Methodist preacher's plan. Arch was, indeed, a keen and eloquent Primitive Methodist preacher, in sympathy with his audiences of agricultural labourers and knowing how to stir them.

Arch himself would never force union on the agricultural labourers.

I was determined not to make any attempt to start the Union myself. I saw it was bound to come; but I also saw that the men themselves must ask me to help them. My part was to sit still and wait; about that I was clear; so I waited.[2]

He waited until early in 1872.

February 7, 1872, was a very wet morning, he recounted,

and I was busy at home on a carpentering job; I was making a box. My wife came in to me and said, "Joe, here's three men come to see you. What for I don't know." But I knew fast enough. In walked the three; they turned out to be labourers from over Wellesbourne way. I stopped work, and we had a talk. They said they had come to ask me to hold a meeting at Wellesbourne that evening. They wanted to get the men together, and start a Union directly. I told them that, if they did form a Union, they would have to fight hard for it, and they would have to suffer a great deal; both they and their families. They said the labourers were prepared both to fight and suffer. Things could not be worse; wages were so low, and provisions were so dear, that nothing but downright starvation lay before them unless the farmers could be made to raise their wages . . . they must join together and strike, and hold out till the employers gave in.[3]

---

[1] *Ibid.*, p. 67.   [2] *Ibid.*, p. 68.   [3] *Ibid.*, pp. 68–69.

So Arch went to Wellesbourne, pondering as he went whether the hour for a forward movement had really struck, or whether a handful of men would batter themselves in vain against the unyielding front of authority. When he arrived he found over a thousand men gathered under the Wellesbourne chestnut-tree.

> The night had fallen pitch dark; but the men got bean poles and hung lanterns on them. . . . I mounted an old pig-stool, and in the flickering light of the lanterns I saw the earnest upturned faces of these poor brothers of mine—faces gaunt with hunger and pinched with want—all looking towards me and ready to listen to the words, that would fall from my lips. . . . I stood on my pig-stool and spoke out straight and strong for Union.[1]

They passed a resolution to form a union then and there. Between two and three hundred men enrolled that night.

Shortly after the meeting under the Wellesbourne tree 200 Warwickshire men resolved to strike for a wage of 16s. a week for a working day from 6 A.M. to 5 P.M. Some of the Press was sympathetic, particularly *The Leamington Chronicle* and *The Daily News*, the latter sending its famous war correspondent, Archibald Forbes, to the scene to write special articles. A meeting in Leamington on March 29, 1872, founded the Warwickshire Agricultural Labourers Union. Several Members of Parliament supported the agricultural labourers, and a sympathizer gave a donation of £100 at the inaugural meeting of the W.A.L.U. Samuel Morley, M.P., later gave them £500. John Stuart Mill pronounced his blessing, and, perhaps most important of all, the organized trade unions gave their active support with funds, propaganda, and personnel. Joseph Arch acted like the revivalist preacher he was. The labourers called him "our man, our Joe, the labourers' hope, apostle, friend." "His influence over them is unbounded," reported a contemporary.

> He has but to speak and it will be done. If he likes to retaliate on the farmers, as they seem inclined to do on him and his men, there will be mischief—mischief for which the farmers will be solely to blame. He has but to urge vengeance, and night after night flaming stacks will illumine the darkness, and the whole country will be laid waste.[2]

---

[1] *Ibid.*, p. 73.   [2] Quoted by A. Clayden, *The Revolt of the Field*, p. 14.

But Joseph Arch had other ideas. At his meetings the enthusiasm of his audiences was given vent in the passionate singing of songs. Labourers in the centre and east of the country were soon marching and singing their own words to popular hymn and song tunes. They sang:

> O workmen awake, for the strife is at hand;
> With right on your side, then with hope firmly stand
> To meet your oppressors; go, fearlessly go,
> And stand like the brave, with your face to the foe.

And

> Come, lads, and listen to my song, a song of honest toil,
> 'Tis of the English labourer, the tiller of the soil;
> I'll tell you how he used to fare, and all the ill he bore,
> Till he stood up in his manhood, resolved to bear no more,
> This fine old English labourer, one of the present time.[1]

Nothing more violent than strike action was in their minds.

In May, two months after the formation of the Warwickshire Agricultural Labourers' Union, the National Agricultural Labourers' Union was formed, with branches all over the country and a central committee at Leamington, of which Joseph Arch was president and Henry Taylor, a carpenter, was secretary. The inaugural meeting was more successful than even Arch had hoped. Papers were read on the Game Laws, Allotments, Education, Co-operative Farming, Co-operative stores, Village Clubs, and Reading-rooms—an indication of the interests of the audience. The subscription was 2d. a week, with a 6d. entrance fee. The concrete demands were for the raising of wages, generally to about 16s. a week for agricultural labourers, and £1 for wagoners and shepherds, a limitation of the working day to nine and a half hours, compulsory education for young farm workers, a gradual nationalization of the land, and a taking over of waste land. Soon the demand for the vote for agricultural labourers was included. George Dixon, Member for Birmingham, presented a petition to the House of Commons from 80,000 farm labourers in favour of household suffrage in the counties. Their meetings continued to have the tone of a religious revival, half the leaders being, like Arch, Methodist local preachers addressing their audiences as "My Christian friends," "Beloved brethren," and the like.

[1] For these and other songs see Arch, *op. cit.*, *passim*.

By the end of 1872 nearly 100,000 men had enrolled in the N.A.L.U. The men were successful in raising wages by about 1s. 6d. to 4s. a week in various parts of the country. Sometimes they struck to gain their end. Sometimes the very appearance of a union in a village was sufficient to effect a wage increase. Unfortunately, however, there were rival unions. There was sufficient sectionalism and jealousy right from the start to cause the formation of several small unions who refused to be absorbed in the N.A.L.U. The London Trades Council did its best to promote unity, but the most it could achieve was a Federal Union of six of these smaller unions.

Who belonged to the unions? There was the carter who came and said:

> My wages are twelve shillings but I have no perquisites; I have to work fourteen hours a day six days out of seven, and on Sunday I have to put in half a day's labour.[1]

And the shepherd who said:

> And look at me, I got ten shillings for a week of seven days, and I lost time in bad weather; out of this I had to pay 1s. 6d. rent for a cottage with two bedrooms, and now here I am, sacked because I've joined the Union.[2]

And the farm labourer who said:

> My poor wages are 7s. a week, and I lose money on bad days; my rent is 1s. 3d. and I have to pay out 1s. 3½d. a month for club money; how is a man to keep alive and going on it? I'm most always hungry, and I can't keep decent clothes on my back, not even of a Sunday, and my family has to make the best shift it can. 'Tisn't life at all, and I often wish I was out of it.[3]

Then there was the old man of seventy who took the chair for Arch at one of the early meetings. He had been a farm labourer for sixty-three years, had worked hard and kept off the parish—dawn till dusk for 11s. a week. Of his numerous children some died in infancy through undernourishment and low fever. Of the rest one son was killed in the Crimea, one in India; a third was lost at sea. Two or three of the girls married agricultural labourers, and were as poor as their parents. One in service was the best off—a good girl, for she remembered her old dad. Other sons were themselves on the

---

[1] Arch, *op. cit.*, p. 133.   [2] *Ibid.*, p. 133.   [3] *Ibid.*, p. 133.

soil. All his children started work at bird-scaring, stone-picking, or the like when very young. There could be no education for them, for schools were scarce and pennies for schooling scarcer. Now the old man had nothing for his old age; his children could help little or not at all. What was in store? "A bit o' stone-breakin' on the roads," he said, "two shillin' a week from the parish, and a loaf or two." He had heard of Wellesbourne and of Joe Arch, and since he was too old to trouble about victimization he had asked Arch down to talk to the men of Grindington.[1]

To most of the farmers and landowners this revolt of the field was outrageous. Bad enough in the industrial worker, unthinkable in the agricultural labourer! They locked out members of the labourers' unions and otherwise victimized them. Assisted by the Bench and the clergy, they sent labourers and their wives to prison. Indelibly stamped on the minds of the labourers was "the shameful Chipping Norton affair."

At Ascot, in Oxfordshire, there was a small local dispute during which Farmer Hambridge got over some men from a neighbouring village. Several Ascot women, whose husbands were locked out, mobbed the men on their arrival and dared them to enter Hambridge's field. The farmer took the matter up, and seventeen women were summoned before the magistrates at Chipping Norton. In their evidence the labourers, strapping fellows not likely to be frightened and hurt by a parcel of women, gave evidence that, so far from being set upon with sticks, they had been invited by the women to come back to the village and have a drink! The two clergymen magistrates nevertheless imprisoned seven of the women with ten days' hard labour, and nine with seven days', despite the fact that several of them had babies at the breast. There was a riot in the town that evening. But the women were driven off at once and lodged in Oxford Gaol.

The Press joined in the indignation which followed. Petitions were forwarded by the Union, £80 was collected from sympathizers, and the farmworkers' demands became definitely more political as they reached out to control the forces which were victimizing them. They reiterated their demand for an extension of the franchise, they demanded the repeal of the Criminal Law Amendment Act, and they asked for the appoint-

---

[1] Clayden, *op. cit.*, pp. 12–14.

ment of stipendiary magistrates, hoping thus to avoid the biased rulings of a Bench comprised of local squires and parsons. When the women came out of Oxford Gaol after serving their sentences they were met with brakes and bands playing, and the £80 was divided between them.

The opposition to the unions continued. Not only did landowners control local justice, but it was easy for the farmers, by their personal intimacy with the labourers, to sow distrust of the union.

The decisive lock-out came in 1874. When Suffolk labourers asked for wage increases from 13s. to 14s. for a fifty-four hour week the farmers responded by a lock-out. The lock-out spread over the Eastern and Midland counties, until 10,000 men were locked out and the National Union had spent over £21,000 in strike pay. The lock-outs continued all over the country. The farmers, the magistrates, the clergy, the publicans—all whose concern it was to keep agricultural wages low, labourers servile, and their pennies directed to the beer-house instead of the union—continued their subversive day-to-day work. Depression set in with the middle seventies: the labourers had no more power to fight, union funds dropped, and everywhere the unions declined. But even as they did so a victory came in another field. The third Reform Act of 1884, like the second Reform Act, owed much to the play of party politics. This time Joseph Chamberlain was a principal champion of Reform, supported by all those to whom the undemocratic county franchise, which had been unaltered by the Act of 1867, was objectionable. After 1884 the agricultural labourers and the miners, as well as the town labourers, at last had the vote. The agricultural labourers responded in fitting fashion by returning Joseph Arch to Parliament the following year. But the long-drawn-out agricultural depression left no hope of trade-union revival, and by 1889 membership had dropped to little over 4000. Many years were to pass before the agricultural workers again organized themselves, but there remained, to keep alive the tradition of an Agricultural Workers' Union, the name of Joseph Arch and the memory of the rally beneath the Wellesbourne tree.

SELECT BIBLIOGRAPHY

Reports of the Royal Commission on the Employment of Children, Young Persons and Women in Agriculture. First Report, 1867–68, XVII. *Second Report*, 1868–69, XIII.

Children's Employment Commission (1862). *Sixth Report of the Commissioners*: on Organized Agricultural Gangs, 1867, XVI.

ARCH, J.: *Joseph Arch, the Story of his Life, told by himself* (Hutchinson, 1898).

CLAYDEN, A.: *The Revolt of the Field* (Hodder, 1874).

FUSSELL, G. E.: *The English Agricultural Labourer from Tudor to Victorian Times* (Batchworth Press, 1949).

HASBACH, W.: *A History of the English Agricultural Labourer* (English translation, P. S. King, 1908).

WEBB, S. AND B.: *The History of Trade Unionism* (Longmans, 1894; revised edition, 1920).

CHAPTER XVIII

THE END OF 'VICTORIAN PROSPERITY'

(a) THE 'LEAN YEARS'

INDUSTRY remained in a condition of prosperity until 1873. In that year began the great depression which, with a temporary and partial lifting between 1880 and 1882 and between 1886 and 1889, lasted until 1896. Its strangest feature was that, while general agreement existed as to the fact of depression, by most of the criteria generally applied to industry it was a period of prosperity. On all sides came reports that the volume of trade was maintained or was increasing. The capital invested at home did not materially decline. The volume of shipping cleared in British ports increased. There was more goods traffic on the railways, more wool used in the woollen industry, more raw cotton in the cotton industry. Fifty-one per cent. more coal was hewn in the early eighties than in the late sixties. In the same period pig-iron production doubled. Taking the country as a whole, there was no diminution in the aggregate of commodities produced by British capital and British labour. There was a growth of Friendly Societies and savings banks, the community drank more tea, consumed more sugar, travelled more miles, employed as many servants, took out as many licences to shoot, had as many carriages. The retail trade remained comparatively prosperous.[1] Yet it was universally agreed that there was a depression, confined to no one industry, but affecting the trade and industry of the country generally.

In what, then, did the depression consist? It was a depression, not of production, but of prices and profits. The price of steel rails slumped from £12 1s. 1d. a ton in 1874 to £5 7s. 6d. in 1883; the price of iron rails from £9 18s. 2d. a ton in 1874 to £5 in 1883; of pig-iron from £4 17s. 1d. a ton in 1872 to £1 12s. 10d. in 1885.[2] In particular, while imports grew,

[1] G. J. Goschen, *Address to Manchester Chamber of Commerce on the Conditions and Prospects of Trade*, June 23, 1885.
[2] L. C. A. Knowles, *The Industrial and Commercial Revolutions in Great Britain in the Nineteenth Century*, p. 144.

THE 'GOOD YEARS' AND THE 'LEAN YEARS'
REFLECTED IN THE VALUE OF BRITAIN'S EXPORT TRADE

Total Value of British Exports (Exclusive of Ships)	
Year	*Million pounds*
1850	71
1855	96
1860	136
1865	166
1868 ⎫	⎧ 180
1869 ⎪	⎪ 190
1870 ⎬ *Spectacular rise*	⎨ 200
1871 ⎪	⎪ 223
1872 ⎭	⎩ 256
1873 ⎫	⎧ 255
1874 ⎪	⎪ 240
1875 ⎪	⎪ 223
1876 ⎬ *Steep fall*	⎨ 201
1877 ⎪	⎪ 199
1878 ⎪ *but still at*	⎪ 193
1879 ⎭ *the 1869 level*	⎩ 192
1880 ⎫	⎧ 223
1881 ⎬ *Recovery*	⎨ 234
1882 ⎭	⎩ 241
1883 ⎫	⎧ 240
1884 ⎬ *Setback*	⎨ 233
1885 ⎪	⎪ 213
1886 ⎭	⎩ 213
1887 ⎫	⎧ 222
1888 ⎪	⎪ 235
1889 ⎬ *Recovery*	⎨ 249
1890 ⎭	⎩ 264
1891 ⎫	⎧ 247
1892 ⎬ *Setback*	⎨ 227
1893 ⎪	⎪ 218
1894 ⎭	⎩ 216
1895 ⎫ *Readjustment*	226
1900 ⎭	283

exports declined in value, and the drop was all the more severe because of the spectacular rise of the previous years. Imports, £355,000,000 in 1872, were £363,000,000 in 1879,

THE 'GOOD YEARS' AND THE 'LEAN YEARS'

REFLECTED IN THE VALUE OF BRITAIN'S EXPORT TRADE

(Total value of British exports, exclusive of ships)

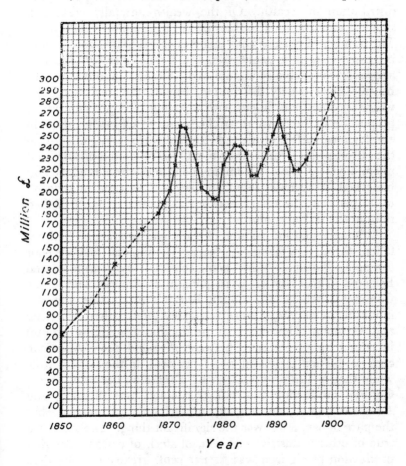

while exports slumped in the same period from £256,000,000 to £192,000,000. After some vicissitudes they were still only £213,000,000 in 1885, when imports were valued at £371,000,000. The effect was seen in a marked diminution of foreign investment, most of the capital which had previously been exported being needed to bridge the gap in the balance of payments. In two of the worst years, 1876 and 1877, Britain even called home some of the interest on earlier investments.[1]

The only people who did not notice the depression were those whose incomes were fixed. These—and they included wage-earners in employment—benefited from falling prices; the rest were the losers. The result was seen in a changing distribution of wealth. Of the wealth annually created a smaller proportion fell to the share of the employers of labour. The number of persons with incomes of less than £2000 a year increased at a more rapid rate, and the number with incomes above £5000 actually diminished. Profits, in other words, became more evenly distributed, leaving the wealthier class, whose incomes had fallen, with a feeling of depression out of proportion to the real state of the country. Of labour, those in employment suffered little reduction of wages and gained from the fall in prices. But employment was becoming erratic, and unemployment grew. Unemployment in the ironfounders' and boilermakers' societies rose from barely 1 per cent. in 1872–73 to 20 per cent. in 1879,[2] and it was greater in the unskilled than in the skilled trades.

Although the total volume of trade and production had not fallen, there were significant signs. Continental markets—for example, Portugal—were being entered by Germans and Belgians. Tariff barriers were going up in America and on the Continent. Above all, though Britain's production was still mounting in volume, it was growing less quickly than American and German. German coal production (excluding lignite) increased by 53 per cent. between 1873 and 1883; American coal production increased by 41 per cent. in the same period, while that of Britain increased by a mere 29 per cent. True, German production was but 55,000,000 tons in 1883, and American 72,000,000 tons, against Britain's 156,000,000,[3] but the pace of expansion was the significant thing. The same was true of other industries—of iron, of steel, of cotton. Britain's production of pig-iron was 31 per cent. greater in 1884 than in 1870, yet other countries had increased their production in

---

[1] L. H. Jenks, *The Migration of British Capital to 1875*, pp. 332–333.
[2] S. and B. Webb, *The History of Trade Unionism*, p. 348.
[3] *Royal Commission on Depression of Trade and Industry*, Third Report, Minutes of Evidence, 1886, XXIII, 206–208.

the same period by 138 per cent.[1] Britain, though still leading
in size of output, was yielding to Europe and America in rate
of development.

What did it all amount to? Hundreds of pamphlets, thousands of speeches, tried to find the answer. There were several
Government Committees and a Royal Commission on the
Depression of Trade and Industry which reported in 1886.
The general conclusion was that there was a depression of a
certain kind. The Royal Commission went so far as to define
it as "a diminution, and in some cases, an absence of profit,
with a corresponding diminution of employment for the
labouring classes."[2] It was also clear that some industries were
more severely hit than others, shipping, iron, and steel being
the most seriously affected.

The apparent over-production of shipping was due to the
quicker journeys of steamships over sailing-ships, to the shortening of sea-routes through the opening of the Suez Canal, so
that each ship could carry more cargoes in the same space of
time. The durability of iron, and later of steel, stronger and
more efficient engines, all gave a longer life as well as greater
speed to ships, and as new ships were produced the amount of
tonnage available became more than was necessary to carry
the world's goods. Britain also suffered in relation to the ships
of other nations by the fact that foreign Governments were
subsidizing their shipping lines and so reducing their freight
rates, making them more effective competitors as world carriers.
Added to this was the fact that the shipping industry had seen
three fundamental changes in construction within a generation
—from sail to steam, from wood to iron, and from iron to steel.
There was considerable adjustment of skill, materials, and plant
and scrapping of existing ships.

The reason for the seeming depression in the British iron and
steel and coal industries was found first in the fact that the enormous demand of the years of the home and foreign railway
booms was slackening. British railway construction was slowing down. So was shipbuilding. Steel rails and steel plates
were lasting longer than iron, and so demand decreased.
America and Europe were not only supplying increasing
quantities of their own iron and steel and coal; they also
invaded neutral markets. Britain was handicapped by the

---

[1] *Ibid.*, Final Report, 1886, XXIII, viii.   [2] *Ibid.*, XXIII, x.

heavy fixed charges loaded into industry—interest rates, royalties, and the cost of railway transport, which was unsubsidized and comparatively high in Britain—above all, by the fact that any industry which has been prosperous for ten years tends to be inelastic. Capital, labour, skill, plant, and to some extent pride in past achievement stand in the way of new methods of production. On the Continent and in America it was different. There was no firmly established industry when the three great steel inventions were made known. Germany, with the great supplies of phosphoric ores captured in Lorraine after 1870, leaped on the basic process, and constructed her industry to it. America, with vast deposits of coal and of phosphoric and non-phosphoric iron-ore, pushed out her railways to link her coal and iron. When the coal of Pittsburgh was thus joined to the iron of Lake Superior she was successfully using the latest forms of all three processes. Belgium early and France rather later were doing the same. The British industry alone needed serious and difficult adaptation. Britain was suffering from having had her industrial revolution first. The inevitable result of foreign competition, falling demand, and comparative inefficiency was a fall in prices, a reduction in profits, the postponement of improvements. The result was seen in the slowing rate of expansion of Britain's exports of iron and steel. In 1870 2,600,000 tons of iron and steel of all kinds were exported; in 1880 3,500,000 tons; in 1890 the volume exported had grown to only 3,800,000 tons.

From iron and steel, coal and shipbuilding, the depression spread to the textile industries, though here it was less severe. Again, although values slumped, production and export were maintained or increased in spite of production behind tariff walls in Germany and the U.S.A. and the beginnings of competition from the Bombay mills. But in textiles, as in the heavy industries, the United States and the Continent were using modern and more efficient methods of production, while Britain was bound to existing plant and machinery.

The challenge to Great Britain had been sounded at the Paris Exhibition of 1867. In toys the Swiss and Germans, in watches and clocks the Swiss and French, in fancy goods the French, had shown themselves superior to the British long before the competition of the end of the century was encountered. Lyon Playfair and the Frenchman Jordan already in the sixties had accused Britain of inefficiency, of neglecting coal economy, of failing to use the trained chemist and the scientist. Inquiries in the sixties had shown a great divergence between the best British producers and the worst. Old processes, it was felt even then, were kept going too long, fuel economies known on the Continent were not practised in Britain. Above all, it was beginning to be said that the British workman was falling behind his overseas counterpart in skill, energy, and adaptability. The Royal Commission on Scientific Institutions of 1867-68 had revealed a backwardness of British labour due to lack of technical education. It was even reported that managers were often illiterate and could not keep acquainted with developments in their industries. Goschen, business-man, economist, and Member of Parliament, nevertheless asserted in 1885 the superiority of British skill and British labour. The Royal Commission the following year reported favourably, though scantily, on the quantity and quality of the work done by British workmen. It pointed out, however, that Britain was falling behind Germany in commercial skill in marketing its goods. In every quarter of the world, it said, "the perseverance and enterprise" of the Germans were making themselves felt. In a knowledge of the markets of the world, a desire to accommodate themselves to local tastes or idiosyncrasies, a determination to obtain a footing wherever they could, and a tenacity in maintaining it, they appeared to be gaining ground upon the British.[1]

Almost every speaker and pamphleteer had his own version of the depression. It was sometimes held that the depersonalization of business through the Joint Stock and Limited Liability Acts, the managing of affairs, not by persons deeply interested and finely skilled, but by more or less salaried managers, had taken the inspiration from commercial life. Goschen included a defect in the machinery of distribution in his reasons for the trouble. Full advantage, he said, was not being taken of increased production because the machinery of distribution was not conveying it to the consumer. Goods were caught up in docks and warehouses instead of finding their way immediately to a customer at home or abroad.[2] The increase in local taxation and the burdens on industry generally, the legislation governing the employment of labour

<hr />

[1] *Final Report*, 1886, XXIII, xx.   [2] Goschen, *op. cit.*

—in particular, trade unions—were often advanced as causes of the depression. But the Royal Commission on the Depression pointed out that taxation, relative to the wealth of the country, was lower than in previous periods, and denied that the trade unions had played a part in the depression of industry.

The price fall was not confined to Britain. There was a world depression of prices whose roots lay outside the field of production. The big gold discoveries in California and Australia at the mid-century had brought a flow of gold which raised prices, quickened production, and oiled the wheels of trade and commerce. But that was more than twenty years earlier. The flow of new gold ceased; increasing goods and services and a growing population had absorbed the metal into its monetary system. Now several countries were discarding silver as a means of exchange and requiring gold. With the demonetization of silver and a growing world production of commodities, the world demand for gold grew at a time when no new supply was forthcoming. There was thus also a monetary reason for the great depression. Britain was affected more than anyone because the price fall came at a time when her Industrial Revolution had passed its peak.

But, explain the depression as one might, there remained the fact that other countries were successfully competing with Britain in face of a world fall in prices which, *ceteris paribus*, would have affected all equally. This, for Britain, was the most serious aspect of the depression. It underlined the basic facts of the situation. While European countries had been torn with their wars of national independence Britain, at peace, had developed her industry. No war but the Crimean War of 1854–56—fought far from her shores—disturbed her calm. Now, newly liberated, actively nationalist, the countries of Europe, particularly Germany, were using their young energy and their enthusiasm to catch up with a somewhat stale Britain. The United States, similarly young and lusty, not only developed her own Industrial Revolution, but was ready to continue where Britain left off.

The solution of the problem was more difficult than its diagnosis. The Royal Commission recommended a cheapening of the cost of production so far as was consistent with maintaining quality—a plan which needed no emphasis to the normal business-man; a greater activity in the search for markets, and particularly—and here the British business-man probably needed some prompting—greater elasticity in accommodating his produce to local tastes; it even suggested changing British weights and measures. It recommended more commercial and technical education, more statistics to show the trends of the commercial world, a development of water transport to cheapen railway carriage, protection against fraud at home and abroad by the marking and stamping of goods, and certain amendments in the law of limited liability.

In other quarters even Free Trade was questioned, 'Fair Trade' being demanded instead, on the argument that there was no equity in allowing imports to enter freely into Britain while her export trade was hampered by foreign tariffs. The import of German goods, in particular, was regarded as a menace. *Made in Germany* was the title of a book published by E. E. Williams in 1896; it listed a whole range of manufactured goods imported into Great Britain from Germany in 1895. Look around your own home, the author urged the householder.

You will find that the material of some of your own clothes was probably woven in Germany. Still more probable is it that some of your wife's garments are German importation; while it is practically beyond a doubt that the magnificent mantles and jackets wherein her maids array themselves on their Sundays out are German-made and German-sold, for only so could they be done at the figure. Your governess's fiancé is a clerk in the City; but he also was made in Germany. The toys, and the dolls, and the fairy books which your children maltreat in the nursery are made in Germany; nay, the material of your favourite (patriotic) newspaper had the same birthplace as like as not. Roam the house over, and the fateful mark will greet you at every turn, from the piano in your drawing-room to the mug on your kitchen dresser, blazoned though it be with the legend, *A Present from Margate*. Descend to your domestic depths, and you shall find your very drain-pipes German-made. You pick out of the grate the paper wrappings from a book consignment, and they also are "Made in Germany." You stuff them into the fire, and reflect that the poker in your hand was forged in Germany.[1]

And so the story continued. But Britain was not ready yet to

[1] Pp. 10–11.

'protect' herself against Germany or any other country. Free Trade had served her well. She still needed to import cheap raw materials and cheap food, and there were still markets where she could send her goods with little restriction. These markets existed in the less highly developed countries of the world, some of which were already within that Empire which was commonly asserted to have been acquired in a fit of absence of mind. Britain now looked at her Empire with new eyes, and, influenced first by Disraeli and then by Joseph Chamberlain, developed that new attitude towards Empire expressed in Imperialism. Already Disraeli in 1875 had made his purchase of a substantial portion of the Suez Canal shares, and Queen Victoria had been proclaimed Empress of India in 1877. With the Colonies Britain now developed stronger ties by the Imperial Federation League of 1884, a Colonial and Indian Exhibition of 1886, and by a series of Colonial Conferences, starting in 1887, at which a system of Imperial Preference was worked out.

Beyond the Colonies Britain and her rivals turned towards other sources of raw materials and other markets, particularly to the great undeveloped lands of the 'backward' peoples, and first to Africa. Here Britain already had some settlements, and in the eighties several Chartered Companies were formed to obtain trading concessions—the British South Africa, the Imperial British East Africa, the Royal Niger. The British flag followed her trading companies, and, as Belgians, Germans, and Frenchmen were all doing likewise, there resulted a rapid partition of Africa in a wild scramble between the Great Powers in which the native interest was secondary. There were thus opened up fresh markets for cotton goods, cheap hardware, tinware, and jewellery, fresh fields for railway construction and the investment of capital. In the process thousands of natives who resisted the intrusion of foreigners were killed in battle. Asia followed Africa as spoil for the white races, and soon there was no possible market unexplored by the Great Powers.

The New Imperialism brought British capitalism a prolonged lease of life. At the same time it forced on the native population the whole panoply of civilization, including clothes, jewellery made in Birmingham, money, wages, taxation, the

moneylender, and a new kind of poverty. Capitalism, when
called to account, must henceforth explain not only the slavery
and degradation of the Industrial Revolution in Britain, but
the second period of slavery in which the coloured peoples
were brought in to arrest a decline which the white races alone
were powerless to stem.

In agriculture meantime there was a similar story of loss of
purchasing power, falling profits, and general depression.

In the seventies came a series of disastrous harvests. The
years 1873, 1875, 1876, 1879, were all very bad years. The
harvest of 1879 was the worst of the century. Almost every
calamity known to farmers took its toll—blight, mould, mildew
in crops; foot-and-mouth disease, pleuro-pneumonia, and liver-
rot in animals. Nearly 70 per cent. of the wheat consumed had
to be imported. Imported corn and imported meat satisfied
the consumer, but prevented the farmer from reaping the comfort of high prices for a small harvest. He was perplexed at the
unusual experience of a small crop and falling prices. As he
tried to economize agriculture slumped into the depression
which lasted from 1875 to 1899, with a partial break between
1884 and 1891. Prices continued falling, with profits and rents
dropping headlong after, farms remained unlet, the average
quantity of wheat per acre fell, agricultural capital diminished,
the land under cultivation began to shrink, and foreign imports
increased. Farmers who in the prosperity period had bought
land and undertaken improvements were faced with ruin.
Improvements and good farming were abandoned; a general
rot set in.

Agricultural distress was general over the whole country,
though there were variations in degree from county to county
and within the same county. In the dairying and mixed-
farming districts, and in areas where a near-by town was a
market for local produce, the depression was least intense.
The main brunt fell on the corn-growing districts, and particularly on the heavy clays and the very light soils which had
needed most care and attention. The Essex clays, the Norfolk
light soils, most of the Central English counties and the
Southern counties were the worst sufferers. Fields chock-full
of thistles became a common sight. Said the Royal Commission
on Agriculture of 1882:

Whatever difference of opinion may exist as to the causes of agricultural depression, or as to remedies which may be suggested for it, it will be observed that there prevails complete uniformity of conviction as to the great extent and intensity of the distress which has fallen upon the agricultural community. Owners and occupiers have alike suffered from it. No description of estate or tenure has been exempted . . . all without distinction have been involved in a general calamity.[1]

Many reasons were advanced for this "general calamity"— the weather, imported food, high rents, insufficient capital for land development, the failure of landowners to compensate tenants for improvements. "For the last twenty-five years," said Joseph Arch, "farmers have farmed to leave instead of to stay."[2] The agricultural labourer blamed the farmer's treatment of his men for the depression. "What has been the policy of the tenant farmers throughout the kingdom for the last twenty years?" they asked.

Their policy has been to do with as little labour as possible, and the labour they did employ was never paid for sufficiently to enable the men to do a good day's work. They have half-paid labour, and the result is half-fed labour.[3]

It was obvious that the sunless, rainy weather of the seventies would affect agriculture. The Royal Commission appointed in 1879 under the chairmanship of the Duke of Richmond, which reported in 1882, laid much stress on the weather. But the weather could not explain the movement in prices, which had normally risen in bad years. When the weather improved in the eighties, but depression continued, the fundamental reason for the decline in British agriculture became apparent. The Royal Commission appointed in 1893 laid more stress on foreign competition, which was the constant factor in the situation, and less on the vagaries of the weather. The real position is best seen in relation to wheat and meat.

The opening of the Middle West of America had produced easily and cheaply great quantities of grain from virgin soil. Moreover, these supplies were not affected by weather conditions prevailing in Europe. Prices in Britain and the Continent had moved more or less together. Now a source of supply

---

[1] The Richmond Commission, XIV, p. 24.
[2] Joseph Arch, *Joseph Arch, the Story of his Life, told by himself*, p. 336.
[3] *Ibid.*, p. 309.

subject to far different and more favourable conditions was open. More than that—it was linked by rail and sea to Britain, and competition in freight rates had by 1884 brought the cost of transport of grain from New York to the United Kingdom down to 4s. a quartern.

Meat followed wheat. The railway could bring animals rapidly across the continent of America to the ports, steam shipping could bring them quickly to Europe. When to the railway was added the refrigerator car and to the steamship the cold-storage room, carcasses instead of live animals were brought. As the canning and compressed-meat industries in the U.S.A. rapidly developed, corned beef and similar products were added to the commodities which brought down the price of British meat. American meat firms formed combines, and by large profits on by-products such as hides and bristles were able to reduce meat prices. Foreign meat was necessarily inferior to home-killed in a way that imported grain was not inferior to British, but even so the competition was formidable and increased the depression. Australia, New Zealand, and the Argentine followed. Fertilizers and animal feeding stuffs followed wheat and meat. More cheese, bacon, eggs, and other dairy produce came from overseas, the imports of butter doubled, of cheese rose by one-third.[1] The most fundamental adjustment of British agriculture was obviously necessary.

British farmers had at first turned to dairy farming as a means of lessening the effect of imported wheat and bad harvests, and the result could be seen in the increase in pasture over arable land. Between 1871 and 1901 the corn area of England and Wales decreased from just over 8,000,000 acres to just under 6,000,000 acres.[2] But laying land down to grass was expensive, and when dairy land also became subject to foreign competition arable farmers were left nonplussed.

The Government helped a little. One of its first actions was in 1875, by the Agricultural Holding Act, to recognize the principle of compensation to departing tenants for unexhausted improvements to their farms. But a merely permissive Act provided little incentive to better farming, and it was not until 1883, following a recommendation by the Richmond Commission, that compensation for unexhausted improvements became compulsory on the owner. The farmer was helped by

[1] Lord Ernle, *English Farming, Past and Present*, p. 378. [2] *Ibid.*, p. 378.

the State in a number of other ways, including a reduction in rates through a grant in aid of local taxation, and measures to stamp out disease in livestock and check the adulteration of feeding stuffs. In 1889 a Minister of Agriculture was appointed in charge of a Department of Agriculture. There was a brief hope that the tide would turn with the better seasons of 1883 to 1890. But cold summers in 1891 and 1892, drought in 1893, and a further bad harvest in 1894 quenched the hope. For underlying the agricultural depression were the fundamental and unalterable facts of world economy. Britain was exporting large quantities of manufactured goods which had to be paid for. The only way in which payment could be met in the long run was by foodstuffs. In the open spaces of the New World were farmers with the triple advantage of excellent natural conditions, the accumulated skill and experience of the Old World, and cheap transport. Britain could not compete. At the same time, if no longer the Workshop of the World, she was still a busy and efficient industrial state with a large export trade. The logic of the situation was inescapable. An international division of labour gave to Britain the factories and the manufactures, to other countries the large-scale raising of food.

(b) READJUSTMENT

Britain found the answer to industrial depression largely in a new attitude to her overseas possessions expressed in Imperialism, by means of which she was able to substitute new markets for those captured by her rivals. She found it partly in technical education; in a greater flexibility of her industry; and in such minor Acts as the Merchandise Marks Act of 1887, which compelled foreign goods to be marked with their country of origin, to prevent the fraudulent selling of foreign goods as British. External events helped to stem the price fall, for gold was discovered on the Witwatersrand in 1884, and the mines were in production five years later. In the nineties more American and Australian gold was being mined, and from the late nineties to 1914 a steady rise in prices set in. By the twentieth century Britain's flow of overseas investments had been resumed, although on a smaller scale than in the sixties and seventies. She was investing in China and Japan, in India and Africa, Canada and Australia, South America and the U.S.A.

Britain did not cease to be prosperous and eminent. Her working classes in the last two decades of the century were better off than ever before, measured both by the standard of real wages and by the percentage of unemployment. Her middle classes remained rich and powerful, even although the distance between rich and poor, measured in money terms, had lessened. Her total wealth increased, but less rapidly than before. She was still eminent, even if no longer pre-eminent.

Her economy, nevertheless, was vulnerable. Cotton goods were her chief exports. A long way behind came woollens, iron and steel, coal, and an increasing quantity of machinery. Her chief imports were still raw cotton, raw wool, timber, and food. Dangers clearly lay in the disproportionate size of the cotton export; in the increasing export of machinery, including cotton machinery, and of coal—which could only in the long run increase the competitive power of her rivals; and in the growing quantities of her food produced abroad.

More immediately obvious was the fact that by the end of the century Britain had yielded to the U.S.A. in the quantity of coal mined, and to both the U.S.A. and Germany in the production of steel. Britain's annual output of coal had increased from about 160,000,000 tons in 1883 to 225,000,000 tons in 1900. But the United States was then producing 241,000,000 tons a year.[1] In steel production Britain had advanced from nearly 2,000,000 tons in the eighties to 5,000,000 tons in 1901.[2] Yet both Germany, with a production of 6,500,000 tons of steel in 1901, and the U.S.A., with a production of 13,500,000 tons in the same year, were ahead. Belgium, Bohemia, Silesia, France, were also active competitors by the twentieth century. Similarly, British pig-iron production was growing less rapidly than American or German, while her wrought iron continued to decline.

In spite of the efforts made at the time of the depression, British industry, compared with that of other nations, was still insufficiently vigorous and elastic. Britain was slow to introduce improvements. She wasted power. She continued, in spite of Gilchrist-Thomas, to use largely the non-phosphoric ores, both her own and an increasing import. In mining she remained conservative. The textile industries, despite some

---

[1] *Fiscal Blue Book*, 1903, LXVII, 441, 491
[2] Sir John H. Clapham, *An Economic History of Modern Britain*, iii, 147.

improvements, were fundamentally as they had been for a century. In cotton, for example, though there was an increase both in output and in the size of the unit, twentieth-century Britain, with its maximum of four looms an operative, compared adversely with America, where twenty looms were supervised by a single worker. In light chemicals and dyeing Germany was well ahead of Britain.

Above all, Britain lagged far behind America and Germany in the use of electricity as a source of power, heat, and light; in electric metallurgy, in electrical transport, and in the manufacture of electrical equipment. To Michael Faraday, a Briton, had fallen the distinction of propounding the principle of the modern dynamo, or electric generator. That was in 1831. In 1884 Sir Charles Parsons produced the modern turbine, a powerful engine which, motivated by steam or water, generated electricity and drove ships and machinery. Britain, nevertheless, with her strong interests in steam-power, was slow to change her ways. She had little of the water-power which is a chief source of the supply of electricity, while vested interests were strong to guard coal and coke and gas as the generators of energy. As a means of lighting, gas indeed, after the introduction of the incandescent burner in the eighties, was generally considered more efficient than the electric lighting which had been introduced in 1875. Moreover, the procedure of getting a Private Bill to start an electricity concern was long and expensive, and resulted in a number of small, self-centred companies, unsuited to the large-scale development of electric power, which requires uniformity and centralization. Tyneside was the only area before 1914 where electric power was used on a large scale, and here factory-owners had united to obtain a centralized supply of power. In electrical equipment the whole British output in 1913—including cables, which were her speciality—was little more than one-third of the German production.

In transport and communications the coming of electricity in Britain was at first more revolutionary than in industry. One after another the great towns electrified their tramways, beginning with Leeds in 1891. Ten years later the last horse-tram disappeared from Leeds streets. Bristol had electric tramcars in 1895; Glasgow, Hull, and Liverpool in 1898; Plymouth and Bolton followed at the turn of the century.

Finally, early in the twentieth century, London electrified her tramway system. Her last horse-trams disappeared slightly before her last horse-buses. She also electrified her Underground railway, the first segment of which had been opened in 1863. In 1900 her electrified "Tuppenny Tube," running from the Bank to Shepherd's Bush, was opened by the Prince of Wales. Even more important was the use of electricity in the communication of messages by means of telegraph, telephone, and wireless. Telegraphic communication had been practised since the late thirties. In 1876 Graham Bell, a Scotsman resident in America, had sent the first telephone message. In 1901 a wireless station in Cornwall, erected by the Italian Marconi, transmitted the Morse Code letter S across the Atlantic to Newfoundland. Soon ships were communicating by wireless, and the human voice itself was transmitted.

The use of electric power was one of the revolutionary developments of the end of the nineteenth century. Ranking beside it was the invention of the internal-combustion engine. Again Britain followed the lead of America and Europe. It had long been realized that steam was a wasteful source of energy, and several experiments had been made before Dr Otto's silent gas engine—the first internal-combustion engine—appeared in 1876. In 1895 the diesel engine was invented by Dr Rudolf Diesel, a German who had helped his fellow-countryman Otto with the engine of 1876. The internal-combustion engine ran on the principle of supplying the power of the fuel direct and internally to the engine. Diesel used heavy oils like petroleum, but there was also being produced in the eighties the smaller, light-oiled internal-combustion engine of Gottlieb Daimler, another German, highly suitable for light road vehicles.

Nowhere was the effect of the internal-combustion engine more revolutionary than on transport. A steam-engine on a road is clumsy as well as wasteful, and the highway in no way rivalled the railroad until Daimler's light, efficient engine appeared. In 1887 Daimler operated the first light-engined motor-car on a road. In 1895 the first motor exhibition was held in London. But the mechanically propelled car could make little headway in England while legislation of 1865 still restricted the speed of mechanically propelled vehicles on roads to four miles an hour in the country and two miles an hour in the towns, requiring them to be driven by not less than three persons and to be attended by a man with a red flag. In 1896 this legislation was repealed; in the same year a motor-car made its appearance in the Lord Mayor's Show, and fifty-four mechanically propelled vehicles set out on the first London-to-Brighton trip. In 1903 mechanical vehicles were allowed to travel at twenty miles an hour.

Up to this point the supremacy of the railway had continued unchallenged, with higher speeds, greater safety, the building of new bridges, uniform freight rates, and reduced passenger fares. After 1896, as road surfaces were improved and private motor-cars and commercial vehicles increased, the challenge was sounded, although it was not until after the First World War that roads became the acknowledged rivals of the railways, offering cheaper fares, often better service, sometimes even speedier transport. In London, where the London General Omnibus Company had been founded in 1888, hundreds of horse-drawn omnibuses were operating, and the twentieth century opened with the horse-bus still supreme. In 1904 the L.G.O.C. obtained its first licence for the provision of mechanical traction, and in 1910, after much experimenting, produced a standardized omnibus driven by petrol.

Besides improved transport on the roads, the internal-combustion engine provided an engine light enough to be used in the air, and so made possible effectively controlled flight. Experiments in flight had been attempted as early as the eighteenth century, but had been confined chiefly to balloons. But balloons could not be steered. Not until the frame of an aeroplane was provided and the internal-combustion engine lifted it from the ground did controllable flight begin. In 1905 the two American brothers Wilbur and Orville Wright stayed in the air for half an hour in such a machine, and covered twenty-four and a half miles. The English Channel was crossed in an aeroplane in 1909 by the Frenchman Blériot. Already in the First World War the aeroplane was being used as a weapon of war.

Thus there developed what was no less than a second Industrial Revolution, the iron, coal, and steam transport of the first Industrial Revolution being paralleled by steel, electric power, and the internal-combustion engine. Nothing, perhaps, so much emphasized Britain's changing position among the nations as

DEVELOPMENT OF ROAD TRANSPORT

Top: Model of Shillibeer's Omnibus, 1829
Bottom: Model of Horse-drawn Omnibus, 1911

[*See pp.* 304, 382–384]

Crown Copyright. From exhibits in the Science Museum, South Kensington

DEVELOPMENT OF ROAD TRANSPORT

Top: L.G.O.C. 'B' type Motor Omnibus, 1910
Bottom: English Daimler Motor-car, 1898

[*See pp.* 383–384]

Crown Copyright. From exhibits in the Science Museum, South Kensington

the fact that she was no longer the nerve centre of this second phase. The great steel inventions go to her credit, but other countries were as quick as she in their utilization; in the development of transport Britain no longer set the standard for countries overseas, as she had done in the railway age, while in the inventions relating to the new power, as well as in their utilization, Britain was out-paced.

In the world of 1914, where Britain, formerly predominant, now stood among equals, space and time were yielding before mechanical and scientific invention. The timorous, the very wise, might still point out the dangers of an unbalanced economy. But the majority, in regarding a world so obviously interdependent, were troubled by no doubts when it became finally clear that Britain had abandoned hope of balance between her farming and her industry.

In 1911 there were more miners in Britain than agricultural labourers. The whole agricultural group was still larger than the whole quarrying and mining group, but, whereas it had accounted for over 12 per cent. of the occupied population in 1881, it was only 8 per cent. in 1911.[1] The agriculture that survived was mostly devoted to stock, only 5,000,000 acres in England and Wales producing corn in 1914, of which less than 2,000,000 acres were for wheat.[2] On the eve of the First World War Britain supplied all her fresh milk, a high proportion of other dairy produce, and nearly three-fifths of her meat, but relied on considerable quantities of imported feeding stuffs for her animals, and imported four-fifths of her bread. She did, however, produce 58 per cent. of the barley consumed and 79 per cent. of the oats, so that, taking cereals as a whole, she produced in 1914 almost exactly half her cereal consumption.[3] Moreover, care in breeding for meat, butter, and milk, better processes in cheese- and butter-making, in feeding, and in milking increased the weight of carcasses, the quality and quantity of milk and other products of the dairy, while careful experiment increased the yield of crops. Research and education were beginning to make headway. Besides the Rothamsted Experimental Station there were founded agricultural schools

[1] Sir John H. Clapham, *op. cit.*, iii, 1.
[2] J. A. Venn, *The Foundations of Agricultural Economics*, Appendix Tables I, II and III.
[3] *Ibid.*, p. 480.

and colleges, some attached to universities, while the Board of Agriculture developed educational functions.

The overall picture was not gloomy for a peace-time agriculture combined with a vigorous exporting industry, particularly since half the imported wheat came from the Empire. The incipient danger of the changing proportions of arable and pasture lay in the fact that fewer people can be fed from a given acreage of pasture than from the same area of arable. An acre of potatoes or wheat has more food value than an acre of land which grazes cattle. But within the limits imposed by world movements the adaptation of British agriculture had been satisfactory.

It had not, however, been accomplished painlessly. It had brought ruin to many farmers, unemployment and lower wages to the labourers, and the break-up of their trade unions. It accelerated the decline of a healthy rural community life based on the villages. When Britain abandoned the idea of a balanced economy she was yielding to the logic of events, but she lost something of infinite value when she let her village life decay.

SELECT BIBLIOGRAPHY

Report of the Royal Commission on the Depressed Condition of the Agricultural Interest (the Richmond Commission), 1882, XIV.

Report of the Royal Commission on the Depression of Trade and Industry, 1886, XXIII.

Final Report of the Royal Commission on Agricultural Depression, 1897, XV.

Fifth and Final Report of the Royal Commission on Labour, 1894, XXXV.

Memoranda, Statistical Tables and Charts prepared in the Board of Trade with reference to Various Matters bearing on British and Foreign Trade and Industrial Conditions, 1903, LXVII (the *Fiscal Blue Book*).

CLAPHAM, SIR JOHN H.: *An Economic History of Modern Britain*, vol. ii, *Free Trade and Steel, 1850–1886* (1932); and vol. iii, *Machines and National Rivalries, 1886–1914*, with an Epilogue, 1914–29 (1938) (Cambridge University Press).

——: *The Economic Development of France and Germany, 1815–1914* (Cambridge University Press, 1921).

DUNCAN, H. O.: *The World on Wheels* (Author, 1926).

ERNLE, LORD: *English Farming, Past and Present* (Longmans, 1912; revised edition, 1927).

JERVIS, F. R. J.: *The Evolution of Modern Industry* (Harrap, 1960).

KNOWLES, L. C. A.: *Economic Development in the Nineteenth Century in France, Germany, Russia, and the United States* (Routledge, 1932; revised edition, 1927).

——: *The Industrial and Commercial Revolutions in Great Britain during the Nineteenth Century* (Routledge, 1921).

——: *The Economic Development of the British Overseas Empire, 1763–1914* (Routledge, 1924).

LIPSON, E.: *The Growth of English Society*, Part III (fourth edition, Black, 1959).

SHERRINGTON, C. E. R.: *A Hundred Years of Inland Transport, 1830–1933* (Duckworth, 1934).

VENN, J. A.: *The Foundations of Agricultural Economics* (Cambridge University Press, 1923; revised edition, 1933).

CHAPTER XIX

THE LABOUR MOVEMENT: 1875–1914

(a) TRADE UNIONISM AND SOCIALISM IN THE POLITICAL FIELD

WHEN the worst of the depression had passed the curtain went up on a new scene in the world of labour. The Amalgamated Societies still held the centre of the stage. They had accepted the principle of political representation, and the period of the Lib-Labs was in full swing. At the same time they had declared themselves against legislative interference with hours or wages, preferring direct negotiation with the employers. But the great depression had taught many lessons. The unskilled workers had learned that, whereas they might be quite prosperous in times of plenty if they went with the grain of capitalism, in times of distress they were bound to suffer. In the kind of language they were beginning to use, they were prosperous when capitalism was expanding and the margin of concession was high, but they were the first to be sacrificed when capitalism contracted and the margin of concession was low. The logical outcome of this reasoning was a questioning of the policy of conciliation in both the political and the industrial field, together with a more profound questioning of the whole relationship of capital and labour and of the basis of capitalist society, which led to a revival of Socialism. In practice the issue was expressed first in the formation of new unions.

The new unions were distinguished from the Amalgamated Societies by low rates of subscription and a less skilled and less highly paid membership; by a concentration on industrial activity rather than Friendly Society function; by a fighting policy in the industrial field which was favourable to strike action; by a Socialist outlook and, in the political field, by opposition to the Lib-Lab alliance. They further differed from the Amalgamated Societies in their desire for explicit protection and regulation of the conditions of their work by law. The Amalgamated Societies, having received their overall sanction at law by the Acts of 1871 and 1875, now wished to proceed by means of negotiation with the employers. The New Unions, having no faith in negotiation, wanted reform expressed in the black and white of legal enactment. Hence, while they would strike for an immediate objective, their long-term policy was to amend the law through the work of their representatives in Parliament to cover hours, wage-rates, and conditions of labour.

Among the unions which now burst into vigorous life were those of unskilled workers who had hitherto remained virtually unorganized, unions which had been at variance with the Amalgamated Society leadership but had been powerless to act, and those which had accepted the official policy of the sixties but now extended their membership and changed their tune.

Of the unskilled, Ben Tillett's Tea-porters' and General Labourers' Union was formed among the dock workers at the Port of London in 1887. In 1888 the match-girls of Bryant and May's formed a union.

At a Fabian Society lecture attention had been drawn to the contrast between the low wages and high dividends paid by Bryant and May. Herbert Burrows and Annie Besant thereupon interviewed several of the girl workers, got lists of their wages and fines, and examined their general conditions of work. They found adults getting 8s. or 9s. a week, young girls 4s. They published an article called *White Slavery in London*, and called for a boycott of Bryant and May's matches. The article was read avidly by the match-girls and many others. Annie Besant was threatened by the firm with libel. When the girls refused to sign a paper declaring they were well treated one of them was dismissed, and the others, some 1400, struck work and sent a deputation to Annie Besant in Fleet Street. For two weeks Annie Besant and her friends worked indefatigably raising subscriptions, writing articles, spreading propaganda. Finally arbitrators were called in, and a settlement was reached which gave the girls higher wages and abolished the system of fines. As a result a Match-girls' Union was firmly established. Annie Besant for a time was secretary, until pressure of work compelled her to resign.

The victory of these hitherto unorganized and lowly girls struck a spark all over the lower ranks of labour, and gave an impetus to the further organization of the unskilled. The following year the Gas Workers' and General Labourers'

Union was formed in London under Will Thorne's guidance, and won the eight-hour day without doing more than present the demand. Stimulated by this victory, Tillett's men at the West India Dock came out on strike.

The docker suffered many burdens, chief of which were low pay, long hours of work, and, for a considerable section, casual employment. Each morning, in the first light or before, crowds of 'casuals' could be seen at the dock-gates struggling for the jobs which were too few to go round. Those who failed in the daily struggle were turned away unemployed, hungry and bitter, to break the news of another workless day to their families. Even when employed the earnings of the 'casuals' were so little that they were immediately consumed in food. One or two workless days meant nothing to eat, and re-employment meant work on an empty stomach. A few hours' work in this condition and the docker was compelled to 'pay himself off' in order to get a little cash to stay the pangs of hunger. Thus, even when work was available, he earned less than he might have done, and set up the whole vicious circle anew. Now, the dockers were demanding a minimum wage of 6d. an hour, the abolition of subcontracting and of piecework, a minimum engagement of four hours, and extra payment for overtime. Nearly the whole of Dockland followed the West India men; Tom Mann and John Burns came to help Ben Tillett; the traffic of the great port was at a standstill.

The dock strike of 1889, taking place in the heart of London and affecting the food and other vital supplies of the Metropolis, focused the attention not only of the whole country, but of people overseas. Public opinion nearly everywhere was instinctively favourable. Subscriptions in this country to help the strikers amounted to nearly £49,000. Australia was kept informed by telegraph of the day-to-day developments, raised a subscription, and telegraphed no less than £30,000 to the strike fund. Thus supported, the leaders paid generous strike pay to the dockers, and even bribed the dockyard casuals to refrain from blacklegging.

Apart from the money raised the moral effect of the support of public opinion was considerable. Chief among the public figures who came to the strikers' aid was Cardinal Manning. Day after day he swept down to the docks to attempt mediation in the little dockland committee-room. With the weight of

public opinion behind them, he and the dockers were successful. The dockers' tanner became a reality, and most of their
other demands were granted.

Everywhere the dockers' victory provided a stimulus. A
Sailors' and Firemen's Union, established in 1887, enrolled
thousands. Tillett's Union was transformed into the Dock,
Wharf, and Riverside Labourers' Union, with branches at the
chief ports. There were similar unions at Liverpool, Glasgow,
and Belfast. Even the black-coated workers for the first time
organized. There were National Unions of Clerks and of
Teachers in 1890, a Shop Assistants' Union in 1891, an Amalgamated Union of Co-operative Employees in the same year.
Older unions enrolled new members. The miners, who had
lost ground after Macdonald's death in 1881, had formed the
Miners' Federation of Great Britain in 1888. By 1893 it had
200,000 members. From not more than 750,000 before 1888
the number of trade unionists in Great Britain grew to over
1,500,000 in 1892.[1] With the growth of trade unions more
trades councils came into existence, and here, and at the annual
Trade Union Congress, New Unionism and Old clashed year
after year, the strong element of Socialism in the New Unionism
being reinforced by the influence of other Socialists who now,
of definite policy, were joining the trade unions whenever
possible.

The rebirth of Socialism was the second significant feature
of the time. Its coming was due partly to the fact that with the
passing of prosperity men naturally began again to question
the basis upon which their society was built. Such questions
had seemed out of place in the security and solidity of the fifties
and sixties. The years of depression were the time when widespread discussion began—not only among workers, but among
intellectuals who seriously questioned the chance of survival of
capitalist society. Socialist ideas were encouraged by the
French Socialist movement which followed the Paris Commune
of 1871, by the German Social Democratic Party of 1875, and
by the influence of Karl Marx and other Continental revolutionaries who were still living in London. Land reform, which
had been popular in Chartist days but had slid into the background during the Good Years, received fresh recruits whose

[1] S. and B. Webb, *The History of Trade Unionism*, p. 428.

zeal was augmented by Henry George's *Progress and Poverty*, which was published in America in 1879 and became popular in Britain a little later, and by Alfred Russel Wallace's *Land Nationalization*, published in 1882.

These were the circumstances in which a new party was formed in 1881—the Democratic Federation. Its founder was Henry Mayers Hyndman, a wealthy Radical influenced by Marx. Its aims were wide, ranging from projects for immediate reform to the large-scale reorganization of society, embracing a political programme not unlike the People's Charter and the demand for self-government for Ireland.

The political section of its programme was straightforward, including universal suffrage, equal electoral districts, payment of Members, the abolition of the House of Lords, and triennial Parliaments. Another section envisaged widespread State action in the interests of the working classes. This included universal free education with school feeding, a legal eight-hour day, State-aided housing schemes, public works for the unemployed, the redemption of the national debt, and a system of graduated taxation in the interests of the poorer taxpayers. A third section embraced the Socialist demands for nationalization of the land, of the railways, and of the mines. An impetus was given to this section—particularly to the demand for land nationalization—when Henry George himself came to England in 1882, even the T.U.C. passing a resolution (against the platform) in favour of nationalization of the land—a resolution which was promptly reversed the following year.

In 1883 William Morris joined the Federation. In 1884 its newspaper *Justice* was started. Industrial gloom was settled on the country, and the Democratic Federation began to work among the rising numbers of unemployed, changing its name to *Social* Democratic Federation. But in this same year, and before it really made its mark, the S.D.F. split. Its wide programme had attracted many diverse elements—Socialists, anarchists, those who hoped to reform the trade unions, those who had no use at all for trade unions, those who relied on political action, those who aimed at a social revolution. But it had not yet attracted the organized core of the working class. Hyndman himself was predominantly political, and was not the man to harmonize the conflicting and soon bitterly hostile elements of his team. At the end of 1884 William Morris and

Belfort Bax and others, including the anarchists, broke away and formed the Socialist League.

Of all the men who turned to Socialism at the end of the nineteenth century perhaps the most remarkable was William Morris. First and foremost he was a poet, a craftsman, and an artist, and largely because of this the effect of his joining the Democratic Federation was stimulating beyond the ordinary.

It would seem that by nature, nurture, and temperament William Morris would be the last to embrace Socialism—let alone devote his energies to it to the detriment of the ruling passion of his life. A substantial legacy had been left him; he had a beautiful home on the upper Thames and a house in Hammersmith; a happy family life with his wife and two children; numerous acquaintances and many friends. His life was rich with the writing of poetry and prose, with painting, designing, and managing his workshops. His hatred of Victorian art and design was expressed not only in the decoration of his house at Kelmscott, but even in the articles of everyday use which he designed himself. He went on not only to design but to manufacture wallpapers and fabrics at his own mills at Kelmscott, where he experimented with new patterns and dyes. He was doing creative work and helping to make the world a more beautiful place. Yet it was from the very fullness of his own life and from its abounding interests that his Socialism took birth. He wrote clearly enough to a Liberal friend in 1883:

> I believe that the whole basis of Society, with its contrasts of rich and poor, is incurably vicious; . . . art has been handcuffed by it, and will die out of civilization if the system lasts. That of itself does to me carry with it the condemnation of the whole system, . . . but furthermore in looking into matters social and political I have but one rule, that in thinking of the condition of any body of men I should ask myself, "How could you bear it yourself?" "What would you feel if you were poor against the system under which you live?" . . . Nothing can argue me out of this feeling, which I say plainly is a matter of religion to me: the contrasts of rich and poor are unendurable and ought not to be endured by either rich or poor. Now it seems to me that, feeling this, I am bound to act for the destruction of the system which seems to me mere oppression and obstruction; such a system can only be destroyed, it seems to me, by the united discontent of numbers; isolated acts of a few persons of the middle

and upper classes seeming to me . . . quite powerless against it: in other words the antagonism of classes, which the system has bred, is the natural and necessary instrument of its destruction.[1]

Morris did not enter public life to any extent until 1877, when he was forty-three years old and protested against the threatened 'restoration' of Tewkesbury Abbey. It took him six years to reach the Democratic Federation. From this time onward Socialism took up ever more of his time. He practised public speaking with growing enthusiasm, until he became a familiar figure at London street-corners. In May 1883 he was put on the executive of the D.F. Soon he was practically running *Justice*, editing it and writing for it, paying its debts. After the break with the S.D.F., when Morris and others formed the Socialist League, he started the *Commonweal*, which then had the money and writing that had previously gone to *Justice*. Above all, it had *A Dream of John Ball* and *News from Nowhere*, two of the finest essays in descriptive Socialism in the language.

The open-air meetings continued. Morris was in Trafalgar Square in 1886 when the police charged the mob. He arrived in the square towards the end of proceedings on 'Bloody Sunday,' in November 1887. He wrote the *Ode to Linnell*, the workman killed by the police in the demonstration of 1888. In 1889 he went as delegate to the International Congress of Socialists in Paris.

The Socialist League, unlike the S.D.F., opposed Parliamentary action, some of its members doing so absolutely, others thinking it premature until the working classes were thoroughly imbued with the spirit of Socialism. Most of them had an approach similar to that of the later Guild Socialists, picturing a State built on trade organizations which were thoroughly Socialist in idea and action. The Socialist League allied the gradualism of the Fabians with a dislike of the State characteristic of the Anarchists and with a belief in the revolution of heart and mind typical of the Christian and the artist. Such a combination was in William Morris, but it was too much to expect that it could hold within an organized group. Soon the Anarchists in the Socialist League gained the upper hand. The editorship of *Commonweal* was taken from Morris in 1889, and

[1] Letter to Mr C. E. Maurice, July 1, 1883, included in J. W. Mackail's *Life of William Morris*, ii, 105 (quoted here by permission of Messrs Longmans, Green and Co. Ltd).

in 1890 he resigned from the League, keeping but a small group round him in the Hammersmith Socialist Society until his death in 1896. After the defection of the Socialist League the S.D.F. held on its way, which in ultimate aim was Socialist and in method had become primarily political, involving the immediate fight for representation in Parliament. Its first Parliamentary election was a complete rout, John Burns the most successful of the S.D.F. candidates securing only 598 votes. It was more successful in its continued work among the unemployed. It organized or attended numerous demonstrations; it raised a relief fund; it attempted to turn into an unemployment demonstration a big Fair Trade meeting in Trafalgar Square in 1886. When turned away by the police the S.D.F. and its supporters marched up Pall Mall towards Hyde Park. Members at their club windows jeered at the marchers, who thereupon pelted the windows with stones. Hyndman, Burns, Champion, and J. E. Williams were arrested, but subsequently acquitted. At the 'Bloody Sunday' demonstration in Trafalgar Square the following year concerning the Irish question Burns and Cunninghame Graham were arrested, the latter bleeding profusely, and sent to prison for six weeks. So, in the day-to-day struggle, the S.D.F. made itself conspicuous.

A group of intellectuals, meanwhile, not influenced by Marx, neither wanting nor envisaging a violent upheaval in the social order, yet conscious of social wrong and desiring change, were meeting in one another's rooms and exchanging views. In November 1883 this small group proposed "that an association be formed whose ultimate aim shall be the reconstruction of Society in accordance with the highest moral possibilities."[1] Such a society was actually founded on January 4, 1884, and called the Fabian Society, after the Roman General Fabius, who, in his wars against Hannibal, patiently waited the right moment to strike, and was content to make his progress step by step. Permeation was the policy of the Fabians, "the inevitability of gradualness" their watchword. They took part in local affairs, getting elected to local councils and education committees, joining trade unions. Always their aim was to spread the idea of Socialism and to take any practical step in local

[1] E. R. Pease, *History of the Fabian Society*, p. 31.

or national government that would improve social conditions. So they wrote and lectured and debated among themselves.

Their early talks and debates were abstract and Utopian. But in the spring of 1885 they began the patient fact-collection and analysis of existing conditions which became so marked a feature of Fabian activity. The membership of Sidney Webb, dating from this time, gave a stimulus to this side of their work. Annie Besant joined them in the same year, making her distinctive contribution in public speaking. George Bernard Shaw was already a member and serving on the Executive Committee. It was a select society, prospective members having to be proposed and approved before being admitted. Consequently there were few inactive members. In March 1885 they started collecting facts on the working of the Poor Law. Then Sidney Webb and Frank Podmore gave their Report on the *Government Organization of Unemployed Labour*. In 1889 the *Fabian Essays* appeared, written by the seven outstanding members of the Society—a group of intellectuals which has rarely been equalled—Annie Besant, Shaw, Sidney Webb, Graham Wallas, Hubert Bland, William Clarke, and Sydney Olivier. The *Essays* were reprinted many times, and were undoubtedly among the formative influences of the period.

At various conferences as well as at their own meetings their discussions continued. One of the earliest conferences was the Industrial Remuneration Conference, to which Shaw made a characteristic contribution. "It was," he said,

> the desire of the President that nothing should be said that might give pain to particular classes. He was about to refer to a modern class, the burglars, but if there was a burglar present he begged him to believe that he cast no reflection upon his profession, and that he was not unmindful of his great skill and enterprise: his risks, . . . his abstinence; or finally of the great number of people to whom he gave employment, including criminal attorneys, policemen, turnkeys, builders of gaols, and it might be the hangman. He did not wish to hurt the feelings of shareholders . . . or of landlords . . . any more than he wished to pain burglars. He would merely point out that all three inflicted on the community an injury of precisely the same nature.[1]

But perhaps the greatest practical achievement of the Fabians was the Minority Report of the Poor Law Commission

[1] Pease, *op. cit.*, pp. 45–46.

of 1905-9. The Fabians Beatrice Webb and George Lansbury were on the Commission and among the signatories of this decidedly Fabian document, afterwards giving it publicity far exceeding that which Government Reports normally achieved.

Thus have the actors assembled for the next big scene. There are the older trade unionists, typified by the Amalgamated Societies; the New Unionists; the Socialists. The story to be unfolded is that of labour representation in the House of Commons.

It had started several years earlier with the second Reform Bill agitation and the perennial resolutions of the T.U.C. in favour of Labour representation. It was carried farther by the third Reform Act of 1884. But Labour representation still meant little except collaboration with the Liberals. In the General Election of 1885 eleven, in that of 1886 ten, working-class candidates were returned to Parliament. All sat with the Liberals. The Lib-Lab era lasted until the nineties. It was ended by a combination of forces which had been at work since the seventies—the forces of the New Unionism and of Socialism.

At demonstrations of Ayrshire miners in 1887 on Irvine Moor and Cragie Hill the resolution was carried that

> the time has come for the formation of a Labour Party in the House of Commons, and we hereby agree to assist in returning one or more members to represent the miners of Scotland at the first available opportunity.[1]

The following year James Keir Hardie stood as Labour candidate in Mid-Lanark against a Liberal and a Tory—the first independent candidate to stand. He took his position as a working-man. "I ask you . . . to return to Parliament," he said, "a man of yourselves, who being poor, can feel for the poor, and whose whole interest lies in the direction of securing for you a better and a happier lot."[2] He gave content to his promise to represent his class by naming his proposals for reform, of which the minimum were: the eight-hour day for the miners; an insurance and superannuation fund for miners supported from royalties; courts of arbitration; and a Ministry of Mines—all practical, immediate proposals. Hardie polled 617 votes.

---

[1] W. Stewart, *J. Keir Hardie: a Biography*, p. 24.   [2] *Ibid.*, p. 41.

In August of the same year, 1888, the Scottish Parliamentary Labour Party was formed, with Hardie as secretary, with the object of returning working-men to the House of Commons. In the same eventful year Hardie went for the second time as delegate to the T.U.C. It was the year of the match-girls strike; events were working up to the dock strike of the following year. The Scottish Parliamentary Labour Party was followed by similar Labour Parties in Lancashire and Yorkshire and the North-east, all having as their object the return of Independent Labour men to the House of Commons. The Scottish Labour Party soon had thirty branches.

While workmen were thus forming their own parties to forward independent working-class representation the Fabian Society was announcing in 1887, "The chief aim of our plan is the formation of a distinct Labour party in Parliament," the New Unionism was making its mark on the T.U.C. in many ways, and the trade unions were being permeated by the S.D.F., the Fabians, and the unattached Socialists according to the avowed policy of the leaders of the new movement.

Then, in the 1892 General Election, three Independent Socialists were returned to Parliament—Keir Hardie for West Ham, John Burns for Battersea, and Havelock Wilson for Middlesbrough. Asked if he would join the Liberal and Radical Party in the House, Hardie replied that "he expected to form an Independent Labour Party." And so it was. In the following year the Independent Labour Party was born.

The motion which came up year by year at the T.U.C. for the formation of an Independent Labour Party was passed again in 1892, and with an increased majority. This time it was no longer allowed to stand as a dead letter. An informal meeting of sympathetic delegates decided to summon a conference to give it effect.

On January 13 and 14, 1893, at the Labour Institute, Bradford, 121 delegates from Labour Clubs, the S.D.F., the Fabian Society, the Scottish Labour Party, and the trade unions elected Hardie chairman and proceeded to business. They decided to call their party the Independent Labour Party rather than the Socialist Labour Party, as expressing more clearly their immediate aim of independent representation in the House of Commons. They put on record at the same time, however, that their object was the "collective ownership and

control of the means of production, distribution, and exchange."
The Labour Leader, the Scottish Labour Party organ, was taken
over as the newspaper of the I.L.P., Hardie continuing to be
its editor. By January 1894, when it held its first annual conference at Manchester, the I.L.P. had 280 affiliated branches.
Hardie was again chosen as Chairman, Tom Mann as Secretary. At the 1895 General Election twenty-nine I.L.P. candidates went forward.

So now there is an additional actor on the stage—a party
not explicitly Socialist, though ready to pass Socialist resolutions; not avowedly trade-unionist, though many of its members belong to their trade unions; but explicitly and avowedly
standing for the independent representation of Labour in
Parliament with the object of securing better conditions for
the working class.

James Keir Hardie, the man who founded the I.L.P., was
the son of a ship's carpenter and general labourer and of a
domestic servant, and was born and spent much of his childhood among the miners of Lanarkshire. Illness and strikes
kept the family poor, and Hardie went to work at seven years
old as messenger-boy for various firms. At ten he went down
the pit as trapper. His mother taught him to read, and he
went to night school. He joined the temperance movement,
became one of the miners' spokesmen, was victimized, and,
with his brother, dismissed from the colliery. Thereupon he
took up small-scale journalism for a living, while he threw himself heart and soul first into the miners' movement and later
into the movement for Parliamentary Representation. Like
many of the early Labour leaders, he was a teetotaller, with a
simple Nonconformist religion, and was an ardent pacifist.
The Socialism of men like Hardie was a simple creed, with
clear blacks and whites expressed in language that was both
plain and uncompromising.

The I.L.P. had no official connexion with the T.U.C., nor
had it attempted to organize a distinct party in the House of
Commons. For some years after the formation of the I.L.P.,
therefore, Hardie and his friends continued to urge the necessity for forming a political party based upon or closely connected with the trade unions, and resolutions to this effect were
passed annually by Congress. In 1899 certain of the delegates
agreed informally to hold a conference of interested persons.

On February 27 and 28, 1900, in London, a special delegate meeting, representing the trade unions, the S.D.F., the Fabians, and the I.L.P., met together and formed the Labour Representation Committee. There were two currents of feeling at the meeting—one which wanted the new party to declare itself Socialist, the other satisfied with a declaration of immediate objectives. The former was typified by a resolution moved by the S.D.F., which proposed:

> That the representatives of the working-class movement in the House of Commons shall form there a distinct party . . . based upon a recognition of the class war, and having for its ultimate object the socialization of the means of production, distribution, and exchange.

The latter was represented by a resolution put by Keir Hardie:

> That this conference is in favour of establishing a distinct Labour Group in Parliament, who shall have their own Whips, and agree upon their policy, which must embrace a readiness to co-operate with any party which for the time being may be engaged in promoting legislation in the direct interest of labour, and be equally ready to associate themselves with any party in opposing measures having an opposite tendency.[1]

The former proposal was lost, the latter carried. A Labour Party was to be formed in the House of Commons which was to have its own policy and its own Whips and be entirely free from engagements to other parties. The various groups affiliated to the L.R.C. would select any candidates they wished, the sole condition being that if returned to Parliament these candidates would accept the Labour Party Whip.

So a Labour Representation Committee was formed in 1900. Its first secretary was James Ramsay MacDonald. It had refused to embrace the terms 'Socialist' or 'class war' in its constitution, but passed resolutions avowing its prime interests to be the well-being of labour and the ending of inequality of wealth. Trade unionists and Socialists had given it birth. It was a "Union of Socialism and Trade Unionism in the political field."

The L.R.C. was neither a Socialist party nor a trade-union party. It had refused to adopt the Socialist resolutions of the S.D.F. at its inauguration. It still refused the following year,

[1] Quoted by Max Beer, *A History of British Socialism*, ii, p. 328.

with the result that the S.D.F. seceded in 1901. Delegates
from the other bodies who happened to be also members of the
S.D.F. or to hold S.D.F. principles nevertheless continued to
attend the L.R.C. meetings, and repeatedly advanced Socialist
resolutions, which were always defeated.

THE UNION OF SOCIALISM AND TRADE UNIONISM IN THE POLITICAL FIELD

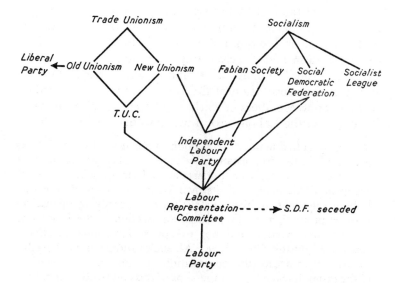

Nor was the L.R.C. a trade-union party, although it gained
much of its strength from the trade unions and its object was
the betterment of Labour. It had no financial assistance from
the T.U.C. which, indeed, still had no political fund. Its
membership was drawn from any sympathetic group or party
which cared to affiliate. Only organizations, not individuals,
were eligible for affiliation.

In 1903 the L.R.C. started its own political fund by making
a levy of 1d. per member *per annum*. As membership increased
the fund mounted, and in 1905–6 the Parliamentary fund, of
the L.R.C. was over £10,000. The trade unions were also establishing political funds of their own. A candidate of Labour
sympathies could at that time stand for election to Parliament under the ægis of a trade union, the I.L.P., or the L.R.C.

If returned for the I.L.P. he would naturally sit in the House with the L.R.C. nominees. If returned for a trade union he would be independent, probably leaning closely to the L.R.C., but perhaps still inclining to support the Liberals. There was nothing to prevent the L.R.C. itself from pursuing a Lib-Lab policy. The influx of trade unionists into its ranks, indeed, emphasized the tendency to Lib-Lab compromise. The I.L.P. members of the L.R.C. consequently felt it necessary to reassert the L.R.C. position of complete independence, and at the 1903 Conference of the L.R.C. brought forward a resolution to that effect. Any departure from that principle, declared Hardie, would ruin their Labour movement. "Let them have done with Liberalism and Toryism and every other 'ism' that was not Labourism." Finally a resolution was carried and embodied in the constitution of the L.R.C. forming the 'pledge' which Labour Members of Parliament were required to take. The object of the Labour group was thus declared to be to

> secure, by united action, the election to Parliament of candidates promoted, in the first instance, by an affiliated society or societies in the constituency, who undertake to form or join a distinct group in Parliament, with its own Whips and its own policy on Labour questions, to abstain strictly from identifying themselves with or promoting the interests of any section of the Liberal or Conservative parties, and not to oppose any other candidate recognized by this Committee. All such candidates shall pledge themselves to accept this constitution, to abide by the decisions of the group in carrying out the aims of this constitution or resign, and to appear before their constituencies under the title of Labour candidates only.[1]

In 1906 the L.R.C. became simply the Labour Party.

Early in the life of the L.R.C. an issue of major importance developed in Wales. In 1901 the Taff Vale Railway Company of South Wales sued the Amalgamated Society of Railway Servants on two counts. The first was to restrain it and its officers from any action calculated to damage the company in its business; the second was for damages already caused by such action. On both counts the railway company was successful. An injunction was granted to restrain the Society of Railway Servants from acts likely to damage the business of the com-

---

[1] *Ibid.*, ii, 338.

pany; and, for injury already done, the Society of Railway Servants was ordered to pay to the Taff Vale Railway Company the sum of £23,000.

The action arose out of a local dispute in South Wales for which the Amalgamated Society of Railway Servants provided the strike pay. The beginnings of the dispute were speedily lost to sight. The overwhelming issue was the fact that, in spite of the Labour Laws of 1871 and 1875, trade-union funds were apparently unprotected by law, so that a few successful actions by employers could deprive them of all accumulated reserves.

The outcry from the trade unions, who thus found their very existence threatened, was loud and immediate. For assistance they turned naturally to the newly formed Labour Representation Committee; and, by the help it was able to give, the L.R.C. established its position as an indispensable part of the machine of Labour organization.

The General Election of 1900 had come too soon for the young L.R.C. to make an ambitious show. But it gave its endorsement to such candidates as the affiliated bodies put up, and in this way fifteen L.R.C. candidates went to the poll, of whom two were successful—Keir Hardie at Merthyr Tydfil and Richard Bell at Derby. The next six years saw a steady growth of the L.R.C., due in large part to the determination of organized Labour to override the Taff Vale decision. In the year 1902 the affiliated membership nearly doubled. Several L.R.C. candidates were returned in by-elections, including Arthur Henderson for Barnard Castle in 1903.

In the 1906 General Election twenty-nine members of the L.R.C., including Hardie, J. R. MacDonald, Philip Snowden, and Fred Jowett, were returned to a Parliament overwhelmingly Liberal. It was this Liberal Parliament which the Labour Members had to persuade to reform trade-union law. On their side was the fact of their remarkable growth in six years, which could not go unnoticed by even the most powerful Government; and the fact that many unattached Members, Lib-Labs, miners' representatives, Liberals, and even Tories had pledged themselves during the election contest to reverse the Taff Vale Judgment. A Royal Commission on Trade Disputes and Trade Combinations had already been appointed by the Tories in 1903, and reported in 1906. The Liberal Government prepared a Bill on the basis of its findings which was

unsatisfactory to Labour. It was then that the full strength of
Labour's position was revealed. The powerful Liberal Government abandoned its own Bill, and introduced another, giving
the trade unions almost exactly what they wanted. The three
most important provisions were: first, peaceful picketing was
made clearly permissible, even to the end of inducing another
person to break his contract of employment, and even although
it was in interference of a man's right to dispose of his capital
or his labour as he wanted; second, no trade union or official
or member of a trade union was henceforth to be actionable at
law in respect of any civil wrong committed by or on behalf of
the union; third, when contemplating or committing an act in
furtherance of a trade dispute a man could not be charged in
combination for a misdemeanour which would not be chargeable were he acting alone.

The Trades Dispute Act of 1906, which became part of the
Charter of Trade Unionism, was remarkable as having been
granted so easily by a powerful Liberal Government to Labour
and trade-union interests, and also for the extent of the privilege granted. It gave to trade unions "an extraordinary and
unlimited immunity" from legal proceedings in respect of civil
wrong, which meant that they could not be charged at law
however considerable the damage caused by any act for which
they were responsible. Individual trade unionists were also
given considerable protection in picketing and in carrying on
the activities essential to a strike. Altogether the Act of 1906
was a triumph for the trade unions and the Labour Party.[1]
To the trade unions it meant an assured freedom in their work;
to the Labour Party it brought an enhanced prestige, confidence and support in contesting elections, and increased power
in the House of Commons.

Resentment at the Act of 1906 and alarm at the powerful
alliance of political Labour and trade unionism led to a further
attack upon the trade unions. The drive was strengthened by
the attitude of certain trade unionists themselves who revived
the Lib-Lab tradition, and even tried to exclude the Socialist
and independent bodies from the Labour Party by a resolution of 1907 confining membership to trade unions only. Then

---

[1] For a full discussion of the Trades Disputes Act of 1906 see S. and B. Webb,
The History of Trade Unionism, pp. 606–608.

objections began to be voiced to the employment of trade-union money to finance independent candidates or Socialist candidates, or, indeed, any political activity whatever. At this point capitalist influence and capitalist money was brought to bear. The agitation came to a head when in 1908 W. V. Osborne, a branch secretary of the Amalgamated Society of Railway Servants, brought a case at law seeking to restrain his union from spending its funds on political objects on the grounds that such expenditure was *ultra vires*. Judgment was given against Osborne, who then appealed. The appeal was upheld, and the House of Lords in 1909 gave judgment in Osborne's favour.

Through the intricate details of their ruling the Lords made it clear that all trade-union political action was illegal. They based their judgment largely on the Act of 1876 which had brought trade unions within the scope of the Friendly Society Acts and, in so doing, had enumerated some of their functions. This enumeration had in no sense been intended as exhaustive. But in 1909 the Law Lords held that, because political action was not one of the functions therein mentioned, trade unions could not legally engage in political activity. No one could reasonably believe that the framers of the 1876 Act had in mind the exclusion of trade unionists from politics. Yet the Law Lords of 1909 were of that mind, and their judgment was a victory for every capitalist interest.[1] It meant that trade unions could be restrained from contributing to a political fund in general, to funds for national or local elections, even to funds for educational purposes which could be held as 'political.'

The Osborne Judgment took the Labour and trade-union movement completely by surprise. It was contrary to much contemporary legal opinion, including that of the court which had in the first place given judgment against Osborne. It was a shattering blow at the finances of the Labour Party, for by cutting off the subscriptions of trade unionists it deprived it of the bulk of its income. The only hope was an overriding Act of Parliament, and this meant a fresh approach to the Liberals. Meanwhile up and down the country injunctions were restraining trade unions from giving to any fund held to be political.

The introduction of Payment of Members in 1911 eased matters a little for the Labour Party, for this meant that their

---

[1] For a discussion of this judgment see Webb, *op. cit.*, pp. 608–631.

successful candidates would be supported from the Exchequer while they were in the House. On the other hand, two general elections had to be fought in 1910 while the Osborne Judgment was operative. Several unions withdrew their candidates through lack of funds, though the reserve still in the central pool enabled the Labour Party to put out a fairly strong field. In most constituencies where it fought, however, it did so with Liberal support. Including the miners' representatives, who had joined the Labour Party in 1909, it returned forty Members to the Parliament of January 1910 and forty-two to that of December 1910.

The Liberal Party was occupied with crises over the Budget and the House of Lords, and it was three years before Labour pressure induced it to agree to the compromise Act of 1913 which partially reversed the Osborne Judgment. The Trade Union Act of 1913 allowed a trade union to undertake political activity provided, first, that a majority of its members had by ballot agreed to do so; secondly, that all payments destined for political use should be put in a separate fund; and, third, that all and any members of the union who wished could contract out of the political levy by signing a form to that end. The effect was that each unionist's contributions were divided into two—one for general purposes and one for political purposes—and that unless he said otherwise the political contribution would be used for the support of Parliamentary candidates, who, in most cases, would be Labour Party members.

The chief objection of the Labour Party and the trade unionists to the Act of 1913 was that it placed them under a disability not applied to other organizations. They held that they should be as free to devote their funds to such purposes as they pleased as any other voluntary organization. In actual fact, however, the Act made little difference to trade-union political funds. Only those most violently opposed to the Labour Party took the trouble to obtain the necessary form and 'contract out' of the political levy; the result was that the number of actual objectors was relatively small and that Labour Party funds were not seriously depleted.

While the Labour Party, under its secretary, James Ramsay MacDonald, had been building up its political machine and pursuing what was necessarily a policy of compromise, steering clear of a Lib-Lab policy which would make its very existence unnecessary, but at the same time taking such aid as the Liberals could give, it was being violently attacked from the left for an abandonment of Socialist principles. The S.D.F., though it had seceded in 1901, never ceased to urge the adoption of a Socialist policy by the Labour Party or, if not by them, by a new party. In 1908 Victor Grayson, calling himself an Independent Socialist, stood for Parliament, pledging himself to subordinate all issues to that of the relief of unemployment. He was returned to the House, was ruled out of order when he made his protest on behalf of the unemployed, and was suspended without any support from the Labour Party. Thereupon he toured the country, gathering considerable support, forming Socialist Committees in several towns, and raising angry debates throughout the Labour and Socialist Parties. The S.D.F. was solidly with Grayson. So were Blatchford's *Clarion*, a weekly newspaper founded by Robert Blatchford in 1891, and various Socialist groups based upon it. The I.L.P. was split on the issue. The Fabian Society held heated discussions. Finally the S.D.F., the *Clarion* groups, part of the I.L.P., and several smaller Socialist groups and unattached persons formed the British Socialist Party in 1911.

(b) INDUSTRIAL STRUGGLE

Labour's political aims from the eighties to the First World War present a logical attempt to achieve political power by a class which for long had suffered from the effects of political power wielded by the master class. They continue a story which had begun incoherently in the early days of the Industrial Revolution, and had continued with increasing purpose through the Reform Bill struggle and Chartism. At the same time, however, in the trade unions the day-to-day struggle was continuing.

Trade-union membership had been rising but slowly between 1897 and 1907, partly because the working class was concentrating on political rather than industrial action, partly because the Taff Vale decision of 1901 threatened the funds of any trade union showing fight. Real wages were rising during part of the period, and only slowly falling during the remainder, so that there was no immediate urge to strike. The unions were loosely and badly organized, with much duplication and overlapping. The engineers were defeated in 1897, the South

Wales miners in 1897–98, the North Wales quarrymen in 1896–98, and again in 1902–3. Moreover, the atmosphere of these years was not favourable to trade-union activity, sympathy with Labour being swallowed up by the rising wave of patriotism associated with the Queen's Jubilee, Imperialism, and the Boer War.

Then, with the reversal of the Taff Vale decision in 1906, trade-union funds were safeguarded. After 1907 real wages were falling heavily, giving the incentive to strike. The National Insurance Act of 1911 brought many members to the Approved Society sections of the unions. The Osborne Judgment of 1909, in making political action more difficult, encouraged industrial activity, while the long delay in getting this judgment reversed by the Act of 1913, the apparent strengthening of the Lib-Lab alliance in those years, led to distrust of politics and to one of those swings of the pendulum from political to industrial action which characterize the development of the working-class movement. Between 1910 and 1913 1,500,000 trade unionists were enrolled. Organization among the unskilled workers continued; women began to swell the men's unions as well as to found their own; and there was a steady advance of organization among the black-coated workers. Most prominent were the transport workers, the railwaymen, and the miners, all of whom substantially increased both their membership and their influence in the period. The builders and the cotton-workers became less influential, although their membership increased. The great model society of the mid-century, the Amalgamated Society of Engineers, went steadily forward in strength, together with allied unions like the Boilermakers and Shipwrights. In 1919 the A.S.E. had a membership of 320,000—five times that of 1892. The agricultural labourers formed a new union in 1906, and many of them joined General Workers' Unions. By 1920 more than 300,000 of them were in some kind of organization.[1]

Accompanying the swing from political to industrial action in the early years of the twentieth century was a profound reconsideration of the whole basis of industrial organization. Established forms of trade unionism were taken up by the roots and examined. In the first decade of the twentieth century

[1] Webb, *op. cit.*, IX, *passim*, and appendix.

there grew up again the idea of One Big Union, representing the workers of all industrial groups and in fundamental opposition to the capitalist state.

The essential features of this industrial unionism were first that the workers' organizations should cover their whole industry and not merely a craft. There should be one Railwaymen's Union—not separate unions for engine-drivers, platelayers, railway clerks, porters; one union to embrace all miners, one for all cotton operatives, one for all engineers. Secondly, these unions should be self-governing bodies functioning for all aspects of the industry's activity—production and sale as well as labour conditions. Thirdly, representatives of these self-governing trade unions or guilds should form the government of the country. Government would thus be based on industrial representation instead of on geographical constituencies. Men would send representatives to Parliament in their right as producers, not through the accident of residence. No longer then would the paradox exist of a political state legislating in economic affairs. Economic power, which had always in reality been basic and whose pressure on the political state had always been decisive, would be recognized as fundamental. "It is an axiom," said James Connolly, the Irish Labour leader, "enforced by all the experience of the ages, that they who rule industrially will rule politically."[1] The function of Industrial Unionism, Connolly declared, was

> to build up an industrial republic inside the shell of the political State, in order that when that industrial republic is fully organized it may crack the shell of the political State and step into its place in the scheme of the universe.[2]

The specialized forms taken by these theories in the early twentieth century were Syndicalism, Industrial Unionism, and Guild Socialism. The first two were virtually the same, and both were revolutionary in tactics. Guild Socialism was a more characteristically British conception, differing from the others in two respects. It envisaged the control of industry by *all* producers and not merely by wage-earners; and it did not associate its aims with violent upheaval.

Syndicalism in France and Industrial Unionism in America were already popular, and exercised considerable influence

---

[1] *Socialism made Easy* (1905), p. 13, quoted by Webb, *op. cit.*, p. 656.
[2] *Ibid.*, pp. 16–17.

over the British movement. In 1905 James Connolly was popularizing Industrial Unionism on the Clyde. Tom Mann, returning in 1910 from Australia, where the influence of the American Industrial Workers of the World was strong, set about organizing the British Syndicalist movement, which he found widely preached though not effectively organized. He started the *Industrial Syndicalist*, and rallied the trade unions as class organs to oust the capitalists and govern the country.

Existing trade-union organization did not lend itself to such a scheme. Among the transport workers, in textiles, in building, there were many craft unions, each with its own separate organization. To rectify this, and as a first step towards Industrial Unionism, an Amalgamation movement gained ground. The National Transport Workers' Federation was formed by Tom Mann and Ben Tillett in 1910 to unite all transport workers on land, sea, and river, except railwaymen, into one organization. There were similar movements in building, printing, engineering, and other trades, and among the railway workers. In their famous pamphlet *The Miners' Next Step*, published in 1912, the miners of South Wales declared for "one organization to cover the whole of the Coal, Ore, Slate, Stone, Clay, Salt, mining or quarrying industry of Great Britain, with one Central Executive." Every man working in or about the mine should be required to join the Union and observe its decisions. It should "engage in political action, both local and national, on the basis of complete independence of, and hostility to, all capitalist parties," with an avowed policy of wresting whatever advantage it could for the working class. It was to be an organization to fight rather than to negotiate; its ultimate aim was the union of all workers in one national and international union.

In 1913 three of the four manual railway workers' unions amalgamated to form the National Union of Railwaymen, whose object was to bring within one union every type and grade of railway worker. The N.U.R. became a powerful exponent of Industrial Unionism, though its efforts to be all-inclusive brought it into conflict with various sectional and craft unions. Guild Socialist propaganda, which had started before the War, continued throughout, directed by a group of young and able intellectuals, but the War turned the energies of Labour into other channels. After the War a series of Building Guilds amalgamated to form the National Building Guild. The Guilds began with some success, making direct contracts for work and returning to their clients any profit made. Undoubtedly their initial success was due, as in Owen's day, to the fact that they could work with small capital and needed no elaborate machinery. They also owed much to the Co-operative Wholesale Society and the Co-operative Insurance Society, who helped with money. But perhaps they were successful chiefly because of the great housing shortage and the Government's willingness to sanction any scheme which would produce houses. With the onset of the post-War slump the Builder's Guild perished, and with it Guild Socialism. The influence of Syndicalism and Industrial Unionism was already waning, and by 1922 had ceased to count.

The railwaymen had their own special problems in these years, foremost among which was overcoming the employers' refusal to recognize railway trade unions of any kind. The attitude of the employers was typified by the statement of the General Manager of the London and North-western Railway: "You might as well have a Trade Union or any 'Amalgamated Society' in the Army where discipline has to be kept at a very high standard, as have it on railways." Throughout the disputes of these years the railway management refused to recognize or to negotiate with the railwaymen's representatives, until compelled to do so by Government pressure. The two famous cases of the period—the Taff Vale case and the Osborne Judgment—were concerned with railway unions, and the unions lost money heavily.

The stage for large-scale activity had been set in 1910 with the organization of the National Transport Workers' Federation. The trouble actually started with the seamen, whose union, the National Sailors' and Firemen's Union, the employers had refused to recognize, and whose demands for a National Conciliation Board and a minimum wage had been refused. The Sailors' and Firemen's Union, after a period of preparation and propaganda, thereupon declared a national strike in June 1911. Attempts to introduce blackleg labour caused the strike to spread and consolidate, and soon the principal ports were at a standstill. The employers were compelled to yield. But even as they were doing so dockers, carters, coal-porters, and other waterside workers were coming out all over the country—at Hull, Manchester, Liverpool, Cardiff—stimulated by the newly formed National Transport Workers' Federation.

In London the Port of London Authority and other employers were threatened with strike action, and agreed to negotiate. On July 27, 1911, the "Devonport" Agreement was provisionally drawn up. This was deemed unsatisfactory, and as a result the whole of London's dockland ceased work, unionists as well as non-unionists. Simultaneously at Liverpool a transport stoppage became general. Starting with a small group of railwaymen, it spread to include dockers, public employees, tramwaymen, and the rest of the railwaymen. Tom Mann arrived to organize the workers there, while Ben Tillett took charge in London. Winston Churchill, the Home Secretary, paraded troops in London and Liverpool and sent them in all directions where disturbance threatened. The Town Hall was burnt by crowds at Liverpool. Great meetings were held on Tower Hill, in London. Clashes between the police and demonstrators, in which many were wounded, occurred at Hull, Cardiff, and Manchester. "It is a revolution; the men have new leaders, unknown before; and we don't know how to deal with them," said an employer.[1]

For both London and Liverpool port workers victory was achieved at the end of August. In the Port of London wages were increased from the 'dockers' tanner' of 1889 to 8d. an hour; there were increases also for the higher paid workers, and the unions were recognized by the employers. But the following year the employers turned the tables. A dispute at the London docks developed into a fierce struggle between the Federation and the employers, and the Federation called on all transport workers in all ports to strike in sympathy. But this time the response was insufficient, and the employers won.

Meantime the railway stoppage of 1911 at Liverpool had spread to other railwaymen. The companies refused to meet the unions, the Government intervened, and appointed a Royal Commission of Inquiry. On Cabinet instructions the railway companies for the first time met representatives of the trade unions, although they still refused them recognition. When a settlement was finally reached it was in the men's

---

[1] E. Halvéy, *A History of the English People in 1905–1915*, p. 448.

favour generally; but most important was the fact that they had made a substantial step forward in their relationship with the employers. Railway unionism continued to grow. By 1914 the N.U.R. had a membership of over 300,000. In that year, after being widely discussed for twelve months, a triple alliance of railwaymen, miners, and transport workers was formed. It was intended that each union should negotiate simultaneously for agreements covering wages and working conditions, and that if any one of the three failed to reach a settlement the others should support it. In practice this meant that a strike or lock-out concerning one section of the Triple Alliance would automatically involve the others. The Triple Alliance was actually ratified in 1915, during the War.

The coalminers, the third group in the Triple Alliance, had been growing steadily in importance. The eighties had been characterized by the miners' growing dissatisfaction with the sliding-scale agreements which then dominated their wage-rates and by the consolidation of their numerous unions into federations. In 1908 the Miners' Federation of Great Britain numbered nearly 600,000. By 1920 it had a membership of nearly 900,000.[1]

In 1908 the Eight Hours Act gave the miners a nominal, though not an actual, eight-hour day, for the eight hours did not include the time taken in travelling from the top of the pit to the coal face—a distance which in some cases took as long as two hours to traverse. At the end of February 1912 nearly a million miners came out on strike on a wages issue. The men wanted to end the system of governing wages by individual output, for this meant that a man in a very bad place, an 'abnormal place,' as it was termed, could never achieve a living wage. The miners therefore wanted a prescribed daily minimum wage. The Government intervened and suggested district minima, together with a joint board and impartial chairman to settle disputes. The miners agreed to try the compromise, which was embodied in the Act of 1912. It proved of considerable benefit to them, and consequently enhanced the prestige of the Miners' Federation.

While the unions were battling with authority the Co-operative movement was making steady though less spectacular

[1] Webb, *op. cit.*, p. 512.

progress. Its chief enemies were the private traders, who in a variety of ways tried to arrest the progress of the Co-operative Societies. At one time they objected, fruitlessly, to Government employees holding office in Co-operative enterprises. In 1910 Lever Brothers prosecuted several Co-operative Societies for selling C.W.S. soap flakes and Parrot Brand soap-powder on the grounds that they were not what customers asked for— those customers being supposed to want Lux and Monkey Brand. The case and an appeal were lost, and Co-operative progress continued. Membership of the Retail Co-operative Societies grew from 500,000 in 1881 to 3,000,000 in 1914. The net annual sales of the C.W.S. grew from £52,000 in 1864 to £35,000,000 in 1914. Its capital and reserves in the same period grew from £2000 to £10,000,000.

From the prosperity period onward the story of Co-operation had been one of all-round expansion and a reaching back from retail to wholesale to production and so to the acquisition of land, machinery, and raw materials. In 1902 the two Wholesale Societies bought tea estates in Ceylon. Plant for handling imported wheat was built early in the twentieth century at Manchester and Newcastle. Ships were bought to eliminate the private carrier; but this venture failed largely because, while the Co-operative Societies could bring them in loaded with goods, they had little with which to load them for the outward journey. So the ships, bought in 1876, were sold in 1906. Constantly reaching out to supply their own needs, they had started an insurance company in 1867, chiefly for fire insurance. At the end of the century activities spread to all insurance, including life insurance. Under the National Health Insurance Act of 1911 the Co-operative movement undertook national health insurance. By 1918 the Co-operative Insurance Company was covering a similar field and working on similar principles to the big commercial companies.

In 1871 the Co-operative Wholesale Society opened a loan and deposit department which it shortly afterwards formed into a bank for the benefit of the Co-operative Societies, for whom it acted as a kind of clearing house in their transactions with one another and with the Wholesales. Then it undertook to deal with trade-union funds, Friendly Society funds, and the funds of other working-class bodies, and also began to take deposits from individual Co-operators. The C.W.S. bank was not, however, independent of the capitalist banks, the Westminster Bank acting as its clearing agent and its agent for foreign business.

Labour in 1914 had its own political party, its own Members in the House of Commons, its own newspaper, *The Daily Herald*, which had been founded in 1911, and was flourishing under the editorship of George Lansbury. Transport workers, railwaymen, and miners had steadily advanced their position in a series of tenacious disputes with authority. The Triple Alliance of these three groups promised to be a powerful anti-capitalist bloc. Syndicalism and Guild Socialism were still spreading, and the Co-operative movement was growing. Everything seemed set for a strong forward move on all fronts of labour. But across the pattern of the period broke the First World War.

SELECT BIBLIOGRAPHY

ARNOT, R. PAGE: *The Miners: A History of the Miners' Federation of Great Britain, 1889-1910* (Allen and Unwin, 1949).
——: *A History of the Scottish Miners* (Allen and Unwin, 1955).
BEALEY, F. AND PELLING, H.: *Labour and Politics 1900-06* (Macmillan, 1958).
BEER, MAX: *A History of British Socialism* (Bell, 1920), vol. ii.
BLATCHFORD, R.: *My Eighty Years* (Cassell, 1931).
BROADHURST, H.: *The Story of his Life . . . told by himself* (Hutchinson, 1901).
COLE, G. D. H.: *British Working-class Politics, 1832-1914* (Routledge, 1941).
COLE, MARGARET: *The Story of Fabian Socialism* (Heinemann, 1961).
ELTON, G.: *England, Arise!* (Cape, 1931).
Fabian Essays in Socialism (sixth edition, Allen and Unwin, 1962).
GRUBB, A. P.: *The Life Story of the Right Hon. John Burns, P.C., M.P.* (Dalton, 1908).
HALÉVY, E.: *A History of the British People in 1905-1915* (1934).
HUMPHREY, A. W.: *A History of Labour Representation* (Constable, 1912).
HYNDMAN, H. M.: *The Record of an Adventurous Life* (Macmillan, 1911).

LANSBURY, G.: *My Life* (Constable, 1928).

LLOYD, ERIC GREY: *William Morris, Prophet of England's New Order* (Cassell, 1949).

MACKAIL, J. W.: *The Life of William Morris* (Longmans, 1899).

MCBRIAR, A. M.: *Fabian Socialism and English Politics* (Cambridge University Press, 1962).

MANN, T.: *Memoirs* (Labour Publishing Company, 1923).

PEASE, E. R.: *The History of the Fabian Society* (third edition), with new introduction by Margaret Cole (Frank Cass, 1963).

PELLING, H. M.: *The Origins of the Labour Party 1880–1900* (Macmillan, 1954).

STEWART, W.: *J. Keir Hardie, a Biography* (Cassell, 1921).

THORNE, W.: *My Life's Battles* (Newnes, 1925).

WEBB, S. AND B.: *The History of Trade Unionism* (Longmans, 1894, revised edition, 1920).

The History of the T.U.C. 1868–1968 (centenary year-book; T.U.C., 1968).

JAMES KEIR HARDIE
[*See p.* 399]
By courtesy of Messrs T. and R. Annan and Sons, Ltd, Glasgow

WILLIAM MORRIS
G. F. Watts
[See pp. 393-394]
National Portrait Gallery

CHAPTER XX

THE END OF AN EPOCH

(a) THE ECONOMIC SCENE, 1914–39

THIS period began and ended with deadly war. Between the Wars Britain suffered the worst trade depression of her history. From both wars she emerged victorious, but in each case with a loss of political influence and economic strength. In both wars the chief enemy of Britain was Germany. In both wars imperialist rivalries and the struggle for markets and raw materials played an important part.

In 1914 Britain adapted her economy to fight the First World War. Men were taken from industry and agriculture for the armed forces. The Government instituted measures of centralization and control to ensure the rapid and uninterrupted production of munitions. It controlled railways, mines, and the basic industries. The Munitions of War Acts of 1915 and 1916 gave the Government compulsory powers for the dilution of industry, and abolished restrictions on the employment of women. It denied the right to strike to industries necessary to the war effort, substituting compulsory arbitration, and abolished overtime restrictions. Winston Churchill went to the Ministry of Munitions, and described the pitch the organization had reached by the end of the War:

> Nearly all the mines and workshops of Britain were in our hands. We controlled and were actually managing all the greatest industries. We regulated the supply of all their raw materials. We organized the whole distribution of their finished products. Nearly five million persons were directly under our orders, and we were interwoven on every side with every other sphere of the national economic life.[1]

Agriculture, faced with an intensive submarine campaign at a time when Britain was largely dependent upon imported food, turned desperately to increase home production. Working through County War Agricultural Committees, it stimulated

[1] *The World Crisis: The Aftermath*, p. 32 (1929 edition).

417

conversion to arable, reduced the arable area devoted to hops, bulbs, and other unessential crops in order to grow more cereals, helped to maintain existing cornland. Farmers were guaranteed a minimum price, the raising of rents was prohibited, wages boards were established to provide a minimum wage for agricultural labourers. Prisoner-of-war labour, interned alien labour, and a Women's Land Army were organized. The number of allotments in the United Kingdom grew to 1,400,000 by 1918.

Results were satisfactory. There was a substantial increase in the production of wheat, barley, oats, potatoes, roots, and hay. The area under hops was reduced by half. By 1918 nearly 3,000,000 acres had been added to the area cultivated for crops other than grass, and the fierce submarine campaign was weathered. The year 1918 had promised a bumper harvest, and, although the weather broke in the North before the crops were gathered, the increase of 1918 over the 1904–13 average was still substantial. There was 58 per cent. more wheat, 36 per cent. more oats, 59 per cent. more potatoes, but small decreases of beans, peas, and barley. There was a necessary reduction in meat, but in terms of human food the change-over had been worth while.[1]

Britain emerged from the War in 1918 as one of the victorious Powers, only to find magnified all the tendencies which had previously threatened her eminence—foreign competition, imperialist rivalries, tariffs, a changed relationship between Britain and the Powers, and an abandonment of balance between her industry and her agriculture, which made her more than ever dependent upon imported food.

It was soon apparent that the First World War had dislocated world economy. It speeded the change which already had been taking place in the economic relationships of nations. Japan, India, and the countries of Central Europe and South America were no longer willing customers for Britain's cotton goods and raw materials. Economic and political upheavals followed the War, and reduced the purchasing power of European peoples. Economic nationalism and tariff barriers reduced world trade. The years between the Wars were a period of world crisis, of declining trade and commerce, of unemployment, of production in excess of purchasing power, of the

---

[1] Lord Ernle, *English Farming, Past and Present*, p. 415.

destruction of stocks which the world needed. The comparative stability of the pre-War years was never reached again. It seemed in retrospect as though 1914 had marked the end of an epoch.

The pattern of the inter-War years in Britain may be roughly drawn. There was first a mild boom, which continued for eighteen months, followed from the middle of 1920 by rapid collapse, rising unemployment, and general depression. The winter of 1921–22 was one of hardship and misery, with unemployment at the 2,000,000 mark. From the middle of 1922 to the summer of 1924 there was a slow recovery in industries supplying the home market, but the export trades continued heavily depressed. There was an improvement from the end of 1924 to 1929 in the world as a whole, but it was barely marked in Britain. World export trade increased, but Britain's share shrank. There followed a period of world crisis, involving Britain as well as Europe and America, during which the number of British unemployed rose to nearly 3,000,000. Only at the end of the thirties, partly under the stimulus of re-armament, did the depression begin to lift. As it did so the world was plunged into the Second World War.

The characteristics of the period between the Wars in Britain were mass unemployment; movements of population resembling those of the Industrial Revolution, but in an opposite direction; a pronounced drift of manpower from the older industries to new ones; the abandonment of Free Trade in an effort to save Britain from world competition; and a general encroachment upon *laissez-faire* by State action made necessary as economic life became more complex and the social services more widespread.

The export industries were most seriously affected by the slump. In value United Kingdom exports fell from £801,000,000 in 1924 to £729,000,000 in 1929, and slumped to £365,000,000 in 1932. In volume Britain in 1924 was exporting only 80 per cent of the 1913 figure. But in the same year she was importing 106·4 per cent. of the 1913 volume.[1] Britain, then, was taking more from the rest of the world in return for less. Her imports included four-fifths of her wheat and flour, three-fifths of her meat, the whole of her raw cotton, nine-tenths of her wool and timber, over one-third of her iron-

[1] *Report of the Committee on Industry and Trade: Survey of Overseas Markets*, 1925, p. 4.

ore. Coal was the only important raw material in which she was self-supporting. Exports continued to be the old staples—cotton goods, woollen goods, iron, steel, and coal. Cotton and coal, the industries upon which Britain's industrial supremacy had been built, were hardest hit. Particularly, the dangerous preponderance of the cotton industry in Britain's oversea trade stood revealed. The First World War did greater harm to this industry than to any other, for it was the most dependent upon

THE SLUMP BETWEEN THE WARS EXPRESSED IN THE VALUE OF EXPORTS AND NUMBERS UNEMPLOYED

YEAR	U.K. EXPORTS OF MERCHANDISE (EXCLUDING RE-EXPORTS)[1]	REGISTERED UNEMPLOYED IN G.B.[2] (TOTALS)
	Million pounds	Millions
1920	1334·5	0·9
1921	703·4	1·2
1922	719·5	1·9
1923	767·2	1·5
1924	801·0	1·3
1925	773·3	1·2
1926	653·0	1·4
1927	709·1	1·1
1928	723·6	1·2
1929	729·3	1·2
1930	570·8	1·9
1931	390·6	2·7
1932	365·0	2·7
1933	368·0	2·5
1934	396·0	2·2
1935	425·8	2·0
1936	440·6	1·8
1937	521·4	1·5
1938	470·8	1·8

[1] From the annual Statement of the Trade of the United Kingdom.

[2] From the Ministry of Labour Gazette; the figures from 1925 onward are based upon the quarterly averages of registered unemployed in Great Britain. These averages are available for Great Britain only. The figures for 1921–24 were given by the Minister of Labour in a written reply to a Parliamentary question on March 3, 1926, and published in the Ministry of Labour Gazette, March 1926, p. 97. The exclusion of Northern Ireland does not appreciably affect the picture.

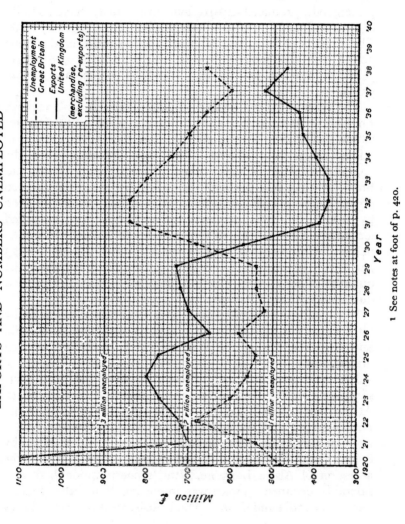

exports. By 1925, when the world consumption of raw cotton had returned to pre-War level, Lancashire was producing and exporting far less than she had done before the War. The 1,900,000,000 lb. of yarn, the 8,000,000,000 square yards of piece goods, produced in 1912 had shrunk to 1,200,000,000 lb. of yarn and 3,000,000,000 square yards of piece goods by 1935. The exports of yarn and of piece goods shrank in the same period from 244,000,000 lb. and nearly 7,000,000,000 square yards to 140,000,000 lb. and nearly 2,000,000,000 square yards.[1]

The reasons for the decline in cotton exports were various. Erstwhile customers, for several reasons, were consuming less cotton goods; they were producing more themselves; they were taking more from sources other than Britain. Thus the 10,000,000 cotton spindles worked in India, Japan, China, and Brazil in 1913 had become 18,000,000 by 1924; the 120,000 power looms in India and Japan in 1913 had become 200,000 by 1922.[2] By 1934 increased Indian production accounted for nearly 70 per cent. of Great Britain's loss in the Indian market, while imports from Japan accounted for another 25 per cent.[3] Japan herself had by 1933 caught up Britain in the quantity of her exports of cotton piece goods, and by 1935 had outdistanced her.[4]

Wool, subject to similar conditions to cotton, was less badly hit because less dependent upon exports, although both India and Australia during the War increased their own woollen manufacture.

Iron and steel suffered. These industries had been overstimulated by the War, but all in the direction of armaments. At the War's close it was found that old markets had shrunk. Between 1913 and 1923 British exports of pig-iron to France decreased by 63 per cent., to Italy by 38 per cent., to Japan by 87 per cent.[5] France had turned to local production with the accession of Alsace-Lorraine. Italy's consumption had considerably declined. Japan was importing from other sources —notably India and China. The British iron and steel industry

[1] *Britain in Recovery*, prepared by a Research Committee of the Economic, Science, and Statistics Section of the British Association, 1938, p. 458.
[2] *Report of the Committee on Industry and Trade: Survey of Overseas Markets*, p. 10.
[3] *P.E.P. Report on the British Cotton Industry*, 1934, p. 32.
[4] *Britain in Recovery*, p. 458.
[5] *Report of the Committee on Industry and Trade: Survey of Overseas Markets*, p. 6.

tried by technical improvement to make up what it had lost during the War, particularly by increasing its output per furnace. The result was increased production side by side with unemployment.

But the industry which suffered most from the world depression and the decline in British exports was the coal industry. Coal supplied in 1926 four-fifths of British exports in volume, one-tenth in value. But both volume of exports and total output were falling. In 1913 287,000,000 tons of coal were produced in Great Britain and 94,000,000 tons exported. In 1934 220,000,000 tons were produced, of which 53,000,000 tons were exported.[1] Not only the volume of British exports, but the proportion of the world's coal demand (apart from her own) supplied by Britain was falling. Britain met about 9·8 per cent. of the world's coal demand between 1909 and 1913; only 7 per cent. in 1925.[2]

The chief losses to Britain were in the German, Russian, Italian, and South American markets. With Russia the reason for the decline was the general economic dislocation of the country following the 1917 Revolution. Italy, instead of taking 90 per cent. of her coal, as formerly, from Great Britain, was taking more from Germany, and took only 63 per cent. of her needs from Great Britain. In the case of Germany, Britain's second largest pre-War customer and the one whose demand had fallen most considerably, the reasons were mixed: she was using more lignite; she was a debtor nation trying to pay her debts, and was therefore reducing her imports; she was paying her reparations partly in coal. South America was taking a little more coal from the United States, but the chief reason for her decline as a customer for British coal was her change to oil fuel. Of the rest of the world, those who had no deposits of their own were importing from Germany or Poland rather than from Great Britain. Others, with their own deposits, had considerably increased their rate of output during or since the War. At the same time the decline in international trade and the increasing use of oil fuel by ships decreased the quantity of British coal shipped in foreign bunkers. Only 51 per cent. of the world's tonnage was coal-fuelled in 1935, compared with 96 per cent. in 1914. In 1913 21,000,000 tons of British coal

---

[1] P.E.P. *Report on the British Coal Industry*, 1936, pp. 31, 157.
[2] *Report of the Royal Commission on the Coal Industry*, 1926, XIV, 9.

were shipped in foreign bunkers; in 1935 13,500,000 tons only.[1]

In face of falling exports and unemployment the industry began to survey the home market. It was found that the consumption per head of the population in hundredweights had decreased from 89 in 1913 to 71 in 1934; that the iron and steel industry had consumed 31,400,000 tons in 1913, but only 17,210,000 tons in 1934; that the Royal Navy, followed by the merchant marine, was changing from coal to oil; that electricity concerns, although based on coal, were learning economy, so that between 1918 and 1936 a threefold increase in electric power was available from a 50 per cent. increase of coal consumption.[2] There was nothing in the home situation to compensate for the loss of oversea markets.

If Britain had been more efficient in her coalmining and had reduced her costs of production she might have held on to her markets more firmly. Before the War no country but Polish Upper Silesia had exceeded the British production of 21·5 units per man shift. Between 1913 and 1934 Britain increased her output per man-shift by 7 per cent., Belgium by 63 per cent., the Ruhr by 77 per cent., Holland by 105 per cent.[3] Even allowing for the lower output and later start of these other countries, British output per man-shift was then substantially below that of the Ruhr, Polish Upper Silesia, and Holland.

Most of the progress on the Continent and in America was due to mechanization. In the U.S.A. in 1924 70 per cent. of the coal mined was already being cut by machine. Britain's progress had been uneven, partly owing to the varying nature of her coalfields. The thin seams of Scotland and the Northeast coast were difficult to get and suitable to machine-cutting. The thicker seams of South Wales, Warwickshire, and South Staffordshire were easier to get, and there was less inducement to mechanization. Over the whole country the average quantity of coal cut by machine was in 1937 only 57 per cent., although there were districts, notably Fife, Northumberland, South Derbyshire, North Staffordshire, and Lanarkshire, adapted to mechanization, where over 80 per cent. of the output was machine-cut.

The second obvious need of the British coal industry between

[1] *P.E.P. Report on the British Coal Industry*, 1936, p. 9.
[2] *Ibid.*, p. 111.   [3] *Ibid.*, p. 11.

the Wars was reorganization. Both the Sankey Commission of 1919 and the Samuel Commission of 1926 recommended the nationalization of royalties, and the Sankey Commission also advocated the ultimate nationalization of the mines themselves. But nationalization of neither royalties nor mines, nor any material reorganization, was effected, though royalties were costing £4,800,000 annually in 1934, an average of 5·86d. per ton,[1] and the industry as a whole was loosely and badly organized. In 1936 there were more than 2000 mines worked by over 1000 companies. Most units were small, only one producing at an annual rate of more than 10,000,000 tons, only six at more than 3,000,000 tons, only twenty at more than 2,000,000 tons per annum.[2] Outside South Wales concentration had not proceeded far, although interlocking directorships and intermarriage often provided links between the various colliery undertakings.

The mine-owners and the Government tried the only remedies that came natural to them. The former cut wages and dismissed men; the latter appointed Commissions, and in 1925–26 granted a subsidy to the industry. But, besides its own inherent weakness, the condition of industry as a whole and the world situation in general were against immediate recovery.

Most of the factors affecting Britain's export trade were outside her control. But in one respect Britain, for reasons largely of prestige, probably injured herself. In common with the other gold-standard countries she had abandoned the gold standard shortly after the outbreak of war, leaving the pound to find its own level of value. The Bank of England was no longer obliged to pay gold for its notes, and the Treasury issued its own notes, not fully backed by gold. These continued to circulate in increasing numbers alongside Bank notes until 1928, when Bank notes and Treasury notes were amalgamated. By the Act of 1928 control of the note issue reverted to the Bank of England, and the fiduciary issue, which before the War stood below £20,000,000, was increased to £260,000,000, Parliament being authorized to increase or decrease it in emergency. Though its limits were widely increased, the volume of money in circulation was still controlled by Bank and

[1] *Ibid.*, p. 5.   [2] *Ibid.*, pp. 2–3.

Parliament. It was not here, but in returning to the gold standard in 1925, that Britain did herself less than justice.

In the middle twenties European countries stabilized their currencies and linked them again to gold. Most of them stabilized by devaluation. But Britain, through reasons partly of prestige, went back to gold at a rate which devalued her currency very little below its pre-War rate.

The ratio of the pound to gold may have been too high absolutely. It certainly was high compared with other countries'. In consequence British exports were dear and sales declined. The British producer could compete in foreign markets only by lowering costs of production and raising his efficiency. In lowering costs of production he found himself met by the rigidity of wage-rates which had been raised during the War. Wages nevertheless were reduced at the cost of unemployment and social friction. The output of man and machine was increased by harder work; by further division of labour; by the substitution of machinery for labour; and by a general tightening up of control to eliminate waste in both machine and worker. 'Rationalization' became the key-word in industry, standing for general all-round efficiency. To the workers it meant unemployment for some, harder and more monotonous work for others, and a general reduction in wages. As machinery upon its introduction had seemed the enemy of the workers, so now 'rationalization,' in itself a desirable thing, became synonymous with oppression.

Rationalization was one way by which British industry attempted to ride the storm of depression. Another was by abandoning a century's practice of Free Trade.

Foreign tariffs, the Fair Trade League, and Joseph Chamberlain's crusade for Empire Preference had left British Free Trade virtually unshaken. It took the First World War and the subsequent depression to turn Great Britain into a Protectionist country.

Throughout the slump of the twenties Protectionist feeling was growing. A tariff could keep out articles which competed with British products, or at least would raise their price so that they were bad competitors. In so far as it kept out foreign goods it would help to reduce the British adverse balance of trade. In so far as it let them in it would augment British revenue. A tariff would be an excellent bargaining weapon for use against other countries. It was essential to building up a scheme of Empire Preference. All round, it was likely to decrease unemployment and restore British prosperity. The arguments for Protection ignored several things, particularly the fact that the return to the gold standard kept British prices high to her foreign customers and that no British tariff could affect this; and that the deepest British depression was in those very export industries which a British tariff at best could only indirectly assist.

Events moved faster than argument. In the world crisis which began in 1929 the balance of payments swung so decisively against Britain that she could not meet her obligations, and was compelled to abandon the gold standard. When the pound sterling was free to find its own level it settled at a point considerably below its gold-standard level, and the corresponding reduction in the price of British goods encouraged the export trade. But, without waiting for these effects to work themselves out, the Government in February 1932 passed the Import Duties Act, which made the first breach in the British Free Trade system.

The Import Duties Act of 1932 provided for a general 10 per cent. *ad valorem* tariff on most imports, including many raw materials and foodstuffs. Higher tariffs were made possible by the setting up of an Import Duties Advisory Committee, on whose recommendation the Government would have power to impose higher duties. In practice most imported manufactured goods were subject to a 20 per cent. duty, iron, steel, and some other goods to an even higher duty. The Act did not apply to Empire products, and so the way was clear for the introduction of a system of Imperial Preference covering Empire food for Britain and British manufactures for the Empire which began with the Dominions by the Ottawa Agreements of 1932, and was extended to the Crown Colonies in 1933.

Thus Britain abandoned a century's practice of Free Trade, yielding before the onslaught of world depression, domestic crisis, and economic nationalism. Instead of the Free Trade world of Cobden's dreams there were growing the angry rivalries of nation states. These states, with expanding populations, increasingly complex economies, and growing public services, including unemployment charges, were compelled to take an ever more active rôle in social and economic life. The British State, in common with most others, could no longer fulfil the chief function which Bentham had assigned to the State—that of keeping quiet.

The introduction of Protection, the expansion of the social services, the increasing cost of government, and the liabilities of war were matched by increased taxation. Total public expenditure grew from £342,200,000 in 1913 to £1,323,000,000 in 1936. The standard rate of income tax, which before 1914 had stood at 1s. 2d. in the pound, was in 1937-38 5s. and in 1941-42 10s. in the pound. The surtax on higher incomes grew rapidly. Estate duties had begun in 1889 with a 1 per cent. duty on estates over £10,000. In 1914 20 per cent. was payable on estates of £1,000,000 and over. By 1930 40 per cent. was payable on estates of £1,000,000, while estates of £2,000,000 and over paid 50 per cent. Under pressure of war, in 1941-42, these estates paid 52 per cent. and over 65 per cent., respectively.

Certain commodity taxes had also risen considerably, particularly those on alcohol and tobacco, motors and oil. But the increase of direct taxation was the most significant, not only as indicating the growing scope of public service, but in its effect on the distribution of wealth. The rich and the very rich had more taken from them, the poor had less taken away, and reaped at the same time benefits in social service which were equivalent to an increase in income—free education, hospital and dispensary services, old-age pensions, unemployment and sick benefit. By these services and by the taxation which made them possible, as well as by the reintroduction of Protection, the *laissez-faire* dream was completely shattered. The wheel had come full circle, and the period of *laissez-faire* stood as less than a century's interlude in British economic history. It had not even been a complete interlude, for even as it reached its zenith the social services were beginning to grow, and with them the activity of the State.

One characteristic of the period between the Wars was the continued depression of the export trade, even when industries catering for the home market improved. The South and the South-east, which were least dependent upon the export industries, showed a general improvement when the North and

the North-east and South Wales, where the great export industries were located, experienced dismal depression and
unemployment. As a result there followed a drift of population
from the depressed areas to the South and South-east, and
particularly to Greater London, round whose perimeter were
growing up a host of industries, mostly supplying the home
market.

The reasons for the location of factories here were many
and varied. In the first place, even before the drift from the
North there was a large centre of population, which meant a
market. Secondly, the growth of electric power had freed the
lighter industries from the dependence upon water and coal
which had determined the location of industry in earlier times.
Thirdly, on the London outskirts and in the South-east
generally, rents and rates were still low enough to attract business-men; raw materials were often of a kind that could be as
easily supplied in the South as the North; good roads and railways could bring materials to the factory and carry away the
finished goods. There was scope for factory building and for
employers' houses. And from every point of view, social as
well as economic, the proximity to London was an advantage.

To London this meant that her outer ring grew in resident
population to a startling extent. The population of Wembley
grew by 205 per cent. between 1921 and 1931; Hornchurch,
in Essex, increased its population in the same time by 166 per
cent.; Merton and Morden, in Surrrey, by 141 per cent.;
Hendon by 106 per cent. Welwyn Garden City, which had
only just been founded, grew in the period by 1059 per
cent.[1] It was a mixed group of light industries round and for
which this population grew, including paper manufacture,
glass manufacture, mechanical engineering, electrical engineering and manufactures, miscellaneous products of clay and
sand, soap, candles, glycerine, scent, matches, white lead, glass
bottles, cycle and motor accessories, saddlery and harness-
making, small-arms, millinery, photographic plates, films and
papers, photographic and cinema apparatus, scientific and
surgical instruments, pencils and penholders.

Where industries flourish the service trades follow. Shops and
distributing services; gas, electric, and water undertakings;
trains, buses, taxis; hairdressing and tailoring establishments;

[1] *P.E.P. Report on the Location of Industry in Great Britain*, 1939, p. 294.

cinemas and dog-racing, doctors and dentists—all the complex services of modern life multiplied in the South and South-east. Between 1923 and 1937 the insured population in the Ministry of Labour's three Southern Divisions increased by 41 per cent.; that in the Midlands by 27 per cent.; but over the rest of Britain it increased by only 10 per cent. Between 1923 and 1931 the Ministry of Labour's three Southern Divisions gained 650,000 inhabitants, between 1931 and 1936 510,000 more by net immigration. Meanwhile Scotland, Wales, and the North of England lost 950,000 by net emigration between 1923 and 1931, and 260,000 more between 1931 and 1936, allowing for a small gain in Scotland.[1] It was almost the reversal of the movement associated with the Industrial Revolution.

It was notable that there was least unemployment in the centres of mixed industry and of light industry, where there was more scope for adaptation and less dependence upon exports. The areas of high unemployment were the coalfields and the centres of heavy industry—South Wales, Cumberland, the North-east coast. Birmingham and Bristol suffered less than Jarrow and Clydeside.

In 1937 a Royal Commission under Sir Montague Barlow was appointed to inquire into the causes which had influenced the existing geographical distribution of the industrial population of Great Britain,

> to consider what social, economic or strategical disadvantages [arose] from the concentration of industries or of the industrial population in large towns or in particular areas of the country; and to report what remedial measures if any should be taken in the national interest.[2]

The Barlow Commission reported in 1940 that the continued drift of the industrial population to London and the Home Counties "constituted a social, economic and strategical problem" which demanded immediate attention.[3] The remedies suggested were a decentralization or dispersal of both industries and industrial population from overcrowded urban areas by means of satellite towns, trading estates, the further development of existing small towns, the encouragement of

---

[1] M. P. Fogarty, *Prospects of the Industrial Areas of Great Britain*, pp. 1–2.
[2] *Royal Commission on the Distribution of the Industrial Population:* terms of reference, 1939–40, IV.
[3] *Ibid.*, 1939–40, IV, 202.

garden cities or suburbs. At the same time the Barlow Commission envisaged a planned industry over the country as a whole which should endeavour to obtain a "reasonable balance of industrial development . . . throughout the various . . . regions of Great Britain."[1] To give effect to the measures they suggested they recommended the appointment by the President of the Board of Trade, after consultation with the Ministers of Health, Labour, and Transport and the Secretary of State for Scotland, of a National Industrial Board, with activities distinct from and extending beyond those within the powers of any existing Government Department. The Board should consist of a Chairman and three other members; and, because of the urgency of the problem in London and the Home Counties, should have power from the outset to regulate the establishment of additional factories or workshops within those areas.

When the Barlow Commission's report was published the Second World War had already begun. After the War the problems of the location of industry and the distribution of the industrial population were complicated by questions of war damage, shortage of houses, of labour, of raw materials, and by the urgent need for maximum production. Slowly after the War plans began to take shape for the restoration and re-planning of bombed cities under the direction of a newly formed Ministry of Town and Country Planning and the re-settlement of industries and of population. But there was inevitably indecision and conflict, and the outcome is yet to be seen.

The population of Great Britain meantime continued to grow, although the rate of expansion diminished. The 41,000,000 of 1911 were 43,000,000 in 1921 and 46,000,000 in 1937. Between 1871 and 1880 the average birth-rate had been 35·4 per thousand and the average death-rate 21·4 per thousand—a margin of births over deaths of 14. Between 1919 and 1924 the average birth rate was 21·3 per thousand and the average death-rate 12·7 per thousand—a margin of only 8·6.[2] By 1939 there was a total working population of 19,750,000, of whom 1,270,000 were unemployed. About 1 in 21 of the working population was engaged in agriculture or fishing.

[1] Ibid., 1939–40, IV, 202.
[2] Report of the Committee on Industry and Trade: Survey of Industrial Relations, p. 3.

Twice as many people were employed in textiles and clothing alone as on the land. The number of coalminers was smaller even than the number of agricultural workers—about 1 in 26 of the working population. The biggest single group was not any industrial group, but 'distribution,' and running close was a group of consumers' services covering entertainment and sport, hotel and catering, laundering, commerce and finance, professional and personal services. The non-productive groups employed nearly half the working population. Of the productive groups proper, metals and engineering was the largest.

The industries which declined most between 1923 and 1938 were cotton and coal, certain sections of the iron and steel industry, the boot and shoe and slipper industry, and the jewellery and watchmaking trades. In contrast to the decline of these old-established industries, certain new ones expanded rapidly in the same period. All kinds of electrical work—electrical engineering, wiring and contracting, cables, lamps, apparatus, head the list, indicating that Britain was beginning to follow the lead of the U.S.A. and Germany; heating and ventilating apparatus, certain types of constructional engineering; silk and artificial silk, the latter being one of Britain's most successful new industries; stationery and typewriting requisites, significant of the trend of the age; explosives, reflecting the growing fear of war. Many of them are those same industries whose growth in the South-east has been noticed.

The most conspicuous trend of British economy revealed by these statistics was one common to all highly developed industrial communities—its dependence upon distributive and personal services of all kinds to such an extent that the proportion of non-productive to productive workers was more than 8 to 10. More significant, perhaps, was the trend away from the heavy industries basic to the life of an industrial state. They were still head and shoulders above the rapidly growing newer industries, yet they had the appearance of being past their prime.

The First World War had provided the first experiment in the central control of agriculture. After the War agricultural prices for the first three years were high. In 1918 and 1919 margins over costs were large and farmers were prosperous. The years 1919 and 1920 saw wages and the price of land rising also, so that agricultural prosperity was shared by all classes on the land. In these post-War years, with land rising in value, and keen competition for farms, large areas changed hands. Many farmers, often ex-Service men, bought with borrowed capital. The Government passed in 1920 the Agriculture Act, which contained a much-needed clause for compensation to tenants for unexhausted improvements. In spite of earlier Acts, a tenant's position had never been really satisfactory. The 1920 Act laid down that a tenant, if required to leave his holding for any reason other than bad farming, must be given a full year's notice, and compensation for unexhausted improvements to the amount of not less than one year's and not more than two years' rent.

But within twelve months the Government had changed its policy. When prices began falling steeply in 1921 farmers lost their guaranteed minimum price, labourers their Wages Board. Many farmers who had bought land on the promise of high prices found themselves in debt. Only the compensation clause of the 1920 Act remained. Wheat, which stood at 86s. 4d. a quarter in 1920, had slumped to 40s. 9d. in 1922. There was then a steadying for two or three years, then a slower fall to 1930, quickening as agriculture was caught up in the world crisis, and reaching its lowest in 1933.

The natural reaction of agriculture was to turn back to its pre-War balance of more pasture and less arable. By 1926 it had already swung farther back than before, the acreage under the plough being then nearly half a million acres below the level of pre-War years. In that year was recorded the largest number of cattle—6,252,400—ever known in the country.[1] Since pasture takes on an average nine to seven men less per thousand acres than arable, agricultural policy added to the rising total of unemployed.

The Government was compelled to take fresh action. Faced with the lag in agricultural wages, it re-established agricultural wages boards, but they were county boards, not national boards, consisting of six employers, six labourers, and three independent members. It continued also to help settle small-holders on the land by means of a series of small-holders' Acts. But, in face of the inexperience of the men and the breaking market, the Exchequer lost heavily, and the Government's

---

[1] Lord Ernle, *English Farming, Past and Present*, p. 418L.

small-holding policy met with little success. In 1929 it relieved agricultural land and buildings from the burden of rates by a Derating Act. It devoted much attention and money to establishing a native sugar-beet industry. In 1921 sugar-beet factories were already open at Cantley, in Norfolk, and Kelham, in Nottinghamshire. The factories were helped from public funds, and by 1934 over 400,000 acres were under sugar beet. In 1935 the existing sugar factories were amalgamated into the British Sugar Corporation, three of whose directors represented the Government. In 1932 the Wheat Act gave a subsidy to growers of wheat, the Act of 1937 to growers of oats and barley.

But the most important steps taken by the Government to assist agriculture, as well as the most significant departure from *laissez-faire*, were through the Agricultural Marketing Acts of 1931 and 1933. The schemes established under these Acts were compulsory, provided that two-thirds of the producers concerned, who were also responsible for two-thirds of the productive capacity, voted in their favour. They were to set up boards for the more rational marketing of various products under a centralized scheme. There were boards for hops, potatoes, pork, bacon, and milk.

Although heavily subsidizing agriculture between the Wars, the Government never went so far as to direct it, and in effect did nothing to stem the broad movements which had been conspicuous before the First World War. The change from arable to pasture continued. The exodus from the land was unchecked. Even in the depression between the Wars, when there was little likelihood of gain by leaving the country for the towns, migration continued at the rate of about 10,000 a year.[1] Between 1871 and 1931 the number of farm labourers declined by nearly 50 per cent. from nearly a million to just over half a million.[2] All the time the decline of the village as a social centre continued.

Economically the decline of British agriculture is bound up with world developments which have moved the centre of gravity of agriculture away from Britain. Technically it is associated with the size of the unit. The British farm, on an average from 5 to 150 acres, is too small to make full use of mechanical inventions and modern farming technique, or

[1] C. S. Orwin, *Problems of the Countryside*, p. 8. [2] *Ibid.*, p. 7.

even to be a well-balanced farm combining effectively several branches of agriculture. At the same time it is generally just too large to be run solely by the labour of the farmer and his family.

Socially the roots of this decay are found in the urban civilization which has been permitted to usurp the real values of the countryside instead of existing side by side with them; in the mental malaise of modern society, which prefers the vicarious pleasures of cinema, wireless, and professional sport to the local dramatic society or village football ground. All these factors—economic, technical, and social—combined in the years between the Wars to make a top-heavy civilization centred on London and the towns, dangerously dependent on foreign agriculture, foolishly ignorant of the sources of health and beauty available in its countryside, careless of the values which were being lost as British agriculture decayed.

(b) LABOUR BETWEEN THE WARS

The uneasy ferment of Labour which marked the opening of the twentieth century was ended by the First World War. Labour in general co-operated with the Government, the measure of its importance being that two Labour Members sat in the War Cabinet. The chief opponents of the War were the I.L.P., but Keir Hardie, having opposed the War before it broke out, announced after its outbreak the necessity of bringing it to a successful end. He died, however, in 1914 shortly after it began.

The device of the War bonus to increase wages as the cost of living rose was practised first by the railways and then by other industries. Strikes nevertheless occurred. The strike on the Clyde in 1915 under the leadership of the shop stewards won a larger increase in wages than the employers had at first offered. In South Wales 200,000 miners won a national wage advance. In all, in spite of Government control and compulsory arbitration, some two million working days were lost by strikes in 1915, two and a half million in 1916, five and a half million in 1917.[1]

Part of the reward of Labour for its co-operation during the War was an extension of the vote to cover all adult males over

[1] J. B. Seymour, *The Whitley Councils Scheme*, p. 9.

twenty-one and women over thirty. The Representation of the People Act of 1918 thus quite quietly completed what had begun as so stormy a struggle more than one hundred years earlier. The workman had the vote; no lack of property qualification prevented his sitting in Parliament; he was paid a salary from the Exchequer while there. The only people not completely satisfied were the Suffragettes, who noisily, and with much suffering to themselves, had been demanding votes for women on an absolute equality with men. This came in 1928, when women as well as men had the right to vote at twenty-one. In the General Election of 1918 the Labour Party put up 361 candidates, and 61 were successful. The Independent Liberals were completely defeated, and the Coalition Government continued in office with Labour having advanced to the position of His Majesty's Opposition.

After the War unrest spread over the whole country, much of it concerned with demobilization and some of it led by the newly formed Communist Party, which was inspired by the Russian Revolution. There was mutiny at Folkestone, and lorry-loads of men drove to London to demand satisfaction. Units of the Army Service Corps at Grove Park and Kempton Park Mechanical Transport Depots formed Soldiers' Councils and attempted to fraternize with the nearest townspeople. At Calais it required two divisions to quell mutiny among fighting men dissatisfied with demobilization arrangements. There was rioting in Glasgow and Belfast. When demobilization began to work more smoothly and the inevitable post-War dislocation began to clear, attention was focused on the railwaymen and the miners.

The Government had controlled both railways and mines during the War. The railway workers had received a considerable cost-of-living bonus, and on February 1, 1919, the eight-hour day came into operation. Later in 1919, while the Government still exercised control, occurred a nine days' strike of over half a million railwaymen.

In 1919 the cost of living was 115 per cent. above that of 1914. Consequently, when new standardized rates of pay were to be introduced, the railway workers expected them to include the war bonus. The Government agreed so far as the locomotive drivers and firemen were concerned—thus separating these grades from the rest of the railwaymen. For these others

it proposed all-round deductions for every grade, ranging from
1s. to as much as 16s. a week. A porter, under these reductions,
would find his wages reduced from about 53s. a week to 40s.,
a drop too severe to be taken without protest. The Government afterwards stated that these reductions were intended to
come into force only if the cost of living fell. But throughout
the negotiations, in a letter written by the President of the
Board of Trade, and on the eve of the strike itself, no mention
was made of this intention.

The railwaymen were unprepared for a strike. They had
insufficient cash available at the various centres for strike pay.
Nevertheless the N.U.R. and the Locomotive Engineers and
Firemen, who joined them, were nearly solid when they came
out at midnight on Friday, September 26, 1919. The Co-
operative Society and the C.W.S. Bank rendered prompt
assistance by making N.U.R. cheques payable at local Co-
operative stores so that strike pay was forthcoming. The
Government was prepared to be unscrupulous. Arbitrarily,
and without justification, it withheld the week's wages due to
the railwaymen. It considered the confiscation of Union funds.
It advised local authorities to form "Citizen Guards." It sent
troops to certain of the railway stations. It had a scheme for
withdrawing strikers' ration cards or withholding the food
supplies which the Government still controlled. Some shopkeepers, indeed, refused food to the strikers. But again the
Co-operative Societies came into action by honouring vouchers
for food issued by the Strike Committee.

The railway stoppage was virtually complete until the
Government, with volunteers and non-Unionists, contrived to
organize a skeleton service. Even so, by the end of a week
heavy goods traffic was seriously disorganized and workers unemployed in mines and factories. The Government put fleets
of lorries on the roads, without opposition from the strikers, to
supply the towns with milk and foodstuffs.

The Government had with it the national Press, the strikers
only *The Daily Herald*. Nevertheless, after the first few days,
the Labour Research Department (which had been created in
1912) and the Publicity Department of the N.U.R. mobilized
such a team of effective writers, cartoonists, and statisticians
that not only the *Herald* but the rest of the Press was glad to
publish their articles. Further, the strikers bought whole-page

advertisement space in the national Press in which to contradict the Government and to state the strikers' case. They even managed to make a film, so that Lloyd George denouncing the strikers was followed by J. H. Thomas denouncing Lloyd George. Public opinion, even newspaper editorials, showed a subtle change by the end of a week. Finally, patient and painstaking negotiations bore fruit, and the dispute was settled on Sunday, October 3. There was to be a stabilization of wages until September 30, 1920, and an immediate rise to 51s. a week for any adult railwayman earning less than that wage. Negotiations for ultimate wage-rates were to be begun again. The Railwaymen's Unions had won a considerable victory over a State prepared in advance for the struggle.[1]

The fact that the Government controlled the mines, the railways, and the basic industries during the First World War naturally gave increased weight to the demand for nationalization. In February 1919 the miners presented the demand not only for a nominal six hours' day and a 30 per cent. advance in wages, but for the nationalization of the mines. They were in a strong position to fight, for coal stocks were low and the Government was harassed by the general post-War unrest. The Government therefore temporized by offering a Royal Commission, and promising to accept its findings. After much consideration the miners accepted, provided that their representatives sat on the Commission together with the mine-owners, and that of the independent Commissioners one-half should be their nominees; and that a Report be issued within three weeks. The Government agreed. Three miners and three intellectuals sympathetic to Labour sat on the Commission together with three mine-owners and three independent capitalists nominated by the Government. The Chairman was Mr Justice Sankey. The Commission duly presented its first Report on March 20, 1919. By this time the miners were uneasy at their decision to substitute negotiation for direct action, but the Cabinet reassured them by pledging itself in writing to carry out "in the letter and in the spirit" the recommendations of Sankey's Report.

The Chairman's Report which the Cabinet had pledged

---

[1] For a detailed account of this strike see S. and B. Webb, *The History of Trade Unionism*, pp. 535–546.

itself to implement was signed by four members of the Commission, including Mr Justice Sankey. It recommended a reduction of miners' hours to seven after a lapse of four months, and to six after a lapse of two years, subject to the condition of the industry at that time. It recommended an increase in wages of 2s. a day (or 20 per cent.) for adults, and 1s. a day for those under sixteen. Concerning ultimate policy it declared that, even upon the evidence already given,

> the present system of ownership and working in the coal industry stands condemned, and some other system must be substituted for it, either nationalization or a method of unification by national purchase and/or joint control.

These were the findings that the Government was pledged to carry out "in the letter and in the spirit."

A larger group of six Commissioners, including the miners' leaders, recommended the immediate reduction of hours to six a day and the 30 per cent. increase in wages for which the miners were asking. This group recommended that nationalization "ought to be, in principle, at once determined on." The three mine-owners recommended no reduction of hours beyond seven a day and much smaller increases in wages.

Impressed by Sankey's Report, the Cabinet's promise, and an offer of further consideration by the Commission of the nationalization issue, the miners agreed that the Commission should continue its sittings. The second Report of the Sankey Commission was presented in July. All the Commissioners then agreed to the nationalization of royalties. The chairman by this time had accepted in full the principle of nationalization of the mines also, and in a special Chairman's Report recommended that "the principle of State ownership of the coal mines be accepted," and that after three years from the date of the Report "Parliament be invited to pass legislation acquiring the coal mines for the State . . . paying fair and just compensation to the owners." The miners' group was in substantial agreement with the Chairman, making seven supporters, including the Chairman, for nationalization. A minority group of five recommended, instead of nationalization, certain improvements in organization. The other Commissioner produced a separate scheme of his own.

Meantime the Government, which still retained its wartime control of the mines and which should, therefore, have been taking steps to raise wages and shorten hours in accordance with the findings of the first Sankey Report, had done nothing, leaving the trade unions and mine-owners to make the necessary adjustments, which, after some friction, they succeeded in doing. Still less did the Government try to implement the 'spirit' of the Sankey Report by inaugurating or considering any changes in organization in the mines. In vain the miners called on the Government to fulfil its promise. Lloyd George agreed in the House of Commons in August that the Government had accepted in the letter and the spirit the Interim Report of Mr Justice Sankey. "In that Report," he said, "there is a recommendation in favour of the unification and reorganization of the industry." But, Lloyd George continued, in his Final Report

> Mr Justice Sankey proceeded with his interpretation of that principle. We accept the principle, but we cannot accept Mr Justice Sankey's final interpretation. His scheme for carrying that out we cannot accept.[1]

A special meeting of the T.U.C. called in December 1919 launched a big propaganda campaign demanding the mines for the nation, but it had little effect. When Congress decided against a strike on the miners' behalf and in favour of political action instead, it was clear that the issue was ended for the time being in favour of the employers and the Government. Royalties were not nationalized, nor was any reorganization effected.

In 1921 the Government gave up its war-time control of the mines. The owners, as they reassumed full control, announced a reduction in wages. The miners resisted, were locked out, and the Triple Alliance failed to respond on what became known in trade-union annals as "Black Friday." The miners were defeated after a long struggle of many weeks. All-round unemployment continued to rise—1,355,000 by the end of March 1921; 2,171,000 by the end of June 1921; nearly 2,000,000 by December 1921. Trade-union membership declined. Agricultural labourers' wages fell to 25s. a week, and poverty enveloped large numbers of the working classes, while acute distress fell on many middle-class families through unemployment and wage reductions. The unemployed organized marches through the streets of London. 'Hunger marchers' came in

[1] House of Commons, August 18, 1919 (Hansard, fifth series, 119, 2003).

orderly fashion from the North as the Blanketeers had marched a century earlier. At big demonstrations in Hyde Park and Trafalgar Square the police used their batons and their horses as a century earlier the yeomanry had used their horses and their sabres at Peterloo. The Communist Party of Great Britain identified itself with the unemployed as the Democratic Federation had done in the eighties, and its influence grew, although it remained small. The Government already in 1920 had passed the Emergency Powers Act in order to be forearmed with a weapon against Labour revolt. By this Act the Government could restore order by "Regulation" in any "state of emergency" which interfered with "the supply and distribution of food, water, fuel or light, or with the means of locomotion." The Act was loosely worded, the powers it gave wide and indefinite, the intention obviously to prevent or to break any large-scale industrial action by the working classes. But for the time being the workers were weak. In 1922 a strike of engineers was defeated and the funds of the A.S.E. were seriously depleted. In 1923 builders, seamen, dockers, and miners all suffered falling wages without being able to organize effective resistance. Only in the political field Labour influence continued to grow. The Labour Party in the General Election of 1922 returned 142 Members of Parliament. Two years later it returned 192 Members. There were then 258 Tories and 157 Liberals. Labour and Liberal together formed a majority of 91 over the Tories. The Labour Party, on the promise of Liberal support, therefore agreed to form a Government, and Labour for the first time held the reins of office. But it was an unsatisfactory arrangement. The uneasy interlude of Labour in office but not in power lasted a few months only. Thereafter followed a period of strong reactionary Tory Government.

At the beginning of this period the miners came again into the centre of the picture, when the coal-owners once more tried to reduce wages and lengthen hours. It was feared that the action of the mine-owners was a prelude to an all-round attack, and a strong movement of Labour consolidated round the miners. In July 1925, accordingly, the T.U.C. pledged support to the miners to the extent of a sympathetic strike if necessary. The Government consequently temporized. Baldwin appointed a Commission of Inquiry under Sir Herbert Samuel, and while it was sitting gave a temporary subsidy to the coal-owners to prevent cuts in wages. In 1926 the Samuel Commission reported. It recommended a wage reduction—but less than the employers had asked for; no increase in the working day—unless this was in place of a wage reduction; the organization of research; the encouragement of colliery amalgamations; the nationalization of royalties; and the discontinuance of the subsidy. Miners and owners alike rejected this compromise Report. "Not a penny off the pay, not a second on the day," declared the men, and called on the trade-union movement to implement its promise of support. But the mine-owners acted first. On April 30, 1926, the coalminers were locked out. The next few days were passed in fruitless negotiations. At midnight on May 3–4 the trade-union movement came to the miners' assistance by calling a general strike.

The T.U.C. had done some preliminary organization. It had decided to call out 'first-line' workers on the first day and 'second-line' workers later. Accordingly, on the morning of May 4 there were no railway or other transport services; printing works, iron and steel works, were silent; building operations were at a standstill. The response of the first-line workers was remarkable. In many cases nearly 100 per cent. solidarity was reported. On the following day the printers' strike was effective, and The Times appeared as a single duplicated sheet. On the 6th and until the 17th it was printed again, but on four sides only. No other national newspaper appeared. But the Government on Wednesday the 5th had its British Gazette ready. The strikers countered with The British Worker, and local workers' committees up and down the country issued their own duplicated strike sheets.

The Government as well as the T.U.C. had prepared for a general strike. On the eve of the T.U.C. declaration it opened a recruiting station, and special constables and volunteers for essential work flocked in. Emergency food depots were opened, volunteers brought supplies from the docks through a hostile Dockland. Previously prepared emergency transport schemes were brought into operation, and skeleton services on roads and railways were running on the second day of the strike.

On May 11 the T.U.C. called out its second line, including shipyard workers and engineers. In the localities, in spite of

Government counter-action, it seemed that experience was giving strength and that the strike was gaining momentum and solidarity. But from headquarters came no definite guidance, no clear call to stimulate and sustain the vast body of men who for the first time came near to the 100 per cent. general strike of which working-class leaders had long dreamed as the supreme weapon of their class.

The Government, on the other hand, under the Prime Minister, Stanley Baldwin, and ably backed by the attenuated *Times*, was skilful not only in emergency organization, but in the still more important task of propaganda. The strikers, in calling out the printers, had done more harm to themselves than to the Government. The Government made full use of the powerful new weapon of radio. The T.U.C. had no way of counter-acting radio propaganda except in their news-sheets and by the use of dispatch-riders. *The British Gazette* echoed and enlarged on the Prime Minister's broadcast statements. Baldwin's unemotional "Keep Steady!" was matched by the "Stand Fast!" of *The Times*. Baldwin was, indeed, master of the art of winning British middle-class opinion. From the first the position was represented as being Strikers versus the Community. "Constitutional Government is being attacked," announced Baldwin on May 6 through *The British Gazette*.

> Let all good citizens whose livelihood and labour have thus been put in peril bear with fortitude and patience the hardships with which they have been so suddenly confronted. . . . The laws of England are the people's birthright. The laws are in your keeping. You have made Parliament their guardian. The general strike is a challenge to Parliament, and is the road to anarchy and ruin.

On the 8th Sir John Simon emphasized the illegality of the general strike on the grounds that men had left work without notice, regardless of their contracts. On the 12th *The Times* leading article declared, "After a full week's experience of a general strike we know the worst; and we know also that the worst is past." *The Times* was right. The following day it announced "The Nation's Victory." The T.U.C. had sur-rendered unconditionally. On the 12th the Council of the T.U.C. had called on Baldwin, and without obtaining any concession agreed to end the strike.

The localities were aghast. The miners were incredulous,

angry, and indignant. Most districts asserted that the strength of the strikers was still growing, and that a few more days' stoppage would have compelled submission by the Government. But it was too late. Once the word had been given by the T.U.C. to resume work the solidarity of the strike was gone. An unofficial general strike could not succeed. Only the miners held out—again alone, bitter and disillusioned, knowing they were beaten.

It is difficult to gauge the strength of the opposing forces on the day the T.U.C. surrendered. The strikers asserted that their strength was increasing with experience. On the other hand, *The British Gazette* was rapidly increasing its range, boasting a circulation of over 2,000,000 by the time the strike ended, the B.B.C. remained at the Government's disposal, volunteers for food distribution and essential services were not slackening, and one-third of London's buses were running on the last day of the strike. That the issue was not put to longer test was due partly to the timidity of the strike leaders and their dislike of so powerful a weapon as the General Strike: they were half in agreement with Baldwin that it was wrong thus to hold the community to ransom. But the General Strike was defeated at least partly by public opinion, skilfully worked upon by the Government. A general strike, of its nature, must cause such widespread hardship that, unless it is cemented by a strong, universal resentment against the Government, it is bound to be generally condemned. In 1926 the Government from the outset astutely identified itself with a peaceful nation assailed by disruptive forces. When Baldwin came to the microphone on Saturday evening May 8 and announced, "I am a man of peace. I am longing and working and praying for peace, but I will not surrender the safety and the security of the British Constitution," the nation devoutly cried "Amen!"

While the strike was on *The British Gazette* had announced, "Either the country will break the General Strike, or the General Strike will break the country." When it was over the Government proceeded to break the miners, who alone remained on strike. It repealed the Seven Hours Act of 1919, it refused to comply with the suggestions of the Samuel Report, the miners' wages were reduced, their working hours lengthened, their leaders victimized. The Russian as well as British trade unions helped them with money. But the Government made full use of the Emergency Powers Act, miners' pickets were arrested, boards of guardians were prevented from using public money for the relief of strikers or their families. By November 1926 the miners were almost literally starved back to work. Unemployment benefit was cut by the assertion that applicants were "not genuinely seeking work." Trade-union membership fell.

In 1927, to underline its victory, the Government passed the Trades Disputes and Trade Union Act. This Act tried to prevent the repetition of a general strike by pronouncing any sympathetic strike illegal. It reversed the political levy clauses of the 1913 Trade Union Act: henceforth a trade unionist wishing to contribute to the political fund of his union had to contract in by signing a special form saying he wished to do so; otherwise no political contribution could legally be taken from him. This effort to maim the political funds of the trade unions, though bitterly resisted, proved less harmful than was expected. Contracting in was generally practised, and the trade unions' income suffered little. A third clause was aimed at conserving the loyalty of civil servants, who were not to be permitted to join a union in which other than civil servants were employed, or which was affiliated to the T.U.C. The 1927 Trades Disputes Act remained for nearly twenty years the ignominious mark of Labour's defeat in the General Strike of 1926.

Two years later the Second Minority Labour Government of 1929–31 was returned to office by an electorate swung against the Tories because of their failure to deal with unemployment. This Government did little more than scratch the surface in its attempts at social reform. Unemployment continued to rise, and in the world financial crisis of 1931 leapt up. The Labour Government was split by the impact of the crisis, the Prime Minister, Ramsay MacDonald, and others remaining in office to form with Tories and Liberals a National Government. This Government appealed to the country, and was returned with an overwhelming majority at the General Election of 1931, the Labour Party suffering a decisive defeat. For the next few years unemployment remained high and trade-union membership fell. In 1932 the I.L.P., under James Maxton, seceded from the Labour Party it had helped to create, itself being split by the decision.

The Co-operative movement continued to grow in numbers and to expand its enterprise. In West Africa between 1914 and 1920 oil and cocoa properties were acquired, a tallow factory was established in Australia, bacon factories in Denmark. Interests in Canadian wheat and Irish butter were developed. Shilbottle Colliery, in Yorkshire, was bought as an effort at Co-operative mining; an additional purchase here in 1930 brought 10,000,000 tons of coal within the C.W.S. area. The installation of coal-cutting machinery was begun in 1924, and Shilbottle Village was built on model lines for the mining population and their families. By 1924 the Wholesale Societies owned nearly 72,000 acres of land in Great Britain. In 1925 the C.W.S. Bank held total assets of £31,000,000.

The net annual sales of the C.W.S. grew from £52,000 in 1864 to £35,000,000 at the outbreak of the First World War. They were £108,000,000 in 1937. Its capital and reserves grew over the same periods from £2000 to £10,000,000 to £113,000,000. The membership of retail societies was 3,000,000 in 1914 and over 6,800,000 in 1936, out of a total population in England and Wales of 40,800,000. One-sixth, or about 17 per cent., of the population were then Co-operators, as against one-twenty-second, or about 4 per cent., at the beginning of the century. Retail Co-operative trade grew from over £50,000,000 in 1900 to £217,000,000 in 1930.

The Co-operative movement in theory kept to the grand ideal of the Rochdale Pioneers—"to arrange the powers of production, distribution, education, and government." The belief of the ardent Co-operator was that by constantly encroaching upon the fields of capitalist enterprise, by learning the machinery of insurance and banking, by establishing trading contacts with foreign countries, the movement would spread until its membership was so large, its interests so wide, and its power so great that the Co-operative Commonwealth would peacefully supersede the Capitalist State. This is Owenism in full modern dress.

More practical Co-operators were compelled to turn to the political action which Owen decried. There was considerable discussion and much disagreement before the Co-operative Congress in 1917 decided to seek Parliamentary representation through its own candidates as the only way of effectively voicing its demands and safeguarding its interests. The following year a working agreement with the Labour Party was reached, which remains, however, loose and somewhat unsatisfactory.

From the middle of 1935 unemployment, though still remaining over the million mark, began to decline, partly in response to the threat of war with Germany, and trade-union membership rose a little. But no section of Labour was ready to renew the conflict with capital. The standard of living of those in work had risen with the price fall of the thirties. Political Labour was bewildered by the events of 1931 and disturbed by internal dissension. Moreover, eyes were being turned anxiously to the countries where Fascism, the arch-enemy of Labour, was gaining influence. After Hitler's return to power in Germany in 1933 Labour prepared itself spiritually to join forces with its own capitalists to fight the greater of two evils. In 1939 there were few dissentient voices when all branches of Labour formed a united front against Fascist Germany.

(c) POSTSCRIPT: THE SECOND WORLD WAR AND AFTER

When the Second World War broke out a radical redistribution of total resources became necessary. In proportion as the effort was more intense the subordination of the individual was more complete than in the First World War. The Ministry of Labour and National Service allocated labour under the Essential Works Order as other Ministries allocated raw materials and food. Agriculture was controlled. Consumer goods were rationed. The total working population of Great Britain grew during the War from 19,750,000 to 21,649,000 by the inclusion of those who had not worked before, of women, of retired workers who came back to industry. Unemployment was eliminated. The struggle to wage total war was so intense that everything was thrown into the effort. Long-term capital investment, replacements not absolutely essential to output, had to wait. The capital equipment of the country deteriorated. Overseas investments were pledged to provide food and the raw materials of war.

When victory was won Britain stood in a position un-paralleled in her history. Long before the War she had accepted the fact that she was not self-supporting in food, but spoke with pride of the coal and manufactures she sent abroad in exchange. Now she had insufficient coal for her own needs. The goods she exported were sacrificed at heavy cost by the home consumer, and even so were insufficient to pay for the imports of corn and other foods essential to life. Her ships and shipping services which could have earned foreign exchange were short, the 17,400,000 gross tons of 1939 having shrunk to 13,900,000 in 1947. Dollars were borrowed from America and Canada, but only partly bridged the gap. The running down of capital equipment during the War was beginning to show. Railways were wanting timber for sleepers, metal for all purposes, coal for running, labour for working the complicated network. All were short. In factories machines broke down or worked inefficiently through want of maintenance. The defeated countries became the liabilities of the victors, for in Europe destruction had temporarily paralysed economic life. In Britain the allocation of goods in short supply meant continued rationing and careful control of industry. Planning became the keyword, as Rationalization had been twenty years earlier.

The War had once more forced on agriculture a swing from pasture to arable. County War Agricultural Committees were again formed and prisoner-of-war labour and women's labour again recruited. The net output of British agriculture during the War increased by about 35 per cent. Mechanization was speeded up. Where there had been 60,000 tractors before the War there were now 190,000, making British agriculture among the most highly mechanized in the world. But no effort on the part of the British could eliminate the need to import food; and the world wheat shortage, due to the War and bad weather and her own disastrously wet harvest of 1946, caused the rationing of bread in Britain. The dependence upon imported dairy produce, feeding-stuffs, and fertilizers continued. Britain was self-sufficient in no food but potatoes; and a bad season brought a great shortage and the rationing of potatoes in 1947. The Government's general policy was to return to a balanced farming of arable and pasture. But until the world wheat position improved the additional area put under crops for direct human consumption during the War could not be reduced.

Shortly after the outbreak of the Second World War in 1939 the Tories, under Neville Chamberlain, were replaced by a coalition of Tory, Liberal, and Labour under Winston Churchill. Throughout a victorious war, bitterly and hardly won, the working classes were recognized as indispensable. Their representatives were in the War Cabinet. They agreed to the direction of labour and the lengthening of working hours. After the War a Labour Government with a clear majority was swept into power in 1945 on a wave whose momentum surprised the working classes as much as anybody. It was clear that the workers, and a considerable section of the middle classes, were distrustful of Tory social policy and ready for the large-scale reorganization of economic affairs in the direction of central planning.

This time Labour in power in the House of Commons with a clear majority had control of the law-making machine. With obvious satisfaction Ernest Bevin, of the Transport and General Workers' Union, saw the repeal of the Trades Disputes Act of 1927. The Government proceeded with the longer-term programme of Labour—the nationalization of the Bank of England, of the coalmines, of transport, of electricity. Organized Labour, after a century and a half of struggle, had at last made its mark. There had been landlord rule, middle-class rule, and now there was Labour rule. In each epoch an economically powerful class was enabled to control the legislature and fashioned it for its own advantage. The landowners, their power based on the land, supported Corn Laws, Game Laws, the free export of wool. The industrial manufacturing classes rose to power with trade and manufacture, and abolished taxes on food and raw materials and exports, and introduced Joint Stock and Limited Liability Acts. The working classes achieved political power as they grew increasingly indispensable to large-scale economy, and proceeded to abolish private ownership of the most important means of production. But they were not allowed to go too fast or too far, as they found when they turned to nationalize iron and steel. The Labour Party ended its first term of power and went to the polls in 1950 with the question of further nationalization still at issue.

While economic and social relationships within Britain have been changing Britain's position in the world has also been undergoing change. All the factors challenging her supremacy which have been perceptible from the seventies onward, which were accentuated by the First World War, and which wrought her great harm between the Wars, have been intensified by the Second World War. This survey began nearly two hundred years ago, with Britain a largely peasant community, feeding itself, excelling in a few manufactures, particularly of wool. A hundred years later Britain was the world's supreme manufacturing and trading nation, her investments flung round the earth. Another hundred years have brought the end of the epoch of British supremacy. How well or ill the new order will be for her people depends upon what emerges from the dislocation of the post-War world. One thing is certain. An epoch has ended just as surely as, two hundred years ago, a new age was about to be born.

SELECT BIBLIOGRAPHY

Reports of the Royal Commission on the Coal Industry (the Sankey Commission), 1919, XI; 1919, XII.

Report of the Royal Commission on the Coal Industry (the Samuel Report), 1926, XIV.

Final Report of the Committee on Industry and Trade (the Balfour Report), 1928–29, VII.

Report of the Royal Commission on Population, 1949 (Cmd. 7695).

Political and Economic Planning (P.E.P.) Reports:
  The British Coal Industry (1936).
  The British Cotton Industry (1934).
  The Location of Industry in Great Britain (1939).

Britain in Depression: Prepared by a Research Committee of the Economic, Science, and Statistics Section of the British Association (1935).

Britain in Recovery, ibid. (1938).

Economic Survey for 1947 (Cmd. 7046).

Economic Survey for 1949 (Cmd. 7647).

Report of the Royal Commission on the Distribution of the Industrial Population (the Barlow Report), 1939–40, IV.

Report of the Committee on Land Utilization in Rural Areas (the Scott Committee), 1942 (Cmd. 6378).

The Industrial Future of Great Britain: a series of lectures arranged by the University of London and the Institute of Bankers, November 1947–March 1948 (Europa, 1948).

ABEL, DERYCK: *A History of British Tariffs, 1923–1942* (H. Cranton, 1945).

CLAPHAM, SIR JOHN H.: *An Economic History of Britain*, vol. iii, *Machines and National Rivalries, 1886–1914*, with an Epilogue, 1914–29 (Cambridge University Press, 1938).

COLE, G. D. H.: *The Post-War Condition of Britain* (Routledge, 1956).

ERNLE, LORD: *English Farming, Past and Present* (Longmans, 1912, revised edition, 1927).

FOGARTY, M. P.: *Prospects of the Industrial Areas of Great Britain* (Methuen, 1945).

HANCOCK, W. K. AND GOWING, M. M.: *British War Economy* (History of the Second World War, United Kingdom Civil Series) (H.M. Stationery Office, 1949).

HICKS, U. K.: *The Finance of British Government, 1920–1936* (Oxford University Press, 1938).

JERVIS, F. R. J.: *The Evolution of Modern Industry* (Harrap, 1960).

KEYNES, J. M.: *The Economic Consequences of the Peace* (Macmillan, 1919).

——: *The End of Laissez-faire* (Hogarth Press, 1926).

LIPSON, E.: *The Growth of English Society*, Part III (fourth edition, Black, 1959).

McCALLUM, R. B. AND READMAN, A.: *The British General Election of 1945* (Oxford University Press, 1947).

McNAIR, JOHN: *James Maxton: The Beloved Rebel* (Allen and Unwin, 1955).

ORWIN, C. S.: *Problems of the Countryside* (Cambridge University Press, 1945).

——: *Speed the Plough* (Methuen, 1942).

——: *A History of English Farming* (Nelson, 1949).

POLLARD, S.: *The Development of the British Economy 1914–50* (Edward Arnold, 1962).

SAUL, S. B.: *The Myth of the Great Depression in England, 1873–1896* (Studies in Economic History, Macmillan, 1969).

SEYMOUR, J. B.: *The Whitley Council's Scheme* (P. S. King, 1932).

SHERRINGTON, C. E. R.: *A Hundred Years of Inland Transport, 1830–1933* (Duckworth, 1934).

VENN, J. A.: *The Foundations of Agricultural Economics* (Cambridge University Press, 1923; revised edition, 1933).

WEBB, S. AND B.: *The History of Trade Unionism* (Longmans, 1894; revised edition, 1920).

WORSWICK, G. D. N. AND ADY, P. H. (ed.): *The British Economy, 1945–50* (Oxford University Press, 1952).

YOUNGSON, A. J.: *The British Economy 1920–57* (Allen and Unwin, 1960).

Annual Economic Surveys published by H.M.S.O.

PART III

1851–1950

A CENTURY OF SOCIAL REFORM

CHAPTER XXI

FACTORY, MINE, AND WORKSHOP

No ill-effects followed the Ten Hours Act of 1847 and the amending Acts of 1850 and 1853. There was no reduction in output, and Factory Inspector Horner testified to the improved health, appearance, and contentment of the workpeople. Thereafter factory legislation developed along two lines. It extended from textiles to other industries and to workshops; and it refined and improved upon its own regulations—sometimes with the co-operation but sometimes in face of the opposition of factory-owners.

The first extension of the Factory Acts was to the industries allied with textiles. The Print Works Act of 1845 had already given some protection to the women and children employed in print-works, but bleaching and dyeing works were not included. In 1853 various bleachers consequently followed the example of the cotton operatives and formed Short-time Committees. The House of Lords, under Shaftesbury's impetus, in 1854 approved a Bill for regulating bleaching works, but the Commons threw it out, and instead appointed a Commissioner—H. S. Tremenheere—to report on the industry in Lancashire and the West of Scotland. Although Tremenheere found women and boys working fourteen, fifteen, and sixteen hours a day and recommended the inclusion of bleaching works within the scope of the Factory Acts, Parliament refused to legislate. In 1857 a Select Committee of the Commons was hearing more evidence. Three years later the matter was raised again, and between 1860 and 1864 bleaching and dyeing, calendering and finishing, were brought under the Factory Acts. There seems no reason why this should not have been done ten years earlier.

Lace-making next received attention, and Tremenheere proceeded to the lace districts, issuing a Report in 1861. In the same year the Lace Works Act placed lace factories, with certain exceptions, within the scope of Factory Law.

Progress had been slow indeed since the winning of the Ten

Hours Act in 1847. How slow was revealed when a new Children's Employment Commission, appointed on the motion of Shaftesbury, began in 1863 to issue its Reports on the working conditions of children and young persons outside the scope of the Factory Acts.

There was every reason for bringing the children in these trades within the law, for their work was unpleasant, unhealthy, dirty and dangerous, the hours long, and the wages small. Each subsequent Report of the Commission told a similar tale —whether in percussion-cap making, paper-hanging, or paper-staining, fustian-cutting, bootmaking; in the hookers', tailors', hatters', glovers', glass-makers' crafts; in metal manufacture, tobacco, indiarubber, artificial-flower making. The Commissioners also drew attention to the scandalous plight of little chimney-sweeps—still climbing from an early age in spite of the Act of 1840 prohibiting it. Pottery manufacture, Lucifer-match making, and lace-making were among the worst of these unregulated trades.

In the Pottery district about 180 factories employed 19,000 adults and 11,000 children and young persons of both sexes under eighteen. Most of the boys were employed as mould-runners, jigger-turners or dippers; most of the girls and women as painters, burnishers or scourers, or as printers' assistants. Hours of work were irregular. Slacker periods would be followed by long hours—from 6 A.M. to 9 P.M.—and irregular and curtailed meal-times. Children started work while very young, commonly at seven years, often at six. They were frequently in the direct employ of a worker. Their wages might be 1s. 6d. to 2s. 6d. a week until they were eleven, 3s. to 5s. at twelve to fourteen, and 6s. from fourteen to fifteen years old. Their education consisted occasionally of Sunday school, still more rarely of night school. The amount of illiteracy was considerable.

All this was reminiscent of the unregulated factory labour of the first half of the century. To parallel the dangers of the moving machinery in the factory the potters had the dangers peculiar to their craft—not so sudden, but insidious and equally destructive. The potters were termed by the senior physician to the North Staffordshire Infirmary "a degenerated population, both physically and morally . . . stunted in growth, ill-shaped, and frequently ill-formed in the chest." They suffered from many disorders of liver and kidneys, from rheumatism, and from scrofula; but most particularly were they prone to chest diseases—pneumonia, phthisis, bronchitis, and what was known as potter's asthma or potter's consumption.

It was the jiggers and mould-runners (boys), the dippers (men, with boys in attendance), and the scourers (women and girls) who were engaged in the most dangerous sections of the trade. The jiggers and mould-runners were described as "pale, weak, diminutive, and unhealthy," many dying of asthma, consumption, and acute inflammation. The dippers, with "dull and cadaverous countenances," were subject to paralysis and nervous diseases in aggravated forms. The scourers were especially prone to pulmonary disease. What was the nature of the work that led to such serious illness?

Jiggers and mould-runners were employed by the flat pressers.

> Each man employs two boys, one to turn the jigger, or hori-zontal wheel, from morning to night; the other to carry the ware just formed from the 'whirler' to the hot house, and the moulds back. These hot houses are rooms within rooms, closely confined except at the door, and without windows. In the centre stands a large cast-iron stove, heated to redness, increasing the tempera-ture often to 130 degrees.[1]

The boys were constantly running to and fro into the open air, in all weathers.

In the dipping-rooms the danger was usually from lead poisoning. Here one or two adults with their attendant boys dipped the ware in the rough into a solution of borax, soda, potash, with whiting, stone, and carbonate of lead, finely ground and mixed together with water; for coarse goods a larger proportion of lead was used, and in some cases arsenic. The hands and clothes of the workers were saturated with the solution, yet they rarely changed their clothes, took their meals in the dipping-room, and were content merely to wipe their hands on their aprons.

China scouring was described as the most pernicious branch of the manufacture. The Commissioners described the process:

---

[1] *First Report of the Children's Employment Commission*, 1863, XVIII, ix. The Commissioners were quoting from a Report of 1842, which they still considered applicable to the industry.

When china ware is to be fired, it is first placed in coarse earthen vessels called 'jaggers'; these contain a quantity of finely pulverized flint; this, during the firing, attaches itself strongly to the china; some two, three, or more young women are employed to scour it off with sand paper and brushes; the particles float abundantly in the atmosphere of the room, and cover their persons just as plentifully as flour does the miller. . . . The fine flint dust diffused through the air of the workshop and inhaled into the lungs very soon produces discomfort, and a sense of oppression in the chest.[1]

A scourer who had worked for eight years in a pottery at Hanley, and who was suffering from chronic bronchitis, said that four other scourers in the same room had died from the effects of the work.

Let us hear a potter's boy speak to the Commissioners of 1863 as Elizabeth Bentley spoke to the Committee of 1832. James Doyle, mould-runner at E. and C. Challinor's Earthenware Manufactory at Fenton, told an Assistant Commissioner:

I am thirteen. My father is an Irishman. I do not know how long I have worked. I wedge clay for a thrower. I come at 6. At Baker's I used sometimes to come at 5.30 A.M. About two or three days a week I used to come at 5.30. I sometimes give over at 6.30; sometimes at 7 and 8. It was 8 last night. I came at six yesterday morning. I go to dinner at one. I always go home to dinner. I come back at two. I get 4s. 6d. a week. I can't read. I go to school sometimes on Sundays.[2]

In spite of the injurious nature of the work, the potter's health could be much improved by shorter hours and better premises. Floors could be swept regularly to keep down the dangerous dust; workrooms could be less crowded and better ventilated; stove temperatures could be reduced by keeping the flat-presser more plentifully supplied with moulds, so that there was no need to hasten the drying of the finished moulds taken by the mould-runner to the stove-room. But, as with the cotton mills earlier in the century, the best employers preferred compulsory regulation of all workshops to one-sided action by the more enlightened. It was, in fact, a memorial from the Wedgwoods and others to the Home Department which caused the Commissioners to direct their attention first to the Potteries.

[1] *Ibid.*, XVIII, xxvi. Again the Commissioners are using the Report of 1842.
[2] *Ibid.*, XVIII, Minutes of Evidence, 16–17.

A particularly dangerous trade had developed since the inquiry by the Commission of 1842, and now was taking great and serious toll of its workpeople. This was the Lucifer-match manufacture, established some time after 1833, when the discovery of applying phosphorus to the end of the match itself had finally superseded the old flint, steel, and tinder method of kindling flame. Most of the match factories were in the poorest and most thickly peopled parts of London, particularly Bethnal Green and Whitechapel, and in some of the largest provincial towns. The number employed was small, there being about 1800 children and young persons and 850 adults concerned.

Match manufacture yielded a quick return for little capital outlay, and was consequently frequently carried on in small garret-like buildings, themselves unhealthy apart from the nature of the work conducted. Although by the sixties the very worst premises had already disappeared, many one-roomed workshops remained.

Of all the diseases to which workers were liable none was so terrible as the necrosis of the jaw, "phossy jaw," as the workers termed it, which the match-makers contracted from contact with the phosphorus composition of the match-heads. If a man recovered from the disease he might have lost his entire lower jaw, and men thus afflicted were actually found by the Commissioners at work in the match factories risking further contagion.

In the process of match manufacture the cut splints were tied in bundles and placed on hot iron, the ends thus scorched being dipped, while hot, in melted sulphur or, in the case of the better sort of matches, in stearine or some fatty matter. The scorching wood was pungent to the eyes; the sulphur caused irritation to the throat and coughing. The bundle was then 'rolled out' or 'dusted out' violently with the hand to knock off superfluous sulphur—a task commonly performed by boys. The air, filled with dust, covered the face and clothing of the workers, and was taken in by the throat and nose, causing coughing and choking. After the matches had been put in clamps by children came the most dangerous part of all—the dipping in the lighting composition, commonly called 'compo' or 'stuff.' It was described thus by an Assistant Commissioner:

Phosphorus is added, in small quantities at a time, the amount being greater in proportion to the cheapness of the match, to glue, which has been soaked and heated as for other common uses, and the whole stirred constantly till the phosphorus is finely divided. . . . The operation of thus 'mixing' the materials is attended with danger not only from the fumes given out, but from the risk of explosion unless carefully conducted. Little boys are often employed to stir the composition, a tedious but light labour, and have their faces for a long time, perhaps half an hour at a time, close by or actually over the composition.[1]

For use the composition was spread evenly upon a stone slab or iron plate, heated by steam or a stove. The tips of the matches were then dipped in the mixture. The 'dipper'— usually, though not always, an adult—was exposed to the vapour plentifully given out by the large heated surface, and the bundles or frames were usually 'handed' or put on the slab for him, and carried away after dipping by boys, who were thus exposed to the same vapour, and who were frequently burned by splashes of the composition on their flesh and clothes. While drying, the matches still continued to give off vapour, which could be seen rising even in daylight. The whole manufacture was rendered more pernicious by the fact that all the processes were frequently carried on in the same room, the poisonous vapour consequently spreading to all persons working in it. Even where several rooms were in use, the vapour spread, and its disagreeable smell was apparent immediately a match manufactory was approached.

The Commissioners in 1863 examined the sections of the lace trade not covered by the Act of 1861. These were the parts of the industry which used no mechanical power, and comprised pillow-lace making and the various processes which came under the head of lace-finishing. In all these trades women, children, and young persons worked for very long hours in overcrowded and unhealthy conditions, sometimes in warehouses, often in private houses, so that it was impossible to estimate their number, except that it was several times greater than the 10,000 persons of all ages and sexes employed in making lace on machines. Lace-finishing proper consisted of separating breadths of lace, of joining lengths together, of

[1] *Ibid.*, XVIII, Appendix, 43.

clipping edges, scalloping, and similar 'finishing' processes. It was done in premises which varied from large new warehouses to rooms in private houses, all of which were hot with steam or gas and inadequately ventilated. Private houses were the worst, excessive overcrowding aggravating all the other evils. Since the work was often simple and mechanical, many children were employed, and where private houses were used as workshops, and the neighbours were similarly occupied, there was no one to raise an objection. A witness described the scene in one such cottage work-room—small and close, lighted by gas placed very low, no means of ventilation but by the windows, which could not often be opened for fear of the damp's spoiling the lace, as many people as possible crowded into the room, so that there was space for the children on their little stools, and for the lace on the ground or on the clipping frames, but not for any furniture or for anyone to move about.

It was the bonnet-front making which was the most injurious section of the lace-finishing trade. The chief trouble was the excessive steamy heat both of the machines which did the gauffring and, more particularly, of the machines which made up into bonnet fronts the lace so prepared. Sarah Parnell, aged thirteen, described Sanders and Francis's, bonnet-front makers, where she worked:

There were from 240–260 women and girls, besides about a dozen men. The youngest girls were about ten years old, and about half of the whole number were under fifteen. In one large room were either five or six gauffring machines, and 30 making-up machines, the latter heated by steam pipes, and standing some of them very close together. In this room were about 150 people altogether. In another room were six making-up machines of the same kind. . . . It was very hot. . . . Could hardly stand it, it was so hot. There was hardly a day passed but what some one fainted. Sometimes three fainted in a day. It was chiefly those at the making-up machines, and generally of as much as twenty years of age. . . . All, women and girls both, complained of the heat very much. When they were working late at night they could hardly work in the room, it was so hot.[1]

The increase in consumption among young women working the gauffring and making-up machines was noted. It was said to have increased from 1 in 45 in 1852 to 1 in 8 in 1861. In

[1] *Ibid.*, XVIII, Minutes of Evidence, 205.

all branches of lace manufacture there was the danger of eye-strain. This was particularly evident in pillow-lace making, so called from the work being made on a kind of pillow, over which the worker needed to stoop to the danger of the eyes and the encouragement of chest diseases. In the Honiton and Buckinghamshire districts, where most of the pillow-lace making was done, it was the regular practice for children to go to a lace 'school' to learn the craft, the 'school' being kept by a woman in her cottage. Here, in winter without heat, always without ventilation, the children crowded together, much as the lace-finishers did, to learn their skill. When proficient—generally at about twelve to fifteen years old—they either worked at home or, more commonly, congregated in neighbours' houses for the sake of companionship and mutual help, and to save light. They worked to what hours they pleased, sometimes all through the night.

What the non-mechanized lace manufacture might mean to its workers is given in Ann Camm's story of her life, as reconstructed by the Assistant Commissioner who examined the conditions of the lace-making industry in 1863.

Ann Camm began lace-work, Brussels and fancy net, and silk edgings, at a mistress's when she was about eleven. The time was called sixty hours a week, all beyond that being reckoned as overtime. Often she worked fourteen or fifteen hours a day, and as much as eighty-five hours a week. Breakfast, dinner, and tea-time were shortened by ten or fifteen minutes each. The children nearly always worked till 10 or 10.30 P.M. Sometimes their mistress went to bed, setting them so much to finish, which kept them till 1 or 2 A.M. They then went to bed in spare beds, which the mistress, who was a widow, had ready for them. She often dropped asleep in her chair, and so did the others. For the first month she was a learner and got nothing. Then she got 6d. a week. At the end of a year she was getting 1s. 9d. When she was about thirteen she had to give over work for a bit, because she could not see any longer. She used to see things like a mist before her eyes, and by fourteen was quite shortsighted. At fifteen she went into a warehouse. The hours were called from eight till seven, but in busy times she had always to stay till nine. She worked at home now. Ann Camm declared she would not know the Assistant Commissioner again if she saw him, although he was sitting only about seven feet from her, with the light full on his face. "I would have to come nearer a bit for that," she said. She was about thirty, but looked fifty—"utterly worn out, her face wrinkled as with age, and her eyes glazed and watery."[1]

The effect of the first *Report of the Children's Employment Commission* can be measured by the fact that the following year six of the manufactures with which it dealt were brought under Factory Law. The Factory Acts Extension Act of 1864 embraced pottery manufacture, Lucifer-match making, percussion-cap making, cartridge-making, paper-staining, and fustian-cutting. The last was carried on as a domestic industry as well as in workshops, and the 1864 Act took a big step forward when it included the home-work fustian-cutters within the scope of the Act. Bringing these industries under the Factory Acts meant that they were subject to inspection, that hours of work were prescribed, and the minimum age of starting work laid down. In addition, masters in these industries were empowered to make rules for ventilation and cleanliness, and women and children and young persons were forbidden to take meals in rooms in which certain specified processes were carried on.

The Commissioners continued their work, and by 1866 had issued five Reports covering a wide range of metal, hosiery, printing, and other trades not yet subject to factory law. The final Report of 1867 dealt with agriculture. In that year were passed a further Factory Acts Extension Act and a Workshops Regulation Act. The Factory Act of 1867 was one of considerable intricacy, but it made a substantial advance in bringing within the scope of factory law all premises in which fifty or more persons were at work in a manufacturing process. The complementary Workshops Regulation Act brought under control all premises in which fewer than fifty persons were employed, defining "employed" as "occupied with or without wages," and thus including home industry. Although admirable in intention, neither Act was effective in operation. The Factory Act of 1867 had much of its good annulled by a series of exceptions which confused the issue and nullified the intention of universal regulation. The Workshops Act was, in effect, merely permissive besides being extremely vague. It

[1] *Ibid.*, XVIII, Minutes of Evidence, 222.

repeated all the weaknesses of the early Factory Acts: although hours were regulated they were not compelled to be taken within a set period, nor were meal-times fixed; stipulations concerning education and the age of employees were vague; and, above all, it relied upon a system of inspection by local authorities. The last was so obviously unsatisfactory—town councillors, it was said, did not care to make themselves obnoxious by interfering with their fellow-tradesmen—that in 1871 the administration of the Workshops Act was passed to the factory inspectorate.

Factory and workshop law was very complicated at this time. Mr Baker, a factory inspector, had written a little manual in 1851 entitled *Factory Acts made Easy*. In 1867 he revised it under the title *Factory Acts made as Easy as Possible*. Ten years later the position was even worse, and a Commission set to work in 1876 to examine the whole body of factory law with a view to its consolidation. On its recommendation the Factory Acts of 1864 and 1867 and the Workshops Regulation Act of 1867 were repealed, and a consolidating Factories and Workshop Act became law in 1878.

The Act of 1878 first and foremost abolished the arbitrary distinction between factories and workshops as places where more or less than fifty persons were employed. Instead the distinction was to be the use or non-use of mechanical power. A workplace using mechanical power was a factory; a workplace not using mechanical power was a workshop. The Act was applied to five divisions of workplaces: textile factories; non-textile factories; workshops employing women, children and young persons; women's workshops; and domestic workshops, in which only the members of a family were employed. Conditions in non-textile factories and workshops were brought into line; textile factories still retained rather shorter hours than either of these; women's workshops and domestic workshops were still inadequately regulated, because, although a ten-and-a-half-hour day was prescribed, the margin within which it might be taken was still left as wide as between 6 A.M. and 9 P.M. To certain listed trades and processes relaxations were permitted, and the Secretary of State had power to extend those relaxations and modifications to trades and processes with similar conditions.

There was another set of children to whom the Report of 1863 called attention, though it was outside its terms of reference to do so. These were the little chimney-sweeps. A Committee of 1853 had already revealed that the Act of 1840 was largely inoperative, and witnesses had brought sensational evidence to that Committee to prove that the chimneys of two of the most vehement opposers of reform—Lord Beaumont and Lord Hardwicke—were among the most difficult and dangerous. A Bill introduced into the Lords by Shaftesbury was there carried, but met its defeat in the Commons. When the Children's Employment Commission reported in 1863 conditions were as bad as they had been at the beginning of the century, and the number of climbing boys was actually increasing. All the evils relating to chimney-sweeping, which it was the object of the legislature to suppress, reported the Commissioners, were reappearing in their worst form, the provisions of the Acts of Parliament being "systematically violated, and almost with entire impunity."[1]

After the passage of the Act of 1840 the number of climbing boys had at first decreased, largely because philanthropic persons either themselves kept a watchful eye on master sweeps or employed a paid agent to do so. Peter Hall was one of those who travelled about the country on his own initiative trying to enforce the Act.

He was . . . much dreaded by the sweeps, and as soon as his arrival became known by the railway policeman or any one seeing him at the station, the sweeps were all on their guard, and he had to employ a person unknown to watch the sweeps for him.[2]

Even so, it was extraordinarily difficult to convict, for magistrates required evidence which it was almost impossible to procure, such as seeing the boy actually in or just leaving the chimney. Entering a house with the bags and brushes of the trade, or leaving it covered with soot, was generally not accounted sufficient evidence to convict a master of having used the boy in the chimney. Nevertheless, in the twenty years after the passage of the 1840 Act, twenty-three cases of irrefutable evidence were on record in the form of twenty-three little boys stifled and found dead in chimneys.[3] In 1862 a

---

[1] *First Report of the Children's Employment Commission*, 1863, XVIII, lxxxiv.
[2] *Children's Employment Commission*, Reports and Evidence, 1863, XVIII, 297.
[3] *First Report of the Children's Employment Commission*, 1863, XVIII, lxxxvii.

child of seven was found badly burned through being compelled to ascend flues on fire. His master was fined £7. In
1861 a child in the West End of London stuck in a chimney and
lost his life. The Coroner for Nottingham reported a case where
a boy was sent up a chimney when the fire was still burning,
and something had to be put over the still hot fireplace for
him to rest his feet on at starting. A hole had to be broken in
the wall to get the boy out, and he was found to be dead. In
another case the master lit straw under the chimney to get
down his boy, whom he had supposed to be asleep, but in
reality he was dead.[1]

This cruel use of boys continued, in spite of the fact that time
and again it was demonstrated that chimneys could be swept
effectively with machines, and that even difficult chimneys
could, with trifling alterations costing a few shillings, be
adapted to the use of machines. There is on record, however,
the prompt action of Lord Ebury in ordering his chimneys to be
altered. A little chimney boy who had worked to the top of
one of his lordship's chimneys could not get back because of
accumulated soot. He climbed out of the top and wandered
about the roof for some time, but was unable to find a way in.
He afterwards managed to descend part of the chimney, rap-
ping with his brush to attract attention. He then discovered
an iron slide in the chimney, which, opening, precipitated him
on the floor of the white damask drawing-room of the house.
Lord Ebury, his butler, and the master sweep came running in.
Lord Ebury, having asked if the boy were hurt, then demanded
of the master sweep why a machine for sweeping was not used.
On being told that his chimneys were not suitably constructed
he immediately ordered the necessary alterations.

This same chimney-sweep had gone through the tortures
of having his bleeding knees rubbed with brine to harden them.
On the whole, however, his lot was better than some. He
describes how he washed on Saturday, and how on Saturday
evening and Sunday he and his friends "were quite gentlemen,
dressed out in blue suits of clothes and high hats." They then
slept "over the house," but during the week four boys together
slept in a kind of cupboard, where the dust was almost choking.
This sweep was the son of a sweep who had apprenticed him
to the trade. At one period he changed his work to vege-

[1] *Ibid.*, XVIII, lxxxvii.

table-hawking, but found he preferred the chimney-sweep's life. He saved some money, set up for himself, bought a sweeping machine, married, prospered, and became a devout Methodist.[1]

The champion of the chimney-sweeps, as of so many other unfortunate children, was Lord Shaftesbury. After the 1863 *Report of the Children's Employment Commission* his Act of 1864 tried again to regulate their employment. But, like the Acts of 1834 and 1840, it failed to specify an enforcing authority, and a further Report from the Children's Employment Commission in 1866 demonstrated its failure. "Years of oppression and cruelty have rolled on," wrote Shaftesbury in his diary in 1872, "and now a death has given me the power of one more appeal to the public."[2] The particular case which Shaftesbury took up by a letter to *The Times* was that of a boy of seven and a half who was sent up a flue and taken out dead fifteen minutes later. The master was sentenced to six months' hard labour. Three years later Shaftesbury brought his long campaign to a successful end. The Act of 1875 forbade a sweep to carry on his trade without a licence from the police, which had to be renewed annually. For offences against the Acts of 1840 and 1864 sweeps could be deprived of their licences. And at last it was made the business of the police to enforce the law.

In the eighties attention was sharply drawn again to the tailoring trade. There was an increasing demand for cheap clothes, irrespective of quality. To meet it wages were being driven down in sweat-shops, while the processes of the trade became more and more subdivided as each wretched worker toiled at the same repetitive process for longer than his physical frame could stand, never learning to make a whole suit, never earning sufficient to keep him well. Instead of the complete tailor were men who made only coats or waistcoats or trousers, cutters, basters, machinists, pressers, fellers, buttonhole workers. In this way apprenticeship was dispensed with—a man could learn his task in all but a few branches of the tailoring trade in a few weeks—and the supply of labour was kept high. At the same time various middlemen appeared between the customer and his finished suit—the master tailor, the contractor, various

---

[1] *Life of a Chimney Boy* (anon., edited Turner).
[2] J. L. and B. Hammond, *Lord Shaftesbury*, p. 234.

subcontractors. Thus in a double way the tailoring trade was cut up. It was cut up vertically according to a man's particular section of the trade, and it was cut up horizontally according to which rung of the ladder the man was on—sweated worker at the bottom, one of the middlemen contractors, contractor-in-chief, or master tailor.

To the native poor were added the influx of pauper foreigners, chiefly German and Russian Jews, who flocked to London driven by starvation conditions and persecution in their own countries, and attracted by the ease with which they could be assimilated into the cheap-clothing trade and by the provision made for them by their co-religionists through such organizations as the Jewish Board of Guardians. The majority of the sweated workers in the East End of London were Jews, many of them unable to speak English. Their hope of a decent livelihood was frustrated, and the majority of them passed lives of misery in a strange land with an unlearned language in direst poverty and dirt. Yet most of them were able to stand these things because of the lowness of the standard of living from which they had come; and in doing so they dragged down the standard of the English workers.

It was the desire of nearly every sweated worker to become himself a sweater. And the ease with which this was done itself attracted into the industry many who hoped for quick gain. But the hope that being a sweater would mean better conditions and higher wages was often illusory. The smaller sweaters had to work with their men, and their own remuneration was driven down as the number of sweaters grew and sweater competed with sweater to get the job from the contractor or subcontractor. There were some streets in Whitechapel and St George's-in-the-East in which almost every house contained one or more sweating dens. Only those who were the "princes of the sweating system," employing forty to fifty people, were able to take things easy with cheap labour and large profits.

The smaller sweat-shops, generally rooms in private houses, provided the worst accommodation. In the majority of cases work was carried on under conditions in the highest degree filthy and insanitary. In small rooms not more than nine or ten feet square, heated by a coke fire for the pressers' irons, and at night lighted by flaring gas jets, six, eight, ten, and even a dozen workers might be crowded. The Public Health Act and the Factory and Workshop Acts were utterly disregarded. The existing system of inspection was entirely inadequate. Barely one-third of the East End sweaters were known to the factory inspectors, the majority being hidden in garrets, back rooms, basements, backyards, wash-houses. At an unexpected visit from an inspector women were tumbled into a bedroom, where the inspector had no right of entry, and word of his coming was passed down the street from sweat-shop to sweat-shop. In abominable sanitary conditions men and women, sometimes ill, carried on their work. Sometimes they wore half-finished garments to keep them warm—a child with measles was seen wearing one. They worked all hours and any hours for next to nothing for the simple reason that next to nothing seemed better than nothing. Forty years of factory and work-shop reform had passed them by. They were no better off than the companions of Alton Locke.

What was true of the East End of London was true of the provincial towns, where the system was repeated in its essentials. Nor was the sweating system confined to tailoring, though here it was found in its most concentrated form. Boot-making, cabinet-making, chain- and nail-making, cutlery and hardware knew the sweaters' den and the sweaters' victims. Though it was clear that the Factories and Workshops Acts had touched but the fringe of the problem, no comprehensive Act was passed until the beginning of the twentieth century.[1]

The Factory and Workshop Consolidation Act of 1901 brought together all that was best in existing legislation as well as adding a 'Particulars Clause.' This clause could not prevent sweating, but it gave certain classes of workers a limited protection in providing that they should be furnished with written particulars of rates of wages and of the work to be done. It applied to all classes of workers except men in men's workshops, a limitation in line with the general policy of factory legislation.

While the Factory Acts had been reaching from one industry to another existing Acts were being amended, tightened, and extended largely owing to the combination of zeal and patience exercised by the factory inspectors.

[1] *Reports of the Select Committee of the House of Lords on the Sweating System*: especially First Report, 1888, XX, and Fifth Report, 1890, XVII.

The introduction of safety measures was at first painfully slow. There was no substantial progress until the passage of the Employers' Liability Act of 1880 recognized the responsibility of the employer for insuring his workpeople against the risks of their calling. After that the principle of fencing machinery was extended from textile to non-textile factories and workshops. An Act of 1891 required adequate fire-escapes. In 1906 the Workmen's Compensation Act made clearer the workman's right to compensation for accident received at work. The first thirty years of the twentieth century saw a lengthening list of regulations dealing with dangerous trades. Old industries like shipbuilding, woodworking, and building were more closely regulated. New industries were brought within a safety code. The growing electrical industry was embraced by the Factory Act of 1901; in 1902 a special Electrical Inspector was appointed; and in 1907 a Code of Safety Regulations governing electrical generating works was issued. Celluloid Regulations received statutory form in 1921; the cinematograph film industry was regulated by Statute in 1928.

By the end of 1932 there were over forty codes of regulations made under the powers conferred on the Secretary of State by the 1901 Act, dealing with health and safety. Most of these were the result of agreement between masters, men, and inspectors. Now, the Medical Inspectorate, the Electrical Inspectorate, and the Inspectorate for Dangerous Trades are each a branch in themselves containing several inspectors and a chief, and safety and the prevention of disease are closely linked. The Home Office Industrial Museum, opened in 1927, displays safety devices, means of ventilation, and other aids to health and the reduction of accidents.

Neither the hours of adult men nor the wages of any persons were regulated by the Factory Act of 1901, nor, indeed, had they been by any Factory Act. The working hours of adult male labour were, however, in most cases indirectly regulated by the working hours of females and young persons, without whom the factory machinery could not be kept working. But the men did not rely on this alone. In the second half of the nineteenth century there developed a method of bargaining between masters and men for regulating hours of work and wages by committees of conciliation and arbitration which became known variously as joint boards, wages boards, or trade boards.

Among the earliest were the Nottingham Hosiery Board and a Building Trades Joint Committee, both established in the sixties. There was arbitration machinery at different times in the pottery, silk, and printing trades. In the iron and steel trade there was a continuous history of arbitration and conciliation from the time of the formation of the North of England Iron and Steel Board of Conciliation and Arbitration in 1869 and the Midland Iron and Steel Wages Board in 1876. These Iron and Steel Boards developed a system of regulating wages by a sliding-scale based on selling prices. Soon the whole iron and steel industry was covered by conciliation machinery and regulated by sliding scales. A similar system spread through the coal industry. The cotton workers, engineers, and boot and shoe operatives developed their own negotiating machinery.

By the end of the nineteenth century there were similar District Boards acting for a number of small and generally unorganized trades within a given locality. These District Boards of Conciliation consisted normally of representatives of the local Chamber of Commerce (employers) and of the local trades council (workmen), and worked with considerable success. In this way a substantial part of British industry was subject to collective agreements made in a formal way between highly organized trade associations. It was the culmination of the policy of the New Model trade unions.

The fist statutory trade boards, as opposed to these voluntary ones, developed not from those already established in the more highly developed industries, but as a consequence of the very bad conditions in the 'sweated' industries. It was to deal expressly with wages in the ready-made and wholesale bespoke tailoring, with paper box-making, with machine-made lace and net finishing and with chain-making, that the first Trade Boards Act of 1909 was passed, establishing trade boards for each of these industries. In addition, the Act empowered the Board of Trade to apply the Act to other trades where they considered wages to be "exceptionally low" compared with those in other industries. As a consequence by 1913 there were also trade boards for linen and cotton embroidery, for hollow-ware making, for tin-box making, sugar confectionery, and food-preserving, and for shirt-making. There also developed a series of Acts applying directly to certain industries. The miners had always favoured this kind of statutory regulation, and now they won the Coal Mines Regulation Act of 1908, which limited the hours of miners to eight a day, the Coal Mines Act of 1919, which brought them down to seven a day, and the Coal Mines (Minimum Wage) Act of 1912. The Shops (Hours of Closing) Act of 1928 statutorily limited the hours of shop assistants. Meanwhile in 1918 an amendment to the Trade Boards Act of 1909 changed the *raison d'être* of a trade board from one in which very low wages obtained to one where "no adequate machinery for the effective regulation of wages" existed. This widening of the scope of the Act, together with the stimulus of the War, increased the number of trade boards so that by the end of 1922 there was a total in the United Kingdom of sixty-three trade boards, covering thirty-nine trades, governing the wages of about three million workers.[1]

In 1916 a Sub-committee of the Cabinet Committee on Reconstruction was appointed, under the Chairmanship of J. H. Whitley, to develop this machinery further. The four Reports of the Whitley Committee appeared between March 1917 and July 1918. For each well-organized industry the Whitley Committee recommended a National Joint Industrial Council, representing both sides of industry, employers and employed, and meeting frequently and regularly. The Joint Industrial Council would consider the wide and general questions concerning the industry. Local matters would be considered by district councils organized on a similar basis. Below these again were to be the Works Councils, functioning for factories and workshops. Over all would be a Standing Arbitration Council.

The State played its part by the 1919 Industrial Courts Act, which established the first permanent Arbitration Court in Great Britain, but most of the better-organized trade unions held aloof. The sixty-four Whitley Councils which were functioning by 1932 in, for example, pottery, road transport, building, wool, were little different from the Conciliation Boards already in existence. But it is significant of the part that joint discussion played in the regulation of industry that when a new Factory Act was under consideration in 1937 it was submitted in draft to the National Confederation of

[1] Dorothy Sells, *The British Trade Boards System*, pp. 5–6.

Employers' Organizations and to the Trade Union Council for comment.

The 1901 Factory Act remained the governing Act until the Factories Act of 1937. There were then some 6000 textile factories, 160,000 non-textile factories, and 75,000 workshops for an inspectorate of about 250, including women inspectors. The Act of 1937 abolished the distinction between factory and workshop, textile and non-textile factory, and it included the men's workshops which had hitherto been excluded. It did away with certain anomalous distinctions such as those between ships under repair in dry docks (which had been subject to the Factory Acts) and those in wet docks (which had not), between builders using mechanical power (who were under the Factory Acts) and those not using mechanical power (who had been outside their scope); between buildings in course of construction and those in course of demolition, between buildings above ground, and excavation and other works below ground. All were brought within the Factory Acts.

Women and young persons were by the 1937 Act given a forty-eight-hour week in place of the sixty hours (or fifty-five and a half hours in textile factories) then operating. On no day were they to work more than nine hours (the outside limit was then ten and a half or ten in textile factories). There was to be no work after one on Saturdays (shops could still substitute a half-day's holiday on another day of the week). For women and young persons the earliest hour of starting work was to be 7 A.M. (in place of 6 A.M.); and young persons under sixteen were not to work beyond six o'clock at night (in place of eight o'clock). While no person under sixteen could in any circumstances work longer than the statutory forty-eight hours a week, women and young persons over sixteen might work overtime up to a maximum of a hundred hours in a calendar year, but not more than six hours in one week. In seasonal trades the maximum overtime limit for women was 150 hours. Other regulations required the extension of medical supervision, the increase of working space per operative, the improvement and control of lighting, temperature, ventilation, and cleaning. To enforce the Act the inspectorate was to be increased.

It is significant, and in line with all preceding factory

legislation, that the Act legislated for women and young persons and not for adult men. The position was all the more anomalous since by this time men's hours were already regulated by trade agreements, by Special Orders, and by the ratification by Parliament of international conventions.

Before the 1937 Act could get properly working the Second World War broke out. Again the national emergency, demanding the highest possible output, was overriding. The only question was—which combination of hours, rest, and welfare would yield the greatest production? So, while working hours were lengthened, social amenities were improved, the factory inspectorate increased, and there was a considerable extension of the principle of joint control of industry by employers, employed, and the State.

It took one and a half centuries to make conditions tolerable, although far from perfect, in the great factories and workshops which fed Britain and much of the world with manufactured goods. As with all movements of social reform in the period, it is not the reform itself which is remarkable, but the length of time needed to effect it.

SELECT BIBLIOGRAPHY

First Report of the Children's Employment Commission, 1863, XVIII.
Reports of the Select Committee of the House of Lords on the Sweating System, 1888, XX; 1890, XVII.
Fifth and Final Report of the Royal Commission on Labour, 1894, XXXV.
Reports of H.M. Factory Inspectors. (These are issued annually. Reports may be obtained from H.M. Stationery Office; older ones may be consulted in libraries, the correct reference number being obtained from *Parliamentary Lists and Indexes* for the required year, under 'Factory.')
Hansard, 1936–37, Fifth Series, Vol. 320.
HAMMOND, J. L. AND B.: *Lord Shaftesbury* (Longmans, 1923).
HUTCHINS, B. L. AND HARRISON, A.: *A History of Factory Legislation* (P. S. King, 1903; revised edition, 1911).
MESS, H. A.: *Factory Legislation and its Administration, 1891–1924* (P. S. King, 1926).
SELLS, DOROTHY: *The British Trade Boards System* (P. S. King, 1924).
SEYMOUR, J. B.: *The Whitley Councils Scheme* (P. S. King, 1932).

CHAPTER XXII

HEALTH AND HOUSING

THE Board of Health, established in 1848 with Chadwick and Southwood Smith, the two paid Commissioners, on a Board of four members, was never popular. Ratepayers were afraid of increased burdens; the localities resented dictation from the centre; a group of people continued to extol the parish as historically and actually the ideal unit of local administration; the dominant *laissez-faire* school was against it on principle. The Board nevertheless continued on its way. Parliament granted it additional powers for dealing with epidemics and contagious diseases. Chadwick drew up a Report on Interments. By 1854 the Board of Health Act had been applied to 214 places. No one can deny, said a reliable reporter,

> the great ability which was exhibited in many of the important documents, statements, and reports, which emanated from the Board upon the epidemic cholera, the practice of quarantine, the burial of the dead, the supply of water, its impurities, the proper modes of drainage, and the removal, deodorizing and utilizing the sewage of towns; while the greatest zeal, activity, and energy characterized their labours.[1]

But after a year's renewal of life beyond the prescribed five years, the Board was dissolved and Chadwick pensioned off. *The Times* and all who opposed the central direction of health affairs were free to take their chance of cholera and the rest rather than be bullied into health by a Public Health Board.

A new Board of Health was immediately appointed in place of the old, and, though its constitution was altered, its powers and duties remained much the same as those of the original Board of Health. The loss of Chadwick was serious. No greater enthusiast, harder worker, or more keenly selfless devotee of the cause of public health was alive. But the appointment the following year of John Simon[2] as Medical Officer to the new

---

[1] Lumley, *English Sanitary Law* (1871), pp. 6 and 7 of Introduction, quoted by Redlich and Hurst, *Local Government in England*, i, 147 (1903 edition).
[2] He received the K.C.B. in 1887.

Board did all that could be done to compensate for the loss of Chadwick. The Board was renewed yearly until 1858, when it was dissolved, and its functions were divided between the Home Office and the Privy Council.

With neither guiding principle nor central control, the public-health service continued in haphazard and piecemeal fashion. Particularly glaring evils were met by the passage of Acts and the creation of authorities to deal with them. The Common Lodging Houses Acts of 1851 and 1853 aimed at controlling the appalling conditions of dirt and overcrowding in workmen's lodgings; the comprehensive Nuisance Removal Act of 1855 repealed earlier useless legislation; the cholera outbreak of 1854 led to the Diseases Prevention Act of 1855, which gave the Privy Council power to take action during any "formidable" epidemic. In 1855 the Metropolitan Local Management Act created a Board of Works for London which replaced the old Commissioners of Sewers. There were Local Government Amendment Acts, Sanitary Acts, Nuisance Removal Acts, Sewage Utilization Acts in the sixties. There was an Artisans' and Labourers' Dwellings Act in 1868 by which an authority had in theory the power to enforce the improvement of premises dangerous to health. A Contagious Diseases Act of 1866 related to venereal disease. In 1860 an Act for Preventing Adulteration of Articles of Food and Drink empowered local authorities to appoint analysts who, for a small payment, would analyse any article of food, and to enforce penalties for adulteration. There were Acts in 1858 and 1866 relating to smoke nuisance; there were Burial Acts, Workshop Regulation Acts, and Factory Acts—all touching public health. Much confusion was caused, each group of Acts designating a new authority for their purpose, so that there were Local Boards, Local Authorities, Nuisance Authorities, Improvement Commissioners, Sewer Authorities, Town Councils, Vestries, Guardians, Overseers. Sometimes a new authority was simply an old authority under a new name. Sometimes its powers were in conflict with the general law of the land. When the confusion was so bad that it could not possibly be overlooked a Royal Sanitary Commission was appointed in 1869 to sort out the tangle.

This Commission reported in no uncertain voice that nearly everything was wrong with the public-health system. The law itself was at fault in being "casual and experimental," "isolated and tentative," where it should have been firm and comprehensive. It had become unusually complex by additions, enlargements, parallel enactments, wholly, partly, or not at all adopted, with no attempt at arrangement, let alone consolidation, with the result that the law was either unknown or misunderstood. The multiplication of authorities had led to doubt as to where responsibility lay, and resulted "either in inaction, litigation, or frustration." On top, responsibility for public health, "after wandering through a labyrinth of Local Authorities," found itself vested in no fewer than three chief offices— the Home Office, the Privy Council, and the Poor Law Board. None of these had any overall powers of compulsion, for the Public Health Acts took effect only by the voluntary adoption of ratepayers.

The result was seen in the condition of the country. There might have been no Chadwick, no Southwood Smith, no Public Health Act. Sometimes ignorance vitiated goodwill. Many towns carried out large schemes of drainage, but unthinkingly discharged their sewage into the nearest river, thus polluting their drinking-water and poisoning men and cattle downstream. "The mere money-cost of public ill-health," said the Sanitary Commissioners, echoing Chadwick's reiterated assertion of forty years earlier, "whether it be reckoned by the necessarily increased expenditure, or by the loss of the work both of the sick and of those who wait upon them, must be estimated at many millions a year."[1]

The Commissioners' overall recommendation was

> that the present fragmentary and confused Sanitary Legislation should be consolidated, and that the administration of Sanitary Law should be made uniform, universal, and imperative throughout the Kingdom.[2]

Their detailed proposals could, under their terms of reference, apply only to England and Wales, excluding London. These were clear-cut and decisive. The Report was greeted favourably, the more so since in 1871 there was a smallpox epidemic and the threat of a fifth invasion of cholera. The legislature acted quickly, and the same year the Local Government Act became law.

---

[1] *Second Report of the Royal Sanitary Commission* 1871, XXXV, 16.
[2] *Ibid.*, XXXV, 3.

The Act followed closely the Report. Poor Law, public health, and the small Local Government Act Department were brought together under one Minister as the Local Government Board. So far so good. But the Act then departed from the Commissioners' explicit recommendation that there should be one Permanent Secretary responsible for Poor Law and one responsible for public health. Under the President of the Local Government Board a Parliamentary Secretary sat in the House, and under him there was one Permanent Secretary only. The emphasis of long practice, the natural bent of public opinion and the Parliamentary mind, was on the Poor Law and Poor Law methods, on deterrence rather than prevention, on relieving destitution rather than preventing disease, on organizing workhouses rather than clearing slums. As a consequence public health found itself subject to Poor Law methods. Poor Law inspectors became general inspectors, including public-health duties in their itinerary, though without the requisite medical knowledge. John Simon, the able and keen Medical Officer to the old Public Health Board, was subordinate to the Poor Law Permanent Secretary.

The following year, the whole country was divided into sanitary districts, each under a sanitary authority. The appointment of a Medical Officer and an Inspector of Nuisances became obligatory on each district.

Having attended to administration, the Government now turned to the law itself, and in the Act of 1875 brought together and consolidated, for areas outside London, the widely spread law relating to public health. Sections of the Public Health Act of 1875 are still in force.

After describing the Urban and Rural Sanitary Districts who were the authorities for executing the Act the Public Health Act of 1875 prescribed their duties. They were responsible for sewerage and drainage, and had powers to enforce the drainage of undrained houses, in urban districts to stop the building of houses without drains, and in all districts the building of houses without privy accommodation. They had powers to provide public lavatories, to enforce their provision in factories, to see that all drains and privies were properly kept, and to make an examination on complaint of a nuisance. They were responsible for scavenging and water-supply, and had certain further powers concerning housing—new cellar dwellings were prohibited, existing ones strictly controlled, lodging-houses controlled, offensive trades strictly curtailed. They had powers of inspection and destruction of unsound food. In the case of infectious diseases the local authority, where necessary, could cleanse and disinfect and destroy bedding. Hospitals could be provided by the local authority.

Some initiative, meantime, was being shown by local authorities. Liverpool, to her great credit, was the first town in the country to appoint a Medical Officer of Health, which she had done in 1847. London followed, John Simon becoming her first Medical Officer in 1848. Manchester followed in 1869, Birmingham, after another interval, in 1875. Here Joseph Chamberlain was mayor from 1873 to 1876, and under his vigorous guidance Birmingham embarked on a big slum-clearance project involving forty to fifty acres of land. London in the seventies similarly set to work to clear some of her worst slums, but she allowed the private contractor virtually free play in rehousing the poor. At Liverpool, Manchester, Bradford, Glasgow, municipal enterprise built docks and town-halls, streets and exchanges, and relieved congestion in some places, though sometimes only at the cost of making it worse elsewhere. On the whole there was a slow move from slum tenements to better houses. But before it had gone far a pamphlet was published which stirred the whole country. *The Bitter Cry of Outcast London* told again the story of slum life which had been told many times before in the Reports of the thirties and forties, and more recently by the Royal Sanitary Commission. Conditions were worse now because they had gone on longer, and seemed worse to the age because it had believed that its social legislation had attended to the evils of overcrowding, dirt, and poverty. Yet here was George R. Sims in 1883 thrusting a penny pamphlet under their noses which told of degradation and immorality in the heart of London, in

pestilential human rookeries . . . where tens of thousands are crowded together amidst horrors which call to mind what we have heard of the middle passage of the slave ship.

The dwellings were described in detail:

To get into them you have to penetrate courts reeking with poisonous and malodorous gases arising from accumulations of sewage and refuse scattered in all directions and often flowing beneath your feet; courts, many of them which the sun never penetrates, which are never visited by a breath of fresh air, and which rarely know the virtues of a drop of cleansing water. You have to ascend rotten staircases. . . . You have to grope your way along dark and filthy passages swarming with vermin. Then, if you are not driven back by the intolerable stench, you may gain admittance to the dens in which these thousands of beings . . . herd together. . . . Eight feet square—that is about the average size of . . . these rooms. Walls and ceilings are black with the accretions of filth which have gathered upon them through long years of neglect. It is exuding through cracks in the boards overhead; it is running down the walls; it is everywhere. What goes by the name of a window is half of it stuffed with rags or covered by boards. . . . As to furniture—you may perchance discover a broken chair, the tottering relics of an old bedstead, or the mere fragment of a table; but more commonly you will find rude substitutes for these things in the shape of rough boards resting upon bricks, an old hamper or box turned upside down, or more frequently still, nothing but rubbish and rags.

Every room in these rotten and reeking tenements houses a family, often two.

Such was life in the London slums in spite of the Local Government Act, in spite of the Public Health Act of 1875, in spite of half a century of denunciation and appeal, in spite of much philanthropic work. Government action took the inevitable form of a Royal Commission. The Royal Commission on Housing sat during 1884 and 1885. Serving on it—an indication of the earnestness with which the question was regarded—were the Prince of Wales and Cardinal Manning.

The Report of the Royal Commission on Housing confirmed the findings of George R. Sims. Improvement was always qualified. In London, for example, a system of house drainage had taken the place of the cesspool system, and a marked improvement was shown in the death-rate and in the habits of the people. Yet the work had been imperfectly done, and the connexion with the sewers was often faulty. There had been much building, moreover, on bad land covered with refuse heaps and decaying matter. Builders were legally obliged to cover the refuse with concrete so far as the house extended, but since the concrete was generally of bad quality it cracked, and the noxious gases escaped into the house.

The water-supply had similarly improved, yet was still

JOSEPH ARCH
[*See pp.* 358–362]

WILLIAM EDWARD FORSTER

H. T. Wells

[See p. 510]

National Portrait Gallery

appallingly inadequate. The poor still kept it in tubs, sometimes in their sleeping-rooms. Sometimes water was supplied from the same cistern for drinking and for flushing the closet, and was sometimes kept, uncovered, close to the closet pan and the dust-heap. Lavatory accommodation remained most defective in spite of the power conferred on local authorities by the law. There might be one closet to sixteen houses, one for all the houses in the street, where thirty or forty people inhabited a single house.

Further sources of insanitary conditions and disease were the noxious trades carried on in already unhealthy and overcrowded dwellings. Rag-pickers, sack-makers, and matchbox-makers often did all their business in the room in which their families lived and slept. The most pernicious trade was rabbit-pulling in which the fur was pulled from the animals' skins and flew freely round the room. Also objectionable to his customers as well as his family was the costermonger's habit of curing and smoking haddocks in his room and storing under his bed his unsold stock, watering it in the morning to give it the appearance of freshness.

The tenements and houses of the slums were in a shocking state of repair. Middlemen—house-jobbers, house-farmers, or home-knockers—acted as rent-collectors for the owners, and on them generally devolved the fixing of the rents and the undertaking of repairs. They passed a fixed sum on to the owner; the rest was their profit. So nothing was spent on even the most elementary improvement. Rooms so damp that the paper hung in shreds were common. There were houses rotten with age in Southwark, so that a man could enter through holes in the wall. Walls alive with vermin, rain driving in, no window glass, were common sights. Many rooms were always dark because a so-called 'cottage' three stories high had been built where the backyard should have been. Houses completely back to back were common all over the country. The tenement house was chiefly characteristic of London, but there were many also in Bristol, Liverpool, and Newcastle. New houses were often little better than the old, the jerry-builder doing almost as he pleased, and his pleasure being profit. "The old houses," said the Commissioners, "are rotten from age and neglect. The new houses . . . are rotten from the first."

The death-rate in the worst slums remained very high. In

part of St Pancras in 1882 in a non-epidemic season the death rate was over seventy a thousand. In the slums of Liverpool there were areas which were always the seat of some infectious disease. The poverty that was part cause, part effect, of these shocking conditions of life was represented by wages which, on an average, were 8s. to £1 weekly. Rents for unfurnished rooms in London were from 3s. 11d. to 5s. for one room, 6s. for two, 7s. 6d. for three. In the Provinces rents were lower, but so also were wages.

As earlier Reports had done, the Royal Commission on Housing reported the inadequacy of the legislature to deal with the problem:

> There was much legislation designed to meet these evils, yet
> . . . the existing laws were not put into force, some of them
> having remained a dead letter from the date when they first
> found place in the statute book.

This was to be the fate of subsequent legislation. An Act of 1885, the Housing of the Working Classes Act of 1890, the Housing and Town Planning Act of 1909, effected little. When the next big inquiry was made into the conditions of the poor the reader was once again transported to the beginning of the century.

Charles Booth's monumental inquiry, set on foot in 1886, into *Life and Labour in London* covered housing, employment, wages, health, and religion. Booth described the tenements, courts, and back-to-back houses of London's slums, foul, insanitary, sunless, their inhabitants the "occasional labourers, street-sellers, loafers, criminals and semi-criminals" of the great city. Their life was "the life of savages, with vicissitudes of extreme hardship and occasional excess." Booth and others, like Beatrice Potter, were beginning to study the problems of slums, poverty, ill health, and working conditions as related subjects. Already the practical experience of doctors, and particularly of Poor Law Medical Officers, testified to their close relationship. As a result of the unremitting and unpretentious work of these men the Poor Law infirmary had been considerably improved, dispensary services, and sometimes the infirmary, had been open to all the poor, whether on poor relief or not. There nevertheless persisted right into the twentieth century the belief that medical relief to the poor led inevitably to pauperism, and that it should be given only under strictly Poor Law conditions. A general medical service for the poor was therefore hampered at the outset, and preventive treatment for them was rare. The medical men of the end of the century were still fighting Chadwick's battle.

The weight of medical opinion given before the Royal Commission on the Poor Law of 1905–9 was overwhelmingly in favour of seeking out sickness among the poor and treating it at once, instead of waiting for the sick to become paupers and then treating them under the Poor Law. This Commission decided, therefore, to test the old assumption that medical treatment encouraged pauperism, and sent Dr M'Vail to investigate. He found the proportion of paupers who had begun their careers of pauperism through sickness to be negligible. He found, on the other hand, that everything was done to turn the applicant for sick relief into a pauper. The sick poor were treated by Poor Law District Medical Officers to whom they had access only through the relieving officer, who would generally grant medical assistance only in cases of complete destitution. In this way treatment was not given until complete destitution was established, and could therefore not be preventive of pauperism, and often not of severe illness. The Poor Law District Medical Officers were paid badly, worked under bad conditions, and yet had often themselves to provide the medicines they prescribed for their destitute patients. The only possible solution to the problem, concluded Dr M'Vail, was to combine in one authority the medical services of the Poor Law and those under the Public Health section of the Local Government Board.

Dr M'Vail's recommendation was not immediately carried out, but in 1908 Dr Newsholme became Chief Medical Officer at the Local Government Board, and his work at the centre, coupled with that of Medical Officers of Health in the districts, began to make a mark on public health. Particularly in these years was infant welfare advanced. Infant Welfare Centres were introduced for distributing free milk to poor mothers, the first being opened in 1899 at St Helens. By 1906 there were over a dozen. The M.O.H. Manchester spread the idea of 'Health Visitors' who advised and instructed mothers. A 'School for Mothers' was opened at St Pancras. The result was an immediate and substantial drop in the infant mortality rate from an average of 138 a thousand under a year old in 1901-5 to 95 in a thousand in 1916-18.

In 1911 the Government undertook a comprehensive measure to raise the standard of health by making a medical service available to all. The National Insurance Act was modelled on Bismarck's famous health-insurance scheme for Germany. It was contributory and compulsory on employers and employees, covering all between the ages of sixteen and seventy employed as manual workers or in non-manual employment not exceeding £160 a year. The National Health Insurance Act of 1919 raised this limit to £250 a year, which was further raised to £420 a year in January 1942. The Act provided for the payment of sickness, disablement, and maternity benefits, and for certain medical benefit, including the services of a general practitioner. The preamble of the Act of 1911 was significant of the development of a new spirit—"an Act to provide for insurance against loss of health and for the prevention and cure of sickness." The numbers of persons within the Health Insurance scheme rose from 13,689,000 in 1914 to 19,706,000 in 1938.[1]

Finally, a Ministry of Health was established by the Ministry of Health Act, 1919, whereby, in the words of the Act, a Minister was appointed "for the purpose of promoting the health of the people throughout England and Wales." Health was no longer to be hampered by Poor Law activities or methods; nor was there to be a division between the sick and the sick pauper. The Poor Law functions of the Local Government Board went to the Home Office, while the new Ministry of Health took over the health functions of the Board. Nor was the new Ministry to suffer by the dispersal of various aspects of Public Health under different authorities. It was given the health and medical inspection duties hitherto in the province of the Minister of Education, and control of the vast health-insurance organization. All other matters relating to health—housing, sanitation, treatment of epidemics, sewerage—naturally fell to it.[2]

Looking back from 1919, one could mark a considerable improvement in the essentials of public health. Typhus had

1 Sir W. Beveridge, *Social Insurance and Allied Services*, 1942, Cmd. 6404, p. 213.
2 See "Into the Sixties," p. 554.

been virtually eradicated, there was in most places a pure water-supply, a purer food-supply, more adequate scavenging, drainage, sewerage, and sanitation. Housing conditions were better. Municipal slum-clearance schemes were taking workers to newly built estates, and private enterprise was building rows of small, comparatively cheap houses in the suburbs. Most of these were ugly, in monotonous rows, and built without consideration of the general amenities of a district. In contrast, at Port Sunlight in 1888 and at Bournville in 1895, model villages were built by employers for their workpeople, while a general Garden City movement resulted in the planning of Letchworth in 1903, and of Hampstead Garden Suburb in 1906. Welwyn Garden City was started in 1920. But no general plan followed. Between the Wars a ribbon development of ugly houses of varying size and cost was allowed to spread from most of the large towns, erected by speculative builders, bought by people of large and small incomes for whom living in the suburbs and working in the town was made possible by quicker and cheaper transport. These dormitory suburbs reduced congestion, and, although many black spots remained, there was a gradual cleaning out of slums. At the same time industrial hygiene showed a considerable advance, and the spread of education was bringing children and parents within the scope of school medical services, while increasing their knowledge of the elements of health and hygiene.

Between the Wars several social surveys were made of conditions in the great towns on the lines of Charles Booth's Survey of London. All showed improvement. The crude death-rate had fallen from 18·6 a thousand in 1900 to 11·4 in 1935, and the infant mortality rate from 159 to 58 a thousand. Public Health Officers were devoting more attention to malnutrition as one of the causes of ill health. The Education (Provision of Meals) Act of 1926 started the process, which the Second World War carried still further, of supplying free or cost-price milk and meals to schoolchildren. A comprehensive Public Health Act in 1936 re-enacted and consolidated many existing regulations, repealed others, and prescribed new ones for areas outside London; while in the same year a Public Health (London) Act consolidated existing health legislation for the Metropolis. Finally, there was inaugurated in 1948 a comprehensive National Health Service which applied to every one in the country. It covered doctors' services, hospital treatment, maternity and child welfare, and dental care. Money contributions were compulsory, services were free. In this way every one contributed to a service which was practically the same for all. But, even while it was being treated, the problem of public health had become more acute as the population grew and became more industrialized. In 1948 the pressure upon the newly-founded health service was greater than existing institutions and personnel could deal with. But when adjustments have been made and new people trained, and when the first inevitable pressure upon the new service has eased, it may be that at last, a century after its conception, Chadwick's dream of an integrated national health service will have been realized.

SELECT BIBLIOGRAPHY

Second Report of the Roval Sanitary Commission, 1871, XXXV.

Report of the Royal Commission on Housing, 1884–85, XXX.

Social Insurance and Allied Services: Report by Sir William Beveridge, 1942 (Cmd. 6404).

Report of the Royal Commission on Population, 1949 (Cmd. 7695).

The New Survey of London Life and Labour, vol. i, *Forty Years of Change* (P. S. King, 1930).

BEVERIDGE, LORD: *Full Employment in a Free Society* (New Statesman, 1944).

BOOTH, C.: *Life and Labour in London* (Collected edition, Macmillan, 1904).

CLARKE, J. J.: *The Local Government of the United Kingdom* (Pitman, 1922).

FINER, S. E.: *The Life and Times of Sir Edwin Chadwick* (Methuen, 1952).

FOGARTY, M. P.: *Town and Country Planning* (Hutchinson, 1948).

HART, W.: *Introduction to the Law of Local Government*, edited by D. J. Beattie (Butterworth, 1946).

LAMBERT, ROYSTON: *Sir John Simon, 1816–1904* (MacGibbon and Kee, 1963).

LEWIS, R. A.: *Edwin Chadwick and the Public Health Movement, 1832–1854* (Longmans, 1952).

MACFADYEN, D.: *Sir Ebenezer Howard and the Town Planning Movement* (Manchester University Press, 1933).

NEWSHOLME, A.: *The Ministry of Health* (Putnam, 1925).

SIMS, G. R.: *The Bitter Cry of Outcast London* (1883).

CHAPTER XXIII

THE END OF THE POOR LAW

RIGHT through these chapters of history there is an under-current—a constant stream of vagrants, unemployed, children, infants, the aged, and the sick—all who are destitute. While workers in industry and agriculture were fighting their battles for existence there were always those who, for one reason or another, had already lost the battle. They and their dependants formed the host with whom the Poor Law dealt.

In 1847 the Board of Poor Law Commissioners with Chadwick as Secretary, which had existed since 1834, gave place to a Poor Law Board which lasted until 1871, when the Local Government Board replaced it. The Poor Law Board of 1848–71 consisted of five members of the Privy Council, including a President. It never met as a Board, and it was, in fact, the President who carried on the functions of Poor Law Authority. He and his Parliamentary Secretary were Members of Parliament, the President often being a Cabinet Minister. Like other Ministers, he was therefore an impermanent head of the department in which he had so much power while in office. Only less powerful were the inspectors upon whose Reports the headquarters staff had necessarily to rely.

In 1871, less through any development in Poor Law policy than because of the public-health position, Poor Law, public health, and the small Local Government Act Department were merged in the Local Government Board, with a President, Parliamentary Secretary, and three permanent secretaries.

In the localities parishes had been grouped into unions after 1834, and Poor Law policy was carried out by boards of guardians who had to be ratepayers elected by other ratepayers and of whom there were about 25,000 over the country. The rating qualifications governing the election of guardians were removed by the Local Government Act of 1894, and women became eligible to act as guardians, many, in fact, being elected. Responsible to the guardians were a salaried clerk to each board and a staff of relieving officers, together with

Workhouse Masters, Assistant Overseers, and Poor Rate Collectors. Then there were the District Medical Officers. All these were directly responsible to the local boards of guardians, though the central authority had the power of defining their powers and duties, and even of dismissing them.

The duties of all these officials, from the Poor Law Board and from the Local Government Board downward, were until the end of the century the provision of relief in accordance with the Principles of 1834, as amended by practice and by the various Orders of the Central Authority. Relief, generally speaking, was to be given in the workhouse, except in the case of physical infirmity. In the workhouse the classes of paupers and the sexes were to be segregated, and the conditions of life were to be less favourable than those of able-bodied persons outside the workhouse.

Let us see what was happening to the men, women, and children whose problems were dealt with by this machinery. For a long time very little was known about this submerged section of the population. Although many of the inspectors did their work well, there was no major Report on the Poor Law between 1834 and the Royal Commission of 1905–9. It was then found that 14,000 children under sixteen were in the general mixed workhouse, that the large lunatic and idiot population mixed freely with the other inmates, including children and pregnant women, that infants, the sick, and the aged were looked after by fellow-paupers. Thus Crabbe's picture of the mixed workhouse of more than a century earlier was repeating itself. It was found that the number of children on out-relief on any one day varied between 200,000 and 300,000, that the sick formed about 30 per cent. of the total pauper population, that outdoor relief was not, as commonly alleged, given indiscriminately, but primarily to the sick, the aged, and the infirm, and to mothers with young children. But no one, not Poor Law Commissioners, Poor Law Board, or Local Government Board, had ever before 1906 inquired into the conditions of life of these people on out-relief—how they lived, what use they made of the relief money, the causes of their destitution, their need for medical attention.

A later generation has been able to build up a picture of what was happening both inside and outside the workhouse.

Babies and infants, a category scarcely noticed by contemporaries, were taken into the workhouse and separated from their mothers. About one-third of them died each year. These infants were often in the charge of nursing mothers, of the aged or the infirm. Sometimes the feeble-minded were set to care for the babies. One such was told to wash a baby. She did so in boiling water, and the child died.

At three or four years of age the children went to the workhouse school, or were farmed out to some professedly educational establishment, where the children were taken for a fixed sum per head. After a number of scandals concerned with illness, particularly cholera, fire, and general neglect, the farm school, which had been confined chiefly to the Metropolis, faded out, and from about 1838 onward larger unions, or groups of smaller unions, began to build their own Poor Law schools. The size of these buildings, the large numbers of children thus brought together, and their general appearance soon brought them the name of 'barrack schools.' Here as many as 2000 children would be herded together under inadequate supervision as to cleanliness, let alone health and education. The painful and often sight-destroying disease of ophthalmia was prevalent, and the disease was spread from child to child without any attempt at segregation. Often the children were permanently at school, for there was no provision for holidays, and in any case no place where they might go.

In the workhouse the title 'school' was a meaningless courtesy. Either it was looked after by another pauper—infirm, aged, often feeble-minded, and occasionally a lunatic—or, if an attempt were made to get a teacher for reading and writing, the salary offered was from £10 to £20 a year, no equipment was provided, the teacher had to live in the workhouse, and the children were expected to spend a considerable part of each day on domestic work. It was long before workhouse authorities would send their children to the public elementary schools. Even after 1870, when school attendance at five years old became compulsory, Poor Law authorities still maintained workhouse schools for their pauper children, on the grounds, presumably, that the parish child must be kept apart.

The aged and infirm, in accordance with the spirit of the 1834 Report, were often granted out-relief at the discretion of the guardians. But round about 1870 a stiffening of attitude, particularly by the inspectors, resulted in guardians being urged to 'offer the house' to their aged poor. For twenty years this hardening continued, but before the end of the century there was a change of spirit. There was a Royal Commission on the Aged Poor in 1895. Charles Booth and others advocated old-age pensions, which, after several Committees had considered the subject, were granted by the Old Age Pensions Act of 1908. Pensions of from 1s. to 5s. a week were given at seventy years of age, subject to a means test, but not subject to the stigma of poor relief. By the end of March 1909 there were already 500,000 old persons receiving old-age pensions. Similarly, about 1885, and especially from 1892 onward, there developed a more lenient policy towards the old in workhouses. Married couples over sixty were given a separate bedroom. They were allowed newspapers, books, tobacco, a little tea, and a better diet, to go for walks, to visit and be visited.

Thirty per cent. of the pauper population were sick people. This elementary statistical calculation was not made until the beginning of the twentieth century. One of the most surprising features in the development of Poor Law administration was, indeed, the continual failure to link destitution with public health. Chadwick had emphasized the need for cleanliness as the most effective method of reducing the poor rate, but the lack of inspection of out-relief paupers, the continued herding together of all kinds, ages, and conditions in the workhouse, was the expression of the refusal of those concerned to take Chadwick seriously. Sick paupers remained virtually uncared for—dirty, receiving but occasional medical visits, with no nurses to care for them, inadequate food, and scanty medicine ignorantly administered. The central authority never inquired after them, nor asked their numbers, and was interested in their ailments only when epidemics broke out.

The movement for reform was from the pauper population outward. An outbreak of infectious diseases in the sixties— diphtheria, typhus, and cholera, with many deaths—caused much alarm, and compelled attention to the sick paupers. Sir John Simon, who was then Medical Officer to the Privy Council, issued several reports by medical men on the condition of the Metropolitan workhouses. The provincial Press and Charles Dickens took the matter up. In 1864 William Rathbone sent a staff of trained nurses at his own expense into the Liverpool workhouse at Brownlow Street, where confirmed drunkards were known to be nursing, to show what could be done. Agnes Jones, who went as matron, died of fever contracted there while nursing. In 1865 the Treasury agreed to the appointment of a Medical Officer, who at once inspected the Metropolitan workhouses and infirmaries. Gradually the slovenly, ignorant, feeble-minded pauper nurse was replaced by a trained nurse in the sick-room, although not until 1897 was pauper nursing of the sick prohibited, and even then paupers acted as assistants. Sick-rooms and wards were cleaned and brightened; sometimes special buildings for the sick were erected. The workhouse infirmary was often the most efficient part of the workhouse. Where it was good its effect on the growth of a general medical service was profound, and deeply influenced the allied question of public health.

At the same time, from the view that sickness in paupers is dangerous to the rest of the population, there was developing the conception of prevention rather than cure, which meant a preventive medical service available to all the poorer classes. This was given official expression in the annual Report of the Poor Law Board for 1869–70, which discussed "how far it may be advisable, in a sanitary or social point of view, to extend gratuitous Medical Relief beyond the actual pauper class . . . to the poorer classes generally." In cases requiring isolation it became the definite policy to remove all the sick of small means to the infirmary. The use of the infirmary by all the sick poor soon followed, the stigma of pauperism fell from the infirmary, and it became the hospital of the poor. Bad cases of unreformed workhouse sick-wards nevertheless still remained. At the beginning of the twentieth century the feeble-minded could still be seen there helping to nurse the sick. But improvement was widespread and considerable. So began a reform of hospitals and a development of dispensary services in which, strangely enough, the workhouse led the way. Better inspectorate, trained nurses, improved or new buildings, transformed the workhouse infirmaries into what the Poor Law inspectors themselves began to call "State hospitals."

The Poor Law authorities were as unmindful of the lunatic as of the sick. There was no separate accommodation for those of infirm mind within the workhouse. County lunatic asylums were full; lunatics could be relieved outside the workhouse only when some one could look after them. The Lunacy Acts Amendment Act of 1862 therefore expressly authorized the creation of well and suitably equipped wards within the workhouse for the housing of the mentally unfit. No local authority, however, availed itself of the Act, and the Poor Law Board was never insistent. In 1904 a Royal Commission on Mental Deficiency recommended that all mental defectives should be removed from the Poor Law and dealt with by special authorities. But five years later Poor Law Commissioners reported on the "terrible sights" they had witnessed. "We have," they said,

> seen feeble-minded boys growing up in the Workhouse year after year untaught and untrained, alternately neglected and tormented by the other inmates, because it had not occurred to the Board of Guardians to send them to (and to pay for them at) a suitable institution. We have ourselves seen . . . idiots who are physically offensive or mischievous, or so noisy as to create a disturbance by day and by night with their howls, living in the ordinary wards. . . . We have seen imbeciles annoying the sane, and the sane tormenting the imbeciles. We have seen half-witted women nursing the sick, feeble-minded women in charge of the babies, and imbecile old men put to look after the boys out of school hours. We have seen expectant mothers, who have come in for their confinements, by day and by night working, eating and sleeping in close companionship with idiots and imbeciles of revolting habits and hideous appearance.[1]

Meantime what of the able-bodied? The successive trade fluctuations of the century and the increasing incidence of unemployment made seasonal out-relief in the big towns a matter of necessity. At such times 'offering the house' became meaningless, since 'the house' could not accommodate all the unemployed. To avoid giving out-relief too lightly the device of the labour yard was used. Out-relief was then given in return for a task of work performed in the labour yard attached to the workhouse. Sometimes the task was light. Generally it

---

[1] *Royal Commission on the Poor Laws and Relief of Distress*, Minority Report 1909, XXXVII, 894.

was heavy and monotonous work like wood-chopping, corn-grinding, oakum-picking, or, most commonly, stone-breaking. Flint, sandstone, and granite were in this way broken up for use on the roads.

To some men the labour task in return for a shilling or two a week was no bad proposition, and they came back again and again so that the labour yard became their place of employment. Many boards of guardians objected to this attitude, and the labour task was made increasingly hard and disagreeable. It was in the Poplar workhouse in the seventies that conditions became notorious. The Poplar guardians sent away their sick and infirm, their aged, and their young to neighbouring work-houses and themselves received the able-bodied men. It became a test put by magistrates for miles around to those requesting relief as to whether they would go to Poplar. Many weary men and women, asking for help, were made to walk several miles without rest or refreshment to Poplar. The men did various tasks of hard work. The women were put to oakum-picking. Seven days' to twelve months' imprisonment was the usual punishment for insubordination when an inmate was brought before a police magistrate. Solitary confinement or short diet was a constant punishment by the overseer. The result was inevitable. Somehow the numbers coming to Poplar decreased, to the satisfaction of the guardians, who thought their device of the separate task workhouse the solution to the pauper problem. But the numbers of sick, infirm, and aged grew, so that the Poplar guardians were compelled either to build fresh accommodation for these or to put them in the now emptying workhouse. They chose the latter course, with the result that the idea of segregation was abandoned and the Poplar experiment ended.

In the seventies unemployment and pauperism mounted. It became clear that Poor Law principles could no longer be separated from questions of trade fluctuations and seasonal employment. Socialist groups in the eighties were calling for the relief of the unemployed and for municipal and State enterprise to provide work. Joseph Chamberlain, as President of the Local Government Board, issued in 1886 a circular to local authorities calling for relief works for the unemployed. But, although there was considerable municipal activity, in terms of reducing unemployment it amounted to little. In the nineties Committees were reporting on Distress from Want of Employment. The Labour group in Parliament demanded relief. In the winter of 1904–5 there was a great increase in out-relief. The Unemployed Workmen Act of 1905 was intended to advance more municipal enterprise, but was no more successful than other municipal schemes. Poplar, in that bad winter, was compelled to give out-relief in kind to all able-bodied men who appeared genuinely unemployed. Poplar smarted under the feeling that it was financially responsible for so many of the unemployed through causes outside its control while other richer cities and districts, housing wealthier people, had few unemployed. The Poplar guardians accordingly repeated in 1905 their proposal of ten years earlier, that the burden of dealing with unemployment should be taken off the shoulders of particular unions and transferred to a central body.

At this time it was becoming abundantly clear that in respect of poor relief in its various aspects there was great confusion between the duties and functions of the various local authorities and the boards of guardians. A growing population and the multiplication of services required by modern society had inevitably brought about a reorganization of local government. The Local Government Act of 1888 created county councils, with powers similar to those of municipal corporations, thus giving the country powers commensurate with those of the town. In 1894 urban and rural district councils were created to take their share of the growing burden. But neither Act had superseded the boards of guardians, which continued to operate all their varied Poor Law functions side by side with the new organs, whose duties often overlapped with theirs, while the actual areas of administration were confusingly intertwined. Joseph Chamberlain, speaking on the Local Government Bill of 1888, put the case for the inclusion of Poor Law administration in the work to be given to the new county councils. "Otherwise," he said,

you will have a state of things anomalous in a high degree, which no one can look upon as permanent. You will have, on the one hand, thoroughly representative popular councils dealing with local government, sanitation, and other important matters, and their work would constantly increase—for, of course, there will be a tendency to throw all new work on the councils—and, on the other hand, you will have a body, elected by an anti-quated process, dealing with a considerable expenditure and an important branch of local administration.[1]

The county councils were not given Poor Law functions in 1888, and the boards of guardians stayed while unemployment continued and the unequal division of the burden remained. In these circumstances a Royal Commission was appointed in 1905 to examine the question of the Poor Law in all its aspects. The immediate cause of the appointment appeared to be alarm in responsible circles at the departure from the 'Principles' of 1834 which had been taking place. Less eligibility and the workhouse test had been gradually abandoned in face of growing unemployment, and a slowly dawning realization that harsh workhouse conditions could not make the sick well, the infirm agile, or the workless employed. The lot of the sick, the aged, and the infirm had been improved, unemployed men were given out-relief. At the same time the figures of pauperism —both absolute and compared with the population as a whole —had been rising since the beginning of the century, and in particular the number of adult men in the towns on poor relief was growing.

To re-enforce the principle of less eligibility J. S. Davy, the principal officer of the Poor Law Division, wanted the applicant for poor relief to suffer

firstly ... the loss of personal reputation (what is understood by the stigma of pauperism); secondly, the loss of personal freedom which is secured by detention in a workhouse; and thirdly, the loss of political freedom by suffering disfranchisement.[2]

When questioned by one of the Commissioners as to the disfranchisement of men out of work through no fault of their own, the Chief Inspector replied: "the unemployed man must stand by his accidents; he must suffer for the general good of the body politic." Davy favoured the able-bodied-test workhouse, where work "both irksome and unskilled" should be the test of relief. Not only the able-bodied but the sick and the children should also be subject to the principle of less eligibility. Conditions had become so agreeable for the old in the workhouse that saving for old age was discouraged; children's

---

[1] House of Commons, April 16, 1888 (Hansard, third series, cccxxiv, 1360).
[2] *Royal Commission on the Poor Laws and Relief of Distress*, Minutes of Evidence, 1909, XXXIX, Question 2230.

homes were so pleasant that they encouraged parents to send their children away; workhouse infirmaries were so efficient that they threatened the voluntary hospital system.

In the expansion of society Poor Law principles had become more and more closely intertwined with other social services, with education and the conditions of labour. But Davy had not yet realized that the emphasis had changed since the days of the famous Poor Law Report, when the object of society was to intimidate the pauper into not being a pauper. Now people were beginning to ask why he was a pauper. Among those who asked were some of the members of the Royal Commission of 1905–9 and their special investigators. What, they asked, was the effect of outdoor relief on wages and conditions of employment? What happened to those applicants for poor relief who were 'offered the house,' but who refused to enter the workhouse? It had occurred to some people that it might perhaps not be a matter of congratulation that a man had failed to pass the workhouse test. Miss G. Harlock, who carried out this investigation, reported that neither relatives nor charity organizations were able to deal with the situation, that even spasmodic gifts were few, that there was

> no evidence to show that the applicants themselves had been stimulated by the refusal of relief to greater personal efforts. On the contrary, the denial of assistance appeared to have discouraged and disheartened many whose energy might have been roused by wise guidance, accompanied by sufficient temporary aid to enable them to maintain physical efficiency. . . . In more than half of the cases the refusal of Out-Relief led to a gradual dispersal of the household furniture and wearing apparel, often not even excepting the most necessary clothing.[1]

When the *Report of the Poor Law Commission* was published in 1909 it was found that all but four of the Commissioners recommended the abandonment of the conception of a *deterrent* Poor Law and of the principle of less eligibility. The Poor Law, they said, must in future be "preventive and curative" of destitution, and should not merely "relieve" it. The old-age pensions, begun in 1908, were approved, the extension of free hospital and infirmary treatment was recommended, the removal of all mental defectives from the Poor Law and their care in special institutions was urged. For the young all the

[1] *Royal Commission on the Poor Laws and Relief of Distress*, Appendix, XXI, 60–61.

Commissioners advocated the extension of residential schools for the children of poor or bad parents, as well as for orphans, and the parallel development of the foster-parent or boarding-out system.

For able-bodied men an effort was made to treat the causes of unemployment as well as destitution itself. Government orders of various kinds should be smoothed out to help regularize trade; boys' employment in 'blind-alley' jobs should be reduced; there should be a universal provision of employment exchanges to bring work and workmen together, and an insurance system, to which the State, the employer, and the workman all contributed, should make 'out-of-work' pay available to the unemployed. Finally, it was recommended, there should be penal measures against those persons persistently refusing to work. As to administration, it was agreed that the boards of guardians should be abolished, together with the union areas and the general mixed workhouse. The county or the county borough council was recommended as the local authority.

In spite of this measure of agreement the Commissioners nevertheless issued a Majority and a Minority Report, each sympathetic to the poor yet showing a profoundly different approach to the subject. The Majority Commissioners wished to replace the Poor Law authority by a Public Assistance Division of the Local Government Board, alongside whom would work Voluntary Aid Committees—"knots of local philanthropists"—who would be given statutory recognition. It would be the duty of the Public Assistance Committee to deal with no application that could be dealt with equally well or better by the V.A.C.[1]

The Minority Commissioners summed up their findings thus:

> We have seen that it is not practicable to oust the various specialized Local Authorities that have grown up since the Boards of Guardians were established. There remains only the alternative . . . of completing the process of breaking up the Poor Law, which has been going on for the last three decades.[2]

Thus the children of school age would go to the Education Committee; the sick and permanently incapacitated, the

---

[1] *Report of the Royal Commission on the Poor Laws and Relief of Distress*, 1909, XXXVII, 520.
[2] Minority Report, 1909, XXXVII, 1007.

infants under school age, and the aged needing institutional care would go to the Health Committee; the mentally defective of all ages and grades to the Asylums Committee; the aged, to whom pensions were awarded, to the Pensions Committee. All these committees would function under county and county borough councils, who would work through Registrars of Public Assistance.

The only section of either Report that at first received favourable consideration by the Government was that for the establishment of labour exchanges. In 1905, under the Unemployed Workman Act, public labour exchanges had been formed alongside municipal schemes for absorbing the unemployed. The labour exchanges in London had had some success, and the Labour Exchanges Act of 1909 now established a national labour exchange, with a network of branches all over the country, with obvious advantages both to workmen and to employers. In two years the whole kingdom was covered. Well over a million vacancies were being filled annually in 1914, over a million and a half by 1927.[1]

Two years after the labour exchanges the Government introduced a scheme of unemployment insurance. It had been studying the health-insurance scheme sponsored by Lloyd George, and attached a similar partial measure of unemployment insurance to the Act which became law in 1911, thus implementing a second proposal of the Poor Law Commission.

Insurance against unemployment on such a scale was a remarkable innovation. Unemployment pay, covered or partly covered by contributions, had been undertaken by trade unions and by some Friendly Societies, but never, and in no country, had the attempt before been made by the State itself to insure compulsorily large numbers of workers against the accident of unemployment. The scheme was largely the work of two permanent civil servants at the Board of Trade—Sir William Beveridge and Sir Hubert Llewellyn Smith; it was sponsored first by Winston Churchill and then by Sydney Buxton, who had succeeded Churchill as President of the Board of Trade. As first applied in 1911, unemployment insurance was made compulsory on the masters and men in seven industries most subject to periodic unemployment, and covered about two and a quarter million workers. In the slump of 1912 the experiment

[1] S. and B. Webb, *English Poor Law History: The Last Hundred Years*, vol. ii, p. 663.

was extended, and again in 1916, by which time about three and three-quarter million workpeople were covered.

The Maclean Committee, appointed in 1918 to try to reconcile the views of the Majority and Minority Reports of 1909, again recommended the transfer of power from the boards of guardians. There the matter rested until 1928. The country then heard from the Minister of Health, Neville Chamberlain, of the confusion, waste, and inefficiency resulting from the continued existence of boards of guardians among other local authorities, their functions and areas of administration overlapping and cutting across one another. The Minister pointed out again that, while on the major local authorities devolved the duty of preventing and treating certain diseases like tuberculosis, of caring for the lunatic and the mentally deficient, of organizing the great maternity and child-welfare services, yet every one of these things had to be dealt with also by the guardians in the discharge of their duties. There existed as a consequence the "remarkable and paradoxical circumstance" that the question of whether a person should receive treatment at the hands of the county borough or the county council, or whether he should receive it under the Poor Law from the guardians, depended not upon the nature or need of his infirmities, but merely upon whether he was destitute or not.

While Poor Law duties were thus confused the burden of paying for their services was as unevenly spread as when Poplar had complained at the end of the nineteenth century. Poor Law charges in 1928 varied in the county boroughs from 5d. in the pound at Blackpool to 10s. 5d. in the pound at Gateshead; in rural unions from 2½d. in the pound at Howden to 5s. 4½d. in the pound at Pontardawe; within the same county they varied so that in Brecon 11¼d. in the pound was the rate at Brecon Union and 7s. 0½d. at Crickhowell.[1]

Finally, in 1928 the mixed workhouse still remained, with all its sordid misery. An institution taken at random was then found to contain seven acutely sick persons, fifty-five infirm and senile persons, six epileptics, eight certified lunatics, eighteen certified mental deficients, nine uncertified mental deficients, one able-bodied man, and three healthy infants.[2]

The Local Government Act of 1929 at last, nearly a hundred

[1] Hansard, Fifth Series, 1928–29, 223, 71.   [2] Ibid., 223, 74.

years after their creation, abolished the boards of guardians, and gave to the councils powers to deal with all destitute persons, either under the Poor Law or under a number of special Acts which they might adopt. In moving the Bill that superseded the guardians, long after it had become clear that their presence was a hindrance rather than a help in administering the social services, the Minister of Health paid tribute to the unpaid men and women who had given their time and energy to serve as guardians of the poor. Many were hard-working, intelligent, and public-spirited, with strong social consciences, anxious to help the distressed. It was not so much the men and women who had served as guardians who needed replacing, but the obsolete machinery through which they worked.

Unemployment insurance meantime was growing of its own momentum, but it was not until the depression following the First World War that a comprehensive Act was passed. Whereas in 1914 two and a half million workers were insured, the Unemployment Insurance Acts of 1920 and 1927 extended the scope of insurance to over twelve million workers. By 1940 the scheme had been extended to all manual workers and to non-manual workers receiving up to £420 a year, and there was a special scheme for agricultural workers. Under the provisions of the Acts workers, employers, and the State each paid contributions to an Unemployment Insurance Fund. Unemployment pay was normally made after not less than four weeks' contributions had been made. In times of low unemployment the Unemployment Insurance Fund accumulated a surplus, in bad times it borrowed from the Treasury. In 1917 a special Ministry of Labour had been set up to deal with the able-bodied unemployed, and it was this Ministry which administered the Fund. The numbers insured against unemployment in Great Britain rose to over fifteen million in 1938.

In 1930 a comprehensive Act was passed consolidating existing Acts concerning the relief of the poor. The aged and impotent could be accepted into the workhouse. Out-relief could be granted in cases of sudden calamity or, in return for a task of work, to able-bodied men when the workhouse was full. Children whose parents were unable to keep and maintain them should be set to work or apprenticed. Local authorities were empowered to send Poor Law children to school, and to take over the rights and powers of a parent in cases where the child's own parents were deemed unfit.

In the Second World War unemployment was eliminated, the vagrants fell to infinitesimal numbers, even the numbers of the aged and infirm on Poor Law relief fell. But during the War attention was focused on the case of Denis O'Neill, a little boy who was boarded out with foster-parents and treated so brutally that he died. In response to indignant inquiries a Parliamentary Committee was appointed in March 1945

> to inquire into existing methods of providing for children who from loss of parents or from any cause whatever are deprived of a normal home life with their own parents or relatives.

The widespread evacuation of children from danger areas, the loss of parents and homes during the War, added a special interest to the Curtis Report which was published in September 1946.

The first impression on reading the Report is that it was published fifty, or even a hundred years ago, and slipped into the wrong cover. The idiot is there in the workhouse with the normal children. So are the senile old men, the adults of questionable habits, the pregnant and nursing mothers confined with the sick and infirm. Drabness and dirt, barrack-like buildings, inadequate and harassed staff, scanty inspection, little action by higher authority even after the report of bad conditions, remain. The Care of Children Committee found

> one century-old Poor Law institution providing accommodation for 170 adults, including ordinary workhouse accommodation, an infirmary for senile old people and a few men and women certified as either mentally defective or mentally disordered. In this institution there were twenty-seven children, aged six months to fifteen years. Twelve infants up to the age of eighteen months were the children of women in the institution, about half of them still being nursed by their mothers. In the same room in which these children were being cared for was a Mongol Idiot, aged four, of gross appearance, for whom there was apparently no accommodation elsewhere. A family of five normal children, aged about six to fifteen, who had been admitted on a relieving officer's order, had been in the institution for ten weeks. This family, including a boy of ten and a girl of fifteen, were sleeping

in the same room as a three-year-old hydrocephalic idiot, of very unsightly type, whose bed was screened off in a corner.[1]

Workhouses, cottage homes, 'barrack' homes, institutions of various kinds assisted by public subscription and State donation, were all, with few exceptions, open to severe criticism. Standing apart were a group of homes not subject to inspection. These were maintained by independent funds, not by public subscription. The ordinary powers of the Home Office and the Ministry of Health stopped short of these homes. Until 1944 even the Ministry of Education had no right to inspect a school maintained on such premises. But even where inspection was the accepted rule it was infrequent, often haphazard. There might be a gap of many years between workhouse inspections. Recommendations and criticism were not followed up. There was a similar story concerning homes where children were boarded out. Visitors were clerks from the local office or other untrained officials, or voluntary workers equally untrained. Visits were irregular and infrequent as well as often perfunctory. On top of all this was the confusion of central authorities, the Ministry of Health and the Home Office in particular often duplicating orders, or each refraining from giving any orders at all. Both these departments, for example, had issued boarding-out rules which were not identical but which both had the force of law, one set under the Poor Law Act of 1930, the other under the Children and Young Persons Act of 1933.

In a chapter headed Poor Law, starting from 1848 when the Poor Law Board was reorganized and finishing at the present day, it has been necessary to speak as much of sickness and unemployment and their treatment as of pauperism and the Poor Law. The very term 'pauper' becomes less used as the story advances. A person is 'unemployed,' 'sick,' 'homeless,' rather than a pauper. In short, the term used describes the reason for his destitution as well as just recording his condition. This is significant of the course that has been run. The modern world is concerned more with finding the cause of a person's distress and less with blaming him for becoming dependent upon society. Nevertheless the cumbersome machinery of modern government has left pockets of ugly distress like those

[1] *Report of the Care of Children Committee*, 1946, Cmd. 6922, 38–39.

revealed by the Curtis Report, while at the same time economic development produces cyclical unemployment, and with it a problem of helping the destitute far vaster than has been dealt with by previous generations.

The Second World War brought to a head the growing feeling that social distress of all kinds must be a State responsibility. The War was fought to ensure freedom. Freedom was something positive as well as mere freedom from restraint, and must be given content by the State.

> What art thou, Freedom? Thou art bread
> And a comely table spread. Thou art clothes and fire and food
> To the trampled multitude.

Or, as it was expressed by Sir William Beveridge, man required Five Freedoms—Freedom from Want, from Disease, from Ignorance, Squalor, and Idleness. For their attainment a policy was outlined by Sir William Beveridge in a Report on *Social Insurance and Allied Services* published in 1942. Health, Housing, and Education services, backed by advances in medicine, town-planning, and teaching, would give much of the desired freedom. Beveridge pointed the way to Freedom from Want in underlining what had been shown by various surveys which had been made between the Wars of conditions of life in some of the great towns, including London, York, Bristol, Liverpool, Plymouth, Southampton, and Sheffield.

> Of all the want shown by the surveys, from three-quarters to five-sixths, according to the precise standard chosen for want, was due to interruption or loss of earning power. Practically the whole of the remaining one-quarter to one-sixth was due to failure to relate income during earning to the size of the family.

The conclusion was therefore that the "abolition of want requires a double re-distribution of income, through social insurance and by family needs."[1] In the first case, to

> prevent interruption or destruction of earning power from leading to want, it is necessary to improve the present schemes of social insurance in three directions: by extension of scope to cover persons now excluded, by extension of purposes to cover risks now excluded, and by raising the rates of benefit.[2]

In the second case some kind of family allowances were necessary.

[1] Sir W. Beveridge, *Social Insurance and Allied Services*, 1942, p. 7.   [2] *Ibid.*, p. 7.

The nation had the resources to end this want. The plan advanced by Beveridge to utilize them was summarized by himself as "all-embracing in scope of persons and of needs," but "classified in application."[1] His six classes covered employees and employers, traders, independent workers, housewives, children and the old, and those who, though of working age, were not gainfully employed. Various benefits and pensions were to ensure all against want, all were to be covered for medical treatment and for rehabilitation after the War. There was to be no stigma of pauperism about the pensions and allowances, for all were to contribute. For the first time social insurance was to be universal and compulsory, administered by a Ministry of National Insurance.

The Beveridge Report was given much publicity and greeted with great enthusiasm. In June 1945 the Coalition Government introduced a system of family allowances. In July the Liberals fought the 1945 General Election largely on the Beveridge Plan. The Labour Government was pledged to carry into effect many of its provisions, and did in fact do so. The old-age pension was raised to 26s. a week. Contributions to social insurance were extended to cover self-employed workers. By July 1948 nearly two million self-employed workers ranging, as *The Times* put it, "from street-hawkers, hedgers, and chimney-sweeps to doctors, company directors, and, apparently, Members of Parliament" had become "comprehensively insured for the first time."[2] A State Medical Service came into operation in 1948. Finally, a National Assistance Act in the same year completed the main pattern of the new social legislation.

This Act not only completed the process of breaking up the Poor Law, as the Minority Commissioners of 1909 advocated, but wiped it out completely, thus, as *The Times* said, winding up half a millennium of English social history.[3] On the one hand, it took from the local authorities all responsibility for the outdoor relief of destitution and made this a function of national government. On the other hand, it gave to the local authorities the important new function of providing residential accommodation for the aged, the infirm, and others who required care and attention in this way. A charge on local rates with Exchequer assistance met this service. It was emphasized that

---

[1] *Ibid.*, p. 9. [2] *The Times*, November 6, 1947. [3] *Ibid.*, November 1, 1947.

it was not concerned with the relief of destitution—this being the function of the central government—but with making comfortable homes for certain classes of persons who would contribute from their old-age pensions or other sources of income according to their ability. "The measure," said *The Times*,

embodies a simple, logical, and civilized conception of the assistance and welfare services required to complete the comprehensive social security system . . . introduced.[1]

For the first time the problems of sickness, old age, unemployment, health, housing, and destitution had been viewed as a whole. It was clear that there had come into operation, in fact if not in name, a Ministry of Social Security fulfilling more completely than they had ever hoped the dream of Chadwick and the Benthamites.

[1] *Ibid.*, November 1, 1947.

SELECT BIBLIOGRAPHY

Report of the Royal Commission on the Poor Laws and Relief of Distress: especially 1909, XXXVII, containing Majority and Minority Reports.

Social Insurance and Allied Services: Report by Sir William Beveridge, 1942 (Cmd. 6404).

Report of the Care of Children Committee (the Curtis Report), 1946 (Cmd. 6922).

Old People: Report of a Survey Committee on the Problems of Ageing and the Care of Old People (Nuffield Foundation: Oxford University Press, 1947).

WEBB, S. AND B.: *English Poor Law History: The Last Hundred Years*, (Longmans, 1929), vols. i and ii.

CHAPTER XXIV

EDUCATION

(a) THE PUBLIC EDUCATION SYSTEM, 1851-1902

In 1857 a Conference on Elementary Education, presided over by no less a person than the Prince Consort, dispelled any complacency which ignorance of the condition of elementary education might have encouraged. It then appeared that only 2,000,000 children were at any kind of elementary school, and that of these nearly 50 per cent. attended for less than a year. At the same time the Government Inspectors, whose number was increased to twenty-one in 1850, were doing their work with zeal. The Reports which they issued, the increasing public expenditure on education, which by 1851 had risen to £150,000, combined with the figures of the Prince Consort's Conference to cause the appointment of a Royal Commission in 1858, under the chairmanship of the Duke of Newcastle, to consider "the extension of sound and cheap elementary instruction to all classes of the people." These terms of reference indicate the advance which had been made in the attitude towards education. The need is admitted. The expenditure of public money is recognized. What is required is that the need shall be met by "sound" instruction and that expenditure shall be practised with economy.

The Newcastle Commission sent ten Assistant Commissioners to representative sections of the country—agricultural, manufacturing, mining, maritime, and metropolitan areas. It also sent questionnaires to practical educationists, examined many witnesses, and collected statistics from education societies, public departments, and private and endowed schools. The result, while by no means a complete survey, gave a general picture of considerable value.

The evidence before the Commission revealed that about one person in eight of the population was at school. This figure compared satisfactorily with the proportions in France and Austria (where a compulsory State system of education was in operation), and showed an increase from the 1818 figure of 1 in 17 at school. But of the number of children at school nearly a quarter were at private schools, which the Commission classed as "ill-calculated to give to the children an education which shall be serviceable to them in after-life." Of the remainder at elementary day schools, over 80 per cent. left before reaching the age of twelve, and did not receive therefore an adequate amount of education. More than half attended school for less than a hundred days in the year, while inefficient teaching retarded the progress of even the more regular scholars.[1]

It was a moderate enough standard of learning which the Newcastle Commissioners required. They asked that a child should be able to spell ordinary words correctly, to write a letter that was legible and intelligible, to make out or check a common bill, to have sufficient geographical knowledge to know the position of the countries of the world; above all, to be sufficiently acquainted with the Scriptures "to follow the allusion and arguments of a plain Saxon Sermon." Yet two-thirds to three-quarters of the children at school left without attaining this standard, and afterwards relapsed "almost entirely into the condition of the uneducated." This was in the heyday of 'Victorian Prosperity,' twenty-four years after the accession of Queen Victoria, ten years after the Great Exhibition, and thirteen years after Chartism's final flare-up.

Faced with this grave deficiency in the quantity and quality of education provided, the Newcastle Commission nevertheless declared a universal compulsory system of education "to be neither attainable nor desirable." Instead they wished to incorporate into the existing system two important changes. They wanted part of the cost of education transferred from the taxes to the local rates; and they wanted to distribute all public grants for education on the principle which became known as "payment by results." The suggestion of rate-aid for education was not new, but as always before met with hostility, and was not adopted. The system of payment by results was approved by the Committee of Council and Parliament and embodied in the Revised Code of 1862.

Under the Revised Code teachers were to receive payment from management committees, and not from the Education Department, the amount paid being dependent upon the

[1] *Report of the Royal Commission appointed to inquire into the State of Popular Education in England*, 1861, XXI, Part I, 293–294.

attendance of pupils and their individual success in passing an examination in the three R's. The test was to be given by specially appointed visiting examiners, who were to conduct a one-day examination. This uncongenial invention, smacking of factory piece-work, became law under the auspices of Robert Lowe, Vice-President of the Council, who has been described as applying Darwin's theory of the survival of the fittest to educational practice, and who urged the Code upon the House of Commons in these words:

> I cannot promise the House that this system will be an economical one, and I cannot promise that it will be an efficient one, but I can promise that it shall be one or the other. If it is not cheap, it shall be efficient; if it is not efficient it shall be cheap.[1]

In the same speech Lowe specified that the State still regarded education as a means of keeping the poor "in their stations." Education was not to be the ladder to success, but the guy-rope to tie the child to its station. "We do not profess," said Lowe,

> to give these children an education that will raise them above their station and business in life—that is not our object—but to give them an education that may fit them for that business.[2]

Payment by results was widely condemned both before the Code became law and afterwards. In practice it succeeded in fulfilling the promise of economy, for the annual grant for education fell by £176,000 between 1861 and 1865—from £813,000 to £637,000.[3] Efficient it certainly was not. The system in operation before the Code of 1862 favoured the bright child at the expense of the dull; this one penalized the bright child while teachers laboured to bring the slower ones up to the required grant-earning standard in the three R's. Teachers themselves declared that the method of 'pricing' subjects provided a stimulus not to good teaching, but to 'cram.' "The Code drives the teacher, and the teacher must then drive the child," as one teacher put it. The system was bad not only for the children. Teachers became demoralized. The profession was debased by the kind of question asked by appointment boards: "What percentage have you passed?"

---

[1] February 13, 1862 (Hansard, third series, clxv, 229).   [2] *Ibid.*, clxv, 238.
[3] *Final Report of the Royal Commission appointed to inquire into the Elementary Education Acts (England and Wales)* (the Cross Commission), 1888, XXXV, 18.

and by the devices which many of them in sheer self-defence adopted, such as sending round examination questions from school to school, shipping dull or backward children to some other school on examination days so as to avoid bringing down their percentage of passes; and marking up absent scholars in order to improve their attendance figures. Managers of schools mostly disliked 'payment by results' because it gave no incentive to attendance beyond the age of eleven, that being the age at which grants ceased. Inspectors condemned it; they noted how rapidly children lost the learning that had been crammed into them, and reported, what was fairly obvious, that the system threatened to destroy the love of knowledge for its own sake. Religious bodies objected to it because religion was not a grant-earning subject, and because Bible lessons were often diverted to last-minute cramming in the three R's.

The system of payment by results nevertheless lasted for thirty years. The reasons for the continuance of a system whose weaknesses were so obvious can be found partly in the fact that it reflected the outlook of the age. In 1862, when he promised cheapness or efficiency, Robert Lowe was promising for education what industry had already achieved, and it was not unnatural that an industrial age should apply to education its own formula for success. In the industrial world success was measured by money, and money was too often the sole incentive to effort. To those whose mental horizons were bounded by such standards there could be no recipe for efficient education save that which embodied the principle of industrial success. Translated, that principle was payment by results.

The principle had in addition, however, the reluctant and partial support of a Government Commission which examined the effects of the system more than twenty years after its inception. The Cross Commission, which reported in 1888, exposed very fully the evils of the system of payment by results. Yet while the Minority Report condemned it wholeheartedly, the Majority, while concluding that the system was carried too far and was too rigidly applied, were convinced that the distribution of the Parliamentary grant could not be wholly freed from dependence on the results of examination. They thererore recommended that the fixed grant for each child in average attendance should be increased, while the variable grant should depend on the good character of the school and the quality of the acquirements of the majority rather than the exact number of passes in the three R's. The Code of 1890 reflected these variations, and payment by results in its worst form was ended. By 1900 the system was ended entirely, and inspection by Government inspectors had replaced grant-earning examinations.

The Report of the Newcastle Commission gave rise to loud factional controversies. On the one hand, the National Education League, founded in 1869 in Birmingham, spoke for those who wanted universal, free, unsectarian compulsory education —the complete Radical formula. It believed the voluntary system to be inadequate, and called on the Government to provide and maintain out of the rates and taxes sufficient schools for the whole population. The National Education Union, formed in 1869 in Manchester, believed, on the other hand, in the denominational system, and urged that the Government should supplement and not supersede it. It was amid the considerable clamour caused by the propaganda of these societies that William Edward Forster, Vice-President of the Council, introduced in 1870 a new Education Bill, which became law only after long and heated debates.

The Act of 1870 was avowedly a compromise. The need for increased education was generally admitted, and in endeavouring to supply it Forster frankly attempted to make the best of the two agents—the national and the voluntary. "Our object," he said in introducing the Bill, "is to complete the present voluntary system, to fill up gaps . . . not to destroy the existing system in introducing a new one."[1]

The Act divided the country into school districts, the units being boroughs, parishes, or groups of parishes, and London being a unit on its own. The first principle of the Act was that in each of these districts there should be school accommodation adequate for the population. Existing—that is, voluntary or denominational—schools were the first source of supply. Where, after a given period of time, this source proved inadequate, the Education Department could call for the election by the ratepayers of a school board. The school board was empowered to build new schools, or otherwise provide school accommodation, and to compel attendance where it thought fit. In order that

[1] House of Commons, February 17, 1870 (Hansard, third series, cxcix, 443-444)

children of all religious views might attend the board schools a clause proposed by Mr Cowper-Temple was incorporated in the Act. This laid down that such schools should exclude from their teaching any "catechism or religious formulary distinctive of any particular denomination." The board schools were to be aided by grants from local rates as well as from the Education Department. In this way they had the advantage over the voluntary schools, which would receive no local assistance. Voluntary schools were to continue to receive Exchequer aid, but in order to do so had to introduce a time-table conscience clause. This stipulated that doctrinal lessons should be given either at the beginning or end of a particular school session, so that those who wished might absent themselves with as little disturbance as possible. The form of the grant was also altered; the building grant was to be abolished within a specified time and an increased grant for maintenance substituted.

The principle of universal free education was not incorporated in the Bill on the grounds that parents had a duty to their children which the State should not encourage them to neglect. But in cases of proved necessity school fees were remitted. Nor was the principle of compulsion incorporated in the Bill, though Matthew Arnold had asserted nearly twenty years earlier that education would never, any more than vaccination, become universal in this country until it was made compulsory.[1] Instead it was left to the discretion of the school boards to compel attendance where they thought fit.

The principles of the Bill which occasioned most discussion were those of rate-aid for education, the permissive compulsion to attendance granted to the school boards, the insistence on unsectarian teaching in board schools, and the time-table conscience clause in denominational schools.

Round the religious clauses, in particular, the debates turned for hours. Many were alarmed at the power for good or ill which the insistence on the omission of any denominational interpretation of the Bible would give to the schoolmaster. Hear Disraeli:

> You are contemplating the establishment of a class who must be endowed with great abilities, and who certainly will have to perform most important functions and to exercise great powers.

[1] *Reports on Elementary Schools*, 1853, p. 27.

. . . You will not intrust the priest or the presbyter with the privilege of expounding the Holy Scriptures to the scholars; but for that purpose you are inventing and establishing a new sacerdotal class . . . which will . . . exercise an extraordinary influence upon the history of England and upon the conduct of Englishmen.[1]

There was some evidence, however, that the religious difficulty was more a debating than a real issue. A conference of schoolmasters which assembled while the debate was taking place believed it was so. In the House of Commons schoolmasters and a clergyman were instanced who from their own practical experience asserted that a conscience clause worked smoothly and unobtrusively in their schools.

In the long debates on the Bill of 1870 the speeches reveal a temper far different from that of the early part of the century. The desirability of universal education and the use of public money to effect it are generally recognized. We approach the question of education, said Forster in moving the Bill,

with the hope of doing great good, by removing that ignorance which we are all aware is pregnant with crime and misery, with misfortune to individuals, and danger to the community.[2]

While the attitude of leading educationists had mellowed, many of the particular reasons for urging educational reform remained. Forster and Mundella argued that it was no use trying to give technical teaching to our artisans without elementary education, and without technical training they would be "overmatched in the competition of the world." It was also important that three years previously the second Reform Act had extended the franchise. As Forster remarked, "Now that we have given them political power we must not wait any longer to give them education."[3]

There were obvious weaknesses in the Act of 1870. It was a compromise through and through. The Act failed to establish a national system of education, yet, while sanctioning the existence of the voluntary schools, it weighted the scales against them. It left the system of payment by results. It applied no direct compulsion to school attendance, yet gave this weapon to school boards to use at their discretion. It laid down no mini-

---

[1] House of Commons, June 16, 1870 (Hansard, third series, ccii, 289).
[2] House of Commons, February 17, 1870 (Hansard, third series, cxcix, 438).
[3] *Ibid.*, cxcix, 465.

THE CRINOLINE, 1855

From "Early Victorian England," edited by G. M. Young
by courtesy of Oxford University Press

DRESS OF THE NINETIES

mum number of attendances expected from each child, but left the number to be decided by the school board. It did not approve free education, yet gave school boards the power of remitting fees in cases which appeared to them necessitous. There were to be, complained Professor Fawcett, "permissive compulsion, permissive school aid, and permissive time."[1]

In respect of compulsory attendance it was indeed impossible for the 1870 Act to be definitive, for there were not schools enough for the whole population of school age. Of a population of over twenty-two million, estimating one-sixth as of school age, over three and a half million required schooling, whereas there was accommodation for only 1,878,000. Six years later, in a population of over twenty-four million, the number of school places had been increased to nearly three and a half million—a higher proportion, though not yet reaching the required one-sixth. By 1886 the target had been passed. There were then over five million school places for a population of nearly twenty-eight million.[2]

By this time Sandon's Act of 1876 and Mundella's Act of 1880 had made compulsory the school attendance of children under thirteen. Sandon's Act was notable in declaring, for the first time, that it was the duty of every parent of a child between five and thirteen, subject to penalty, "to cause such child to receive efficient elementary instruction in reading, writing, and arithmetic." The enforcement of the Act was, however, for the most part indirect and unsatisfactory, being directed at the employer and not the parent. No employer, under penalty not exceeding 40s., was to take into employment a child under ten or a child between ten and thirteen who had not reached a specified proficiency in the three R's. To provide for the child who could not learn, the device of the "dunce's pass" allowed a child between ten and thirteen to be employed if it could produce a certificate of regular school attendance for a specified time previously.

So·the optional compulsion of 1870 became the indirect compulsion of 1876. Both proving ineffective, universal, direct compulsion was for the first time applied in the Act of 1880. Mundella's Act did not repeal the indirect provision of Sandon's Act, but it converted what had, under the Act of 1870, been an

[1] House of Commons, July 11, 1870 (Hansard, third series, cciii, 59).
[2] Report of the Privy Council on Education for 1886, 1887, XXVIII, ix.

option on the part of school boards to enforce the attendance of children at school into an obligation. Henceforth it was the duty of every school board to get to school all its children of school age. Six years later nearly all the children who ought to be there were on the registers of the elementary schools. But this was not always the same as being in regular attendance. Fewer than three and a half million were in average attendance in 1886, when there were four and a half million on the registers and there was accommodation for over five million scholars.[1] There were then still many thousands of children over five who had "never been inside a schoolroom."[2]

The reasons attendance fell "lamentably short" of provision of school places were partly the uneven distribution of schools, partly the continued growth of certain areas and the failure of school boards to keep up with the growing requirements of an expanding population. The chief reason for the discrepancy between numbers on the register and in attendance was the continued evasion by parents of the "school-board man" whenever there was money to be earned by their children.

After 1870 educational administration occupied a larger part of the picture than before. Although circumstances had compelled the State to take a more direct interest in education, it could not overcome its reluctance firmly to incorporate the voluntary system within its own. This led to a confusion after 1870 which became worse before it got better. The growth of State responsibility for education was of two kinds—legislative and administrative. But, instead of the legislature's laying down a policy which the administration put into operation, it was frequently in the administering bodies—the school boards in particular—that policy originated. If policy is to be uniform, it must originate from one body; the well-meaning activity of the various local administrative groups added further variety and confusion to the already tangled development of educational policy and practice.

In 1886 a Royal Commission under Sir Richard Cross was appointed to consider the working of the 1870 Act. It reported two years later. Its general conclusion was that the existing expenditure on education did not receive commensurate results. The legacy of the monitorial system remained in over-emphasis

[1] *Ibid.*, XXVIII, vii–viii.
[2] Report by Mr. Blakiston on the North-east Division of England for 1887, *Ibid.*, XXVIII, 262–263; and other Inspectors' Reports.

on the spelling lesson and insufficient opportunity through new books and school libraries to acquire fluency in reading. The Cross Commission made many suggestions for essential and optional subjects, some of which were already being embodied in the New Code of 1887. Under this Code reading, writing, arithmetic, and, for girls, needlework were compulsory subjects. Optional class subjects throughout the school were singing, English, geography, history, and elementary science. In the upper classes individual children might also take any of several specific subjects, including mathematics of various kinds, chemistry, physics, Latin, and French.[1]

The 1870 Act had been concerned entirely with elementary education, with getting children to school and wiping out illiteracy. Subsequently the needs of children who did well in the elementary schools, or whose parents were ambitious for them, led to the development of what was a distinctly higher type of elementary education in the upper classes of elementary schools. The school boards introduced new subjects and extended old, and founded a new advanced standard in their schools—the seventh—for which they obtained a Parliamentary grant. Later they set up "ex-standard classes," and even new schools for advanced children where history, grammar, French, mathematics, and physical science were taught. It was thus that the school boards began to provide what was virtually a secondary education within the elementary-school ambit. At the same time instruction was being given in evening classes to older children who had left school. The teaching thus given was tending to become more scientific and practical. From early days British educationists had urged increased technical efficiency as one of the reasons for extending educational opportunity, and the Science and Art Department, founded after the Great Exhibition, had sponsored classes in technical subjects. In 1867 complacent British manufacturers had been brought up sharply by Dr Lyon Playfair's letter to the Schools Inquiry Commission calling attention to the technical advance of our foreign competitors, as demonstrated by the Paris Exhibition of that year. There followed Select Committees of the House of Commons to investigate the matter, and finally a Royal Commission on Technical Instruction which was appointed in

[1] *Report of the Committee of Council on Education, 1886–87*, 1887, XXVIII, 119–120.

1881 and reported from 1882 to 1884. Its description of the technical high schools, the classes for artisans, the schools of arts and crafts, the museums and public galleries of the Continent—all provided at State expense—caused British manufacturers and educationists to pay serious attention to the recommendations of the Report. These included the extension of drawing lessons from models and casts in all elementary schools, and the encouragement of handwork in wood and iron; for country children a compulsory course in the principles and practice of agriculture; the establishment of free technical classes for artisans, and of technical schools and colleges of secondary standing; and the opening of art galleries and museums on Sundays for the benefit of working-men and their families. But the law gave no help to technical education until the Technical Instruction Act of 1889 authorized the levy of a penny rate to aid technical education under the supervision of the Science and Art Department. The following year certain money which had been intended for compensation to publicans whose licences had not been renewed—'whisky money'—was given instead to local authorities to use at their discretion either in relief of rates or for technical education. Various schools, institutes, polytechnics, and colleges in this way received aid towards technical instruction; but the instruction given was scientific rather than technical, intellectual rather than manual; and in any case the Technical Instruction Act had excluded public elementary schools from aid. So instead of the general technical education required by the Royal Commission there developed a special form of scientific secondary education to add to the general confusion of the educational system.

It was characteristic of English educational development not only that its secondary education grew without form or plan, but that in 1894 a Royal Commission was appointed to find out what had been happening. This Commission, under Sir James Bryce, found five separate authorities connected with secondary education in England. There were the Charity Commissioners, the Science and Art Department, the Education Department, the Board of Agriculture, the local authorities. Each one of these had been

called into being, not merely independently of the others, but with little or no regard to their existence. Each had remained in its working isolated and unconnected with the rest.

"The problems which Secondary Education presents," they reported,

> have been approached from different sides, at different times, and with different views and aims. . . . This isolation and this independence, if they may seem to witness to the rich variety of our educational life, and to the active spirit which pervades it, will nevertheless prepare the observer to expect the usual results of dispersed and unconnected forces, needless competition between the different agencies, and a frequent overlapping of effort, with much consequent waste of money, of time, and of labour.[1]

The Commission recommended the reduction of the five Authorities for secondary education to two—a central authority to concentrate the powers and duties of the existing authorities for secondary education, which would have little direct executive power, but be "stimulative and helpful"; and local authorities, who would have large powers of supervision but little coercive control, and who would utilize to the utmost private and proprietary schools, in order not to make secondary education a purely State affair. In accordance with its terms of reference, these recommendations covered secondary education only. Nevertheless the Commissioners had covered much general ground, and they urged that the central authority should be headed by an Education Minister who would be responsible for both elementary and secondary education. They did, in effect, advocate a central authority for public education in England.

In 1899 effect was given to this idea by the creation of the Board of Education, which was formed by amalgamating the Science and Art Department and the Education Department. But shortly afterwards the confusion into which the whole educational system had fallen was demonstrated by the Cockerton Judgment. Mr Cockerton was a district auditor of the Local Government Board, and at the instance of a school of art he brought a case at law against the school boards for teaching certain branches of science and art and for instructing adults. The Judgment of 1900, upheld in 1901, was against the school boards and for Cockerton. It asserted that the school boards were acting contrary to their powers in undertaking any teaching other than the strictly elementary. Any secondary instruction by the school boards was *ultra vires*. One of

---

[1] *Report of the Royal Commission on Secondary Education*, 1895, XLIII, 17–18.

the most useful branches of education thus being lopped off, confusion was worse confounded. In these circumstances Arthur Balfour steered into law the Education Act of 1902.

In administration the Act was distinctly an advance. School boards were abolished. County boroughs and county councils became the local education authorities, London again remaining a separate unit. In most cases the county borough or the county council was responsible for both elementary and secondary education within its area; but in districts of a certain size the borough council or district council was enabled to take powers for elementary education. In such cases there was a regrettable division of authority in the direction of the educational process. The actual work was to be done by education committees, which were to include members elected from the council and others co-opted to serve because of their special qualifications. In accordance with the sentiment both of the Cross and Bryce Commissions, the Act of 1902 extended rate-aid to the voluntary schools. Henceforth maintenance and the payment of teachers in both "provided" (State) and "non-provided" (voluntary) schools were to be met by the local education authority. The non-provided schools were allowed to teach their religious creeds subject to the operation of a time-table conscience clause, but their secular teaching was within L.E.A. control: on their boards of management representatives of the L.E.A. were to sit; while the appointment and dismissal of their teachers became subject to the consent of the L.E.A., on the understanding that it would be withheld only on educational and not on religious grounds.

The Act of 1902 put upon the local education authority the duty of training teachers. The status, payment, and training of teachers was still little better than when Kay-Shuttleworth had written in the middle of the century:

> There is little or nothing in the profession of an elementary schoolmaster, in this country, to tempt a man having a respectable acquaintance with the elements of even humble learning to exchange the certainty of a respectable livelihood in a subordinate condition in trade or commerce, for the mean drudgery of instructing the rude children of the poor in an elementary school.[1]

[1] Sir James Kay-Shuttleworth, *Four Periods of Public Education* (1862 edition), p. 474.

Training colleges for intending teachers had been instituted by 1860, and were later supplemented by Pupil Teacher Centres for special training. But until pupil teachers could be relieved of the pressure of school duties they could study only in the evening. When in the later eighties the actual teaching hours of pupil teachers were reduced by half so that they had time during the day to pursue their studies the first real step in teachers' training was made.

The second forward step was taken by the institution of day training colleges attached to the universities. By 1886 many teachers were taking the teachers' certificate by examination, but fewer than half of those employed had been through a training college. This weakness was overcome by the institution of colleges which were for day students, as opposed to the residential colleges, which could not accommodate all intending teachers and which were too expensive or otherwise inconvenient for most. The Code of 1890 gave effect to this scheme, and day training colleges were attached to King's College, London, to the provincial universities, to Cambridge in 1891, and to Oxford in 1892. No longer were teachers spare-time instructors or the "dregs of other callings." They became an organized profession. The Headmasters' Conference, consisting of the headmasters of the chief public schools, and the National Union of Teachers, consisting of elementary-school teachers, were founded in 1870, and other teachers' organizations followed. Nevertheless in 1902 36 per cent. of the existing teachers had never passed the examination for the teachers' certificate; 55 per cent. had never been to a training college of any kind.[1] Under the Act of 1902 provision for their training was made part of the duty of the local education authority, and fresh regulations for the training of pupil teachers followed, no one being able to start the course under the age of sixteen, or fifteen in rural districts.

Among the specified powers given to the L.E.A.'s by the Act of 1902 were some which reversed the Cockerton Judgment. The L.E.A.'s were empowered to "supply or aid the supply of higher education," to provide or assist in the provision of scholarships or allowances, or to pay or assist the payment of fees of scholars to secondary schools of any kind. The L.E.A.'s

[1] Arthur Balfour, House of Commons, March 24, 1902 (Hansard, fourth series, cv, 853).

did, in fact, build and maintain new secondary schools; they aided others; they assisted scholars both to their own schools and to grant-aided schools, and to schools outside their control. In 1904 there were about 86,000 secondary-school children in England and Wales. In 1943 there were 514,000, more than half of them in schools provided by the L.E.A.'s.[1]

(b) HIGHER EDUCATION, 1851–1902

These secondary schools modelled themselves largely on the grammar schools. They gave, therefore, a general, academic education oriented towards the universities and the professions rather than the bench and the workshop. Fortunately, by the time they were thus taken as models, the grammar schools had considerably improved their organization, their standards of teaching, and their curricula.

In 1861 a Commission under the chairmanship of the Earl of Clarendon had been appointed "to inquire into the Revenues and Management of Certain Colleges and Schools, and the studies pursued and instruction given there." The schools concerned were those which had become known as the nine public schools—Eton, Harrow, Westminster, Winchester, St Paul's, Merchant Taylors, Shrewsbury, Charterhouse, Rugby. In 1864 a further Royal Commission under Lord Taunton was appointed to inquire into those schools covered neither by the Clarendon nor the Newcastle Commissions. Both Commissions found little advance since the beginning of the century, apart from the reforms in discipline and general 'tone' carried through by individual headmasters like Arnold of Rugby. The emphasis was still on the classics. Yet still classical teaching was inefficient. As Lord Clarendon, who, besides being Chairman of the Commission, was head of a house at Oxford, remarked to the headmaster of Eton:

> We find modern languages, geography, history, chronology, and everything else which a well-educated English gentleman ought to know given up, in order that the full time should be devoted to the classics, and at the same time we are told that the boys go up to Oxford not only not proficient, but in a lamentable state of deficiency with respect to the classics.[2]

[1] *Educational Reconstruction*, presented by the President of the Board of Education to Parliament, July 1943, 1942–43, XI, 9.
[2] *Royal Commission appointed to inquire into the Revenues and Management of Certain Colleges and Schools . . .*, Minutes of Evidence, 1864, XXI, 115, Question 3554.

Still science and history and mathematics were regarded as 'inferior' subjects, still the schools were understaffed. But still the boys trained there were those who aiterwards naturally filled the important places of government and administration. Most of the evils of the nine public schools were present in the smaller grammar schools. The Taunton Commission summed up the position:

> Untrained teachers, and bad methods of teaching, uninspected work by workmen without adequate motive, unrevised or ill-revised statutes, and the complete absence of all organization of schools in relation to one another.[1]

Endowments still continued which had lost all connexion with reality. The master of Whitgift Hospital, Croydon, had no pupils during the thirty-odd years he was master. At Ottery St Mary's, where the terms of the endowment stipulated the taking of boarders, there were six day boys and no boarders at all. "The boarders' dining room was occupied as a coach-house by two of the master's carriages, the night study was a laundry, and the large dormitory a billiard room." At Netherbury the master carried on simultaneously the school, a flour-mill, and a spinning-mill. In a Suffolk school the master did no work whatsoever, but supported his old age in the comfortable schoolhouse. It often happened that the master of a school was vicar of a parish. One schoolmaster "was incumbent of one parish, curate of another, and chaplain to a workhouse besides."[2]

But even while the Clarendon and Taunton Commissioners were sitting a change was taking place which had produced results by the end of the century.

Talk was of a "liberal education," of the inclusion of scientific subjects in school and university curricula, of the value of education as a whole. People tried to define education. They drew up schemes, expounded theories, rounded on existing educational institutions with stern criticism and practical suggestions. From Ruskin the medievalist artist, through Thomas Huxley the scientist, to practical teachers and scholars like Dean Farrar, Whewell, and Jowett, the talk was of education.

[1] *Report of the Royal Commission appointed to inquire into the Education given in Schools not comprised within Her Majesty's Two Former Commissions*, 1867–68, XXVIII, Part I, 139.
[2] *Ibid.*, XXVIII, Part 1, 224–227.

Meredith featured education in his novels. Matthew Arnold, man of letters, son of Arnold of Rugby and Inspector of Schools, made a detailed study of Continental as well as of British systems of education.

Ruskin spoke of education as the "general elements of human discipline,"[1] which every child should be required by law to receive. He denied that it was connected with mere knowledge. "You do not," he said, "educate a man by telling him what he knew not, but by making him what he was not."[2] "That man, I think, has had a liberal education," said Thomas Huxley,

> who has been so trained in his youth that his body is the ready servant of his will . . . whose intellect is a clear, cold logic engine, with all its parts of equal strength, and in smooth working order; ready, like a steam-engine, to be turned to any kind of work—to spin the gossamer as well as forge the anvils of the mind; whose mind is stored with a knowledge of the great and fundamental truths of Nature and of the laws of her operations; who, no stunted ascetic, is full of life and fire, but whose passions are trained to come to heel by a vigorous will; the servant of a tender conscience who has learned to love all beauty, whether of Nature or of art, to hate all vileness, and to respect others as himself.[3]

In 1854 a series of lectures on education was delivered at the Royal Institution of Great Britain before the Prince Consort. The lecturers included Faraday; Whewell, the Master of Trinity College, Cambridge; Charles Daubeny; Professor Tyndall. All pleaded for a scientific education. Whewell advocated the teaching of geometry, jurisprudence, natural science, and the physical sciences. "The knowledge of which I speak," he said,

> must be a knowledge of things, and not merely of names of things; an acquaintance with the operations and productions of nature, as they appear to the age, not merely an acquaintance with what has been said about them; a knowledge of the laws of nature, seen in special experiments and observations, before they are conceived in general terms; a knowledge of the types of natural forms, gathered from individual cases already made familiar. By such study of one or more departments of inductive

---

[1] *Time and Tide*: Letter XVI, 1867 (*Collected Works*, xvii, 397).
[2] *Munera Pulveris*: *Ibid.*, xvii, 232.
[3] "A Liberal Education; and where to find it." An Address to the South London Working Men's College (*Collected Essays*, 1893 edition, p. 86).

knowledge, the mind may escape from the thraldom and illusion which reigns in the world of mere words.[1]

A few years later the Rev. F. W. Farrar edited several *Essays on a Liberal Education*, the very title of which was significant. Farrar's own contribution was an essay which advocated "the immediate and total abandonment of Greek and Latin verse-writing as a *necessary or general* element in liberal education."[2] The chief subject which would take its place would be science. "At present," he wrote,

> we send forth a few fine scholars and a multitude of ignorant men: I am convinced we might send forth the same number of scholars, and a large number of men who, while they would know as much or *more* Latin and Greek than the paltry minimum to which they now attain, should not at the same time startle and shock the world by the unnatural profundity of their ignorance respecting all other subjects in heaven and earth.[3]

We require, Farrar concluded,

> the knowledge of *things* and not of *words*; of the truths which great men have to tell us, and not of the tricks or individualities of their style; of that which shall add to the treasures of human knowledge, not of that which shall flatter its fastidiousness by frivolous attempts at reproducing its past elegancies of speech; of that which is best for human souls, and which shall make them greater, wiser, better; not of that which is idly supposed to make them more tasteful, and refined.[4]

At the same time Benjamin Jowett, then tutor of Balliol College, Oxford, was planning wider courses of lectures which would include early Greek history and philosophy and Latin and Greek literature. John Henry Newman in 1852 gave his lectures on the *Idea of a University*, which were published in 1859, with their two cardinal requirements of the unity of all teaching and the necessity of a liberal teaching in the universities as an end in itself.

Thus within the universities and from the universities, as well as outside, the need was being felt for an education that would be more liberal and less narrow in scope, more scientific and less rigidly academic in outlook. The movement for a liberal education was not one which forcibly reformed the

---

[1] W. Whewell, *On the Influence of the History of Science upon Intellectual Education* (1854).   [2] P. 206.   [3] P. 208.   [4] P. 239.

universities and the grammar schools from outside: it was a joint movement in which many of the keenest reformers were themselves university or grammar-school teachers. The universities by their entrance examinations influenced teaching in the grammar schools; the grammar schools by the men they sent up to the universities exercised a reciprocal influence. The influence of both percolated through the educational system to secondary and elementary schools, to inspectors of schools, and to education committees. Both became increasingly susceptible to outside opinion as the scope of education became wider. The State showed its interest in the universities, as it did in other branches of education, by a series of Commissions. In 1850 separate Royal Commissions sat on Oxford and Cambridge. In 1872 a Royal Commission considered the two universities jointly. In 1877 there was a further Commission on the two universities followed by the Universities of Oxford and Cambridge Act, which required colleges to contribute more to university funds, especially for better instruction in art and science. By this time the oligarchy of heads of houses had been modified by putting greater power into the hands of the M.A.'s —of Convocation at Oxford and the Senate at Cambridge— while the executive of each university became a council elected by the graduate university residents. Many colleges followed suit, and oligarchies of older Fellows gave way to more democratic college government in which younger Fellows obtained an influence which helped the development of the liberal and scientific outlook.

The universities and colleges, thus administratively reformed, had been given the power to alter their own statutes, provided no objection was raised in Parliament and that the Privy Council assented. Thus they were able to free themselves of restrictive statutes. The rules governing Fellowships were drastically amended. The taking of Holy Orders and celibacy had ceased to be conditions of Fellowships. 'Close' Fellowships, non-residential Fellowships, and consequently most sinecures were abolished. In 1871 the Universities Tests Act abolished the religious test in Oxford, Cambridge, and Durham, except in the divinity degrees or chairs of divinity.

While the older universities had been coming into line with the greater liberalism of the period new universities and colleges were being formed in London and elsewhere. The newer universities tended to lay greater emphasis on the teaching of science and politics than Oxford and Cambridge, while the numbers of students receiving financial aid from university or college funds, from private trusts or the State, steadily grew in the older universities as well as in the new, with a consequent enlargement of the sphere from which the universities received their entrants.

The subject of women's education was first officially aired before the Schools Inquiry Commission. Until the middle of the century there had been little occasion to treat girls' education apart from that of boys. The daughters of the poor went to a 'National' school or a similar institution. The daughters of the well-to-do had governesses at home, and, if they went to school, went to a private establishment for young ladies which was quite as bad in its way as the corresponding boys' schools. The Commissions of Inquiry into elementary schools covered girls as well as boys; the Public Schools Inquiry was, by its terms of reference, confined to boys' schools. It was when the Schools Inquiry Commission was appointed to examine all other schools that women felt it necessary to ensure that girls' schools should not be omitted. Accordingly there was presented to the Commission a request bearing many signatures that the education of girls should be included within the Commission's scope. The Commissioners agreed, and, besides much written evidence, examined many girls' schools, which thus came within the range of the educational reform movement.

The further demand for the opening to women of education as far as the universities was more controversial. But a number of determined intellectual women of the middle class had by the end of the century achieved much of their aim of equal educational opportunity for men and women. In 1847 Mrs Reid started the classes for girls in her own home which in 1860 became Bedford College. Anne Clough organized a series of lectures for women by well-known scholars which in 1871 gave rise to Newnham College, Cambridge. The varied activity of Emily Davies was crowned by the establishment of a women's college at Girton, outside Cambridge, in 1869. Oxford followed this lead by the opening of Lady Margaret Hall and Somerville Hall (later College) for women in 1879. The

Cambridge local examinations had been opened to girls in 1865, and finally university degrees were opened to women, first by London in 1878, then by the newer universities, but by Oxford not until 1920 and by Cambridge not until 1948.

(c) THE TWENTIETH CENTURY

The Act of 1902 provided an administrative framework for the development of education which has not been substantially altered. The chief developments of the twentieth century have been concerned with the scope and duration of the different stages of education; with raising the school-leaving age; with reducing the size of classes and improving buildings; with supplying an adequate stream of well-qualified teachers to the schools.

In the year 1926 a Committee under the chairmanship of Sir Henry Hadow published a Report on the *Education of the Adolescent*. The Report, after weighing much evidence, recommended that there should be a distinct break in the educational process at the age of eleven, and that all children, regardless of ability, should at that age be drafted to new schools which should supply a grammar-school education, or a combination of the academic and the technical, or be simply a 'senior' school catering for the least bright of the elementary-school children. This recommendation was put into effect wholly or partially in most areas, and the break at the age of eleven-plus became an accepted principle of school life. Obvious defects led to a Report by Mr Will Spens and his Committee in 1938 on the organization and integration of schools catering for children beyond the age of eleven, and a further Report by Sir Cyril Norwood and his Committee in 1941 on suggested changes in the secondary-school curriculum and the question of school examinations.

The school-leaving age was the second problem which exercised the mind of educationists in the twentieth century. By the Education Act of 1918 it was raised to fourteen. By the Education Act of 1936 it was raised to fifteen, and was to have been enforced from September 1, 1939, but this was prevented by the outbreak of war.

The climax of earlier legislation came in 1944. The Education Act of 1944 had two main objects: the provision of conpulsory, free education for all from the ages of five to fifteen, with extensions downward and upward to cover all children and young people from two years old to eighteen; and a reorganization of the stages of education. Before 1944 the educational process tended to divide into two—elementary, for the period covering compulsory school attendance, and higher, including all education beyond this and some from the age of eleven onward. The eleven-plus, or secondary stage, generally divided in accordance with the Hadow Report into central, secondary, and technical. The 1944 Act, having raised the school-leaving age to fifteen, divided the whole educational process into three—primary, secondary, and further education. Above the primary stage there was to be a further division in accordance with the recommendations of the Spens and Norwood Committees into grammar, modern, and technical schools. The grammar schools were to be what their name implied, and continue the best tradition of the grammar and secondary schools; the modern schools were to provide an education more general, and closely linked to the interests of the pupils, following the lines of the best senior schools; the technical schools were to link a general education with the teaching of some industry, of agriculture or commerce. No fees might be charged for tuition in any type of primary or secondary school maintained by a local authority.

In reorganizing the educational process as a whole from two to eighteen the Board of Education found itself faced with the various anomalies consequent upon the haphazard growth of the English education system. It had to decide questions relating to Church schools, denominational schools, other private schools, and the public schools, as well as to resolve problems of authority, delegation, administration, and execution. In trying to solve these problems it attempted, in the words of Mr Butler, who moved the adoption of the Bill in the House of Commons, a

> synthesis . . . between order and liberty, between local initiative and national direction, between the voluntary agencies and the State, between the private life of a school and the public life of the districts which it serves, between manual and intellectual skill and between those better and less well endowed.[1]

[1] January 19, 1944 (Hansard, fifth series, 396, 232).

The Act of 1944 replaced the Board of Education by the Ministry of Education. The function of the President of the Board had been loosely defined as "the superintendence of matters relating to education in England and Wales." The function of the Minister of Education was

> to promote the education of the people of England and Wales and the progressive development of institutions devoted to that purpose and to secure the effective execution by local authorities, under his control and direction, of the national policy for providing a varied and comprehensive educational service in every area.

The development of the English educational system has been marked and marred by denominational quarrels and the uneasy partnership of the Dual System. The State came into the picture with the first grant for education in 1833, but until 1870 it was no rival to the denominational schools. After 1870 voluntary, or non-provided, schools and board, or provided, schools continued side by side. In 1902 the majority of children were still educated in voluntary schools—there were over 3,000,000 of them, as compared with 2,600,000 in board schools[1]—but after the Act of 1902 the decline of the voluntary schools became more pronounced. The concession of rate aid proved less real than it seemed, since upkeep and repair, as well as compulsory alterations to structure, had to be carried out by the funds of the voluntary societies. The State had not killed the voluntary schools, but had pronounced their death sentence. By 1938 there were only 10,553 voluntary schools, as against 10,363 council schools; they housed only 1,374,000 pupils to the council schools' 3,151,000, and many of their buildings were in such a bad state of repair that, of the 753 schools on the Board of Education's black list in 1925, 541 were non-provided schools.[2]

The history of the Dual System has been fraught with bitter controversy which time and again has retarded the development of education. The provisions of the 1944 Act relating to voluntary schools hope to still that controversy once and for all. They were framed with the double purpose of incor-

---

[1] Arthur Balfour, House of Commons, March 24, 1902 (Hansard, fourth series cv, 855).

[2] *Educational Reconstruction*, July 1943, 1942–43, XI.

porating the voluntary schools more firmly into the general
system of education, while allowing sufficient freedom of conscience and freedom for initiative to break what might otherwise
prove to be a sterile uniformity of instruction. For in the past
the danger was that the quarrels of interested parties would
prevent the breath of life from being infused into the educational system. For the future the danger is lest too few people
will be interested in education, and that individuality—even
freedom—may be sacrificed to a State-administered uniformity.

(d) CHILDREN'S READING

The scope and nature of children's reading has widened and
altered immeasurably since the days when Catechisms, carefully vetted Bible stories, a spelling book and a 'primer,' a
few moral tales and *The Fairchild Family* were the range of the
average child's reading. In 1847 the Committee of Council
on Education published a *List* bringing elementary books,
whose names were supplied by the publishers, to the attention
of managers of schools and at the same time gave a grant to
assist in the purchase of books. This and the extension of education after the Act of 1870 gave a stimulus to the writing and
publishing of school books and children's books. Lindley
Murray continued to be popular. Butter's *Spelling*, which had
reached its twenty-second edition in 1839, was still being
revised and reprinted in 1897, having attained a boasted
circulation of nearly two and a half million copies. Mavor's
English Spelling-Book had been equally popular since the beginning of the century, and in 1885 was published in an edition
charmingly illustrated by Kate Greenaway. The child who
had missed the rudiments at school could study at home by
means of numerous little books. Early in the second half of
the century, for example, *Chambers's Minor Educational Course*
could be bought for 2*d.* a volume. A collection of these would
cover reading, grammar, arithmetic, geography, history. Older
children might enjoy at home a page or two of *Cassell's Popular
Educator*—or even of *Cassell's Technical Educator*—or there might
fall into their hands one of Mrs Sewell's "Household Tracts
for the People," three million of which were said by the publishers to have been in circulation in Great Britain and the
Colonies at the mid-century.

In 1882 an official *Instruction to Inspectors* laid down the general lines of school reading:

> In Standards V, VI and VII, books of extracts from standard authors may be taken, though such works as *Robinson Crusoe*, Voyages and Travels, or Biographies of eminent men (if of suitable length) are to be preferred. In Standards VI and VII a single play of Shakespeare, or a single book of one of Milton's longer poems, or a selection of extracts from either poet equal in length to the foregoing may be accepted. As a rule, ordinary text-books or manuals should not be accepted as readers.[1]

According to Lord Morley, by far the most popular of school textbooks in the eighties was Macaulay's *Essays*. They "have done more than any other writing of this generation to settle the direction of men's historical interest and curiosity," wrote Morley in 1881. "From Eton and Harrow down to an elementary school in St Giles's or Bethnal Green, Macaulay's *Essays* are a text book."[2]

All the time the S.P.C.K. was sponsoring books of many kinds, mostly 'improving' stories. One of its most popular authors was Mrs Carey Brock, who was writing from the fifties with speed and enthusiasm through to the eighties. Her stories usually contained one strong-willed, headstrong, and selfish girl and one good, gentle, submissive girl who was the heroine. "You know, Edith," remarked one of the latter, a schoolgirl, uttering a sentiment common to her type,

> "I have not had a prize, yet I am sure I could scarcely feel happier than I do this evening. I think it is the knowing that we have done our best that makes us happy, . . . for I am sure I should not care at all about praise if I felt I did not deserve it, should you?"[3]

Home Memories, Sunday Echoes in Weekday Hours, Arthur; or The Chorister's Rest, Little Susie and her Blind Brother, were the kind of titles which still went to press. A *Children's Annual* of 1869 has the same 'improving' tone. *Childhood*, a monthly magazine started in January 1892, contained such titles as *Darling Little Agnes: a True Tale of Lovely Christian Piety in Early Childhood*. On the other hand, a *Children's Journal* of 1863 contained

[1] *Report of the Consultative Committee on Books in Public Elementary Schools*, 1928, p. 10.
[2] Quoted by D. C. Somervell, *English Thought in the Nineteenth Century*, p. 91.
[3] Mrs Carey Brock, *Home Memories* (1859), p. 81.

modern verse by Tennyson and Coleridge and some fables as
well as the inevitable moral tales. *Little Folks*, for the young,
and *Sunshine*, for rather older children, which were both popular
in the eighties, still resembled in format and style their predecessors. There was the 'moral' story of the untidy girl whose
punishment and consequent reform were automatic, and of the
untruthful boy upon whom retribution falls swift and certain.
But there is less grimness in such stories, and there are fewer
of them.

The Fairchild Family tradition continued to the end of the
century. There was even in the sixties a Roman Catholic
priest, the Rev. I. Furniss, who published a series of children's
books in which the punishments for transgression were made
even more horrific. In *The Terrible Judgment and the Bad Child*
the Devil opens the Book in which the child's sins are written
down.

> He reads up all the sins the child committed in thoughts,
> words, or actions, during all its life . . . behaving bad in chapel
> —disobedience to parents—quarrels, fightings . . . immodesties
> in thought, word, and action—reading bad books—going into
> bad company—stealing if it was only a pin—the number of times
> of each sin will be given exactly, and the child will remember
> that it is the true number.[1]

More than this, writes the priest exultantly, each *place* will
testify:

> In this street, a voice cries, the child committed such a sin—in
> this room, another voice cries, the child committed such a sin
> —in this field, in this dark entry, cries another voice, the child
> committed a great, a terrible sin.

The terror of the small child, vainly trying to imagine what so
great a sin could be—the thought that, perhaps, all unknow-
ingly, he had already committed it—the consequent dark hours
of misery in bed—were apparently the object of the book, whose
mission seemed only to terrify. Even good works helped little.
For, although these would be listed, the Devil comes in again
to point out that some good works had been done by the child
because it pleased him to do them, and that therefore they
didn't count! Poor child! Under Father Furniss's guidance
he could be sure of nothing but pain. Any pleasure he had

[1] P. 13.

would be sure to count against him and lead him to the torment of the damned, such as the Reverend Father loved to describe.

Luckily, Father Furniss was not typical, and in general literature in the second half of the nineteenth century the child was garnering a harvest never before equalled. *Eric; or, Little by Little* (1859) now brings a tolerant smile, and even *Tom Brown's Schooldays* (1857) seems over-pious, while *Little Lord Fauntleroy* (1886) is too good to be tolerated, but children will still laugh and weep over *Uncle Tom's Cabin* (1852) and travel *Westward Ho!* unquestioningly with Amyas Leigh. Alice began her *Adventures in Wonderland* in 1865. There came *Tom Sawyer* in 1876, Ballantyne's books of the sea in the seventies, *Treasure Island* and *King Solomon's Mines* in the eighties, historical adventures by Stanley Weyman in the nineties, *The Jungle Book* in 1894. Kate Greenaway in the eighties was brightening children's books with delightful illustrations. In the twentieth century the writing of children's stories became an increasing vogue, with the multiplication of books, weekly magazines, newspapers, and annuals of various kinds.

The Consultative Committee of the Board of Education on Books in Public Elementary Schools had to report in 1928 that the books at the disposal of the elementary schools had been too few, and that some of those supplied to them had not been of a kind either to cultivate the children's tastes for reading or to teach them how books should be rightly used. In the country as a whole the situation was, even then, "often serious and sometimes deplorable."[1] Nevertheless there had been a marked improvement from 1850 in the quality and quantity of both school books and books for general reading. In the thirties the improvement continued with the development of school libraries and the increased use of public libraries. The increasing accessibility of books affected children, teachers, and the general public alike. If much trash was published there were more and cheaper classics and better textbooks. At the same time radio, with the various devices of imagery and action at its disposal, was supplementing the textbook and providing the teacher with a new teaching device.

[1] P. xv.

(e) ADULT EDUCATION

The Education Act of 1944 made it incumbent upon the local authorities to secure full-time and part-time education for persons over compulsory school age, and leisure-time occupation of a cultural and recreative nature for those over school age able and willing to profit by it. The provision of adult education, which had previously been permissive to the local authority, thus became a duty. But adult education had already proceeded far by its own momentum.

By the middle of the nineteenth century most of the earlier experiments had died, though not without leaving their mark. Thenceforward there were several lines of development. The Committee of Council for Education for the first time in 1851 made grants in aid of evening schools. These classes were originally for the elementary instruction of adults, generally for the teaching of the three R's to those who had not attended school in their youth. Later, when most children went to school and imbibed at least a smattering of reading and writing, the evening classes gave more advanced instruction. But adult education continued in the main to develop as a result of private initiative. The schools and classes thus started showed a marked difference from those of the earlier part of the century. They stressed the need for a liberal education, at the same time aiming at fostering a sense of social responsibility, whereas the earlier classes had aimed at teaching a variety of largely scientific and technical subjects. They tried to integrate teaching into a whole rather than organize a number of disconnected lectures. The Sheffield People's College, founded in 1842, offered such a liberal education. The London Working Men's College, founded in 1854 by a group of Christian Socialists and others, aimed at furthering social ideals by a liberal, integrated course of study for working-men, during which tutors and classes should realize something of the corporate life of the residential college. A new Adult School movement developed under the guidance of the Society of Friends. Joseph Sturge, the Chartist, William White, a bookseller, and other Quakers started an Adult School in Birmingham in 1852 which has continued to the present day.

In the seventies came the notable development of university-extension classes. University-extension work had been mooted by both Jowett and Sewell, who urged that college and university endowments could not be most profitably spent in being devoted entirely to the comparatively few students who came up to the universities. They should partly be employed in taking the university to those who could not come up. James Stuart, of Cambridge, with his "peripatetic university," set the idea in motion. In 1873 the University of Cambridge arranged three courses of twenty-four lectures each at Derby, Nottingham, and Leicester. The scheme was outstandingly successful, and had the double result of establishing the University Extension movement and of causing new university colleges to be opened in the towns where the classes had been held. London followed Cambridge's lead in 1876, Oxford in 1878.

Towards the end of the century the idea of tutorial classes for adult students was being mooted—small classes with a high standard and a close relationship between tutor and students. Classes on these lines were started at Toynbee Hall in 1899. The general difficulty in organizing them was expense, since the classes were to be small and students' fees must necessarily be low. The movement was really launched when Oxford granted money in 1907–8 for two university tutorial classes, one at Rochdale, in Lancashire, and one at Longton, in North Staffordshire.

The agencies of adult education were by this time many, including the trade unions and the Co-operative Societies. In 1903, under the inspiration of Albert Mansbridge, the Workers' Educational Association was formed to unite the existing organizations for adult education. Four years later a conference of working-class and educational organizations was held at Oxford under the auspices of the W.E.A. to consider the relationship of Oxford University to working-class education. The outcome was the formation of a Joint Committee of the University and the W.E.A. and a Report recommending that Oxford should promote the establishment of tutorial classes and should pay half the cost, and that their management should be in the hands of a Joint Board. Thus form and momentum were given to the organization of tutorial classes. They came to be organized as three-yearly courses consisting of twenty-four meetings each year. Each meeting of two hours was part lecture, part discussion, and each student had to submit a given number of written essays. The University, besides meeting half the cost, provided a small library, or book box. Other universities followed Oxford and advanced classes for adult working-class students were jointly sponsored by the universities and the W.E.A. In the following year (1908) the Plebs League was formed for entirely independent working-class education to be run without financial assistance from the universities or any non-working-class body.

There thus grew up a network of classes for adult students ranging from simple terminal courses of twelve meetings, or even fewer, sponsored by a Co-operative Society, a trade union, or an Adult School, but generally under the auspices of the W.E.A., to ambitious three-yearly tutorial classes organized by the Joint Committee of a university and the W.E.A. The weakness of such classes was a lack of the corporate life provided by the residential college. It was partially overcome by institutions like the London Working Men's College, the City Literary Institute, and Morley College, which had their own buildings and organized their own social life apart from the class subjects which were taught; by summer schools organized at university colleges and elsewhere, by residential working-men and women's colleges, of which the chief was Ruskin College, founded at Oxford in 1899 by two American disciples of Ruskin. The adult education movement continued through the First World War and after. On the eve of the Second World War nearly 58,000 students were enrolled in over 3000 classes of all kinds.[1]

These students were served by specially qualified instructors, small class libraries, the public libraries, most of which had student sections, and parts of university libraries such as the Goldsmith's Library of the University of London, which was open to them as a lending library. The adult student no longer needed *Chambers's Minor Educational Course* at 2d. a volume, nor the *Popular Educator* and *Scientific Educator* and other publications of John Cassell which, at a penny each, had served him so well in the second half of the nineteenth century, and which he had sought with such avidity that Cassell was reported to have issued between 25,000,000 and 30,000,000 of these penny publications annually.[2] The adult student, who

---

[1] *Report of the Board of Education for 1938*; 1938–39, X, 180.
[2] J. W. Adamson, *English Education, 1789–1902*, p. 347.

was now not necessarily the working-man in the sense in which the mid-century had understood the term, turned for his reading to the classics and standard texts of his subject.

In addition, newspapers, periodicals of all kinds, from the technical and scientific to pictures with a caption, were universally read and spread knowledge or information. The cinema, largely entertainment, partly instruction, spread to every town. Above all, radio sets became nearly as universal as the daily newspaper, and provided in every home news, information, and entertainment. The cinema and the radio are the new, and as yet only partly assessed, instruments of culture and entertainment. They are bad to the extent that they supply ready-made ideas and in so far as their values are at fault. They are bad in fostering the modern tendency to vicarious emotion and the spectator rather than the actor mentality. But their educational value is potentially great: their best use is one of the vital problems of the age.

The development of education over nearly two hundred years has been marked by an enlargement of scope and a change of attitude. Nowhere is this development clearer than in the language of official documents. There is less talk of "educating young persons according to their stations" and more of "education for life," of the functions of citizenship, the development of character. In 1878 inspectors were instructed that the object of education should be

> over and above the acquisition by every child of the bare ordinary rudiments of education, to promote the development of the general intelligence of the scholars rather than to seek to burden their memories with subjects which, considering the early age at which the majority of children leave school, would not be likely to be of use to them.[1]

The Introduction to the Code of 1904–1926 pronounced that the "purpose of the Public Elementary School" was

> to form and strengthen the character and to develop the intelligence of the children entrusted to it, and to make the best use of the school years available, in assisting both girls and boys, according to their different needs, to fit themselves, practically as well as intellectually, for the work of life.

[1] *Final Report of the Royal Commission appointed to inquire into the Elementary Education Acts*, 1888, XXXV, 42.

Hannah More and Sarah Trimmer wanted to train children "in habits of industry and piety." The Code of 1926 aimed at training them

> in habits of observation and clear reasoning, so that they may gain an intelligent acquaintance with some of the facts and laws of nature; to arouse in them a living interest in the ideals and achievements of mankind, and to bring them to some familiarity with the literature and history of their own country; to give them some power over language as an instrument of thought and expression, and, while making them conscious of the limitations of their knowledge, to develop in them such a taste for good reading and thoughtful study as will enable them to increase that knowledge in after years by their own efforts.

Finally, the Education Act of 1944 describes the object of education to be "to contribute towards the spiritual, moral, mental and physical development of the community." Compared with the sayings of Sarah Trimmer and Hannah More, this is the measure of the progress of two hundred years.

SELECT BIBLIOGRAPHY

Report of the Royal Commission appointed to inquire into the State of Popular Education in England (the Newcastle Commission), 1861, XXI.

Report of the Royal Commission appointed to inquire into the Revenues and Management of Certain Colleges and Schools, and the Studies pursued and Instruction given there (the Clarendon Commission), 1864, XX; 1864, XXI.

Report of the Royal Commission appointed to inquire into the Education given in Schools not comprised within Her Majesty's Two Former Commissions (the Taunton Schools Inquiry, or Endowed Schools Commission), 1867–68, XXVIII.

Report of the Royal Commission on Technical Instruction, 1884, XXIX.

Report of the Royal Commission appointed to inquire into the Elementary Education Acts (England and Wales) (the Cross Commission), 1888, XXV.

Report of the Royal Commission on Secondary Education (the Bryce Commission), 1895, XLIII.

Final Report of the Adult Education Committee, 1919, XXVIII.

Report of the Consultative Committee of the Board of Education on Secondary Education (the Spens Committee), 1938.

Educational Reconstruction: presented by the President of the Board of Education to Parliament, July 1943. Cmd. 6458, 1942–43, XI.

Report of the Committee on the Curriculum and Examinations in Secondary Schools (the Norwood Committee), 1943.

Report of the Committee on Public Schools and the General Educational System (the Fleming Committee), 1944.

A Guide to the Educational System of England and Wales: Ministry of Education Pamphlet No. 2.

Report of a Committee on Post-war University Education, 1944 (British Association for the Advancement of Science).

ADAMSON, J. W.: *English Education, 1789–1902* (Cambridge University Press, 1930).

ARNOLD, M.: *Report on Elementary Schools, 1852–1882* (Macmillan, 1889).

CURTIS, S. J.: *History of Education in Great Britain* (third edition) (University Tutorial Press, 1953).

CURTIS, S. J. AND BOULTWOOD, M. E. A.: *A Short History of Educational Ideas* (Chapters X or XI onward) (University Tutorial Press, 1953).

FARRAR, F. W. (Ed.): *Essays on a Liberal Education* (Macmillan, 1867).

JONES, M. G.: *The Charity School Movement* (Cambridge University Press, 1938).

LOWNDES, G. A. N.: *The Silent Social Revolution: an Account of Public Education in England and Wales, 1895–1935* (Oxford University Press, 1937).

CHAPTER XXV

EPILOGUE

IN the years 1760–1851 Britain had been in transition economically and socially. As the period ended she emerged as the Workshop of the World, her middle classes and her aristocracy united by many ties in a ruling class whose strength was economic, political, and social.

The following period, 1851–1950, underlined the economic changes begun in the previous century. Life became more urban, industry more highly mechanized; speed of production, transport, and communication increased; Britain became more completely dependent upon imported food. But there was nothing essentially new in kind until the revolution associated with electricity. And here Britain no longer led the way.

In this second period the social changes were more revolutionary than the economic. As the first period saw the rise of the middle class, so the second saw the rise of the working class. As in the first the middle classes had fused with the aristocracy, so in the second the working classes and the middle classes became more closely identified through the extension of the franchise, the spread of education, the common bond of reading the same newspapers and some of the same books, and sharing the same entertainment; through the expansion of the social services and, in the twentieth century, by a cheapening and improvement of ready-made clothing, especially for women, so that the clothes of all classes became more alike.

The economic and social scene in 1851 presented a picture of some unity. There had been many sides to the story, but it had built up steadily to the climax of 1851. The following century presents no such unity. At some point the continuity is broken. The period starts with unchallenged material prosperity, certainty, and optimism, which continues for a quarter of a century. It ends with impoverishment, uncertainty, and a mood which, if not pessimistic, is cautious and doubtful.

The watershed was not the seventies and the period of falling trade variously estimated as "the Lean Years" and "the Great Depression." It was not the publication of *The Origin of Species* in 1859; though Darwin's work shook the Victorians profoundly, it took some decades for the challenge of evolution to make itself felt. It was not the death of Queen Victoria in 1901, for a decline had set in before that. It was not the Boer War, which broke out in 1899, though this was considerably disquieting. It was not the foreign rivalries, which clashed louder as the twentieth century opened. Nor was it the growing force of organized labour and the extension of the social services; for the Victorians on the whole believed with Lord John Russell that there is nothing so conservative as progress. Nor does the end of Victorian optimism date from the movement for the emancipation of women, the coming of the bicycle and the motor-car, or the week-end habit, though all these dealt a hard blow at churchgoing and a strictly regulated family life. None of these in themselves mark the end of Victorian Prosperity and all that went with it in life and thought and ideas. It was the cumulative effect of many things, economic, social, political, spiritual—even personal, for the influence of Victoria's long reign must not be discounted—which had brought about a perceptible change in atmosphere by the end of the century.

Security, certainty, a unity shaped by authority, continued to characterize the life of Britain until almost the end of the nineteenth century. It ran through all walks of life. Socially there was a hierarchy from the Queen downward. In private life the family constituted a similar unity, graded from father downward. In religion the Victorian recognized the authority of God the King and Father, and, whether he was High Church, Low Church, or Chapel, continued to regard Sunday as a day devoted to religious observation on which churchgoing or chapel-going was both a social obligation and a spiritual necessity. In political and economic affairs the expected parallel from the State downward was becoming increasingly apt as the State assumed more functions, but the Victorian continued to be an individualist, and resented the enlargement of the sphere of political or economic control.

Material prosperity continued to bear evidence to the rightness of the Victorian's way of life. "The Lean Years" were a warning to a few rather than a shock to many, and in the subsequent readjustment it seemed that all had come right again. To balance the competition from Europe and America Britain had exalted her empire, and to the concept of empire went much of the fervour of patriotism which had previously concentrated on the Workshop of the World. No major war other than the Crimean troubled her conscience or her resources until the Boer War of 1899 awoke an uneasy feeling that all was not well. There was progress in medicine. The second half of the century began with the work of Pasteur, saw the widespread use of chloroform, the discovery of X-rays by Röntgen, and ended with Ronald Ross's discovery that the malarial parasite was carried by mosquitoes; the new century opened with Marie Curie's isolation of the element of radium. If the great medical research-workers were not always British, Britain shared in the development of their discoveries, and herself continued, by the progress, slow but unchecked, of the social services, to demonstrate the justice and mercy of her social system.

Their spiritual and economic values being in accord, the Victorians knew little of inner or outward conflict; they had neither spiritual nor worldly doubt as to the rightness of things:

> God's in his heaven—
> All's right with the world!

was a statement of fact. So the Victorians worshipped God, continued their profitable business enterprises, accepted their positions in society, and faced life with optimism.

The arts continued to express their mood. Architecture became more ornate; inside their homes the Victorians collected more knick-knacks, their furniture and articles of everyday use became more heavily decorated. Only size and quantity could fittingly bear witness to their continued prosperity. Giants among the poets and novelists continued to supply the quality their own genius dictated as well as the quantity their age required, Tennyson, the Poet Laureate, with *Maud* and *The Princess*, Browning with *The Ring and the Book*, Morris with his medieval and Nordic sagas. Among the novelists were not only Dickens, Thackeray, and those who have become classics, but a host of best-sellers whose vogue was great in their own day. Trollope has had a modern revival, but few now trouble about Charlotte Yonge's *Heir of Redclyffe*, which, from the time of its publication in 1853, was read avidly, while Ouida's books of the sixties and Marie Corelli's of the nineties are remembered chiefly as novels which Victorian mamas could not allow their children to read, and which, incidentally, helped to sap the custom, so beloved of the Victorians, of reading aloud. There was a continued delight in tales of mystery and imagination, and Mrs Archer Clive, with *Paul Ferrol* and *Why Paul Ferrol killed his Wife* (both best-sellers), set in train the modern detective story, which was developed by Wilkie Collins in *The Woman in White* and *The Moonstone* (again, best-sellers). But also the Victorians were sentimentalists, with their feelings, for all their hard exteriors, near the surface. Even stern fathers of families were alleged to have wept over Little Nell and Paul Dombey. The vogue of issuing books in 'parts' or serial form continued. Though illiteracy was still extensive, many who could not read themselves were drawn to reading parties by Dickens's novels in serial form.

By the end of the century the growing vogue of the music-hall and of the country week-end were the two chief innovations in Victorian social life. Cricket, tennis, bicycling, and motor-car riding were becoming established. Holidays by the sea had become a regular feature of the life of the well-to-do, and were spreading rapidly among the poorer classes.

The classical economists continued to be the accepted exponents of British capitalism, John Stuart Mill being their chief living representative, and at the same time the expositor of the new Liberalism which developed after the passage of the first Reform Bill. This Liberalism became increasingly concerned with the rôle of the State and its relationship with individuals. The individualism of the early Victorians had happily blended with the idea of an ordered society, but the increasing power of the State made a synthesis less easy, and the great Liberal writers of the end of the nineteenth century showed their preoccupation with the question. T. H. Green lectured and wrote on the *Principles of Political Obligation*, Bosanquet on the *Philosophical Theory of the State*. These acknowledged the necessity of the increasing functions of the State in a complex society. But Herbert Spencer feared the State as destructive of liberty.

For all their optimism, the Victorians were sometimes

reminded, as with *The Bitter Cry of Outcast London*, that there were still uncharted depths of misery and humiliation in their midst. The comparative few to whom social and spiritual conditions in the second half of the century cried for redress found their own ways of action. William Booth founded the Salvation Army in 1865. Toynbee Hall was founded in 1884. Ruskin in 1867 unburdened himself massively to the two religious groups, both Low and High Church:

"Suppose," he said to the first group,

> only for a little while . . . you were to make it a test of conversion that a man should regularly give . . . half his goods, to the poor, and at once adopt some disagreeable and despised, but thoroughly useful, trade? You cannot think that this would finally be to your disadvantage; you doubtless believe the texts "He that giveth to the poor lendeth to the Lord" and "He that would be chief among you, let him be your servant." The more you parted with, and the lower you stooped, the greater would be your final reward, and final exaltation. You profess to despise human learning and worldly riches; leave both of these to *us*; undertake for us the illiterate and ill-paid employments which must deprive you of the privileges of society and the pleasures of luxury. You cannot possibly preach your faith so forcibly to the world by any quantity of the finest words, as by a few such simple and painful acts.

Then, turning to the second group:

> To you, on the other hand, gentlemen of the embroidered robe, who neither despise learning nor the arts . . . as you have certainly received no definite order for the painting, carving, or lighting up of churches, while the temple of the body of so many poor living Christians is so pale, so mis-shapen, and so ill-lighted; but have, on the contrary, received very definite orders for the feeding and clothing of such sad humanity. . . . Do not burn any more candles, but mould some; do not paint any more windows, but mend a few where the wind comes in, in winter time, with substantial clear glass and putty. Do not vault any more high roofs, but thatch some low ones; and embroider rather on backs which are turned to the cold, than only on those which are turned to congregations.[1]

Carlyle continued his fulminations. Matthew Arnold turned on the middle classes violently, terming them Philistines. William Morris joined Ruskin in his plea for beauty, his passionate denunciation of ugliness as sinful, and went on with a

---

[1] *Time and Tide*, 1867 (*Collected Works*, xvii, 407–09).

group of friends to design houses and articles of everyday use, to make wallpapers and curtains and even to design loose-flowing garments for women, in opposition to the tight-waisted and distorted fashions of the time.

Criticism deepened as the century closed. Gilbert and Sullivan mocked the Victorians, but so merrily that the laughter was infectious. Bellamy's *Looking Backward* was as influential in England as in America. Shaw in his *Plays* and *Prefaces* was satiric, mocking, half serious, and never quite understood by most Victorians. Still less did they understand the massive work of the German Communist Karl Marx, who for so many years had laboured among them at the British Museum. Marx's *Das Kapital* and the more popular *Communist Manifesto*—the one partly translated into English in 1886, the other translated in 1888—expressed a theory of class struggle inevitable because based on the economic contradictions of capitalist society. It became the professed basis of belief of a section of the British working-class movement—notably of the Social Democratic Federation and later of the Communist Party. But the British Labour Party and the trade unions, the strongest sections of British Labour, never had more than a fraction of Marxism or Communist membership. Instead of the inevitability of class war they believed in the inevitability of gradualness. It was *Fabian Essays* rather than the *Communist Manifesto* which influenced them.

As the new century opened the social onslaught quickened. Among the books which made most stir Chiozza Money's *Riches and Poverty*, published in 1905, showed that one-third of the national wealth was in the hands of fewer than one-thirtieth of the population. Four years later Charles Masterman published *The Condition of England*. Galsworthy and Wells joined Shaw in social criticism through plays and novels. But perhaps nothing contributed to the failing optimism of the turn of the century more than the feeling that even where they had been most conscious of virtue the Victorians had not conspicuously succeeded. Neither the Empire nor democracy was proving quite such a good thing as it had seemed. The Boers had fought a stubborn war in South Africa, there were signs that the Empire was not popular with other countries. As for democracy, those who thought deepest were not at all sure that it was yet a success. Political enfranchisement had perhaps marched ahead of educational development and intellectual enlightenment. The ha'penny daily newspaper ensnared the half-educated and prevented their advance to reading of worth. The suburbs where they lived trapped them in a vacuum free from political or social life or corresponding obligation. The 'man in the street' had become important politically before he was fit to bear his responsibilities. "The man-in-the-street," said Leonard Hobhouse in 1904,

> is now the typical representative of public opinion, and the man-in-the-street means the man who is hurrying from his home to his office, or to a place of amusement . . . the man who has not time to think and will not take the trouble to do so if he has the time. He is the faithful reflex of the popular sheet and the shouting newsboy. . . . To this new public opinion of the streets and the tramcars it is useless to appeal in terms of reason; it has not time to put the two ends of an argument together; it has hardly patience to receive a single idea, much less to hold two in the mind and compare them.[1]

For a few years, coinciding partly with the reign of King Edward, a brighter spirit developed, but after the First World War the mood of pessimism and uncertainty deepened. There came an unsure feverishness in literature and the arts. Though the revolt against Victorian ugliness was complete, there was nothing to put in its place. The younger poets and novelists reflected the horror that war had wrought and the failure of the peace to give them stability or hope. Spiritually men were at a loss. Churchgoing had ceased to be an accepted duty or even a social obligation. But the breakdown of the concept of religion as the Victorians understood it had been followed by the erection of no commonly accepted spiritual value. Scientific knowledge became ever wider and far outdistanced any plans man had made for its utilization. Politically, as the power of the State grew stronger, rival forms of totalitarianism disputed its control in the forms of Communism and Fascism. In Britain Liberalism and individualism grew weaker, but after the Second World War it was the Labour Party which found itself at the head of the State, with an enormous concentration of power in its hands, which it attempted to use not in the form of crude dictatorship, but of Socialist democracy. It was helped by the fact that the continued spread and improvement of

---

[1] *Democracy and Reaction*, pp. 70–71.

education, the extension of adult education of many kinds, was shaping a democracy that in its capacity to put the two ends of an argument together belied the fears of Hobhouse.

So far the chronicle. The story has yet no ending. Strife and endeavour lie before as well as behind. Stupendous sources of power are about to be released which will dwarf the achievements of earlier years. For less than a century and a half has Britain been an industrial power. In that time production of all kinds has multiplied, her middle classes have risen to power, her working classes follow; the State has become stronger, all-embracing, scarcely any social or economic activity being outside its orbit. *Laissez-faire*, so newly achieved, is already an outworn dogma. Not the position of classes, but the control of the State, is the vital question. A new way of life has emerged, different from the past in its nature, its values, its pleasures. We know more, we can do more. May the story of our past help us to do it better.

SELECT BIBLIOGRAPHY

BRINTON, C.: *English Political Thought in the Nineteenth Century* (Benn, 1933).

CRUSE, A.: *The Victorians and their Books* (Allen and Unwin, 1935).

——: *After the Victorians* (Allen and Unwin, 1938).

GRETTON, R. H.: *A Modern History of the English People, 1880–1922* (Secker, 1929).

HEARNSHAW, F. J. C. (Ed.): *Edwardian England, 1901–1910* (Benn, 1933).

—— (Ed.): *The Social and Political Ideas of Some Representative Thinkers of the Victorian Age* (Harrap, 1933).

HOBHOUSE, L.: *Democracy and Reaction* (Unwin, 1904).

LAVER, J.: *Taste and Fashion from the French Revolution to the Present Day* (Harrap, 1937; revised edition, 1945).

QUENNELL, MARJORIE AND C. H. B.: *A History of Everyday Things in England*, vol. iv, 1851–1942; revised edition (Batsford, 1942).

SWINNERTON, F. A.: *The Georgian Literary Scene* (Heinemann, 1935).

WEYMOUTH, A.: *This Century of Change, 1853–1952* (Harrap, 1953).

YOUNG, G. M. (Ed.): *Early Victorian England, 1830–1865*, 2 vols. (Oxford University Press, 1934).

PART IV

THE AGE OF AFFLUENCE

CHAPTER XXVI

INTO THE SIXTIES

THE general pattern of the fifteen years 1950–65, in spite of some fluctuation, is one of continued improvement in our economic position, in our social relationships, and in the standard of living of the majority of our people. The Welfare State is firmly established, the nationalization of the basic industries and services (with some modifications) is an accepted fact, the necessity of economic and social planning is not disputed. On July 3, 1954, consumer ration books were consigned to the bonfire, and as other legacies of the War went the same way the nation turned its back on austerity and entered a period characterized by expansion in every direction.

The population rose by a million between 1945 and 1951 and by a further 2 million in the next ten years, the census of 1961 giving a total of 51 million people for Great Britain, 5 per cent. more than in 1951; there were an estimated 52 million in 1965. The total working population meantime grew from 23.5 million in 1951 to some 25 million in 1965. The numbers employed in the basic occupations have shown a steady decline since the War. In agriculture and fishing they have fallen from about 1 in 23 of the working population in 1954 to 1 in 26 in 1960; in coal-mining from 1 in 27 or 28 to 1 in 36 over the same period; in the ancient trade of shipbuilding and marine engineering only 1 in 98 of the working population was employed in 1960.

The group producing electrical and engineering goods, meanwhile, was the biggest single productive group, comprising 1 in 11 or 12 of the working population in 1960. Taken with Metal Manufacture, Vehicles, and Other Metal Goods, it comprised 1 in 5 or 6 of the working population.

The trend away from the old heavy industries to the new continued into the sixties, and was paralleled by the spectacular growth of the group comprising services of various kinds. Those classified by the Ministry of Labour as employed on "Financial, professional, scientific and miscellaneous services" numbered nearly 5 million persons in 1960, just about the same as the total employed in all heavy industry, 1 in under 5 of the working population. If to these are added workers in direct national government and local government service, the total of 6,204,000 in 1960 was by far the biggest single group—1 in 4 of the working population. The distributive trades had risen substantially also, from 2,802,000 to 3,335,000—more than those employed in the engineering and electrical trades, and not far short of the whole of heavy industry taken together—about 1 in 7 of the working population: the whole of the increased civil working population of nearly a million between 1954 and 1960 went to the non-productive sector of industry; and there was an additional transfer from the productive sector of nearly 400,000 persons, making something like 1,400,000 more persons engaged on non-productive work. The ratio of non-productive to productive workers was then about 6¾ to 10, or 2 to 3—and this

DISTRIBUTION OF MANPOWER IN 1954[1]

Total Working Population		23,816,000	
Civil Employment		22,714,000	
Metals, engineering, and vehicles	(M)	4,487,000	
Transport and communications	(B)	1,692,000	
Miscellaneous manufactures	(M)	1,590,000	
Building and contracting	(M)	1,438,000	
Agriculture and fishing	(B)	1,022,000	
Textiles	(M)	995,000	Productive
Food, drink, and tobacco	(M)	905,000	14,564,000
Mining and quarrying	(B)	865,000	
Clothing, including footwear	(M)	685,000	
Chemicals and allied trades	(M)	509,000	
Gas, electricity, and water	(B)	376,000	
Professional, financial, and miscellaneous		4,037,000	
Distribution		2,802,000	Non-productive
Local Government service		728,000	8,150,000
National Government service		583,000	
·Total of Basic Industries	(B)	3,955,000	
Total of Manufacturing Industries	(M)	10,609,000	

[1] *Economic Survey, 1955* (Cmd. 9412), p. 29.

DISTRIBUTION OF MANPOWER IN 1960[1]

Total Working Population		24,557,000
Civil Employment (excluding armed forces)		23,711,000
Engineering and electrical goods	(M)	2,103,000
Transport and communication	(B)	1,667,000
Other manufactures	(M)	1,639,000
Construction	(B)	1,548,000
Agriculture, forestry and fishing	(B)	939,000
Vehicles	(M)	909,000
Textiles	(M)	853,000
Food, drink, and tobacco	(M)	819,000
Coal-mining	(B)	675,000
Metal manufacture	(M)	633,000
Clothing and footwear	(M)	589,000
Metal goods not elsewhere specified	(M)	564,000
Chemicals and allied industries	(M)	538,000
Gas, electricity, and water	(B)	377,000
Shipbuilding and marine engineering	(M)	250,000
Other mining and quarrying	(B)	69,000

Productive 14,172,000

Financial, professional, scientific, and miscellaneous services		4,964,000
Distribution		3,335,000
Local Government service		738,000
National Government service		502,000

Non-productive 9,539,000

Total of Basic Industries	(B)	5,275,000
Total of Manufacturing Industries	(M)	8,897,000

excludes those in the armed forces. The trend, which is typical of a highly populated industrial country with rising wage rates and a rising consumer demand, continued unabated into the middle sixties, forming one of the major social as well as one of the major economic characteristics of our time.

Production was seen to rise throughout the period, although automation, nuclear power, and liquid gas by no means reached their full potential, and the continued spectacular

[1] *Economic Survey, 1961* (Cmnd. 1334), p. 55.

rise in incomes of all kinds outstripped the rate of increase in the product of industry. One result of this was a continued inflation which checked Britain's exports and threatened her economy, and it became a major task of government to curb it by an 'incomes policy' or a 'prices policy.' To this end—and also to pay for the rising cost of the social services—taxation was high and wage restraint repeatedly urged. Meanwhile the working classes, helped by high wages, full employment, the National Health Service, pensions, family allowances, and other social services, were better off than ever before.

In spite of the overall progression, the fifteen years have had their crises. In 1951 the balance of trade fell sharply against us to the tune of £521,000,000.[1] This was partly because of a rise in imports. In 1951 they were £3,497,000,000, compared with the 1949 figure of £1,974,000,000, and the increase was due not only to higher prices, but also to about 16 per cent. increase in the *volume* of imports. This increase in volume was due partly to increased home consumption, but partly to the replacement of commercial and other stocks which had heavily depreciated.

There was nothing to set against these increased imports. On the contrary, the adverse balance was augmented by a fall in world demand for textile and other consumer goods which we exported; by a fall in British 'invisible exports,' particularly shipping services; by the fact that interest on the United States and Canadian loans became payable at the end of the year; and by an increase in military expenditure due to commitments in Europe, the Korean war, and trouble in Malaya and the Middle East.

The Government had to act quickly and drastically. It announced a cut in imports amounting to £600,000,000, falling mainly on food consumption, and on the stockpiling of food, tobacco, and raw materials. The measures were effective. By 1952 the balance of payments crisis was checked, largely by a reduction of imports, which fell to £2,927,000,000 in 1952, and partly by an increase of exports, which rose from £2,748,000,000 in 1951 to £2,836,000,000 in 1952.[2] Expressed in the volume of goods imported, the cuts were not so acute as they sounded. Taking 1950 as the basic year, they were:

---

[1] *Economic Survey, 1952* (Cmd. 8509), p. 10.
[2] *Economic Survey, 1953* (Cmd. 8800), p. 9.

Goods	1950	1951	1952[1]
Food, drink, and tobacco . .	100	110	98
Raw materials	100	111	104
Manufactured goods . . .	100	121	111

In 1953, to the accompaniment of a world revival in trade, we were able to restore many of our import cuts, particularly food, tobacco, and animal feeding stuffs. The quantity of tobacco increased by 50 per cent. over the 1952 level.[2] Exports of capital goods, such as machinery, remained relatively stable, but the export of consumer goods, particularly aircraft, refined petroleum, arms and ammunition, showed a large increase. Coal exports, at 14,000,000 tons, were the highest since the War.[3]

Two years later there was again a worsening of the terms of trade. Coal production did not fulfil the bright hopes of 1953, and did not rise in line with the increased demands of home consumption and export. Exports of coal had, in fact, fallen, and imports of coal risen. In addition, the demand for steel was running ahead of production. With practically full employment at home the increased demand could be met only by longer hours of work, which trade unions were often unwilling to permit. Further, full employment and high wages provided a buoyancy to home demand which failed to give the manufacturer stimulus to increase his export trade.

The year 1955 ended on a note of uncertainty. Higher production and greater exports were still needed. Against this, wages and salaries were high enough to create a very large consumer demand and an unwillingness to work overtime. In spite of increased purchase-tax on goods of many kinds, announced in an emergency budget at the end of 1955, the Christmas spending of that year reached a record height, and resulted in the withdrawal of very large sums from National Savings.

Full employment, rising prices, and rising wages gave, at the beginning of 1956, a feeling of buoyancy to the country as a whole, but the inflationary situation still caused anxiety. Unless the cost of living could be pegged down it would be impossible

[1] *Ibid.*, p. 11.
[2] *Economic Survey, 1954* (Cmd. 9108), pp. 10–11.
[3] *Ibid.*, p. 14.

to resist the trade union demands for ever higher wages, and the spiral would continue to ascend.

This is, in fact, what happened, wages, salaries, and consumer spending all continuing to rise faster than national productivity.

The annual average wage per head of those employed, including salaried workers, increased by 6½ per cent. between 1948 and 1958, by a further 2½ per cent. in 1958, and a further 3½ per cent. in 1959. In the second half of 1960 earnings per head were 7 per cent. higher than in the second half of 1959. Between these last dates consumer spending, after all taxes and personal savings had been allowed for, increased from under sixteen million pounds to nearly sixteen and three-quarter million.

National productivity was not keeping pace with these increases. After three years of little change, industrial production rose rapidly between October 1958 and April 1960, but then levelled off and changed little during the rest of the year. In a few industries output even fell—notably in the motor industry in the second half of 1960, which suffered a fall in export demand and a sharp decline in home demand. So while domestic incomes rose between 1959 and 1961 at an average annual rate of 6¼ per cent., the value of domestic output rose by only 3¼ per cent.[1] By the beginning of 1961 a familiar inflationary cycle was in operation, with an increasing pressure of home demand upon goods of all kinds pushing up both prices and costs, including wages, and resulting in a serious deficit in the external balance of payments. The Budget of 1961 provided for a net increase in taxation largely by an increase in profits tax and higher indirect taxation, but a shortage of labour, particularly skilled, served to push wage rates up even more rapidly. By the middle of the year inflation and adverse trade balances threatened the value of the £ all over the world.

Emergency measures announced on July 25, 1961, included an increase in Bank Rate from 5 per cent. to 7 per cent., a restriction of credit, and a pay pause which would stop or materially restrict wage, salary, and dividend increases in order to bring the rise in incomes more into line with the growth of national production. Even so, the index of retail prices was 4¼ per cent. higher in the fourth quarter of 1961 than a year earlier.[2]

[1] *Economic Survey, 1962* (Cmnd. 1678), pp. 19, 21.
[2] *Economic Survey, 1962* (Cmnd. 1678), p. 22.

By the end of 1961 the upward pressure of demand had been considerably reduced, and on January 29, 1962, the Government announced that the pay pause would end on March 31. To underline the lessons, not only that spending and production must keep in step but that a Government must plan to this end, it issued a White Paper on incomes policy[1] which expressed the view that increases in incomes in 1962 should not exceed 2½ per cent. It also set up a National Economic Development Council to consider ways of improving economic performance. 'Neddy' had its first meeting in March 1962.

The removal of restrictions was immediately followed by the wage demands held in check over the previous months. In all, about 12¾ million manual workers received an increase in 1962 of about £5¼ million in their basic full-time weekly wages, and the increases continued all round in the following years, in wages, salaries, dividends, profits. The increases were spent on food, alcohol, tobacco, housing, fuel and light, clothing and footwear, cars and durable household goods, on petrol, travel, entertainment. Nothing, perhaps, gives so vivid a picture of the modern family's consumption as the new Index of Retail Prices announced by the Minister of Labour's Cost of Living Advisory Committee on March 16, 1962. Here appeared for the first time, roasting chicken, fish fingers, sherry, electric cookers, refrigerators, motor-scooters, nylon underwear—all far beyond the imagination of the families who lived at the level of the 1914 cost-of-living index, which merely included the bare subsistence items necessary to a working-man's family. A daily newspaper, underlining the items which appear in the cost-of-living index for the first time, drew this picture of the housewife of 1962:

> This week-end the lady of the house should be lounging in *jeans* and *thick-knit sweater* over her *nylon panties* and *girdle*, sipping a glass of *sherry* and nibbling *potato crisps* in her *gloss-paint* lounge with its *oil heater* and *latex-backed carpet* before taking the *roast chicken* or *fish fingers* out of the *refrigerator*, and popping it into the *electric cooker* while her man should be cleaning his *motor-scooter* from a *plastic bucket* and keeping an eye on his *wrist-watch*.[2]

Such a rosy picture of Britain in the nineteen-sixties should not obscure the fact that this is Mrs Average Housewife, and

[1] *Incomes Policy: The Next Step* (Cmnd. 1626), February 1962.
[2] The *Daily Express*, March 17, 1962.

that many people in Britain were not only below this level, but well below it. There were low-paid workers, and pensioners whose incomes lagged far below prices, to whom such a picture would appear derisory. Nor should it obscure the fact that, although Britain still enjoyed a higher income per head than any major country except the United States, her annual economic growth was lower than that of almost any other European country.

INDICES OF INDUSTRIAL PRODUCTION (1950=100)[1]

	1952	1953	1954	1955	1956	1957	1958	1959
W. Germany	126	139	156	179	193	204	211	225
France	110	112	122	131	144	156	165	170
Italy	117	128	140	153	164	177	181	202
Netherlands	103	114	125	134	140	143	143	158
Belgium	109	108	114	125	132	132	124	129
Luxembourg	122	112	116	130	139	142	136	142
U.S.A.	111	119	111	124	127	127	119	133
U.K.	101	106	115	121	121	123	121	129

The share borne by co-operative trading in what, despite some contrary indications and not a few forebodings, must be regarded as a period of prosperity, is still substantial, whether reckoned by increasing membership, growing sales, building activity on new stores and the reorganization of old, a larger share and loan capital, or a greater average sale per member. But growth has failed to keep up with the increased spending of the population, a larger proportion of whose money goes to stores other than the co-operative.

Trade-union membership also grows, but not as fast as the population. Of a total working population in civil employment in 1954 of 22·7 million, there were 9·5 million trade unionists. Of a total working population in civil employment in 1963 of 24·4 million, there were 9·9 million trade unionists. Out of the 1¾ million new workers in civil employment less than half a million joined a union. Yet it is these trade unionists who are the spearhead of organized labour, keeping wages up and hours of work down. They are partly responsible for the difficulties

[1] P.E.P. (Political and Economic Planning), "Planning," Vol. XXVI, No. 445, p. 287.

of successive Governments in operating a prices and incomes policy.

Unemployment over the period was practically eliminated, though there remained—and always will—a small core of virtually unemployable labour and a fluctuating number of temporarily unemployed—mostly people changing jobs or school-leavers looking for the right niche. There were one or two bad periods—all-round demand, for example, ceased to rise in the second half of 1962 and left its legacy in rising unemployment figures. And on top of this came the disastrous snow and ice of the record cold winter of 1962–63 when all building work stopped and unemployment grew. At the end of 1962 492,000 persons were wholly unemployed, and 40,000 temporarily: a total of 532,000, not counting the 34,000 school-leavers under eighteen who were knocking at the door. Almost no areas were without unemployment. Scotland and the North of England were very badly hit; so were London and the South-east. Through the first months of 1963 the figures rose—815,000 in January, 878,000 in February.

Reductions in purchase-tax on motor-cars and other commodities, a lowering of the Bank Rate, and an improvement in the weather helped a slow but steady economic recovery. Unemployment declined from March onward, being down to 475,000 in October.[1] In that month, too, signs of a full recovery were apparent in the outstanding success of British cars at the Motor Show and the general development of this industry which, in many ways, has come to be a pointer to economic health generally. But Scotland and the North still lagged, and the Government was sufficiently alarmed to send a representative to the North-east and then, in the Government reconstruction of October 1963, to create the post of Secretary of State for Industry, Trade, and Regional Development and to set on foot a series of regional Enquiries. There followed efforts to entice industry and Government departments to the North, but the pull of the South remained strong, and the trends had not been reversed by 1965. But by that time the expanding economy was clamouring for more labour than it could get, and immigrants of many nationalities were crowding to our shores, the West Indians and Pakistanis, in particular, creating pressure upon housing and schooling that frequently led to friction.

[1] The monthly *Ministry of Labour Gazette* provides these figures.

REGISTERED UNEMPLOYED IN GREAT BRITAIN

ANNUAL AVERAGES	TOTAL
1939	1,513,600
1951	252,900
1952	414,300
1953	342,000
1954	284,800
1955	232,200
1956	257,000
1957	312,500
1958	457,400
1959	475,200
1960	360,400
1962 (Dec.)	566,000
1963 (Feb.)	878,000
1963 (Oct.)	475,000
1964 (April)	412,000
1965 (April)	341,000

It was recognized that Britain needed to encourage her scientists, to speed the use of automation and apply greater energy to selling overseas. She also endeavoured to join the European Common Market of France, Belgium, Italy, Luxembourg, Germany, and Holland. Home opinion was much divided on the benefits of this move, and her 'rebuttal at the gates of the Common Market' in 1963 caused little economic dislocation.

More serious was the extent of the trade deficit which became apparent during the course of 1964. A Labour Government won office at the end of the year partly on the promise to speed automation and efficiency in British industry and to re-vitalize the export trade, and partly because the worst trade-balance figures we had had—a deficit of some £700,000,000 for the year —was laid at the door of the Tories, who had held office for thirteen years. By the middle of 1965, although the immediate crisis had been averted, it was not clear that the general position had materially altered, either in terms of the trade balance, the position of sterling, the inflationary situation, or the much-vaunted incomes or prices policy.

A still unknown factor is the speed with which nuclear energy will be harnessed for industrial use, the extent to which this will change existing social and economic patterns, and the role to be played by Britain. In the first Industrial Revolution, Britain was in a uniquely favourable position. In science she led the world, and it was from Britain that most of the inventions came. These inventions her wealth enabled her freely to develop. Beneath her soil there were what seemed to be inexhaustible reserves of coal, the basic raw material on which progress was to depend. In the middle of the twentieth century the position is far different. For the basic raw materials on which nuclear power depends—uranium and thorium—Britain is comparatively well placed, for though she has negligible resources herself, there are in the Commonwealth, and especially in Australia, large reserves. But many other factors are involved: capital, scientific manpower, the relationship of nuclear to conventional forms of power, especially in the light of newly discovered large reserves of natural gas in Holland and Africa, which by 1964 were reaching Britain in liquid form in ships specially built for the purpose. Meanwhile in February 1955 the Government presented to Parliament its *Programme of Nuclear Power*,[1] declaring that "Nuclear energy is the energy of the future," and proposing a ten-year programme which would be started about the middle of 1957, and bring into operation eight nuclear power stations by 1965. This is a modest programme, and, even so, perhaps over-optimistic.[2] But although the cost would be high, the reward would be great. Once capital expenditure had been made, running costs would be lower than for other types of power station. Above all, the heat from one ton of fuel in a nuclear power station would be the equivalent of that provided by 10,000 tons of coal.[3]

The programme was trebled in 1957, in spite of the fears of some people that even the original programme was over-optimistic. But the more cautious estimates proved correct, and there was first a 'deferment' in October 1957 and then, on June 20, 1960, the Minister announced a 'cutback' in the rate of acceleration. This was partly due to the fact that, in spite of fears, an acute coal-shortage did not develop; that supplies of oil were more abundant than had been estimated; and that

[1] Cmd. 9389.   [2] H. W. B. Skinner, *op. cit.*   [3] Cmd. 9389.

although technical advances allowed a decrease in the cost of power from conventional stations, the cost of power from the first nuclear stations was higher than forecast. The modified programme allowed for nine atomic reactors at nuclear power stations by 1969, and three were actually completed by the early part of 1964 and the others all under construction.

Of the other nationalized concerns electricity and gas were doing spectacularly well. The coal-mining industry, since its nationalization on January 1, 1947, has undergone at least two distinct phases. For the first ten years the problem was one of raising production to meet increasing consumption. In 1947 about 190,000,000 tons of coal were being mined—about the same as before the War. In 1956, 228,000,000 tons were being mined, and demand was so high that domestic coal was rationed and other uses were 'programmed.'

But before the year was out a new phase had been introduced which resulted in a rapid decrease of consumption. The figure for 1957 was 221,000,000 tons; for 1958, 208,000,000 tons; and for 1959, 195,000,000 tons. The reasons for the earlier expansion of demand are found in post-War reconstruction and the needs of the heavy industries. The recession is explained partly by the fact that this demand was falling, partly by the fact that industry generally was hit by the transient national recession of 1957–58, partly in a greater efficiency in the use of coal, partly in the mild weather of 1959 which caused domestic demand to fall. It is also relevant that in 1958, while the consumption of coal fell by 13,000,000 tons, the consumption of oil rose by 6,500,000 tons of coal equivalent. By 1965 both electricity and gas were also formidable rivals on every front, while the Clean Air Act of 1956, making provisions for the establishment of smokeless zones, hindered an increase in domestic coal consumption.

The Coal Board rose splendidly to the challenge. It introduced smokeless fuels of several kinds, it modernized and mechanized its pits, improved the working and living conditions, as well as the pay, of its miners, and planned output at about 200,000,000 tons a year to meet the expected level of demand and maintain a capacity for expansion if needed.

British Railways presented an equally difficult problem. The mergers and amalgamations which had taken place over the years had resulted in a mixture of good, bad, and indifferent services within a near-monopoly organization. Nationalization had not appreciably changed the picture, and a modernization of equipment in the middle fifties had taken place without any basic change in the scope of the railway system or of the services it provided. By 1953 profits were declining, and by 1955 they had turned into a rising loss. The Prime Minister, speaking in the House of Commons on March 11, 1960, foreshadowed the reshaping of the whole system, and it was with this in mind that an inquiry was set up under the chairmanship of Dr Richard Beeching, which reported in 1963.[1]

The general conclusions of the Beeching Report that traffic should be built up on the well-loaded routes, and that routes and stations which did not pay their way should be closed down, was not, superficially, objectionable. But the list of proposed closures was very long. Not only were familiar lines and stations with sentimental attachments to be closed, but people wondered about some of the holiday peak traffic discussed in the Board of Trade's report on holidays. There were fears of complete road blockages if more travellers were forced on to the roads. There were difficulties over compensating staff who would be redundant. By and large, there is a general recognition that a large public service like the railway system must be forced into greater efficiency, but a note of warning has also been sounded against committing our future too squarely to roads and abandoning a system, or parts of a system, of transport whose permanent obsolescence has by no means been proved.

Steel, nationalized by the Labour Government in 1949, was denationalized by the Tories three years later. The Labour Government proposed renationalization in a White Paper[2] published in 1965: in no case did the Government's action appear to be supported by any strong economic reason.

At the end of December 1958 it was possible to look back upon the first ten years of the National Health Service. The task which faced those responsible for the new service when it was inaugurated, on July 5, 1948, was herculean—three thousand hospitals to be taken over, many of them old, all of differing sizes, capacity, standards, and traditions; extensive war damage to be made good; a population encouraged to be

[1] *The Reshaping of British Railways* (H.M.S.O., 1963).
[2] *Statement on Steel Nationalization*, April 1965 (Cmnd. 2651).

increasingly disease-conscious, and ready to swamp existing surgeries and hospitals; medical men to be persuaded not only of the rightness of the system but of the necessity of swallowing the large quantity of paper-work which is the regrettable adjunct of any public service. That it was undertaken in such comprehensive fashion was a magnificent demonstration of the way in which Britain had become one nation. Naturally the cost was high. Naturally there were mistakes. Initially there was concern over what seemed like over-spending. In the first complete year, 1949–50, £403,000,000 were spent on the National Health Service in England and Wales. In 1957–58 £626,000,000 were spent. In 1959 the cost was £726,000,000. Yet, as a written answer to a Parliamentary question on March 18, 1960, showed, no higher percentage of the gross national product was being spent:

Gross Cost of National Health Service for Great Britain
as Percentage of the Gross National Product

1949	3·7
1951	3·5
1952	3·6
1953	3·4
1954	3·3
1955	3·3
1956	3·3
1957	3·3
1958	3·4
1959 (est.)	3·6

Yet, with the Exchequer meeting 68 per cent. of the cost, the burden of the State was heavy. Patients' charges in respect of dental treatment, dentures, spectacles, hospital appliances, were increased; so were National Health Insurance contributions. But rising costs continued to be alarming, and in 1953 a Committee was appointed to inquire into the finances of the whole Service. The Guillebaud Committee reported in 1956, concluding that there was no foundation for the charge of widespread extravagance, that it could not make any recommendation which would reduce the Health Service cost in a substantial degree, and that no major change was needed in its general administrative structure. The Committee also pointed out that the increasing cost was due, to the extent of 70 per cent., to the inflationary trend of the economy. The cost continued to rise, augmented by increases in doctors' salaries and in the rising costs of everything that contributed to the Service from bandages to buildings, from medicines to meals, from surgical instruments to nurses' aprons. For the year 1963–64 the total cost was £1,028,000,000, National Health contributions were £146,000,000, patients' charges were £68,000,000 and the Exchequer contributed £690,000,000. Yet in 1965 the Labour Government abolished prescription charges, so lowering patients' contributions and increasing the Exchequer payment.

The return for this expenditure was seen in a steadily expanding hospital intake, the reduction of waiting-lists, the immediate admission of urgent and emergency cases; it was seen in crowded doctors' surgeries and in the dispensing of more than 200,000,000 prescriptions in a year: it is not always easy to assess the improvement that these facts represent. The hospitals embarked on a large building programme estimated to cost about £500,000,000 for England and Wales between 1961 and 1971, and £70,000,000 for Scotland over the same period. This capital re-equipment was long overdue, and many other deficiencies have not yet been tackled—for example, the relationship between the general practitioner and the hospital technician is not close enough, while the Health Centres which might bring nursing and secretarial assistance as well as diagnostic aid to the doctor are not coming into operation quickly enough. And, as the report of the Ministry of Health for 1960 remarked, it would still be a great gain to the country, "if instead of preoccupation with disease and drugs and hospitals, people thought more of preserving good health and acting on the advice available to them on how this may best be done."

One of the aids to preventive medicine is undoubtedly good housing. While a National Health scheme had been dealing with one aspect of Chadwick's problem, and making progress in spite of the pressures upon available buildings, equipment, and personnel, the housing position was proving very difficult.

During the War bombing had destroyed houses, factories, offices, hospitals, all of which could claim priority in a reconstruction programme. But when it came to rebuilding after the War the British Government had to consider not only these claims but those of general maintenance, of reconditioning, and of new schemes, such as those connected with atomic research. It had also to consider the relation of builders and building materials to other workers and other industries, especially in view of the emphasis which had necessarily to be put on the export industries. When all these factors had been taken into account the resources available for new houses or reconditioning old ones were not very substantial.

Of the £6½ billion which was, in fact, spent on fixed capital objects in the period 1948–51, three-quarters was spent on industrial projects and one-quarter on social and administrative. Of this quarter, three-quarters went to new houses, and the rest to hospitals, schools, Government offices, and the like.[1]

To deal with the housing problem, and to leave the Ministry of Health free to concentrate upon the administration of the National Health Service, alterations were made in the Government departments dealing with these matters.

In January 1951 the Minister of Town and Country Planning became the Minister of Local Government and Planning, and during the year were vested in him, besides his planning functions, all the responsibilities of the Minister of Health, except the administration of the National Health Service, which remained the Ministry of Health's sole function. This gave to the Ministry of Local Government and Planning 'environmental public health' such as water-supply, sewage disposal, and public cleansing, as well as planning. In May 1951 the name of this Ministry was again changed, and it became the Ministry of Housing and Local Government. It still maintained its planning function, but the change in its title underlined the emphasis which the Conservative Government was putting on its rehousing programme. As a Government White Paper expressed it, "The pressing need for house building and the many other demands upon the resources available have led to the assumption by the Central Government of responsibility for directing housing as a national campaign."[2]

In 1950, 1951, and 1952 the Labour Government had planned to complete 175,000 new houses in England and Wales each year. The actual figures fell rather below this in 1950 and 1951, when about 172,000 houses were provided. The public was getting restless. In the election of 1951 the Conservatives promised a higher priority to housing in allocating national

[1] D. H. Robertson, *Britain in the World Economy*, pp. 13–14.
[2] *Report of the Ministry of Housing and Local Government for the Period 1950/51 to 1954* (Cmd. 9559), p. 4.

resources, and, largely on the strength of this promise, were returned to office. They were nearly as good as their word, and
in 1952 nearly 209,000 new houses were completed in England
and Wales (240,000 in Great Britain); in 1953, 279,000 new
houses were completed in England and Wales (319,000 in Great
Britain); and in 1954, 309,000 in England and Wales (348,000
in Great Britain).[1]

Most of this building was done by local authorities heavily
subsidized by the Government, but private building, again
encouraged by the Government, increased. But although the
avowed target of 300,000 new houses a year was reached and
passed, the end of the housing shortage was not in sight. Early
marriage, larger families, better wages, immigration, all continued to build up a demand greater than the supply—and all
the time older houses were needing repair, and slum areas still
remained uncleared. To deal with this situation a slum-clearance programme was launched in 1956 with a target of 375,000
houses to be cleared in five years—some 45 per cent. of the total
estimate of unfit houses. The following year the Conservative
Government by the Rent Act removed the upper limit to rents
imposed by war-time legislation, believing that higher rents
would encourage more letting. There was no spectacular rise
either of accommodation offered or of rents, but the Labour
Government in 1965 proposed to re-impose restrictions. By this
time, however, attention had been riveted upon the Report of a
Committee on Housing in Greater London under the chairmanship of Sir Milner Holland which revealed gross conditions
of overcrowding, lack of amenities, and slum conditions in
houses in multiple occupation which yielded high profits to
unscrupulous landlords.

As part of its task in providing new houses, as well as in reducing the congestion in our great cities, the Ministry, under
the New Towns Act of 1946, was empowered to approve the
construction of new towns to take the 'over-spill' from London
and other big cities. To supplement these, the Town Development Act of 1952 was to help the expansion of any small town
willing to take population from overcrowded cities. Under the
first Act twelve new towns came into being. By the end of 1954
in these new towns more than 27,000 houses had been built,
and 131 factories with an employment potential of over 17,600

[1] *Ibid.*, p. 5.

had been completed. As the population continued to grow more towns were planned, more spaces scheduled for building, and the problems of diverting population from the South became more urgent, but no more easy of solution.

NEW TOWN	COUNTY	DATE OF DESIG- NATION	PRO- POSED POPULA- TION	AREA[1] DESIG- NATED
London New Towns				*Acres*
Stevenage	Herts	1946	60,000	6,100
Crawley	Sussex	1947	50,000	5,920
Hemel Hemp- stead	Herts	1947	60,000	5,910
Harlow	Essex	1947	80,000	6,320
Welwyn Garden City	Herts	1948	50,000[2]	4,230
Hatfield	Herts	1948	25,000	2,340
Basildon	Essex	1949	80,000	7,834
Bracknell	Berks	1949	25,000	1,850
Provincial New Towns				
Aycliffe	Durham	1947	10,000	880
Peterlee	Durham	1948	30,000	2,350
Corby	Northants	1950	40,000	2,675
Welsh New Town				
Cwmbran	Monmouth	1949	35,000	3,160

The 'cleaning-up' functions of the Ministry of Housing and Local Government are those necessary to a healthy environment, both in new and older towns. They include an attempt to deal with the smoke-laden fog which is a growing menace in our big cities. After the particularly virulent 'smog' of December 1952, when the death-rate suddenly increased by 4000 in a week, and illness mounted alarmingly, a Committee was appointed, and, as the Air Pollution Committee, published its report in November 1954. It urged the strengthening of the law for the control of air pollution, not only in respect of the smoke and grit and harmful gases from factory chimneys, but also in respect of the ordinary domestic coal fire.

[1] Cmd. 9559, p. 100.   [2] Increase under consideration.

In line with the general expansionary trend, National Insurance and Health benefits were raised from time to time—a fact which helped particularly the non-contributory, fixed-income class like widows and the old, whose weekly pension reached £4 in 1965. It is also in line with the development of the Welfare State that holidays should become a matter of public concern. Both the increasing number of holiday-makers, and those who cater for them, suffer from the present concentration of holidays on to one or two months—largely because of works holidays and school holidays. In 1937 about 15 million people took a holiday, by 1956 23 million (about half the population), by 1962 30 million, or 60 per cent. of the population, were leaving home in the summer. Of these about 26½ million people spent holidays in Britain. There were in addition some 7 or 8 million day trippers, and travellers abroad frequently spent a night at each end of their holiday in this country, so increasing the pressure generally upon home resources.

Of all these holidays in 1962, 63 per cent. were taken in July or August, and nearly a quarter of these were taken in the single fortnight at the end of July and the begining of August, not counting the day trippers, of whom there were about 3 million in the period round August Bank Holiday. The resulting crowds, packed trains, traffic jams, poor service, and high prices led to a survey by the Board of Trade and suggestions that the school General Certificate Examination should be taken in June, and that works, factory, and office holidays should be staggered.[1]

In a healthy community mental and intellectual development goes side by side with physical well-being. The opening paragraph of the Report of the Ministry of Education for 1960 indicates that the educational services are not lagging. "Whether the yardstick is the number of children in school, the number of serving teachers, the total of building work in progress, or the growth of technical education the record of expansion is there to see; but education is a service where the more that is done the clearer becomes the need to advance even further."

In the period under review no change was made in the basic pattern laid down by the Butler Act of 1944; but there was a growing ferment within the pattern. At the bottom of the scale

---

[1] *Staggered Holidays*, a Report of the Board of Trade (1963) (Cmnd. 2105).

comprehensive schools which aimed at bridging the gulf between the more clever and the not so clever were still viewed with considerable suspicion in 1955: by 1965 they were no longer bold experiments. Their number had grown substantially, and the Labour Government announced its acceptance of the comprehensive principle. But it is still too early to anticipate how fast and how widely they will spread. The grammar schools cling tenaciously to their reputation, and confirm their value, but the public schools continue to remain an anomaly within the system. The attempt to make them more representative by introducing a substantial proportion of boys who were not privately paid for, as the Fleming Report recommended, broke down because local authorities could not or would not afford the expense of high fees when they could provide a good education at much less expense in their own grammar schools. But the attacks on the public-school system have displayed less bitterness, and there is more constructive thinking about the practical problems involved.

In the general field of secondary education the accent on science became considerably more pronounced during these years, and at the same time there developed a growing dissatisfaction with the high degree of specialization in sixth-form studies that had so long been taken for granted. But attempts to introduce radical changes met with little response, and most educationists continued in typical British manner to prefer gradual change. Meanwhile there was a tendency throughout public schools and grammar schools for boys and girls to stay at school beyond an age when they would previously have left to earn a living. The number of university students increased sharply, but considerably less sharply than in some of the other countries of Europe. In 1958 there were in Great Britain 19·9 per 10,000 of the population at universities; but in Holland, West Germany, Italy, Belgium, Switzerland, Sweden, and Austria the figure was over 30, and in France it had risen to 43·3. Nevertheless by 1970 with a university population of nearly 220,000 Britain had passed her target and was closing the gap. 'New' universities like Sussex, York, East Anglia, Essex, Warwick, Kent, and Stirling were being joined by still more, many technical colleges were being upgraded to university standing, while the older universities were expanding rapidly.

The expansion of education, as of other public services, turns on the ability of the nation to meet the cost. The size of the fund available in future years will turn largely on how rapidly the economy can grow. It will not grow as much as it could, and should, without a sure and suitable foundation in the schools and colleges.[1]

With a population growing and a school population growing even more rapidly—in 1962 there were over two million more children on the registers of maintained schools than there were when the 1944 Education Act was passed—public expenditure on education was higher in 1962 than on any other public service except defence,[2] and questions of the size of classes, and of numbers and training of teachers, remained urgent, as did the suitability of various forms of classification and curriculum both to give to the children, and to get from them, the best that is possible. There were still not enough teachers to reduce classes to manageable size, and the wastage of women teachers particularly was high because of the earlier age of marriage and childbearing. Though some of these teachers return to their profession when their families are grown up, the immediate problem had to be faced, and the solution was to find as many part-time teachers as possible, while increasing by all conceivable means the flow from the universities and training colleges. Within this problem was the further one, emphasized by the Newsom Report,[3] that the shortage of teachers drew all but the most devoted away from the secondary moderns to the grammar schools, from the ramshackle, bad buildings that still existed in many pockets to the brighter, better-equipped schools, so loading the scales still further against the not so bright and the bad-area children.

The Newsom Committee began its work in March 1961, its terms of reference being "to consider the education between the ages of 13 and 16 of pupils of average or less than average ability." These pupils constitute the secondary-modern and the non-grammar school section generally, and comprise about half the pupils of all the secondary schools—*Half Our Future* in the expressive words of the title of the Report. The Newsom Committee endorses the necessity of raising the school-leaving age to

[1] *Report of the Committee on Higher Education* (The Robbins Report), October 1963 (Cmnd. 2154).
[2] *Annual Report of the Ministry of Education for 1962* (Cmnd. 1990).
[3] *Half Our Future*, a report of the Central Advisory Council for Education (England) (H.M.S.O., 1963).

sixteen for all pupils entering secondary schools from September 1965 onward. But at the same time the report draws attention to the deplorably inadequate school buildings still existing, and strongly urges more public expenditure on improvements as a vital background to staffing and curricula.

Many schools themselves are also concerned with the problems of curriculum and organization. The 'eleven plus,' already abolished in some areas, remains in disrepute, and there are indications that "the kind of intelligence which is measured by the tests so far applied is largely an acquired characteristic."[1] Although 'streaming' in junior schools has become fairly common, some teachers who have tried this are now returning to the older system of keeping the children of an age group working together regardless of their differing abilities. A major inquiry into the effects of 'streaming' was set on foot.

For secondary schools in general the problem is one of adapting curricula and teaching methods quickly enough to meet the changing needs of society, and to take full advantage of new knowledge about the processes of learning. A Curriculum Study Group was set up by the Minister of Education to help with this work.

In higher education the most important event was the Report, published on October 23, 1963, of the Robbins Committee, which was appointed in December 1960 to review the pattern of full-time higher education in Great Britain.

The general conclusion of the Committee is that "Both in general cultural standards and in competitive intellectual power, vigorous action is needed to avert the danger of a serious relative decline in this country's standing." They therefore recommend an expansion in university places to provide for all candidates who can reach a required standard of ability.

This expansion means providing, in the long run, for 560,000 students in 1980–81 as against 216,000 in full-time education in 1962–63; and, in the short run, for the taking in of the 'bulge' students of 1966–67 by a short-term, emergency programme which would increase the present plans by 10 per cent. and provide about 390,000 places in 1973–74.

The short-term programme requires immediate building for both teaching and residence, and emergency measures to maintain the student/staff ratio.

[1] The Newsom Report, p. 6.

The long-term policy—which in part overlaps with the immediate—envisaged the establishment of six new universities at once, and the expansion of existing ones, the promotion to technological universities of four of the most important technical colleges and the establishment of one new one, and the similar promotion of other institutes of higher education. In charge of higher education generally should be a Minister of Arts and Sciences.

In general, the Committee recommends that more students should receive a broader education for their first degrees, and that there should be more courses involving the study of more than one subject. Technical and scientific subjects could be linked to a social subject that concerned the student in his career or could be related to the social and æsthetic implications of his work, or the history of the science he was studying. At the same time, the Committee would like to see an increase in the proportion of graduates proceeding to post-graduate work, both in the social sciences and humanities and in science and technology.

The Government immediately accepted most of the targets set out in the Robbins Report and announced a ten-year programme for the 390,000 full-time higher-education places recommended for 1979. Of these, they estimate that 217,000 will be in university institutions. Responsibility rests with a Minister of Education and Science.

Meanwhile, it is worth considering some of the dangers—as well as the manifest advantages—of expansions as rapid as those envisaged both in the next few years and over the longer period. The pressure on university teachers will reflect on the schools whose sixth forms will find their staffs attracted to the universities, and on the schools whose case is so feelingly put by the Newsom Committee. Grants for junior and secondary education—for the children of the Newsom Report "whose spirit needs education as much as the body needs nourishment"—will have to compete with the universities, for the central pool is not bottomless. Is there not, moreover, a danger of pouring too much material into moulds which have served well in the past but which may well need more drastic reshaping than the Robbins Committee has given them? The university system as we know it, with high selectivity and products which compare well with those in any part of the world, is not necessarily the same system—or even the best system— if it is enlarged by more than 150 per cent. One or two years' study—not sufficient for a degree on present standards—may be the best provision for many young men and women who will be swept uncritically into the university orbit. Art students, nurses, physiotherapists, and others are training now for useful work, and growing intellectually and spiritually as well in their own centres as at universities. The emphasis on the degree-giving university—whatever attempts are made at diversity—tends to repeat a similar pattern. Diversity in diverse institutions may well be a better answer, as well as preventing the sheer size, which in itself tends to inflexibility. Large organizations—educational as well as others—can only run if all their parts are centrifugally geared. The Robbins proposal for a Ministry of Arts and Sciences to control higher education is not without danger: it draws too sharp a distinction between the schools and the rest of the educational process, and by bringing all university teaching under the control of a central body it may discourage initiative as well as inefficiency.

There is excitement in the Robbins Report. Its promise of intellectual fulfilment to an expanding population matches the material advances of the Welfare State. There will be dangers to avoid, principles to balance, and claims to assess. Above all there will be work to be done at many levels. But it is 'thinking big,' and 'thinking big' is right in an expanding society.

The large majority achieved by the Labour Party in 1945 carried it through five years of government which saw the rapid development of the Welfare State. Before the end of its term of office it steered into law the Representation of the People Act of 1949, which claimed to complete "the progress of the British people towards a full and complete democracy begun by the great Reform Bill of 1832."

The Act ended plural voting, abolished all two-Member constituencies by breaking them into single-Member seats, and redistributed seats in accordance with population movements since the previous redistribution in 1918.

The most important, as well as the most controversial, of these changes was the abolition of plural voting. There were two kinds of plural voting, the 'business premises' vote and the 'University' vote. The first gave a person the vote in the constituency in which his business premises were situated as well as in his place of residence. The University vote gave graduates the right of returning a Member for their university as well as voting in their homes. The latter roused the greater feeling. It was felt, on the one hand, that unbiased and 'unpolitical' voting at the universities returned Independent Members to the House who were a refreshing stimulus to the political parties. On the other hand, it was argued that a university man generally voted at his university in the same way as he voted in his home, and therefore merely doubled his vote. The 'Left' felt, in addition, that even a so-called University Independent was a 'Right' under the skin.

The net result of the Act of 1949 probably gave Labour an advantage. Nevertheless, at the General Election of February 1950 Labour's position was considerably weakened. It polled about ¾ million votes more than the Tories, returning 315 Members against their 297. With 9 Liberals and 3 others, this gave them a certain overall majority of only 6—too narrow for effective government.[1] The Labour Government's stay in office of eighteen months was longer than was expected, but at the next General Election in the autumn of 1951 the Conservatives were returned with a majority of 26 over Labour and a clear majority of 17, although they did, in fact, poll 231,000 fewer votes than Labour.[2] They did not conclude their five-year term of office, but, having surmounted the economic crisis of 1951, checked the development of nationalization by de-nationalizing the iron and steel industry and part of the road transport services, and made a conspicuous success of the housing campaign, they went to the country in May 1955, and were returned with an overall majority of 59.

When the Tories, after eight years of continuous office, went to the country at the end of 1959, at a time when consumption was booming and Macmillan's light-hearted remark that we had never had it so good was seized upon to become a party rallying-point and slogan, they were returned with an increased majority, Labour's share of the poll dropping from 46·4 per cent. to 43·8 per cent. Only in Scotland, Lancashire, and Cheshire, where there was much unemployment, did Labour improve its position.

[1] H. G. Nicholas, *The British General Election of 1950* (Appendix by D. E. Butler), p. 306.
[2] D. E. Butler, *The British General Election of 1951*, Appendix, p. 251.

It was significant that in this election the Liberals' share of the poll more than doubled. A sweeping victory for the Liberal candidate at the Orpington by-election in March 1962 was being hailed as an even more significant pointer to a Liberal revival.

It could hardly have been foreseen that before another Election peak publicity and first-class news space would have been devoted to a spy trial—the Vassall case[1]—and the Profumo/Ward case which personally discredited the Minister for War, causing his resignation, while shaking the whole Government on moral and security issues.[2] Nor could it have been foretold that these scandals would result in calls for the resignation of a Prime Minister and party leader successful by most of the canons of his party, that his actual resignation—sudden and unexpected when it came as the result of illness—would produce unprecedented confusion in the Conservative Party as a new leader was sought in a blaze of publicity without parallel, that the final choice of Prime Minister would fall on a man who could not take his seat in the House of Commons because he was not a Member of that House, and that there would be a consequent unprecedented delay of two weeks in the reassembly of Parliament until the Earl of Home had renounced his peerage and fought and won a by-election in a constituency specially offered to him.

The Labour Party, too, changed its leadership after the sudden death of Hugh Gaitskell in 1962. The voting of the Parliamentary Labour Party for a new leader was again carried out in full publicity, though, of its nature, it was not fraught with such excited speculation as accompanied the more widespread soundings of the Tory Party. All three parties at the end of 1963 lined up for the expected General Election of 1964. The Liberals had lost some of the promise that seemed theirs after Orpington, the by-elections at the end of 1963 indicating a swing from Conservative to Labour, the extent and duration of which were the subject of much speculation as each political party groomed itself for the public appearances which have become part of the political scene. For politicians, indeed, publicity

<hr />

[1] *Report of the Tribunal appointed to inquire into the Vassall Case and related matters* April 1963 (Cmnd. 2009).
[2] *Lord Denning's Report*, September 1963 (Cmnd. 2152).

has become essential. This means subjecting themselves to a series of newspaper and television interviews by men who have become professional questioners. The new technique assumes that a man is accountable not only to the public, but publicly, for the trust he bears, and must not only answer for his political conduct but reply to more personal questions; that he must answer not only face to face but in face of television cameras trained to detect shades of meaning or embarrassment which words can hide. Such ordeal by interview calls for qualities not necessarily associated with statesmanship or integrity. The showman's art is equally important. Yet so anxious is every public figure to promote a favourable 'public image' of himself that he dare not refuse to be interviewed—and lucky the man whose temperament and training enables him lightly to turn the embarrassing or impertinent question. But a third dimension has in this way been added to public life, and in particular to the political fight.

The General Election of 1964 gave the Labour Party a majority of four over all other parties combined. To implement its assertions that Britain needed a technological revolution to enable her to take her place in the world, it made two administrative changes. In April 1964 it replaced the Ministry of Education by a Department of Education and Science under a Secretary of State who was responsible for two administrative units—the schools on the one side, and civil science and the universities on the other. Six months later it created a Ministry of Technology. In the same year, emphasizing the importance of economic matters, a Department of Economic Affairs was created. In 1966 it appealed for a more decisive mandate, and the General Election of March gave it an overall majority of 96. True to its ideology, the Labour Government re-nationalized the iron and steel industry by an Act of March 1967. In August it swept away the National Assistance Board and the Ministry of Pensions and National Insurance, amalgamating assistance, pensions, and national insurance in a Ministry of Social Security—thus fulfilling, in name at least, the vision of Beveridge. Two years later the Ministry of Labour became the Ministry of Employment and Productivity—though whether, or why, it was better to be employed and to produce than to labour no-one explained.

SELECT BIBLIOGRAPHY

The Reshaping of British Railways (The Beeching Report) (H.M.S.O., 1963).

Half Our Future: a Report of the Central Advisory Council for Education (England) (The Newsom Report) (H.M.S.O., 1963).

Report of the Committee on Higher Education (The Robbins Report) (H.M.S.O., Cmnd. 2154, 1963).

Annual Economic Surveys until 1962, for that year and thereafter Economic Reports (H.M.S.O.).

Political and Economic Planning: British Trade Unions, Five Studies (new and revised edition, 1955).

ADAMS, J. W. R.: *Modern Town and Country Planning* (Churchill, 1952).

ASHWORTH, W.: *The Genesis of Modern British Town Planning* (Routledge and Kegan Paul, 1954).

BUTLER, D. E.: *The British General Election of 1951* (Macmillan, 1952).

———: *The British General Election of 1955* (Macmillan, 1955).

BUTLER, D. E. AND ROSE, R.: *The British General Election of 1959* (Macmillan, 1960).

BUTLER, D. E. AND KING, A.: *The British General Election of 1964* (Macmillan, 1965).

———: *The British General Election of 1966* (Macmillan, 1966).

CLEGG, H. A. AND CHESTER, T. E.: *The Future of Nationalization* (Blackwell, 1953).

H.M.S.O.: *Design in Town and Village* (1953).

NICHOLAS, H.: *The British General Election of 1950* (Macmillan, 1951).

PEDLEY, R.: *Comprehensive Schools To-day* (Council of Education Press, 1955).

———: *The Comprehensive School* (Penguin, 1963).

PELLING, H.: *A Short History of the Labour Party* (Macmillan, 1961).

ROBINSON, JOHN A. T.: *Honest To God* (S.C.M. Press, 1963).

TOWNSEND, P.: *Family Life of Old People* (Routledge, 1957).

———: *The Last Refuge: A Survey of Residential Institutions and Homes for the Aged in England and Wales* (Routledge, 1962).

WORSWICK, G. D. N. AND ADY, P. H. (Eds.): *The British Economy in the Nineteen-fifties* (Oxford University Press, 1962).

YOUNGSON, A. J.: *The British Economy 1920–57* (Allen and Unwin, 1960).

CHAPTER XXVII

OUT OF THE SIXTIES

In many directions growth remained the keynote. The population increased alarmingly. The estimated 52 million for 1966 turned out to be 52·3 million. A mid-year estimate for 1969 was 54 million.[1] Of these, some 24½ million people were in civil employment in the middle of 1970, of whom over 14 million were manual workers and over 9 million white-collar workers. The agricultural population continued to decline, amounting to fewer than 395,000 in June 1970.[2] A disturbing note, in a society supposedly geared for maximum expansion, was the fact that unemployment was the highest since the War, reaching over 600 thousand by the middle of 1970, not counting the school-leavers.[3] Some unemployment was caused by people changing jobs, by redundancy, while increased social service benefit made the finding of work less imperative. But the figure was too high to be explained away in this fashion and was linked with the repeated crises which shook Britain at the end of the sixties.

Externally these were expressed in repeated adverse balance of payments and by foreign borrowing; internally, by mounting costs (£1600 million were spent on the National Health Service in 1968–69), by high taxation (the 1966 Budget increased taxation by £375 million and instituted the Selective Employment Tax), and by the attempted freezing of wages. But in 1967 a balance-of-payments deficit for the fifth year in succession brought the inevitable devaluation of the pound. On November 18, 1967, sterling was devalued by 14·3 per cent., making its exchange value with the dollar 2·40. Measures to reduce home consumption followed—a reduction in the defence programme, cuts in public expenditure, further increases in taxation, a reduction of bank lending, a tightening of hire-purchase restrictions, an increase in bank-rate to 8 per cent.

None of this was sufficient to damp down consumer spending

---

[1] *Monthly Digest of Statistics*, August 1970, Table 10, p. 14.
[2] *Ibid.*, Table 19, p. 21.   [3] *Ibid.*, Table 22, p. 23.

to the required degree, yet, helped by certain extraneous factors such as the German re-valuation of the Deutschmark, the British balance of payments was in surplus by 1969. But no-one was happy about the general economic situation. Unemployment was high, taxation was high, prices were high, strikes were long and frequent, wages were erratically high in some places and low in others, productivity was low, and Britain's growth rate of some 3 per cent. was the lowest in Western Europe.

The Index of retail prices continued to rise. Taking 1962 as 100, by mid-1970 the Index for all items was 140, for food of all kinds 142.[1] Consumers responded by spending even more—in spite of taxation—on consumer goods. ·They stepped up their spending on these items and food from £17½ million in 1962 to £20 million in 1967 at constant 1958 prices.[2] They were able to do this partly by cutting back on personal saving. This mattered less to them since State social and welfare services gave at least a cover to old age and to most misfortunes; it mattered more to the economic system, which required savings if it was going to expand.

The second way in which consumers maintained their purchasing power was by the old weapon of the strike. Average weekly earnings of manual workers had increased from an index figure of 68·1 in 1950 to 130·1 in 1960 and 224·4 at the beginning of the seventies. Corresponding salary earnings were 133·4 in 1960 and 222·9 in 1970. In January 1970 this gave an average weekly wage, including overtime, to a skilled iron-and-steel maintenance worker of nearly £32; an unskilled engineering worker got £19 11s. 0d.[3] Some 90 or 95 per cent. of the strikes that had been largely responsible for achieving this had been 'unofficial'—that is, strikes arising from an immediate grievance taken up without resort to trade-union leadership or to any negotiating machinery or existing agreements. "The bargaining which takes place within factories is largely outside the control of employers' associations and trade unions. It usually takes place piece-meal and results in competitive sectional wage adjustments and chaotic pay structures. Unwritten understandings and 'custom and practice' predominate."[4]

[1] *Employment and Productivity Gazette*, August 1970, p. 752.
[2] *Economic Report*, 1967, p. 42.
[3] *Employment and Productivity Gazette*, August 1970, Table 128, p. 745.
[4] Donovan Report, p. 261.

Whether increased wages pushed up prices, or rising prices pulled wages up after them, the overall picture was of a spiralling inflation which the Government desperately tried to stem. Refusing to be committed as to first causes, it spoke of a "prices and incomes" policy. The whole life of the 1966–70 Labour Government was dominated by its efforts to enforce such a policy. Its failure to do so was the prime cause of its defeat in the Election of June 1970. The sixties are strewn with its failed endeavours—Prices and Incomes Board (established in 1965); the National Plan (September 1965); the Prices and Incomes Bill (July 1966). Whatever lip-service they paid to the need to stem inflation, the trade unions either would not or could not implement any wage restraint, and massive strikes continued.

A Royal Commission on Trade Unions and Employers' Associations was appointed in 1965 under Lord Donovan—the fifth body to inquire into industrial relations in a hundred years. Its Report in June 1968[1] recommended the extension of collective bargaining and particularly of productivity agreements, the appointment of an Industrial Relations Commission with which agreements reached by workmen and employers should be registered, and the reduction of the number of unions, particularly when several operated in the same industry.

Hardly was the ink dry on this not very dynamic Report than the Government came forward with another attempt to bridle the unions. *In Place of Strife* was a White Paper with the subtitle "A Policy for Industrial Relations" and was published in January 1969.[2] It proposed, like the Donovan Report, a Commission on Industrial Relations to look into disputes; a Register of Collective Agreements to which reference should be made when a strike threatened; a secret ballot of union members before a strike was called; and a cooling-off period of up to two months between the threat of a strike and its actual implementation. But trade union opposition was firm and uncompromising. When it came to the point loyalty to the Labour Party—*their* party—counted little, and appeals to the public good fell on deaf ears. The unions had narrowed their sights to wage increases, and they were so strong that the whole prices-and-incomes policy collapsed in the middle of 1969 as it became

[1] Cmnd. 3623. [2] Cmnd. 3888.

necessary to placate the unions before the General Election that could not be far away.

The Labour Government was scarcely less happy with the various social questions that were never far below the surface. Immigration and race relations remained points of conflict, and in 1968 a Race Relations Act was thought necessary to end alleged race discrimination; how far it exacerbated a conflict which might more easily resolve itself if left alone had not been ascertained. A loosening of social and moral standards associated with what has come to be called the Permissive Society was even more serious. It was connected with the increase in population, which itself has led directly not only to the acceptance but to the advocacy of a birth-control pill, and the legalization of abortion in the Abortion Act of 1967 in such terms that London found itself virtually the abortion centre of the world. Crime increased, drug-taking increased as the sixties gave way to the seventies. Student riots, demonstrations of all kinds against established institutions, whatever their merit and with or without a worthy cause, supplied a small section of young people with an outlet that no ideal appeared able to channel. This malaise, this being out of joint, is common to the whole world. It is a world where men land on the moon (in July 1969), Concorde breaks the sound barrier, noise increases, the motor vehicle takes control of cities and eats up the countryside, while pollution of the atmosphere and of rivers and seas arises from man's own activities.

Britain has to deal with these, as well as with her economic problems. A Royal Charter for the Open University in 1969—a University of the Air to be conducted through broadcasting channels—showed that her mind was still on education; though at the other end of the scale there was trouble as the Labour Government's insistence upon 'comprehensive' education for all schoolchildren aroused growing opposition. One way and another, at the opening of 1970 the standing of the Labour Government in the country was abysmally low. Yet surprisingly, with a good balance-of-payments surplus in the spring, Public Opinion Polls began to show a swing to Labour and, intent on seizing the opportunity, the Government fixed Thursday, June 18, 1970, as General Election day—nine months before it was bound to dissolve.

The Labour Party fought a muted and undistinguished

Election campaign, seemingly content to let it rest upon the personalities of the two leaders, Harold Wilson, the Prime Minister, and Edward Heath, the leader of the Conservative Opposition. They felt assured of victory on the showing of the Public Opinion Polls, which were allowed to intrude blatantly into the electoral scene and destroy the dignity that Britain's hard-won democratic system was entitled to. The Tories similarly—through their own desire or because the media of public opinion wanted it so—were represented mainly through their leader. Edward Heath played an unemotional campaign, promising to keep prices down, to check the incomes boom without statutory wage-restraint, and to reduce unemployment. He indicated that he would make the trade unions subject to the law of contract; he also promised sober, efficient government without gimmickry.

At least three Opinion Polls were published on the very day of the Election, showing a Labour lead of 7 per cent., 4·1 per cent., 2 per cent., which would give a Labour majority ranging from a hundred to twenty seats. In the event the figures were:

Conservative	330
Labour	287
Liberal	6
Others	7
	630

The swing to the Conservatives was decisive, the Opinion Polls had been damned, the Liberal group in the House was further reduced, many well-known Labour figures were toppled, and the Labour Party retreated to lick its wounds.

Within four months the Conservative Government gave State pensions to all then over eighty years of age who were too old to have entered the existing insurance scheme and who, for some reason, the Labour Government had always bypassed; it produced the text of a proposed Industrial Relations Bill in October 1970, which the trade unions prepared to tear apart; it continued the negotiations for Britain's entry into the Common Market which had been proceeding spasmodically for years. On October 15 it announced a reorganization of government.[1] The Ministry of Technology, monument to Wilson's

---

[1] *The Reorganisation of Central Government*, October 15, 1970, Cmnd. 4506.

'technological revolution', was to go—merged with the Board of Trade into a new Department of Trade and Industry. The Overseas Development Ministry was to be incorporated into the Foreign Office. The Department of Employment and Productivity was to lose its productivity connotation and be simply the Department of Employment; and the demise of the Prices and Incomes Board was announced at the end of October 1970. An attempt was to be made to bring all Departments and Ministries within a central framework of policy and control, and to this end two central bodies were created: a 'Central Capability Unit' of experts, based on the Cabinet Office, was to oversee, question, and, where necessary, challenge, departmental policy. Another central unit was to analyse and keep under constant surveillance public expenditure.

The Conservative Government announced also, at the same time, the creation of a Department of the Environment formed from the Ministry of Housing and Local Government, the Ministry of Transport and the Ministry of Public Works and Buildings. It is a bold title and envisages control of the major nuisances of noise, smell, smog, oil-slick, industrial waste and effluent, fouled rivers, traffic-jammed cities, ill-planned housing, overrun countryside. It is a welcome creation to deal with a problem made all the more difficult through being delayed too long.

The Government made it clear from the beginning that its attitude to social and industrial problems was to be one of non-intervention wherever possible. It also indicated that it would not allow the social services to be either a cushion for the lazy and well-off or a dis-centive to self-help. But it was prepared to supplement the incomes of the lowest paid to bring them up to an agreed minimum level.[1] This is throwing down the gauntlet to the Welfare State with a vengeance! Either Beveridge is turning in his grave or he is wryly admitting that no principles endure for ever and that changing circumstances require changing attitudes.

But, whatever it does, and however it does it, the success—and the very life—of the Conservative Government of 1970 will be bound up with the same set of problems which bedevilled the life of the Labour Government—how far it can keep down prices and taxes, curb wages and salaries, and

[1] *New Policies for Public Spending*, October 27, 1970. Cmnd. 4515.

negotiate a realistic agreement with the trade unions. There is little doubt not only that it will stand or fall by its success in these matters, but that the role of the trade unions in society and the whole relationship of capital and labour will be involved in the issue.

CHAPTER XXVIII

INTO THE SEVENTIES

MR. HEATH came to power committed, as he said, to a "quiet and total revolution" based upon "less government". For the first three months of the life of the Conservative administration there was, indeed, little to mark a change of government: prices continued to rise, investment to lag, a dispute in the shipbuilding industry, inherited from the time of the Labour Government, continued until July 10, a stoppage in the docks occupied the rest of the month. Before the end of the year there had been unspectacular wage increases for more than two million workers in such disparate occupations as coal-mining, cotton-weaving, bespoke tailoring, sawmilling and local-government service and the balance-of-payments surplus continued to rise.

By this time, however, a pattern was emerging in Government policy.[1] To curb price rises it attempted to restrict wage increases to 8 per cent.; but, while it had some control over the public sector, it had little over private enterprise. Car workers, in particular, had set a standard which left the workers in public enterprise far behind. The electricity supply workers were among the first in the public sector to press for a wage increase in excess of what they were offered and in the early weeks of December 1970 they operated a 'go slow' resulting in serious power cuts. The Electricity Supply Authority, backed by the Government, was not prepared to give way but in the end both sides agreed to arbitration, electricity supplies were restored in time for Christmas, and the Wilberforce Committee reported on February 10, 1971 with recommendations which amounted to wage increases of rather over 10 per cent.[2] Both sides accepted the proposals; the electricity workers, indeed, claimed that the findings had given them nearer 15 per cent. and so blown the Government's wages policy sky high.

Next to claim higher wages were the workers in the Post

---

[1] And see *supra*, pp. 581–82.

[2] *Report of a Court of Inquiry into a dispute between the parties represented on the National Joint Industrial Council for the Electricity Supply Industry*, February 1971, Cmnd. 4594 (The Wilberforce Report).

Office whom the Government, perhaps fearing that it had conceded too much to the electricity workers, fought in a bitter
struggle for 47 days in the early months of 1971. This time the
Government's weapon of 'no action' was used relentlessly as the
postal workers and the Post Office Authority wrangled day after
day without compromise. Perhaps because it was easier to do
without the postal services than without electrical power, but
partly because their union funds ran out, the postal workers
were beaten. They consented to the appointment of a Committee to consider their claim and had no alternative but to
agree to the 9 per cent. increase offered.[1] The postal strike left a
legacy of bitterness. The Government had, indeed, scored a
near victory for its 8 per cent. but at the expense of one of the
weaker and less well-off sections of the working population.

As though to emphasize that it had two policies—one for the
strong and one for the weak—the Government at the end of the
same year, 1971, doubled the Queen's official income and
increased the annuities paid from public funds to other members
of the Royal Family.[2] Almost at the same time it substantially
raised the salaries of all Members of Parliament. The Prime
Minister's salary was increased from £14,000 to £23,000 a year
—£5,000 of it tax free; the Leader of the Opposition was to get
£9,500 a year; Ministers and office holders got substantial increases and the ordinary Member of Parliament had his salary
raised from £3,250 a year to £4,500 a year—an increase of
nearly 40 per cent. In addition there was a considerable increase in the amount of expenses allowed from public funds. It
is true that there had been no increase for M.P.s since 1965 and
that their pay was still not high compared with members of the
business and professional classes. But the timing was wrong,
there was the question of extra-Parliamentary income received
by Members, a feeling that dedication to their work or service
to the community might have induced a smaller increase, or
even that the opportunity might have been taken to set an
example to the rest of the community by taking less. As it was
there was not one dissentient vote from any part of the House to
the proposed salary increases, the Bill was rushed into its Second
Reading, on December 10, 1971 and pushed with equal speed

[1] *Report of the Committee Appointed by the Post Office and Union of Post Office Workers to
enquire into the circumstances of a Dispute arising out of the Union's claim for pay increases and
shortening of incremental scales*, April 30, 1971 (The Hardman Report).
[2] The Civil List Act, 1972.

through Committee where there was no amendment. The Queen's approval was immediately obtained and the clauses of the Act became operative from January 1972.[1]

This, in contrast to the 9 per cent. so recently given to the postal workers, may have affected the timing of the next move. The miners, still very powerful in spite of pit closures and labour redundancy, were by this time spoiling for a fight—more particularly since the fight would now be against the traditional enemy, a Tory Government, and there would be no need to pull punches as there might have been if Labour had been in power. The miners, who considered themselves the aristocracy of the working world, doing work at once the most important and the most dangerous, had improved their position so much since the War that, in spite of pit closures and the effects of redundancy, their wages had been well up among the highest in the country. But by 1970 they found themselves both hit by rising prices and slipping down the national wage table as workers in private industry, particularly car workers, won big increases. They had given warning that they would strike unless given a substantial rise and, activated no doubt partly by the determination to vindicate the claims of labour after the postal workers defeat, they came out in an all-out strike in the early weeks of 1972. For six weeks the industrial situation went from bad to worse. The miners were resolute in picketing not only the mines but the power stations where coal was used and in this way the disruption of the economy and the disturbance to private life were at the maximum. The strike also revealed most potently that, in spite of the use of other forms of power, coal still was basic to the country's needs. It became a vital question as to whether or not it was legal to picket any place other than the mines but the Government had no wish for a confrontation on this issue and coal was resolutely kept from the power stations by miners' pickets. After weeks of pursuing the policy of inaction which had helped to defeat the postal workers the Government found itself driven into another policy as industry, deprived of power, was left high and dry. At the same time it was apparent that, though public exasperation at the long power cuts was growing, much of the resentment was directed against the Government and not against the miners, whose work was recognized as being both difficult and dangerous.

[1] *Ministerial and other Salaries Act*, February 10, 1972.

The miners did not agree to arbitration until they sensed they had won. The tactic paid and they drove a hard bargain even after the Wilberforce Committee had reported. When their leaders emerged from No. 10 Downing Street with the terms which both sides had accepted it was found that they had won a general average increase of about 21 per cent. which gave face-workers a wage of £34.50 a week.[1]

"Wanted—An Incomes Policy" cried *The Times* in its leading article of February 22, 1972. The Government tried to save face by re-iterating the miners' own arguments that mining was a just case for special treatment. But, taken with their own salary increases, it was clear that their policy of inertia and their limitation of wage increases to 8 per cent. was broken into frag-ments. But there was nothing to put in its place, for the Government had emphasized its policy of non-intervention by winding up the National Board for Prices and Incomes on March 31, 1971. And other workers had their claims, too: before the middle of 1972 transport workers were lining up for increases, the pilots and crews of British airlines, the postal workers, the teachers and others were again in the field.

The Labour Government had retreated from an Incomes Policy in face of trade-union opposition. The Conservative Government, as a matter of principle, never accepted an in-comes policy. Yet successive strikes and wage increases in both the private and the public sector continued to indicate the need for one. Though the full effect of restrictive action by workmen is difficult to reduce to statistics, the bald figures show that the aggregate number of working days lost, which had remained from 1964 to 1967 at between 2,200,000 and 2,900,000 a year, jumped in 1968 to 4,690,000; in 1969 to 6,846,000; in 1970 to 10,980,000; and in 1971 to 13,558,000.[2] The industrial position has, moreover, become such that the whole community can be held to ransom by any group operating an essential service. Sectional interests show a complete disregard for other people or for the community as a whole. There have for long been gross inequalities in British society, much selfishness and sectional greed. The Labour pioneers who brought their people up out of the abyss of oppression and inequality knew all about this.

[1] *Report of a Court of Inquiry into a dispute between the National Coal Board and the National Union of Mineworkers*, February 18, 1972, Cmnd. 4903 (The Wilberforce Report).

[2] *Department of Employment Gazette*, January 1972, p. 68.

But they would not have condoned action which in essence is sheer anarchy, disrupting the whole economic system and bringing the maximum distress to the public, who are very largely their own fellow workers. Labour's dream was of justice and dignity. Neither is possible where any sectional interest thinks only of itself, not hesitating to wreck society in an effort to get more for itself alone from the general pool. But if the sectional strike is to be outlawed and an incomes policy is not accepted, something fair and constructive, and something seen to be fair by all concerned, must be put in its place.

The Conservative Government, in its Industrial Relations Bill, produced a piece of legislation which it hoped would serve as just such an automatic regulator of wages and labour conditions, giving freedom to the trade unions without giving their members the licence to blackmail society by unregulated strikes. The Second Reading of the Act was introduced into the House of Commons on December 14, 1970 by Robert Carr, the Secretary of State for Employment, who emphasized the antithesis between liberty and licence: Anybody looking objectively at the industrial scene in Britain to-day, he said, "must agree that new rules are needed, that liberty has in some areas degenerated into licence, that the balance between order and chaos is in need of being redressed in favour of a more orderly and disciplined system and that the freedom of the ordinary industrial worker will be increased and not diminished by a change which brings that about".[1] In effecting such a change the Industrial Relations Bill would rely basically upon collective bargaining, the historical core of wage settlement, but would endeavour to ensure that workers' action was always the result of the majority will, freely arrived at, and that a strike was a last resort. "Orderly procedures in industry" for the peaceful settlement of disputes by negotiation, conciliation, or arbitration were the aim. A free association of workers in independent trade unions and of employers in employers' associations were, as before, to be the "representative, responsible and effective bodies for regulating relations between employers and workers."

Effective control was to be exercised by a strengthened Registry of Trade Unions and a new Industrial Relations Court. When a trade union registered it was at the same time to file its method of procedure in industrial disputes, and notify

[1] *Hansard*, Vol. 808, c. 963.

any special agreements entered into. Strikes called by registered unions within the limits of such procedures and agreements would not be illegal. Strikes called by unauthorized persons or groups, or outside those limits, could be liable for damages; where such rules did not exist the Registry could recommend certain procedures as, for example, in the case of lightning strikes.

The worker retained his complete freedom to join a trade union and take part in trade union activities, and in the case of infringement of these rights by an employer he could take his case to the Industrial Tribunal for redress. The worker was to have, also, the right *not* to belong to a union. In the case of the dismissal of a workman the employer could be asked to show the Tribunal what his reasons were—redundancy, incapacity, conduct—and to show that he did not act unreasonably. The Tribunal could allow compensation of up to £4,160 and could recommend, though not enforce, a man's re-instatement. At the same time the employee was to have the right to information concerning the undertaking in which he was employed to the same extent as a shareholder in the business.

The Bill was given its Second Reading in the House of Commons on December 15, 1970 by 324 votes to 280[1] to the accompaniment of one-day strikes by the unions—strikes which, however, were considerably less enthusiastic and effective than strikes for pay claims. The Bill became law in August 1971. In the same year trade union membership topped the ten million mark.

Apart from fearing that the Industrial Relations Act would interfere with the right to strike, which since the inception of trade unions had been regarded as their basic weapon, the labour world was uneasy in many ways. The Industrial Relations Tribunal would be bound to act as a brake upon union activities and its right to fine for contempt would subject union funds to crippling fines for what the men could not regard as offences. And the liberty given by the Act for a man *not* to join a union would jeopardize that unanimity which was essential to successful trade union action. It would, moreover, entitle a non-participant, without contributing in any way, to reap all the advantages of industrial action. The unions had taken their stand against this for years and now a Tory Government was

[1] *Ibid.*, pp. 961–1250 *passim.*

forcing their hand. Many, nevertheless, were at first willing to register under the Act and some internal disputes were actually brought before the Court.

The fight, which came within six months of the passage of the Act, concerned the right of the Court to fine for contempt, and its right to call for a 'cooling-off period' and a compulsory ballot in order to avert a strike.

The first issue involved the dockers. The core of the dispute concerned the pre-packaging in containers of goods which the dockers had previously handled themselves; it was held that lower-paid, and therefore 'scab' labour was used for this and the dockers refused to handle the cargoes concerned. When summoned before the Industrial Relations Court they refused to appear and their union, the Transport and General Workers' Union, was fined a total of £55,000 for contempt—thus implementing the worst fears of the opponents of the Act. When the trade union leadership attempted to compromise certain militant shop-stewards continued the 'blacking' of firms concerned with containerization thus raising the question of how far the union was responsible for the acts of its own shop stewards. But the T.G.W.U. had meanwhile appealed against the fine and, in a shattering blow to the authority of the Court and the prestige of the Government, the Court of Appeal rescinded the fine. But the whole issue was left unsolved, the threat of a national dock strike hung over the country, and the basic question was left unanswered: how to treat an occupation like that of dock work which is inevitably declining as the rational alternative of containerization grows all over the world.[1]

Parallel with the dockers' fight was that of the railwaymen. The railway workers' demand for higher pay was reinforced by a 'go-slow' or 'work-to-rule' which was notable for the amount of public antagonism generated (in contrast to the sympathy won by the miners) as transport services, particularly commuter services in and out of London, were cut to a trickle causing the maximum of delay and discomfort. Arbitration failed, the compromise suggested by Jarratt, as an independent tribunal of one, was turned down by the railwaymen, and the Industrial Relations Court stepped in to rule the railwaymen guilty of "wilful disruption" and a breach of contract in failing to operate a full service. When agreement was still not reached the

Court called for the "cooling-off" period laid down in the Industrial Relations Act followed by a ballot of railwaymen on the issue of whether they would accept the proposed settlement or continue to work to rule for a higher one. It was a gamble which failed. The result gave a nearly six to one majority for a continued work-to-rule. When a 14 per cent. wage increase was finally conceded it was a bitter blow to government policy.

Wage and salary increases had not helped the Government to keep its Election pledge and reduce or contain prices. On the contrary, the general index of retail prices continued to rise steeply. Taking January 1962 as 100 by mid-December 1970 the Index for all items had been 140[1] and the monthly average for the whole year stood at 140·2. In 1971 the monthly average was 153·4 and at December 1971 it stood at 158·1. By the same date the Index for food of all kinds had risen to 162·8 of which fish showed the steepest rise, standing at 181, butter, lard and margarine at 175, meat, bacon and sugar at 170, milk, cheese and eggs at 168. Housing at the same date had risen to 178·6, fuel and light to 167·7, services of all kinds to 174·8, clothing to 135·9, durable household goods to 137·4, motors and cycles to 135, and fares to 197. All these compared with the figure of 100 in January 1962. There were signs that the rate of increase might be slowing down in the spring of 1972, but in April the general Index for all items stood at 161·8 and for all food stood at 164·6. Of food, fish stood at 191, butter, margarine, lard and cooking fats at 176, vegetables and fresh and canned fruit at 177.[2] At the same time the most spectacular increases in house prices that had ever been known both emphasized the shortage of housing and blew sky-high any pretence that inflation was being contained.

A reduction in taxation and an increase in the flow of credit were integral to Conservative Government policy and, though suffering a severe blow by the death of Iain Macleod shortly after his appointment as Chancellor of the Exchequer, the Conservative Government continued a policy of easing restrictions under the Chancellorship of Anthony Barber. By the time of his first full Budget in May 1971, cuts were already in operation and by the end of 1971 included income tax relief, reduction in

[1] *Supra*, p. 578.   [2] *Department of Employment Gazette*, passim and May 1972, p. 514.

Selective Employment Tax, in Corporation Tax and in purchase tax. The Budget of March 1972 added much more relief in the form of reduced income tax and lower purchase tax and other benefits to business. At the same time restrictions on consumer and bank credit were being lifted and Bank Rate had been cut. An unknown quantity was the Value Added Tax announced in the 1972 Budget, to become operative in 1973.

The Government had also been driven, against its announced policy, to restore the grants for development programmes in backward areas which it had previously withdrawn. This was partly because of the continually rising unemployment figures, which had passed the million mark, and the spectacular collapse of two of the bastions of British enterprise—Rolls-Royce and Clyde Shipbuilders. Both these organizations were given State loans. The Government made further inroads into its policy of non-intervention—its "anti-lame-duck-policy"—by creating in a Cabinet re-shuffle announced on April 7, 1972, a Ministry of Industrial Development with Christopher Chataway as Minister. Several Members of Parliament wanted to know in what way, and how far, this policy differed from that of the Labour Government.

In the social services the Government furthered its aim of selectivity. It continued and increased the prescription charges for medicines and dental treatment but encouraged the claiming of exemption; pensions were increased and special benefits for invalidity and attendance allowances were introduced and widely taken up. It also introduced a Family Income Supplement to be claimed by the lowest-paid workers. The purpose of this was to discriminate between the better-off and the worse-off and to bring all incomes up to an acceptable level. The fact that claiming it involved a statement of means got it off to a slow start. To balance this, and to prevent the better-off from taking advantage of free and cheap facilities which it was felt should be diverted to the less well-off, the charges for school dinners and for welfare milk were raised and free milk withdrawn in schools for children in the seven to eleven age-group.

In education the school-leaving age was raised to sixteen, and comprehensive schools seem to be accepted, although there are signs that the Education Minister would like to see the largest of them reduced in size as well as a reduction in the size of classes.

Teachers' training was the subject of a Report published early in 1972 which was notable for recommending a three-tier course of teacher training. The first tier would consist of a two-year general course of higher education, suitable to civil servants and others besides intending teachers, which would lead to a Diploma of Higher Education. The second tier would consist of two years of professional education of which the first would normally be spent in a College, or Department, of Education. Students who completed this year would become 'licensed teachers' and would proceed to a second year of school-based experience during which they would be paid. They would work in the schools to a reduced time-table and be released for further study for the equivalent of not less than one day a week. At the end of this training they could qualify for a B.A. (Education) degree awarded by the Regional Council. The third tier would consist of release for re-training and refresher courses for at least the equivalent of one term in every seven years.[1]

Violence, insubordination, and lack of discipline in schools is meanwhile a subject of very real concern and the Minister is proposing an Inquiry. Students in Universities had their grants increased; there was less student rioting in 1971 than in 1970, but protests over the financing of Students' Unions caused the proposals to be held back for re-consideration. Notably successful was the first year of the Open University, not only in the quality of its teaching but in its high success rate, over 60 per cent. of students passing their first Examination. In the world outside violence of all kinds causes the gravest anxiety while crimes, and particularly crimes of violence, increase. In spite of Conservation Year (1970) and the Department of the Environment,[2] seas, rivers and lakes and the natural life within them are threatened by the waste materials of man and his industries; the vehicles which jam the roads continue to pollute the atmosphere with fumes and noise; visually, standards of building, of shop-fitting, of lettering degrade both towns and villages.

The Conservative Government held throughout to its resolution to take Britain into the European Economic Community. Its positive determination to do so has, indeed, been at variance with its aloofness on the labour front. It resolved European

[1] *Report of a Committee of Inquiry on Teacher Education and Training*, January 1972 (The James Report).
[2] *Supra*, p. 582.

differences on points of detail but still had to face considerable opposition in its own ranks, as well as from the Labour party. In the event it won the support of sufficient Labour Members of Parliament to balance the loss of the votes of its own people, and on October 28, 1971, with both Parties in the House divided amongst themselves, the motion in favour of the principle of entering the Common Market was carried by 356 votes to 244. The Conservative victory was, however, accompanied by a Labour announcement that it would fight the detailed clauses of the European Communities Bill one by one and at whatever length necessary. The fight continued until July 13, 1972 when the Third Reading went through the Commons by 301 votes to 284. The Prime Minister and the Foreign Secretary had signed the treaty of Britain's accession to the Common Market on January 22, 1972 at Brussels but the whole issue has split, and continues to split the country as it has split the Parliament and the political parties. But meanwhile Britain "went decimal" on February 15, 1971 when the distinguished and distinguishing £s, shillings and pence, their origins embedded in centuries of British history, gave way to featureless decimalization.

While Britain was in the middle of her Common Market controversies a new pattern of international exchange rates was agreed to comparatively quietly after a period of wild speculation and deep dismay as the dollar slipped from its pre-eminence to suffer a *de facto* devaluation. At a meeting of the Group of Ten countries in Washington in December 1971 the position was formalized and the dollar/sterling relationship fixed at a medial point of $2·6057 to the pound sterling in place of the former $2·40. Exchange rates would be permitted to fluctuate within a $4\frac{1}{2}$ per cent. band—$2\frac{1}{4}$ per cent. on each side of the medial rate. But the arrangement lasted a very short time. Pressure on the pound caused the Government to allow a floating exchange rate from the end of June 1972, in which it dropped to a lower parity thus bringing about a virtual devaluation.

Underneath it all the population continued to rise, the Preliminary Report of the Census carried out on the night of April 25/26, 1971 giving the estimate of 48·7 million persons in England and Wales and 5·2 million in Scotland. The unprecedentedly numerous and detailed questions asked on the Census form were disquieting to many people who feared an infringement of privacy, if not of liberty, but were justified by the requirements of social workers and others concerned with statistics. The continued upsweep of the population caused concern because of its pressure on space and resources and methods of birth control and the advantages of family planning were widely advertised. More acceptable reasons for abortion than those often put forward were at the same time canvassed.

The people, meanwhile, continued to spend more money and to save less. Consumers' expenditure grew from nearly £23 million in 1965 to over £34 million in 1971. Even discounting inflation and revalued at constant 1963 prices it grew from £21·243 million in 1965 to £23·396 million in 1970 and was rising even faster in 1971. Of personal disposable income, saving in 1965 amounted to 8·3 per cent., in 1970 to 7·8 per cent., and further decreased in the third quarter of 1971 to 5·7 per cent. Expenditure of all kinds increased—food and household, housing, drink and tobacco, clothing and footwear, cars, motor-cycles, radio and television sets. Though there remain pockets of poverty and areas of distress caused, notably by unemployment and by housing shortages, there is every encouragement to spend more to 'expand' to 'grow' and an unflagging determination by the population to respond to the appeal. Unemployment is a dark cloud getting larger and coming nearer. Increased unemployment benefit, the making of redundancy payments where these are appropriate takes the very worst sting out of the situation but cannot minimize the effect on the unemployed themselves. A great deal of the unemployment is deep seated in the slowing down of older industries, particularly in the north and north-west, in technical improvements of various kinds, in the recruitment of young labour and the easing-out of others before retirement age. Even so, much would be eliminated if the slack were taken out of the economy and this is what the Government is attempting to do by the encouragement of investment and the making of development loans. More effective competition in foreign markets is also needed, but this is possible only if wage increases are matched with productivity increases. Basically, it would seem that society's whole attitude to work and production needs to be changed. A society with unemployed labour while houses are desperately needed and many areas derelict is only one aspect of a strangely disintegrated economy. A Planned Economy was at one time offered as a panacea for all our economic ills. Curiously little has been said about it recently. But perhaps a Plan drawn up jointly by labour and management and the politicians is the only way out of our difficulties?

The Labour Party had many issues to face, besides that of its defeat at the General Election of June 1970. It could not but regard the incessant use of the strike weapon as a threat to the economy yet could not dissociate itself from the unions whose child it is. The very fact that it stands as an alternative government means that it cannot condone the anarchy which appears only too likely on the industrial front. In particular, it was placed in a difficult position concerning the Government's attempt to introduce order through the Industrial Relations Act. It could not but remember, too sadly, how its own Incomes Policy, Four Year Plan and Industrial Relations Bill went down before trade union pressure: the cooling-off period, the strike ballot, could have been lifted from their own document *In Place of Strife*.[1] On top of all this it has found itself deeply divided on the issue of the Common Market. A massive split in the Labour Party as its Deputy Chairman and other leading Members of the House of Commons resigned on April 10 and 11, 1972— largely on the Common Market issue—involved other questions as well, including that of the party leadership.

The spring of 1972 was uncertain, precarious, and anomalous. With over a million people unemployed total consumer spending was higher than ever before; with Britain poised to enter the Common Market and the Treaty of Accession signed, the issue split one of the two major political parties and no-one knew whether the majority of people wanted to become part of Europe or not.

In May 1972 local elections showed a sweep to Labour when the Conservatives suffered a net loss of 884 borough seats; in the summer, with the Conservative Government to some extent discredited, the Labour Party published a new policy document. In September 1972, on the eve of the Trades Union Congress, there was continued speculation on Britain's industrial future but no clear political or economic pattern had emerged.

[1] *Supra*, p. 579.

CONSUMERS' EXPENDITURE[1]
£M

| | 1965 | | 1970 | |
	Current prices	Re-valued 1963 prices	Current prices	Re-valued 1963 prices
Total	22,943	21,243	31,238	23,396
Food and Household	5,065	4,770	6,363	4,984
Alcoholic drink	1,466	1,282	2,178	1,548
Tobacco	1,428	1,224	1,720	1,248
Housing	2,586	2,273	3,904	2,641
Fuel and Light	1,087	1,035	1,489	1,274
Clothing and Footwear	2,099	2,026	2,634	2,195
Cars and Motorcycles	697	706	980	839
Furniture and floor covering	574	532	626	467
Radio and Electrical, etc.	504	486	661	540

SELECT BIBLIOGRAPHY

Some books of documents useful for the period covered by this book are:

COLE, G. D. H. AND FILSON, A. W. (Eds.): *British Working Class Movements: Select Documents 1789–1875* (Macmillan, 1951).

FLINN, M. W.: *Readings in Economic and Social History, Parts II and III* (Macmillan, 1964).

HARVEY, C., MARTIN, G. AND SCHARF, A. (Eds.): *Industrialization and Culture 1830–1914* (Open University Edition; Macmillan, 1970).

PELLING, H. M. (Ed.): *The Challenge of Socialism* (documents) (A. and C. Black, 1954).

[1] *Economic Trends*, No. 219, January 1972, Table 12, p. xxiv.

Note from p. 590

After this edition went to press the Law Lords of the House of Lords, constituting the ultimate Court of Appeal, re-imposed the fine on the T.G.W.U. by holding that a trade union *was* responsible for the acts of its shop stewards. Other developments too late for more than a passing mention here, were the publication of the Jones-Aldington Report, the imprisonment of five dockers for contempt of the Industrial Relations Court, the dock strike, and the acceptance of the terms of the Jones-Aldington Report modified in the dockers' favour.

APPENDICES

TABLES OF DATES

AGRICULTURE

1767. Arthur Young sets out on his 'Tours.'

1784. Arthur Young begins publication of *Annals of Agriculture.*

1793. Board of Agriculture.

1801. First General Enclosure Act.

1815. Corn Law prohibiting import of foreign wheat until the price of English had reached 80s. a quarter.

1830. "The Last Labourers' Revolt."

1834. Sentence of the Dorchester Labourers.

1836. Tithe Commutation Act.

1838. Royal Agricultural Society.

1846. Repeal of the Corn Laws.

1867. Report of the Children's Employment Commission on Organized Agricultural Gangs.

1867–69. Reports of the Royal Commission on the Employment of Children, Young Persons, and Women in Agriculture.

1868. The Gangs Act.

1872. (March). Warwickshire Agricultural Labourers' Union founded.

1872. (May). National Agricultural Labourers' Union founded.

1882. Final Report of the Royal Commission on the Agricultural Interest.

1885. Joseph Arch returned to Parliament.

1889. Department of Agriculture created under Minister of Agriculture.

1897. Final Report of the Royal Commission on Agricultural Depression.

1920. Agriculture Act.

1929. Agricultural Derating Act.

1931. Agricultural Marketing Act.

1932. Ottawa Agreements.

1932. Wheat Act.

1933. Agricultural Marketing Act.

1937. Subsidy for oats and barley.

1942. Report of the Scott Committee on Land Utilization in Rural Areas.

1947. Agriculture Act (price guarantees).

1958. Agricultural Marketing Act (to consolidate the Agricultural Marketing Acts 1931–49).

INDUSTRIAL INVENTION

1719. Lombe's silk factory at Derby.
1733. Kay's flying shuttle.
1740. Huntsman produced cast steel.
1760. Spinning by rollers—Wyatt and Paul.
1767. Hargreaves's spinning jenny.
1769. Arkwright's water-frame.
1779. Crompton's mule.
1782. Watt's steam-engine with rotary movement.
1783. Puddling iron—Cort and Oliver Onions.
1785. Cartwright's power-loom.
1828. Neilson's hot-air blast.
1831. Faraday enunciates the principle of electromagnetic induction.
1839. The steam-hammer.
1851. Beginnings of precision-tool making.
1856. Bessemer's hot-air blast for the making of steel.
1861. Siemens's open-hearth method of making steel.
1867–68. Royal Commission on Scientific Institutions.
1875. Electric lighting introduced.
1879. The Gilchrist-Thomas 'basic' method.
1884. The turbine—Sir Charles Parsons.
1943. Atomic Energy.
1950. Automation and the use of computers.
1960. Natural gas.

TRANSPORT AND COMMUNICATIONS

1761. Bridgewater Canal.
1763–73. Manchester Ship Canal.
1802. First steamship (on Forth and Clyde Canal).
1825. Stockton–Darlington railway opened.
1827. Gurney's steam-coach.
1829. Shillibeer's omnibus.
1830. Liverpool–Manchester railway.
1836–37. 'Little railway mania.'
1838. Steamship service across the Atlantic.
1839. The electric telegraph.
1844. The 'Parliamentary train.'
1845. First iron ship crosses the Atlantic.
1846. 'Railway mania.'
1851. Channel under-water cable for telegraphic communication.
1863. First segment of London's Underground railway.
1866. Atlantic under-water telegraph cable.
1874. The modern bicycle.

1876. First telephone message.
1876. Internal-combustion engine.
1887. Daimler's light-engined motor for road travel.
1888. London General Omnibus Company.
1895. First Motor Exhibition—held in London.
1895. Diesel engine.
1890–1900. Electrification of tramways.
1900. Electrified 'Tuppenny Tube.'
1901. Marconi's first wireless message.
1905. First aeroplane flight—the Wright Brothers.
1909. Blériot crosses the Channel by air.
1910. Standardized omnibus driven by petrol.
1914. Electrification of the railways.
1920. Automatic telephone.
1937. Jet engines.
1947. Nationalization of the railways and other transport services.
1963. The Beeching Report on the railways.

THE POOR LAW AND PUBLIC HEALTH

1795. 'Speenhamland System' introduced.
1834. Report of Royal Commission on the Poor Law.
1834. Poor Law Amendment Act.
1847. Poor Law Commission replaced by Poor Law Board.
1848. Public Health Act establishing Board of Health.
1854. New Public Health Board—dismissal of Chadwick.
1858. Public Health Board dissolved.
1869. Royal Sanitary Commission appointed.
1871. Local Government Act.
1875. Public Health Act.
1883. *The Bitter Cry of Outcast London* (George R. Sims).
1884–85. Royal Commission on Housing.
1886. *Life and Labour in London* (Charles Booth).
1903. Letchworth Garden City.
1905–9. Royal Commission on the Poor Laws.
1908. Old Age Pensions Act.
1911. National Health Insurance Act.
1917. Ministry of Labour established.
1919. Ministry of Health established.
1920. Unemployment Insurance Act.
1929. Local Government Act.
1930. Poor Law Consolidating Act.
1936. Public Health Acts.
1942. Beveridge Report on Social Insurance and Allied Services.
1944. Establishment of Ministry of National Insurance.
1945. Family Allowances.

1946. National Insurance Acts.

1946. Report of the Care of Children Committee.

1948. The end of the Poor Law (National Assistance Act).

1948. Inauguration of National Health Service.

1949. Report of the Royal Commission on Population.

1956. Report of the Committee of Inquiry into the cost of the National Health Service (The Guillebaud Report).

1966. Ministry of Social Security.

FACTORY AND MINING

1802. Health and Morals of Apprentices Act.

1819. An Act for the Regulation of Cotton Mills and Factories.

1830. *Letters on Yorkshire Slavery* (R. Oastler).

1831–32. Report of Select Committee on Factory Children's Labour (Sadler's Committee).

1833. An Act to regulate the Labour of Children and Young Persons in Mills and Factories.

1833–34. Reports of Commissioners on Employment of Children in Factories.

1840. Chimney-sweeps Act.

1842. Children's Employment Commission: First Report, Mines.

1842. Employment of Women and Children in Mines Act.

1844. An Act to Amend the Laws relating to Labour in Factories.

1845. Print Works Act.

1847. An Act to limit the Hours of Labour of Young Persons and Females in Factories (the Ten Hours Act).

1850. Act for the Inspection of Coal Mines in Great Britain.

1861. Lace Works Act.

1863–66. Reports of the Royal Commission on the Employment of Children in Trades and Manufactures not already regulated by Law.

1864. The Factory Acts Extension Act.

1864. Chimney-sweeps Act.

1867. The Factory Acts Extension Act.

1867. The Workshops Regulation Act.

1875. Chimney-sweeps Act.

1878. Factory and Workshops' Consolidating Act.

1880. Employers' Liability Act.

1891. An Act to Amend the Law relating to Factories and Workshops.

1895. An Act to Amend and Extend the Law relating to Factories and Workshops.

1901. Workmen's Compensation Act.

1906. Factory and Workshop Consolidation Act.

1908. Coalmines Regulation Act.

1909. Trade Boards Act.

1912. Coalmines (Minimum Wage) Act.
1917–18. Whitley Committee Reports.
1919. Coalmines Act.
1937. Factory Act.
1946. Nationalization of the Coal Mines.

EDUCATION

1780. Robert Raikes's first Sunday school.
1798. Samuel Butler becomes Headmaster of Shrewsbury.
1802. *The Fairchild Family* (Mrs Sherwood).
1808. The Lancasterian Society.
1811. National Society for Promoting the Education of the Poor in the Principles of the Established Church.
1814. British and Foreign School Society.
1816. Robert Owen starts his school at the cotton mills at New Lanark.
1823. Glasgow Mechanics' Institute.
1823. London Mechanics' Institute.
1828. Thomas Arnold becomes Headmaster of Rugby.
1828. Foundation of University College, London.
1831. Foundation of King's College, London.
1833. First Government grant to education.
1839. Committee of the Privy Council appointed to organize the distribution of public money for education.
1850. Royal Commission on Oxford.
1850. Royal Commission on Cambridge.
1851. First Government grant to evening schools.
1854. London Working Men's College.
1860. Foundation of Bedford College for Women.
1861. Report of the Newcastle Commission into the State of Popular Education in England.
1862. The Revised Code (instituting Payment by Results).
1864. Report of the Clarendon Commission.
1867–68. Report of the Schools Inquiry Commission.
1869. The National Education League.
1869. The National Education Union.
1869. Foundation of Girton College, Cambridge.
1870. The Education Act.
1871. Universities Tests Act.
1871. Foundation of Newnham College, Cambridge.
1873. University Extension Classes (Cambridge).
1877. Royal Commission on Oxford and Cambridge.
1879. Opening of Lady Margaret Hall, Oxford.
1879. Opening of Somerville Hall (later College), Oxford.
1880. Mundella's Act—universal, compulsory school attendance

1884. Report of the Royal Commission on Technical Instruction.
1888. Final Report of the Cross Commission on the Elementary Education Acts.
1895. Report of the Royal Commission on Secondary Education.
1899. Foundation of Ruskin College.
1899. Establishment of Board of Education.
1900–1. Cockerton Judgment.
1902. Education Act.
1903. Formation of Workers' Educational Association.
1907. Joint Committee of Oxford University and the W.E.A.
1907–8. First University Tutorial Classes.
1918. School-leaving age raised to fourteen.
1926. Hadow Report (the Adolescent).
1931. Hadow Report (the Primary School).
1936. Education Act.
1938. Report of the Spens Committee on Secondary Education.
1941. Report of the Norwood Committee on the Curriculum and Examinations in Secondary Schools.
1944. Report of the Fleming Committee on Public Schools and the General Educational System. Education Act.
1954. Report of the Committee on the Organization and Finance of Adult Education in England and Wales (The Ashby Report).
1963. Report of the Committee on Higher Education (The Robbins Report). *Half Our Future* (The Newsom Report).
1969. Charter for Open University.
1972. School-leaving age raised to sixteen.
    Report of the Committee on Teacher Education and Training (The James Report).

HEALTH AND HOUSING

1943. Ministry of Town and Country Planning.
1946. New Towns Act.
1947. Town and Country Planning Act.
Jan. 1951. Ministry of Local Government and Planning.
May 1951. Ministry of Housing and Local Government.
1952. Town Development Act.
1954. Report of the Air Pollution Committee.
1954. Housing, Repairs and Rent Act.
1956. Clean Air Act.
1957. The Rent Act (rent de-control).
1965. The Rent Act (restoring rent control).
1965. Milner Holland Report on Housing in Greater London.
1970. Department of the Environment.

THE POPULATION OF GREAT BRITAIN

Year	England and Wales	Scotland	Great Britain
			(*Millions*)
1760 (*estimate*)	6,736,000		8·0
1801 (*first census*)	8,892,536	1,608,420	10·5
1811 (*census*)	10,164,256	1,805,864	12·0
1821 (*census*)	12,000,236	2,091,521	14·0
1831 (*census*)	13,896,797	2,364,386	16·0
1841 (*census*)	15,914,148	2,620,184	18·5
1851 (*census*)	17,927,609	2,888,742	21·0
1861 (*census*)	20,066,224	3,062,294	23·0
1871 (*census*)	22,712,266	3,360,018	26·0
1881 (*census*)	25,974,439	3,735,573	30·0
1891 (*census*)	29,002,525	4,025,647	33·0
1901 (*census*)	32,527,843	4,472,103	37·0
1911 (*census*)	36,070,492	4,760,904	41·0
1921 (*census*)	37,886,699	4,882,497	43·0
1931 (*census*)	39,952,377	4,842,980	45·0
1951 (*census*)	43,744,924	5,096,415	49·0
1961 (*census*)	46,071,604	5,178,490	51·0
1971 (*census–prov.*)	'48,593,658	5,227,706	54·0

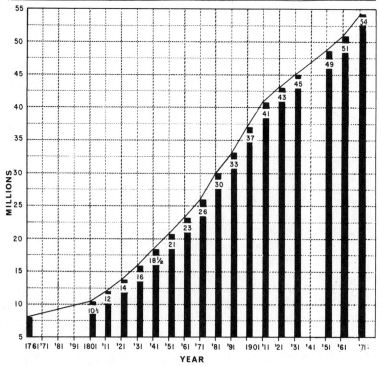

GROWTH OF TRADE-UNION MEMBERSHIP
IN THE UNITED KINGDOM[1]

Year	Membership in Millions	Year	Membership in Millions
1892	1·6	1927	4·9
1893	1·6	1928	4·8
1894	1·5	1929	4·9
1895	1·5	1930	4·8
1896	1·6	1931	4·6
1897	1·7	1932	4·4
1898	1·8	1933	4·4
1899	1·9	1934	4·6
1900	2·0	1935	4·9
1901	2·0	1936	5·3
1902	2·0	1937	5·8
1903	2·0	1938	6·1
1904	2·0	1939	6·2
1905	2·0	1940	6·6
1906	2·2	1941	7·1
1907	2·5	1942	7·8
1908	2·5	1943	8·1
1909	2·5	1944	8·0
1910	2·6	1945	7·8
1911	3·1	1946	8·8
1912	3·4	1947	9·1
1913	4·1	1948	9·32
1914	4·1	1949	9·27
1915	4·4	1950	9·24
1916	4·6	1951	9·48
1917	5·5	1952	9·53
1918	6·5	1953	9·46
1919	7·9	1954	9·50
1920	8·3	1960	9·80
1921	6·6	1963	9·92
1922	5·6	1965	10·18
1923	5·4	1967	9·97
1924	5·5	1969	8·9
1925	5·5	1971	10·0
1926	5·2		

[1] *Ministry of Labour Gazette.*

DEVELOPMENT OF CO-OPERATIVE TRADING
IN UNITED KINGDOM[1]

RETAIL SOCIETIES				
Year	No. of Societies	Membership	Share and Loan Capital in £s	Total Sales in £s
1844	1 (Rochdale)	28	28	—
1875	1,266	437,000	4,412,000	13,218,000
1900	1,439	1,707,000	21,967,000	50,054,000
1914	1,385	3,054,000	45,318,000	87,980,000
1925	1,289	4,111,000	100,854,000	183,584,000
1935	1,118	7,484,000	168,682,000	220,430,000
1945	1,070	9,402,000	310,841,000	361,000,000
1950	1,019	10,691,543	295,939,000	613,765,000
1954	973	11,486,726	285,070,000	792,981,000
1960	859	12,956,839	294,117,050	1,032,749,334

WHOLESALE SOCIETIES (*English and Scottish*)		
	Share and Loan Capital in £s	Total Sales in £s
1875	401,000	2,677,000
1900	2,486,000[2]	21,508,000
1914	10,431,000	44,336,000
1925	56,973,000	94,301,000
1935	114,176,000	116,929,000
1945	247,226,000	221,919,000
1954	137,086,000	483,947,000
1960	106,845,672	562,952,644

[1] Figures from annual reports of the Co-operative Congress and from *Co-operative Statistics* (Co-operative Union, Ltd.).   [2] 1901 figure.

INDEX OF SUBJECTS

INDEX OF PERSONS

INDEX OF PLACES